Making Sense of WAR

Making Sense of WAR

THE SECOND WORLD WAR AND THE

FATE OF THE BOLSHEVIK REVOLUTION

Amir Weiner

PRINCETON UNIVERSITY PRESS · PRINCETON AND OXFORD

Library of Congress Cataloging-in-Publication Data

Weiner, Amir, 1961–
Making sense of war : the Second World War and the fate of the
Bolshevik Revolution / Amir Weiner.
p.   cm.
Includes bibliographical references and index.
ISBN 0-691-05702-8 (alk. paper)
1. World War, 1939–1945—Psychological aspects. 2. World War,
1939–1945—Soviet Union. 3. World War, 1939–1945—Social as-
pects—Soviet Union. 5. World War 1939–1945–Ukraine—Vinnytsia
Region. 6. World War, 1939–1945—Propoganda. 7. Propoganda, So-
viet—History. 8. Communism—Soviet Union—History. 9. Vinnytsia
Region (Ukraine)—History—20th Century. I. Title

D744.44 .W45 2001
940.53'1–dc21   00-044125

This book has been composed in Janson

The paper used in this publication meets the minimum
requirements of ANSI/NISO Z39.48-1992 (R1997)
(*Permanence of Paper*)

http://pup.princeton.edu

Printed in the United States of America

10   9   8   7   6   5   4   3   2   1

Contents

Illustrations

Unattributed photographs are by the author.

Figures

Maps

Tables

Acknowledgments

THE PUBLICATION of a first book gives the opportunity to thank a number of individuals and institutions whose invaluable support and input into this project helped to bring it about.

The idea of writing about the impact of the Second World War on the Soviet polity was conceived during my studies at the Hebrew University of Jerusalem at a time when the study of the post-1941 era in the Soviet Union was still considered the pursuit of political scientists, not historians. There I was fortunate to be trained by a unique group of scholars, especially Jonathan Frankel, Theodore Friedgut, Israel Getzler, Ezra Mendelsohn, and Yehoshua Arieli. Their broad intellectual horizons and interdisciplinary scholarship shaped my approach to history.

At Columbia University, where I wrote my doctoral dissertation, I benefited greatly from the teaching and scholarship of Mark von Hagen, Richard Wortman, and Leopold Haimson. Without doubt, the versatility and unmatched intellectual intensity of the Russian history program at Columbia helped define my work. I also had the great fortune to be part of a fascinating group of graduate students whose work has ushered in a new dimension in Soviet studies. Ongoing dialogue with Fred Corney, Igal Halfin, Jochen Hellebck, David Hoffmann, Peter Holquist, and Yanni Kotsonis has enriched my work, and I thank them all.

At Stanford, where I have taught since 1995, I have enjoyed the friendship and scholarship of a remarkable group of colleagues. Many thanks to Norman Naimark, Terence Emmons, and Nancy Shields-Kollmann for their constant support and friendship, and their unparalleled knowledge of Russian history. Aron Rodrigue and Steven Zipperstein read large segments of the text and offered incredible insights and nuanced interpretations of history in general, and Jewish history in particular. James Sheehan and Keith Baker provided invaluable commentary on my introduction. Philippe Buc and Brad Gregory refined my notion of religious-like zeal that pervaded the Soviet enterprise and introduced me to sources that would otherwise have escaped my attention.

Several colleagues and dear friends deserve special mention. Stephen Kotkin taught a seminar at Columbia University in the spring of 1991 that left a deep impact on my conceptualization of the Soviet phenomenon (and, I dare say, that of my fellow graduate students as well). Since then, Steve has been a constant source of inspiration and encouragement, penetrating criticism, and intellectual challenge. Omer Bartov has been a terrific mentor and friend, whose pathbreaking work on modern mass violence and the Nazi phenomenon have greatly influenced my own thinking.

Special thanks to Yuri Slezkine for his subtle reading of Russian and Soviet history, and especially for his thoughtful criticism on the final draft of this book; his critique helped to tighten numerous arguments in the text. Roman Szporluk brought to this project his superb command of Ukrainian and modern European intellectual histories. It is my hope that this work will help him in his crusade to reinstate Ukrainian history to its deserved place in European history. Hiroaki Kuromiya has been a loyal friend, and a source of common-sense criticism and unparalleled knowledge of the Soviet era in Ukraine. Many thanks as well to Peter Holquist for endless hours of discussion and stimulating intellectual companionship and friendship throughout the years; to Ben Nathans for always being there with unsparing criticism and enthusiastic support; and to Reginald Zelnik, who read the entire manuscript, for his support and help even when disagreeing with my approach to Soviet history.

In Vinnytsia I was lucky to befriend Valerii Vasil'ev, a remarkable historian and person. Valerii opened his home to me, helped in every step of my research in the region, and shared with me his unmatched knowledge of the local archives and insights into Ukrainian history.

My thanks to Blair Ruble and Dan Orlovsky for unfailing encouragement and support; to Francine Hirsch and Daniel Gordon for their most helpful comments on the introduction and on chapters 3 and 4; to Pieter Lagrou and Luc Huyse for furnishing me with information from the Western European perspective; to Karel Berkhoff and Serhy Yekelchyk for constant advice and help. Their pioneering works on wartime and postwar Ukraine, respectively, often challenged and enriched my argument; to Andrei Rus for helping with working out the statistical data; and to Steven Barnes, Stuart Finkel, Andrew Jenks, and Ann Livschiz for their assistance in my research and their clarifying questions and comments.

At Princeton University Press I would like to thank Brigitta van Rheinberg for her enthusiastic support of this project; to Rita Bernhard for her meticulous and patient editing that greatly improved the manuscript; and to Mark Spencer for prompt assistance in all technical matters. I would also like to thank Chris Bert for designing maps and David Dineen for assistance with photography.

Parts of this manuscript were presented in conferences and workshops in Chicago, Toronto, and Georgetown. I thank Michael Geyer, Sheila Fitzpatrick, Richard Stites, Lynne Viola, and Paul Magocsi for their insightful comments. Thanks to Tony Judt as well for offering me the opportunity to be present at a stimulating conference on the legacy of World War II, which expanded my notion of the postwar settlement in Europe.

This manuscript was completed during a sabbatical at the National Fellow Program at the Hoover Institution on War, Revolution, and Peace at Stanford University. Special thanks to Charles Palm and Tom Henriksen, who enabled me to have a year free of obligations, and to Wendy Minkin who made that year a most pleasant one.

In my research in the Russian and Ukrainian archives, I was greatly helped by a number of excellent professionals and generous people. Special thanks to Sergei Mironenko and Dina Nokhotovicha of the State Archive of the Russian Federation (GARF) in Moscow; Larisa Malashenko and Larisa Rogovaia of the Russian State Archive of Socio-Political History (RGASPI) in Moscow; Ruslan Pyrih and Iryna Komarova of the Central State Archive of Civic Organizations of Ukraine (TsDAHOU) in Kiev; Larysa Iakovlieva of the Central State Archive of the Highest Organs of Authority and Government of Ukraine (TsDAVOVU) in Kiev. In Vinnytsia Kateryna Synytsia literally opened the state and party archives for me. The research for this book would not have been complete without her courageous support and enthusiastic guidance. John Taylor of the National Archives in Washington, D.C., and the staff of the Yad Vashem Archive in Jerusalem were most helpful.

Research for this project was funded by the Harriman Institute of Columbia University; the American Council of Teachers of Russian Language; the Davies Center for Russian and East European Studies of Harvard University; the Kennan Institute for Advanced Russian Studies of the Woodrow Wilson Center in Washington, D.C.; the School of Humanities and Social Sciences of Stanford University; the Tad Taube Faculty Fund of Stanford University; and the Krater Research grant of Stanford University.

A section of chapter 1 appeared in *Russian Review* 55 (October 1996): 638–60. I am grateful for the journal's permission to reproduce it here. Sections of chapters 3 and 4 appeared in *American Historical Review* 104, no.4 (October 1999): 1114–1155, under the title "Nature, Nurture, and Memory in a Socialist Utopia," and I thank that journal as well for allowing me to use this essay. The University of Toronto Press has granted me permission to publish Maps 1 and 2.

Finally, my greatest thanks go to my wife, Julia Erwin-Weiner. She accompanied this project from research to publication, read numerous drafts, and offered the most pointed commentary. Her unfailing patience and generosity, humor and love, have sustained me through the long and winding road of research and writing.

This book is dedicated to the memory of my late parents, Moshe and Tsipora Weiner. They taught me the love of the polemical, political, and ideological, and I hope this book reflects these values.

Making Sense of WAR

GERMANY

○Minsk

Nowogrodek○

Torun

Bialystok○

Buh

BELORUSSIAN
S.S.R.

P O D L A C H I A

Warsaw○

Brest

P O L I S S I A

Pripet

Lodz○

Kielce

Lublin○

Chelm

V O L H Y N I A

P O L A N D

Luts'k

○

.Zhytomyr

Katowice

Vistula

San

G A L

Cracow

L'viv

C

A Ternopil'○

Vinnytsia

LEMKIAN REGION

PRESOV REGION

CZECHOSLOVAKIA

Stanyslaviv○

Dniester

Kamianets'
Podil's'kyi

SLOVAKIA

Uzhhorod

SUBCARPATHIAN
RUS

Chernivtsi

MOLDAVIAN
A.S.S.R.

Budapest

Tysa

MARAMAROSH

BUKOVINA

BESSARABIA

Prut

H U N G A R Y

ROMANIA

DOBRUDJA

Bucharest○

Danube

BULGARIA

International boundaries, 1921

Soviet Socialist Republic boundaries

Autonomous Soviet Socialist Republic
boundaries

Boundaries of Polish papatinates (1921),
Czechoslovak provinces (1928), and
Soviet oblasts (1932)

⊙   State capitals

○   Administrative centers of palatinates,
    provinces, and oblasts

·   Selected cities

Ukrainian ethnolinguistic boundary, 1930

Post-1945 borders

0   150 miles

0   150 kilometers

Homel

U.   S.   S.   R.

Tambov

Don

Voronezh

Kursk

RUSSIAN

Chemihiv

Desna

Sumy

S.F.S.R.

Kiev

Kharkiv

Dnieper

Poltava

Donets

UKRAINIAN   S.S.R.

Luhans'k

(to 1924)

Kirovohrad

Dnipropetrovs'k

Shakhty

Kryvyi Rih

Zaporozhia

Stalino

Don

Rostov

Taganrog

Southern Buh

Mykolaiv

Kherson

Odessa

Sea of Azov

KUBAN

Kuban

CRIMEAN
A.S.R.

Symferopil'

BLACK   SEA

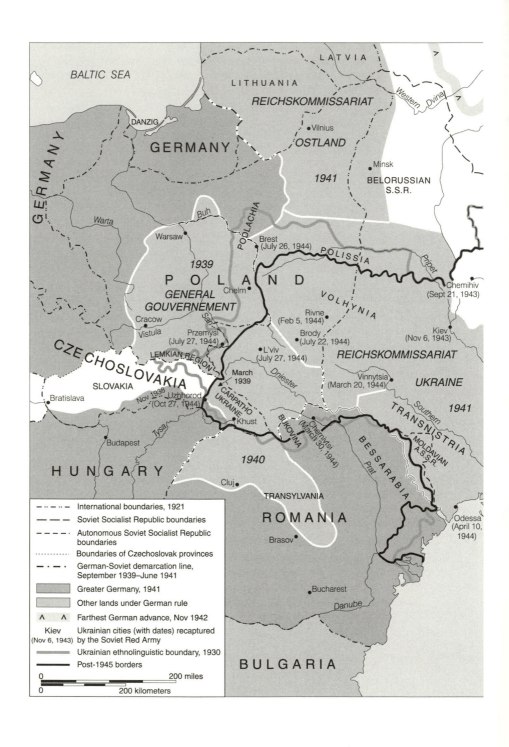

BALTIC SEA

LATVIA

LITHUANIA

REICHSKOMMISSARIAT

DANZIG

GERMANY

•Vilnius

OSTLAND

•Minsk

1941

BELORUSSIAN
S.S.R.

GERMANY

Warta

Buh

PODLACHIA

Warsaw

Brest
(July 26, 1944)

POLISSIA

Pripet

1939

P O L A N D

Chelm•

VOLHYNIA

Chemihiv
(Sept 21, 1943)

GENERAL
GOUVERNEMENT

Rivne
(Feb 5, 1944)

Cracow

Vistula

Przemysl
(July 27, 1944)

San

Brody
(July 22, 1944)

Kiev
(Nov 6, 1943)

CZECHOSLOVAKIA

LEMKIAN REGION

•L'viv
(July 27, 1944)

REICHSKOMMISSARIAT

SLOVAKIA

March
1939

Dniester

Vinnytsia
(March 20, 1944)

UKRAINE

•Bratislava

Nov 1938

Uzhhorod
(Oct 27, 1944)

CARPATHO
UKRAINE

TRANSNISTRIA

1941

Southern

•Khust

BUKOVINA

Chernivtsi
(March 30, 1944)

MOLDAVIAN
A.S.S.R.

Tysa

BESSARABIA

•Budapest

1940

Prut

H U N G A R Y

Cluj•

TRANSYLVANIA

R O M A N I A

Odessa
(April 10,
1944)

Brasov•

•Bucharest

Danube

B U L G A R I A

Western Dvina

	International boundaries, 1921
	Soviet Socialist Republic boundaries
	Autonomous Soviet Socialist Republic boundaries
	Boundaries of Czechoslovak provinces
	German-Soviet demarcation line, September 1939–June 1941
	Greater Germany, 1941
	Other lands under German rule
∧ ∧	Farthest German advance, Nov 1942
Kiev (Nov 6, 1943)	Ukrainian cities (with dates) recaptured by the Soviet Red Army
	Ukrainian ethnolinguistic boundary, 1930
	Post-1945 borders

0   200 miles
0   200 kilometers

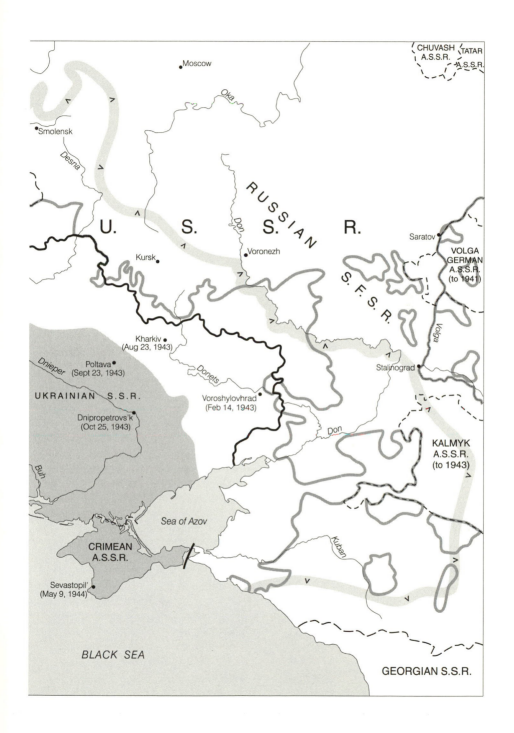

CHUVASH A.S.S.R.

TATAR A.S.S.R.

Moscow

Oka

Smolensk

Desna

R U S S I A N

U. S. S. R.

S. F. S. R.

Kursk

Don

Voronezh

Saratov

VOLGA GERMAN A.S.S.R. (to 1941)

Volga

Kharkiv (Aug 23, 1943)

Donets

Dnieper

Poltava (Sept 23, 1943)

UKRAINIAN S.S.R.

Dnipropetrovs'k (Oct 25, 1943)

Voroshylovhrad (Feb 14, 1943)

Stalinograd

Buh

Don

KALMYK A.S.S.R. (to 1943)

Sea of Azov

CRIMEAN A.S.S.R.

Kuban

Sevastopil' (May 9, 1944)

BLACK SEA

GEORGIAN S.S.R.

THE SECOND WORLD WAR was an unprecedented cataclysm that rocked the entire European continent. It shook institutions, identities, and convictions that, until then, appeared to be solidly entrenched. This book explores the war's impact on the ideology, beliefs, and practices of the Soviet regime and its subjects by examining the ways in which various segments of the polity strove to make sense of this traumatic event.

The "Great Patriotic War," as the war was heralded within the Soviet Union, transformed the Soviet polity physically and symbolically. It served to validate the original revolutionary prophecy while at the same time almost entirely overshadowing it; it appeared as proof—and perhaps the cause—of both the regime's impotence and its legitimacy; it redefined the party according to the ethos of veterans' sacrifices; it advanced the ethnicization of the Bolshevik "purification drive"; it rearranged the "fraternal family of Soviet nations"; it forced and inspired individuals to reassert themselves, take up new roles, and make new claims; and it forever divided Soviet history and life into two distinct eras.

Not surprisingly, an event of this magnitude invited different interpretations from Soviet citizens. Some saw the war as the Bolshevik Armageddon, a final cleansing of elements that had intruded on the desired socialist harmony, ushering in the era of communism. Others considered it a bloody sacrifice necessary to redeem the regime's past evils. Still others viewed the war as the long-awaited death blow to an evil enterprise. But for all, the war signaled the climax in the unfolding socialist revolution, sanctioning the ever changing methods employed to reach the ultimate goal of a homogeneous and harmonious society.

Understanding the ways in which Soviet people coped with the experience and legacy of the war requires an in-depth look at the institutions that informed their world. To begin, the Soviet world was not an anomaly, nor did it emerge in a vacuum. Soviet contemporaries, party-state officials, and ordinary people alike were always attentive to the universal roots of their world even when they carved their own path to socialism and communism. The Soviet ethos was ingrained in the politics that shaped the modern era where states sought the transformation of societies with the help of scientific models and a myriad of institutions charged with managing all social spheres. The Soviets co-opted or juxtaposed their ideology and practices to this phenomenon, and often did both, but never lost sight of it. The war reinforced the Bolshevik enterprise as part of the modern political universe. The direct encounter with competing ideologies and movements, the prolonged exposure of large segments of the population to alternative rules, and the increasingly apparent proximity between the Soviet methods of social engineering in the wake of the war and that of its rivals, particularly the Nazis, compelled both the regime and its citizens to reassess the state of the Revolution and its distinct features at the very same time that socialism had finally managed to break its isolation.

Second, contemporaries could not conceive of the war as detached from the permanent, unfolding socialist revolution. For Soviet citizens, the war was a crucial, integral link in the ongoing Bolshevik revolutionary enterprise. The war reinforced key institutions of the Soviet system, primarily the socioeconomic order, the endurance of the party, and the drive to purge the polity of elements that hindered the desired social and political harmony. But it also shifted conceptions and practices of the Revolution, superimposing a new set of tropes onto prewar categories. Social origin no longer served as the dominant criterion of sociopolitical status, as former class enemies were allowed to redeem themselves through wartime exploits. The unprecedented deportations of entire ethnic groups, the replacement of temporary incarceration with eternal exile, and the extermination of separatist nationalist movements qualitatively altered the postwar drive for purity along ethnic lines.

Within the pantheon of myths that endowed the permanent revolution with legitimacy and historical relevance, the Great Patriotic War loomed large. Juxtaposed against other heroic tales within the Bolshevik narrative of the Revolution, the war superseded other foundational myths, such as the civil war and the collectivization of the countryside, which were increasingly viewed as distant, irrelevant, and, in some cases, too controversial because of their traumatic legacy. Yet like the myths it displaced, the myth of the war defined criteria for legitimate membership in and exclusion from the Soviet family. As many discovered, Communists included, the stigma of passivity in the struggle against the Nazi evil was detrimental to one's standing in the community. Similarly, being perceived as intruding on or challenging the official universal version of the war experience could lead to collective exclusion, as Jews who sought to advance their own version of the genocide and wartime contribution learned.

Finally, the war in the Soviet world also derived its meaning from the powerful presence of two key institutions. The first was that of personal networks of veterans of the Red Army and of the partisan movement. Personal bondings had been the primary mode of political association in the Soviet system, and as the war became the focal point in the lives of the majority of the population rather than the civil war or building socialism, these networks evolved around shared wartime experiences. Already during the war, veterans were taking over in localities throughout the Union, turning their understanding of the war into a litmus test for political legitimacy. A second and closely related institution was the regime's creation of particular entities that were formed to advance the politicization of every sphere of life, yet often produced unintended results. I focus on the commemoration of the war in literature, where veterans successfully struggled to articulate their own narrative of the war; the collective farm assemblies, where peasants used their wartime sacrifice and exploits to assume more control over their lives and to integrate themselves as legitimate members in the polity; and the ethnonational territorial units, the Ukrainian Republic in this case, where indigenous populations made the most of the war cult, often co-opting it in the cultivation of their own particularistic identities.

These themes are examined as experienced in the rural western-central Ukrainian region of Vinnytsia. The history of the region offers a unique insight into the evolution of the Soviet experience vis-à-vis the war. The pastoral tranquillity of this relatively small region—a little more than twenty-seven thousand square kilometers stretched along the banks of the Southern Buh River—did not shield it from becoming the ultimate testing ground for the evolution of Soviet mythology and the quest for purity or a laboratory for social engineering for every political movement that gained the upper hand there.[1]

The tale of wartime experience and legacy in Vinnytsia is told in three parts. Part 1 examines the impact of the war on the articulation of Soviet political identities. The first chapter traces the local political elite's quest for a legitimate historical past in a region whose history offered no easy answers, if only because of the legacy of Soviet prewar policies. At the height of the Terror in 1937–38, Vinnytsia was the site of mass executions by the People's Commissariat of Internal Affairs (NKVD), with more than nine thousand people shot and dumped into mass graves on the outskirts of the town. The massacre destabilized the local scene. The exhumation of mass graves by the Germans made the assessment of the Soviet past, the Nazi present, and a possible Soviet future an unavoidable dilemma. The massacre also reshuffled the local party organization, bringing to the fore a new generation of local leaders who would endure the ordeal of war shortly thereafter. The tension between the traumatic past that was all but erased from official memory and the cataclysm of war were largely responsible for shaping political identities in the postwar Soviet world. Local politics also witnessed a harsh battle over what the legacy of the war should be and who would define it—Red Army veterans or local partisans—a conflict with deep roots in Soviet history. Chapter 2 pursues the cleansing of the Communist Party rank and file when wartime conduct emerged as the key criterion in the evaluation of "party-worthiness." Subjected to

---

[1] In spite of its tendentious tone, the historical survey of the region in *Istoriia mist i sil URSR: Vinnyts'ka oblast* (Kiev: Hol. Red. Ukrainskoi rad. entsyklopedii AN URSR, 1972), 9–75, is still a valuable and informative source for the pre-Soviet era in particular.

inquisitorial verification that raised questions such as "Where were you during the German occupation, and how did you survive?" (which often implied "Why did you survive?"), thousands of Communists saw their careers and beliefs assessed through the prism of the new legitimizing myth of the war.

Part 2 follows the evolution of the Soviet purification drive as it applied to the population at large and compares it to postwar settlements in other European countries that coped with similar problems. By war's outbreak, the region's inhabitants had already been exposed to mass cleansing acts. Like the rest of Europe, the modern era in Vinnytsia started with the Great War. By the end of 1915, Vinnytsia (then still part of Podillia Province) witnessed mass deportations of German settlers and Jews by the tsarist army.[2] This was followed by the upheavals of the civil war, collectivization, and the ensuing famine that hit this rural region hard; hundreds of thousands were deported or killed, or starved to death. Starting in the early 1930s, the population was subjected to consecutive waves of deportations, particularly the Polish and German minorities.[3] But the worst was yet to come. On 19 July 1941 the invading German army occupied the city and remained there until 20 March 1944. A month after the invasion the region was partitioned: The territory between the Dniester and the Buh rivers was turned over to Romania and renamed Transnistria, and the remaining territory, including the city, became part of the Reichskommissariat Ukraine and was subjected to direct rule by the SS. Nazi policies of genocide, deportation, and starvation decimated the region. When the Red Army liberated the city, the population numbered less than one-quarter of its nearly 100,000 residents on the eve of the war. Barely one-seventh of the 140,000 Jews in the region survived the occupation. The ethnic German community practically ceased to exist. Twelve years after the war ended, the population had yet to recover its prewar level of approximately 2.3 million. Against this background, chapter 3 tells the story of the eradication of the Ukrainian separatist nationalist movement in Vinnytsia. What set this political-military movement apart from other insurrectionary forces was the Soviet application of punitive measures reserved for enemy nations during and after the war. The permanent exile imposed on all ethnic groups deported during and after the war by the 26 November 1948 decree of the Presidium of the Supreme Soviet of the USSR was extended

---

[2] An estimated twenty thousand German settlers were deported from the region by the end of 1915. See Ingeburg Fleischhauer and Benjamin Pinkus, *The Soviet Germans: Past and Present* (London: Hurst, 1986), 67 n. 5; Eric Lohr, "Enemy Alien Politics within the Russian Empire during World War I," Ph.D. dissertation, Harvard University, 1999, 163–64, 168.

[3] See Valerii Vasil'ev and Lynne Viola, eds., *Kollektivizatsiia i krest'ianskoe soprotivlenie na Ukraine (noiabr' 1929–mart 1930 gg.)* (Vinnytsia: Logos, 1997); Ivan Shl'ha *Holod na Podilli* (Vinnytsia: Prym, 1993); Vasil'ev, ed., *Politychni represii na Podilli (20-30-i rr. XX st.)* (Vinnytsia: Logos, 1999).

to members of the movement and their families in April 1950, as was done to the Baltic nationalist guerrillas a year before. This was in stark contrast to the rank and file of the Russian Liberation Army ("Vlasovites"), who, along with other collaborationist groups, were treated in a similar fashion to Red Army officers who fell in German captivity. They were sentenced to six-year terms, and most were released upon completion of their term in 1951–52.[4] The extent of the pacification campaign and the introduction of the irredeemability of certain categories of Soviet citizens reflected a shift in the pattern of Soviet cleansing, namely, indiscriminate and irreversible excision of those stigmatized as wartime collaborators.

The radicalization of Soviet state violence triggered comparison with its Nazi racial counterpart, especially regarding the Jewish minority, who, in the wake of the war, found themselves targeted as the ultimate enemy within. Chapter 4 traces the war's impact on Soviet-Jewish relations, and examines the specific forms of extinction the Soviets used against the Jews that differed from those employed by the Nazis. The presence of a substantial number of local Jews, who either survived the Romanian occupation or returned from evacuation to the Soviet rear and to service in the Red Army, guaranteed a fierce battle over the commemoration of the war and the Jewish genocide. The integration of the unique Jewish tragedy into the universal narrative of Soviet suffering and the simultaneous denial of Jews' contribution at the front highlighted the process and outcome of the delineation of particularistic realms within the Soviet polity.

Part 3 analyzes the viability of the Soviet system during the trials of war and its aftermath. As a border region until 1939, Vinnytsia was the prime focus of the powerful separatist nationalist movement across the border. With the unification of the eastern and western regions under Soviet rule following the Molotov-Ribbentrop agreement, the region witnessed a clash between Soviet-style Ukrainianhood and separatist ethnocentric nationalism. Chapter 5 traces this struggle from the collapse of Soviet power in the region during the initial phase of the war to the power vacuum that

---

[4] Viktor Zemskov, "Spetsposelentsy (po dokumentatsii NKVD-MVD SSSR)," *Sotsiologicheskie issledovaniia* 11 (1990): 17 nn. 18, 22. It appears that Soviet leaders, most notably Nikita Khrushchev, believed that Stalin would have liked to turn the postwar eradication campaign in western Ukraine into an anti-Ukrainian crusade per se. Throughout 1956–57 Khrushchev repeatedly suggested that only the sheer number of forty million Ukrainians prevented Stalin from deporting all Ukrainians after the war. Without doubt, Khrushchev was appealing to Ukrainian party officials for support in the leadership struggles at the time, but the scale of postwar repression in the Ukrainian Republic and the precedent set by the complete deportations in the Caucasus insinuated that somehow his claim was credible. See Khrushchev's "Secret Speech" on 20 February 1956, in his *Khrushchev Remembers*, trans. and ed. Strobe Talbott (Boston: Little, Brown, 1971), 652; and his comments during the special session of the Central Committee in June 1957 (Vladimir Naumov and Terence Emmons, eds., *Rossiia XX vek: Dokumenty; Molotov, Malenkov, Kaganovich, 1957* [Moscow: Mezhdunarodnyi fond "Demokratiia," 1997], 452).

existed throughout the first postwar year and exposed large segments of the population, for the first time in their lives, to a rival cohesive movement. First were the young activists of the Organization of Ukrainian Nationalists (OUN), then the two factions OUN-M (Mel'nyk faction) and OUN-B (Bandera faction), and, later, the large and well-organized detachments of the Ukrainian Insurgent Army (UPA)—each sustained by a coherent ideology that placed the rural Ukrainian populace at its center. The presence of competing alternatives turned Vinnytsia into a testing ground for the viability of the three decades of sovietization in the face of a formidable challenge. Chapter 6 studies the war's role in inculcating a workable framework of Soviet patriotism and Ukrainian particularism in the Vinnytsia countryside and bringing about a thorough sovietization of the peasantry, the Achilles' heel of Soviet society.

Finally, I conclude the discussion by posing two questions fundamental to the Soviet experience in general, and to the aftermath of the war in particular: Was there a venue for Soviet citizens to make sense of the war with tools other than those offered by Soviet power? Could the powerful myth of the war survive the Soviet trademark yet tenuous coexistence between universal and particularistic identities? The afterword answers these haunting questions and, in doing so, sheds light on the strengths and weaknesses of the Soviet system in the wake of the war.

The Making of a Revolutionary Myth: War and Thermidor

The Revolution has a beginning. It has no end.[5]

The Second World War affected every Soviet individual, family, and community. The sheer magnitude of this unprecedented cataclysm touched all, whether at the front or in evacuation, anti-German resistance or collaboration. It is no surprise that participants from all walks of life set out to record their experience, and Soviet historians responded in kind by producing many memoirs and histories. One community, however, seemed determined to avoid the subject of the war: American students of Soviet history. Among the voluminous writings on the October Revolution, the civil war, the Great Break, the Terror, and the cold war, the few social and political histories of the Soviet-German conflict reflected a reading of this event as an inexplicable intrusion on more important processes that shaped the Revolution and the Soviet polity.

---

[5] *Nikto ne zabyt, nichto ne zabyto: iz opyta raboty komiteta komsomola Vinnitskogo meduchilishcha imeni akademika D. K. Zabolotnogo po voenno-patrioticheskomu vospitaniiu uchashchik-*

This was not always the case. During the first postwar decade, students of the Soviet Union seemed well aware of the centrality of the war in Soviet politics and in the lives of Soviet citizens. Already in the first major study of the Soviet postwar polity, Julian Towster highlighted the impact of the recent war on the makeup of political and social institutions.[6] The study of the war and its consequences appeared to be off to a promising start, with Towster's work followed by several seminal monographs that have stood the test of time, and all written, not incidentally, by a now practically extinct school of political scientist-historians.[7] The impact of the war and its emerging cult were too powerful to be ignored by scholars. Remarkably enough, however, they soon were. When the fiftieth anniversary of the war's end was commemorated in 1995, the dearth of publications by Western scholars about the Soviet theater stood in glaring contrast to the avalanche of monographs and memoirs on practically all other theaters of the war. This disparity was only magnified by the fact that some of the best of these few works were written by outsiders to the Soviet field, British specialists in German and European wartime history who do not even command any Slavic languages.[8]

An effort to recover the war as a central theme in Soviet history requires an inquiry into the reasons it was relegated to the margins of historiography. Lack of sources could hardly account for this drought in the study of the war and its aftermath. On the contrary, the Soviets as well as émigré

---

hsia (Vinnytsia, 1986). This is a slogan from a propaganda brochure prepared by a Komsomol cell in Vinnytsia.

[6] Among other things, Towster noted that the awards for wartime performance turned the Soviet people into the greatest title-bearing nation in the world. By 1 October 1944 there were already nearly 2.9 million people decorated with government orders and medals (Julian Towster, *Political Power in the USSR, 1917–1947* [New York: Oxford University Press, 1948], 329 n. 52).

[7] See John Armstrong, *Ukrainian Nationalism, 1939–1945* (New York: Columbia University Press, 1955); John Armstrong, ed., *Soviet Partisans in World War II* (Madison: University of Wisconsin Press, 1964); Alexander Dallin, *German Rule in Russia, 1941–1945: A Study of Occupation Policies* (London: Macmillan, 1957); Merle Fainsod, *How Russia Is Ruled* (Cambridge, Mass.: Harvard University Press, 1953); and Barrington Moore, *Soviet Politics: The Dilemma of Power* (Cambridge, Mass.: Harvard University Press, 1950). Alexander Werth's classic *Russia at War* (New York: Avon, 1964) is still an indispensable study of the private and public sentiment during the war years.

[8] See Antony Beevor, *Stalingrad* (London: Penguin, 1998); and Richard Overy, *Russia's War: A History of the Soviet War Effort, 1941–1945* (London: Penguin, 1997). One unfortunate caveat about these otherwise superb studies, especially Beevor's study, is the lack of a rounded, nuanced examination of the Soviet soldier at the individual level. One cannot escape the thought that, despite the impressive use of a wide range of sources, both authors were limited by the lack of command of the Russian language (and their primary specialization in German and European history), requiring them to rely on selective material and the good will of Russian colleagues. The result is a much fuller account of the German side.

communities have produced a multitude of histories and memoirs of the war, and the contemporary Soviet press and government decrees were available to Western researchers. The same types of sources that furnished the voluminous literature on the first two decades of the Bolshevik Revolution were there for interested scholars, and in a much greater number.[9] Moreover, the Germans left voluminous and meticulous documentation of Soviet society under their occupation, ranging from an analysis of local power structures and politics to populations, moods, and reactions to Soviet power, their own policies, and wartime changes.

Alas, few were interested. The dominant voices in Western historiography have argued for the primacy of socioeconomic structures and have subscribed to the view that the experiences of the 1920s and early 1930s constituted the formative and enduring moments in the Soviet polity. Within the dichotomy drawn between socioeconomic structures and political-ideological domains, the war was accorded the status of a mere *événement* in the *longue durée*. It was thus relegated to studies of military operations devoid of social, political, or ideological context,[10] and to a handful of monographs mainly by students of Soviet high politics, science, and literature. In this light, it was not surprising that the 1985 publication of a collection of essays on the impact of the war on Soviet society and politics hardly made an impact on Soviet historiography—largely because of the interpretive thrust of some of the contributors' other writings.[11]

---

[9] A guide for Soviet publications between 1941 and 1967 dealing with the war cited more than eight thousand items (A. I. Babin et al., *SSSR v gody Velikoi Otechestvennoi voiny [iiun' 1941–sentiabr' 1945]*, 3 vols. [Moscow: Nauka, 1977–81]). In 1950 alone, the Soviets published 7,831 newspapers, 1,408 journals and periodicals, and 40,000 books, a rather impressive body of literature on contemporary politics and society (Timothy Dunmore, *Soviet Politics, 1945–1953* [New York: St. Martin's, 1984], 3).

[10] See, for example, the immense body of work by David Glantz, such as *When Titans Clashed: How the Red Army Stopped Hitler* (Lawrence: Kansas University Press, 1995); and the more rounded study by Albert Seaton, *The Russo-German War, 1941–1945* (New York: Praeger, 1971).

[11] Compare, for example, Sheila Fitzpatrick's incisive "Postwar Soviet Society: The Return to Normalcy, 1945–1953," in Susan J. Linz, ed., *The Impact of World War II on the Soviet Union* (Totowa, N.J.: Rowman and Allanheld, 1985), 129–56, to the main body of her work, where the war and its aftermath are either beyond the realm of the revolutionary narrative or, when dealt with, are dismissed as merely an era of continuities of prewar policies and structures (Sheila Fitzpatrick, *The Russian Revolution* [New York: Oxford University Press, 1982; 2d ed., 1994]; Fitzpatrick, "Stalin and the Making of a New Elite," *Slavic Review* [September 1979]: 377–402; Fitzpatrick, *Stalin's Peasants: Resistance and Survival in the Russian Village after Collectivization* [New York: Oxford University Press, 1996], 313–20). The same applies to Moshe Lewin's *The Gorbachev Phenomenon: A Historical Interpretation* (Berkeley: University of California Press, 1988). Interestingly, in his review of Lewin's writings, Roland Lew noted that despite Lewin's having experienced the war personally and having been motivated by the war to study Soviet history, he nevertheless downplayed the significance of this event in his analysis of the Soviet experience (Roland Lew, "Grappling

The study of the war and its aftermath turned out to be another casualty of the paradigm of *Thermidor*, the term assigned to the demise of the revolutionary drive in late-eighteenth-century France and applied to all subsequent revolutions. Reluctant to accept the legitimacy of the Stalinist claim of having enacted the fundamentals of the revolutionary premise— the abolition of the market, the establishment of partocracy, and the destruction of alien classes—historians followed Trotsky's footsteps in declaring the Revolution over by the mid-1930s, when the Stalinist regime enacted a series of policies in favor of consolidation and stability at the expense of radical experiments on both the domestic and international fronts. The Revolution was pronounced dead, too young and innocent to bear the responsibility for the atrocities that were later committed in its name.[12] Thus the Soviets were informed by foreign scholars that the Revolution was over at the very time it was gathering momentum and consequently that the impact of the war the Soviets were so keen to highlight actually amounted to nothing.[13] Nor did the turn to "cultural" history or the rediscovery of ideology, both of which extended the chronological boundaries of Soviet historiography, encourage a reevaluation of the war and its legacy. The war has still been viewed as an isolated event, albeit interesting, bereft of any long-standing impact on the structures of Soviet life and irrelevant to the evolution of socialist ideology.[14]

Nevertheless, when read closely, the Thermidorian framework is critical to the reintegration of the war into the history of the Revolution. Thermi-

---

with Soviet Realities: Moshe Lewin and the Making of Social History," in Nick Lampert and Gabor Rittersporn, eds., *Stalinism: Its Nature and Aftermath: Essays in Honor of Moshe Lewin* [Armonk, N.Y.: M. E. Sharpe, 1992], 11).

[12] Leon Trotsky, *The Revolution Betrayed: What Is the Soviet Union and Where Is It Going?* (New York: Doubleday, Doran, 1936); and Nikolai Timasheff, *The Great Retreat: The Growth and Decline of Communism in Russia* (New York: Dutton, 1946).

[13] The war's impact is, of course, examined in the few monographs that treat popular reactions to mobilization, evacuation, and siege. However, these studies limit their assessment of the impact of the war to the war years and assign an unconditional primacy to social conditions and survival over the political-ideological domain in daily life. The result is that contemporary Soviet citizens, party members included, are deprived of the very beliefs and biases that largely shaped their reactions to the calamity of the war. See John Barber and Mark Harrison, *The Soviet Home Front, 1941–1945: A Social and Economic History of the USSR in World War II* (New York: Longman, 1991); Richard Bidlack, *Workers at War: Factory Workers and Labor Policy in the Siege of Leningrad, The Carl Beck Papers*, no. 902 (March 1991); Richard Brody, *Ideology and Political Mobilization: The Soviet Home Front during World War II, The Carl Beck Papers*, no. 1104 (October 1994).

[14] Richard Stites, ed., *Culture and Entertainment in Wartime Russia* (Bloomington, Ind.: Indiana University Press, 1995). The war does not figure prominently in the two main works that have done more than any others to dismantle the paradigm of Thermidor. Martin Malia's *Soviet Tragedy: A History of Socialism in Russia, 1917–1991* (New York: Free Press, 1994) loses its narrative momentum at this particular time, regaining it only with the begin-

dor in history has gained a dual meaning. For French contemporaries, it meant merely the end of the revolutionary terror. Not surprisingly, the renunciation of mass terror as an alien phenomenon to France's original cause in 1793 and that of the Soviet Union in 1953 were literally identical. "This cannibal horde / Which hell vomits from its womb / Preaches murder and carnage! It is covered with your blood!" proclaimed a Thermidorian song in France.[15] "A meat-mincer, butchery, and blood bath," echoed Nikita Khrushchev, referring to the terror of 1937.[16] In both representations the terror was excised from the revolutionary myth, hand in hand with the reaffirmation of the rest of the revolutionary principles. The removal of the terror was the ultimate affirmation of the just Revolution. Neither the French nor the Soviets advocated a return to the prerevolutionary world; instead, both claimed to salvage the Revolution and continue its progress, only on a more popular and civil basis. In neither case, however, was a pluralistic political arena imagined. The mythology of a homogenized sociopolitical and national body, the most acclaimed achievement of the terror, continued to be the pillar for the post-terror order. For contemporaries, in a word, ending the terror did not imply the end of the Revolution.

As Bronislaw Baczko aptly observed, the terror in France had an afterlife in which, as institutions and personnel were further dismantled, the question shifted from *how to finish with the Terror* to *how to terminate the Revolution*? This, however, required the articulation of a new, positive institutional and constitutional order, an inconceivable notion for Soviet rulers and ruled alike until the very end of the Soviet polity. Thermidor could not be partial. The moderation of certain revolutionary concepts and means did not alter the fundamentals of a single-party system, a nonmarket economy, a welfare system from cradle to grave, and, not least of all, the obsession with the purification of the polity. And as long as the outside world was perceived as an actively hostile antithesis to the socialist utopia, there was hardly any room for a substantive change in the domestic arena.[17]

---

ning of the Soviet decline, and Stephen Kotkin's *Magnetic Mountain: Stalinism as a Civilization* (Berkeley: University of California, 1995) ends on the eve of the war.

[15] Bronislaw Baczko, *Ending the Terror: The French Revolution after Robespierre*, trans. Michel Petheram (Cambridge: Cambridge University Press, 1994), 212.

[16] Khrushchev, *Khrushchev Remembers*, 82, 89.

[17] Baczko, *Ending the Terror*, 224, 251. This was bound to change when external ethical and political systems turned from antitheses into sources of inspiration. It was an irony of history that in both France and the Soviet Union the revolutionary order was on its way out once the American arrangement of a bicameral, representative system was invoked in debates over the future order of society, instead of the usual mimicking of American production methods and popular culture. In this sense, Thermidor as a full-blown alternative could not have occurred before December 1991, when the communist leadership acknowledged that

The war, in this light, was not only a part of the revolutionary era but, in more ways than one, the postwar and the post-Stalin eras epitomized the undiminished impetus for revolutionary transformation. These decades were marked by grandiose plans to transform nature and to abolish the last residues of market relations in the national economy. Khrushchev, in turn, launched the Virgin Lands campaign in 1954–56, revived the late Stalinist concept of "communism in our lifetime," advanced communal surveillance to an unprecedented degree, and set out to convince the collective farm peasants to give up their household plots. The war and its aftermath could not be distinguished from the Revolution at large. As long as the revolutionary ethos retained its viability, it was the prism through which Soviet contemporaries made sense of the cataclysmic events that shaped their lives.

The Revolution, as experienced by contemporaries, members of the political elite, and ordinary citizens alike, was a constantly unfolding enterprise with the imposition of a linear evolution toward the ultimate goal of communism. The road to communism was punctuated by a series of traumatic events that both shaped and were shaped by the revolutionary project. Within this chain of cataclysms, the war was universally perceived as the Armageddon of the Revolution, the ultimate clash dreaded yet expected by the first generation to live in a socialist society, the event that would either vindicate or bring down the system, depending on one's views and expectations.[18]

---

the Revolution had exhausted itself and that they, the revolutionaries, were unwilling to start it all over again or even try to resuscitate it. The myth of social and political harmony and partocracy gave way to political and economic pluralism as the pillars of any future arrangement. For an insightful analysis of the final exit of the Soviet regime, as witnessed by political insiders, see Stephen Kotkin, "In Search of the Nomenklatura: Yesterday's USSR, Today's Russia," *East European Constitutional Review* 6, no. 4 (December 1997): 104–20.

[18] The present argument contrasts with the sole book-length study of the cult of the war, Nina Tumarkin's *The Living and the Dead: The Rise and Fall of the Cult of World War II in Russia* (New York: Basic Books, 1994). Tumarkin views the cult as a typical heavy-handed Soviet attempt to impose a single meaning onto a complex and diverse human experience. The state-orchestrated veneration of the war is depicted as a manipulation designed to mobilize support for a failing political and economic system steadily losing its legitimacy. This crude and increasingly bombastic enterprise erased the blunders of early defeats, desertion, collaboration, and the sense of emancipation in the trenches of the front, and the unique Jewish fate at the hands of the Germans. All true, except that such an explanation deprives the articulators of the war's myth of any belief but for holding on to power. Similarly the dichotomy drawn between the public and the private domain is rather tenuous for a system that endured for such a long time to a large degree because of an effective fusion of personal and public imagination. Such an admission, however, was unlikely from Tumarkin's main sources: Moscow and Leningrad intellectuals during the swan song of the Soviet polity. One is left wondering what their view was at the time of the event and its immediate aftermath. Nor, as we shall see below, was the Soviets' belated engagement of the traumas of defeat and

Hence the first step in understanding the role the war played in the articulation of Soviet political identities entails a shift in focus to the politics of myth. Whereas Marxist eschatology and millenarianism provided the Soviet polity with historical meaning by situating it in the context of a perceived human destiny, that polity was legitimized by certain myths, such as those of the civil war, the collectivization and industrialization drives, and the Great Patriotic War, which related it to concrete historical situations. These mythical representations were often referred to as historical turning points and constituted frameworks for meaning that ordained them with a structure for both understanding and accepting change.[19] Significantly these myths have been major tools in the perennial rearrangement of social and political hierarchies within the Soviet world. The narration of Soviet myths, like practically all other political myths, was rather simple, yet politically explosive. To paraphrase the colorful words of Isaiah Berlin, since mankind was assumed a priori to be divided between good sheep and dangerous goats, social and political life was propelled by evil conspiracies and cataclysmic struggles in which the liquidation of the irredeemable goats was viewed as a service to humanity.[20] And each triumph brought the millennium closer, none more than the Great Patriotic War.

The ordination of the war as a climactic watershed in the Soviet epic originated from none other than the Soviet authorities. In a speech to the Tenth Plenary Session of the Union of Soviet Writers on 15 May 1945, Nikolai Tikhonov, the Union's secretary, went out of his way to mark the war as a transformative event for Soviet Man. "The war is over," Tikhonov told the writers. "The man of our country confidently looks to the future. Each tied his fate to the cause of the victory, each was at his military post.... This man with weapons in hands marched the long road from Stalingrad to Berlin on the roads of the war. Not only did the landscape change along

---

collaboration unique when compared to other societies that went through even less traumatic experiences. Finally, if one can infer from the adoption of the day Minsk was liberated from German occupation as Independence Day in Belarus or the centrality of the 9 May (V-Day) in present day Ukraine and Russia, the myth of the war is alive and well.

[19] For an incisive treatment of the structure and role of myth, see Leszek Kolakowski, *The Presence of Myth* (Chicago: University of Chicago Press, 1989). See also the excellent studies in Katerina Clark, *Petersburg: Crucible of Cultural Revolution* (Cambridge, Mass.: Harvard University Press, 1995); Richard Wortman, *Scenarios of Power: Myth and Ceremony in the Russian Monarchy*, 2 vols. (Princeton, N.J.: Princeton University Press, 1995 [Vol. 1]; 2000 [Vol. 2]); and Yael Zerubavel, *Recovered Roots: Collective Memory and the Making of Israeli National Tradition*, (Chicago: University of Chicago Press, 1995).

[20] Isaiah Berlin, "Marxism and the International in the Nineteenth Century," in Berlin, *The Sense of Reality* (London: Chatto and Windus, 1996), 116–67, esp. 139, 141–42. See also David Kertzer, *Politics and Symbols: The Italian Communist Party and the Fall of Communism* (New Haven: Yale University Press, 1996), 16–40.

these roads, but so, too, did he. His inner world came to light." If Tikhonov focused on the impact of this singular event on the makeup of the Soviet Man, he by no means viewed it in isolation from the Soviet experience as a whole. "The Soviet Man, the soldier-liberator, created by the great land of the Soviets, molded by the party of Lenin-Stalin, carries in him the high principles of our progressive Bolshevik idea, embodies the best features of a man of the Stalinist era."[21]

The theme was picked up by Andrei Zhdanov in his famous speech on 21 September 1946, which became the canon for the rest of the Stalinist era. Zhdanov's lecture, in Katerina Clark's observation, elevated the war "to the status of a second revolution in the roster of Great Moments—a revolution that had wrought a *qualitative* change in Soviet man."[22] "With each day our people attain an ever higher level," stated Zhdanov. "Today we are not the people we were yesterday, and tomorrow we will not be as we were today. We are already not the same Russians we were before 1917. Russia is not the same, and our character has changed too."[23] The war, in Zhdanov's formulation, had its own singular input into the shaping of the New Man, but it derived its meaning from the revolutionary eschatology. It was, in a word, a weighty link in the revolutionary chain.

Bolshevik myths, however, were subjected not only to periodic redefinition but, as happened to most prewar myths, to repudiation. To understand the changing fate of core Soviet myths, we must examine how a myth is made, starting with the experience and expectations of those on whom it was supposed to operate, as well as the mechanisms that sustained and subverted its hold on the population. Thus the myth of the war built on the evident failure of civil war methods during the early days of the war, the ambiguous legacy of collectivization, and the absence of exposure to a viable and attractive alternative from without. By no means were these unprecedented circumstances in history. Unlike most other movements and regimes, however, the Soviets operated for an extensive period in a thoroughly Manichean world, endured long enough, and preserved an undiminished will to carry the logic of their enterprise to its conclusion.[24]

[21] Nikolai Tikhonov, *Pered novym pod"emom: Sovetskaia literatura v 1944–45 gg.* (Moscow: Literaturnaia gazeta, 1945), 2, 4.

[22] Katerina Clark, *The Soviet Novel: History as Ritual* (Chicago: Chicago University Press, 1981), 198.

[23] Ibid.

[24] In their discussion of the viability of dominant myths, both Stephen Kotkin and Richard Wortman convincingly establish the link between perceptions of viable competing myths in the international arena and the cohesion of the ruling elites at home. Just as the global crisis of the 1930s elevated the appeal, cohesiveness, and steady course of the Soviet messianic drive at home, so did the rhetoric and imagery of the French Revolution and the diminishing influence of Russia in Europe trigger the erosion of belief among the Imperial Russian elite. See Kotkin, *Magnetic Mountain*; and Wortman, *Scenarios of Power.*

Cataclysmic events are naturalized and integrated into the lives of men and women through an elaborate set of rituals, many of them so banal that they are hardly noticeable. This is also the source of their tremendous power. Almost from the moment of commencement the myth of the war became a central feature in the world of Soviet citizens through a myriad of rites and rituals that shaped daily calendars from cradle to grave and constantly reminded people of the war, turning them into ex post facto participants in this event. The Soviet landscape was plastered with monuments, choreographed cemeteries, collective farms, and streets that bore the names of battles, heroes, and dates of the great event. Literature, music, and cinema witnessed an avalanche of war anthologies, memoirs, poems, albums, and films that celebrated this epic event.[25] The war was impossible to ignore.

Finally, if the initial appeal of a new myth draws its power from the erosion of old ones, its endurance depends to a large degree on the political power of the social group with whom it is associated. Changes in the political fortunes of the articulators and transmitters of the myth often lead to its reevaluation, or at least some of its components, as seen through the fate of the Soviet civil war ethos and heroes.[26] The hegemonic status of the myth of the war cannot be traced solely to the Soviet state and its propaganda machine, but at least as much to the identity of the articulators of the myth in the localities, the peasant-soldiers, for whom the war turned

[25] The Commission for the History of the War was established by a decree of the Presidium of the Academy of Sciences of the USSR as early as 15 January 1942, under the supervision of a Central Committee's commission. The gathering of commemorative material on the war was initiated by Shcherbakov in the wake of the battle of Moscow in the winter of 1941 (A. A. Kurnosov, "Vospominaniia-interv'iu v fonde komissii po istorii Velikoi Otechestvennoi voiny Akademii Nauk SSSR," *Arkheograficheskii ezhegodnik za 1973 g.* (1974): 118–32; and N. S Arkhangorodskaia and A. A. Kurnosov, "O sozdanii komissii po istorii Velikoi Otechestvennoi voiny AN SSSR i ee arkhiva," *Arkheograficheskii ezhegodnik za 1981 g.* (1982): 219–29.) For original studies of the commemoration of the October Revolution, see Frederick Corney, "Rethinking a Great Event: The October Revolution as Memory Project," *Social Science History* 20, no. 4 (1998): 12–28; and James Von Geldern, *Bolshevik Festivals, 1917–1920* (Berkeley: University of California Press, 1993). Following George Mosse's pioneering *Nationalization of the Masses* (New York: Fertig, 1975), scholars of Italian history in particular point the way in a series of remarkable studies of rituals. See especially Simonetta Falasca-Zamponi, *The Fascist Spectacle: The Aesthetics of Power in Mussolini's Italy* (Berkeley: University of California Press, 1997); Emilio Gentile, *The Sacralization of Politics in Fascist Italy* (Cambridge, Mass.: Harvard University Press, 1996); and Kerzer, *Politics and Symbols*.

[26] Such a phenomenon modifies Karl Mannheim's influential paradigm in which he identified the formation of sociological generations, as distinguished from biological ones, as the reaction of young people as a group to cataclysmic events in their youth. The inapplicability of traditional means to solve a given crisis forced the articulation of a new and distinctive reaction that shaped the worldview of the group for the rest of their lives (Karl Mannheim, *Essays on the Sociology of Knowledge* [London: Routledge & Kegan Paul, 1952], 276–322).

into an autobiographical point of reference and point of departure.[27] This
somewhat populist assumption, less than obvious at first glance in the
context of the highly stylized Soviet system, points to a powerful institution that allowed for particularistic expressions: personal bonding in the
making of elites. Students of the non-Russian republics, in particular, noticed that the Soviet system was marked by weak (impersonal) structures
and strong (personal) ties. Power was often exercised on a personal, familial, and clan level. Common background and experiences prevailed in the
formation of elites and political alliances.[28] The powerful presence of the
war in the lives of so many guaranteed that the myth would eventually
outlive the Soviet polity itself.

The Armageddon of Revolution:
Aesthetic Violence and Soviet Millenarianism

If they will not understand that we are bringing
them a mathematically infallible happiness, we
shall be obliged to force them to be happy.[29]

This book situates the Second World War firmly within the overarching
feature of the Soviet enterprise: the revolutionary transformation of society from an antagonistically divided entity into a conflict-free, harmonious
body. The war was followed by an acceleration in the continuous purification campaign that sought the elimination of divisive and counterproduc-
tive elements. Exclusion and violence, in this light, were not random or
preventive policing measures that delineated the boundaries of the legiti-

[27] Referring to the impact exercised by "the kind of history that common men carry in
their heads," Carl Becker noted that it was particularly noticeable "in times of excitement,
in critical times, in time of war above all. It is precisely in such times that they form (with
the efficient help of official propaganda!) an idealized picture of the past, born of their emo-
tions and desires working on fragmentary scraps of knowledge gathered, or rather flowing
upon them, from every conceivable source, reliable or not matters nothing" (Carl Becker,
"What are Historical Facts?" in Phil L. Snyder, ed., *Detachment and the Writing of History:
Essays and Letters of Carl L. Becker* [Ithaca: Cornell University Press, 1958], 61–62).

[28] See John A. Armstrong, *The Soviet Bureaucratic Elite: A Case Study of the Ukrainian
Apparatus* (New York: Praeger, 1959); Jan Gross, *Revolution from Abroad: The Soviet Conquest of Poland's Western Ukraine and Western Belorussia* (Princeton, N.J.: Princeton University Press, 1988); Boris Lewytzkyi, *Die Sowjetukraine, 1944–1963* (Cologne: Kiepenheuer
and Witsch 1964); T. H. Rigby, "Crypto-Politics," *Survey* 50 (1964): 192–93; and Michael
Urban, *An Algebra of Soviet Power: Elite Circulation in the Belorussian Republic 1966–1986*
(Cambridge: Cambridge University Press, 1989).

[29] Yevgeny Zamyatin, *We* (New York: Penguin, 1993), 3.

mate and the permissible; rather, they were integral parts of the ongoing enterprise of community structuring.[30]

I trace the rationale of the Soviet Marxist quest for purity through three crucial components: the correlation between the progression of the revolutionary time line and the measures taken to realize the socialist utopia, the impact of Nazism and capitalism on the Soviet political and social calculus, and the forms of excision employed. Undoubtedly, circumstances such as the brutal experiences of civil war, collectivization, famines, Terror, and, above all, world war exerted an undeniable impact on the evolution of the Soviet purification drive. As each campaign charged ahead, new enemies were created and eradicated. Similarly, institutions such as the political police and its GULAG empire had a vested interest in a permanent and ever expanding purge, if only because of the self-serving motives of increasing their budget, manpower, economic clout, or all three. Yet neither circumstances nor institutional interests explain why the Soviets reacted in the unique way they did to the same circumstances experienced by other polities, why their unique punitive organs were created in the first place, and why the regime pursued its purification campaigns well after the conditions that initiated them had dissipated.

The answers to these haunting questions lie in the ethos that shaped Soviet beliefs and practices. As early as 1896 Georg Simmel drew attention to the aesthetic nature of the socialist enterprise. Placing socialism firmly within the modern tendency to organize "all of society symmetrically and equally structured according to general principles," Simmel pointed to the dual functions of socialism, that of control and coordination along with aesthetic urges and desire for harmony. Rejecting the popular view that reduced socialist utopia exclusively to the needs of the stomach, and consequently to the ethical dimension, Simmel pointed instead to the conflict between socialistic and individualistic tendencies as the origin of socialist aesthetics:

[30] For insightful treatments of the inherent relationship between violence and attempts to implement utopian enterprises, see Hannah Arendt, *The Origins of Totalitarianism* (New York: Harcourt, Brace, 1951); Zygmunt Bauman, *Modernity and the Holocaust* (Ithaca: Cornell University Press, 1991); Saul Friedländer, *Nazi Germany and the Jews*, Vol. 1: *The Years of Persecution, 1933–1939* (New York: HarperCollins, 1997), chap. 3; Peter Holquist, "To Count, to Extract, to Exterminate: Population Statistics and Population Politics in Late Imperial and Soviet Russia," paper presented at the workshop "Empire and Nation in the Soviet Union," University of Chicago, 24–26 October 1997; Kotkin, *Magnetic Mountain*; Leszek Kolakowski, *Main Currents of Marxism*, 3 vols. (Oxford: Clarendon, 1978); Claude Lefort, *The Political Forms of Modern Society: Bureaucracy, Democracy, Totalitarianism* (Cambridge: Polity Press, 1986), chaps. 8–9; Malia, *The Soviet Tragedy*; and Andrzej Walicki, *Marxism and the Leap to the Kingdom of Freedom: The Rise and Fall of the Communist Utopia* (Stanford: Stanford University Press, 1995).

That society as a whole should become a work of art in which every single element attains its meaning by virtue of its contribution to the whole; that a unified plan should rationally determine all of production, instead of the present rhapsodic haphazardness by which the efforts of individuals benefit or harm society; that the wasteful competition of individuals against individuals should be replaced by the absolute harmony of work—all these ideas of socialism no doubt meet aesthetic interests . . .[31]

Simmel prophetically concluded that "this general trait of socialistic plans attests to the deep power of attraction in the idea of a harmonious, internally balanced organization of human activity *overcoming all resistance of irrational individuality.* This interest, a purely, formal aesthetic one, *independent of all material consequences*, has probably always been important in determining the social forms of life."[32] The logic of the quest for harmony would crystallize when socialism crossed the threshold from being a protest movement into becoming a political power. The construction of a harmonious society in the Soviet Union would be defined by a constant and relentless campaign to eradicate the intruding elements.

In the wake of the cataclysmic war, social and political harmony became the motto in Stalinist self-representations. The party's leading theoretical and political journals credited the war with forging a kinship of blood between Communists and nonparty people that was proclaimed to be the most important feature of a society already displaying communist characteristics. Yet the celebration of the liquidation of antagonistic contradictions and the establishment of *moral-political unity*—the favored Soviet term for harmony—was accompanied by an ominous warning. The serenity of the postwar world was still being violated by individuals who retained vestiges of the old world in their conscience, and, to make matters worse, were entrusted with leading positions. Hence postwar cleansing would acquire an additional edge.[33]

---

[31] Georg Simmel, "Soziologische Aesthetik," *Die Zukunft* 17 (1896): 208, 209–10.

[32] Ibid., 210–11 (my emphasis). For pioneering studies on the aesthetic context of the Soviet experience, see Boris Groys, *The Total Art of Stalinism: Avant-Garde, Aesthetic Dictatorship, and Beyond* (Princeton, N.J.: Princeton University Press, 1992); and Katerina Clark, *Petersburg.* It seems no accident that both authors are literary critics and not historians by discipline.

[33] V. Ozerov, "Obraz bol'shevika v poslevoennoi sovetskoi literature," *Bol'shevik* 10 (May 1949): 60–61, 66. In postwar Soviet literature, the doctrine of "conflictlessness," though not beyond contemporaries' criticism, paraded social structures and incidents in which conflicts involved people who operated within the system, not outside or against it, and consequently were resolved in the establishment of harmonious relations. See Clark, *The Soviet Novel*, 189–209; and Vera Dunham, *In Stalin's Time: Middleclass Values in Soviet Fiction* (Cambridge: Cambridge University Press, 1976). Similarly political art conveyed the message that the polity was entering a classless world of serenity, beauty, and harmony. Soviet political posters advanced the notion of a climax, a final destination on a linear path that

Several years after the triumphant conclusion of the war, with the prospect of reaching communism seeming brighter than ever, a leading Soviet theoretician concurred with Marx and Engels:

> A communist revolution is necessary not only to overthrow the rule of the exploiting classes and to liberate the working masses but also for the cleansing of people from the filth of the old world. The history of the Great October Socialist Revolution and the socialist construction in the USSR shows how systematically, step by step, this vital cleansing process is taking place, how in the course of desperate class struggles between the exploiters and exploited a new man is born—a man of the communist society, with a totally new worldview and a new moral-political makeup . . . Under the conditions of socialism the personality is molded, developed, and functions in the historically unprecedented atmosphere of the moral-political unity of Soviet society.[34]

We shall soon return to the war. But even well before the outbreak of war, it became evident that the road to purity and harmony would be extremely violent, both reflecting and leading the way for cleansing policies in other political systems while carving its own unique path. Unlike Italian fascism, the Soviet aesthetic enterprise was much more than an urge to stylize social life; it literally cut into the flesh of its own subjects.[35] And unlike German Nazism, Soviet aesthetics did not gloss over residues of the old world in the souls and minds of the subjects. All had to be engaged in the purifica-

---

progressed through hardship, violence, and crudity until it reached its goal (Victoria Bonnell, *Iconography of Power: Soviet Political Posters under Lenin and Stalin* [Berkeley: University of California Press, 1997], 243–44).

[34] M. D. Kammari, *Marksizm-leninizm o roli lichnosti v istorii* (Moscow: Gos. izd-vo. polit. lit-ry, 1953), 235. Looking back at the fate of the Revolution, Viacheslav Molotov, Stalin's most loyal lieutenant, observed with unconcealed disdain the false pretense of the post-Stalin leadership to reach communism via an evolutionary, peaceful path:

> The task of elimination of social classes is arduous and revolutionary. But 'we are building communism' is only a lame excuse for avoiding this question and an effort to escape revolutionary tasks. Communism, they say there [at the top], springs on its own as classes are eliminated. This is a typical rightist position. There is no need to eliminate the kulak, he will do it himself. Here we have the morality of the rightists: 'Let us find an explanation for needless cruelty; we must be humanists, and laws must be obeyed.' But this morality is not revolutionary . . . The whole point is that you cannot arrive at communism without having resolved this question. (*Sto sorok besed s Molotovym: iz dnevnika F. Chueva* [Moscow: Terra, 1991], 483, 490)

[35] In her fascinating study of fascist aesthetics, Falasca-Zamponi, who projected Simmel's observations on socialism onto fascism, proceeds to discuss the central role of violence in Italian fascist aesthetics. Without downplaying the domestic brutality of Italian fascism, the fact remains that the most systematic violence was applied against external foes, as occurred in the Ethiopian campaign, rather than against internal opponents of the regime (Falasca-Zamponi, *The Fascist Spectacle*, 28–38).

tion campaign, either as purgers or purged and often as both. It was practically inconceivable to expect in the Soviet Union anything like Himmler's
speech in Posen in October 1943, in which the architect of the "Final
Solution" emphasized the historical necessity of the extermination of the
Jewish vermin—side by side with the acknowledgment of the survival of
inhibitions among the perpetrators ("And then they come 80 million worthy Germans, and each has his decent Jew. Of course the others are vermin,
but this one is an A-1 Jew"), the need to accommodate these inhibitions,
and, above all, the need to maintain integrity and decency in their bourgeois sense ("We had the moral right, we had the duty to our people, to
destroy this people . . . But we have not the right to enrich ourselves with
so much as a fur, a watch, a mark or a cigarette or anything else").[36] These
were not merely generalizations. Himmler was well aware of complaints
by none other than SS officers against excessive brutalities in the course
of deportation of Jews. The best way to prevent such excesses and the
impression of blindly raging sadists, wrote one such officer in Berlin,
would be adherence to form ("This does not exclude that, when time
comes, with all due form, one can occasionally give a Jew a kick in the
rear, but even then it should be done with decency") and compassion for
certain categories ("Among the [beaten] Jews there were Jewesses with
small children on their arm. This sight was both degrading and shameful").[37] In the Soviet polity entertaining much milder thoughts, let alone
expressing them, marked people as internal enemies.

Long before the war, under the auspices of formidable state punitive
institutions and extensive legislation, Soviet society evolved into a self-
policing organ; a large part of the Terror was conducted in public deliberations, with citizens attaching their signatures to denunciations of their
fellow citizens and having direct access to the coercive apparatus of the
state in exercising such acts.

Each and every member of the Soviet polity was expected to be an active
agent in the purification of himself and his surroundings. Power in the
Soviet polity was privatized, in the apt definition of Jan Gross. When the
regime launched its periodic cleansing operations, it invested both individuals and communities with the power to select the individuals who
would fill the imposed quota for imprisonment, deportation, or execution. The community, observed Gross, was condemned to be all powerful
and powerless at the same time. It could ruin a life or grant a stay of

---

[36] Office of United States Chief of Counsel for Prosecution of Axis Criminality, *Nazi
Conspiracy and Aggression* (Washington, D.C, 1946), 4:563–64.

[37] See the complaint of an SS officer against the beating of Jewish deportees in Berlin,
dated 4 March 1943, in John Steiner, *Power, Politics, and Social Change in National Socialist
Germany: A Process of Escalation into Mass Destruction* (Atlantic Highlands, N.J.: Humanities Press, 1976), 418–21.

execution in any individual case, but it could not lift the sentence: A certain number of its members had to be destroyed. The war, as we shall see below, was critical in advancing this policy.[38] Hence the Soviet drive to reconfigure society acquired its meaning not only from the unfolding logic of the party-state ideology and policies but equally from the daily practices of ordinary citizens who constantly sought to integrate themselves into the body politic via the institutions offered to them by the Soviet state.

Marxist regimes struggled with whether to assign primacy to either the "objective" category of class origin or the "subjective" criteria of conduct and experience. In polities founded on the Marxist premise of the primacy of acculturation, but simultaneously engaged in the constant eradication of social strata presumed to be illegitimate, the tension between nurture and nature was a constant.[39] It intensified as the Soviet polity advanced along the road to socialism and communism, and radicalized its purification policies both qualitatively and quantitatively. Following the Second World War, social and ethnic categories and practices were totalized in a marked shift: Enemy groups previously considered to be differentiated, reformable, and redeemable were now viewed as undifferentiated, unreformable, and irredeemable collectives. This totalization of the Marxist sociological paradigm challenged the commitment to the primacy of nurture over nature in the ongoing social engineering project, inviting comparison with contemporary biological-racial paradigms, most notably that

---

[38] Gross, 115–16, 120. See also Oleg Kharkhordin, *The Collective and the Individual in Russia: A Study of Practices* (Berkeley: University of California Press, 1999), for a fine discussion of communal surveillance during the Khrushchev and Brezhnev years; and Jean-François Lyotard, *The Postmodern Explained: Correspondence 1982–1985* (Minneapolis: University of Minnesota Press, 1992), 55–58, for an incisive commentary on the deliberative operation of Stalinist terror in comparison to the Nazi counterpart. For a similar phenomenon in Nazi Germany that resulted in a further increase in the capacity of the state to pursue its racial policies, see Robert Gellately, *The Gestapo and German Society* (Oxford: Clarendon, 1990); and Eric Johnson, *Nazi Terror: The Gestapo, Jews, and Ordinary Germans* (New York: Basic Books, 1999).

[39] On the prevalence of this dilemma in Stalinist Russia and the struggles of individuals to cope with it, see Kotkin, *Magnetic Mountain*, chaps. 5–6; Igal Halfin, "From Darkness to Light: Student Communist Autobiography during NEP," *Jahrbücher für Geschichte Osteuropas* 45 (1997): 210–36; and Jochen Hellbeck, "Fashioning the Stalinist Soul: The Diary of Stepan Podlubnyi," *Jahrbücher für Geschichte Osteuropas* 44 (1996): 344–73. On the tension between "class as political behavior" and "natural redness" in Communist China, see Lynn T. White III, *Policies of Chaos: The Organizational Causes of Violence in China's Cultural Revolution* (Princeton, N.J.: Princeton University Press, 1989), 222–25, 267; Richard Curt Kraus, *Class Conflict in Chinese Socialism* (New York: Columbia University Press, 1981), 89–141; and the contributions by Stuart Schram, Susan Shirk, Jonathan Unger, and Lynn White III, in James L. Watson, ed., *Class and Social Stratification in Post-Revolution China* (Cambridge: Cambridge University Press, 1984). See also Arendt's suggestive chapter "Race-Thinking before Racism," in her *Origins of Totalitarianism*, 150–84.

of Nazi Germany—a comparison the Soviets were well aware of yet wanted to avoid at all costs. The absence of genocidal ideology and institutions allowed for different modes and sites of total excision from the socioethnic body within the socialist utopia. Still, Soviet contemporaries continued to confront the ever-present shadow of the biological-racial ethos.

The Soviet purification drive operated on a universal-particularistic axis, combining the modern European ethos of social engineering with Bolshevik Marxist eschatology.[40] Their fusion created a stable menu of categories and practices, and a dynamic mode of applying them. The Soviet state emerged and operated within an ethos aptly named by Zygmunt Bauman the "gardening state," which appeared ever more universal in the wake of the Great War. This cataclysm brought to fruition the desires for a comprehensive plan to transform and manage society, one that would create a better, purer, and more beautiful community through the removal of unfit human weeds. It was, in a word, an aesthetic enterprise. The unprecedented increase in the capacities and aspirations of the state went hand in hand with the view of society as raw material to be molded into an ideal image. The transformation—or removal—of the individual and the community became the accepted goal of the state in both its welfare and punitive policies.[41]

[40] For overdue and successful attempts to contextualize Soviet population policies within the ethos of the Enlightenment era, see, on the welfare state, Kotkin, *Magnetic Mountain*; on the role of social-scientific disciplines, Yuri Slezkine, *Arctic Mirrors: Russia and the Small Peoples of the North* (Ithaca: Cornell University Press, 1994); Francine Hirsch, "Empire of Nations: Colonial Technologies and the Making of the Soviet Union, 1917–1939," Ph.D. dissertation, Princeton University, 1998; on the emerging "gardening" state, Peter Holquist, "Information Is the Alpha and Omega of Our Work: Bolshevik Surveillance in Its Pan-European Context," *Journal of Modern History* 69 (September 1997): 415–50; and, on the cross-ideological phenomenon of Romantic anticapitalism, Clark, *Petersburg*. In his intriguing analysis of political religion, Philippe Burrin concluded that totalitarian regimes (the political religions of communism, fascism, and Nazism) were incompatible with the course and demands of modernity, and were bound to disintegrate if only because their attempt to impose unanimity and undifferentiation went against the grain of centuries of European cultivation of the individual as an agent of his or her own salvation (Philippe Burrin, "Political Religion: The Relevance of a Concept," *History and Memory* 9, nos. 1/2 [fall 1997]: 342). However, one cannot gloss over the fact that the social, political, and economic institutions employed by totalitarian regimes for managing their populations were the epitome of modernity.

[41] See Giorgio Agamben, *Homo Sacer: Sovereign Power and Bare Life* (Stanford: Stanford University Press, 1998), 119–80; and Bauman, *Modernity and the Holocaust*, 65, 91–93. For a recent impressive treatment of the "gardening state" in various societies and ideologies, see James C. Scott, *Seeing Like a State: How Certain Schemes to Improve the Human Condition Have Failed* (New Haven: Yale University Press, 1998). Scott, however, approaches the "gardening state" as a starting point in the practice of social engineering schemes, glossing over the ways in which multiple agencies—including those conventionally considered liberal and progressive—initiated and often launched transformative schemes. This pattern was particularly noticeable in pre-Soviet Russia before the party-state consolidated its role as the

The impetus to sculpt society developed boundlessly and across ideologies. From Russia, Maxim Gorky observed in late November 1917 that "the working class is for Lenin what ore is for a metalworker . . . He [Lenin] works like a chemist in a laboratory, with the difference that the chemist uses dead matter . . . [whereas] Lenin works with living material."[42] But Bolshevik Marxism was not alone in its refusal to accept human nature and society as they were. Rather, the premise of the primacy of nurture over nature was encoded within the larger pan-European view of modernity whereby increasingly omnipresent political authorities sought to define and manage virtually all critical public and private spheres. The expanding welfare state and the cleansing state were opposite ends of the inclusionary-exclusionary axis, which became the trademark of transformative modern politics.[43] Beginning in the second half of the nineteenth century, the remapping of Europe evolved around so-called voluntary resettlement, population exchanges, or the unmixing of peoples, a rather polished, ex post facto legitimization of ethno-religious cleansing.[44]

---

sole organ of transformation. For the role of ethnographers in the shaping of population policies in Imperial Russia, see Slezkine, *Arctic Mirrors*, 95–129; Holquist "To Count, to Extract, To Remove"; and, for the role of military reformers, David Alan Rich, *The Tsar's Colonels: Professionalism, Strategy, and Subversion in Late Imperial Russia* (Cambridge, Mass.: Harvard University Press, 1999), esp. 29–64. For the continual impact of ethnographers in the Soviet polity during the prewar era, see Francine Hirsch, "The Soviet Union as a Work-in-Progress: Ethnographers and the Category *Nationality* in the 1926, 1937, and 1939 Censuses," *Slavic Review* 56, no. 2 (1997): 251–78.

[42] *Novaia zhizn'* 10, 23 November 1917, as cited in Maxim Gorky, *Untimely Thoughts: Essays on Revolution, Culture, and the Bolsheviks, 1917–1918*, trans. Herman Ermolaev (New Haven: Yale University Press, 1995), 89.

[43] Between 1935 and 1975 none other than the Swedish welfare state forced the sterilization of nearly sixty-three thousand people, mostly women, often because they were considered racially or socially inferior. About forty-five hundred mental patients were forced to undergo lobotomies under officially encouraged eugenics programs that started in the 1920s (Gunnar Broberg and Mattias Tyden, "Eugenics in Sweden: Efficient Care," in Broberg and Nils Roll-Hansen, eds., *Eugenics and the Welfare State: Sterilization Policy in Denmark, Sweden, Norway, and Finland* [East Lansing: Michigan State University Press, 1996], 109–10; *The Economist*, "A Survey of the Nordic Countries," 23 January 1999; *New York Times*, "Sweden Plans to Pay Sterilization Victims," 27 January 1999).

[44] The systematic uprooting of Muslims patterned after the conscious urge to reorder society and the increasing desire for ethno-religious homogeneity in the course of Imperial Russian consolidation of rule over Crimea and the Caucasus, along with the disintegration of the Ottoman Empire and the rise of Balkan nationalism, is considered a turning point in modern population policies. See Willis Brooks, "Russia's Conquest and Pacification of the Caucasus: Relocation Becomes a Pogrom in the Post-Crimean War Period," *Nationalities Papers* 23 (1995): 675–86; Rogers Brubaker, *Nationalism Reframed: Nationhood and the National Question in the New Europe* (Cambridge: Cambridge University Press, 1996), 152–56; Holquist, "To Count, to Extract, to Exterminate"; and Kemal Karpat, *Ottoman Population, 1830–1914* (Madison: University of Wisconsin Press, 1985), 65–75. For a stimulating discussion on the emergence and evolution of corporate expulsions carried out by the secular

By the late 1930s the chronological starting point of our discussion, the transformation of society, had already been established as a cross-ideological phenomenon, involving liberal, socialist, and fascist polities alike.[45] Thus in 1942 Eduard Benes, the figurehead of liberal democracy in Central Europe, could state as a matter of fact that "national minorities are always a real thorn in the side of individual nations" and that the ideal state of linguistic and national homogeneity could be reached only by extensive population transfers.[46] About two years later, in a meeting with Stalin, Benes concluded that "the defeat of Germany presents us with the singular historical possibility to radically clean out the German element in our state," a policy that was faithfully executed at the end of the war.[47] Tellingly, both American and British leaders who endorsed this massive population transfer were concerned mainly with its potential economic impact and orderly conduct. The uprooting of millions of people had already become an integral part of the political game, with everyone pointing to the successful Turkish-Greek precedent in the early 1920s as the proper example. Moral concerns were nowhere to be found. This powerful ethos would wane only in the mid-1950s, when exhaustion, exposure to the full magnitude of wartime atrocities, fears of continuous, limitless purges coupled with uprisings in the camps, and the rise of consumerism compelled European regimes and parties to accept some limits on their transformative powers.[48]

---

state striving for purity of its realm, see Benjamin Kedar, "Expulsion as an Issue of World History," *Journal of World History* 7, no. 2 (1996): 165–80.

[45] For an insightful analysis of this phenomenon, see Michael Geyer, "The Militarization of Europe, 1914–1945," in John Gillis, ed., *The Militarization of the Western World* (New Brunswick, N.J.: Rutgers University Press, 1989), 65–102; and Brubaker, *Nationalism Reframed*, 148–78. Whereas the origins and frequent use of mass population transfers were unmistakably European, they were soon adapted by postcolonial non-European regimes as well. Despite the passage of time and the new research on individual cases, Joseph Schechtman's work is still a good starting point. See his *European Population Transfers, 1939–1945* (New York: Oxford University Press, 1946); *Postwar Population Transfers in Europe, 1945–1955* (Philadelphia: University of Pennsylvania Press, 1962); and *Population Transfers in Asia* (New York: Hallsby Press, 1949). Also see István Deák, "Trying to Construct a Productive, Disciplined, Monoethnic Society: The Dilemma of East Central European Governments, 1914–1956"; Gordon Chang, "Social Darwinism versus Social Engineering: The Education of Japanese Americans during World War II"; and Norman Naimark, "Ethnic Cleansing between Peace and War," in Amir Weiner, ed., *Landscaping the Human Garden* (Stanford: Stanford University Press, forthcoming 2001).

[46] Benes vowed that the mistake of 1919, when "idealistic tendencies" were governing, would not be repeated. This time it would be necessary to carry out population transfers on "a very much larger scale than after the last war" (Eduard Benes, "The Organization of Post-War Europe," *Foreign Affairs* [January 1942]: 235–39).

[47] Benes to Stalin, 16 December 1943, quoted in Naimark, "Ethnic Cleansing."

[48] The renunciation of mass terror in the Soviet Union, the abandonment of collectivization, and the acceptance of a modus vivendi with the church in East-Central Europe, along

Whatever its ideological coloring, social engineering possessed a tremendous capacity for violence. The mobilization of the legal and medical professions for the goal of perfecting society shifted the political discourse to new realms. The pretense of scientific criteria and measures to study and work on the population meant that the state would employ the most advanced and radical tools in its quest for a purer, better society. The urge to maximize the management of society gave birth to myriad institutions for activities such as passportization, surveillance, and physical and mental cataloguing, without which the radical transformation of the population could not have taken place.[49] And it was perfectly logical that the most radical forms of mass extermination were preceded by smaller-scale destruction of groups categorized as incompatible and irredeemable both medically and legally, then supplemented by military-industrial methods of operation.[50]

---

with the abandonment of integral socialism by the German Social Democratic Party, were key markers of this shift. The various origins of the scaling down of state ambitions—self-imposed limitations by Stalin's successors fearing another endless cycle of terror in the Soviet Union and the rise of effective civil societies in liberal democracies—pointed to a common reluctance to accept without challenge the costs of transformative drives. However, collectivization and the Cultural Revolution in China and the Khmer Rouge regime in Cambodia, to cite two examples, were powerful reminders that elsewhere the urge for violent transformation still resonates.

[49] See, for example, the Nazis' use of the meticulous Dutch registering and mapping of the population for the implementation of their anti-Jewish policies in Bob Moore, *Victims and Survivors: The Nazi Persecution of the Jews in the Netherlands, 1940–1945* (London: Arnold, 1997), 194–99; and Scott, *Seeing Like a State*, 78–79. For the Soviet use of passportization in executing deportations in the annexed territories in 1939, see Gross, *Revolution from Abroad*, 188–89. And for the defining and persecuting of internal enemies throughout the prewar era, see Holquist, "State Violence as Technique," in Weiner, *Landscaping the Human Garden*.

[50] For the Pan-European discourse of degeneration, see Daniel Pick, *Face of Degeneration: A European Disorder, c. 1848–1948* (Cambridge: Cambridge University Press, 1989). Among the voluminous literature on the lethal combination of legality and biological-medical science in the service of modern extermination campaigns, see especially Omer Bartov, *Murder in Our Midst: The Holocaust, Industrial Killing, and Representation* (New York: Oxford University Press, 1996), esp. 67–70; Ingo Müller, *Hitler's Justice: The Courts of the Third Reich* (Cambridge: Cambridge University Press, 1987); Michael Stolleis, *The Law under the Swastika: Studies on Legal History in Nazi Germany* (Chicago: University of Chicago Press, 1998); Michael Burleigh, *Death and Deliverance: "Euthanasia" in Germany, 1900–1945* (Cambridge: Cambridge University Press, 1994); Henry Friedlander, *The Origins of Nazi Genocide: From Euthanasia to the Final Solution* (Chapel Hill: University of North Carolina Press, 1995); and Detlev Peukert, "The Genesis of the 'Final Solution' from the Spirit of Science," in Thomas Childers and Jane Caplan, eds., *Reevaluating the Third Reich* (New York: Holmes & Meier, 1993), 234–52. For the culpability of the legal ethos and the legal profession in the persecution of French Jewry, see Richard Weisberg, *Vichy Law and the Holocaust in France* (New York: New York University Press, 1996); and, on the employment of reproductive policies and technologies in the service of social engineering in interwar

Where the paradigm of modernity falls short is by not providing a satisfactory explanation for the *evolution* of purification drives within totalitarian systems. If the urge to perfect societies stemmed from a universal axis of modernity, its implementation acted on clearly particularistic urges and a sense of limitation. First, "gardening states" blossomed throughout Europe, just as in the Soviet Union. In the wake of the Great War, the European political landscape was marked by planned economies, elaborate surveillance systems, and thoroughly politicized eugenics research. Yet the intrusions on public and private lives coexisted, albeit tenuously and reluctantly, with the acceptance of autonomous spheres, whose violation was considered either too costly, futile, or unethical, and often all three. The discourse on individual rights, the cultivation of institutional buffers between citizen and state, and the acceptance of the insurmountable complexity of the economy effectively tamed the aspiration for unhindered perfection throughout Europe. Undoubtedly the colonial experience left a deep imprint on the European policies and ideologies in providing a sense of limitless possibilities and the power to pursue them, and, not least, by introducing the racial factor into the gardening enterprise. It was not merely symbolic that during the liquidation of the Warsaw Ghetto uprising in April 1943, SS foreign troops, such as the Ukrainian and Baltic police units and the Trawniki men, were referred to as *Askari*, the Swahili term for African soldiers and policemen in the service of the German and successive British powers during the colonial era. Still, nontotalitarian "gardening states" reserved their most violent schemes for their colonial domains, while displaying considerably more restraint at home.[51]

Hence it was the Soviet polity that ended up with teleology as its economic modus operandi alongside a system of concentration camps, mass deportations, and killings.[52] Indeed, the Soviets went out of their way to

---

Italy, see David Horn, *Social Bodies: Science, Reproduction, and Italian Modernity* (Princeton, N.J.: Princeton University Press, 1994).

[51] For an eloquent discussion of the self-imposed restraints of the liberal state, see Scott, *Seeing Like a State*, 101–2. On the conscious removal of restraints on violence in colonial wars, mainly the erasure of the distinction between combatants, noncombatants, and prisoners of war, ideologically based dehumanization of the enemy and its culture, and a concerted effort to destroy the socioeconomic structure of the foe, see Sabine Dabringhaus, "An Army on Vacation? The German War in China, 1900–1901"; Trutz von Trotha, "The Fellows Can Just Starve: On Wars of 'Pacification' in the African Colonies of Imperial Germany and the Concept of 'Total War' "; and Robert Utley, "Total War on the American Indian Frontier," in Manfred Boemeke et al., eds., *Anticipating Total War: The German and American Experiences, 1871–1914* (Cambridge: Cambridge University Press, 1999).

[52] Tim McDaniel's interpretive essay, *The Agony of the Russian Idea* (Princeton, N.J.: Princeton University Press, 1996), esp. 86–117, is an excellent starting point for a discussion of the tenuous relations among modernization, communist ideology, and the Russian heritage. Unlike McDaniel, however, I am inclined to view the totalitarian-revolutionary ethos

underline this difference. Unlike the Philistines, who constantly lament brutality and the loss of lives and preach reconciliation, the ultimate goal of the social engineering project—a genuine moral-political unity of society—could be reached only through an irreconcilable and violent struggle, declared Soviet ideologues.[53] Second, the campaign to eradicate internal enemies within the totalitarian state intensified *after* all residues of political opposition had been crushed, and, in the Soviet case, following the declaration that socialism had been built.[54] Terror becomes total, Hannah Arendt noted, when it becomes independent of all opposition.[55]

The key to the distinctive development of the Soviets' purification drive lay in the volatile fusion of Bolshevik millenarianism and the ultimate goal of creating a conflict-free and harmonious society. It was an eschatological worldview insofar as it anticipated an end to history; it was apocalyptic in its belief in the imminence of the end of time and that, in the wake of reaching socialism, Soviet people were living in the final stages of history; it was millenarian in its belief that the final cataclysm would be followed by the kingdom of communism, namely, a conflict-free and harmonious society, the very feature that set it apart from other totalitarian enterprises that espoused cyclical conceptions of time and envisioned an endless struggle for domination and survival.[56] The quest for purity was neatly tied

---

as one ingrained in pan-European modernity, though one that acted on particularistic ideologies, largely because of its aspiration for a total transformation of society. The Russian heritage was certainly crucial for the evolution of Soviet communism, yet similar patterns in Nazi Germany and Marxist regimes in Asia and Africa point to a supranational, cross-cultural ideological phenomenon. In this sense, and despite its underlying teleological reasoning, Jacob Talmon's magisterial trilogy is on the mark in identifying the issue as a primarily ideological phenomenon rooted in the Enlightenment era. See Talmon, *The Origins of Totalitarian Democracy* (London: Secker & Warburg, 1952); *Political Messianism—the Romantic Phase* (London: Secker & Warburg, 1960); and *The Myth of the Nation and the Vision of the Revolution* (London: Secker & Warburg, 1981). See also Bernard Yack, *The Longing for Total Revolution: Philosophic Sources of Social Discontent from Rousseau to Marx and Nietzsche* (Princeton, N.J.: Princeton University Press, 1986), for emphasis on the attempts of various European thinkers to overcome the dehumanizing spirit of modern society and their dissatisfaction with the limited scope and impact of a political insurrection such as the French Revolution.

[53] Georgii Glezerman, *Likvidatsiia ekspluatatorskikh klassov i preodolenie klassovykh razlichii v SSSR* (Moscow: Gos. Izd-vo polit. lit-ry, 1949), 229.

[54] In his speech at the meeting of SS major-generals at Posen on 4 October 1943, when the extermination process was reaching its maximum intensity, Heinrich Himmler stated that no danger was expected at that point from Communists in the Reich since "their leading elements, like most criminals, are in our concentration camps" (*Nazi Conspiracy and Aggression*, 4:560).

[55] Arendt, *Origins of Totalitarianism*, 464.

[56] For an excellent introduction to these concepts and the tensions they created in the early medieval era, see Richard Landes, "Lest the Millennium Be Fulfilled: Apocalyptic Expectations and the Pattern of Western Chronography, 100–800 C.E.," in Werner Verbeke et

to *the* distinguishing aspect of the Bolshevik utopia: From the moment its power was established, the Soviet regime imposed a time line marking concrete stations on the road to realization of the communist utopia. Following Stalin's speech at the Eighteenth Party Congress, in which the Soviet leader celebrated the homogeneity and unity achieved in the wake of the Terror, Soviet legal theoreticians established a concrete time line for reaching communism. With the triumph of socialism codified in the Stalin Constitution of 1936, one author asserted that "on the basis of the victory [of socialism] achieved over the period of the first two five-year plans, the Soviet Union in the Third Five-Year Plan enters a new period of development, a period of the conclusion of building a classless socialist society and the gradual transition from socialism to communism."[57] With the war over and reconstruction under way, the drive was resumed full steam. Thus, in 1947, the draft of the party program set the goal of "building a communist society in the USSR in the course of the next twenty to thirty years," and, in 1948, a leading political theoretician could declare confidently:

If it were possible to organize a socialist society on the whole within twenty years from the moment of the triumph of Soviet power under the most difficult circumstances, then it is entirely possible to assume that, after the triumphant conclusion of the Patriotic War and the restoration of the ruined people's economy, two more decades will be enough to roughly erect the highest stage of communism. *Therefore, the generation that in 1920 was fifteen to twenty years old will live in a communist society.*[58]

---

al., eds., *The Use and Abuse of Eschatology in the Middle Ages* (Leuven: Leuven University Press, 1988), 137–211. Both fascism and Nazism aimed at the creation of militaristic societies living off war, and, in the case of the Nazis, final victory was not necessarily viewed as the only possible outcome. Here I concur with Burrin who emphasizes Nazism's, and particularly Hitler's, "sense of its own fragility" (Burrin, "Political Religion," 339–40; Geyer, "The Militarization of Europe," 101; and Falasca-Zamponi, *The Fascist Spectacle*, 40). Ironically, in this light the Soviet Union, which is a marginal addendum to the Nazi state in Zygmunt Bauman's account, appears as the ultimate expression of the gardening state, as it was the only totalitarian enterprise with a certain vision of its final goal (Bauman, *Modernity and the Holocaust*).

[57] I. Trainin, "Kommunizm i gosudarstvo," *Sovetskoe gosudarstvo i pravo* 2 (1939): 109.

[58] Indeed, this confident prediction was presented as a "scientific answer to the question on the historical epochs of building communism [that] we find in the writings of Lenin and Stalin" (Tsolak Stepanian, "Usloviia i puti perekhoda ot sotsializma k kommunizmu," in F. Konstantinov et al., eds., *O sovetskom obshchestve: Sbornik statei* [Moscow: Gos. izd-vo poli. lit, 1948], 539, 540, 542). The political importance assigned to this intriguing collection of essays was underlined by its large circulation: some 120,000 copies printed for the 1948 and 1949 editions. Stepanian's elaboration on his essay was published in 1951 under the title *O postepennom perekhode ot sotsializma k kommunizmu*, and 200,000 copies were printed. For the 1947 draft of the party program, see Elena Zubkova, *Obshchestvo i reformy, 1945–1964* (Moscow: Rossiia molodaia, 1993), 93. The program envisioned that, based on accelerated

A year later communism was said to be around the corner, each day bringing further affirmation of the triumphant march to communism. As the first secretary of the All-Union Communist Youth League (Komsomol) assured the delegates to the Eleventh Congress of that organization in March–April 1949, this included evidence of communist harmony—an end to the great schisms between mental and physical labor, and between town and village. The "overwhelming majority" of Soviet youth, noted another secretary, already possessed "all the elements of character of the man of Communist society." By now, the kinship of blood forged at the war fronts between party and nonparty people alike displayed itself in the common struggle of building communism.[59] Society as a whole, then, was preparing to enter the communist era. On the eve of the Nineteenth Party Congress in October 1952 Stalin threw his personal weight behind the matter. In his last major work, *Economic Problems of Socialism in the USSR*, he sought to rush the march toward communism by creating a central barter system to replace collective farm property and commodity exchange in the countryside, both of which he viewed as the last obstacles to a full-blown communist economy.[60] And with the addition of the new socialist "shock brigades"—the people's democracies in East Asia and Europe—which altered the prewar isolation, the "mighty motherland" was said to be in the flower of her strength, possessing "everything necessary to build a complete communist society."[61]

These indications of communism's rapid approach directly impacted how the "weeds" intruding on the harmonious garden were viewed and

---

productivity and investment in heavy industry, the Soviet Union would surpass the productivity level per head of the leading capitalist countries, including the United States. Khrushchev's invocation of these principles, under different conditions, underlined their deep roots in Soviet political culture (RGASPI [Rossiiskii gosudarstvennyi arkhiv sotsial'no-politicheskoi istorii], f. 17, op. 125, d. 476, ll. 190–91).

[59] The heroic sacrifice of the Krasnodon Komsomols (the doomed youth underground in this German-occupied region) was celebrated as a proper example, side by side with the tale of the non-Komsomol partisans whose dying wish was that they be posthumously enrolled as Komsomol members (*Komsomol'skaia pravda*, 30 March and 2 April 1949).

[60] "Ekonomicheskie problemy sotsializma v SSSR" and "Otvet tovarishcham Saninoi A.V i Venzheneru V.G," in I. V. Stalin, *Sochineniia*, ed. Robert McNeal (Stanford: Stanford University Press, 1967), 3 (16): 205–7, 294–304. Indeed, this was how the work was presented to the delegates of the Nineteenth Party Congress. In his speech Lavrentii Beria celebrated Stalin's work not only as an innovative theoretical statement but mainly as a concrete political program for the realization of communism. "Undoubtedly, our congress and our entire party will adapt Comrade Stalin's statements on the conditions for and the ways of accomplishing the gradual transition from socialism to communism as their program of struggle for building communism," declared Beria (*Pravda*, 9 October 1952).

[61] See the speeches by Georgii Malenkov and Stalin at the Nineteenth Party Congress (*Pravda*, 6 and 15 October 1952). The linkage between the favorable change in the international arena and the construction of communism was celebrated throughout the postwar

the measures needed to uproot them. Groups and individuals perceived to be hostile were now referred to in biological or hygienic terms—for example, vermin (*parazity, vrediteli*), pollution (*zasorennost'*), or filth (*griaz'*)—and were subjected to ongoing purification.[62] The implications of this rhetoric were profound. The declaration that socialism had been achieved, the victorious outcome of the Great Patriotic War, and the sense that communism was on the horizon made eradication of "this weed that in some way sprouted between the stones of our bright and well-constructed edifice"[63] even more urgent. In his speech at the February–March 1937 plenary session of the Central Committee, Stalin identified a new type of adversary in this age of socialism, the elusive enemy, a theme he had already begun to develop at the completion of collectivization. Since official ideology and its institutional implementation were infallible, errors and failures could be attributed only to the ill will of individuals. After several decades of socialism, accompanied by continual purges, the fact that these human "weeds" still existed had to be the result of their devious and elusive nature. Like a cancer, they mutated in different forms and various locations. And because this vermin was unrepentant, it had to be excised in its entirety. The only question was how to achieve this. The former brand of internal enemies, argued Stalin, was openly hostile to the Soviet cause by virtue of social origin and professional orientation; they could not be mistaken for anything other than what they were. The new saboteurs, on the other hand, were "mostly party people, with a party card in their pocket, that is, people who are not formally alien. Whereas the old vermin turned against our people, the new vermin, on the contrary, cringe before our people, extol our people, bow before them to win their trust."[64] These highway brigands were devoid of ideological belief, claimed Stalin, and would resort to any imaginable crime in their struggle

---

era. See I. T. Goliakov, "Ocherednaia vekha na puti k kommunizmu," *Sovetskoe gosudarstvo i pravo* 11 (1950): 1, 15.

[62] On Soviet preoccupation with the purity of the collective body, particularly in the 1920s, see Eric Naiman, *Sex in Public: The Incarnation of Early Soviet Ideology* (Princeton, N.J.: Princeton University Press, 1997).

[63] *Komsomol'skaia pravda*, 12 February 1953.

[64] I. Stalin, "O nedostatkakh partiinoi raboty i merakh likvidatsii trotskistskikh i inykh dvurushnikov. Doklad na Plenume TsK VKP (b) 3 marta 1937," *Bol'shevik* 7 (1937): 7. See Kuromiya, *Freedom and Terror*, 184–85, for an examination of the appearance of the term in 1933. Note the identical logic advanced by Heinrich Himmler in a speech before Waffen-SS troops in Stettin on 13 July 1941, in which he concluded that for the last one thousand years the Aryan race had fought the same struggle against the same enemy who reincarnated itself, each time appearing under a different name, whether Huns, Magyars, Tartars, or Mongols. "Today they appear as Russians under the political banner of Bolshevism," stated Himmler (quoted in Richard Breitman, *The Architect of Genocide: Himmler and the Final Solution* [Hanover, N.H.: University Press of New England, 1991], 177).

against the Soviet state. Thus the Soviet state must guarantee the annihilation of this vermin from its midst. With anxiety over the approaching war increasing daily, the long-held principle of verifying an individual's guilt was sacrificed in favor of collective punishment.[65] "We could not pause to investigate thoroughly an individual [case] and study it objectively. Action could not be deferred," admitted Molotov.

> Of course, had we operated with greater caution, there would have been fewer victims, but Stalin insisted on making doubly sure: Spare no one, only guarantee stability for a long time—through the war and the postwar years . . . let innocent heads roll, but there will be no wavering during and after the war.[66]

Stalin's warning was repeatedly invoked in the purge campaigns that followed. By then, the war had already been established as a modern-day Armageddon. Addressing the Nineteenth Party Congress in October 1952, Lavrentii Beria noted that nothing less than the mass slaughter and destruction of modern civilization was prevented by the Soviet Union, which "battled for its independence, routed the enemy who had terrorized the armies of Europe, and saved mankind and its civilization through tremendous sacrifice and supreme exertion, mobilizing all the material and spiritual resources of the people."[67] The purification drive, in this light, acquired an additional edge. The moral-political unity gained by a relentless and thorough purge was juxtaposed to the proliferation of "fifth columns" in the rest of Europe, which, in the Soviet view, was a major factor in Europe's rapid collapse beneath the Nazi onslaught.[68]

"We have no ready-made pure people, purged of all sins," reflected Molotov. The revolutionary purification had to be sustained despite the general exhaustion and desire for relaxation, which Molotov admitted engulfed both the party and the population at large. Herein lay the core of the Bolshevik ethos. Revolutions age and make people old, quipped Bronislaw Baczko. And no one was more aware of the aging process and more intent on delaying it than the Bolsheviks. In a comment that spoke to both the Stalin and Khrushchev eras, Molotov remarked: "It is 'living calmly' that the Bolsheviks cannot accept. When people's lives are calm, the Bolsheviks are absolutely unnecessary. They are always in the thick of

---

[65] Note the remarkable similarities between the Soviet and Nazi articulation and pursuit of elusive enemies. For a fascinating account of the German obsession with the Jew within, starting at the fronts of the First World War, cultivated during the Weimar era, and finally culminating under the Nazis, see Omer Bartov, "Defining Enemies, Making Victims," *American Historical Review* 103 (June 1998): 771–816, esp. 772–81.

[66] Molotov, *Sto sorok besed*, 407, 416.

[67] *Pravda*, 9 October 1952.

[68] See the announcement on the uncovering of the "Doctors' Plot" in *Pravda*, 13 January 1953; L. Smirnov, "Neustanno povyshat' politicheskuiu bditel'nost' sovetskikh liudei," *Bloknot agitatora* 3 (January 1953): 11, 15–17; and Glezerman, *Likvidatsiia*, 193–94, 219–20.

the fray, advancing, overcoming obstacles, but when life is calm, who needs the Bolsheviks?"[69] And so the quest for purity charged ahead. On 1 December 1952 Stalin cautioned members of the Presidium of the Central Committee that "the more successes we have, the more the enemy will try to harm us. Our people forgot about this because of our great successes."[70] With the announcement, in mid-January 1953, of the "Doctors' Plot," when a group of physicians, mostly Jews, were accused of plotting to murder Soviet leaders, *Komsomol'skaia pravda* reminded Soviet youth that it was the impenetrable, homogenized home front that frustrated the fascist invaders in the recent war. But even in defeat, the enemy does not rest. A call went out for vigilance:

> Having won the war we again turn to construction, because we love life and youth, because we want to make our land a flourishing garden. But as we build, we must remember that enemy spies will continue to invade our home front, that our enemy will recruit all kinds of scum to undermine our strength, to poison our joyous, happy life . . . the greater our success in building communism in the USSR, the more active and vile the operations of the imperialists and their myrmidons.

Like the biblical serpent, these enemies were the most elusive imaginable. "The spies and saboteurs sent to us by the imperialist intelligence services or recruited by them within the country from among incompletely routed anti-Soviet scum do not operate with visors up. They operate 'on the sly,' masking themselves in the guise of Soviet persons in order to penetrate our institutions and organizations, to worm their way into our confidence and conduct their foul work," stated *Izvestiia*'s editorial from the same day. An unwavering vigilance was required to "ensure the cleansing of people's minds from the survivals of capitalism, from the prejudices and harmful traditions of the old society," the editorial concluded.[71]

The arrival of socialism ordained new sites of excision. With the destruction of antagonistic classes, internal enemies became enemies of the people and were to be sought in new realms.[72] By then, the nationality question harbored the clearest and most present danger to the moral and political

[69] Molotov, *Sto sorok besed*, 391, 312.

[70] Entry for 1 December 1952 in the diary of V. A. Malyshev, then a member of the Presidium and the minister of the shipbuilding industry, *Istochnik* 5 (1977): 140.

[71] *Komsomol'skaia pravda*, 15 January 1953; *Izvestiia*, 15 January 1953.

[72] The new category of "enemies of the people" was codified in Article 131 of the 1936 Constitution. A year later, on the occasion of the twentieth anniversary of the October Revolution at the time when the Terror was reaching its climax, Molotov pointed to the "unprecedented inner moral and political unity of the people" that was forged through wrenching the country free from the rotting capitalist society and in the ordeal of heroic struggle against the exploiting classes and foreign intervention. This unity also meant that by now the enemies of the Communist Party and the Soviet government had become enemies of the people, declared Molotov (*Pravda*, 7 November 1937).

unity of the Soviet people, Stalin declared at the Seventeenth Party Congress in 1934, underlining the increasing ethnicization of the Soviet social body and the shift in the search for the enemy within. The fight against recurrences of nationalist views had become the most critical task in the struggle against the last vestiges of capitalism in the people's consciousness, Dmitrii Chesnokov, a prominent party ideologue, declared in 1952. The residue of *zoological chauvinism* (the Soviets' favored term for racism), especially in regions temporarily exposed to fascist propaganda during the German occupation, represented a stubborn intrusion on Soviet harmony and called for the severest measures if harmony was to be maintained, Chesnokov concluded.[73] Another leading ideologue pointed to the unprecedented high stakes of the current campaign. Unlike the "Great Turn" of the early 1930s, the postwar collision involved a Soviet state at the height of its power and a shrewd enemy armed with an articulate ideology developed under conditions of statehood and capable of conducting a well-organized military campaign.[74]

Yet Soviet relations with parallel, modern politics across the European continent were not merely phenomenological. Rather, the Soviets were constantly examining their methods in the European mirror. Soviet contemporaries were extremely anxious regarding the potential for degenerating into a "zoological" ethos. Throughout the 1930s Soviet leaders, and notably Stalin, reacted vehemently to any suggestion that their sociologically based model of the human subject could be equated with any biologically based, genetically coded enterprise, whether the racial Nazi polity or contemporary policies of eugenics and euthanasia, which enjoyed widespread acceptance during that decade. When, in the wake of war, the Soviets' indiscriminate and irreversible punishment of enemy groups drove home the inevitable comparison with Nazi racial ethos, the Soviets persistently maintained that their destruction of internal enemies was not genocidal, that their penal system, unlike the death camps in the capitalist world, remained true to its corrective mandate.[75]

---

[73] Dmitrii Chesnokov, *Sovetskoe sotsialisticheskoe gosudarstvo* (Moscow: Gos. Izd-vo. poli. lit-ry, 1952), 209. The necessity for coercion in the age of harmony and socialist democracy was hammered out by Chesnokov throughout the entire exhaustive text (see 246, 556).

[74] Glezerman, *Likvidatsiia*, 362–63, 372–74.

[75] "In contrast to the capitalist countries, where concentration camps are sites of torture and death, the correctional labor camps of the Soviet state are a distinctive school for the reeducation of a worldview bequeathed to us by the capitalist society," claimed a 1944 brochure of the Cultural-Educational Department of the GULAG (M. Loginov, "Vozvrashchenie k zhizni," in Gosudarstvennyi Arkhiv Rossiiskoi Federatsii [GARF], f. 9414, op. 4, d. 145, l. 3. Notably, a decade earlier, it was the Western penal system that was the favorite point of reference (Maxim Gorky et al., *Belomor: An Account of the Construction of the New Canal between the White Sea and the Baltic Sea* [New York: Smith and Haas, 1935], 328).

The Soviets' acute sensitivity to being equated with the Nazi racial enterprise and their awareness that efforts to excise certain groups did not imply complete physical elimination necessitated other means of purification in addition to deportations and executions. Memory was a key political arena where the exclusion of certain groups from official representation of the Soviet fighting family, along with the denial of their unique suffering, left those groups politically invisible, without official recognition of their distinct, collective identities.

Such was the ethos that shaped and was shaped by the experience of the Great Patriotic War.

Part I ———————————————————

DELINEATING THE BODY POLITIC

One

Myth and Power: The Making of a Postwar Elite

The holy blood of this war cleansed us of the innocent blood of the dekulakized and of the blood of 1937.[1]

ON 24 AUGUST 1942 the readers of *Pravda* were treated to a rather unusual literary event. With the war approaching a decisive moment, the leading newspaper of the country found the time and space to serialize a new play by the leading Ukrainian writer Oleksandr Korniichuk. There was, indeed, nothing ordinary about the play, entitled simply *The Front*.[2] Initiated by Stalin and unmistakably reflecting real-life personalities and policies, the play instantly created major political waves.[3]

The Front was a direct attack on the way warfare was conducted by army commanders of the civil war generation, who were portrayed as those responsible for the Red Army's initial defeats. Simply put, they were remnants of bygone years who could not successfully confront the realities of modern warfare. The conclusion was inevitable. The civil war generation had to step aside and give way to the very people it despised most—the new cadres of professional officers who had emerged from the Soviet military academies.

Plenty of motives were at hand behind the publication of the play in *Pravda*. One was to shift blame for the humiliating military defeats early on in the war from Stalin and the party to the military command; another was the genuine dissatisfaction with those commanders' performance, es-

---

[1] Vasilii Grossman cited in Semen Lipkin, *Stalingrad Vasiliia Grossmana* (Ann Arbor: Ardis, 1986), 15; and *Zhizn' i sud'ba Vasiliia Grossmana* (Moscow: Kniga, 1990), 9.

[2] Shortly after its serialization, *The Front* was staged with the best-known actors of the day cast in leading roles. The text used here is from the original edition, published by the *Iskusstvo* publishing house in August 1942, in pamphlet form, with a circulation of twenty thousand copies. Korniichuk wrote the play in Ukrainian, as the publishers noted on the front cover.

[3] Alexander Werth related that Korniichuk, soon after the play was published, told him that he had gotten the "general idea" of the play from Stalin himself (Werth, *Russia at War*, 423). The earlier removal of Voroshilov and Budennyi, both prominent civil war commanders, from their posts did not escape comparison with the events in Korniichuk's play.

pecially after the crushing defeats of 1941–42. In the long run, however, *The Front* had major implications for the entire Soviet polity. Intentionally or not, the play forcefully laid out a basic dilemma confronting the Soviet Union—the uneasy coexistence of conflicting myths as the core of its social and political legitimacy.

Although *The Front* took aim at Red Army commanders of the civil war era, it was not the individual commanders who bore the brunt of the criticism. The play mercilessly attacked pillars of the prewar revolutionary myth, of which the civil war was a major component, to such a degree that its viability was called into question. It virtually renounced the civil war as a romantically naive, irrelevant, and outdated model for the Soviet polity. The character of Ivan Gorlov, the old front commander, was a vehicle to delegitimize some cherished values of the early revolutionary era such as spontaneity, intuition, and courage as the answers to the problems of modern warfare. In the same vein, the characters in Gorlov's entourage of lackeys serve to mock another long-held principle of class origin. "Take me, for example," exclaims one of them. "I didn't work very long in a factory, only three years and two weeks. Even I am amazed that I've managed to sustain enough proletarian instinct for the rest of my life."[4] When confronted with charges of a lack of military professionalism, they immediately invoke the myth of proletarian supremacy. So when the intelligence chief is criticized by the chief of staff of the front, he rushes to check on the latter's class origin. "Listen," he says, when he calls the party bureau, "don't you remember the file of Blagonravov, what sort of family does he come from? Origin? Aha! The son of a deacon? I see."[5]

Equally intriguing were the criteria of generational demarcation. The lines between the groups in *The Front* were not necessarily chronological. Rather, these were the different experiences of individuals and the lessons they drew that set people apart or solidified them as collectives. The play concludes with a veteran commander of the cavalry group embracing Vladimir Ognev, a young professional officer, newly appointed as commander of the front, citing Stalin's call for applying professional criteria in the promotion of both young people and veterans. Another character supports this generational demarcation. Miron Gorlov, the brother of protagonist Ivan Gorlov and a factory manager, makes the argument for the overhaul of leadership in the civilian sector. Like Ognev, he is a beneficiary of the most recent cataclysmic event of the Soviet scene, namely, the purges. Without spelling out the very word, both characters endorse the Terror that removed their predecessors and paved their way to commanding positions in the army and industry. "Remember how it was in industry," Miron reminds a member of the Military Council:

[4] Oleksandr Korniichuk, *Front* (Moscow: Gos. izd-vo khudozh. lit-ry, 1942), 50–51.
[5] Ibid., 50.

At first many factories and trusts were run by managers with an honorable past and authority—old comrades who boasted of their callused hands, their loud voices, their use of swear words. But the business of management they did not know and did not want to know. They did not know how to run a plant. At each step they chattered about their humble origin . . . And what came of it? The plants worked extremely badly because almost everywhere the people in charge were "authoritative" and vain ignoramuses.[6]

Class credentials thus produced a deadening hold over the lifeline of the country. It was left for the Central Committee (not even the party as a whole) to break this tangle. Apparently referring to the Terror, Miron pursued his line of reasoning:

> Had the Central Committee not taken a sharp turn, had it not appointed engineers, technicians, and people who knew their jobs to head the enterprises, the workers undoubtedly would have said: "go to hell with your old authoritative people, if you can't manage properly." That's a fact. No matter how the ignoramuses screamed, no one supported them. The people love and demand only smart leaders who know their job.[7]

But even the transformative drives of the 1930s are not given full credit for the formation of the New Soviet Man. Indeed, they produced the academies where the future Soviet officers and managers were trained to conduct and lead in a rational "Stalinist scientific" manner, but that alone counted for nothing. The civil war buffoons and the anarchic ethos of that era continued their reign over the Soviet scene, bringing about disasters at the military and home fronts. Seemingly the Terror alone could not and did not remove them. But where the Terror failed the current purgatory of the war would succeed.

The Front exposed, if unintentionally, a rather acute dilemma. For Stalin, using Korniichuk as his mouthpiece, the war was the ultimate purgatory of the Revolution and confirmation of an already well-placed system. Four years later, in his election speech of 9 February 1946, he would articulate this view in his own words. It remained to be seen, however, whether such clarity was also shared by the cohort of professional commanders and managers themselves. What could be the point of reference of the now celebrated heroes who only yesterday were the very victims of the Terror? What could be the point of reference of the real-life Ognevs?[8] What con-

---

[6] Ibid., 22.

[7] Ibid.

[8] As Werth points out, a figure that immediately comes to mind is Marshal Konstantin Rokossovskii. Following a meteoric rise through the ranks of the Red Army, Rokossovskii was arrested and jailed in August 1937. He was released in March 1940 and reinstated to the high command. Rokossovskii's highly successful performance in the war was symbolically rewarded when he was chosen to lead the Victory Parade in Moscow on 24 June 1945. The

crete past did the war validate? In a word, how could they fit their new formative experience into the revolutionary ethos that molded their world? With this in mind, let us examine the way these people were shaping their identities in the midst and the aftermath of this cataclysmic event.

The Right Story

On 2 October 1945 the secretaries of the raikoms (Communist Party district committees) in the Vinnytsia region received an unusual letter from Mykhailo Stakhurs'kyi, the first secretary of the obkom (party regional committee). In his letter Stakhurs'kyi wholeheartedly recommended the public reading of Valentin Ovechkin's novel, *With Greetings from the Front*, with party activists at the first meeting of each raikom. These activists were expected to familiarize themselves immediately with the story, and Stakhurs'kyi recommended picking a reader who could speak clearly so that all present would understand. "It would be good," he wrote, "if one of the leaders acquaints himself with the story in advance and is prepared, if needed, to comment."[9]

What could be the appeal of a novel that was distinguished by its call for compassion for a party boss with a reputation of rudeness and vengeance, who was notorious even by current standards?[10] The publication of Ovechkin's short novel was indeed a major literary event but unlikely to be a major concern for a party boss busy with the restoration of the regional economy and the party machine in the wake of war.[11]

Stakhurs'kyi's initiative apparently sprang from the biographies and conduct of both himself and Ovechkin's fictional hero, Captain Spivak. The resounding similarity between the real-life and fictional heroes pointed to a phenomenon whose implications went beyond the narrow

---

sudden stature of officially celebrated hero that the play cast upon him and those like him was nothing but awkward for Rokossovskii, to say the least (Werth, *Russia at War*, 425).

[9] Partiinyi arkhiv Vinnyts'koi oblasti (PAVO), f. 136, op. 13, d. 35, l. 9.

[10] See the consistent complaints of officials in the lower ranks against Stakhurs'kyi's rude conduct, and the Central Committee's comments, in PAVO, f. 136, op. 12, d. 202, l. 71; Tsentral'nyi derzhavnyi arkhiv hromads'kykh ob'iednan' Ukrainy (TsDAHOU), f. 1, op. 23, d. 2681, ll. 114–16; d. 2727, ll. 1–6; op. 46, d. 2285, l.9; and d. 3817, ll. 2, 6, 8.

[11] Valentin Ovechkin, *Z frontovym pryvitom* (Kiev: Ukrainse derzhavne vyd-vo, 1946). The novel was originally published in Russian in the journal *Oktiabr'* (May 1945). The Russian edition was circulated in one hundred thousand copies, and the Ukrainian edition in twenty-five thousand. The novel triggered a wide response in the press, though it is unclear whether other leading officials followed Stakhurs'kyi's initiative. However, on the occasion of the announcement of the first wave of demobilization, the republic's paper, in its editorial, cited the heroes of the novel as models for the expected conduct of demobilized servicemen in the era of postwar reconstruction (*Pravda Ukrainy*, 23 September 1945).

Figure 1.1. Lieutenant-General Mykhailo Stakhurs'kyi, soon to be appointed first secretary of the Vinnytsia Party Regional Committee.

literary boundaries. From July 1945 until March 1951 Stakhurs'kyi ruled Vinnytsia with an iron fist.[12] In spite of a successful career in the Central Committee in Kiev on the eve of the war, it was his military career and exploits that Stakhurs'kyi chose to advance in public and private alike. Unquestionably Stakhurs'kyi was distinguished by the wartime rank of lieutenant-general that he held as a member of the Military Council of the First Belorussian and Second Ukrainian fronts, but he was never a career officer (Figure 1.1).[13] He often referred to himself as a "general in reserve" and, for a while after his arrival in the region, was addressed as "secretary of the obkom, lieutenant-general Stakhurs'kyi."[14] The highly visible military profile that Stakhurs'kyi cultivated became so pronounced that his

---

[12] Stakhurs'kyi was sent to Vinnytsia to restore order in the party organization and to revive its viability as an administrative organ in the countryside after the indecisive tenure of Havrylo Mishchenko. For accusations leveled at Mishchenko on the occasion of his demotion from the position of delegate to the Supreme Soviet SSSR, 29 October 1945, see RGASPI, f. 17, op. 45, d. 2007, l. 221.

[13] Except for the period of the Second World War, Stakhurs'kyi served in the Red Army only in 1919–23 and 1925–27. In 1937 Stakhurs'kyi already headed the Department of Agriculture of the Central Committee in Kiev, and in 1939 he was appointed a deputy in the People's Commissariat of Agriculture of Soviet Ukraine (TsDAHOU, f. 1, op. 46, d. 3786, l. 56).

[14] See, for example, the letter written by the regional chief of the NKVD, August 1945, in PAVO, f. 136, op. 13, d. 48, l. 23; TsDAHOU, f. 1, op. 23, d. 4170, ll. 13–14.

Figure 1.2. Stakhurs'kyi delivering a public address. Stakhurs'kyi's blunt language and manners, and his aura of a general-in-reserve, rattled party and state officials in the region throughout his reign from 1945 to 1951.

rivals in the party complained that he presented himself at conferences as "a member of the Military Council of the Front and not as a representative of the party organization."[15] Throughout his reign in Vinnytsia, Stakhurs'kyi systematically cultivated the image of an ideal-type Bolshevik: an iron-fisted general, defender of the motherland, and electrifier of the countryside (Figure 1.2).[16]

Stakhurs'kyi found his popular counterpart in Ovechkin's fictional hero, Captain Spivak. Of peasant origin, Spivak began as a shepherd, a tractor driver, a kolkhoz party organizer and, on the eve of the war, worked as a raikom instructor in Poltava. The war brought not only hardship but also an officer's rank. Even more relevant was Spivak's resolve to return to his native village instead of pursuing a military career.[17] Throughout long monologues and discussions with Petrenko, his battalion commander and an agronomist in his village, Spivak advanced the notion of army veterans

[15] The verification of these specific allegations, which was sent to the Central Committee in Kiev in January 1946, refuted the charge that Stakhurs'kyi did so in all conferences and meetings, yet it cited at least one such occasion, a meeting with the command of the Twenty-seventh Army stationed in Vinnytsia (TsDAHOU, f. 1, op. 23, d. 2727, l. 3).

[16] See the biographical sketches of Stakhurs'kyi in the regional newspaper during the election campaign of January–February 1946 (*Vinnyts'ka pravda*, 12, 19, and 30 January 1946; and TsDAHOU, f. 1, op. 23, d. 2740, l. 43). Such was also the perception of rank-and-file Communists who, as late as 1949, still viewed Stakhurs'kyi as "a general in civilian uniforms, one who inspired fear" (interview with Boris Halfin, 18 February 1994, Kiryat Gat, Israel).

[17] Ovechkin, *Z frontovym pryvitom*, 19.

as those most suited for postwar tasks. In his kolkhoz, for example, all three field brigadiers were lieutenants and senior lieutenants. "They departed as privates and sergeants but returned as officers. One lost his hand, another is on crutches, but they maintained their dignity. They wear uniforms. When answering questions in the management meetings, they stand up shaved, smart. And the chairman, a captain, is also an invalid."[18] Furthermore, the demobilized officers had practical answers to the formidable tasks that lay ahead. When Spivak and Petrenko decided to write a letter to the raikom secretary to offer their thoughts and advice, they were motivated by the belief in their ability to jump-start the stalled system quickly and efficiently. Relating to new inexperienced cadres "who need help in every step," the two concluded: "It is possible to speed things up. It is possible to return people to prewar life within ten years, but it is also possible within three years."[19]

Finally, Ovechkin's heroes conveyed an intentional rejection of prewar memories and habits as a guiding past. The war was a conscious point of departure from this past. Reflecting on their own qualifications as civilian leaders ("From one battalion one can enlist kolkhoz chairmen and brigadiers for three districts"), the *frontoviki* (front-line soldiers) concluded that one should "take a look at how many new names showed up with us during the war. People who led regiments and battalions at the beginning of the war now lead armies and fronts. One cannot live all the time by old memories."[20]

That the Ovechkin episode was the rule rather than the exception is made even clearer when we turn to works that were conventionally considered more typical of the postwar "kolkhoz literature." Stakhurs'kyi's self-image did not evolve in a vacuum. In fact, it intersected with an ideal type from popular literature to such a degree that one can hardly distinguish between the two. A barrage of popular novels on the postwar countryside celebrated a new hero: the demobilized officer who transferred his zeal from the front to pursue the electrification of the backward countryside. As a rule, the character of the relentless veteran was contrasted with that of a laid-back bureaucrat, most likely one who avoided the front and adapted a "soft" and conservative approach to the tasks of reconstruction. Also predictably, the veteran cut through the red tape with a display of iron will and voluntarist enthusiasm. This genre of kolkhoz literature came under harsh scrutiny by contemporary Soviet literary critics, even before Stalin's death. The pastoral and romanticized portrayal of kolkhoz life was charged with detachment from reality, deliberate ignorance of ac-

---

[18] Ibid., 40.
[19] Ibid., 55–56.
[20] Ibid., 51, 127–28.

tual difficulties, and encouragement of bullying methods in the country-side.[21] Although the validity of this line of criticism was never in doubt, it ignored a crucial point. Such works had a large and receptive real-life constituency. Just as these literary propagandist products aimed at the creation of new ideal types, they simultaneously reflected a popular self-image of many of the veteran-turned-civilian leaders. As such, these textual representations of the war codified major political phenomena of the postwar scene.[22]

The acuteness of this phenomenon is highlighted when we examine Semen Babaevskii's *Cavalier of the Golden Star*, the epitome of the genre and the novel that drew the harshest criticism. One is struck by the almost identical collisions between Babaevskii's fictional Sergei Tutarinov, the decorated veteran-turned-chairman of a district soviet executive committee, and his predecessor Khokhlakov, and between the real-life Stakhurs'kyi and Dmytro Burchenko, the chairman of the Regional Soviet Executive Committee.

In his story Babaevskii juxtaposed a young and enthusiastic demobilized officer with an aging and cautious apparatchik. The worldview and practices of the young veteran, Sergei Tutarinov, were drawn solely from the front. For his opponent, Khokhlakov, who got used to cozy formalism and the network of cronies, such a phenomenon was an assault on his secure environment. When the two clashed over an ambitious plan to build a hydroelectric station, Khokhlakov snapped: "I think that the noise of war is still filling your head. You seem to think you have only to want something and you'll get it." Sometime later Khokhlakov complained of the combat-like style of Tutarinov, who "simply drove down to that kolkhoz and started giving orders as if he were in his tank company. But this is not a tank company, this is a kolkhoz!" Tutarinov's response was anything but apologetic: "Where did you get such a convenient theory of 'don't worry, don't bother.' Every slacker will smother you with kisses for this! What more could he want? A quiet life."[23]

The rhetoric and politics of Babaevskii's Kuban Cossack settlement found its real-life counterpart in Vinnytsia. Although Stakhurs'kyi was not a novice to party life, he, like the fictional Tutarinov, owed his meteoric

[21] See the sarcastic comments by Aleksander Shtein at a writers' conference in 1947, as cited in Konstantin Simonov, "Zadachi sovetskoi dramaturgii i teatral'naia kritika," *Novyi mir* 3 (1949): 191; Vladimir Pomerantsev, "Ob iskrennosti v literature," *Novyi mir* 12 (1953): 218–45; and Fedor Abramov, "Liudi kolkhoznoi derevni v poslevoennoi proze," *Novyi mir* 4 (1954): 210–31.

[22] This aspect of Soviet literary discourse is best treated in Katerina Clark, *The Soviet Novel: History as Ritual* (Chicago: Chicago University Press, 1981).

[23] Semen Babaevskii, *Kavaler zolotoi zvezdy*, in his *Sobranie sochinenii* (Moscow: Khudozhestvennaia literatura, 1979), 1:221, 462–63.

rise to a high commander who spotted his talents.[24] The unusual promotion to the rank of lieutenant-general was perceived as confirmation of the view of civilian life as a military front and approval of the corresponding methods of leadership, combining harsh discipline and the ability to adjust to constantly changing circumstances. Stakhurs'kyi charged his arch-rival Burchenko, who objected to the electrification campaign on practical grounds, of being a "reactionary character, a Potemkin-village ideologue," and the *oblispolkom* (Regional Executive Committee) of being "an institution where conservatism flourishes and every stimulating initiative is killed."[25] In a damning letter addressed to Khrushchev personally, Stakhurs'kyi implicitly contrasted his own combative and effective style with Burchenko's spineless and indecisive conduct. "[Burchenko] does not lead the oblispolkom and the departments," retorted Stakhurs'kyi,

> but, on the contrary, the fulfillment of the directives of the Central Committee of the party and the government is objectively delayed by his spinelessness and liberal approach to any deficiencies. He guides the meetings of the ispolkom in such a manner that any combat resolution is allowed to drop. . . . There is no precision, purposefulness, and energy in his work. [Burchenko] tends to follow rather than lead [*sklonen k khvostizmu*]. In speeches he often resorts to demagoguery, seeks to exert cheap authority. All the so-called offended find shelter and sympathy with him.[26]

In the aftermath of the war it was the Stakhurs'kyi-Tutarinovs who carried the day as the officially endorsed ideal type of political leader. Whether fiction imitated politics or vice versa, the resounding similarity suggests that they combined to create and propagate a powerful political myth. For party leaders who returned from the front, representations of war were the prism through which they viewed civilian life and a major instrument with which they cemented their political power and authority. The story, however, did not end there. In the following years veterans persistently proceeded to carve their own space within the highly stylized parameters of

---

[24] Vasyl' Kostenko, then the secretary of the Ukrainian Komsomol, described Stakhurs'kyi as a "natural force." According to Kostenko, Marshal Rokossovskii was so impressed by Stakhurs'kyi's indefatigable working capability at the Stalingrad front that he asked Stalin to appoint the latter, who was at the rank of captain at the time, to lieutenant-general. Stalin consented (interview with Vasyl' Kostenko, 23 March 1993, Kiev, Ukraine). For Rokossovskii's praise of Stakhurs'kyi's wartime performance, see his memoirs entitled *A Soldier's Duty* (Moscow: Progress, 1985), 214.

[25] TsDAHOU, f. 1, op. 23, d. 4170, l. 14; and f. 1, op. 46, d. 2285, l. 9.

[26] Ibid., f. 1, op. 62, d. 1739, l. 185. When a Central Committee instructor looked into the rivalry between the two in June 1947, he concluded that because of his long tenure in Vinnytsia, Burchenko [like the fictional Khokhlakov], "got used to people, to the situation, and began to lose his edge in work" (ibid., op. 46, d .2284, l. 33).

the Soviet polity, a phenomenon that invites a look at the mechanism that allowed for the preservation and promotion of particularistic interests and images in this world. This phenomenon is clarified by the following tales.

Their Soviet War, Their Soviet Story

In March 1950 the Vinnytsia obkom recommended that Ivan Bevz be awarded the Order of Lenin posthumously . The obkom's official account of the underground activity during the occupation identified Bevz as the organizer and leader of the first Bolshevik underground organization in Vinnytsia. On 21 July 1955 the City Soviet Executive Committee proceeded to name a street after Bevz (Figure 1.3).[27] These actions would have seemed natural but for one fact: By that time Bevz was still a former party member in disgrace. He had become a party member in 1928, after seven years of service in the Red Army for which he volunteered in 1919 at the age of sixteen. In 1938 he was expelled from the party for concealing his father's past as a White officer and for writing a recommendation for a person exposed as an "enemy of the people." But on the eve of the war Bevz accepted an offer by the party and the NKVD to stay in the soon-to be-occupied town of Vinnytsia and organize underground activity. Sometime later the underground was exposed by the Germans, and by the end of 1942 Bevz, his wife, and other underground activists had been executed.[28] At the time of his death, Bevz had still not been reinstated in the party or even rehabilitated. Only a year before his posthumous award as Hero of the Soviet Union, granted by the Supreme Soviet of the USSR in 1965, Bevz was rehabilitated and reinstated into the party.[29]

[27] The final version of the obkom report on partisan and underground activity in the Vinnytsia region was issued on 16 April 1950 and sent to the Central Committee in Kiev (TsDAHOU, f. 1, op. 22, d. 153, ll. 2–3; PAVO, f. 425, op. 1, d. 25, ll. 66–67; Derzhavnyi arkhiv Vinnytskoi oblasti (DAVO), f. 151, op. 9, d. 673, ll. 10–11.

[28] Bevz's father served in the Red Army in 1918, but after being captured by the Whites in 1919 he joined them at the rank of officer. For his service with the Whites, Bevz's father was convicted and imprisoned between 1922 and 1924 and again in 1931 for eight years. According to the rehabilitation protocols, Bevz lost contact with his father after 1919. This account draws on materials from the files of Bevz's expulsion and posthumous rehabilitation and reinstatement in the party in April 1964 (PAVO, f. 136, op. 10, d. 151, ll. 2, 5–6; f. 136, op. 59, d. 173, ll. 1–14; and the biographical sketch of Bevz in the memoirs of Dmytro Burchenko, *Reid k iuzhnomu Bugu* [Kiev: Politizdat Ukrainy, 1978], 19–20).

[29] *Vedomosti Verkhovnogo Soveta SSSR*, no. 20 (1263), 19 May 1965, 4. A note from 1962 argued that Bevz was reinstated into the party before his assignment to underground work "in order to enhance . . . his fighting spirit and enable him to deal with the remaining Communists as equals" (DAVO, f. 5243, op. 1, d. 111, l. 8). This claim appears unfounded in light of the elaborate process of Bevz's posthumous reinstatement into the party in April 1964.

Figure 1.3. A monument on Vinnytsia's main street commemorating Bevz, who was purged during the Terror in the late 1930s. Bevz had volunteered to lead the anti-German underground in the city on the eve of occupation, was subsequently executed by the Germans, and, posthumously, was named Hero of the Soviet Union.

What could induce the obkom to take such risky measures, and, more-over, what was it that enabled it to pursue policies in defiance of the central line? Searching for signals from above does not take us too far. Indeed, in the summer of 1942 a score of popular plays by leading Soviet writers already conveyed the message of a possible redemption for an imperfect political past. At the center of short stories by Tolstoy and Leonov were characters who redeemed their political crimes by volunteering for the patriotic cause. In Leonid Leonov's *Invasion*, an embittered murderer re-cently released from prison is plainly advised that the best cure for him is "a soldier's greatcoat. Jump right into the firing line head first." In *A Strange Story*, Aleksei Tolstoy went even further. The hero of Tolstoy's tale is Petr Philipovich Gorshkov, who comes from a wealthy family of Old Believers. Gorshkov has served a ten-year sentence in a concentration camp as an enemy of the Soviet power. Even though the Germans force him to serve as the village burgomaster, with the additional temptation of regaining the property confiscated by the Soviets, Gorshkov nevertheless voluntarily acts as an informer for the Soviet partisans who are active in the region. In his first encounter with the partisans, Gorshkov delivers a brief monologue that underscores the idea of the war as a means of per-sonal and national transformation. To make his point, Gorshkov invokes the name and teaching of Avvakum, the founder of his sect. "Then [in Avvakum's day] there was one truth," Gorshkov tells the partisans. "Today there is another, but truth nevertheless. And this truth is Russia . . . The Soviet government armed the people, led them into battle to stop those damned Germans from mocking us. The Soviet government is our government, the government of us Russians, us peasants (*russkaia muzhit-skaia*). I have written off and forgotten about my personal grudge long ago." The war at that point had already transcended class and personal cleavages. Significantly, however, both authors kill off their heroes at the end. For the time being, one still had to be dead in order to rejoin the political body.[30] Moreover, although Stalin assured the delegates of the Eighteenth Party Congress in March 1939 that "the edge of our punitive organs and intelligence service is no longer turned to within the country but to without, against external enemies," the reading of the Terror as a legitimate tool for the eradication of undesirable segments of Soviet soci-ety had not yet been altered. To the contrary, the Terror, as we shall see below, was just reaching its climax.

A partial answer is found in another affair that was developing simulta-neously on a national scale. In the summer of 1952 the journal *Zhovten'*, based in L'viv in the center of western Ukraine, published several chapters from Dmitrii Medvedev's book on the Vinnytsia underground, *Na bereg-*

---

[30] Leonid Leonov, "Nashestvie," *Novyi mir*, 8 (1942): 50–85; Aleksei Tolstoy, "Strannaia istoriia," *Krasnaia Zvezda*, 28 August 1942.

akh iuzhnogo Buga. There was nothing exceptional in the publication of this literary-documentary account, already a leading genre on the Soviet literary scene, except that its real-life heroes had all been expelled from the party as collaborators and impostors. Moreover, the author was well aware of this and of the risks he undertook in pursuing this line. In a barrage of protest letters, former underground activists advanced charges that could well have been fatal to the accused in the political environment of the *annus horribilis* of 1952.[31] Medvedev and *Zhovten'* were accused of deliberately advancing a personal counterversion of the party's official line. Medvedev had found it unnecessary to study the decisions of party organizations that studied the work of the underground, and *Zhovten'* ignored the Central Committee's decrees regarding the journal *Leningrad* and others. That was the only way to explain the irresponsibility of the journal in deciding to publish the chapters, exclaimed the authors.[32] And the Vinnytsia gorkom secretary who looked into the matter noted that his own wish was that, instead of Medvedev's worthless tales of falsification, "a good book about the patriots who gave their lives in the struggle against the occupiers, a real documentary novel, had been published, one that would have been a memorial to the fallen comrades and educational for future generations."[33]

Shortly after that criticism, on 24 January 1953, the attack on Medvedev turned public. The political significance attached to the case was evident when the original attack, which appeared in the local *Vinnyts'ka pravda*, was reissued on 10 February in *Literaturnaia gazeta*. Medvedev, charged the authors, chose to rely on the accounts of certain "rogues," who had nothing to do with the actual struggle against the Germans, a fact that did not stop them from fabricating accounts, portraying themselves as the organizers and leaders of the underground. The hero of the book, Trohym Kychko, was expelled for these actions from the party. Moreover, followed the allegation, in Medvedev's account, "the activity of the Vinnytsia underground [was] depicted in isolation, apart from the guiding influence of party leadership." Medvedev refused to re-

---

[31] The disbelief in the possibility of expressing particularistic views in 1952 is shared by a great many of the observers of the Soviet scene at the time. Dismissing any deviation from orthodoxy in Vasilii Grossman's *For a Just Cause*, Shimon Markish, the son of Perets Markish, the Soviet Jewish author executed in 1952, argued that "it is absurd to think that in the terrible year of 1952 someone would dare to praise a book that differed one iota from the ideological and aesthetic standard of those in power" (Shimon Markish, "A Russian Writer's Jewish Fate," *Commentary* 81, no. 4 [1986]: 42–43). For a convincing rebuttal of Markish's assessment of *For a Just Cause*, see Frank Ellis, *Vasiliy Grossman: The Genesis and Evolution of a Russian Heretic* (Rhode Island: Berg, 1994); and Edith Rogovin Frankel, *Novy Mir: A Case Study in the Politics of Literature, 1952–1958* (Cambridge, Mass.: Cambridge University Press, 1981), 4–19.

[32] PAVO, f. 425, op. 1, d. 88, ll. 17, 29.

[33] TsDAHOU, f. 1, op. 46, d. 3215, l. 31.

cant, however, or to change his account. Despite his reputation as a brave, independent thinker, dating back to his career as a Chekist and commander of a partisan parachute detachment, Medvedev was politically savvy enough to realize the danger of his actions.[34] The suppression of Fadeev's *Molodaia gvardiia* was all too recent to be ignored.[35] Posthumous eulogies by former comrades-in-arms attributed Medvedev's persistence to his civil courage and honesty, traits that should not be dismissed offhand.[36] Medvedev himself, however, offered a hint toward a more institutional direction. It seems more than just coincidence that Medvedev, in his preface to the novel, mentioned *Molodaia gvardiia* as the sample of books on the war that "are eagerly snatched up by readers of the new generation, who have no recollection of themselves in the year 1941; for many of them, *Molodaia gvardiia* was the first book they read on their own."[37] When Medvedev protested the party's handling of the Vinnytsia affair in a series of letters to the Central Committee throughout 1950–51, he concluded that the doubts cast on the real-life heroes of his story were nothing less than heresy. "To charge that because Hitler's staff was in Vinnytsia there could not have been an underground is an insult to Soviet people, and most of all to Communists," charged Medvedev.[38] In letters to relatives of the fallen underground activists, Medvedev went so far as to compare the tactics of the denouncers to those of foreign agents, a rather politically charged term in Soviet political vocabulary.[39] About a year later, and in spite of the unchanged status of those in disgrace, the

[34] In his review of the first edition of Medvedev's book, which also served as Medvedev's obituary, Petro Vershyhora, the famous partisan commander and author, emphasized that Medvedev was well aware of the probable consequences of his actions. See P. Vershyhora, "Zhizn' v bor'be," *Literaturnaia gazeta*, 17 December 1957.

[35] In 1945, Aleksandr Fadeev, a prominent writer and at the time the secretary of the executive board of the Union of Soviet Writers, published a novel about the Komsomol underground in Krasnodon, Donbas. Although the book was well received and won a First-Class Stalin Prize in 1946, a year later it was subjected to harsh criticism, mainly for its alleged downplaying of the party's role in planning and guiding the underground organization in favor of spontaneity and youthful enthusiasm. Fadeev was obliged to introduce corrections in this spirit in the second edition, issued in 1951. The affair drew broad attention and is well documented. See Harold Swayze, *Political Control of Literature in the USSR, 1946–1959* (Cambridge, Mass.: Harvard University Press , 1962), 42–45, 148–49; Werth, *Russia: The Post-War Years*, 338–39.

[36] In 1961 an editorial preface to Medvedev's book admitted that the work had "required not only great labor but also civil courage; when Medvedev went to work on the book, much was unclear on the history of the Vinnytsia underground, and several of its participants were subjected to unjustified accusations" See the 1961 edition, p. 2, and the 1962 edition, p. 2, of Dmitrii Medvedev's *Na beregakh iuzhnogo Buga* (Kiev: Radians'kyi pys'mennyk).

[37] Dmitrii Medvedev, *Na beregakh iuzhnogo Buga* (Moscow: Molodaia gvardiia, 1957), 5. This comment was omitted from the preface to the 1962 edition, published in Kiev, yet fully restored to the 1987 edition.

[38] TsDAHOU, f. 1, op. 84, d. 4042, l. 31.

[39] DAVO, f. 5243, op. 1, d. 128, l. 2.

editorial board of one of the leading Ukrainian-language journals decided to publish Medvedev's tale. When Medvedev finally gained a partial rehabilitation for Kychko and company, he paid a visit to Vinnytsia, where, according to his biographer, he was recognized in the streets, and "strangers approached him, shook his hands, and thanked him for all that he had done to restore the good reputation of hundreds of people from the lies of a small group of slanderers."[40]

Although in his letter Medvedev made every effort to emphasize that the affair was not of a personal nature but, rather, was essentially one of "political principles," these aspects appeared institutionally intertwined. The focus on personal bonding and the sense of power that accompanied it was underscored by another Hero of the Soviet Union, Petro Vershyhora, who, like Medvedev, was a partisan commander who turned to writing after the war. In 1948 Olga Dzhigurda, who served as a military doctor on a battleship during the war, published her diary, entitled *Teplokhod "Kakhetiia,"* in the literary journal *Znamia*.[41] Dzhigurda's recollections were realistic to the point of challenging some of the official myths of the wartime experience. Panicked soldiers, pregnant servicewomen, and other unflattering moments of the war were openly discussed. Not unexpectedly, the diary's initial publication attracted an outpouring of criticism. Less expected was the equally spirited defense of Dzhigurda by veterans, high-ranking officers, and rank-and-file soldiers. Dzhigurda's account, which was harshly condemned in the pages of *Literaturnaia gazeta* and *Zvezda*, gained support in a series of meetings that one observer appropriately portrayed as "not simply a literary meeting but a broader public demonstration."[42] When Vershyhora defended Dzhigurda in the pages of *Zvezda*, he asserted the moral right of veterans to describe the history of the war as *they* had seen it. "I shed enough blood for our people," Vershyhora quoted one *frontovik* as saying, "to have the right to see their shortcomings and defects."[43] The writing and publication of unfiltered memoirs were, according to Vershyhora, nothing less than a political right exercised by those who had earned that right with their blood:

[40] Teodor Gladkov, *Ostaius' chekistom!* (Moscow: Izd-vo polit. lit-ry, 1987), 124.

[41] Olga Dzhigurda, "Teplokhod 'Kakhetiia': zapiski voennogo vracha," *Znamia* 1 (1948): 3–86; 2:22–79.

[42] Matthew P. Gallagher, *The Soviet History of World War II: Myths, Memories, and Realities* (New York: Praeger, 1963), 121. Among the speakers who stood up for Dzhigurda were the editor of *Krasnyi flot* and the deputy chief of the political administration of the navy.

[43] Petro Vershyhora, "O 'byvalykh liudiakh' i ikh kritikakh," *Zvezda* 6 (1948): 106. To sharpen this point, Vershyhora implicitly drew the distinction between veterans baptized by fire and servicemen who worked behind a desk. Criticism of Dzhigurda's portrayal of panic and fear under fire could only come from those who have never experienced it. "Besides, they [the fighters] often became scared under bombs. I don't know about comrades Lifshits and Knipovich [Dzhigurda's critics], but I, for example, until the very end of the war, did not forget how to be afraid when facing enemy bombs" (ibid.).

Understandably, such a huge movement of force, will, and characters, as was the war, led millions of people—true patriots of our motherland—to reflect a lot. The defenders of the fatherland have the moral right to share these thoughts with contemporaries . . . It is difficult to overestimate the significance of books, such as *Kakhetiia*. Besides the direct conscious use and aesthetic satisfaction, they could play a significant role in the formulation of the history of the Great Patriotic War.[44]

Vershyhora's rebuttal, in this light, did not amount to, nor was it intended as, a subversion of the hegemonic discourse. Rather, carving a space for veterans to voice their own versions of the wartime experience was designed to prevent the marginalization of their experience; it was also an expression of their desire to belong and participate, a dilemma and solution not unlike those encountered by their counterparts overseas.[45] The realization of this urge would find its most viable mechanism in personal networks, the predominant form of Soviet political association.

Personal and Ethnic Bonding

The study of the Vinnytsia elite yields two main patterns of socialization through wartime experience and ethnicity.[46] These two patterns coincided to produce two clearly demarcated groups.[47] The first and numerically

---

[44] Ibid., 108.

[45] For a similar and futile attempt by American veterans to convey the war story as they experienced it and in defiance of the sanitized version advanced by an overwhelming propaganda machine at home, see the splendid account by Gerald F. Linderman, *The World within War: America's Combat Experience in World War II* (Cambridge, Mass.: Harvard University Press, 1997), 300–344, 358–62. However, this failure, noted Linderman, was also a partial result of the veterans' own desire to acquire a positive view of their wartime experience, one that would facilitate an easier assimilation into civilian society. In the process, the inevitable happened and the veterans' vision of combat drifted away from that of the combat soldier (362).

[46] The steady Ukrainization of the leading cadres in the midst of an official crackdown on the slightest perceived expressions of Ukrainian separatist sentiments attracted the attention of observers of the postwar Ukrainian scene. Interpretations referred to this phenomenon as one of inertia, resulting from the return of a critical mass of ethnic Ukrainians from the front. Armstrong and Bilinsky agree that the war played a major role in setting this course either by mass influx of demobilized Communists or the entrenchment of partisan leaders whose familiarity with the local conditions seemed useful for postwar tasks (John A. Armstrong, *The Soviet Bureaucratic Elite: A Case Study of the Ukrainian Apparatus* [New York: Praeger, 1959], 16–17; Yaroslav Bilinsky, *The Second Soviet Republic: The Ukraine after World War II* [New Brunswick, N.J.: Rutgers University Press, 1964], 233). These valid assumptions, however, gloss over the strong prescribed ethnic undertone that shaped the local political arena.

[47] The study is based on the analysis of 138 *spravki* of all obkom and raikom secretaries, following the elections of October 1948 (TsDAHOU, f. 1, op. 46, d. 3786, ll. 25–162).

TABLE 1.1
Wartime Service of Local Elite by Ethnicity

	Ukrainians	Russians	Others	Row Total
Active service at the front	72	20	2	94
	75.0%	52.6%	50.0%	
Soviet rear	24	18	2	44
	25.0%	47.4%	50.0%	
Column Total	96	38	4	138
	69.9%	27.5%	2.9%	100.0%

TABLE 1.2
Year of Joining the Local Elite in Vinnytsia by Ethnicity*

	Ukrainians	Russians	Others	Row Total
1929–35	13	1	3	17
	13.5%	2.6%	75.0%	
1936–40	41	2	0	43
	42.7%	5.3%	.0%	
1941–45	27	23	0	50
	28.1%	60.5%	.0%	
1946–48	15	12	1	28
	15.6%	31.6%	25.0%	
Column Total	96	38	4	138
	96.6%	27.5%	2.9%	100.0%

* *The party regional nomenklatura consisted of all raikom secretaries, heads of raikom depart-ments, chairmen of raispolkom and planning committees, secretaries of the Komsomol, newspaper editors, prosecutors, and directors of Machine Tractor Stations and sovkhozes.*

larger group consisted of ethnic Ukrainians, who served at the front during the war. About half the Ukrainian veterans joined the party after the onset of the Terror but had already joined the elite circle before the war (Table 1.1).[48] The second group consisted of ethnic Russians of whom only half saw active service during the war. These officials were party veterans but new to the local scene. Two-thirds joined the party before the commencement of the Terror, and almost all arrived in Vinnytsia after the liberation of the region in March 1944 (Table 1.2).[49]

The marginalization of noncombat service coincided with the resentment of the officials who returned after being evacuated to the Soviet rear.

[48] Of ninety-six ethnic Ukrainians, seventy-two fought in the war, forty-two joined the party after 1935, and fifty-four held positions at the level of at least department head of raikom/raispolkom before the war.

[49] Of thirty-eight ethnic Russians, only twenty fought in the war, twenty-five joined the party before 1935, and only three held a leading position in Vinnytsia before the war.

Early on, denunciation of party officials who had not spent the war years at the front or in the underground became a main component of party life. At times, even raikom secretaries did not hesitate to denounce their superiors if they believed that the latter had dodged combat activity. When two raikom secretaries who had returned from the occupied territory spotted three secretaries of the obkom in Moscow, they charged that the latter had

> formed and then abandoned four groups for underground work in the Vinnytsia region in various locations near the front. Even worse, they told everyone that they, too, remained in underground work in order to lead the underground raikoms, which means that they either lied or displayed cowardice. This disgraceful behavior is not proper party conduct.[50]

Eventually this resentment amounted to a tacit criticism of Russian officials who arrived from the Soviet rear. As one might suspect, direct expressions of ethnic resentment among the party elite could not be voiced publicly. Yet the single piece of evidence available is a telling one. On 2 February 1947 the first secretary of the Vinnytsia obkom was informed of a conspiracy to remove Kalashnikov, the first secretary of the Iaryshiv raikom. The leader of the plot, the second secretary, Andrii Lupokh, was quoted as telling other secretaries who supported him: "We'll kick out all the Russians and install our own people."[51] If the first secretary of the obkom, Havrylo Mishchenko, could not be as blunt, his attitude toward the Russian evacuees differed from that of Lupokh only in its more restrained tone. When Mishchenko addressed the plenum of the obkom in December 1944, the tacit criticism of the outsiders was clear enough:

> Every single Communist must understand that the methods of work we employed before the war, or those we have been using during the war in the eastern regions of the Soviet Union, where there were no Germans [are of no use in the present conditions]. Nevertheless, many comrades among us, arriving from the eastern regions, are familiar [only] with the kinds of work and leading party organizations in circumstances that differ from those we face now in the territory previously occupied by the Germans. It must be understood that the implementation of mechanistic methods of work from Sverdlovsk, Novosibirsk, Chkalovsk, and Cheliabinsk is absolutely impossible, and at this time they are absolutely unacceptable for us in Ukraine.[52]

---

[50] TsDAHOU, f. 1, op. 22, d. 165, l. 104. Ironically the accused secretaries, Burchenko and Nyzhnyk, did take an active part in the partisan movement, serving as commissars of the two largest formations.

[51] PAVO, f. 136, op. 13, d. 124, l. 8. Lupokh himself was Ukrainian, a native of a village in the Iaryshiv district. He joined the party only in May 1941 and served as a commissar in the war (TsDAHOU, f. 1, op. 62, d. 231, ll. 152–54, 165).

[52] RGASPI, f. 17, op. 44, d. 1651, ll. 119–20.

A report from the cadres department in July 1947 showed that this division within the party between Ukrainian veterans and Russian evacuees had become institutionalized. Newly arrived veterans, who comprised the majority of the regional *nomenklatura*, were portrayed as inexperienced but "quick to learn." In contrast, the second group of officials who arrived from evacuation and had longer tenure in their jobs were described as unsuitable for the tasks of the postwar era.[53]

The regeneration of the party proceeded along the lines of ethnic affiliation and combat exploits. The annual reports by the cadres departments at the obkom and raikom levels regularly recorded their share of decorated veterans in the *nomenklatura*.[54] Party officials repeatedly demonstrated that inner-party hierarchy and status had come to be defined by public recognition of their wartime exploits. When two of them protested the delay in bestowing the duly deserved governmental awards for their partisan past, the personal injury and anxiety over their political status could not be exaggerated:

> In what way are we worse than others? Our formation had done far more than the Stalin formation. Why isn't our performance as commander and commissar rewarded? We are hurt to the depth of our souls. Our partisans are also troubled by this fact. Someone here deliberately degrades the dignity that we won in the harsh struggle against the fascist aggressors. No one will deprive us of it. Our contribution should be honored truthfully and deservedly.[55]

In line with this, the obkom continued to address itself to similar incidents well into the 1960s and 1970s. Repeatedly the regional leadership took time off from the daily operations of the party-state machine to respond to the complaints of prominent officials who sought to correct the wartime record. The Kychko affair alone was brought to a closure in

---

[53] TsDAHOU, f. 1, op. 23, d. 4423, l. 71.

[54] Ibid., f. 1, op. 23, d. 4422, l. 33. In 1946 the obkom cadres department emphasized that more than half the obkom *nomenklatura* fell into the new category: 850 were decorated once, 488 twice, and 851 three times. The lower the hierarchical level, the higher the rate, especially with the wave of demobilization under way. In late May 1947, 281 of the 304 members of the *nomenklatura* in the Koziatyn raikom were decorated veterans (ibid., d. 1562, l. 29).

[55] TsDAHOU, f. 1, op. 22, d. 160, l. 32. To be sure, the quest for public recognition had its lighter side, as in the case of one S. A. Kuznetsov, a charlatan who launched a successful literary career by presenting himself as a Hero of the Soviet Union and the recipient of five government awards. Before being exposed as a fraud—neither a Hero of the Soviet Union nor a writer—Kuznetsov managed to publish a novel, in Kiev, in the Ukrainian language, *Formula muzhnist'*. The Russian-language edition was published by none other than the Ministry of Defense as *Rasskazy o perezhitom*. Apparently that was not the first time Kuznetsov falsely identified himself as a Hero of the Soviet Union in order to publish stories in journals such as *Krasnoflotets* and *Pioner* (TsDAHOU, f. 1, op. 23, d. 4979, ll. 3–8).

early 1963, and as late as April 1975 the party rehabilitated posthumously another member of the disgraced Vinnytsia underground.[56] But the regional organization's obsessive engagement of the war's legacy was hardly unique. Five years after the region was liberated, the war generation had established itself as the single largest group in the regional *nomenklatura*. The newcomers' visibility was demonstrated publicly at the Eighth Regional Party Congress in January 1949, where 52 percent of the delegates had joined the party during and after the war, and 63.4 percent were participants in the war.[57] At the same time, the relative share of Ukrainians in the *nomenklatura* increased steadily from 58.5 percent in 1945, to 72.2 percent in 1949. The share of ethnic Russians dropped by more than one-half from 33.3 percent to 16.3 percent. Five years after the region was liberated, representations of the war had already defined a lasting self-image and model of regeneration for the local elite. At the regional and district levels, which were less prone to direct intervention from Moscow, these images were both a means of expressing ethnonational pride within an identifiable political culture and of fortifying political status (Table 1.3).

Reconstructing the Pantheon of Heroes

Although the Soviets maintained an uncompromising adherence to several iron principles, mainly the rejection of a capitalist market economy and the establishment of one-party rule, they refrained from fixing a static set of cultural representations. Repudiation of certain myths, policies, and celebrated ideal-type figures, on purely pragmatic grounds, had been institutionalized in Soviet political culture. In the mid-1930s this elasticity, which owed its presence partially to the absence of authoritative definition of what constituted capitalist culture, allowed for the introduction of a new set of cultural codes.[58]

Less pronounced, however, was the impact of the constant reshaping of the pantheon of heroes on the inner world of the true believers. Like other Soviet citizens from all walks of life, Communists had to reconcile their entrenched belief in the existence of elusive and irredeemable enemies in their midst with the professed inability to accept the guilt of certain individuals and groups they either admired or knew personally. Signs of

---

[56] PAVO, f. 425, op. 1, d. 107, ll. 1–5; d. 113, ll. 1–10.

[57] PAVO, f. 136, op. 29, d. 1, ll. 247–51.

[58] For the vagueness, though not to be confused with impotence, of the codification of "socialist culture" owing to the imprecision in conceptualizing its "bourgeois" counterpart, see Kotkin, *Magnetic Mountain*, 180–92.

TABLE 1.3
Composition of the Vinnytsia Party Elite
(Raikom and Gorkom Secretaries)

Categories of Members		1947		1948	
		N	%	N	%
Gender	Male	139	97.2	131	95.0
	Female	4	2.8	7	5.0
Age	< 30	—	—	8	5.8
	30–35	22	15.4	27	19.8
	35–40	43	30.1	32	23.2
	40–45	53	40.6	57	41.3
	40 +	20	13.9	14	10.2
Nationality	Ukrainian	96	67.0	101	73.2
	Russian	44	30.9	35	25.3
	Others	3	2.1	2	1.5
Education	Higher	18	12.6	23	16.6
	N.C. Higher	12	8.4	18	13.1
	Middle	71	49.7	77	55.7
	N.C. Middle	31	21.6	18	13.1
	Elementary	11	7.7	2	1.5
Admission Date to Party	pre–1930	52	36.6	37	26.8
	1930–34	50	35.1	39	28.3
	1935–38	8	5.8	18	13.6
	1939–40	24	16.1	23	16.7
	1941 on	9	6.4	21	15.2
Tenure as a Raikom Secretary	0 to 6 mos.	5	3.6	16	11.6
	6–12 mos.	13	9.2	23	16.8
	1–3 years	51	35.6	43	31.1
	> 3 years	74	51.6	56	40.5
Year of Joining the Local Elite in Vinnytsia	1929–35	—	—	17	12.3
	1936–40	—	—	43	31.2
	1941–45	—	—	50	36.2
	1946–48	—	—	28	20.3
Wartime Service	Active	—	—	94	68.1
	Noncombat	—	—	44	31.9

Note: N.C. = incomplete; N.C. Higher = incomplete higher education; N.C. Middle = incomplete high school education.

confusion among the die-hard Communists accompanied the Great Transformation from the outset. In the rural region of Vinnytsia, signs of doubt in the official narrative appeared during collectivization. A zealous party member, voicing alarm at the catastrophic results of the pace of collectivization—a policy he nevertheless endorsed in principle—wrote a letter to the Politburo in Moscow confronting the erosion in belief caused by the incomprehensible reconstruction of the Bolshevik pantheon of heroes. Addressing the exclusion of Trotsky, Zinoviev, Bukharin, Rykov, Rakovskii, Sosnovskii, and others, the devout Communist, who withheld his full name, referred to the former leaders as the wisest people of the country, the vanguard of the Revolution, of struggle, of victory, and the close and beloved colleagues of Ilich [Lenin]. "The question arises," he asserted, "how they could stop being revolutionaries after Ilich's [death]. In my opinion, we should not even entertain such a thought. All the dismissed comrades remained revolutionaries."[59] Shortly afterward, following the suicide of Mykola Skrypnyk, the demoted commissar of education and the driving force behind the Ukrainization policy, teachers in Vinnytsia told their students that "Skrypnyk was not guilty, and that the party and Postyshev had led him to suicide."[60]

The mutual processes of rattling the hitherto cohesive world and the search for a meaningful guiding past and ideal types was punctuated by the Terror. In the February–March 1937 Plenum of the All-Union Central Committee, none other than the zealous Pavel Postyshev expressed his own disbelief that one of his subordinates, an apparatchik with perfect revolutionary credentials, had "suddenly" become a Trotskyist in 1934.[61] On a more intimate level, Stepan Podlubnyi, the Vinnytsia-born son of a dekulakized peasant obsessed with his impure social origin, was tormented by the incomprehensible arrest of admired acquaintances ("So many offspring from the other class are being uncovered, in every corner, its amazing . . . And they are all wonderful people, they are the best—celebrated heroes of labor. One could draw a very interesting conclusion," he wrote in his diary) and his own beloved mother ("To number mama, a halfilliterate woman, among the Trotskyites, that would have never occurred to me. Not even in my dreams would I be able to imagine this, as I know

[59] The yearning for guiding figures found its expression in the eulogization of Lenin, who "as a matter of fact, we do not have figures equal to [Ilich] . . . However you consider it, Comrades, it is my view that if Ilich were alive, the country would not have reached such a desperate situation" (PAVO, f. 136, op. 3, d. 4, ll. 75–78).

[60] PAVO, f. 136, op. 3, d. 219, l. 126.

[61] Postyshev concluded that Karpov, the person to whom he referred, had always been an enemy. This, however, Khrushchev omitted when he cited Postyshev's comment in his de-Stalinization speech at the Twentieth Party Congress, and thus Postyshev entered historiography as a principled opponent of the Terror. See J. Arch Getty, "The Politics of Repression Revisited," in J. Arch Getty and Roberta Manning, eds., *Stalinist Terror: New Perspectives* (Cambridge: Cambridge University Press, 1993), 56 n. 65; Khrushchev, *Khrushchev Remembers*, 629–30. Other accounts cite that the announcement of the trial of the military command on charges of treason, especially of Marshal Tukhachevskii, appeared to be a watershed in the ability of many to suspend disbelief in the official version (Kotkin, *Magnetic Mountain*, 345–46).

her very well").[62] In Leningrad Iuliia Sokolova-Piatnitskaia, a veteran revolutionary and the wife of a prominent party leader arrested at the height
of the Terror, was devastated by her failure to unconditionally accept the
guilt of the man she loved and admired. "It still distresses me that I cannot
hate Piatnitskii," she wrote in her diary.

> although I thought at the beginning that I would absolutely hate him, that
> any other way was impossible . . . Obviously Piatnitskii was never a professional
> revolutionary but a professional bastard—a spy or a provocateur . . . But who
> was he—the one or the other? It is unclear to me, and it is tormenting me. I
> think of the first, and I feel unbearably sorry; I want to die or fight for him. I
> think of the second—it's unbearably disgusting, dirty. I want to live to see that
> they are all caught.[63]

Neither doubted that pernicious enemies could be found even among the
best of their society. But neither could escape the lingering confusion
brought on by the destruction of the close and admired ones.

On the eve of the war the confusion caused by the constant attrition of
the revolutionary pantheon of heroes began breeding blunt cynicism.
"Why is it impossible to refer to Maksim as a present-day hero?" soldiers
asked an officer during a discussion of the popular films *The Youth of Maksim* and *The Return of Maksim* in the summer of 1939. "If Maksim turned
up today, he would be tried and shot, so this doesn't work," answered the
officer. "After all, a few civil war heroes had been shot. At first, they were
heroes but later they were tried and shot as enemies of the people. This
could happen with Maksim as well: Either he is an enemy, or he would be
made into one."[64] A year later party agitators were confronted with certain
questions: "Why are there no heroes in the Soviet Union such as Pechorin,
Evgenii Onegin, and Chatski? And if they were to turn up, would the
NKVD arrest them?"[65] Years later, with another mass purge looming on
the horizon, the probable consequences of such confusion were evident.
Following the announcement of the "Doctors' Plot," some party members in Ukraine were recorded saying that the new affair "reminds me of
1937. Then they also spoke about Gorky and others, saying that their

[62] Jochen Hellbeck, "Fashioning the Stalinist Soul: The Diary of Stepan Podlubnyi,
1931–1939"; *Jahrbücher für Geschichte Osteuropas* 44 (1996): 367, 370.

[63] *Golgofa. Po materialam arkhivno-sledstvennogo dela no.603 na Sokolovu-Piatnitskuiu
Iu.I* (St. Petersburg: Palitra, 1993), 100, 42, respectively.

[64] Rossiiskii gosudarstvennyi voennyi arkhiv (RGVA), f. 9, op. 39, d. 71, l. 267. Along
with *The Vyborg Side*, both films were part of a trilogy directed by Grigorii Kozintsev and
Leonid Trauberg. In a sense, the officer was wrong; during the war, the fictional character
of the revolutionary hero, Maksim, was mobilized to the war effort in patriotic appeals to
the population.

[65] RGASPI, f. 17, op. 125, d. 46, l. 8.

deaths were not from natural causes. Personally I do not believe this." Another declared that he "firmly believes we are witnessing a repetition of 1937, when masses of honest Soviet people were declared enemies of the people . . . another Ezhov has undoubtedly arisen and is engaged in dirty deeds, throwing totally innocent people in jail. I do not believe this group did those things reported in the communiqué. It seems to me that all these repressions have another goal."[66]

For a great many articulators of the myth of the Great Patriotic War, the Terror meant more than the destruction of heroes under whose shadow they were introduced to the Bolshevik idea. The events of 1937 and 1941 constantly fed each other within the inner world of communist veterans who integrated the myth of the war as both a shield from arbitrary violence and a personal redemption from the humiliation of incompetence felt during the Terror. When Stalin turned on the famed Marshal Zhukov in June 1946, he was confronted by a previously inconceivable united front of defiant commanders who defended their comrade. "Today it's him, tomorrow it's me," recalled Marshal Konev. "If we did not defend Zhukov, 1937 would have repeated itself all over again. And besides, during the years of the war we became more courageous."[67] The same was true for the leaders of the Jewish Anti-Fascist Committee (JAFC) on trial in 1952. Subjected to months of beating by their interrogators, the Jewish leaders not only insisted on being innocent but even chose to make the abuse a central issue in the court proceedings. Neither poor health nor old age had an impact on their defiance. Like their predecessors during the Terror of the late 1930s, these veteran Communists were seasoned enough to realize that their fate was sealed long before the actual trial. Unlike those tried during the Terror who confessed to any fantastic charge, they confessed to nothing.[68] Between 1937 and 1952 there was the war and the reflections it triggered on the Soviet system. Mykhailo Stakhurs'kyi is said to have escaped being purged in 1937 by the skin of his teeth.[69] Dmitrii Medvedev, a career member of the NKVD and the author of the Vinnytsia underground story and its disgraced heroes, nearly became a victim of the Terror in the fall of 1937 and was forced into retirement at the age of thirty-nine. Like the fallen Bevz, it was family ties to "hostile elements" that nearly brought down Medvedev.[70] As for two

---

[66] "More about Public Reaction to the Doctors' Plot," *Jews in Eastern Europe* (Fall 1996): 33.

[67] Kuromiya, *Freedom and Terror in the Donbas*, 311.

[68] See, for example, the defiant testimony of Boris Shimeliovich in Vladimir Naumov, ed., *Nepravednyi Sud: Poslednii Stalinskii Rasstrel. Stenogramma sudebnogo protsessa nad chlenami evreiskogo antifashistskogo komiteta* (Moscow: Nauka, 1994), 198–99.

[69] Interview with Vasyl' Kostenko, 23 March 1993, Kiev, Ukraine.

[70] Medvedev's biographer refers to the repression of his brother, Aleksander, also in the NKVD ranks, that had repercussions on Medvedev's career (Gladkov, *Ostaius' chekistom*, 50).

other legendary and better-known heroes of the Soviet Union, Konstantin Rokossovskii and Semen Rudnev, combat exploits were both a reaffirmation of their Bolshevik credentials and a point of departure from a past to which no one could or wanted to refer.[71] It seems that the learning curve of Soviet citizens and wartime experience bred a new assertive citizen.

By wartime, the self-erasure of the Terror among members of the local elite was practically complete. Having returned from a raid into occupied Vinnytsia in August 1943, Dmytro Burchenko, the commissar of the Lenin partisan brigade, composed a report addressed to Khrushchev on the situation in the region. Referring to the political mood of the population, Burchenko wrote Khrushchev that in order to discredit Soviet power,

> the Germans blow the horn about facts allegedly "disclosed" by them of the mass murder by the NKVD organs of the Ukrainian population in the city of Vinnytsia between 1937 and 1939 and in 1941. This propaganda began soon after the seizure of the city of Vinnytsia and continues at the present time. Periodically the excavation of cemeteries and mass graves is carried out, photographs are published, testimonies [are published] of relatives, who allegedly identified their close relatives, their personal belongings, and other materials. All the newspapers published by the Germans in Ukraine spread similar information.[72]

"This propaganda is not successful," Burchenko assured Khrushchev, "since the population is convinced that all the photographs are of victims of the mass extermination of Jewish and other populations, organized by the Germans themselves." Burchenko was referring to the exhumation of the mass graves, which contained some 9,439 corpses, by the Germans and the local authorities in May 1943.[73] As a veteran of the Vinnytsia party

[71] Semen Rudnev, the commissar of the Kovpak partisan formation, was a career serviceman who was jailed for two years before he was released and retired to his hometown in 1939. Rudnev was killed in the famous raid to the Carpathians in 1943 and instantly became one of the most celebrated symbols of the partisan struggle. On Rokossovskii's career, see n. 8, above.

[72] PAVO, f. 425, op. 2, d. 11, l. 6.

[73] The Germans indeed used the exhumation of the mass graves to discredit Soviet power within and without the occupied territories by establishing an international investigation commission, as they had done shortly before in Katyn. However, if Soviet responsibility for at least part of the executions was clearly established, the identification of the victims as solely Ukrainians was misleading. Only 679, a mere 7.2 percent of the corpses, were identified by nationality, of whom there were 490 Ukrainians, 28 Poles, and 161 of "unknown nationality." An editor of *Vinnyts'ki visti*, the local newspaper in occupied Vinnytsia, confirmed that although there were Russians, Ukrainians, Jews, and Poles among the corpses, the published reports spoke only of Ukrainians (Harvard University Refugee Interview Project [HURIP], 1950–51, #548). *Vinnyts'ki visti* began reporting on the exhumations immediately upon their commencement on 24 May 1943 and continued throughout August of that year. See *Vinnyts'ki visti*, May–August 1943, passim. For a brief account by a German reporter, see Tsentral'nyi derzhavnyi arkhiv vyshchykh orhaniv vlady Ukrainy (TsDAVOVU), f. 3206, op.

machine, who was already an obkom secretary at the height of the Terror, Burchenko was familiar with the mass executions and the identity of their perpetrators. Although at the time many of the identified victims were executed as "enemies of the people," by 1943 the Terror had become a nonevent even in a confidential correspondence between two of its perpetrators and beneficiaries. The new pantheon of heroes would be constructed with a fairly clean slate.

Similarly, whereas until the very eve of the war social origin was still the central motif in the articulation of self-identities, in 1944 this urge was virtually gone.[74] Early in the war, the release from the special settlements and bestowing internal passports to families of former kulaks who were serving at the front, as well as other nonpolitical inmates, sent the message that wartime exploits redeemed past sins. Whereas this act, as we shall see below, was in line with the Soviet prewar policies in society at large, its application to party life was truly astounding. By early 1943 one Dmitrii Triastsov, who described himself as a former recidivist who knew the penal system rather well, had already become a company commander in the Red Army. Writing to his former wardens on 11 April 1943, Triastsov implored the Chekists to read his letter to other prisoners as a living example of the possibility to rebuild their lives through service at the front. "Here, each of them can vindicate himself, be a good commander, and also receive high decoration, as I had," wrote Triastsov.

> For my good exploits in the fight against fascism I was awarded not only with the Red Star medal, but I was also admitted to the ranks of the Communist Party. I don't have on me anymore this past, filthy stain of my [criminal] record. It was dropped. Therefore, a bright path for a happy life is open for me. The party opened my eyes that had been blinded by crime.[75]

The adaptation of the war as a self-ordained point of departure was best captured in a letter by Mitia Khludov, a nineteen-year-old soldier, who belonged to a well-known Moscow merchant family that suffered greatly during the early years of the Bolshevik regime. "I am proud to tell you," Khludov wrote to Alexander Werth two weeks before the young soldier's death,

---

2, d. 71, l. 85; and Ihor Kamenetsky, ed., *The Tragedy of Vinnytsia: Materials on Stalin's Policy of Extermination in Ukraine during the Great Purge, 1936–1938* (Toronto: Ukrainian Historical Association, 1989).

[74] For the predominance of the social origin category in the prewar Soviet world, see Hellbeck, "Fashioning the Stalinist Soul"; and Sheila Fitzpatrick, "Ascribing Class: The Construction of Social Identity in Soviet Russia," *Journal of Modern History* 65 (December 1993): 745–70.

[75] GARF, f. 9414, op. 1, d. 325, l. 65. Another decorated former inmate, one V. P. Shekhavtsev, rose to the rank of lieutenant and was readmitted to the party (l. 80).

that my battery has done wonders in knocking the hell out of the Fritzes. Also, for our last engagement, I have been proposed for the Patriotic War Order, and, better still, I have been accepted into the party. Yes, I know, my father and my mother were *burzhuis*, but what the hell! I am a Russian, one hundred percent Russian, and I am proud of it, and our people have made this victory possible after all the terror and humiliation of 1941; I am ready to give my life for my country and for Stalin; I am proud to be in the party, to be one of Stalin's victorious soldiers.[76]

In Vinnytsia, scores of more fortunate servicemen who survived the war lived to experience the institutionalization of Khludov's boast in party life. Many of them were reinstated into the party in spite of having committed various offenses that would otherwise have led to automatic expulsion. Between April 1944 and December 1947 the obkom reinstated at least ninety-one members who had been expelled by the raikoms for violations that ranged from observing religious rites to criminal offenses such as embezzlement and theft of grain from the collective farms. As a rule, Communists who committed such violations and had not served at the front were expelled. The guiding criterion in reversing the raikoms' decisions were service in the Red Army and military awards. Such was the case of Slava Marchuk. A party member since 1925, Marchuk was demoted from the post of kolkhoz chairman and expelled from the party by the Khmil'nyk raikom for poor performance and for profiteering. Reversing the expulsion, the obkom bureau wrote:

> Comrade Marchuk deserves expulsion from the party, but, having learned that he long served in the Red Army ranks, was at the front, and was awarded six orders and medals, [the bureau] orders the reversal of the decision by the bureau of Khmil'nyk raikom from 26 August 1947 and the reinstatement of Marchuk as a member of the CPSU [Communist Party of the Soviet Union].[77]

At a time when the campaign to regain control over the kolkhoz peasantry reached its climax and violators of lesser crimes were expelled, the obkom found it sufficient to attach merely a "severe reprimand" to Marchuk's personal file.

Wartime exploits also compensated for religious offenses. Even though the authorities intensified their antireligious campaign in the region and expelled scores of Communists charged with religious offenses, decorated veterans maintained their party status. At least eighteen veterans who practiced religious ceremonies, mainly the baptism of babies, were allowed back into the party. Grigorii Lutskov, to cite one example, baptized his

---

[76] Werth, *Russia at War*, 763.
[77] TsDAHOU, f. 1, op. 50, d. 377, l. 9; for similar cases, see d. 159, l. 61; and d. 257, ll. 13–14; d. 260, ll. 12–13.

son and was expelled by the Ulaniv raikom in August 1946. Shortly after, however, the obkom overturned this decision and reinstated Lutskov, citing his service in the Red Army between 1936 and 1944 and his discharge as an invalid at the rank of captain.[78]

The primacy of wartime credentials was evident even in cases classified as political violations, particularly ties with people who were categorized as "hostile elements." Ivan Klimov, a demobilized invalid, not only married the daughter of a former *starosta* (village elder appointed by the occupation authorities) but also organized a campaign among the kolkhozniks for the rehabilitation of his father-in-law. As one might suspect, the Chernivtsi raikom expelled Klimov for his "ties to hostile elements, for protecting and defending a former Romanian *starosta*, and for his nonparty conduct."[79] The obkom, referring to Klimov's status as a decorated invalid, reinstated him with only a severe reprimand.

Purifying the Myth, Act I: A Partisan Cult without Partisans

For many others, however, the emerging myth of the war was the exit door from the Soviet elite. The fate of former communist partisans, who for a while came to personify the Soviet popular wartime effort, was particularly instructive. During the first four postwar years regional party politics were dominated by a fierce power struggle between Red Army veterans and the partisan movement. The roots of the friction between the battling camps dated back to the civil war era, but the postwar struggle did more than stir up traditional conflicts. At stake was the appropriate interpretation of the war's legacy in party life and, by extension, what it meant to be a postwar Bolshevik.

Four years after the liberation of Vinnytsia only 2 of the 131 party secretaries had been affiliated with the partisan movement, a striking development in light of the intensive cult of the partisan movement.[80] This is even more surprising if one recalls that until 1947 former partisans occupied

---

[78] TsDAHOU, f. 1, op. 50, d. 199, ll. 16–17. As with criminal and intraparty offenses, there were individual exceptions to this rule, especially when the subjects of verification systematically engaged in religious rites or in additional violations. Vasyl' Krasyl'nyk, a decorated veteran, was not saved by his wartime record after he got married in a church and engaged in selling kolkhoz products in western Ukraine (d. 201, l. 26; and d. 204, l. 14).

[79] Ibid., d. 115, l. 16.

[80] Of the two, Pavlo Lukovs'kyi, the first secretary of Bar district, was only briefly attached to partisan activity in 1944. The other, Nadiia Herzhova, the secretary of cadres of the Vinnytsia gorkom, was young (only thirty-one years old) and female, not a plus in the almost totally male arena (95 percent).

three of the top positions in the region: second secretary of the obkom, chairman of the oblispolkom, and chairman of the presidium of the regional consumers' society (*oblpotrebsoiuz*).[81] Students of postwar Soviet politics have pointed to the emergence of a powerful and enduring political faction during this era, the so-called partisan clan.[82] Indeed, at a time of upheaval in party life, those associated with the partisan movement enjoyed either stability or upward mobility. Although less impressive than the gains of their Belorussian counterparts,[83] a significant number of former partisans in Ukraine reached the top of the regional *nomenklatura*. At the Sixteenth Congress of the Ukrainian Party in January 1949, 66 of the 650 delegates were former commanders or commissars of partisan formations. As late as 1955, according to one observer, nearly three-quarters of the obkom secretaries in the Ukrainian Republic and most members of the Ukrainian Central Committee gained their leading posts during the war as organizers of the partisan movement.[84]

Numerous signs indicated that the former partisans were busy forming a tight patronage network at the local level. During the initial phase of verifying the wartime conduct of Communists who remained on the German-occupied territory, the obkom showed preference to the scores of individuals who served in the partisan detachments or enrolled in the party during their stay there. Of the thirty-two former partisans whose party status was considered by the obkom between March 1944 and December 1947, thirty-one were reinstated—the highest rate for any given group. For one thing, the organized detachments that operated in the region from 1943 on functioned as the combat branches of the Soviet power on the occupied territory and led a full party life. A rejection of their admission to the party could well be interpreted as a challenge to the party's own credo of "baptism by fire." Often, however, the recommenders for the partisan applicants were the postwar obkom secretaries who served as commissars of the detachments. By now these very same officials were in charge of the verification procedure, and the bumpy road to reinstatement into the party was smoothed. One such beneficiary was Mykola Lunev, who had served in the Red Army since 1938 before he was captured by the Germans. Later on, Lunev lived two years on the occupied territory where he worked under the Germans. In December 1943 he joined the partisans with whom he served with distinction until April

[81] The three were Nyzhnyk, Burchenko, and Moliavko, respectively.

[82] Boris Lewytzkyi, *Die Sowjetukraine, 1944–1963* (Cologne: Kiepenheuer and Witsch, 1964), 72–75; "Besonderheiten der sowjetukrainischen Entwicklung," *Osteuropa* 11 (October 1962): 669–75; Armstrong, *The Soviet Bureaucratic Elite*, 131–32.

[83] See Urban, *An Algebra of Soviet Power*.

[84] Boris Lewytzkyi, "Kommunistychna partiia Ukrainy—1955 rik," *Ukrains'kyi zbirnyk* 3 (1955): 129.

1944. In February 1944 the party committee of the partisan brigade requested that Lunev be admitted as a member. His admission was denied
in November 1944 by the Komsomol raikom on the technical ground that
the recommenders knew Lunev less than a year, thus violating the party
statute. For thousands of Communists, a record as murky as Lunev's
spelled nothing but expulsion from the party. The obkom, however, overruled the raikom and reinstated Lunev. That two of his recommenders
happened to be Vasyl' Nyzhnyk, second secretary of the obkom, and
Semen Oliinyk, an aid to the obkom's first secretary, surely had its effect.[85]
Former top commanders readily provided glorifying reference letters on
behalf of lower-ranking commanders, even when their credentials had
been cast in doubt. And so in May 1944 Dmytro Burchenko, then serving
as second secretary of the obkom, showered praises on Semen Oliinyk, a
former underground activist and partisan who was accused at the time of
having betrayed his comrades to the Gestapo and falsifying his wartime
record. Nevertheless Burchenko praised Oliinyk's personal bravery, fear-
lessness, and discipline, as well as his political assets: "[Oliinyk] inculcated
among the partisans the love of the party and of the socialist motherland
[and] under his leadership the party political apparat of the formation
systematically conducted mass party work among the peaceful population;
as a result, all measures taken by the enemy were sabotaged by the population."[86] Vasyl' Nyzhnyk's letter of recommendation for Volodymyr Sliusarenko is even more impressive in this regard, given the suspicion raised
against the latter's cozy relations with Ukrainian nationalist partisans.[87]
Further, the two obkom secretaries placed their former subordinates in
the partisan formations in jobs and secured health care for ailing veterans.
Still, in a few short years the Vinnytsia party elite had literally been purged
of former partisans.[88] How and why?

Once again, the clue lay in the figure of the man who ruled Vinnytsia
in the first postwar decade and the ethos he espoused and embodied. Although there is no direct evidence of explicit hostility on the part of Stakhurs'kyi directed against the former partisans as a group, it was definitely
the impression he conveyed. In May 1949 a report by the Ministry of
State Security (MGB) on one Mykola Iakubov, a former partisan under
investigation for making anti-Soviet comments, noted:

> In a conversation with close acquaintances in January 1949 regarding his search
> for a job, [Iakubov] said that he would wait for the appointment of former chair-
> man of the *oblispolkom* Burchenko and approach him. Harshly cursing the secre-

[85] RGASPI, f. 17, op. 45, d. 2001, ll. 114–15.
[86] TsDAHOU, f. 1, op. 22, d. 160, ll. 33–34.
[87] Ibid., l. 19.
[88] Ibid., op. 13, d. 6, l. 19; RGASPI, f. 17, op. 45, d. 2003, l. 183.

tary of the Vinnytsia obkom [Stakhurs'kyi], Iakubov slanderously asserted that the former sacked every partisan from responsible positions.[89]

Stakhurs'kyi's actions spoke for themselves. His arrival to Vinnytsia in mid-1945 signaled the swan song of the partisan hegemony on the local scene. More specifically, it meant the end of shortcuts in the party career of former partisans and a more pronounced ambivalence toward the partisan movement. The first signs were evident in the verification process. Volodymyr Kulybaba was enrolled as a full member by his party cell in the Stalin partisan brigade in October 1943, without the mandatory tenure of candidacy. On 26 July 1945 the obkom's bureau reduced Kulybaba's party status to that of a candidate.[90] This rule applied to relatively prominent apparatchiks, such as the above-mentioned Volodymyr Sliusarenko, chairman of the Turbiv raispolkom and a decorated partisan commander who had climbed the ranks. Sliusarenko was admitted as a candidate by the primary party cell of his partisan detachment in October 1943, and as a full member in January 1944. Sliusarenko claimed that he had already been enrolled as a candidate in May 1942 by the party primary organization of his army unit. Yet, since his claim was found to be unsubstantiated, the obkom reenrolled him merely as a candidate.[91]

Between 1947 and 1948 all prominent partisans left the region. In March 1947 Vasyl' Nyzhnyk, second secretary of the obkom, left to work in the Central Committee in Kiev. In May of that year Moliavko, chairman of the Presidium of the Vinnytsia *Oblpotrebsoiuz*, was discharged by the Central Committee, and in October 1948, after a long and bitter struggle, Stakhurs'kyi secured the transfer of his nemesis, Burchenko, out of the oblast.[92] Moliavko's case was revealing. Charged with embezzlement, womanizing, drunkenness, and a loose handling of personnel, Moliavko invoked his partisan past as the deputy of Aleksei Fedorov, the famous partisan commander and prominent party official, twice named Hero of the Soviet Union. It was hardly incidental that at the top of the list of Moliavko's defenders was Burchenko, chairman of the oblispolkom and former commissar of the largest partisan formation in the region. In this

[89] PAVO, f. 136, op. 29, d. 191, l. 100.

[90] RGASPI, f. 17, op. 45, d. 2005, ll. 4–5. For a series of similar rulings, see ll. 119–22, 147–50, 206–7; and TsDAHOU, f. 1, op. 50, d. 210, ll. 4–5.

[91] RGASPI, f. 17, op. 44, d. 1654, ll. 56–57.

[92] The archives of the Central Committee in Kiev and the obkom in Vinnytsia contain abundant materials on the bitter struggle between Stakhurs'kyi and Burchenko. The Central Committee addressed the rivalry and its impact on the performance of party and state organs time and again between 1946 and 1948. Burchenko was finally left isolated when his deputy, Lutokhyn, was dismissed for incompetence and he himself was held responsible. See PAVO, f. 136, op. 12, d. 828, ll. 102, 134, 157–58; TsDAHOU, f. 1, op. 23, d. 2681, ll. 114–16; and d. 4213, ll. 29–30; op. 46, d. 2285, ll. 8–9.

light, the obkom bureau's resolution was telling. It charged Moliavko with employing at least twenty-one people (out of a core of thirty-five) who held administrative positions under the Germans and added that the slight improvement in the organization's performance was attributed to the recruitment of demobilized Red Army servicemen.[93] Herein lay the key to the problem as well as the solution.

For the hegemonic group of Red Army veterans now at the helm of the local scene, the former partisans embodied the antithesis of everything they stood for. The shadow of the civil war *partizanshchina* (a term for unruly, anarchic conduct) still loomed. The prevailing feeling of regular army officers toward partisans was one of contempt. The inferior image of partisans, seen as bandits rather than equal comrades-in-arms, found its expression in the retort of Red Army officers: "You [partisans] are bandits. It's better to leave a policeman [who served under the Germans] alive than a partisan scoundrel."[94] In line with this thinking, army officers in Ukraine tried, and in some cases even executed, partisans who engaged in looting and arbitrary revenge after liberation.[95] In the immediate aftermath of liberation, the obkom repeatedly vowed to stop the unruly conduct of partisans who were still armed and launching shooting sprees, and harassing women.[96]

Needless to say, these were not Ovechkin's model Communist servicemen. As viewed by the Department of Cadres and the oblispolkom, the main asset of the army veterans was the ability to instill disciplined enthusiasm in the population at large. Successive reports directly linked combat heroism, discipline, and postwar performance. Such was the case for one Colonel Dakhnovs'kyi, Hero of the Soviet Union, who worked as head of the transportation sector in the region's labor reserve administration and "introduced the appropriate order in its management." At a lower level was Pavlo Boiko, a decorated veteran who worked as chairman of a kolkhoz. In his short tenure as chairman, Boiko, it was claimed, raised the work discipline of the kolkhozniks so that now they all fulfilled their quotas.[97]

In memoirs published immediately after the war, some partisan commanders made an effort to prove that the Second World War partisan was a far cry from his civil war counterpart. Two of the highest-ranking apparatchiks, Fedorov and Kovpak, echoed each other in refuting the image of

[93] TsDAHOU, f. 1, op. 23, d. 4147, ll. 1–7, 8–20, 38–64, 85–86, 195–200.
[94] HURIP, #358, 7.
[95] Ibid., #121, p. 12; #64, p. 3.
[96] TsDAHOU, f. 1, op. 22, d. 161, l. 12.
[97] DAVO, f. 2700, op. 7c, d. 116, ll. 1–3; TsDAHOU, f. 1, op. 23, d. 1562, l. 17.

an anarchic-peasant movement. While Fedorov quoted Rudnev, the famous commissar of the Kovpak formation, urging commanders and officials alike to "view every partisan not only as a warrior but also as a postwar
official,"[98] Kovpak went further in identifying the Second World War partisan as the cream of Soviet society:

> I remember the partisans of the civil war. In those days they used to say: "Look
> here, he's an old soldier, a front-line man. He must, of course, be appointed a
> commander." It was in this way I myself became a commander. But now we had
> plenty of men who were able to command. Army ways showed themselves even
> in men who had never served in the army. If a comrade had been a good chair-
> man of a kolkhoz or sel'sovet, or a brigade leader, it was possible to make a good
> partisan commander of him quickly, just as former tractor drivers in a kolkhoz
> had become our tankmen in Spashchans'kyi Forest. The division into "military"
> and "nonmilitary" had quickly disappeared. By the time we were stationed in
> Stara Huta, all the Putivl' men had become soldiers. This could be said even of
> their external appearance.[99]

For Fedorov and Kovpak, partisans were on equal footing with the role
model of the Soviet society: the army serviceman turned civilian leader.

But, as often happened, it was left to Kovpak's deputy, the blunt and
outspoken Petro Vershyhora, to shed light on a more complex reality. In
Vershyhora's memoirs the partisan spirit was directly juxtaposed to the
ethos espoused by the army and party, and not necessarily as inferior to it.
Vershyhora, who joined the party only in late 1943, wrote sympathetically
about a group of rebellious youngsters in his unit who were "daredevils"
in battle yet resented almost violently the commissar's efforts to inculcate
militarylike discipline. Moreover, Vershyhora admitted that party high officials who arrived at the formation to check its overall performance were
initially met with suspicion. "I cannot say that we felt too comfortable
under this scrutiny. It was the party that was checking up on us," he wrote.
Even harsher words were used to describe the rift between the partisans
and the Red Army. Referring to the dark days of the early military defeats
at the hands of the Germans, Vershyhora conveyed an unmistaken sense
of military and moral superiority regarding the Red Army. The nearly
complete isolation from the Soviet rear and the continued retreat of the
Red Army forged a bitter sense of pride among the partisans. "Let me put
it bluntly," Vershyhora wrote, "before the battle of Stalingrad we all held
the Red Army accountable. Many bitter words were said, many bitter
thoughts thought. After all, we were routing the Germans in their rear

---

[98] Aleksei Fedorov, *Podpol'nyi obkom deistvuet* (Kiev: Izd-vo polit. lit-ry Ukrainy, 1986), 541.
[99] Sydir Kovpak, *Ot Putivlia do Karpat* (Moscow: Gospolitzdat, 1945), 62.

and moving forward, while they kept retreating."[100] This bitterness, however, was not to be confused with despair. Rather, it was an indication of defiant self-reliance. Vershyhora found it appropriate to cite a poem by the well-known poet and partisan Platon Voronko that conveyed these sentiments:

> The partisan does not seek mercy
> He does not call for help.
> He does not call a distant friend
> who is a thousand miles away at the front,
> Behind the Don and the blue Bug
> Relief does not arrive for us.

In a more reflective tone, Vershyhora admitted post factum that the partisans' successes owed more to their having faced the weakest forces of the enemy, whereas the Red Army came against the best of the Hitlerite forces and resources. These conciliatory observations, however, were reserved for the future. As long as the war was raging, he wrote, many, if not all, of the partisans were more likely to view themselves as the motherland's sole true defenders. "They [the Red Army] abandoned towns, villages, rivers," Vershyhora continued.

> They abandoned them with a heavy heart, perhaps, but nevertheless behind them lay a country being filled more and more with the Stalinist will to victory, and they felt it. They had the rear, the mighty Soviet rear. And we, an army with no rear and no flanks, we saw only the bitter results of the retreat, its seamy side. We saw Belorussia turned into dust, we saw Ukraine trampled, bloodstained. And we also knew the thoughts and angry words of a certain order, and more than anybody else, we, the civilians, teachers, accountants, kolkhozniks, and musicians who had taken up arms, we had the right to cast reproaches at the men who were retreating eastward.[101]

The rage against the Red Army was not limited to its poor performance on the battlefield, however. In summing up his observations, Vershyhora openly rejected the military ethos. In words that bore implications for the future, he condemned the mechanical way of thinking of army personnel who joined the partisans' headquarters:

---

[100] Vershyhora, *Liudi s chistoi sovest'iu* (Moscow: Moskovskii rabochii, 1946), 234–35.

[101] Ibid., 235. Vershyhora referred here to the draconian Order number 270, which was issued on 16 August 1941 by the general headquarters of the Supreme Command of the Red Army. The order practically banned surrender to the Germans and called for the execution of commanders who panicked during a battle and the treatment of their families as families of traitors. The order was first published in full only in 1988 in *Voenno-istoricheskii zhurnal* 9 (1988): 26–28. For a discussion of the order and its impact, see Amnon Sella, *The Value of Human Life in Soviet Warfare* (London: Routledge, 1990), 100–10.

Some people think that it is possible to achieve [superiority] by arithmetical calculations, by the simple device of counting bayonets . . . They forget that sometimes a single soldier is a match for ten enemy soldiers, that the spirit of an army is sometimes worth more than a hundred complicated machines . . . In a word, I believe in applying algebra and not arithmetic to war.[102]

The contrast between semi-anarchic improvisation and orderly, routine patterns of action could not be clearer. Vershyhora indeed touched a Soviet raw nerve, as witnessed by the succeeding editions of his book. Although the main thrust of the paragraph was maintained, the direct assault on the Red Army officers was omitted altogether. The "us and them" tone was reduced to an abstract observation about the art of war.[103]

Nor were the traditional patterns of *partizanshchina* absent. A letter written by a young female partisan, who had served in the partisan detachment led by Mychkovs'kyi, portrayed a state of anarchy. In his quest for personal glory (*maniia velichiia ne davala emu pokoia*) Mychkovs'kyi denied requests for help by other commanders in danger, waiting for his force to increase and thus be recognized as an independent formation. In the camp, Mechkovskyi and his cronies led a wild life that violated the basics of military readiness; daily drinking bouts were followed by musical evenings. Partisans were sent to collect food for the parties, needlessly exposing themselves in the villages. Neither party cell nor special department functioned in the formation: "There was no control. Do as you please [*Bylo sploshnoe shirokoe pole deiatel'nosti*]."[104] One could hardly distinguish between the conduct of this Soviet partisan commander and that of the anarchic individuals whom he was supposed to transform into disciplined fighters in the spirit of the Red Army. Aleksei Fedorov, the secretary of the Chernihiv obkom and commander of one of the largest Soviet partisan formations, left a record of an encounter with one such partisan. The latter defiantly countered Fedorov:

I adore the *partizanshchina*, that is freedom—and that's all there is to it! What does it mean—you are a commander? A commander is one whom the people follow into battle! The partisan should not be oppressed! A partisan is like a wild beast in the forest, like a wolf! He joins the flock when there is a need to beat the enemy, but after the fight he is again his own boss![105]

[102] Vershyhora, *Liudi s chistoi sovest'iu*, 412.

[103] Compare the original 1946 edition of *Liudi s chistoi sovest'iu* (p. 412) to the editions of 1952 (p. 342) and 1955 (p. 390).

[104] PAVO, f. 425, op. 1, d. 528, ll. 15–20. Iakuv Mel'nyk, the commander of the largest formation in Vinnytsia, expressed similar charges. In a conversation on 27 January 1945 Mel'nyk accused other partisan commanders with deliberate inactivity and reluctance to engage in battle (TsDAVOVU, f. 4620, op. 3, d. 109, ll. 29–30, 49–53.

[105] Fedorov, *Podpol'nyi obkom*, 246.

This was not exactly the desired product of three decades of revolution, but it certainly was not beyond cure. Immediately on joining forces with the Red Army, the bulk of the rank-and-file partisans were drafted for a second "baptism by fire." Too long out of the party's reach and evidently developing unruly habits, the partisans of the Great Patriotic War could not rejoin the Soviet family as such. Partisan commanders and commissars were the first to acknowledge this problem. An aide to the chief of staff of the Ukrainian partisan movement, Captain Aleksander Ruzanov, was captured by the Germans in mid-1943. In his interrogation, Ruzanov detailed the reasons behind this inherent suspicion. "The partisans [were] poorly informed about the real situation in the Soviet Union," Ruzanov told his interrogator.

> They do not know and do not need to know about the famine in the Soviet Union, the compulsory mobilization of women and teenagers, about the straits and hardships, about the terror. That is why partisans, who incidentally found themselves on Soviet territory as a result of the advance of the Red Army, are not dispatched to the rear and are not left in place but are immediately drafted to the army and sent to the forefront in special units. All measures are taken to isolate the partisans from the rest of the mass of Red Army soldiers. In the [army] units you do not meet partisans among Red Army warriors, except for special propagandists. This measure is justified by considerations such as these: the partisans had been in the German rear, read enemy literature, and had become familiar with criticism of Stalin and Bolshevism. Admittedly they did not believe all that, because vital hardships had reduced them to despair. Conditions dictated (*Shkura meshala soznaniiu*), so to speak. Still there is the danger that, having seen the real situation in the Soviet Union and the terror that rages there, they will remember all they heard while on the German side and start viewing things differently . . . Those who have been on that side, including the partisans, in general do not believe [Soviet propaganda]. They know what they should not know. After five, ten, fifteen years they will be able to remember this. That is why, sooner or later, something must be done with them.[106]

Whatever doubts could be cast at Ruzanov's testimony in captivity—chiefly the wish to please his interrogators with anti-Soviet views—they were echoed by the party leadership immediately upon liberation. When the secretary of cadres spelled out to the obkom's plenum in June 1944 the list of untrustworthy groups that must be drafted at once to the army, he cited partisans side by side with Communists who remained on the occupied territory and those who were taken prisoner by the Germans.[107]

---

[106] *Nezavisimost'* (Kiev), 14–15 August 1992.
[107] RGASPI, f. 17, op. 44, d. 1650, l. 59.

Thus, regardless of their wartime exploits, the rank and file of the partisan movement were officially placed in the company of groups that were suspected of passivity, even cowardice.[108]

Although there are no precise figures on the rate of losses of those partisans, some claim that the majority of those who were poorly trained and armed perished.[109] For the survivors, the prolonged experience of strict military discipline was expected to erase the semi-anarchic habits of their partisan days. According to a Central Committee report from 12 April 1944, three weeks after the liberation of the region, 2,345 of the 3,149 partisans in the largest formations had already been dispatched to the army. While 162 were directed to work in the NKGB (People's Commissariat of State Security) and the NKVD (not necessarily in the region), only 270 were selected for party-Komsomol and state work.[110]

Another sensitive issue that worked against the former partisan leaders was that of relations with the mortal enemies of Soviet power, Ukrainian nationalist partisan formations. Although contacts with the nationalists were often sanctioned by the top command out of tactical necessity, in the immediate aftermath of the war the party turned a suspicious eye toward this practice. In a stormy session of the obkom's bureau, Mychkovs'kyi, a partisan commander, was subjected to intense interrogation by the first secretary of the obkom and the instructor of the Central Committee. Beyond the establishment of contacts, which seemed justifiable in light of the numerical inferiority of the Red partisans in Mychkovs'kyi's territory, the party was interested to know "why comrade Mychkovs'kyi maintained a loyal attitude to the nationalists. He exchanged correspondence with

---

[108] The stigma followed partisans into civilian life and was reflected even in the financial aid policy for veterans of the movement. A Central Committee decree from 4 March 1944 imposed harsh qualifications for allowances to partisans. The only partisans who qualified were those who had joined the formation no later than three months after the capture of their army units by the Germans. If a partisan joined later and served in the rank and file he lost his right to receive aid equal to that of his last salary (TsDAHOU, op. 23, d. 3845, ll. 42–43).

[109] Moshe Kaganovich, *Der Yidisher Ontayl in Partizaner-bavegung fun Sovet-Rusland* (Rome: Osyg. fun der Tsentraler historisher komishe baym Partizanerfarband P.H.H. in Italye,1948), 281–82.

[110] TsDAHOU, f. 1, op. 22, d. 9, l. 3. A detailed account for each of the major formations was reported by partisan commanders in a meeting of the obkom's bureau on 5 April 1944 (TsDAHOU, d. 161, ll. 10–11). For an example of a partisan who was drafted to the NKVD in another oblast, consider the case of Hryhorii Chernen'kyi. Chernen'kyi became a party member only in 1941 and worked as a school director before the war. Following underground and partisan activities in the Tomashpil' and Sharhorod districts, Chernen'kyi was reinstated into the party almost immediately after the region was liberated and recruited to the NKVD as deputy of the head of political affairs of the Proverochnyi NKVD filtration camp (RGASPI, f. 17, op. 45, d. 2004, l. 88).

them, visited them, raised toasts to them."[111] The issue was brought to
Khrushchev's personal attention. The report cited another commander,
Sliusarenko, for cozy relations with the nationalists: "Mychkovs'kyi and
Sliusarenko negotiated with the Ukrainian nationalists, exchanged representatives in their shared location in the forests, and declared a general
amnesty. Mychkovs'kyi and Sliusarenko even enjoyed drinks with leaders
of a nationalist band."[112]

Finally, the cohesion of the former partisans as a political group was
severely undermined by a lack of solidarity. Behind the public pronouncements of comradeship and the advancement of the partisan ethos lay a
bitter rivalry. The thorny relations between former partisan commanders
played a major role in their political demise. The tensions both inside and
outside the units were politicized by the reports sent to the partisan central command and to the Central Committee. Exacerbated by the uncer-
tainties of underground conditions and tensions between professional soldiers, professional apparatchiks, and nonparty personnel, these rivalries
were carried into the postwar era.

No words were spared in exchanging denunciations. Reporting to the
chief of staff of the Ukrainian staff of the partisan movement, Vladimirov,
a career Chekist who was sent to work with the partisans, had this to say
about Burchenko, the commissar of the Mel'nyk formation and secretary
of the Vinnytsia obkom:

> I talked at length with Mel'nyk about our past, saying that he was wrong in
> many cases; he agreed and said that he was worn out by Burchenko, who did
> not know about and didn't want to know about the surrounding enemy, consid-
> ering that he was a cabinet official. Besides, he became gun shy [*puganyi zaiats*].
> He did not care for people, only for saving his own skin. The warriors say that
> when the major and the colonel [Mel'nyk] were cut off from us in front of Slavut-
> s'kyi forest, Commissar Burchenko wept. There are disputes between Mel'nyk
> and Burchenko; they are at odds. Burchenko is often wrong. The command
> does not like him and considers him a fair-weather partisan [*kurortnik*]; he does
> nothing and engages in squabbles. The commanders regret that Burchenko is
> evidently compromised in the eyes of the warriors and is called a coward and
> worse. Burchenko formed a clique with Kuznetsov, Nyzhnyk, and Sivun.[113]

Nyzhnyk, the other secretary of the underground obkom, did not fare
much better. In a letter to Strokach, Nyzhnyk was dismissed by an aide to

---

[111] TsDAHOU, op. 22, d. 161, l. 7.

[112] Ibid, d. 9, l. 4.

[113] In his memoirs Burchenko offers the inverse picture of his own conduct and of his
relations with Mel'nyk and Vladimirov. Moreover, Burchenko wrote the introduction to
Vladimirov's wartime memoirs. See Burchenko, *Reid*, 47, 133, 149; and Mykhailo Vladimirov, *Vohnenna zona* (Kiev: Vyd-vo polit. lit-ry Ukrainy, 1982), 3–4.

Mel'nyk as useless and inactive.[114] Often commanders traded charges of criminality. Medyns'kyi charged that native leaders like Kondratiuk encouraged the murder of commanders like him [Medyns'kyi] who were sent from the rear. The brigade commander, Kondratiuk, was quoted as saying: "Don't let Medyns'kyi get to Kiev, [since] he knows a lot about us."[115] An earlier report that was sent to the Central Committee in late January 1944 corroborated Medyns'kyi's charges. Kondratiuk was portrayed in an even darker light as lacking initiative and being ignorant of military affairs. He did not control the brigade and was often drunk. Medyns'kyi's fears of being murdered were confirmed by the suspicious deaths of two decorated commanders who were shot in the back. Moreover, it was argued, until their unification into one formation, the various groups and detachments struggled for power, and seniority was decided by force and politics.[116]

In a timely and symbolic act in late December 1948 the Central Committee reprimanded the obkom for belittling the role of the Soviet army in the destruction of the German army in its official account of the partisan and underground struggle in the region. The obkom obliged, and the primacy of the army was confirmed in the second edition of the report in 1950. The very first pages of an account primarily designed to record the partisan activity paid homage to the "Red Army [which], led by the genius of Stalin, displayed miraculous heroism, defended every part of the Soviet land, and inflicted tremendous blows on the treacherous enemy—the fascist invaders."[117] The story of the war could finally be told properly.

Four years after the region was liberated one phase in the purification of the myth of the war was complete. The political arena came to be dominated by ethnically Ukrainian veterans of the Red Army. At the same time, a second process involved a much larger group—the entire contingent of Communists who remained on the occupied territory. This process was bound to occupy the party's attention for many years to come.

---

[114] PAVO, f. 425, op. 2, d. 11, ll. 10–11.

[115] Interview with representatives of the Commission for the Compiling of Chronicles of the History of the Patriotic War, 5 March 1944 (Institut istorii akademii nauk otdel rukopisnykh fondov [IIAN ORF], f. 2, d. 9, ll. 3–4). Indeed, one of the parachuted commanders was murdered mysteriously.

[116] TsDAHOU, f. 1, op. 46, d. 327, ll. 1–5. This report was incorporated word for word into the Central Committee report on the partisan movement in Vinnytsia, prepared by Zlenko, instructor of the Organization-Instruction Department of the Central Committee. For investigations into the case of Boiko's death, see TsDAHOU, f. 1, op. 46, d. 3668, ll. 170–71, 185. By October 1946 the issue still had not been resolved.

[117] TsDAHOU, f. 1, op. 22, d. 159, ll. 7–8; and d. 153, l. 5.

Two

"Living up to the Calling of a Communist": Purification of the Rank and File

THE INSTITUTIONS of purge and verification were born with the Bolshevik Party itself. The quest for purity among the revolutionaries' ranks was at the heart of the Marxist-Leninist ethos. As the self-appointed vanguard and guardian of purity of the chosen class, charged with the messianic crusade to transform society in the face of open hostility before and after taking power, the party was keen on maintaining the purity of the chosen few. And as the virus of compromise and self-doubt was deeply rooted in the souls of many members of the chosen class, the party leadership saddled itself with the daunting task of constant and relentless purification of itself and of its rank and file.[1] Purity (*chistota*) was defined mainly on negative grounds, namely, by a list of characteristics and habits that constituted violations of the sacred calling of a Communist. Each cycle of the periodic purges that engulfed the party throughout the prewar era compounded new offenses, but the overall grounds for expulsion remained the same. Personal ethics, political offenses such as association with alien elements or participation in religious rites, passivity in party life, and violation of party discipline were among the more common grounds for expulsion.[2]

"Expulsion from the party is the highest measure of punishment as it entails the civil and political death of the expelled," stated a circular by the Central Committee in the aftermath of the civil war.[3] True, in following years party authorities went out of their way to convey the message

[1] Ironically Trotsky (along with Akimov) was one of the first people to point out this line in Lenin's ideas and politics when, in the wake of the debate over the nature of the party in the 1903 Second Congress, he termed Lenin's modus operandi "substitutionism" (*zamesti-tel'stvo*). Lenin's logic led to a pyramidlike structure in which the base is constantly narrowed by delegitimizing entire segments: The majority of the workers were considered unreliable because of their trade union mentality, the party is infected with the same virus of compromise seekers, and the Central Committee is ridden with factionalism and thus the path to personal dictatorship is paved (Leon Trotsky, *Nashi politicheskie zadachi* (Geneva: Tip. partii, 1904); Leszek Kolakowski, "Marxist Roots of Stalinism," in Robert Tucker, ed., *Stalinism: Essays in Historical Interpretation* (New York: Norton, 1977), 283–98.

[2] For eloquent treatments of the institutional and ideological logic of the purges, see Graeme Gill, *The Origins of the Stalinist Political System* (Cambridge: Cambridge University Press, 1990), 119–21; and Kotkin, *Magnetic Mountain*, 294–96, 298–302.

[3] Tsentr khraneniia sovremmennykh dokumentov (TsKhSD), f. 6, op. 1, d. 15, l. 116.

of possible redemption and reinstatement even for those who had shown themselves to be enemies of the Revolution, but the spirit of the expulsion act from the party remained harsh and uncompromising. Expulsion was meant to be, as indeed it was, a traumatic experience for the expelled.[4]

When the party launched the verification of its members' wartime conduct, procedures of the cleansing act had already been established. These procedures were structured in the most intimidating manner possible. For the individual in question, it was at once an intimate and public affair. In the weeks before the local party organization convened to decide on the party status of those subjected to verification of their wartime conduct, NKVD agents solicited information from anyone willing (or not) to offer such data. The information was hardly gathered in secrecy, and the individuals under interrogation found themselves isolated within their own circle of friends and coworkers until a positive decision was handed down, which, in any case, was a highly unlikely outcome. Often the identity of the accusers was made public, adding a social edge to the already vulnerable position of the accused. When Ostap Levyts'kyi, a party veteran since 1929, stood for verification, he found out that "the partisan comrades Mylymko, Kucheriavenko, and other residents of the village of Felitsianivka characterize [him] as a coward who categorically refused to stand with arms in hands against the German invaders and maintained friendly contact with the village *starosta*."[5] If Levyts'kyi had chosen to refute these charges, he faced the almost impossible task of undermining the credibility of both fellow villagers and people who were already recognized by the party as its armed branch under occupation. When the commission in charge of the verification finally convened, the atmosphere was tense, especially in light of the limited prospects for a positive outcome. All party activists attended, and the Communist under investigation was pummeled by questions from all sides. The opening question was this: "Why did you choose to remain on the occupied territory?" thus conveying the assumption that it was a voluntary choice and not the outcome of wartime circumstances. If found guilty, a person was expelled on the spot; the commission proceeded immediately to the next case, intentionally ignoring the presence of the recent expellee and so adding insult to injury.[6]

---

[4] For a penetrating portrayal of the psychological turmoil of individuals who had been expelled from the party in the mid-1930s, see Jochen Hellbeck, "Laboratories of the Soviet Self: Diaries from the Stalin Era," Ph.D. dissertation, Columbia University, 1998, esp. chaps. 3, 7.

[5] RGASPI, f. 17, op. 45, d. 2001, l. 150.

[6] Boris Halfin, interview, 18 February 1994, Kiryat Gat, Israel. For other firsthand portrayals of the verification process in the late 1930s, see the diary of the writer Aleksandr Afinogenov in Hellbeck, "Laboratories of the Soviet Self," chap. 7; and Victor Kravchenko, *I Chose Freedom* (New York: Scribner's, 1946), 132–47.

As the regime turned to those who had not risen to the occasion during the Great Patriotic War, party members recalled the all too recent memories of the Terror in the second half of the 1930s, which was a culmination, though not the end, of a series of purges. The triumphant conclusion of the "Great Breakthrough" (collectivization and industrialization) and the onset of the Terror saw a qualitative shift in the quest for purity. By then, as we may recall, the focus shifted to a new brand of elusive weeds—enemies of the people "with a party card in their pocket"as Stalin warned at the February–March 1937 plenary session of the Central Committee. NKVD and party investigators reopened old files of Communists, family ties to those deemed hostile elements once again became critical, and the spread of the Terror made it clear that the stakes were higher than ever. As the postwar purge was gathering momentum, ominous references to the Terror and to Stalin's 1937 speech reappeared in party deliberations.[7] And toward the end of the process, the "Leningrad Affair" erupted in a bloody reminder that doubts cast on the party credentials of anyone could be fatal indeed.

However, herein also lay a critical feature that set the verification of wartime conduct apart from any previous cycle of purges: If found guilty of dishonorable conduct under occupation, individuals could offer no repentance or "self-criticism" (*samokritika*) to pave their way back into the party ranks. They could, and did, appeal to the higher bodies of the party, but no proof of inner change or improved performance on the job or in party life could sway the decision. Only irrefutable evidence of active struggle against the German invaders could have an impact, and, given the chaotic wartime conditions, this was hard to produce. Moreover, the stain of failing to rise to the occasion during the war was irremovable. With the polity as a whole realigned on the basis of wartime experience, the stigma was not only a party matter but a social one as well.

Even more than in previous purges, expulsion from the party on the grounds of a murky wartime record often cost people their jobs and governmental awards. If the war was the toughest test for the polity on the path to communism, so, too, were the standards for purity that followed this cataclysmic event. The verification process was at the core of the Communist ethos. Ruling on the wartime conduct of Communists went beyond a decision on membership status. It was a central component in the redefinition of the essence of being a member of the chosen few in the wake of the Bolshevik Armageddon. Party status (*partiinost'*) of rank-and-file Communists had come to be defined by nothing less than indisputable evidence of combat valor. Passivity in the armed struggle against the occu-

⁷ Elena Zubkova, "Kadrovaia politika i chistki v KPSS (1949–1953)," *Svobodnaia mysl'* 4 (1999): 100.

piers disqualified a person from membership regardless of circumstances and personal background. The Communist was measured by the highest standards: With the majority of expulsions grounded on passivity, guilt was based on omission as much as commission.

The verification of the wartime conduct of Communists was launched with the opening shots of the Soviet-German clash. With the calamity of the German invasion still unfolding and the fate of the Soviet Union hanging by a thread, the Communist Party turned to a meticulous verification of the way its members responded to the crisis. Throughout the first year of the German invasion, the Party Control Commission (the body in charge of verifying the conduct and status of party members) began to assemble information. In 1942 and early 1943 the commission reviewed some 464 appeals of Communists who were expelled from the party. It was a small fraction of the overall number, but certain patterns that would shape the course of things to come began to emerge. The absolute majority of this group (428, or 92.2 percent) were expelled from the party on two grounds. Some 285 Communists were expelled for having refused to be evacuated to the Soviet rear in the face of the German advance, compromising themselves under occupation by registering with the occupation authorities or performing certain services for the Germans. Another 179 were expelled by the Main Political Administration of the Red Army for falling into German hands.[8]

The commission's report outlined both procedural ground rules and patterns for decision making. Most important was the adherence to individually based judgments and to elaborate verification and appeal processes. In line with Bolshevik fundamentals, every decision counted; each individual had a file, a story, and a face behind it. Second, a stained wartime record left little room for redemption. The commission approved 93.3 percent of the expulsion of those who fell in German captivity and 91.6 percent of those who remained on the occupied territory. Finally, the few rulings in favor of reinstatement shed light on what constituted redemption and who was most likely to receive it. The twelve Communists still in active duty in the Red Army who were reinstated to the party redeemed themselves on the battlefield by winning governmental awards for heroic exploits in which they were often severely wounded. At the same time, twenty of the twenty-four Communists who remained on the occupied territory and had been reinstated were women. In addition to not having compromised themselves under occupation, these women often had close relatives in the ranks of the Red Army or were saddled with small children, and thus could not be evacuated. Being an able yet inactive male under occupation was practically an insurmountable barrier

[8] TsKhSD, f. 6, op. 6, d. 36, l. 1.

to redemption.[9] The purge was set to go. And so what started as a trickle of individual cases turned into a sustained drive on a mass scale that engulfed the party for most of the following decade and a great many individuals for a far longer time.

On 1 November 1943 the Central Committee of the Ukrainian Communist Party ordered the verification of the conduct of all its surviving members who had remained on the occupied territory. The Central Committee's decision, entitled "On the Creation of Party Organizations in Districts of Ukraine Liberated from the German Occupation and the Improvement of Their Leadership," ordered the gorkoms and raikoms of the liberated areas to register all Communists immediately and weigh the issue of their party status "on a strictly individual basis."[10] The Central Committee condemned the gorkoms and raikoms that employed such Communists and delayed the decision on their party status. None of these Communists was allowed back into the party until a thorough investigation into their wartime conduct was completed.

At the time this decision was handed down, the Ukrainian Communist Party numbered 16,816 Communists, 3.2 percent of its prewar manpower.[11] At the same time, the party, virtually extinguished, had some 114,000 Communists on site who survived the occupation, roughly 22 percent of its total membership before the war.[12] Nevertheless, throughout most of the following decade, the party fiercely pursued verification of the wartime conduct of its rank and file in what became the largest purge in the postwar era. The timing of the verification was key to the entire process. Launching the purge immediately after liberation of the region and well before commencement of the mass demobilization, along with the reluctance to employ Communists on site despite a severe shortage in personnel, underlined the subjugation of all pragmatic considerations to the zealous pursuit to verify party members' conduct both under fire and under occupation. The purge took precedence over other urgent needs, such as rebuilding the virtually extinguished party organization and recruiting experienced cadres.

Throughout the remainder of the decade, party life was overshadowed by the verification process; it marginalized all other issues, including the purging of other categories of people. By the end of 1946 the Ukrainian Party obkoms reviewed 7,938 expulsion decisions by the raikoms and

---

[9] Ibid., ll. 2–9.

[10] TsDAHOU, f. 1, op. 6, d. 698, ll. 1–3.

[11] Theodore Rigby, *Communist Party Membership in the USSR, 1917–1967* (Princeton, N.J.: Princeton University Press, 1968), 263–64.

[12] This figure is based on data from 1 January 1949. Of 142,134 Communists who remained on the occupied territory, the various party organizations in the Ukrainian Republic registered 113,890 Communists for verification. The others were either verified as dead or classified under "unknown location" (TsDAHOU, f. 1, op. 46, d. 5337, l. 98).

confirmed 2,888 of these for reasons such as drunkenness, failure to pay membership fees, criminal offenses, and so on. At the same time, the obkoms reviewed 48,890 decisions by the raikoms on the party status of Communists who remained on the occupied territory and expelled 44,659 of them.[13]

The pursuit of purity was further underscored by the authorities' determined refusal to be swayed by the confusion created by wartime conditions. By the end of 1945 the Communist Party of Ukraine had no information on the whereabouts of some 66,668 members and candidates who accounted for more than 20 percent of the prewar membership. Documents were lost or destroyed, and many Communists did not rush to the raikoms with applications for reinstatement. By the end of that year only 32,456 of the 55,694 said to have remained on the occupied territory without the party's authorization turned in such applications. This number would more than double over the next four years. To complicate matters further, the gathering of verification material was a daunting task, especially when it concerned partisan and underground formations that had long gone unsupervised by the party and the NKVD during the war.[14] Nevertheless, the verification moved forward.

Ironically the impact of the Communists' wartime conduct on the way the party viewed itself was intensified by nothing other than the obscurity of the entire process. Despite its massive scale, the verification process was shrouded in complete secrecy. From its inception to the very end, and even well after its conclusion, the verification of Communists who remained on German- and Romanian-occupied territory was not mentioned in the contemporary press or discussed in any other publication. The secrecy of the verification process contrasted with the simultaneous and well-publicized purge directed at all party organizations in the regions liberated from German occupation. In August 1946 Nikita Khrushchev reported to the plenary session of the Ukrainian Central Committee that a major reshuffling of the leading cadres has been under way, resulting in the removal of more than half "the leading workers" (obkom and Central Committee apparatus), 38 percent of the raikom secretaries, 64 percent of raispolkom chairmen, and 66 percent of Machine-Tractor Station (MTS) directors.[15] Somewhat later, the Central Committee inspector, N. I. Gusarov, openly

<hr/>

[13] TsDAHOU, f. 1, op. 23, d. 4095, ll. 5, 14. The Party Collegium of the Central Committee convened twice a week and reviewed thirteen to fifteen cases on average (f. 1, op. 23, d. 2697, l. 20).

[14] TsKhSD, f. 6, op. 6, d. 37, ll. 1–2; d. 783, l. 3

[15] *Pravda*, 23 August 1946; *Pravda Ukrainy*, 25 August 1946. In comparing the postwar purge to its prewar counterpart, Brzezinski correctly draws attention to the absence from the process of mass hysteria and the participation of the masses (Zbigniew Brzezinski, *The Permanent Purge: Politics in Soviet Totalitarianism* [Cambridge, Mass.: Harvard University Press, 1956], 148–49).

portrayed the purge as one leveled against the raion (district-level) *nomen-klatura*. By November 1946, wrote Gusarov, 9,267 of 19,000 had already been replaced.[16] The figures for Vinnytsia were even more impressive. Throughout 1946 and the first ten months of 1947, 59.5 percent (1,510 people) of the obkom *nomenklatura* were replaced. The main reasons given for their replacement were inadequate policies regarding recruitment, poor qualifications, stagnation of party life, and "bourgeois-nationalistic deviations."[17] By 1947 the purge of the *nomenklatura* had subsided significantly, but the verification process was gathering momentum.[18]

Sixteen years lapsed before the verification decree was briefly mentioned for the first time, and even then only at a scholarly conference.[19] When a

[16] Gusarov, "O rabote s kadrami v Ukrainskoi partorganizatsii," *Partiinaia zhizn'* 1–3 (November 1946): 39.

[17] TsDAHOU, f. 1, op. 46, d. 3212, ll. 130–133. Throughout August and September 1946 *Pravda Ukrainy* published statistics on the purges in various oblasts. Thus, in Kharkiv and L'viv, 57.4 percent of *all* party workers were replaced, while 50 percent and 27 percent were replaced in Voroshylovhrad and Vinnytsia, respectively (*Pravda Ukrainy*, 25 August 1946; 14–15 September 1946). A verification by the Central Committee at the end of 1947 revealed that, in the Vinnytsia region alone, 40.4 percent of the raikom's secretaries for cadres were replaced in 1946, and 36.7 percent in the first ten months of 1947 (TsDAHOU, f. 1, op. 23, d. 4213, l. 26).

[18] Indeed, the mass purge of 1945–46 in the Ukrainian Republic was followed by a period of growing stability for cadres. In 1947 and 1948 only 16.5 percent and 11.4 percent were replaced, respectively. See V. I. Iurchuk, "Vosstanovlenie i ukreplenie partiinykh organizatsii na Ukraine v 1945–1953 godakh," *Voprosy istorii KPSS* 6 (1962): 80. In Vinnytsia, only 244 officials of the obkom *nomenklatura* were replaced during the first half of 1947 compared to 1,098 in the entire year of 1946. See TsDAHOU, f. 1, op. 23, d. 4423, l. 76; op. 46, d. 3212, l. 131. In this light, there was no surprise that contemporary observers of the Soviet scene concluded that the purge was one more effort to confront systemic strains within the Soviet polity that were only intensified by the war. These chronic problems, suggested Moore and Brzezinski, included the formation of bureaucratic cliques at the local level, the consequential decay of "inner party" democracy, and the mass influx into the party during the war, which necessitated the weeding out of politically unreliable elements (Barrington Moore, "The Present Purge in the USSR," *The Review of Politics* 9, no. 1 [1947]: 65, 69–71; Brzezinski, *The Permanent Purge*, 147–48). The sole exception was Holubnychy, who commented that "there are grounds for believing that this 'fluctuation of personnel' actually represented a fairly extensive purge of party members who in one way or another had proved to be unreliable during the war and the occupation." Regrettably Holubnychy left it at that, without further elaboration (Vsevolod Holubnychy, "Outline History of the Communist Party of the Ukraine," *The Ukrainian Review* 6 [1958]: 113).

[19] F. A. Petliak, "Vosstanovlenie i ideino-organizatsionnoe ukreplenie partiinykh organizatsii Ukrainy posle ee osvobozhdeniia ot nemetsko-fashistskoi okkupatsii (1943–1945 gg.)," in F. P. Ostapenko, ed., *Voprosy istorii KPSS perioda Velikoi Otechestvennoi voiny* (Kiev: Izd-vo Kievskogo universiteta, 1961), 135. When Petliak published a monograph on the same issue some twenty-seven years later, he refrained from mentioning the decision in his otherwise detailed account. Instead, in his portrayal of the difficulties that the shortage in personnel posed for the Soviet power in the immediate aftermath of liberation, Petliak merely noted that "many heads of departments in the *ispolkoms* were picked up on the spot

top party official finally referred to this issue, a full year and a half after Stalin's death, his brief comments conveyed the impression of a limited, small-scale verification process, rather than a massive operation that captured the party's attention for years to come.[20] The failure of so many members of the Soviet vanguard to rise to the occasion in the most critical test of the polity was a mark of shame to be kept out of public sight.

What follows is a detailed analysis of the purge. It traces the permeation of the myth of the war into the party's rank and file via this institution, beginning with the prevailing mood in the regional party organization that shaped the process in its initial phases, the bureaucratic mechanism that enforced the verification and kept it focused, the rulings that defined the essence of postwar purity, and, finally, the tension aroused between the universal pretense and the ethnic dimension of the process. The core of the data is taken from protocols of the obkom bureau's rulings that verified the wartime conduct of individual Communists. Each of the available 2,828 protocols consisted of an individual's biographical data, his or her career pattern before the war, the raikom's decision, a detailed description of the individual's wartime conduct prepared by the Party Collegium, and the subsequent ruling of the obkom bureau. This body of data, from March 1944 to the end of 1947, covers almost the entire volume of the obkom's rulings on the issue (89.7 percent of the total number of rulings by January 1951) and allows for analysis of trends and patterns in this prolonged and formidable process. A second body of sources consists of protocols of the obkom's plenary sessions, decisions made by the Central Committee in Kiev, and responses of individuals, ethnic communities, and lower party organs at the district and kolkhoz level to the process and its implications.

Purity at All Costs

On the local level, the purge largely reflected a worldview that had been shaped over the course of the three preceding years at the front, in the forests, and in the underground. The transition of party personnel in the

---

from the population that remained on the occupied territory" (F. A. Petliak, *Partiinoe ruko-vodstvo sovetami na Ukraine v gody Velikoi Otechestvennoi voiny [1941–1945]* [Kiev: Vyshcha shkola, 1986], 68). Rigby, who cited Petliak as a source, confessed ignorance regarding the numbers of Communists who survived the occupation and passed the test of registration (Rigby, *Communist Party Membership*, 263–64).

[20] P. Komarov, "O trebovatel'nosti i chutkosti," *Partiinaia zhizn'* 17 (December 1954): 23. Komarov, the deputy chairman of the Party Control Committee, referred only to the verification of former underground activists and partisans, based on examples from Vinnytsia (*Vinnyts'ka pravda*, 12 December 1954).

partisan detachments into key positions in political organs guaranteed the
continued suspicion toward those Communists who had remained on the
occupied territory. The contempt felt by those who bore the brunt of the
war for those who merely sought survival was unrestrained. Three months
before the liberation of the region, the commissar of a local partisan regiment concluded:

> Many communists, who remained for underground work, left for other districts
> for various reasons. Others simply hid and waited to see "what will happen
> later." Still other "Communists," who somehow happened to be on the Ger-
> man-held territory, even publicly turned to treason against Soviet power and
> began actively to help the Germans restore the war-ravaged economy and actu-
> ally spied for the German intelligence. In Plyskiv district, for example, the for-
> mer "Communists," Comrades Zelyns'kyi, Derdyra, Strelets, and others, turned
> to treason.[21]

Swords had been drawn. The translation of these sentiments into postwar
policy followed shortly thereafter. Only two weeks after the liberation of
Vinnytsia, the obkom bureau convened to outline a policy regarding
Communists who remained on the German- and Romanian-held territory.
All the major commanders and commissars of the regional partisan units
were present. The importance attached to the issue was evident by the
presence of an instructor from the Central Committee in Kiev. In his comments, the instructor stressed the urgent need for a fast yet thorough verification by which no individuals or groups would be spared, including
partisans and underground activists. This choice posed no difficulties for
the partisan commanders. Evidently the partisan leaders carried with
them a deep resentment against the "generation of 1943," namely, those
who joined the partisan wagon only when the tide of war turned clearly
in favor of the Soviets. This sentiment intensified when those who spent
the war on the fence happened to be party members. "It is just very unfortunate that prominent party members joined us only when the Red Army
took over Cherepashyntsi. These people were here all the time but now
come to us and say that they did a lot," complained Mychkovs'kyi, one of
the commanders who attended the meeting.[22] In his comments, Kanilov,
the Central Committee instructor, followed suit and elaborated:

> Many partisan organizations existed in the region. It will be necessary to gather
> materials, which the party raikoms must review immediately. There were many
> people in these detachments. The party raikoms must examine them and decide
> their fate. Many will issue statements such as "I was an underground worker,"

[21] TsDAHOU, f. 1, op. 22, d. 164, l. 88.
[22] TsDAHOU, f. 1, op. 22, d. 161, l. 7.

"I was in a partisan detachment," and so on. The question of deciding people's fate is an acute one . . . all the materials should be collected and sent to the Central Committee. These materials are needed for subsequent use by the bureau. [We must] bring the matter to an end so that people who emerged from the underground will be dispatched to the Red Army and assigned to work. The war rages on, and we must step into battle. The obkom employs the party personnel of the [partisan] detachments. The raikoms and the obkom should take care in counting all those who selflessly fought in the detachments and the underground organizations.[23]

The determination to institutionalize retribution, to launch a mass verification campaign while the war was still raging, to refuse to enroll available Communists who remained on the occupied territory was only magnified by the severe shortage of personnel. Like its counterparts in Ukraine, the Vinnytsia party organization was practically decimated by the war. The core of the existing cadres were the operational groups, each consisting of from five to seven people who followed the returning Red Army and reestablished Soviet power in the liberated areas.[24] Six weeks after the region was liberated the party machine had in hand only 2,724 Communists, comprising 13.6 percent of the prewar total.[25] Nor was the leadership in a much better state. Three weeks after liberation, with the purge already under way, the bodies in charge of the process were still understaffed. Only forty of the forty-four positions of the raikom's first secretaries were filled, barely twenty of the second secretaries, and, even worse, only twenty-three secretaries for cadres. Six months later four district organizations had yet to appoint heads of the organization-instruction departments, nine had no instructors, and seventeen were understaffed.[26]

While the waves of mass demobilization were still a matter for the distant future,[27] the local organization had to cope with another major constraint: the compulsory allotment of cadres to the newly annexed western oblasts. Shortly after liberation, the Ukrainian Central Committee obliged

[23] Ibid., l. 9.

[24] The practice of operational groups that were turned into raikoms immediately after liberation took place in all the liberated territories. See, M. L. Gutin, "Vosstanovlenie partiinykh organizatsii na osvobozhdennoi territorii v gody Velikoi Otechestvennoi voiny," *Voprosy istorii KPSS* 7 (1974): 79.

[25] TsDAHOU, f. 1, op. 23, d. 4076, l. 19. For figures on the entire Ukrainian Communist Party, see Rigby, *Communist Party Membership*, 263–65.

[26] TsDAHOU, f. 1, op. 23, d. 1055, ll. 17–20; d. 811, l. 19.

[27] The first stage of demobilization from the Red Army was launched in June 1945. Even so, by May 1946 demobilized servicemen counted for merely 10,180 Communists in Vinnytsia (V. N. Donchenko, "Demobilizatsiia sovetskoi armii i reshenie problemy kadrov v pervye poslevoennye gody," *Istoriia SSSR* 3 [May–June 1970]: 97, 101).

the major party organizations of the eastern oblasts to allocate leading cadres to the restoration of the virtually extinguished organizations in the western provinces. On 5 August 1944, less than five months after the region's liberation, the Vinnytsia party organization was ordered to allocate its share of cadres in a specific decision of the Central Committee.[28] The pressure that the allocation policy put on the local organization was highlighted by the fact that this category was the largest in the turnover of the obkom *nomenklatura*. In 1944, 51 of a total of 137 officials were replaced. More specifically, 3 of the 13 raikom first secretaries and 5 of the 15 second secretaries were replaced.[29] Throughout 1945 the obkom directed an additional 96 officials to the western oblasts, the largest group from the 338 party and Komsomol officials who were replaced in that year. The number of those directed for permanent work in the western oblasts came to more than one-tenth of the regional *nomenklatura*.[30]

The authorities in Kiev were fully informed about the crisis in personnel in the provinces. A special session of all the obkom secretaries for cadres of the Ukrainian party that was convened in Kiev on 20–22 June 1944 was dedicated to the issue. The secretaries' reports only emphasized the party cadres' dire state. According to the secretary from Vinnytsia, the regional *nomenklatura* was in shambles. Of a total of 2,569 positions that were classified under this category, only 1,768 were selected and working. Of the 975 positions assigned to party-Komsomol work, the obkom had filled only 455. This category consisted of three principal groups: 328 who returned from evacuation in the eastern regions, 99 who arrived from the Red Army, and 28 who emerged from the underground and partisan ranks. To make matters worse, the majority of the party-Komsomol cadres (335 of 455), were new to their job, and another 42 had less than a year of experience. The state of the regional NKVD was equally poor. Of the 250 required personnel, only 138 were working, and 27 of the 44 district branches had no chief. Most of the NKVD personnel were army veterans with little experience in police work.[31]

If one expected that against this background the party would opt to recruit Communists on site, even temporarily, that was not to be. By 1944 the utilitarian practice of temporary employment of "politically untrust-

---

[28] By 1945 the number of party and Soviet workers who were sent to western Ukraine amounted to 49,000, of whom 22,400 were Communists (P. A. Borkovskii, "Vosstanovlenie i organizatsionnoe ukreplenie partiinykh organizatsii zapadnykh oblastei USSR [1944–1945 gg.]," *Voprosy istorii KPSS* 11 [1971]: 66–67).

[29] PAVO, f. 136, op. 21, d. 12, ll. 16–17.

[30] TsDAHOU, f. 1, op. 23, d. 1562, ll. 15–16.

[31] RGASPI, f. 17, op. 44, d. 1649, ll. 53–55. More specifically, only 1,100 of the 1,256 obkom *nomenklatura* were in the region. Of the 158 Central Committee CPSU *nomenklatura*, 139 worked; of the 118 *nomenklatura* of the Ukrainian Central Committee, only 63 were staffed.

worthy elements," prevalent throughout the 1920s, was no longer in the cards. On 1 October 1944, when the regional organization consisted of only 5,470 Communists (about 25 percent of its prewar composition), it also registered 3,546 Communists who remained on the occupied territory for verification. Whereas 776 of them were directed to the army or other regions, the remaining 2,770 were subjected to verification of their wartime conduct and a subsequent ruling on their party status. The slow pace of actual verification and the high rate of expulsions practically guaranteed the exclusion of those Communists from party life.[32]

The deliberate avoidance of recruitment and employment of Communists who remained on occupied territory was repeatedly made clear to the party throughout 1944. During the plenary session of the Vinnytsia obkom that convened on 6–7 June 1944, the issue was addressed by two of the obkom secretaries. In his speech, Zhukovs'kyi, the secretary for cadres, ruled out any compromise:

> None of those people who remained on the occupied territory or were taken prisoner or were with the partisans is permitted to request that the *raivoenkomy* [district military committees] retain them in their positions. Such people must be drafted into the army. Faithful, capable, verified people who can fulfill the tasks should be selected to replace them . . . Those chairmen of collective farms who are not needed, who worked under the Germans, must be replaced by people who are faithful to Soviet power.[33]

Zhukovs'kyi then gave several examples that revealed an alarming gap between the party's aspiration for the purity of its cadres and the reality in the district organizations. "There is, for example," he told the plenum, "a deputy chief engineer, who worked under the Germans, who is now employed and the entire future depends on him. The plan is not fulfilled. His son worked in the Gestapo and still works today. So far he has not been arrested, and no one has inquired about him."[34]

In his summation, Burchenko, the first secretary of the obkom, stressed the point even further. On the one hand, Burchenko, a former partisan leader, could hardly conceal his harbored contempt for those who remained on the occupied territory and survived. "The ranks of our party will not be replenished in the near future," Burchenko told the attendants.

> So who shall we admit? Those who resided on the occupied territory? You cannot expect that Comrade Zhukovs'kyi [the obkom secretary of cadres] will send you

---

[32] TsDAHOU, f. 1, op. 23, d. 811, ll. 16–19. Of the 2,770 cases in hand, the raikoms reviewed 894 cases, expelled 704, and reinstated 190. The obkom that mandatorily reviewed the raikoms' decisions studied only 102 cases, of which 61 Communists were expelled and 38 reinstated.

[33] RGASPI, f. 17, op. 44, d. 1650, ll. 59–60.

[34] Ibid.

sufficient numbers of workers. That is why it is the duty of every Communist to fulfill his duties in the realm of work among the population, to attract the intelligentsia, to attract those who proved themselves patriots during the war. There are underground activists and partisans in every district. Therefore [we] must examine each [case] in its essence and examine its political character. There are cadres on whom the party organization can rely. The issue of enrollment into the party is of utmost importance.[35]

At the same time, Burchenko ruled out exclusion *en bloc* of Communists who survived the occupation and warned against giving up on the entire group. Instead, he called for the intensification of the verification process on individual grounds. Admittedly these Communists were under a cloud, but their potential contribution to the party could be determined only after a thorough examination of their wartime conduct. Burchenko made his point by focusing on the state of affairs in the Komsomol district where there were "all kinds of Communists":

One chairman [of a kolkhoz] has done nothing, another participated in underground work, and a third worked in an organization that was established by the enemy on our territory. There are various categories of these people. There are ninety such people registered in the Komsomol district. Nikolaienko [the raikom secretary] approaches these people the following way: "They submitted a statement but are not ready to decide their party status. Although they are available, they most likely do not want to be in the party." This is wrong. If they do not submit statements [they] must be summoned, and essentially the issue must be resolved without a statement. And if they happen to be scoundrels, traitors, rogues—deprive them of the rights of party members. [We] must examine what these Communists did, but Nikolaienko thinks that, when the time comes, he will find this Communist who will certainly hand in a statement. And if he will not—we shall mechanically consider him gone.[36]

The message was loud and clear. The political fate of Communists, especially those who did not live up to their calling at a time when they were most needed, was not in their hands. Nor could they simply vanish into the night. They had to be engaged by the party.

Initial Steps and Lessons

The verification of Communists who remained on occupied territory had already commenced before the Red Army completed its liberation of the region. In what appeared to be a test case for the future, the party launched

---

[35] Ibid., ll. 79–80.
[36] Ibid., l. 77.

a summary purge of all railway system personnel. Although the authorities provided no specific reasons for focusing on this branch, the logic seemed to combine the traditional perception of the railways as a Bolshevik stronghold, the NKVD jurisdiction over the railway system, and the fear of sabotage of a crucial service while the war was still raging.

The special Railway Verification Commission commenced its work in February 1944 after the liberation of Koziatyn, a major railway junction. With no prior experience to guide its work, the commission had to rely on verification documents of other organs, such as the Verification Commission of the Economic Unit, and on reports by employees of the cadres department of this or that unit."[37]

The improvised manner of verification drew harsh criticism as early as the summer of 1944. The nature of the charges shed light on the purge process at the local level, just as their immediacy foreshadowed major consequences for its future. The thrust of the criticism was the loose manner in which the commission approached the verification of the wartime conduct of individual railway workers. The impression conveyed was that of bureaucratic chaos. The first criticism was the tremendous number of cases reviewed within a short span of time. The commission dealt with cases en masse and not on an individual basis. In a single session on 17 June 1944 the commission reviewed 538 cases, and on 27 July 1944 it decided another 502 cases. Having to examine such a massive number of cases, it came as no surprise that the commission was accused of

> formally stamping the decision of the "verification commission of economic units" without having verified the actual accuracy of the testimonies . . . not a single document was disclosed on which basis those who testified provided a negative or positive reference on the workers and servicemen who remained in the German-occupied territory. According to comrade Butko [the deputy head of the cadres department], a testimony was provided on the basis of the decision of the primary commission. Nor did these primary commissions have a single document that spoke in favor or against the verified person, with the exception of an autobiography and a note signed by the verified people themselves.[38]

Second, several examples pointed to another chronic problem plaguing the institution regarding the purge. Whatever efforts the party invested in monitoring and channeling its procedures, once the gates were lifted, a flood of denunciations soon followed. For some, the commission's proceedings provided an opportunity to settle personal scores. Many cases were based on unverified oral testimonies not even signed by the accuser.

---

[37] PAVO, f. 136, op. 13, d. 18, l. 53. On 30 April 1944 the Central Committee ordered several obkoms to form party organizations in the railway system by 10 May of that year (TsDAHOU, f. 1, op. 23, d. 805, l. 9).

[38] PAVO, f. 136, op. 13, d. 18, l. 54.

Such was the case of one H. S. Antonenko, who was falsely accused, in an oral and unsigned testimony, of registering for work in Romania. This allegation was found to be false. More alarming was the case of one Sadovnyk, a nonparty man, who had worked in the railway system since 1923. Sadovnyk was charged with speculation and trading with the Romanian authorities. The original decision was to turn the case over to the military committee and allow Sadovnyk to keep his job. Sometime later, an official in charge of the verification process again raised the allegation against Sadovnyk, only in harsher terms, and vigorously sought his conviction. The commission revealed the motive behind this move: Sadovnyk apparently exposed incidents of corruption by his superiors. Wishing to get rid of Sadovnyk, commission members revived the charges and again placed him on trial.[39] The final note concerning the attestation in the railway system was reported to the plenary session of the obkom on 28 March 1945 and concluded that no fewer than 96 former policemen, 36 translators, 154 *starosty* (village elders), 55 informers, 112 people who had been awarded by the Gestapo, 9 Ukrainian nationalists, and 857 other "corrupted people" were employed before the verification. They had all been dismissed but somehow appeared in other positions in the region.[40]

Several lessons were learned from the railway episode. The subsequent verification was closely monitored by both the obkom and the Central Committee and tightly documented. Although the inherent problems of a mass-scale purge were abundant, the party's early and decisive intervention signaled its determination to prevent the search for purity from becoming an uncontrolled witch hunt. The main goal and challenge was to maintain the purge as an issue-driven process. At the same time, the verification signaled a major shift from the prewar years when expulsion from the party on the grounds of compromised conduct under occupation resulted automatically in loss of a job.

The determination to tighten control over the verification procedure was evident in the first recorded decisions by the obkom's bureau. The bureau reviewed the decisions of the Koziatyn raikom from 23 March to 1 April 1944 regarding the party status of five Communists who had remained on the occupied territory. It was also the last time the bureau dealt with decisions collectively. The collective ruling, however, allowed the obkom to formulate a clear message to the districts. The bureau overturned all five reinstatements, accusing the raikom of approaching the

[39] Ibid., ll. 56, 58.
[40] TsDAHOU, f. 1 op. 50, d. 7, l. 167. Another body that paid attention to the railway personnel was the obkom's military department. The department's annual report for 1944 noted that in November alone 89 expected draftees, who had no right to avoid the draft, were traced among the railway cadres, most of them former war prisoners (TsDAHOU, f. 1, op. 23, d. 953, l. 187).

issue in a formalistic and mechanical manner. In a supporting commentary, the bureau stated that decisions on the fate of Communists who had
remained in the occupied territory should be based on the latter's "role
in carrying out the orders of Comrade Stalin from 3 July 1941 on the
struggle against the German invaders." Apparently all five Communists
were reinstated in the party, with only fines and reprimands recorded in
their personal files. The Koziatyn raikom's decision conveyed the impression that the lower body either did not understand the goals of the verification, as the bureau implied, or it was determined to retain these people
because of familiarity with them or the evident scarcity of personnel. The
bureau cited the case of one Shcherba, which, it argued, was analogous
to the others. The Koziatyn raikom reinstated Shcherba, who admittedly
displayed cowardice in the occupied territory and destroyed his party card.
Shcherba's cowardice resulted in a strong reprimand and fine. It was the
last case where passivity in the struggle against the occupiers was countered with anything short of expulsion from the party ranks.

Another case was used to establish the hierarchy within the verification
proceedings. Petro Didenko, a member of the Volyn' underground
obkom and a combat commissar of an infantry division, was captured by
the Germans and imprisoned throughout the entire occupation. The bureau overturned his readmission and ordered the raikom's secretary to
submit the materials on Didenko to the main political administration of
the Red Army in Moscow where the matter would be settled. So as to
leave no room for future misinterpretations about who was authorized to
make the final decision on party status, the bureau concluded with the
following: "Explain to the secretary of the Koziatyn raikom, Comrade
Kravchenko, that the institution of party controllers functions only in the
oblasts, territories, and republics, based on the resolutions of the Central
Committee of the CPSU."[41]

Between Kiev and Vinnytsia

The maintenance of a strict inner-party hierarchy was perceived as the key
to keeping the verification process focused. The mass dislocation during
the initial postwar period and the strong suspicion of various groups created fertile ground for bureaucratic chaos and the advancement of agendas
other than wartime conduct. The hand of the Central Committee in Kiev
was evident at every turn from commencement to closure, making it one
of the most closely monitored purges in Soviet history. This was not a
small feat in the wake of the Terror.

[41] RGASPI, f. 17, op. 44, d. 1653, ll. 70–71.

The basic source for the formulation of policy were the continual reports of the Central Committee's regional instructors, which contained both raw data on the purge and recommendations. The first report on the purge in Vinnytsia was submitted nine months after liberation of the region. As of 1 January 1945 the Central Committee was informed that the Vinnytsia obkom had registered 3,544 Communists who had remained on the occupied territory. This figure, however, was under a dark cloud of apathy on the part of both registered Communists and the local party organization. The report cited, in alarm, that only 2,287 (64.6 percent) of those who were registered applied to the raikoms for reinstatement into the party.[42] In the district of Plyskiv, for example, only 28 of the 92 registered Communists applied for reinstatement, and in Chernivtsi and Iaryshiv the figures were 41 of 112 and 12 of 57, respectively.

The actual review of cases revealed an even bleaker picture. The Central Committee reprimanded both the raikoms and the obkom for their lack of interest in the wartime conduct of these Communists, and in the reasons why they had not applied for reinstatement. Whereas the raikoms reviewed 1,265 of the 2,287 statements (55.3 percent), the obkom reviewed only 346 of the 1,022 cases (33.8 percent) submitted for its approval, that is, only one-tenth of the total number of Communists who had remained on the occupied territory without the party's authorization (ll. 10–11).

At the same time, the high rate of expulsion—the raikoms expelled 80 percent of the people they reviewed and the obkom 82 percent—was of no value in itself. The Central Committee condemned the inclination of several raikoms toward across-the-board expulsions, reinstatements, and unspecified charges when handing down decisions. Whereas the Lypovets' raikom was reprimanded for reinstating fourteen of the twenty-two Communists it reviewed, the Komsomol raikom expelled thirty-nine of forty-one and the Turbets' raikom expelled all the thirty-three people who had come before it. The obkom's failure to verify these decisions was identified as a core problem. It led, the Central Committee charged, to the loose and misguided approach of these raikoms. In the same vein, the instructor condemned the mechanistic registration of unfounded reprimands. Such was the case with Hryhorii Troshyn, who had been severely wounded and taken prisoner by the Germans and had destroyed his party card on the orders of his battalion commissar. Based on his heroic struggle as a soldier and later as a partisan, Troshyn was recommended for reinstatement, yet along with a reprimand for the destruction of a party document.

One instructor's comment, however, was particularly illuminating:

> Basically the raikoms and the obkom decided correctly the question of the party status of the Communists who remained on occupied territory. All those who

[42] TsDAHOU, f. 1, op. 22, d. 158, ll. 10–17.

did not live up to their calling as Communists are expelled. Some of them were enrolled into the party by mistake and in a complicated situation [the war] displayed their ideological and political instability. (l. 12)

The trial of the war, in this sense, was the ultimate purgatory that unmasked those elusive weeds about whom Stalin warned the party back in 1937. Lenience, therefore, was out of the question, as seen in the second review of a case described above, that of Comrade Shcherba from Koziatyn. Shcherba lived the war years on the occupied territory and was arrested several times by the Germans. He was released after his wife gathered two hundred signatures from the local population stating that he was not connected with the partisans. Nevertheless, exclaimed the instructor, the raikom ruled that "for display of cowardice and destruction of a party document, and also for passivity in the enemy's rear, enter a severe reprimand in the personal file. Permit Comrade Shcherba to pay membership fees for the proceeding period. Request the bureau of the obkom to approve the decision and issue a new party card for Comrade Shcherba" (ll. 13–14).

The Central Committee instructor concluded with several recommendations for accelerating the pace of the verification process and improving its quality. The thrust of the recommendations called for a hands-on approach by the obkom. The regional Party Collegium was ordered to visit the districts systematically, inspect the preparation of cases there, and send party investigators in advance to prepare cases for meetings. The organization-instruction department of the obkom was ordered to verify several raikoms with regard to their review of Communists who remained on the occupied territory. The raikoms were ordered to summon the Communists who had not applied for reinstatement and decide on their party status. Finally, both the raikoms and the obkom were urged not to lose track of the work and conduct of the Communists who had been expelled from the party (ll. 16–17).

Early in 1945 the pressure on the regional organizations increased significantly. On 14 October 1944 the Main Political Administration of the Red Army issued a directive allowing the admission of sergeants and privates who had remained on the occupied territory or had been taken prisoner only after the raikoms provided a reference about their conduct under occupation. The decree was approved by the Organizational Bureau of the Central Committee in Moscow. On 12 December 1944 the heat was turned up under the Ukrainian Party organizations after the head of the political administration of the Second Ukrainian Front complained that the regional bodies were ignoring repeated requests for material. Several raikoms from Vinnytsia were among those cited in the complaint to the Central Committee. The Ukrainian Central Committee responded by issuing a decree on 21 March 1945 that obliged all the Ukrainian obkoms

TABLE 2.1
Stakhurs'kyi's Impact on Purge Decisions

	Expelled	Reinstated	Total
Before Stakhurs'khyi's Arrival	789	293	1082
	72.9%	27.1%	38.3%
After Stakhurs'kyi's Arrival	1478	268	1746
	84.7%	15.3%	61.7%
Total	2267	561	2828
	80.2%	19.8%	100.0%

to examine those cases and report back to the Central Committee by mid-April 1945 (op. 23, d. 1539, ll. 3–4; d. 2697, l. 25).

The incident with the army's Main Political Administration coincided with another milestone in the verification process—the appointment of Mikhailo Stakhurs'kyi as first secretary of the obkom. As mentioned earlier, a major reason behind the decision to appoint Stakhurs'kyi first secretary was the urge to reestablish firm control over what was perceived to be a loose organization. Indeed, the impact of Stakhurs'kyi's military background and personality was soon evident. At his very first appearance before the Vinnytsia gorkom, Stakhurs'kyi let his subordinates know that tightening control over the conduct of the verification process would be a major concern for him. The gorkom's secretary and the chairman of the City Council were given one month to submit to Stakhurs'kyi personally a list of all those who remained on German-held territory.[43]

Stakhurs'kyi's ascendance unquestionably signaled a rigidification of the decisions on the party status of Communists who remained on the occupied territory. Both the number of examined cases and the expulsion rate rose sharply under Stakhurs'kyi. The already institutionalized suspicion against Communists who remained on occupied territory was translated to expulsion nearly en masse. Before Stakhurs'kyi's arrival, 72.9 percent of the cases brought before the obkom ended in expulsion. In the next two-and-a-half years the rate of expulsions rose by 11.8 percent to 84.7 percent (Table 2.1).

Still, the Central Committee was not content with the pace of the verification process. Less than a year after the appointment of Stakhurs'kyi, the Central Committee in Kiev handed down a decision that specifically addressed the Vinnytsia obkom. On 19 April 1946 the Politburo of the Central Committee issued a decision entitled "On Shortcomings in the Regional Party Organizations of Dnipropetrov'sk and Vinnytsia in the Scrutiny of Personal Cases of Communists Who Remained on the Occu-

---

[43] RGASPI, f. 17, op. 45, d. 2010, l. 41.

TABLE 2.2
The Impact of the 19 April 1946 Central Committee
Resolution on the Purge

	Expelled	Reinstated	Row Total
Before April 1946	1179	366	1545
	76.3%	23.7%	54.6%
After April 1946	1088	195	1283
	84.8%	15.2%	45.4%
Column Total	2267	561	2828
	80.2%	19.8%	100.0%

pied Territory." The brunt of criticism was directed against the slow pace of reviews and the subsequent accumulation of bottlenecks. The Politburo noted that the Vinnytsia raikoms and gorkoms had not yet reviewed 813 cases of the 3,301 Communists who submitted statements on their conduct on the occupied territory. The obkom had yet to review 1,297 of the 2,488 rulings by the raikoms. The Central Committee also condemned the careless examination of cases that resulted either in admission of "bad apples" or unwarranted expulsions. More than eight hundred Communists who had remained on occupied territory did not even submit statements to the party organizations, which were doing nothing about it. The first secretary of the obkom, Stakhurs'kyi, was held personally responsible for this state of affairs. To underscore the severity with which it viewed the issue, the Central Committee obliged the obkoms, raikoms, and gorkoms to report on the tenth of every month about the progress of the verifications.[44]

The Politburo intervention had immediate and weighty consequences. During the next twenty months the obkom's bureau decided an almost equal number of cases as those that had been ruled on in the preceding two years—45.4 percent of all the cases between March 1944 and December 1947. Although the Politburo had not called for more expulsions, this seems to have been the obkom's perception. Following the 19 April resolution the expulsion rate increased by 8.5 percent, from 76.3 percent to 84.8 percent (Table 2.2).

From the Central Committee's point of view, the April 1946 resolution finally put the verification process on the right track. Although it continued to be concerned by the accumulation of cases and arbitrary decisions, by the end of 1946 the Central Committee noted with satisfaction that after the April resolution and the dispatch of instructors to help the obkoms, the pace throughout the entire republic increased significantly—

[44] TsDAHOU, f. 1, op. 6, d. 918, ll. 3–6.

two thousand to twenty-five hundred cases a month compared to one thousand to twelve hundred cases a month before May 1946 (op. 23, d. 4095, ll. 1–9).

The Central Committee interventions did in fact define the parameters of the verification proceedings. The constant pressure on the lower organizations conveyed to them the seriousness attached to the issue and demonstrated the Central Committee's determination to monitor the process and force the lower organs to adhere strictly to the issue of wartime conduct.

However, the pressure to decide a large number of cases individually and in a short time span was more than the conventional problem that dogged previous purges. In light of the collective and irreversible punishment meted out against entire ethnic groups in the wake of the war, adherence to differentiation increasingly appeared as an aberration.

Between Vinnytsia and the Districts: Paralysis and Persistence

The Vinnytsia obkom, as the organ directly in charge of the purge, constantly struggled to enforce the criterion of wartime experience in the verification proceedings. The obkom had to cope with the implications of this process in the daily running of the party machine and with severe personnel shortages. The raikoms' willingness and ability to pursue a thorough mass verification of their veteran Communists were far from evident. The amount and variety of information required to produce a thorough inquiry on each individual overwhelmed many of the raikoms. Faced with meager resources and other pressing problems, some raikoms often adopted a hands-off approach, namely, the mechanical use of code phrases instead of a genuine investigation of each case.

On the one hand, the obkom was more likely than not to uphold the raikoms' rulings on the party status of Communists who remained on the occupied territory. Of the 2,828 decisions made by the raikoms in 1944–47, the obkom confirmed 2,588 (91.6 percent). Yet the overwhelming rate of approval did not disguise some crucial points of friction between the two hierarchies. The obkom opted for expulsions more often than the raikoms, and it signaled this predisposition by overturning many of the raikoms' decisions ruling against expulsion. Of the 238 overturned rulings, 168 (70.6 percent) were overturned in favor of expulsion (Table 2.3).

But there was much more to the obkom's impetus for expulsion than meets the eye. Throughout the purge, the obkom received signals that the purge was not universally endorsed in the districts and on collective farms. Certainly sentiments were strong against the continued employment of Communists who had served under the occupiers, but these attitudes were

TABLE 2.3
Coincidence between Obkom and Raikom Purge Rulings

	Upheld	Overturned	Total
Expulsion	2197	70	2267
	96.9%	3.1%	80.2%
Reinstatement	391	168	559
	69.9%	30.1%	19.8%
Total	2588	238	2826
	91.6%	8.4%	100.0%

more likely to be expressed in official meetings in the presence of representatives of the obkom and Central Committee. Even then, the constraints and stresses of personnel shortages were acknowledged. That was the message conveyed by several secretaries in a meeting of all raikom secretaries and instructors of cadres in the region on 28–29 May 1947. Drawing the link between young and inexperienced specialists and the abundance of experienced cadres who remained on the occupied territory, one secretary admitted:

> The raikom's department of cadres has not studied sufficiently those cadres who are specialists of the rural economy, and it has not yet purged the ones who do not inspire political trust . . . surely we cannot retain them. But so far we have not received anyone to replace them. We have a livestock expert, Tsybulia, and a senior MTS agronomist, Bohebs'kyi, both of whom worked in these positions under the Germans. Maybe we are at fault in retaining them, but we did present the question to the regional department of the rural economy. But they don't send us people, only promises (d. 4422, l. 8).

As the purge gathered momentum and control of the higher party organs tightened, scattered signs of paralysis were traced to the district organizations. The fear of the party's retaliation for the enrollment of those who remained on the occupied territory and who might later be exposed as collaborators or passive by-standers was prevalent. In the Vendychany sovkhoz, the secretary of the primary party organization lamented:

> Among several Communists, party activists included, there is a fear of providing recommendations for enrollment into the party. This is because we study people poorly and barely attract nonparty activists to participate in productive and political work. There is the misimpression that the party does not encourage the admission of those who remained on occupied territory. (d. 4214, l. 23)

A similar opinion came from the Vinnytsia rural raikom:

> A wrong impression has been circulating regarding the admission into the party of comrades who remained on the occupied territory. We have outstanding brig-

adiers and kolkhozniks, who long ago submitted statements for enrollment into the party, but their statements have still not been reviewed only because earlier they had resided on the occupied territory. (d. 4214, l. 23)

In March 1947 the stagnation in enrollment had so escalated that the Central Committee itself addressed the issue. The Committee's instructor clearly emphasized that the party only wanted a genuine evaluation of wartime conduct strictly on an individual basis. The instructor criticized the obkom, whose "individual party workers were misguided in their thinking regarding those who had remained on the occupied territory, believing that their admission to the party was prohibited since they did not inspire political trust" (op. 46, d. 2285, l. 39).

The few examples the instructor cited underscored the emerging problem of the stagnation in party enrollment. The secretary of the primary party organization in the village of Ruban', Nemyriv district, was quoted as saying, "We have no good people; they all remained on the occupied territory and it is essential to withhold their admission to the party." Ushakov, the secretary of the primary cell of Mohyliv-Podil's'kyi MTS, said: "Who can we admit into the party when the tractorist and other MTS workers are people who remained on the occupied territory" (op. 46, d. 2285, l. 39). Consequently this party organization had enrolled only one individual since its establishment in 1944. The secretary of the primary party organization in the village of Iaruha, Mohyliv-Podil's'kyi district, Comrade Boiko, commented on the gorkom secretary's remark regarding the need to select the best people into the party ranks: "Whom shall we admit when all those in the village either remained on the occupied territory or were taken prisoners and released back home?" (ll. 37, 39; d. 4076, l. 20).

Paradoxically, in other districts, the dire need for personnel produced opposite results. One study from July 1947 cited, in alarm, an indiscriminate admission policy throughout the region (op. 23, d. 4075, l. 1). Only 7 of 1,230 applicants were rejected in the first half of 1947. As a result of these random admissions, some bad apples entered the party, notably people who had remained on the occupied territory. The primary party cell Peremoha in the Haisyn district admitted one Kulevs'kyi, the son of a soldier in the White Army and a former kulak who had served under the Germans and was rewarded by them. The primary cell in the village of Kurashivtsi, Murovani-Kurylivtsi district, enrolled an individual who prospered during the occupation, and another cell in the village of Sbodne, Voronovytsia district, enrolled someone who had remained passive throughout the occupation. The primary cell of the Chechel'nyk raispolkom exceeded the others when its second secretary recommended for candidacy a person who had served as a policeman under the occupation (ll. 8–9).

Another troubling phenomenon in the districts was the use of rhetorical codes in the absence of any documents, instead of a genuine inquiry into the wartime conduct of individuals. E. P. Ivanova was expelled by the Vinnytsia gorkom on 13 November 1944 as one "who had not lived up to the calling of a Communist" (op. 22, d. 158, l. 39). The investigation by the Party Collegium revealed that Ivanova had volunteered for the Red Army as a military nurse after the outbreak of war. After taken prisoner, she was released and lived for the remainder of the war in her native residence. For a while Ivanova was inactive owing to illness, but once recovered, she began agitating against the Germans among her relatives and acquaintances. When the Red Army returned, Ivanova nursed wounded soldiers and received a letter of appreciation from the command of the First Ukrainian Front. Based on these incidents and a positive reference from the party cell of her work place, the Party Collegium recommended that Ivanova be reinstated to the party as a "participant in the war of the fatherland."

Several analogous cases underscored the serious breakdown in communication between the various organs in charge of the verification process. When the Khmil'nyk raikom expelled Stepan Dudnyk, a former partisan, on the grounds of passivity in the armed struggle, such an ignorant decision could have been excused by the fact that Dudnyk was active in another district.[45] At the same time, it revealed a failure of communication between the raikom and the central staff of the partisan movement which held such information. Similarly the Koziatyn raikom had no knowledge of the military record of Onysym Dovhaliuk when it expelled him from the party in December 1945. Dovhaliuk, a party member since 1927 and a railway worker, was wounded in a battle and then worked in the rear. He had arrived in Vinnytsia in May 1945. The raikom did not spare insults when it expelled him for "a display of cowardice, faintheartedness, and the groundless destruction of his party card." While the raikom may have been in the dark regarding Dovhaliuk's record, it was all the more surprising that his governmental awards were not acknowledged.[46]

Another general line used frequently by the raikoms to justify reinstatement was "no compromising materials found." This, however, was an open invitation for further interpretation. When the Vinnytsia gorkom reinstated one Shepetovs'kyi on these grounds, the Party Collegium saw it in a different light. Shepetovs'kyi, it charged, failed to establish contact with Soviet partisans. Moreover, one of his relatives was exposed as a policeman under the Germans. His wife, who resided in the Cheliabinsk

---

[45] RGASPI, f. 17, op. 45, 2005, l. 132.

[46] Probable explanations may have been the inherent suspicion against the railway workers and the rush to condemn someone who did not return to the region directly from the army. The obkom eventually reinstated Dovgaliuk into the party (TsDAHOU, f. 1, op. 50, d. 244, l. 3).

region, was informed that he had died heroically and received a pension throughout this period.[47] More intriguing and confusing was the reinstatement into the party of Hryhorii Sverdzelko by the Pohrebyshche raikom in January 1947. A kolkhoz chairman already before the war, Sverdzelko was reinstated without the obligatory explanation. The obkom overturned the decision in an unusually fierce and detailed ruling. Having accused the raikom of a "nonserious approach to the issue of reinstatement into the party,"[48] the obkom followed with a detailed history of public collaboration with the occupiers, thus raising the question of how the raikom could have claimed ignorance in face of such obvious facts. Sverdzelko, according to the obkom, was on close terms with the German commandant, served in a commission that selected people for forced labor in Germany, participated in confiscation of grain from the population, and agitated against Soviet power.

The obkom showed no signs of easing the pressure on the raikoms in the pursuit of genuine verification, and the verification proceedings continued to occupy a central place in party life. Wartime conduct was clearly the main issue in cases that involved a decision regarding party status. Between 1944 and 1946 the Party Collegium of the obkom reviewed the party status of 1,488 Communists in cases ranging from loss of party documents to religious offenses and murder. At the same time, the Collegium registered 4,257 cases of individuals who remained on the occupied territory and reviewed 3,000 of them.[49]

Early on, the obkom signaled the seriousness with which it viewed the purge to the local apparat. Leading officials in the region became vulnerable if they seemed to adopt a lax approach to the verification proceedings. The first secretary of the Komsomol raikom was dismissed from his job on the grounds that he "tolerated the protection of individuals who had served under the Germans."[50] When the first secretary of the Bar raikom came under criticism, which later led to his removal from office, one of the main reasons was his decision to employ one Zozuliak as the head of the propaganda and agitation department.[51] In September 1944 the raikom reinstated Zozuliak, a party member since 1930, on the basis of underground activity and recruiting people to the partisans.[52] Sometime later, the raikom was embarrassed by the discovery of compromising infor-

---

[47] Ibid., l. 38.

[48] A clue to the raikom's decision was the apparent award of a medal "for valiant work during the war of the fatherland," which the obkom now ordered to be investigated (TsDAHOU, f. 1, op. 50, d. 278, l. 7).

[49] Ibid., op. 46, d. 2285, ll. 184–86.

[50] PAVO, f. 136, op. 21, d. 12, ll. 15–16.

[51] TsDAHOU, f. 1, op. 23, d. 2463, ll. 1–2.

[52] RGASPI, f. 17, op. 44, d. 1654, ll. 163–64.

mation about Zozuliak's conduct during his stay on the occupied territory. Zozuliak submitted a statement to the gendarmerie renouncing communism and slandering Soviet power and the Communist Party.[53] On 10 November 1947 the obkom's bureau reversed itself and expelled Zozuliak from the party based on the new incriminating information.[54] For the first secretary of the Bar raikom, however, the damage caused by his association with someone who had compromised himself under occupation was irreversible.

On other occasions top regional leaders were criticized before the rest of the party apparatus. During the plenary session of the obkom in March 1945 the entire body of the regional organization secretaries witnessed the admonishment of their colleagues. The first secretaries of the Lityn and Trostianets' raikoms were criticized for superficial selection of cadres and, as a result, accidental, politically dubious, and alien elements penetrated into the leading posts in these districts.[55]

At the end of the day, the obkom leaders could note with a certain satisfaction that they managed to keep the verification process focused and moving forward despite formidable constraints and pressures. Led by a former Red Army general and veterans of the partisan movement, the Vinnytsia obkom approached the verification of wartime conduct of the party's rank and file as more than a routine cleansing to which it had previously been accustomed. For these individuals, the verification process was an extension of their own personal values and practices that had been born out of the singular defining event in their lives. They were determined to see it through to the end.

Answering the Call: Defining Purity in the Postwar Era

While the constant interventions by the Central Committee and obkom conveyed the unequivocal message that the verification would proceed at all costs, what actually constituted conduct worthy of a Communist under occupation remained unclear. As in all previous purification campaigns, purity was defined, first and foremost, by what it was not. The yardstick for ruling on the party status of Communists who remained on the occupied territory was defined as "living up to the calling of a Communist" (*oprav-*

---

[53] TsDAHOU, f. 1, op. 23, d. 1562, l. 16.

[54] Ibid., op. 50, d. 373, ll. 23–24.

[55] In the Lityn district, the head of the fire department avoided being drafted into the Red Army and during the occupation period housed the German headquarters in his home. The chief accountant of the Raizo managed the Lityn MTS under the Germans. Based on his information and in his presence, the Germans beat tractorists who refused to work for them. Similar scenes occurred in the Trostianets' district (TsDAHOU, f. 1, op. 50, d. 7, l. 6).

dat' zvanie kommunista). A series of individual rulings by the obkom articulated the intent behind this demanding, yet somewhat vague, measure
of devotion.

To begin with, the obkom flatly rejected any claims of extraordinary
circumstances advanced by individual members as an excuse for not answering the party's call for uncompromised struggle against the invaders.
Sacrifice of family ties and concerns in favor of the patriotic cause were
marked as the ultimate feature of the true believer in wartime. When Ivan
Ochyns'kyi opted for passivity in the struggle against the Romanian occupiers in fear of retaliation against his family, the obkom, in agreement with
the Chechel'nyk raikom, expelled the thirty-two-year-old Communist
from the party.[56] In the same vein, the party demanded the severance of
all relations with relatives who collaborated in any form with the occupiers, no matter how close the blood relations were. One reason Mikhailo
Kravets' was expelled from the party was that he concealed his brother's
service as a *starosta* and "maintained contact with him after the liberation
of the district."[57] Another party veteran who had joined the ranks in 1926
was expelled by the Shpykiv raikom in August 1944 for inactivity. His
bigger sin, however, was that his daughter, herself a former member of
the Komsomol, worked as a teacher during the occupation and, in 1942,
participated in a meeting with representatives of the Romanian government where she greeted the attendants in the Romanian language.[58]

Communists who found themselves under occupation were expected to
carry out an active struggle no matter what the circumstances and consequences might have been. The party was well aware of the ruthless German
practices regarding partisan activity, yet it deliberately expressed its scorn
for those who shied away from such activity.[59] Porfyrii Burdiuha, a veteran
Communist who joined the ranks in 1926, was expelled from the party
on the charge that he knew about the existence of an underground organization but made no effort to establish contact with it.[60] In the same spirit,

[56] RGASPI, f. 17, op. 44, d. 1653, l. 92. For similar cases, see ibid., op. 45, d. 2003, l.
236; d. 2004, ll. 149–50; d. 2008, l. 2.

[57] TsDAHOU, f. 1, op. 50, d. 313, l. 30.

[58] RGASPI, f. 17, op. 45, d. 2002, l. 275; see a similar case in d. 2004, l. 147. To be sure,
family ties to those regarded favorably by the party could also help. Two sons at the front,
in addition to pro-Soviet agitation under occupation, helped Ivan Sobol' from Zhmerynka
to tip the balance in favor of reinstatement, despite their registration in the gendarmerie,
which was usually unforgiven (TsDAHOU, f. 1, op. 50, d. 133, l. 20). In the same spirit,
when the obkom reinstated Antonina Todchuk into the party based on her voluntaristic
underground activity, it cited as a positive factor her marriage to a highly decorated Red
Army officer, who served in the army since 1937 (RGASPI, f. 17, op. 45, d. 2006, l. 214).

[59] On the brutality of the German antipartisan war, see Omer Bartov, *The Eastern Front,
1941–1945: German Troops and the Barbarization of Warfare* (New York: St. Martin's,
1986), chap. 4; Matthew Cooper, *The Phantom War* (London: Macdonald and Janes, 1979).

[60] RGASPI, f. 17, op. 45, d. 2005, l. 152.

the obkom expelled Pavlo Pshenychnyi, who the obkom alleged "had all the opportunities to join a partisan detachment and actively conduct a struggle against the Fascists."[61]

In its capacity as the guardian of revolutionary purity, the party consciously relinquished requirements for command of its ideological teachings and puritanical personal ethics in favor of combat valor. The essence of being a Communist was now defined by an individual's performance on the battlefield. Prokip Drahan was expelled from the party for having surrendered to the Germans without a fight. His contribution to the restoration of the ruined economy did not compensate for his murky wartime record.[62] When the Nemyriv raikom explained the reinstatement of the above-mentioned Porfyrii Burdiuha for his good work in the Kiev power station and for his being a kolkhoz chairman, the obkom made no reference at all to these motives when it overruled the raikom. Shying away from underground or partisan activity could not be counterbalanced.[63]

Interestingly enough, there were few charges of active collaboration with the occupiers. The obkom leveled this accusation against only 114 Communists in the Vinnytsia region and charged 24 people with treason (5.02 percent and 1.06 percent, respectively). Nor did the obkom rush to apply the label of collaboration. More than once the protocols of the obkom's rulings cited the charge of collaboration as advanced by the raikom, but dropped that charge in its own conclusion, even if the verdict of expulsion was not changed.[64] This self-imposed restraint was shown also in the display of understanding for some unique circumstances, as evidenced by the expulsion decision of Anastasiia Pidoprihora, a kolkhoznitsa from Stanislavchyk district. Under interrogation by the gendarmerie, Pidoprihora gave the names of Communists in her native village. As a result, those Communists were forced to register and were subjected to repression. But since no executions were mentioned and the information had not been voluntary, Pidoprihora was expelled for "failing to live up to the calling of a Communist and for unworthy conduct," but not for collaboration or treason.[65]

---

[61] Ibid., d. 2003, ll. 22–23.

[62] TsDAHOU, f. 1, op. 50, d. 146, l. 41. For similar expulsions from the party on grounds of "cowardice" [*boiahuztvo*] on the battlefield, see RGASPI, f. 17, op. 44, d. 1654, ll. 213, 222; d. 1655, ll. 6–7, 110.

[63] RGASPI, f. 17, op. 45, 2005, l. 152.

[64] See, for example, the ruling on the party status of Hanna Serhiiva, 28 May 1945 (RGASPI, f. 17, op. 45, d. 2004, l. 160). In some cases, the conduct of those who served as *starosty* or helped the Germans to select people for forced labor in Germany was merely categorized as "unworthy" (TsDAHOU, f. 1, op. 50, d. 122, l. 8 and d. 155, l. 7).

[65] TsDAHOU, f. 1, op. 50, d. 148, l. 7.

When Communists were charged with voluntary collaboration, expulsion from the party was probably the lighter consequence suffered for these offenses. Pimen Bondar was expelled from the party as a traitor and sentenced by a military tribunal to "the highest measure of punishment," namely, execution. Bondar apparently informed the German police of the whereabouts of Soviet partisans, some of whom were subsequently executed.[66] Other cases resulted in prolonged imprisonment.[67] All forms of collaboration, however, could not be compensated by service in the Red Army. Andrei Naumov, a young party member (b. 1921), served as the head of the municipal department of the German police in Kharkiv. After the city was liberated, Naumov joined the Red Army where he was admitted to the party and wounded in battle. His combat background did not save him, however. He was expelled by Khmil'nyk raikom as a traitor against the fatherland and was arrested by the NKGB.[68]

The most prevalent reason for expulsion from the party was passivity in the struggle against the invaders. Of the 2,267 Communists who were expelled from the party between 1944 and 1947 because of their wartime conduct, 2,044 (90.16 percent) were charged with passivity in the armed struggle.[69] However, omission from the armed struggle was given the broadest definition possible. Proven membership in an underground cell did not count for much if not accompanied by a solid proof of voluntaristic activism. The Communist should not to be urged to act but rather should offer himself, as Arsen Zhurakovs'kyi learned. A kolkhoz chairman before and after the war, Zhurakovs'kyi was supposedly in better standing than the majority of Communists under verification, given his role as member of an underground committee in the Haisyn district. Nevertheless, the obkom expelled him, explaining that Zhurakovs'kyi "factually did not carry out any [underground] work before the arrival of the Red Army. [Only] under pressure from the partisans did he distribute Soviet [propaganda] leaflets."[70]

Even when a Communist did take part in underground activity, it had to be consistent and uncompromising, as Pavlo Palamarchuk discovered. Following captivity and three months' imprisonment by the Romanian gendarmerie, Palamarchuk joined an underground cell in December 1942

[66] RGASPI, f. 17, op. 45, d. 2007, l. 95. See also Ibid., d. 2005, l. 260.

[67] See RGASPI, f. 17, op. 45, d. 2007, l. 97; and TsDAHOU, f. 1, op. 50, d. 242, l. 20.

[68] RGASPI, f. 17, op. 45, d. 2001, l. 125. For a similar case of expulsion of a severely wounded serviceman who, under occupation, befriended policemen and enjoyed their protection, see TsDAHOU, f. 1, op. 50, d. 160, l. 11.

[69] This figure includes several dozen cases of registration in the gendarmerie, the destruction of the party card for fear of being exposed as Communists, and fifteen cases of desertion from the Red Army in the initial stage of the war.

[70] RGASPI, f. 17, op. 45, d. 2003, ll. 23–24; for an identical case, see ibid, d. 2003, l. 172.

but was soon arrested, tried, and acquitted. After this experience Palamar-chuk shied away from any underground activity and did not join the parti-sans. The Zhmerynka raikom expelled Palamarchuk and the obkom up-held the decision, adding sarcastically that "his [Palamarchuk's] struggle against the German-Romanian occupiers consisted in that, throughout the period from 1941 to 1944, he once caused a short circuit in the power station [according to his own testimony]."[71]

Nor did service in the Red Army compensate for passivity under occupa-tion, especially if such service was not at the front and was not rewarded with decorations. When the obkom expelled Oleksandr Moskalenko for passivity and registration in the Romanian gendarmerie, it indeed cited Moskalenko's draft to the Red Army in 1944 but also the fact that he had not participated in battles.[72] In the cases of other Communists who were drafted into the army after the liberation of the region, the obkom took care to cite a lack of military decorations as a factor in making a decision on their party status.[73] Recall those Communists whose military awards paved their way back into the party in spite of their having conducted religious rites. The weight of military decorations was demonstrated, when, in their absence, Communists who committed religious offenses were expelled from the party.[74]

Some rulings must have left many Communists wondering whether there was any redemption at all for their stay on the occupied territory. One of those was Petro Sadovnyk. Sadovnyk seemed to correspond ideally to the party's expectations of its members under occupation. Throughout the occupation Sadovnyk received communiqués from the Soviet Informa-tion Bureau and sheltered a person in his apartment who was wanted by the occupiers—offenses punishable by death. The obkom, however, found these actions insufficient, since Sadovnyk "did not join underground orga-nizations or partisan detachments, continued to work, and did not con-duct an active struggle against the occupiers as a Communist."[75]

Often simply surviving the occupation was tacitly marked as a sign of guilt. In some cases the obkom took care to emphasize that the person in question was not persecuted by the Gestapo, inferring that the individual had collaborated.[76] In others, the very survival of a collective arrest by the enemy was a major factor in the decision to expel a member from the party, especially if the other Communists arrested with that individual were exe-cuted. Although the case in point was not prosecuted as collaboration in

---

[71] TsDAHOU, f. 1, op. 50, d. 88, l. 9; for a similar case, see ibid, d. 108, l. 29.
[72] Ibid., f. 1, op. 50, d. 159, l. 53.
[73] See, for example, ibid., d. 153, l. 9; d. 159, l. 46; d. 60, ll. 12–13.
[74] See, for example, ibid., d. 242, l. 9.
[75] Ibid., l. 2.
[76] RGASPI, f. 17, op. 44, d. 1653, l. 10.

the murder of fellow Communists, the deliberate reference to it carried an irremovable stain that led to automatic expulsion.[77] Even when the party reinstated Communists who risked their lives in the struggle against the enemy, it was adamant in condemning anyone who deviated even slightly from a perfect record. Such was the case regarding one Petro Kuzmich Polonchuk, who was reinstated to full membership by the Koziatyn raikom. Polonchuk, who became a party member in 1939, was ordered by the raikom to remain on the occupied territory for underground activity. On 10 July 1941 he was instructed to restore the railway between Borivka and Fastiv. Polonchuk, according to the protocol, considered it dangerous to carry his party card with him since a German parachute unit operated in the area he had to cross. So he hid the party card in his sister's house, where it was later found by a relative who destroyed it for fear of a search by the Germans. On March 1944 Polonchuk, who was eventually evacuated to the rear, was decorated for successfully carrying out the restoration of communications under front-line conditions. Polonchuk was reinstated by the raikom in June 1944, but with a severe reprimand in his file for the careless handling of a party document. The obkom's bureau confirmed both the reinstatement and the reprimand in the personal file, only to add the derogatory charge of "cowardice."[78]

The severity with which passivity under occupation was regarded was hammered into the rank and file by the refusal to redeem this offense even by means of a belated contribution at the front. We have explored earlier the redemption of various violations of party and criminal codes by which individuals were rehabilitated because of outstanding performance in combat. No such venue was open to Communists who lived out the years of occupation waiting for the war's fate to be decided. Hnat Kalachyns'kyi who stayed in his village throughout the war, was drafted to the Red Army in March 1944 immediately upon liberation. Kalachyns'kyi's service did not spare him from expulsion by the Sharhorod raikom on the grounds of his earlier passivity in the armed struggle.[79]

As a rule, military offenses were more difficult to redeem. The obkom was uncompromising in its insistence on a perfect military record. Mykola Sukhodols'kyi, a party member since 1938, was expelled by the party cell of his brigade in January 1942 for concealing a former platoon commander's intention to desert from the battalion and for helping the latter to cover his route. On 20 December 1946 the Vinnytsia gorkom requested that the obkom reinstate Sukhodols'kyi, who was then a high official in the city administration, on the grounds "that Sukhodols'kyi's service in the Red Army and participation in battles against the German invaders

[77] Ibid., d. 1654, ll. 158–59.
[78] Ibid., op. 45, d. 2001, ll. 141–42.
[79] TsDAHOU, f. 1, op. 50, d. 151, l. 14; see also d. 242, l. 15.

redeemed his guilt before the party, and also in consideration of his good performance in his current work." The obkom flatly declined to reinstate Sukhodols'kyi.[80] Those who failed to carry out the mission assigned to them on the occupied territory were also ultimately expelled. Vasyl' Murha, a party member since 1932, appeared to be a model Communist. Murha was ordered by the NKVD to remain on the occupied territory and organize diversionary acts. Murha chose instead to work under the Romanians and failed to establish contact with Soviet partisans. The Mohyliv-Podil's'kyi raikom expelled him almost immediately after the region was liberated on 3 August 1944.[81] The same action was taken against a career member of the NKVD from Khmil'nyk who was dispatched to organize partisan activity; once on the occupied territory, however, he returned to his family in the village where he lived out the rest of the war.[82]

Unlike the Germans, the Romanians did not execute Communists en masse. They did, however, force them to sign an obligation to refrain from struggle against their occupation. The Romanian authorities often organized gatherings of Communists for this goal. In some cases the signatories had to guarantee the maintenance of order in their villages, turning themselves into hostages. Communists who attended those meetings and signed such obligations were automatically expelled from party ranks.[83] So severe was the obkom's view of Communists who registered in the gendarmerie that there was no redemption for this offense, as Borys Basys'tyi learned from both the Tul'chyn raikom and obkom. Preaching Soviet propaganda to the population did not spare Basys'tyi from expulsion when the party learned about his registration.[84] Tykhon Skorokhod, from the district of Iampil', was forced by the Romanians to sign an obligation not to engage in a struggle against them. When the Red Army arrived at his village, Skorokhod joined a partisan brigade where he remained for two days. Whereas the partisan stamp was enough to convince the raikom to reinstate him as a candidate, the obkom disagreed and expelled Skorokhod from the party.[85] At least one Communist who was held hostage by the

---

[80] Apparently a military tribunal sentenced Sukhodol'skyi to ten years in prison but instead he was dispatched to the front. Two years later the sentence was dropped. The obkom's only concession was to allow Sukhodol'skyi to reapply for party membership (TsDAHOU, f. 1, op. 50, d. 251, l. 16).

[81] RGASPI, f. 17, op. 44, d. 1654, ll. 144–45; for a similar case, see op. 45, d. 2009, ll. 275–76.

[82] TsDAHOU, f. 1, op. 50, d. 257, l. 42.

[83] See for example, ibid., f. 1, op. 50, d. 88, ll. 14, 42; d. 151, l. 20; d. 201, l. 8. For a rare case of the use of this tactic by the German gendarmerie, see the decision to expel one Anton Makarevych, who signed a statement that he repudiates the ideology of the Communist Party and would refrain from a struggle against the Germans (d. 218, l. 18).

[84] RGASPI, f. 17, op. 45, d. 2008, l. 48.

[85] Ibid., l. 67.

gendarmerie was drafted to a penal battalion in the Red Army immediately after liberation. According to the obkom, this party member had committed no offense.[86]

A frequent offense was leaving voluntarily for work in the Reich. This offense, as a rule, could not be compensated by a belated contribution to the war effort and led to additional legal repercussions.[87] Demil Chered, who was accused of volunteering for work in an arms factory in Germany, had already been sentenced to five years in prison when the Dashiv raikom expelled him from the party ranks.[88] At times this charge was categorized as nothing less than treason.[89] In this light, obviously service in managerial posts under the occupiers also met with harsh punishment and, in some cases, could mean a person's life. Iosif Dudnyk volunteered to work as sovkhoz manager and employed prisoners of war whom he treated rudely, even including incidents of beating. Dudnyk was brought to trial on treason charges.[90] Another Communist, Il'ia Lozyns'kyi, a party veteran since 1927, served as deacon in a church and as a school director under the Germans. That cost Lozyns'kyi his party membership and an additional five years in prison.[91]

Altogether the series of rulings that defined the requirement of "living up to the calling of a Communist" under occupation constituted an insurmountable challenge. Given the German and Romanian occupation regimes in the region, this essentially meant being willing to die for the Soviet cause. There was no middle ground.

The Universal and the Particular: An Ethnic Purge?

In the increasingly ethnicized postwar Soviet world, ethnicity factored in all major considerations. Moreover, it posed a troubling challenge to the core of the revolutionary ethos: Was the Revolution losing its universal aspirations in favor of the pursuit of particularistic agendas? For many contemporaries, especially members of ethnic minorities, the Revolution was certainly heading in this direction. For ethnic minorities subjected to

---

[86] TsDAHOU, f. 1, op. 50, d. 151, l. 24.

[87] Such was the case regarding Ihor Serkovs'kyi, who signed an obligation not to conduct any struggle against the occupiers and, in November 1942, volunteered to work in Germany, where he stayed for about two months. Serkovs'kyi joined the partisans in November 1943, concealing his stay in Germany. Both the raikom and obkom ignored his partisan past and expelled him from the party (RGASPI, f. 17, op. 45, d. 2005, ll. 214–15).

[88] Ibid., d. 2002, ll. 282–283; see also d. 2003, l. 246.

[89] TsDAHOU, f. 1, op. 50, d. 122, l. 19.

[90] RGASPI, f. 17, op. 45, d. 2005, l. 251.

[91] Ibid., l. 250

attacks for their alleged nationalist separatism, the purge of their individual members appeared intentionally to undermine their communities as a whole. But was it so?

The fate of the Jewish Communists under verification, more than any other group, demonstrated the primacy of the wartime experience and the tension between universal and particularistic concerns. The universal resentment that confronted the Jewish community makes its case all the more instructive. At a time when official anti-Semitism was gathering momentum and popular outbursts against Jews were on the rise, it seems only likely that Jewish Communists would have been driven out of the party en masse. In Vinnytsia such prospects seemed even more likely given Stakhurs'kyi's anti-Semitic views and the stubborn struggle that the local Jewish community conducted against him. Indeed, throughout 1947, the Central Committee repeatedly addressed itself to this matter.

In an unpublished letter to *Pravda*, dated 19 September 1946, a group of local Jews accused Stakhurs'kyi of orchestrating an anti-Semitic campaign and driving Jewish Communists out of the region. The letter emphasized the centrality of the war experience in the articulation of identities and perceptions of individuals and groups alike. The Jews clearly believed that they could use the war experience to shield them from Stakhurs'kyi's wrath. "The seeds of the liquidation of the Jewish nationality, left by the Fascists, develop well in the city of Vinnytsia and in the region," wrote the authors of the letter.

> It must be established that with the arrival of Comrade Stakhurs'kyi incidents of anti-Semitic character assumed a systematic character, and no wonder since Stakhurs'kyi himself, in a conversation with workers of the apparatus of the obkom and raikoms, referred to Jews only as "weevils" and "jackals." Stakhurs'kyi, for some reason, is "deeply convinced" that, to a man, all the Jews were in Tashkent and not one of them fought! It would do him no harm to know that every Jew of draft age was at the front and fought fairly well for the motherland, no worse than other nationalities of our immense motherland. It is a fact that the performance of the Jews was distinguished and that their heroism at the front was not below that of the other peoples of the USSR.[92]

Baptism by fire, then, was perceived to transcend all other categories. The writers of the letter followed with an example of a demobilized Jewish officer, who was declined admission to legal studies on the grounds that only the indigenous population was eligible for admission. "It is not difficult to imagine," they wrote,

---

[92] TsDAHOU, f. 1, op. 23, d. 4170, ll. 2–4. Although the letter was signed in Yiddish and Russian by four people, it was classified as anonymous when it was directed to the Ukrainian Central Committee's secretary for cadres on 10 April 1947.

the bewilderment of this comrade, whose great grandfather, grandfather, father, and he himself were born, lived, and continue to live in the Vinnytsia region. He shed blood for this land, but he is still a Jew, not a member of the "indigenous population." Who knows, after all that, what the standards are for establishing membership in the indigenous population?[93]

The authors continued with additional examples of anti-Semitism, which, they argued, were numerous and included the murder of a demobilized officer. Finally, and probably intentionally, the authors charged that this anti-Semitism from above played into the hands of the worst segments of the Ukrainian polity, namely, those who remained on the occupied territory and served the Germans: "Worthless Black Hundreds, Ukrainian nationalists who [collaborated] with the Germans on the occupied territory, only wait for a call for provocation. [And] not without reason. Scandalous incidents of beatings and even murder have become more frequent."[94]

A year later the perception of a Stakhurs'kyi-guided, anti-Semitic campaign gained support from another source. The charges the Jewish authors raised were echoed in a letter by M. Iakunenko, the *Izvestiia* correspondent in the Vinnytsia region, to the chief editor of the newspaper. The letter from 18 August 1947 was submitted to Lazar Kaganovich, the then first secretary of the Ukrainian Central Committee. "I cannot avoid reporting," wrote the correspondent,

> on the special hostility of Comrade Stakhurs'kyi toward the Jewish population, of whom a large number resides in Vinnytsia and the region. Comrade Stakhurs'kyi literally banishes Jewish party and soviet workers from leading positions, makes them wander unemployed, forcing them to depart to other regions. I know of many instances where decorated *frontoviki* who [wish to] return to their former jobs are not allowed to return to them, on the order of comrade Stakhurs'kyi, only because they are Jews.[95]

Apparently the issue touched a raw nerve and the Central Committee ordered an investigation. The report of Popeliukh, the executive organizer for the Vinnytsia region in the cadres administration of the Central Committee, challenged most of the accusations the Jews raised. He did so, however, in quite ambivalent terms. The report denied the practice of an anti-Jewish agenda in the party by underlining the relatively high presence of Jews in the party ranks. At the time of the report, wrote Popeliukh, Jews accounted for 217 of 2,757 of the obkom's *nomenklatura*, of whom 46 served in party jobs, 78 in Soviet organs, 19 in the judicial and security bodies, and 74 in rural and industrial branches. Furthermore, in 1946 and

[93] Ibid.
[94] Ibid.
[95] Ibid., l. 16.

TABLE 2.4
Change in Ethnic Composition of the Vinnytsia Party
Organization, 1939–1949

Year	Ukrainians	Russians	Jews	Others	Total
1939	13,823	1,095	3,366	805	19,089
1946	18,313	4,493	3,099	655	26,560
1947	21,441	4,942	3,685	690	30,758
1948	22,231	5,264	3,757	737	31,989

Sources: TsDAHOU, f. 1, op. 23, d. 4212, ll. 2–3; op. 46,
d. 3976, l. 1; d. 3977, l.1.

the first four months of 1947 Jews made up 14.5 percent (203 of 1,398) of those admitted as candidates to membership by the entire regional party organization and, more specifically, 23.1 percent of those admitted by the gorkom (63 of 229) (Table 2.4).

What the reporter did not mention was that throughout the preceding period, which overlapped the arrival of Stakhurs'kyi to Vinnytsia, the presence of Jews in the apparatus declined both in relative and absolute numbers. Whereas in 1945 Jews comprised 9.34 percent (242 of 2,590) of regional *nomenklatura*, in 1946 their presence shrank to 7.46 percent (218 of 2,922). The annual report of the obkom's cadres department shows that the relative number of Jews in the *nomenklatura* was singled out and unofficially calculated.[96] At the same time, Stakhurs'kyi's denial of the anti-Semitic connotation of his comments was treated with a grain of salt. In his concluding comment, the reporter confirmed the systematic character of the problem and added that similar anti-Semitic statements were recorded in 1946.[97]

The Ukrainian Central Committee was even more emphatic in its report to the Central Committee in Moscow denying anti-Semitism, highlighting the Jewish presence in party and state organs and justifying individual dismissals on professional grounds. Yet the report to Moscow did confess at least one case of unjustified dismissal of a Jewish official, who remained unemployed over two months. Even more pointedly, the report to Moscow condemned the "insufficient energy of the cadres departments of the obkom, gorkoms, and raikoms in placing Jewish Communists who return from the Red Army in jobs."[98]

---

[96] The decline throughout 1945–47 applied to all individual branches of the regional *nomenklatura* (ibid., d. 4423, l. 8, 69; d. 4212, l. 43).

[97] Ibid., d. 4170, ll. 6–9.

[98] Ibid., d. 3731, ll. 41–53 (here, l. 47). Apparently the anonymous letters of complaint were addressed to the party leaders in Moscow, thus extending the matter beyond local boundaries (ibid., l. 44).

TABLE 2.5
Rulings on Party Status by Ethnicity, 1944–1947

Ethnicity	Expelled	Reinstated	Total*
Ukrainians	2025	449	2474
			88.7%
Russians	62	44	106
			3.8%
Jews	80	32	112
			4.0%
Others	76	20	96
			3.4%
Total %	2243	545	2788
	80.5%	19.5%	100.0%

* No data on the ethnicity of 40 people.

Ultimately, however, the postwar anti-Semitic wave seemed not to have a unique impact on decisions regarding Jewish Communists' party status. The obkom bureau's decisions did not reveal any particular bias. Indeed, following Stakhurs'kyi's appointment, the rate of expulsion of Jewish Communists increased from 66 percent to 75 percent. This 9 percent increase, however, did not exceed the general trend after Stakhurs'kyi again assumed leadership. The overall rate of expulsions in the same period rose by 11.8 percent, from 72.9 percent to 84.7 percent following Stakhurs'kyi's arrival, whereas the rate for ethnic Ukrainian Communists who remained on the occupied territory rose by 14.7 percent, from 71.6 percent to 86.3 percent (Table 2.5).[99]

An examination of individual cases does not reveal any consistent bias for or against Jews. In some instances, the obkom displayed utter indifference to the fate of Jews under occupation. At other times, the wartime experience of Jews clearly played in their favor. On the one hand, there were enough signs to support the argument for either deliberate or tacit discrimination against the Jews. The most common pattern was a disregard of the unique circumstances that the Jewish population faced under the occupation. The party organizations applied to the Jewish Communists the same standards it applied to the rest of the rank and file, regardless of their wartime conditions. Passivity in the struggle against the occupiers was cited in almost all the expulsion decisions, including cases in which individuals under review were locked in ghettos and concentration camps established by the Romanian authorities. Some were expelled from the party for settling in the ghettos voluntarily, despite the admission that

[99] See Table 2.1, below.

they had no alternative after the occupiers drove them from their homes.[100] The party organizations were fully informed of the traumatic experience of the ghettos. The Khmil'nyk raikom expelled one Iudko Grinfeld even though it was cited in the protocol that his wife and two children were murdered in the ghetto of Zhmerynka.[101] At times, the language used revealed utter insensitivity. When the bureau expelled Buzia Kaiser, a party member since 1937, for inactivity and for registration in the gendarmerie, it concluded the detailed verification with a comment that "[he] was not subjected to repressions by the occupiers."[102] Although this could well be a simple use of bureaucratic terminology reserved for those who did not suffer physical repression at the hands of the occupiers, such an interpretation seems less likely given the party's awareness of the plight of the Jewish population under occupation.

Less complicated were the expulsions of people who had served as policemen in the Jewish ghetto and were in charge of recruiting the labor force for the Romanians, as did one Lazar Tsap.[103] Hanna Tkhorzhevskaia, a Jew and party member since 1940, was expelled by the Vinnytsia gorkom for serving as a translator for the Germans. Not only had she refrained from contact with underground organizations, charged the gorkom, but "to the contrary, [Tkhorzhevskaia] had intimate and secret contact with the German occupiers who helped her materially and provided her with documents stating that she was the wife of a serviceman in the German-Fascist army."[104]

Already in 1944, two years before the protest letters against Stakhurs'kyi and the first wave of mass demobilization, it was evident that Jewish veterans viewed anti-Semitism as the driving force behind any decisions that concerned them. When Abram Pogranichnyi was expelled by the Sharhorod raikom in October 1944 for his loose conduct while serving on a people's court, the decorated war veteran fired back with charges of anti-Semitism. The obkom rejected Pogranichnyi's allegations and approved his expulsion, but his accusation only intensified when the obkom reinstated other Red Army veterans who had committed similar offenses and had similar military records to his own.[105]

At the same time, the party occasionally displayed compassion toward the unique Jewish experience during the war. The obkom reinstated Rakhil' Masniak, a party member since 1940, who was expelled for falsification of a party document. After she had been evacuated to the Chkalovsk re-

---

[100] RGASPI, f. 17, op. 44, d. 1653, l. 146; d. 1654, ll. 145–46; op. 45, d. 2004, l. 214.
[101] TsDAHOU, f. 1, op. 50, d. 108, l. 11.
[102] RGASPI, f. 17, op. 45, d. 2008, l. 10.
[103] Ibid., op. 44, d. 1653, l. 149.
[104] Ibid., l. 141.
[105] Ibid., op. 45, d. 2001, ll. 111–12.

gion, Masniak apparently concealed her Jewish name and origin in her personal file and replaced it with Ukrainian ones. Such a violation of party rules led automatically to expulsion, and Masniak was indeed expelled by the Kryzhopil' raikom. In her appeal to the obkom, Masniak explained her action as a result of her "past woes, having lost her sixteen-year-old son and the persecution of the Jews by the Fascists (murdering utterly innocent people and burying children alive)."[106] The obkom then overruled the raikom and reinstated Masniak with a reprimand. Similarly the obkom overturned the Mohyliv-Podil's'kyi raikom's expulsion of Genia Kogan, a party member since 1938, who had been accused of passivity in the struggle against the German-Romanian occupiers. The bureau cited in detail the persecution that Kogan endured at the hands of the Germans and the Romanians, and emphasized her antifascist agitation among the population as well as the fact that her three brothers had served in the Red Army since 1941.[107]

Even more significant was the use of anti-Semitic conduct during the war as a criterion for expulsion from the party. Some Communists were expelled without elaboration beyond the comment of "showing themselves as anti-Semites during the occupation,"[108] and others were expelled for participating in the pillage of property of local Jews who were shot by the Germans.[109] In some cases the obkom employed unambiguous language in its condemnation of Communists who took part in, or made peace with, the persecution of Jews. On 23 January 1945 the obkom reinstated Matvii Karvats'kyi as one who lived up to the calling of a Communist. Yet on 15 November 1946 the Bar raikom expelled Karvats'kyi based on new materials about his conduct on the occupied territory. Karvats'kyi apparently worked as a foreman and skilled worker in the remounting and construction of a road where forced Jewish labor was used. The Jews, the protocol read, were rounded up in a special camp, tortured by the police, and, when the work was concluded, shot. "Karvats'kyi," stated the obkom, "made no effort to avoid this job, [and hence] compromised the title of Communist." On 25 March 1947 the obkom adhered to the raikom ruling, reversed its original decision, and expelled Karvats'kyi from the party.[110] In other cases, aid to the Jewish population during the occupation was cited as a reason for reinstatement into the party, fulfilling the requirement of "living up to the calling of a Communist."[111]

[106] Ibid., d. 2002, ll. 269–70.

[107] Ibid., d. 2007, ll. 192–93.

[108] See, for example, the ruling by the Mohyliv-Podil's'kyi raikom on the expulsion of Iakuv Shkolnik, a party member since 1930, in ibid., op. 44, d. 1654, ll. 55–56.

[109] Ibid., ll. 159–60; op. 45, d. 2005, l. 41.

[110] TsDAHOU, f. 1, op. 50, d. 255, ll. 11–12.

[111] RGASPI, f. 17, op. 45, d. 2002, ll. 3–4; TsDAHOU, f. 1, op. 50, d. 88, l. 35.

The condemnation of anti-Semitism, insofar as military personnel and wartime records were concerned, continued after the war as we learn from at least one incident. On 18 July 1946 the obkom expelled a relatively prominent official who had moved into the apartment of a demobilized Red Army man during the war, but he refused to evacuate the apartment. When this official, Iakov Matviichuk, who served at the time as inspector of military training of personnel of the regional militia, ignored the gorkom's order to move into another apartment, the head of the political section of the regional militia tried to evict Matviichuk himself, at which time Matviichuk burst out with anti-Semitic remarks. The gorkom expelled Matviichuk for a "systematic display of anti-Semitism and lack of discipline," and the obkom upheld the decision. Notably Stakhurs'kyi himself presided over the meeting of the obkom's bureau that dealt with the case.[112]

Finally, the primacy of wartime credentials was evident in the obkom's decisions on the party status of Jewish veterans. Natalia-Sara Ulitskaia joined the Stalin partisan brigade in May 1943, where she became a detachment political instructor and was decorated for "valor and heroism." Ulitskaia was admitted as a candidate to the party in October 1943 and, just two months later, in clear violation of the mandatory candidacy period, was accepted as a full party member. At a time when the obkom moved to reduce the party status of partisans with a similar history back to candidacy, it indeed cited this violation yet proceeded to confirm her admission by the partisan brigade's party cell.[113] Even more instructive was the case of Iosif Groisman, who was expelled by the Tul'chyn raikom for refusing to take a job in the countryside. Following his demobilization in December 1945, Groisman was offered work as either an agricultural agent or a chairman of a kolkhoz board—unlikely jobs for a Jew in the postwar era. Groisman declined, citing a lack of familiarity with rural economic work. The obkom considered Groisman's military record, including his decorations and service throughout the war, and reinstated him with only a reprimand.[114]

It is plausible to assume that, for Jewish Communists, wartime experience prevented a further deterioration in their already fragile political and social status.[115] At a time when the Jewish community as a whole was sub-

---

[112] TsDAHOU, f. 1, op. 50, d. 144, ll. 9–10.

[113] RGASPI, f. 17, op. 45, d. 2002, l. 150. Other cases show that Jews admitted to the party during their stay with the partisans were not subject to discrimination (see d. 2003, ll. 28–29, for the reinstatement of Iosif Isakovich Mali, a staff officer of the Mel'nyk partisan formation).

[114] TsDAHOU, f. 1, op. 50, d. 251, ll. 3–4.

[115] For a discussion on the paradox of a continued and relatively high percentage of Jews in the CPSU, despite the mass influx of non-Jews into the party and the growing official

jected to increasing persecution, its individual members with an irrefutable wartime record could still thrive. For a significant number, combat exploits won recognition. For the less fortunate, those who remained on occupied territory, the traumatic experience brought uneven results. For all Jewish Communists, the absence of a certain bias in the ruling on their party status accentuated the primacy of wartime credentials in the party's calculus.

Closure and Totalization

As the decade drew to a close, the pressure to conclude this painful episode in party life only increased. On 1 June 1948 the Central Committee of the Ukrainian Communist Party ordered all raikoms and gorkoms to conclude the verification of Communists who remained on the occupied territory. By and large, the regional organizations, Vinnytsia included, complied.[116] On 1 January 1948 the Communist Party in Ukraine counted 120,601 Communists who remained on the occupied territory, of whom 16,414 were killed or dead and 86,878 were registered. Up to that point, the obkoms had reviewed 65,279 cases and expelled 58,848 Communists from the party (90.14 percent).[117] A year later the total number of those identified as staying on the occupied territory rose to 142,134. By then the obkoms had reviewed 73,740 cases and expelled 68,032 (92.25 percent).[118]

The tendency for nearly total expulsion as the verification was running its course was noticed in Vinnytsia as well. By 1 January 1947 the regional party organizations registered 4,337 Communists who had remained on the occupied territory, reviewed 2,379 of them, and expelled 1,945 (81.75 percent).[119] A year later the regional Party Collegium recorded 4,957 Communists who had remained on the occupied territory, of whom it registered 4,337, reviewed 2,636, and expelled 2,233 (84.71 percent).[120] Three years later the figures increased: Of 6,214 Communists who had remained on the occupied territory, 923 were killed or dead and 163 could not be located. The obkom reviewed 3,151 cases and handed down 2,764 expulsions (87.71 percent).[121] As late as 1951 Communists who had remained on the occupied territory without the party's authorization still

---

anti-Semitism, see Rigby, *Communist Party Membership*, 385–88; and Benjamin Pinkus, *The Jews of the Soviet Union* (Cambridge: Cambridge University Press, 1988), 181–82.

[116] TsKhSD, f. 6, op. 6, d. 55, l. 5.
[117] Ibid., f. 1, op. 46, d. 5337, l. 211.
[118] TsDAHOU, f. 1, op. 46, d. 5337, l. 98.
[119] Ibid., op. 23, d. 4095, ll. 7, 14.
[120] Ibid., op. 46, d. 5337, l. 211.
[121] Ibid., d. 5336, l. 30.

TABLE 2.6
Number of Rulings on Party Status by Year, 1944–1947

	Expelled	Reinstated	Row Total
1944	269	74	343
1945	775	277	1,052
1946	829	142	971
1947	394	68	462
Column Total	2267	561	2828
	80.2%	19.8%	100.0%

constituted the largest single category of expellees from the regional party organization. That year the obkom approved all 201 expulsions carried out by the gorkom and the raikoms.[122]

Clearly the trend toward total excision ran opposite the premise of a meticulous, individually based review. There were undoubtedly abundant reasons for expulsion en masse. Thorough verification required a great deal of time and resources at a period when the party was facing a new famine and the pressures of collectivization in the western provinces. Yet such obstacles did not prevent the party from launching the verification process in the immediate aftermath of the war, when it was in a far more dire situation. It is also likely that those Communists with a distinguished record under occupation would have come forward early on or have been paraded by the party as model Communists, whereas those with a murky past would have preferred to keep a low profile in hopes of weathering the party's wrath. After the initial phase of the region's liberation, very few partisans and underground activists were left to emerge in public. Indeed, the bulk of reinstatements in the party occurred in the first year-and-a-half after liberation. Whereas the rate of reinstatements in 1944 and 1945 were 21.57 percent and 26.33 percent, respectively, they dropped sharply to 14.62 percent in 1946 and 14.71 percent in 1947 (Table 2.6).

Not every single Communist endorsed the relentless persecution of those who remained on the German-occupied territory and the irremovable stigma attached to them. Some were seemingly frustrated by the application of collective guilt and its crude manipulation by all kinds of people. It was important, in this sense, that army veterans gave voice to these sentiments. No one was more blunt than Viktor Nekrasov, the veteran-turned-writer. In his 1954 novel, *In the Native Town*, which focused on the troubled time of the immediate aftermath of the war, Nekrasov staged a climactic clash between two demobilized Communists, now at a building institute in Kiev. The dean, Captain Chekmen', is trying to remold the faculty's party cell by recruiting "*frontoviki*, real guys," and by

---

[122] PAVO, f. 136, op. 15, d. 12, ll. 57, 60.

getting rid of the seventy-year-old professor Nikol'tsev. And what better way is there than digging into the latter's wartime record. Nikol'tsev, it appears, lived the war years under German occupation. "Didn't he spend three years under occupation?" Chekmen' retorts to Mitiasov, a fellow veteran who questions the practice of such allegations.

> Spent his time there like a good boy. The devil only knows what else he was doing there. He was selling booklets. We know all about these books. I bet they [those who lived on occupied territory] wrote articles in the [German] filthy newspapers attacking the Bolsheviks, but later, when our [forces] approached, these very people suddenly turned out to be fighters for Soviet power. They all lie! . . . Three quarters of them gave up willingly.[123]

Mitiasov, whose wife and close friend survived the German occupation, responds by slapping Chekmen' on his face. When the party cell convenes to discuss Mitiasov's expulsion from the party, he is nothing but apologetic. "No, it is not my friend whom you insulted," he scolds Chekmen'.

> You insulted everyone who was taken prisoner, who was in the fascist camps, or lived under occupation. Everyone, without making distinctions. We know— there were all kinds of people there. There were bustards and traitors among them—we know all that. But how many? And who were they? A bunch of scoundrels. But the people were expecting us. Those who could—escaped to the forest and became partisans. . . I beg your pardon, comrades, but I'll say it upfront: I don't know how any of you here would have reacted if someone in your presence, moreover, a Communist—no, he is not a Communist, he just carries a party card in his wallet—if someone like that had told you that three quarters of the people who were taken prisoners, went willingly, and everyone who had lived under the Germans, are, without distinctions, villains and scoundrels. I don't know what you would have done. I hit him.[124]

In all likelihood, Nekrasov, and his fictional mouthpiece, Mitiasov, knew well what their fellow Communists would have done. Condemning such allegations was not in their repertoire. The opposite. However defiant and emotional was the summation, it was also futile. Mitiasov was not reinstated in the party, which was one of the main reasons the novel could not be made into a film, as one official plainly told Nekrasov.[125] The postwar party was not in a conciliatory mood.

When one views the purge as part of the overall postwar purification campaign, its substantial radicalization appeared to be the rule rather than the exception. As the war emerged as the Bolshevik Armageddon, there

---

[123] Viktor Nekrasov, "V rodnom gorode," *Novyi mir* 10 (October 1954): 3–65; 11 (November 1954): 97–178, here, 161–62.

[124] Ibid., 172.

[125] Viktor Nekrasov, "Slova 'velikie' i prostye," *Iskusstvo kino* 5 (1959): 58.

was less toleration of groups marked as internal enemies and a significant erosion of the long-held principle of differentiation of the enemy within. In this light, it was not surprising that guilt was extended from the conduct of the individual under a cloud to his blood lineage. In spite of Stalin's famous dictum that "sons do not answer for their fathers," the purge's proceedings betrayed the extension of genealogical accountability. Family ties to those who served in the region under occupation were highlighted in the materials provided by the Party Collegium. Although these materials were never the sole reason for expulsion, their very mention spoke for itself. At the district level, family ties to those who remained on the occupied territory were sufficient grounds for expulsion from the party or dismissal from a job. Thus the head of an MGB district branch could accuse the obkom's cadres department of employing a Red Army veteran who, after being demobilized, had married a daughter of a "fervent Petliurite" [i.e., a Ukrainian nationalist]. Both the father-in-law and wife served under the Germans during the occupation.[126] As late as May 1951 the deputy chairman of the oblispolkom, Biriukov, failed to receive final confirmation of his job. Biriukov was initially charged with concealing his father's stay on the occupied territory. His father had worked as an administrator in a sovkhoz under the Germans, treated the workers rudely, and participated in the confiscation of property for the Germans. Only later, when the obkom learned that Biriukov had not lived with his father since 1932 and had been awarded three orders and two medals during the war, did it appoint him to the office.[127]

Seven years after the region was liberated, the purification of the local party organization drew to a close. The stain of a large inactive rank and file was removed by way of expulsion, although the stigma of expulsion on these grounds was humiliating enough to drive individuals to appeal the verdict well into the 1950s and 1960s.[128] The handful of Communists who rose to the occasion of war and survived verification were now joined by a mass of demobilized Communists. On 1 July 1947, 75.8 percent of the 6,263,116 party members and candidates throughout the Union were people who had joined the ranks during and after the war.[129] It was a new party with both elite and rank-and-file members who viewed the war as

---

[126] TsDAHOU, f. 1, op. 46, d. 2284, l. 19. Similarly Porfyrii Cherniak paid the price for his father-in-law's past. Cherniak was discharged from the Red Army as a war invalid. Yet his father-in-law's service as a senior policeman under the occupiers, in addition to his own late enrollment into the Red Army, tipped the balance in favor of expulsion (RGASPI, f. 17, op. 45, d. 2008, l. 35).

[127] TsDAHOU, f. 1, op. 46, d. 5533, ll. 22–23.

[128] In February 1956 alone, some 575 people, who were expelled for having remained on the German-occupied territory, applied to the Twentieth Party Congress requesting that the ruling in their cases be overturned (TsKhSD, f. 6, op. 6, d. 1075, ll. 1, 3–4).

[129] RGASPI, f. 17, op. 122, d. 291, l. 127.

the focal point in their lives. The zealous adherence to the criterion of wartime conduct in defining the essence of the ideal postwar Communist reflected the view of the war as both the ultimate test and the purgatory of the Revolution. But the purge was not limited to the party. Rather, it was a core institution in the remolding of society as a whole in the wake of the war, which takes us out of the party boundaries to the sociopolitical and ethnic groups that populated the region.

Part II

DELINEATING THE BODY SOCIOETHNIC

Three

Excising Evil

Therefore as soon as a spark appears it must be
snuffed out, and the yeast separated from the vicinity of the dough, the rancid flesh cut off, and
the mangy animal driven away from the flock of
sheep, lest the entire house burn, the dough
spoil, the body rot, and the flock perish. [The her-
etic] Arius was one spark in Alexandria; but because he was not immediately suppressed, the entire world was devastated with his flame.

(St. Jerome, *Commentariorum in Epistolam ad
Galatas libri tres*)[1]

THE UKRAINIAN nationalist cause failed to materialize in the Vinnytsia
region. To contemporaries, however, the virtual eradication of the nationalist presence in the region was not a foregone conclusion. At the time,
several factors seemed to play into the hands of the anti-Soviet movement,
powerful enough to induce Soviet authorities to lump the region together
with its western counterparts, where a full-fledged civil war was already
under way.

A by-product of the annexation of the western provinces in the fall of
1939 was the proliferation of nationalist activity in the region. As the
westernmost border region in pre-1939 Soviet Ukraine, Vinnytsia was expected to figure highly in nationalist activity. And that is indeed what happened. The arrival of nationalist activists to the region from western
Ukraine during 1939–40 prepared the ground for an outburst of underground activity already on the eve of the war and surfaced following the
arrival of German troops.[2] And with the looming German retreat, nationalist forces once again emerged as the most powerful in the region. "At

---

[1] St. Jerome, *Commentariorum in Epistolam ad Galatas libri tres*, in J.-P. Migne, ed.,
Patrologia latina, vol. 26 (Turnhout, Belgium, n.d.), col. 430.
[2] *Tsentral'nyi Arkhiv Vnutrennikh Voisk Ministerstva Vnutrennikh Del Rossiiskoi Federatsii
(Arkhiv VV MVD SSSR po Ukrains'koi i Moldavs'koi SSR)* (hereafter, *TsAVVMVDRF*), f.
488, op. 1, d. 51, l. 1. According to a local nationalist memoirist, slogans such as "Get the
Moskali [a derogatory name for Russians] and Muscovite Language Out of Ukraine and Our
Schools" and "Long Live the Independent United Ukrainian State" appeared in schools on

the very beginning," related a Soviet partisan commander from Vinnytsia, "the largest organizations were those of the nationalists, who actually seized all the power in the villages, in the districts, and in the towns."[3] Indeed, nationalist leaders were beaming with confidence in the popularity of their cause in the region. Internal communications between nationalist partisans in Vinnytsia on the popular reaction to their movement were unequivocal:

1. With the exception of individual supporters of the Bolsheviks, the population is following the work of the insurgents with great interest. Every action taken is welcomed with great enthusiasm. Although secretly, people talk about it everywhere. They view the insurgents as their defenders from the bloody regime. One can often hear individual women threaten Bolshevik activists, saying: "Just you wait! Don't think that you are special (*Boha zlovyv za nohy*). There were many like you among us, but they are no more," and so on.

2. The spirit of the population is much undermined when they learn that we are few. Rumors that individual detachments of the UPA [Ukrainian Insurgent Army] marched past various roads in large numbers raise hopes for a quick and decisive victory.

3. The population welcomes and respects the insurgents. One often meets a family who has no means to survive but nevertheless does its best to feed every insurgent with whatever it can, sharing its last crumb of bread.

4. The population desires to see us victorious at every step, wishes the expansion of our activity and that everywhere the NKVD will be met with machine guns and resistance.[4]

Equally definitive was the assessment of the popular rejection of Soviet power. "Almost 99 percent of the population hates the Bolsheviks and views them with hostility," continued the communiqué. "You can learn this by speaking to any peasant. [The population] especially hates the kolkhoz system, the NKVD, and that they confiscate all the bread." The report followed with an optimistic note regarding the healthy skepticism of the local population who "does not believe any of the Bolshevik promises that after the war life will get better and more concessions will be made. For twenty-five years the Bolsheviks ruled, promised a lot, but gave nothing. The population understands this business."[5]

---

the eve of the German invasion (Ievhen Aletiiano-Popivs'kyi, *Z ideieiu v sertsi—zi zbroieiu v rukakh* [London: Ukrains'ka vydavnycha spilka u V. Brytanii, 1980], 159–61).

[3] IIAN ORF, f. 2, op. 9, d. 1, l. 6. On nationalist establishments in the region, see TsDAHOU, f. 128, op. 1, d. 1, l. 98; IIAN ORF, f. 2, op. 9, d. 3, l. 7.

[4] TsAVVMVDRF, f. 488, op. 1, d. 51, l. 43. Similar assessments were recorded by a junior commander following successive raids to four different villages between 12 and 15 May 1944. "The majority of the population appears supportive of the nationalists, is swayed by their propaganda, hates the kolkhozes, and is disposed toward individual property," concluded Hryts, a commander of a five-man squad (ibid., l. 51).

[5] Ibid., ll. 43–43a.

One could expect a somewhat more qualified assessment from the nationalists, especially when, at a time the Red Army's drive westward was already in full swing, the population was also said "not to believe in the victory of the Bolsheviks but to be in complete agreement with our uprising and confident in the victory of the Ukrainians." Yet even when it appeared that the nationalists were reading their own expectations into the local population, one could hardly fault them for assuming that Vinnytsia would be a fertile ground for their message. The bloody legacy of Soviet power in the region, starting from forced collectivization through the famine of 1932–33, mass deportations and the Terror, which hit Vinnytsia particularly hard, were all perceived as powerful mobilizing factors. These events were expected to provide the nationalist cause with a seemingly broad popular base and, indeed, "former people" and their families were targeted during recruitment drives by the region's OUN (Organization of Ukrainian Nationalists), along with former members of repressed nationalist organizations such as the "Defense of Ukraine," led by Mykola Mikhnovs'kyi, the Ukrainian Military Organization (UVO), the Union for the Liberation of Ukraine (SVU), the Union of Ukrainian Youth (SUM), former soldiers of the Ukrainian National Republic (UNR), Free Cossacks (Vil'ne Kazatstvo), and former soldiers of the Ukrainian Galician Army (UHA), who, according to one local activist, could still be found in the region.[6]

Moreover, nationalist ideas appeared to make inroads among local youth. As late as December 1944 the NKVD uncovered networks of students, aged fifteen to seventeen years old, who engaged in the production of weapons and the distribution of anti-Soviet leaflets. All the youngsters came from families of a solid Soviet background, which led the head of the regional NKVD to place the blame on the political education at their school which failed to counter the damage done by two-and-a-half years of exposure to nationalist propaganda. Apparently libraries in Vinnytsia still had nationalist literature on their shelves.[7]

The picture that emerged following the region's liberation from German occupation was one of a power vacuum. Several months after the return of Soviet power to Vinnytsia, the Soviets' control over large portions of the region was still ineffective. The presence of nationalist forces in the region was impressive. Commanders of Soviet partisan units spotted nationalist units of several hundred men each. The Lenin Mounted Brigade reported the arrival of some six hundred fighters from the western provinces to the Black Forest in late 1943. The nationalist unit that settled in the Lityn district felt confident enough to issue an ultimatum to the Soviet partisans to evacuate the region. The nationalists, whom the Soviets

---

[6] Aletiiano-Popivs'kyi, *Z ideieiu v sertsi*, 17; TsAVVMVDRF, f. 488, op. 1, d. 51, l. 4.

[7] TsDAHOU, f. 1, op. 50, d. 1, ll. 208–10.

admitted were better armed, forced the latter to enter into negotiations to clarify the former's position in the event of German raids. Only the approach of the Red Army and another partisan brigade forced them out of the region.[8] Even if these figures were somewhat exaggerated to provide an excuse for the negotiations with the nationalists, they punctuated the perceived threat from the Communists' point of view.[9]

With the approaching withdrawal of the Germans, the UPA increased its activity in the region. In February 1944 several hundred guerrillas were dispatched to Vinnytsia where they joined forces with smaller local units.[10] Despite increasing pressure from the NKVD and the destruction battalions (*istrebitel'nye batal'iony*)—auxiliary detachments of armed civilians charged with hunting down German and nationalist stragglers—Soviet power was admittedly far from in control. Side by side with the NKVD's admission of the virtual lack of basic intelligence regarding the size and command of the nationalist forces in the region, party officials continued to complain about a veritable power vacuum in the region.[11] Several months after the Red Army's triumphant return to the region, large areas of Vinnytsia were prone to daylight activity of nationalist bands, which exposed the absence and impotence of the Soviet power in the region. Frequent nationalist raids on civilian posts sought to humiliate the Soviets publicly. On 3 May 1944 a nationalist detachment interrupted a meeting of kolkhoz activists in the Illintsi district, robbed the raikom representatives who attended the meeting, and mocked a demobilized invalid of the Red Army.[12] A month later a detachment of thirty-five men raided the village of Maidan-Suprunivs'kyi in the Lityn district. The nationalists robbed Red Army servicemen, who were in the village at the time, of their boots, documents, and waist belts.[13] On 12 June 1944 the secretary of the Kalyniv raikom reported to the obkom secretary about the systematic and uninterrupted activity of large nationalist formations in his district. Soviet and party apparatchiks were frequently targeted and killed by the nationalists. On 6 June 1944, reported the secretary, nationalist bands of eighty to one hundred people appeared in the Hushchyntsi rural soviet armed with machine guns, robbed the kolkhozniks in the yard, and injured the chairman of the kolkhoz. On departing for the forest, they took four peasants with them whose fate was still unknown. Two days later a band of twenty to twenty-five people showed up in the village soviets of Ianiv and

[8] Ibid., f. 128, op. 1, d. 1, ll. 18–20.

[9] The official report already inflated the numbers provided by its own intelligence unit, which mentioned 510 nationalists (ibid., d. 5, l. 24).

[10] TsAVVMVDRF, f. 488, op. 1, d. 51, l. 32.

[11] Ibid., ll. 8–9.

[12] This incident was one of many similar in character (PAVO, f. 136, op. 13, d. 35, ll. 31–32).

[13] Arkhiv Sluzhby Bezpeky Ukrainy po Vinnyts'koi Oblasti (ASBUVO), d. 26674, l. 52.

Ianiv-Sloboda. They arrived at the village in daylight in a motor vehicle amid machine-gun and rifle fire. The nationalists also distributed numerous leaflets that threatened the lives of Soviet officials if the latter pursued the collection of grain and loans. The secretary concluded that the destruction battalions in the district could not cope with the nationalist detachments and pleaded with the obkom to take decisive measures.[14]

Five long and bloody years would pass until the obkom secretary could state confidently that Vinnytsia was excised of the nationalist menace. This, however, was not an ordinary pacification campaign. The eradication of the Ukrainian nationalist movement in this region captured the evolution of Soviet state violence in the wake of the war. Conducted in a region that had been subjected to a continuous purification campaign since the First World War throughout the interwar years and simultaneously to similar campaigns across the European continent, the postwar antinationalist drive in Vinnytsia and the neighboring regions displayed a qualitative shift in the Soviet quest for purity that was highlighted by these previous and contemporary points of reference.

In the European Mirror

As the Nazi war machine began to roll back across the European continent, nations appeared determined to exact revenge on those deemed collaborators with the Nazi occupiers. Following humiliating defeats and years of occupation, the purge of the national body became the order of the day. On the surface, the European purification enterprise appeared universal and grappled with common core dilemmas. What would be the criteria for guilt and purity, and who would define them? What would be the arenas and forms of purification: the extrajudicial street justice executed by individuals and groups claiming to be anti-Nazi resistance fighters or the administrative branches of the postwar state? How far should the purification go, or rather what were its ultimate goals? Was its aim the irreversible eradication of collaborators, or was it a redemptive exercise to reintegrate black sheep into the national family? Finally, how long should the purification drive last, or, in other words, would it be subjected to circumstantial constraints or be a goal in its own right, lasting as long as, and as far as, it could reach?

---

[14] PAVO, f. 136, op. 13, d. 8, l. 9. Similar complaints arrived simultaneously from the district of Illintsi. According to the raikom secretary, bands of armed nationalists operated from the surrounding forests. The bands agitated among the kolkhozniks against the delivery of grain to the Red Army (PAVO, d. 35, ll. 31–32). For similar accounts from the districts of Dashiv, Haisyn, Sytkov, Dzhulyn, Trostianets', and others, see TsAVVMVDRF, f. 488, op. 1, d. 51, ll. 5–7, 35–38.

In their search for solutions to these haunting questions, nations referred primarily to familiar paradigms. Indeed, most European countries had had prior experience in mass exclusionary and reintegrative social operations. In the wake of the Great War, during which many of these nations had been occupied, European countries acquired rich experience in the use of amnesty legislation and the resocialization of political opponents and criminal offenders, albeit with different degrees of success and popular approval. This was evidenced by the bitter debates over the reintegration of World War I collaborators in Belgium, which delayed amnesty legislation until 1937, while in the Netherlands the resocialization policy of criminal offenders was enacted methodically through an extensive network of prison and aftercare associations, including churches and trade unions. Not surprisingly, the relapse of some of the rehabilitated collaborators in Belgium into similar criminal behavior during the Second World War worked to toughen attitudes toward amnesty and rehabilitation, while in the Netherlands the resocialization programs and facilities for criminals were easily converted to the reintegration of their World War II black sheep.[15]

Less expected was the early realization that the prosecution of collaborators was not a challenge to the prewar order, but rather a manifestation of its continued power. A full investigation of collaboration—and not merely of those who served in the German punitive and propaganda institutions—threatened to open a Pandora's box of de facto accommodation by many of the sitting bureaucratic, judicial, and economic elites—essentially the entire existing order. And since the latter showed no signs of acquiescence, the debate soon turned into partisan politics. Public life under Nazi occupation was left out of the investigation, as were numerous high officials who fit well into the renewed conservative order.[16] While the postwar European state was busily extending its domain into practically every sphere of society, the temptation to recall strayed, yet seasoned, bureaucrats was easily rationalized. Nor could the impact of the unfolding cold

[15] As late as 1955 some 60,000 Belgians were still stripped of all or some of their political and civil rights. Mass reinstatement of rights was made possible only in 1961 after the intervention of the European court. In Holland, on the other hand, by January 1948 the foundation in charge of the resocialization of political delinquents employed 320 staff members and 16,000 supervisors who oversaw 42,000 former collaborators. See Lucien Huyse, "La reintegrazione dei collaborazionisti in Belgio, in Francia e nei Paesi Bassi," *Passato e presente* 16, no. 44 (1998): 118–19, 123.

[16] Martin Conway, "The Liberation of Belgium, 1944–1945," in Gill Bennett, ed., *The End of the War in Europe 1945* (London: HMSO, 1996), 117–38; here, 125; Conway, "Justice in Post-War Belgium: Popular Passions and Political Realities," *Cahiers d'histoire du temps present* 2 (1997): 7–34; and Luc Huyse and Steven Dhondt, *La repression des collaborations 1942–1952: Un passé toujours present* (Brussels: Centre de recherche et d'information socio-politique, 1993).

war be ignored. In Hungary, a tiny communist party vying for more members opted for mass recruitment of none other than the rank and file of the Arrow Cross, the fascist organization now in disgrace whose class orientation was deemed more important than its political past.[17] On both sides of the European divide, the developing conflict dictated a facade of national unity. Unpleasant and painful reminders were shelved, or rather erased from the official memory of the war.

Wartime experience, however, defied a universal definition of collaboration. In the vengeful atmosphere of devastated Poland, attending concerts at which German music was performed was deemed a collaborative act by the secret courts. At the same time, in a great many countries, from France to Norway to Hungary, the very same people both collaborated and resisted, in accordance with their perceptions and expectations of German policies and the changing tide of the war.[18] Neither martyrs nor evildoers were in the majority in Nazi-occupied Europe.

It was precisely this gray mosaic that stood in the way of national reconstruction because, at its core, the purge of collaborators was not merely about retribution or restoration. Rather, the purge was basically an effort to define the existing order and shape postwar society. Purification was a transitional medium between the imperfect past and the improved— if possible, perfect—society of the present and future. Considering the European experience as a whole, it appears that a precondition for purification to work was an ideal representation of the people as a positive undifferentiated entity. In order to exonerate the "Good People," as a mythic group, from charges of collaboration, the charge was assigned instead to an isolated, narrow circle of weeds. In other words, blame for the initial humiliating defeats and atrocities against segments of one's own society was shifted to an alien element. A dignified future required a heroic past. And if the past was to be a guide to the future, it had to be painted in crisp colors. No shades of gray would interfere with the heroic tale of struggle between good and evil.[19] And so, as quickly as the vengeful spirits

[17] As a result, party ranks swelled from thirty thousand in February 1945 to five hundred thousand in October of that year (Margit Szöllösi-Janze, " 'Pfeilkreuzler, Landesverräter und andere Volksfeinde': Generalabrechnung un Ungarn," in Klaus-Dietmar Henke and Hans Woller, eds., *Politische Saüberung in Europa: Die Abrechnung mit Faschismus und Kollaboration nach dem Zweiten Weltkrieg* [Munich: Deutscher Taschenbuch Verlag GmbH, 1991], 355).

[18] István Deák, "Collaboration/Accommodation/Resistance," a paper presented at a conference entitled "Remembering, Adapting, Overcoming: The Legacy of World War Two in Europe," Remarque Institute, New York University, 24–27 April 1997; Deák, "Civil Wars and Retribution in Europe 1939–1948," *Zeitgeschichte* (25 Jahrgang 1998): 7–8.

[19] Quite likely the most imaginative exercise in the European postwar creation of the "Good People" took place in France under the auspices of Charles de Gaulle. In his contempt for the defeated 1940 generation and the minuscule Resistance, the French leader resur-

arose, so, too, did they abate. All over Europe, retribution against alleged collaboration faded away at a truly amazing pace, and arguments in favor of reintegration of convicted collaborators surfaced shortly after the end of the hostilities.

But such a development was literally inconceivable within the Soviet polity. The Soviet experience, too, pointed to the presence of an earlier paradigm but one that accentuated the sharp distinctions between the totalitarian and other political enterprises. The Soviet policy of purge was not merely reactive nor was it conditioned by tactical requirements. Rather, purification and reintegration were complementary components in the colossal project of building a new socialist polity. Specific developments in both the domestic and international arenas affected the choice of targets, but the goals and methods of dealing with these targeted groups and individuals were subjected to the ongoing endeavor of restructuring. If the study of the horrifying wartime losses and destruction helps to explain the harsh retaliation of the Soviets, then the reading of the war into the progressing revolutionary narrative elucidates the unique choice of methods.

The war was not merely an unpleasant accident, nor was it a customary clash between two major powers. It was the realization of a historical nightmare, one that Soviet power expected from the moment of its inception. Throughout the 1930s Soviet citizens were constantly warned against the evils of German fascism and its implications for the USSR. The dominant theme of the Terror in 1937–38 was excision of fascist agents from the Soviet body politic. If the alleged crimes of the sinners in the late 1930s were presumed to anticipate the forthcoming catastrophe of the capitalist encirclement, then the alleged crimes in the 1940s were perceived as the full-blown actualization of the worst fears of the preceding decade. In the postwar official narrative the war was perceived as the inevitable outcome of historical forces. "It would be wrong," declared Stalin in his election speech on 9 February 1946, "to think that the Second World War was a casual occurrence or the result of errors of particular statesmen, though mistakes were made. Actually the war was the inevitable result of the development of world economic and political forces on the basis of modern monopoly capitalism."[20]

In this light, collaborators were not the by-products of the war but eternal enemies whom the war and occupation helped to uncover. They

---

rected the generation of 1914 as the embodiment of the new France. See Pieter Lagrou, "Heroes, Martyrs, Victims: A Comparative Social History of the Memory of World War II in France, Belgium, and the Netherlands, 1945–1965," Ph.d. dissertation, Catholic University of Leuven, 1996.

[20] I. V. Stalin, "Rech na predvybornom sobranii izbiratelei Stalinskogo izbiratel'nogo okruga goroda Moskvy," in Stalin, *Sochineniia* 3 (16): 2.

were the embodiment of the evil other, not accidental tourists trapped in a cataclysmic event. Their destruction was therefore not merely an act of defense but the execution of the will of history. The passing of time did not work to moderate the punitive policies against those accused of collaboration. Whereas French politicians were quick to interpret public opinion surveys supporting a reconciliation bill as a mandate for enacting amnesty, Valentin Ovechkin's pleas for compassion toward those who went through the hell of occupation remained unheeded. "Solicitude for the welfare of traitors who helped the Nazis lacerate France shows up the present-day collaborationists in their true colors. Birds of a feather," was the bitter reaction of Soviet newspapers when the French National Assembly launched the debate over the final legislation of mass amnesty for convicted collaborators in December 1952.[21] As Europe was moving fast on the road to amnesty and rehabilitation, the Soviet Union, in contrast, intensified its campaign of retribution.

Ultimately Soviet power was never restrained by circumstantial inhibitions in its purification drives. Earlier we saw that the purge of the party— the vanguard of the Soviet polity—was not subject to administrative-managerial requirements, nor did the admission that many Communists did not rise to the occasion form an obstacle to the purge. When the population at large was purged, entire ethnic groups were stigmatized as collaborationist and deported into the Soviet interior. Within the grand scheme of social engineering, loss of face was not a weighty factor. And no external pressure, like that of the European court on Belgium in 1961, was allowed to interfere with the pursuit of purity.

However, the Soviet purification drive was not entirely different from the European purge. If the postwar experience of Belgium, Czechoslovakia, and Yugoslavia is any indication of the European purge, it appears that multiethnic groups in many ways made a distinct effort at purification. Wherever collaboration was presumed to have had an ethnic face, the process of the purge continued well beyond that of more homogeneous polities and assumed a more vindictive character.[22] Indeed, here lay the gravest challenge to the ideal representation of the "Good People," a difficulty that resonated most clearly in the Soviet Union. One might think, and with considerable justification, that the uninhibited savagery of the German occupation of the Soviet territories would perpetuate the myth of the "Good People" and make the purge of the collaborationist weeds a

[21] "Amnesty for Traitors," *New Times* (Moscow) 49 (3 December 1952): 19–20; "Krestovyi pokhod frantsuzskoi reaktsii," *Izvestiia*, 7 December 1952.
[22] Thus, in the ethnically divided Belgium where Walloons constituted the core of the collaborationist movement, 53,005 of the 57,052 (92.9 percent) people prosecuted for various collaborationist offenses were found guilty (Martin Conway, *Collaboration in Belgium. Leon Degrelle and the Rexist Movement* [New Haven: Yale University Press, 1993], 277).

common national enterprise. Finding themselves at the bottom of the Nazi racial hierarchy, the Slavic populations soon discovered that the various distinctions the Nazis applied to each of them mattered little in the new order. But the harmonious representation of Soviet society at war collided with the unintended legacy of Soviet prewar nationality policy. The racially based Nazi ethos had fallen on fertile ground. The principled cultivation of ethnic particularism by the Soviets, be it the creation of ethnonational territories or the ethnicization of the enemy-within category, rendered critical segments of society susceptible to ethnically based visions and practices. In such a milieu, the occupation of the non-Russian Slavic republics for most of the war and the slightest preferential treatment by the Germans triggered contemporaries' reflection on the consequences of the Soviet ethnicized world.[23] In prewar Ukraine the ongoing Soviet nation building had to be reconciled with the ethnic legacy of collectivization, famine, and deportations. Similarly the postwar translation of ethnically based hierarchies of heroism into hierarchies of loyalty was a powerful challenge to the myth of one, indivisible society. With its prewar legacy, geopolitical location, and socioethnic mosaic, Vinnytsia offered itself as a test case for the evolution of the Soviet postwar purification enterprise.

The Prewar Purification: Ethnicization, Differentiation, and Redemption

By the time Soviet power turned to eradicate the nationalist presence in Vinnytsia, the people of the region were already seasoned by consecutive and relentless purification drives. Whereas the concrete targets and reasons for the drives varied according to domestic and international circumstances, their practice was a permanent feature in the shaping of the Soviet community. In a polity built on the premise of "national in form, socialist in content," ethnicity was not expected to become the primary category in social engineering. In any case, this neat distinction proved difficult to maintain. The year 1919 witnessed the first recorded occurrence of conflating the body national and social with the de-Cossackization campaign in the Don region. Notably this was a brief episode as the regime retreated from the practice in fear of denigrating the Marxist enterprise into a "zoological" project.[24] Nevertheless Soviet power continued to

---

[23] An intriguing linkage between the Soviet passportization policy and German racial policies and the impact on the Kiev wartime population is offered by Lev Dudin in his memoirs, *Velikii mirazh*, Hoover Archive, Nicolaevsky Collection, series 178, box 232, folders 10–11, p. 73.

[24] Peter Holquist, "Conduct Merciless, Mass Terror: Decossackization," *Cahiers du monde russe* 38, nos. 1–2 (1997): 127–62.

question the political loyalty of the nonindigenous populations in Ukraine throughout the 1920s. The Polish and German minorities were specifically marked for increased surveillance based on their alleged vulnerability to hostile propaganda by their external homelands, a state of affairs that was only inflamed by the Weimar's blatant interventionist policy. In line with this, in a review of the political situation in the Podillia province in 1925, the discussion of espionage referred only to the large Polish-Catholic minority which, it was argued, had yet to be sovietized and was drawing the attention of the Polish government.[25]

As early as 1932 the downgrading of class structure as an explanatory paradigm and class struggle as a modus operandi entailed the reconceptualization of the various components of the Soviet body as total categories, most notably ethnonational ones.[26] As the Soviet crusade approached the realm of socialism, the tenuous balance between social and ethnic origin increasingly tilted in the direction of the latter. True, class would continue to be the raison d'être of the revolutionary enterprise to the very end, a concept written into the structure of each and every Soviet institution. Stalin, the very person who renounced class heredity as a detrimental factor in determining political legitimacy, had his reasons for scorning party members in the Seventeenth Party Congress who "dropped into a state of foolish rapture in the expectation that soon there will be no classes and therefore no class struggle." But overshadowed by Stalin's oft-quoted remark was the addendum that the survivors of capitalism were "much more tenacious in the sphere of the national problem . . . because they are able to disguise themselves in national costume."[27] The threats to the aspired harmony assumed an ethnic face.

The conflation of class and ethnic categorization resurfaced with a vengeance with the commencement of the collectivization drive. Increasingly the battle lines were drawn on ethnic grounds. In Ukraine, in general, and Vinnytsia, in particular, peasants' protests and eventual uprisings against

[25] PAVO, f. 29, op. 1, d. 172, l. 45. On the tenuous relations between the Soviet regime and the German minority throughout the 1920s, see Harvey Dyck, *Weimar Germany and Soviet Russia, 1926–1933* (New York: Columbia University Press, 1966); *Nimtsi v Ukraini 20–30-ti rr. XX st.: Zbirnyk dokumentiv derzhavnykh arkhiviv Ukrainy* (Kiev: Institut istorii Ukrainy, 1994); and Ivan Kulynych and Nataliia Kryvets, *Narysy z istorii nimets'kykh kolonii v Ukraini* (Kiev: Natsionalna Akademiia Nauk Ukrainy, 1995). For Weimar's policies within the broader framework of an external, active homeland assuming responsibility for its diaspora co-ethnics, see Rogers Brubaker, *Nationalism Reframed: Nationhood and the National Question in the New Europe* (New York: Cambridge University Press, 1996), 112–47.

[26] A key marker in this shift was Stalin's letter to *Proletarskaia revoliutsiia* in which the Soviet leader asserted that an alliance with "oppressed peoples and colonies"—and not with oppressed classes among these peoples—had always been the cornerstone of Bolshevik ideology (Slezkine, *Arctic Mirrors*, 259).

[27] I. V. Stalin, "Otchetnyi doklad XVII s"ezdu partii," in Stalin, *Sochineniia* 13:351, 361.

forced collectivization were often directed against "Russia-Muscovy" and the "Communist Kikes," and in favor of "Independent Ukraine."[28] Similarly Soviet power increasingly drove home the ethnicization of class-enemy categories, especially when applied to the ethnic mosaic of the border regions. Already at the onset of dekulakization (the assault on the allegedly well-off peasants) on 23 January 1930, the obkom—along with other localities—was ordered by the Ukrainian Central Committee to "devise special perspectives regarding the national minorities districts (Germans, Bulgarians, and others)."[29] There the identification of hostile classes with ethnic minorities increasingly guided the local authorities in their dekulakization campaign. And since Poles—as well as Germans and Jews—were perceived as kulaks by nature, they were marked for collectivization regardless of socioeconomic status.[30]

The ascendance of ethnicity within the excision enterprise was further accentuated when the deportations commenced in the spring of 1930. On 5 March 1930 the Politburo ordered the deportation from these provinces, regardless of the stage of collectivization, of an additional ten to fifteen thousand kulak households of all three categories—first in line being those of Polish nationality.[31] The same applied to families of Polish "nobles," disregarding their material position. The 1930 deportation from the border belt of the Republic claimed 4,906 people, of whom only 2,445 were classified as kulaks. The districts that would be lumped together to create the Vinnytsia region two years later accounted for 1,479.[32] With socialism built, ethnic hostility replaced class antagonism as the primary category intruding on harmony, a shift that was underscored when the purification drive accelerated in the mid-1930s.

---

[28] PAVO, f. 136, op. 3, d. 8, ll. 113–14; Valerii Vasil'ev, "Krest'ianskie vosstaniia na Ukraine, 1929–30 gody," *Svobodnaia mysl'* 9 (1992): 74–75; Lynne Viola, *Peasant Rebels under Stalin: Collectivization and the Culture of Peasant Resistance* (New York: Oxford University Press, 1996), 120–21.

[29] PAVO, f. 29, op. 1, d. 577, l. 133.

[30] The conflation of class and ethnicity regarding the Polish minority was captured in the rhyme: *raz poliak—znachit kulak* (All Poles are kulaks) (cited in Terry Martin, "The Origins of Soviet Ethnic Cleansing," *Journal of Modern History* 70 [December 1998]: 837). For complaints by the Vinnytsia obkom about the break of the collectivization drive in the Jewish communities in the region in late 1934 owing to "counterrevolutionary nationalist and clerical" activity, see PAVO, f. 136, op. 3, d. 225, ll. 19–21.

[31] RGASPI, f. 17, op. 162, d. 8, ll. 109–10. The quota for the Belorussian border regions was set at three thousand to thirty-five hundred families. For prewar Soviet policy toward the Polish minority, see Mykolaj Iwanow, *Pierwszy Narod Ukarany: Polacy w Zwiazku Radzieckim w latach 1921–1939* (Warsaw: Panstwowe Wydawnictwo Naukowe, 1991).

[32] Ihor Vynnychenko, *Ukraina 1920–1980-kh: deportatsii, zaslannia, vyslannia* (Kiev: Vyd-vo "Rada," 1994), 24.

Initially the murder of Sergei Kirov appeared as the key event in the escalating purge. In the immediate aftermath of the murder, on 9 December 1934, thousands were arrested within hours and Moscow ordered a thorough review of the German and Polish districts in Vinnytsia and in the neighboring region of Kiev. The communities were warned that Soviet power would not tolerate the slightest display of anti-Soviet activity or agitation and would even deport those who display disloyalty to distant provinces of the country. Lists of deportees were ordered within a week.[33]

But if the murder was a catalyst in escalating the drive, it certainly did not trigger it. The plenipotentiaries, who supervised the review in the wake of the murder, already had in their hands a preformed plan regarding the German minority in the region. Following a directive by the All-Union Central Committee to local authorities throughout the Soviet Union on 5 November 1934, the Vinnytsia obkom ordered the NKVD immediately to "remove the hostile anti-Soviet elements from the German villages and deport them out of the region and to apply the harshest methods against the most active ones." Recipients of material aid from Germany received special attention. At the same time, the "politically unreliable elements" among the leading cadres in the German villages were to be replaced by "staunch Bolshevik cadres." This despite the fact that the survey of the German national village soviets indicated either decline or stagnation in the absolute numbers of ethnic Germans in the region.[34] Moreover, apparently the cataloging of the German rural districts merely complemented that of the industrial urban sector. According to Evgeniia Evelson, who was employed at the time in the National Commissariat of Local and Light Industry, in late 1934 the Central Committee of the CPSU ordered the registration of German nationals. At her suggestion, the mass operation was implemented in complete secrecy and rushed apace through passportization of the entire industrial sector. As a result, claims Evelson, who guided the enterprise along with the head of the cadres division of the National Commissariat for the Forestry Industry and the industry division of the Central Committee, by the end of 1934 "*every German* born in Russia or brought there temporarily or permanently as a worker in the wide field of Soviet industry in the country *was individually registered to the fullest extent* regardless of what branch of industry he belonged to, and this is in each and every National Commissariat, and also

[33] TsDAHOU, f. 1, op. 16, d. 11, ll. 294–95, 316, 318–19.
[34] In December 1934, for example, the German population of the Liudvykovskyi and Sul'-penskyi sel'sovets, both in the Dzerzhinskyi district, declined from 831 in 1933 to 777, and from 602 to 366, respectively (PAVO, f. 136, op. 3, d. 225, ll. 23–31).

all personnel data were listed and collected by the Central Committee of the CPSU."[35]

Notably the deportation order maintained differentiation in the treatment of the population. It approached the ethnic communities as a whole but refrained from collective punishment. The lists of deportees from villages with "concentrated Polish and German populations" were to include "independent peasants who did not fulfill their obligations to the government and unreliable kolkhozniks." They should be replaced by some four thousand "excellent kolkhozniks and activists" from Kiev and Chernihiv regions. Class categories still mattered. The deportees were directed to the eastern regions of Dnipropetrovsk, Kharkiv, and Odessa. By the end of January 1935, 8,329 households were marked for deportation within the Republic's boundaries.[36]

However, the differentiation was accompanied by an intriguing development. When deportations resumed in late September 1935 the Central Committee ordered that Polish leading cadres in the Vinnytsia and Kiev regions be replaced by ethnic Ukrainians and that the affairs in the reorganized village soviets be conducted in the Ukrainian language.[37] On 4 March of that year the Central Committee in Kiev obliged raikom secretaries in the German national districts to "conduct a decisive struggle against the disregard for instruction of the Ukrainian language in schools of these districts," a literal reversal of the official policy up to that point.[38] The Central Committee also ordered an increase in the number of books in the Ukrainian language in the libraries of these schools. One is left to question the motives behind the Ukrainian Central Committee's request to increase the deportation quota for Poles from Vinnytsia. By this time, the local authorities' practice of intensifying the level of repression in their jurisdiction had already become a trademark of Bolshevik political culture.[39] But the identity of the concrete target pointed to additional

[35] Ingeborg Fleischhauer and Benjamin Pinkus, *The Soviet Germans: Past and Present* (London: Hurst, 1986), 90.

[36] TsDAHOU, f. 1, op. 16, d. 12, l. 38; 2,854 households came from Vinnytsia (GARF, f. 5446, op. 16a, d. 265, l. 14).

[37] TsDAHOU, f. 1, op. 16, d. 12, ll. 39, 280.

[38] Kulynych and Kryvets, *Narysy z istorii nimets'kykh kolonii v Ukraini*, 237. For an example of the official line regarding the primacy of the German language in the German national districts, see information note from Zaporizhzhia, 19 December 1930, in *Nimtsi v Ukraini*, 150–57.

[39] Iagoda was not the one to say no to such a request. On 17 October 1935 he supported the increase on the grounds that "there were still significant cadres of counterrevolutionary Polish nationalist elements in a number of districts in the Vinnytsia region. From the viewpoint of fortifying the border, their stay in the border districts must be considered undesirable" (GARF, f. 5446, op. 16a, d. 265, l. 14).

sources. Tellingly those marked for deportation were classified as "unde-sirable elements," and the enterprise was officially characterized as a "cleansing of the mass pollution of the [Polish] national village soviets." The harmonious society to which the Soviets aspired was beginning to look more and more ethnically consolidated. Whether or not it was a back-door Ukrainization several years after the actual termination of this policy in Ukraine, the local population was introduced to an increasingly homo-geneous society.

By now, deportations became a steady feature on the Vinnytsia land-scape. In October the Central Committee in Kiev decreed the deportation of another 1,500 Polish households to Kharkiv, Donetsk, and Dniprope-trovsk, to be carried out in the first half of January 1936.[40] That year saw quantitative and qualitative changes in the purification drive. With the tide of the Terror rising everywhere, the Moscow Central Committee or-dered, on 17 January 1936, the deportation to Kazakhstan of another 2,000 households from Vinnytsia alone and set a target of 15,000 German and Polish households (a total of 69,283 people) for the Kiev and Vinnyt-sia regions together.[41] Between 15 and 20 May 1936, 2,250 households, which included some 9,000 people, were removed from the region, and by August of that year Vinnytsia's share of deportees increased to 8,777 households.[42] By then, the destination of the deportations was no longer the eastern regions of the Ukrainian Republic but Central Asia.

Until this point, the institution of national village soviets for the Ger-man and Polish minorities remained intact. Their number, however, was constantly being reduced. Throughout 1933–35 dozens of Polish village soviets in Vinnytsia were converted into Ukrainian soviets, and, even more critical, the rationale provided for the abolition spelled the impending end of the institution itself. A note dated July 1936 on the state of work among the Polish communities declared that the abolished national village soviets and schools were established as a result of the extensive large-scale coun-terrevolutionary nationalist work of the Polish military organization (POV) [forcing] the artificial Polanization of the Ukrainian popula-tion."[43] The rate of abolished soviets and schools, and the closing of Polish Roman Catholic churches, made it clear that the entire organized Polish

[40] PAVO, f. 136, op. 3, d. 371, l. 8; TsDAHOU, f. 1, op. 16, d. 12, l. 314.

[41] GARF, f. 9479, op. 1, d. 36, l. 23; TsDAHOU, f. 1, op. 16, d. 13, l. 25.

[42] PAVO, f. 136, op. 3, d. 362, l. 7; d. 371, l. 8; TsDAHOU, f. 1, op. 16, d. 13, l. 49. For the 28 April 1936 decree of the Council of Peoples Commissars, see GARF, f. 5446, op. 57, d. 41, ll. 116–20. When the MVD recommended, in September 1953, the release of Polish citizens of the USSR who were deported from Ukraine and Belorussia in 1936, there were 23,559 such people in the special settlements (GARF, f. 9479, op. 1, d. 612, l. 44).

[43] PAVO, f. 136, op. 3, d. 371, ll. 1–5.

minority was under suspicion. Furthermore, the rhetoric and practices of this shift embodied the essence of the ensuing Terror. In the wake of attaining socialism, the reference to any organ as an artificial creation by a foreign organization marked it as a weed to be uprooted from the Soviet garden.[44] The Polish minority was perceived as an alien body obstructing the construction of a harmonious polity. Thus it seemed no accident that the decree ordered district authorities to explain to parents that children should be instructed in the "mother tongue," and so, allegedly at parents' initiative, some 116 schools were converted to Ukrainian.[45]

Ethnic Ukrainians also figured in the Soviet reconstruction drive, although somewhat differently. Since *korenizatsiia* (nativization; indigenization of local power) was put to rest in the early 1930s, charges of nationalism, that is, plots to separate the Ukrainian Republic from the Soviet Union, figured highly in every cleansing campaign both within and outside party ranks. This shift is well documented, yet one aspect of the antinationalist campaign proved critical in shaping future developments. When the Military Collegium of the Supreme Court in Kiev addressed the cases of thirty-seven people accused of nationalist terrorist activity in December 1934, it cited that most of the accused had arrived from Poland and some from Romania. Actually only seven of the defendants were Galicians, who had been legally admitted to the Soviet Union. Of the rest, only two had traveled abroad at any time.[46] The official representation, however, sent an unequivocal message that both the men and their ideology were foreign products, alien to the Ukrainian national body. Later, during and after the war, the message of geographic and ideological alienation would become the core of the Soviet antinationalist drive in much greater magnitude and intensity.

With the Terror, the ethnicization of categories of the enemy within came full circle. In 1937 the Far East region was cleared of all ethnic Koreans,[47] and large numbers of Germans, Poles, and Latvians were arrested or executed regardless of their social origin, occupation, geographi-

---

[44] By 1939 the 16,860 Poles in GULAG camps accounted for 1.28 percent of the inmate population, while their share in the entire Soviet population was only 0.37 percent. With the exception of Russians, the 0.91 percent gap was the largest among the ethnic groups in the GULAG system (J. Arch Getty, Gabor Rittersporn, and Victor Zemskov, "Victims of the Soviet Penal System in the Pre-War Years: A First Approach on the Basis of Archival Evidence," *American Historical Review* 98 [October 1993]: 1028).

[45] PAVO, f. 136, op. 3, d. 371, l. 5; op. 6, d. 591, ll. 2–3.

[46] Hryhory Kostiuk, *Stalinist Rule in the Ukraine: A Study of the Decade of Mass Terror (1929–1939)* (New York: Praeger, 1960), 100; Yuri Shapoval, *Ukraina 20–50-kh rokiv: storinky nenapysanoi istorii* (Kiev: Naukova dumka, 1993), 153.

[47] Nikolai Bugai, *L. Beriia-I. Stalinu: "Soglasno Vashemu ukazaniiu . . ."* (Moscow: AIRO-XX, 1995), 18–25; Michael Gelb, "An Early Soviet Ethnic Deportation: The Far-Eastern Koreans," *The Russian Review* 54 (July 1995): 389–412.

cal location, or citizenship. In some regions, arrests and executions elimi-
nated almost all Germans and Poles.[48] The axe fell on 1 December 1937,
when the Organizational Bureau of the Central Committee (Orgburo)
decreed the liquidation of many national districts and village soviets (German, Polish, Estonian, Finnish, Korean, Bulgarian, and others) throughout the entire union. The rationale given echoed that of the Ukrainian
decree from mid-1936. The Orgburo declared these institutions to be
artificial creations that did not correspond to their national composition
and, even worse, the creations of "enemies of the people led by bourgeois
nationalists and spies." The party authorities in all republics and regions
with national districts were given a month to submit a plan of liquidation
of the national districts and their integration into regular ones.[49] But the
most intriguing reason for the liquidation of the national districts and
soviets was offered by Georgii Malenkov on 29 November 1937. The Spar-
tak German national district in the Odessa region was singled out as an
encroachment on Ukrainian rights. Its borders were repeatedly altered so
as to isolate, artificially, the Ukrainian kolkhozes. Thus the district became
exclusively German. When Malenkov proceeded to condemn the removal
of the Russian language from the curriculum in elementary schools in
these national districts and village soviets, which, he claimed, "practically
deprived the children of kolkhozniks and workers of non-Russian nationality from enrollment into middle and higher educational institutions,"
the message of the harmonious body was complete.[50] Weeding out the
foreign bodies became a precondition for harmony.

Finally, the Terror delivered a brutal message regarding the limits of
redemption in the wake of triumphalistic socialism. In his canonization of
the history of the Communist Party, *The Short Course*, Stalin celebrated
the physical annihilation of the elusive enemies who managed to survive
previous cycles of purification. With socialism built, extermination was the
only way to cope with those who had not yet redeemed themselves.[51] It
seemed no accident that the first salvo of the bursting Terror was directed

[48] For the orders issued by Ezhov, the people's commissar for internal affairs, requesting
the arrest of members of these communities on 25 July and 11 August 1937, see *Butovskii
poligon, 1937–1938* (Moscow: Moskovskii antifashistskii tsentr, 1997), 348, 353–54;
Moskovskie novosti, 21 June 1992. At the height of the Terror in the Stalino region in the
Donbas, 80.2 percent of the 3,777 Poles and 84.6 percent of the 4,265 ethnic Germans
arrested between September 1937 and February 1938 were executed (Kuromiya, *Freedom
and Terror in the Donbas*, 231–33).

[49] The Central Committee approved the resolution on 17 December 1937 (TsKhSD, f.
89, op. 62, d. 6, l. 14; d. 4, l. 1; RGASPI, f. 17, op. 114, d. 829, l. 119).

[50] RGASPI, f. 17, op. 114, d. 829, ll. 123, 125–126. For decrees ordering the reorganization of national schools, see TsKhSD, f. 89, op. 62, d. 7, ll. 1–2; d. 8, ll. 5–6.

[51] *History of the Communist Party of the Soviet Union (Bolsheviks): The Short Course* (New
York: International, 1939), 346–48.

at those who had already been punished and pardoned. Indeed, the latter figured prominently in the Politburo's resolution of 2 July 1937, "Concerning Anti-Soviet Elements." Having been punished and stripped of their hostile class identity, these individuals and groups appeared to redeem themselves through productive labor that won them not only the restoration of voting rights but also, for some, release from the special settlements. Indeed, only two years earlier, the rehabilitation of former kulaks was trumpeted as the triumph of nurture over nature. Celebrating the completion of the White Sea Canal, the authors of the special commemorative volume noted that "on the whole kulaks were the hardest to educate . . . but even in these *half-animals*, the idolaters of private property, the truth of collective labor at last *undermined a zoological individualism*."[52] Accordingly, on 25 January 1935, all former kulaks regained their voting rights.[53] But two-and-a-half years later the Central Committee identified former kulaks, recently rehabilitated, as the principal anti-Soviet element, responsible for a barrage of diversionary acts in the countryside. In spite of regaining their civil rights and permission to return from exile to their homes, these former kulaks had allegedly resumed hostilities against the socialist state. Essentially they had proved to be immune to socialist corrective measures, were therefore irredeemable, and were marked for immediate arrest and execution.[54] In the era of socialism redemption was not offered twice.

Still, the prewar cleansing policies maintained several key features that set them apart from those of the postwar era. First, they aimed at cleansing specific territorial space—mainly border regions populated by minorities with an external active homeland—or politically suspicious segments of these communities, but not entire peoples, which meant that targeted groups were treated as differentiated entities.[55] As noted above, the lists of deportees from Polish and German villages consisted mainly of peasants who did not conform to the collective farm system, just as the arrest and execution lists for these nationalities at the height of the Terror consisted mainly of political émigrés, alleged spies, and people working in sensitive industries. Equally important, deportees often remained within the

[52] Gorky et al., *Belomor*, 341 (emphasis added).

[53] GARF, f. 9479, op. 1, d. 949, l. 77.

[54] For the 2 July 1937 resolution of the Politburo and the Central Committee, see *Trud*, 4 June 1992.

[55] While one should not underestimate the Soviet anxiety over external homelands appealing to their brethren within the Soviet Union or the fear of disloyalty in case of invasion, these concerns have to be squared with a military doctrine that at the commencement of deportations of Poles and Germans from the borderlands outlined a single option of an offensive into the enemy territory. See Raymond Garthoff, *Soviet Military Doctrine* (Glencoe, Ill.: Free Press, 1953), 67–68, 435–36; and Mark von Hagen, "Soviet Soldiers and Officers on the Eve of the German Invasion: Towards a Description of Social Psychology and Political Attitudes," *Soviet Union/Union Sovietique* 18, nos. 1–3 (1991): 95.

boundaries of the Ukrainian Republic. Hence, even after the conclusion of repetitive waves of deportations, border regions were still populated by tens of thousands of members of the deported groups, just as members of the marked groups residing outside the targeted region were often left unharmed, including several thousand Koreans in Iakut.[56] Such exceptions will not repeat themselves when the Soviets opt for total cleansing of nationalities during and after the war. Equally important, Jonathan Bone pointed out that in sharp contrast to exiled kulaks, Korean deportees were categorized as *pereselentsy* (agricultural settlers) and not as *spetspereselentsy* (special settlers), and received financial compensation (admittedly inadequate and often stolen by its handlers) for their property, wage losses, and travel expenses. Compensation alone, as opposed to the use of violence in order to terrorize an ethnic population and induce it to flee an area indiscriminately, challenges the notion of prewar ethnic cleansing regarding even the Far East Koreans.[57]

Second, differentiation often left the door open for possible redemption. The GULAG doors kept revolving, with 20–40 percent of the inmates released annually.[58] Rehabilitation of deported kulaks continued throughout the second half of the 1930s. The Council of People's Commissars' resolution of 22 October 1938 provided children of former kulaks with internal passports and the right to move to their place of choice (with the exception of closed districts), a right that elevated them not only above their previous status but also above the rest of the Soviet peasantry, which was deprived of passports and hence the right of free movement. By wartime, nearly eighty thousand children of kulaks had already been released from the settlements.[59] Surveillance reports on deportees divided them into subgroups corresponding to their potential for redemption. Hence

[56] Gabor Rittersporn, " 'Vrednye elementy,' 'opasnye menshinstva' i bolshevitskie trevogi: massovye operatsii 1937–38 gg. i etnicheskii vopros v SSSR," in Timo Vikhavainen and Irina Takala, eds., *V sem'e edinoi. Natsional'naia politika partii bol'shevikov i ee osushchestvlenie na Severo-Zapade Rossii v 1920–1950-e gody* (Petrozavodsk: Izd-vo Petrozavodskogo universiteta, 1998), 115; Gelb, "An Early Soviet Ethnic Deportation," 406. On the eve of the deportations in early 1935, Polish national soviets in the Vinnytsia region consisted of 77,545 people. Yet some 55,610 Poles were still counted in the Vinnytsia region in the 1939 census, as well as 95,679 in the Kamianets'-Podil's'kyi region and 30,509 in the Kiev region. The census also counted 13,720 ethnic Germans in these regions, many of whom were later drafted by the Germans into the police and civilian administration following the June 1941 invasion (PAVO, f. 136, op. 6, d. 503, ll. 63–65; I. A. Poliakov, *Vsesoiuznaia perepis' naseleniia 1939 goda: Osnovnye itogi* [Moscow: Nauka, 1992], 68–69; and GARF, f. 9479, op. 1, d. 83, l. 3).

[57] Jonathan Bone, "Asia Stops Here: Border-Zone Slavicization and the Fate of the Far Eastern Koreans, 1925–1937," paper presented at the thirty-first annual meeting of the American Association for the Advancement of Slavic Studies, St. Louis, 18–21 November 1999.

[58] Getty et al. "Victims of the Soviet Penal System in the Pre-War Years," 1041.

[59] GARF, f. 9479, op. 1, d. 89, l. 216; d. 925, ll. 282–83.

the ethnic Germans deported in the spring of 1936 were split into three groups: the first was composed mostly of demobilized Red Army servicemen who responded to the resettlement with optimism; the second group felt cheated but could be redeemed with the right dose of propaganda; and the third, whose expectations of a German invasion and unification with their German brethren, was marked as hopeless.[60] Consequently ethnic Germans throughout the Soviet Union were still considered reliable enough to be drafted into the Red Army, a policy, however, that was bound to change when this minority (and others) would be summarily targeted with the outbreak of war. When the Politburo outlined the criteria for conscription into the Red Army and the military units of the NKVD in late August 1940 it reaffirmed its commitment to the political and territorial rather than the ethnic principles of the cleansing paradigm. Members of enemy nations were no longer classified strictly on the grounds of ethnonational affiliation but rather by geographical location. The Politburo allowed the induction of citizens born between 1917 and 1919 residing in the recently annexed western Ukrainian and Belorussian regions (with the exception of former servicemen in the Polish army), as well as Karelians, Finns, Lithuanians, Latvians, Estonians, Germans, Poles, Bulgars, and Greeks, with the exception of those residing in the three Baltic republics, Northern Bukovina, and Bessarabia.[61] Even Koreans residing in Moscow and Leningrad were inducted into the Red Army, and their wartime exploits were recognized and rewarded by the Soviet state.[62]

Notably the war itself soon became a redemptive vehicle for prewar outcasts. On 11 April 1942 the State Defense Committee (GKO) passed a resolution that allowed the drafting of former kulaks into military service. The spouses and children of the draftees were released from the special settlements and given passports. In 1943 alone this cohort amounted to 102,520 people. By March 1945, some 1,068,800 inmates had already been drafted into the army, and 10,000 more were about to join them shortly thereafter.[63] As the head of the GULAG administration observed with unconcealed satisfaction, many of the released served with distinction, including five who received the nation's highest award, Hero of the Soviet Union. Inmates, including "politicals" of the Terror years, were encouraged to follow these examples and win their way back into society.

[60] Ibid., f. 9479, op. 1, d. 36, l. 15.

[61] Other categories of draftees were directed to labor battalions. These included Turks, Japanese, Koreans, Chinese, Romanians, and people with close relatives repressed for espionage and counterrevolutionary activities. Also included were those previously deported or whose parents had been deported but had already regained their civilian rights and were no longer living in the NKVD-controlled districts (RGASPI, f. 17, op. 162, d. 29, ll. 2–3).

[62] Gelb, "An Early Soviet Ethnic Deportation," 406–7: Bugai, *L. Beriia-I. Stalinu*, 22.

[63] GARF, f. 9479, op. 1, d. 140, l. 12; f. 9414, op. 1, d. 330, l. 61.

Moreover, some 43,000 Poles, who had been categorized as members of an "enemy nation" merely two years earlier, were released.[64] In 1944 the NKVD and the USSR Procuracy agreed not to prosecute former kulaks who left the special settlements for various wartime services and failed to return. Mass rehabilitation intensified in the postwar years. In 1946 the regime removed all limitations imposed on the families of former kulaks who had children in the Soviet Army, were participants in the Great Patriotic War, or received governmental awards, and on women who married local residents.[65]

With the war the ethnicization of categories of the enemy within came full circle. An apparent consequence of the wartime redemption was the substitution of ethnicity for class as the dominant inmate category in the Soviet penal system. On the eve of the war 90.9 percent of the 977,000 people recorded living in the special settlements, along with their families, were classified as kulaks.[66] Yet by 1948 their number was already down to 130,463, and on the eve of the final wave of releases in early 1954, members of the 1929–33 generation numbered only 17,348.[67] By then, the vacuum created by the release of 975,000 camp inmates to the front between 1941 and 1944 was filled with inmates from the newly annexed Baltics, western Ukraine, and Belorussia, and with nationalities deported during the war.

The Postwar Purification Drive: Totalization and Irredeemability

The war saw a stark shift in the purge paradigm from cleansing certain areas to cleansing entire groups of people. The prewar partiality and focus on specific border regions were replaced by the targeting of each and every member of a stigmatized group regardless of geographical location or service rendered to the Soviet state. Whatever anxieties and inhibitions that had halted excision campaigns such as the 1919 de-Cossackization

[64] The releases were ordained by decrees of the Presidium of the Supreme Soviet of the Soviet Union from 12 July and 24 November 1941, and GKO special resolutions in 1942–43. The decrees, which affected about 577,000 inmates, ordered the release of those convicted for absenteeism, moral and insignificant malfeasances, and economic crimes. Political categories were not covered by the decrees ("Gulag v gody Velikoi Otechestvennoi voiny: Doklad nachal'nika GULAGa NKVD SSSR V.G. Nasedkina. Avgust 1944 g.," *Istoricheskii arkhiv* 3 [1994]: 64–65). For wartime mobilization and the rehabilitation campaign inside the camps, including the use of letters by former inmates serving at the front, see Loginov, "Vozvrashchennye k zhizni," 4b, 11–12b, 14b–15.

[65] GARF, f. 9479, op. 1, d. 925, l. 283.

[66] Ibid., d. 612, l. 42.

[67] Ibid., d. 925, l. 284; Zemskov, "Spetposeletsy," 17 n. 24.

were now removed. Excision was intended to be total, irreversible, and pursued relentlessly. The treatment of ethnic Germans served as a model for this new stage. Hence the decree on the resettlement of the Volga Germans on 28 August 1941 was followed by decrees that extended resettlement to all ethnic Germans in the Soviet Union and ordered that all ethnic Germans be removed from the ranks of the fighting Red Army.[68] Remarkably the decrees followed an earlier official recognition of the community's voluntary enrollment in the Soviet cause and the heroic fight of some of its members against the Nazi invaders.[69] Once again the regime demonstrated that exigency was not the driving motive in cleansing the ranks. With its very existence hanging by a thread and the Red Army being routed by the invaders, the regime opted for the largest cleansing operation since collectivization, removing from the ranks hundreds of thousands of capable young men. For many, this was a traumatic event. One of them was Gabriel Temkin, a Jewish refugee from the German-occupied Polish territory, going through military training at the time. For this reason alone he found himself a suspect. "One day, together with many such men, I was ordered to appear at the camp's center, where we were told about an impending transfer into military labor battalions," recalled Temkin.

> I was in shock and so were many others. I recall the reaction of a Soviet cadre officer, a lieutenant; Miller was his name, of German ancestry, born in Russia in the city of Engels on the Volga. He knew almost no German. He was now bitterly cursing in pure, juicy Russian. Though he had already been engaged in

---

[68] For the extension of the deportation of ethnic Germans to the rest of the union, see O. L. Milova, ed., *Deportatsii narodov SSSR (1930-e—1950-e gody)* (Moscow: Rossiiskaia Akademiia Nauk, 1995), vol. 2, 54–56, 79–89, 118–30. On 8 October 1941 the GKO ordered the deportation of another 46,533 ethnic Germans from Georgia, Azerbeijan, and Armenia (GARF, f. 9479, op. 1, d. 73, l. 5). For the 8 September 1941 GKO decree no. 35105 on the removal of ethnic German servicemen from the ranks of the Red Army, see Meir Buchsweiler, ed., "A Collection of Soviet Documents Concerning Germans in the USSR," *Research Paper No.73; The Marjorie Mayrock Center for Soviet and East European Research* (Jerusalem, Hebrew University, 1991), 17; and Alfred Eisfeld and Victor Herdt, eds., *Deportation Sondersiedlung Arbeitsarmee: Deutsche in der Sowjetunion 1941 bis 1956* (Cologne: Verlag Wissenschaft und Politik, 1996), 74. On 11 September 1941 the GKO decreed the establishment of labor battalions under NKVD control for all healthy ethnic Germans between the ages of seventeen and fifty (GARF, f. 9414, op. 1, d. 1157, l. 5a).

[69] Tellingly, in the course of a conversation with a correspondent, Genrikh Geiman, one of these Soviet Germans referred to his unit as an "international brigade" consisting of Russians, Ukrainians, Mordavians, and Germans. "Yes, I am a German. And I hate with all my heart he who calls himself the leader of Germany. I will fight him to my last drop of blood," declared Geiman. The interview was published the same day that the authorities issued the deportation decree (*Komsomol'skaia pravda*, 28 August 1941).

front-line battles and wanted to continue fighting the German Fascists, he was removed from his regular military unit and assigned to become a company commander in a labor battalion.[70]

Moreover, as one scholar aptly observed, the deportation resolution was framed as a prophylactic measure rather than a punitive one, whereby the Germans were accused of harboring scores of diversionist and hostile attitudes to Soviet power as opposed to performing concrete anti-Soviet acts. The criteria for deportation were purely ethnic; non-German family members were spared, although they were allowed to follow their relatives into exile.[71] The same applied to all other ethnic groups marked for excision in the wake of the war. Whereas during the prewar era the presence of relatives who had served in the Red Army or partisan detachments was enough to protect entire families from being deported,[72] by the end of the Second World War, officers and soldiers of the deported nationalities were severed from their units and often sent to the newly established special regime camps or work battalions while the war was still being waged.[73] As happened during collectivization, the stigma of collective guilt bred unmitigated brutality. When an NKVD unit charged with herding Chechen villagers was delayed in the mountains, it locked some 730 prospective deportees in a barn, set them on fire, and shot those who tried to escape. During the initial phase of deportations and incarceration, mortality rates among the groups deported in their entirety in the aftermath of the war was devastating, with about 100,000 Chechens and Ingush out of the

[70] Gabriel Temkin, *My Just War: The Memoir of a Jewish Red Army Soldier in World War II* (Novato, Calif.: Presidio, 1998), 39–40.

[71] J. Otto Pohl, *The Stalinist Penal System* (Jefferson, N.C.: McFarland, 1997), 74. The ethnic criteria were spelled out in the NKVD order no. 001158 on 27 August 1941 concerning the resettlement of Germans from the Volga, Saratov, and Stalingrad regions (GARF, f. 9401, op. 1, l. 422).

[72] For the exemption from deportation of kulak families with Red Army relatives in 1930–31, and of Polish and German families in Vinnytsia in May 1936, see *Istoricheskii arkhiv* 4 (1994): 171 and PAVO, f.136, op.3, d.362, 1.6.

[73] By March 1949 some 63,660 former Red Army front-line servicemen from nationalities deported during and after the war were counted in the special settlements. This figure included 33,615 ethnic Germans, 8,995 Crimean Tatars, 6,184 Kalmyks, 4,248 Chechens, 2,543 Karachai, and 946 Ingush (Nikolai Bugai, "40–50-e gody: Posledstviia deportatsii narodov [Svidetel'stvuiut arkhivy NKVD-MVD SSSR]," *Istoriia SSSR* 1 (1992): 134); *Tak eto bylo: Natsional'nye repressii v SSSR 1919–1952 gody* (Moscow: Rossiiskii mezhdunarodnyi fond kul'tury, 1993), 1:312; and Aleksander Nekrich, *The Punished Peoples: The Deportation and the Fate of Soviet Minorities at the End of the Second World War* (New York: Norton, 1979), 83. On the special regime camps established in December 1941 for Red Army soldiers captured by the Germans and those who lived in the German occupation zone, see Nicolas Werth and Gael Moullec, eds., *Rapports secrets soviétiques: La société russe dans les documents confidentiels, 1921–1991* (Paris: Gallimard, 1994), 391.

nearly 500,000 deported dying during the first three years, to cite one case. Like the kulaks immediately after deportation in the early 1930s, the mortality rate superseded the birth rate several times over during the first five years of exile among groups deported during and after the war.[74] In practice, postwar deportations often spelled mass death.

The number of deported nationalities, "kulaks" in the newly annexed territories, repatriated Soviet prisoners of war and forced labor in Germany, and Axis POWs—all political categories by definition—surpassed the total of those deported throughout the preceding two decades, collectivization and the Terror included. Those convicted of political crimes, on completion of their sentences, were exiled indefinitely.[75] Correspondingly, the GULAG population reached its climax in the early 1950s, with more than 2.5 million inmates in the camps and colonies alone, approximately .5 million more than in 1938, including the prison population.[76]

Inside the camps, the postwar era saw the unprecedented rigidification of penal policies. Two years into the war the GULAG witnessed the reintroduction of *katorga* (a hard labor regime), a true blast from the tsarist past. After less than two years of work under the harshest conditions, almost half the *katorga* inmates turned invalids. This, however, prompted the authorities to request "no fewer" than an additional sixty thousand inmates, rather than improving their conditions. The 26 November 1948 decree by the Presidium of the Supreme Soviet imposed twenty years of hard labor on those who escaped from deportation sites and five years of imprisonment on anyone who assisted inmates to escape from deportation sites, sheltered them, helped them to return to their home place, or offered assistance in resetttling them in their former places of residence.[77] This was

[74] Mortality rates in the GULAG camps reached an all-time high in 1942–43 with a ratio of 176 deaths per 1,000 inmates, almost double that of 1938 and six times that of 1937, largely owing to the assignment of this population to the bottom of the social ladder (Getty et al., "Victims of the Soviet Penal System in the Pre-War Years," 1048–49; Norman Naimark, "Ethnic Cleansing between War and Peace," in Weiner, *Landscaping the Human Garden*; and Zemskov, "Spetsposelentsy," 12–13). To these, one should add the 994,270 people tried and convicted by military tribunals during the war, of whom 157,593 were condemned to death ("Sud'ba voennoplennykh i deportirovannykh grazhdan SSSR. Materialy Komissii po reabilitatsii zhertv politicheskikh repressii," *Novaia i noveishaia istoriia* 2 [March–April 1996]: 100–101).

[75] See the 21 February 1948 decree of the Presidium of the Supreme Soviet of the USSR (GARF, f. 7523, op. 36, d. 345, ll. 53–54).

[76] Getty, Rittersporn, and Zemskov, "Victims of the Soviet Penal System in the Pre-War Years," 1039–41.

[77] Steven Barnes, "All to the Front, All for Victory! The Mobilization of Forced Labor in the Soviet Union during World War II," *International Labor and Working Class History* 58 (fall 2000); Viktor Zemskov, "Spetsposelentsy," 9.

the environment within which the campaign to eradicate the Ukrainian nationalist movement evolved.

As indicated by the assault on the communal structure of the above communities as well as the Jewish community, the postwar calculus was indifferent to the security of the borders and the existence of hostile external homelands of stigmatized nationalities. The enemy within was ostracized and treated as a totality. With the building of communism a political goal and a time line in place, the belief in the malleability of humans in general and internal enemies in particular eroded.

As clashes with nationalist forces in the Baltics and western Ukraine turned into extermination campaigns, compromise and partiality were ruled out as a matter of principle. The impetus for the radicalization of practices appeared to engulf every layer of the polity, most notably in the localities.[78] As always, punitive measures were not thought of as simply ad hoc countermeasures but, first and foremost, as didactic practices. Thus in early 1946 Mikhail Suslov, then the first secretary of the Lithuanian Central Committee, vehemently rebuked none other than Georgii Malenkov for the alarming signs of Moscow's "softening" of the pacification campaign in his jurisdiction. In 1945, exclaimed Suslov, the military tribunals of the NKVD in Lithuania tried some 8,675 people for treason and banditry, and, of these, 468 were sentenced to death.

> In light of the aggravation of the political situation in the Republic, this punitive policy of the NKVD's military tribunal should by no means be considered harsh. Quite the contrary. In accordance with the 15 August 1945 decree of the Central Committee of the All Union Communist Party, bandits and terrorists who committed atrocities against the population were given show trials in the county

---

[78] By this time, as we have seen in the party purge, the radicalizing input by the localities has already become a crucial feature in the purification drive. Either a product of literal understanding of purge decrees emanating from Moscow or a calculated tactic of playing it safe, the organs of Soviet power in Ukraine demonstrated zeal in dealing with targeted enemies. On 23 January 1930, in the midst of the collectivization drive, the Ukrainian Central Committee informed the localities that dekulakization quotas for the entire Ukrainian Republic were set at 150,000 households, of which 60,000 were marked for deportation out of Ukraine (the first two categories of kulaks). Alarmingly these figures resembled those set by the Politburo for the entire Union—60,000 for the first category and 150,00 for the second (PAVO, f. 29, op. 1, d. 577, l. 131). For figures for the entire Union, see *Istoricheskii arkhiv* 4 (1994): 145–52. By the time of the Terror, the scene repeated itself with the Ukrainian NKVD (as well as in other regions) requesting and this time receiving permission to increase the number of executions, which amounted to tens of thousands of lives. Throughout 1937–38, the "Special Troikas" in the localities were constantly "overfulfilling plans" for executions and imprisonment in the labor camps (*Moskovskie novosti*, 21 June 1992; and Getty, Rittersporn, and Zemskov, "Victims of the Soviet Penal System in the Pre-War Years," 1036.)

and district centers. Notice of the death sentences for such criminals are printed in the newspapers, eliciting the approval of the population. Yet the Military Collegium of the Supreme Court of the USSR often reverses even these verdicts. The population learns about it through the relatives of the convicted, and our punitive politics invoke bewilderment.[79]

From Kiev the leader of the Ukrainian Republic voiced almost identical concerns. Referring to Soviet officials who appeared lenient in the fight against the nationalists, Khrushchev warned that "this kindliness is foreign to the Bolsheviks."[80] Compromise was not on the agenda of the postwar polity.

Alienation from within and without: The Wartime Milieu and Brutalization

"Many underground organizations existed in the Vinnytsia region, but almost all of them were liquidated," a Jewish senior lecturer in Marxism-Leninism in the Vinnytsia Pedagogical Institute told an MGB informer in early 1949. "Why? Because the patriotic sentiment atrophied among the Ukrainians, and they are willing to sell out. Whatever sentiment was there was a drop in the sea. Still they say that the American papers are wrong when they write that the Ukrainian people did not display the required resistance against the German fascists."[81] Sometime earlier, a visiting Yugoslav leader recorded his Russian chauffeur cursing "the Ukrainians' mothers because their sons had not fought better, so that now the Russians had to liberate them."[82]

If both of these individuals are to be excused for having ignored the service of several million Ukrainians in the ranks of the Red Army, their comments nevertheless conveyed the powerful sense of alienation felt by Communist activists and partisans in the region. The Soviet partisans were both the creators and the subjects of the myth of the war, and their images of the wartime locality within which they operated became a critical component in the articulation of the Soviet ethos in the postwar era. The partisans carried with them, during and after the war, a sense of alienation from the population among whom they operated and for whom they believed to be fighting, inculcating antagonism and further brutalizing the postwar scene. Hnat Rybachenko, the deputy commander of the Second

[79] RGASPI, f. 597, op. 1, d. 24, l. 8.
[80] TsDAHOU, f. 1, op. 22, d. 166, l. 276.
[81] PAVO, f. 136, op. 29, d. 191, l. 83.
[82] Milovan Djilas, *Conversations with Stalin* (New York: Harcourt, Brace & World, 1962), 48.

Stalin Partisan Brigade, a native of Vinnytsia and a career NKVDist, was blunt when he summarized the attitude of the local population toward the Communist partisans in an interview immediately upon liberation. Following the description of his own narrow escape from the Romanian gendarmerie, which almost failed owing to information from collaborators, Rybachenko told the members of the commission gathering materials on the war that from 1942 until the fall of 1943 the population had a very negative attitude toward the partisans. Thus the partisans not only faced great difficulties from the fascists and their servants but also from segments of the population. This population, said Rybachenko, could be divided into two categories. The first consisted of anti-Soviet elements already dissatisfied with Soviet power who, with the arrival of the Germans, entered the service of the fascists as spies, servants, and so on. The second category included those who did not understand the essence of fascism and, in their pursuit of private property and land, sided with the Germans, immediately reporting to German authorities the arrival of partisans in one town or another.[83]

Rybachenko's grim assessment of his native region referred mainly to the peasant population. The peasants, who persisted in their hope that the Germans would eventually dismantle the kolkhozes, not only greeted them with the customary bread and salt but, early in the war, turned over Communist partisans to the Germans.[84] According to some, public executions of partisans at that time were met with general indifference or even approval.[85] The consolidation of power in the villages at the hands of returning "former people" was not a source of satisfaction for Rybachenko and his cohorts either.[86] Hostility was bound to be fueled by the lack of resentment against volunteers to the German army, understood at least by some as a desperate measure to gain decent food and clothing as conditions in the region deteriorated.[87] The hostile environment was supplemented by the proliferation of local partisan detachments whose political orientation was difficult to identify. The severity with which the Soviet authorities viewed this phenomenon was demonstrated in the dispatch of special commissars and commanders into occupied Vinnytsia to unite these units, which had gained the nickname *dikie* (wild), and direct them to fight the Germans and the nationalists.[88]

---

[83] IIAN ORF, f. 2, r. II, op. 9, d. 2, ll. 9, 16, 19. The conversation with Rybachenko took place in Kiev on 6 March 1944, two weeks before the Red Army liberated Vinnytsia.

[84] HURIP, #33, 5. In Chernihiv, according to another informant, a peasant woman turned in a partisan who managed to escape execution by the Germans (#27, p. 2; #548, p. 3).

[85] Ibid., #121, p. 13.

[86] Ibid., #548, p. 3.

[87] Ibid., p. 7.

[88] IIAN ORF, f. 2-II, op. 9, d. 3, ll. 1, 6–7.

The sense of isolation among the Soviet partisans was augmented by the political composition of the partisan units. The Communist core constituted a small percentage within the partisan detachments. On 22 March 1944, two days after the liberation of Vinnytsia, a count of the partisan detachments in the region indicated that of a total of 6,779 partisans, only 1,025 were Communists and another 1,478 were members of the Komsomol. The remaining 4,276 (63 percent) were not affiliated with the party.[89] More specifically, Communists in the Lenin Mounted Brigade numbered 205 (99 party members and 106 candidates) who comprised 14.8 percent of the total 1,378 partisans. In addition, there were 323 Komsomol members and 850 nonparty rank and file. In the Second Stalin Partisan Brigade, Communists accounted for 306 party members and 94 candidates. Of those who were full party members, 161 were readmitted into the party and 115 were new members. According to the brigade commander, the unit was composed at first of locals, a situation that changed with the arrival of POWs and the recruitment of youths who had avoided deportation to Germany.[90] Even this small number of Communists among the partisans was significantly higher than the official postwar estimation for the entire republic; of a total of 220,000 partisans, the overall number of Communists (members and candidates alike) was set at 14,875 (7 percent) and the number of Komsomol members (12 percent) at 26,000.[91] The Vinnytsia partisan units ranked equally with the roving bands, the fighting core of the movement. Of the 25,850 partisans for whom data were available on 25 August 1943, 4,913 were either party members or candidates (19.1 percent).[92]

The political isolation from within was accompanied by ethnic and generational alienation from without. In a region that was nearly 90 percent Ukrainian, the percentage of Ukrainians in the partisan units was significantly lower. Whereas the Mel'nyk formation, the largest partisan unit operating in the region, had 69.7 percent Ukrainians (2,037 of a total

[89] TsDAHOU, f. 1, op. 22, d. 156, l. 277. Other data showed different and lower absolute figures but the same ratio. Of 3, 149 partisans, 476 were party members and candidates, 745 were Komsomols, and 1,928 (61 percent) were not affiliated with the party (d. 9, l. 3).

[90] IIAN ORF, f. 2-II, op. 9, d. 1, l. 10; TsDAHOU, f. 1, op. 22, d. 164, l. 53. Somewhat later, comprehensive data on the Ukrainian partisan formations fixed the number of Communists in this brigade at 506, constituting 18.3 percent of the total number of partisans (2,763). The same source fixed the number of Communists at 464 in the Mel'nyk formation, the largest formation operating in the region, that is, 15.9 percent of the total number of partisans (2,919) (TsDAVOVU, f. 4620, op. 3, d. 102, l. 13).

[91] *Pravda Ukrainy,* 26 January 1949. A Soviet study fixed the number of party members in the Ukrainian partisan movement at 68,245, or 13.6 percent of the total number (Nikolai Starozhilov, *Partizanskie soedineniia Ukrainy v Velikoi Otechestvennoi voine* [Kiev: Vyshcha shkola, 1983], 70).

[92] Zakhar Bogatyr', *V tylu vraga* (Moscow: Sotsekgiz, 1963), 303.

of 2,919), the other two large formations, Kondratiuk and Vladimirov, comprised only 49.8 percent and 48.7 percent Ukrainians, respectively.[93] This state of affairs was only bound to be inflamed by the Germans' initial policies. In cases of sabotage where the culprits were not discovered, German instructions called for reprisals against the Jews and Russians but not the Ukrainians.[94] Awareness of the German policies also penetrated the ranks of the Red Army. German troops who captured surrendering Soviet soldiers in the early days of the invasion recorded the latter screaming "Ukrainians, Ukrainians," when they were laying down their weapons.[95] The preferential treatment of ethnic Ukrainians in jobs and local administration, and the release of hundreds of thousands of Ukrainians from German POW camps between July and November 1941, were in stark contrast to the fate of ethnic Russians. Most of the released POWs returned to their villages where they resumed civilian life under occupation, hardly an endearing act in the eyes of the Red partisans.[96]

Equally important was the age composition of the largest formations. Nearly 80 percent of the partisans in Ukraine were born after 1910, which meant that the decisive majority were products of the Communist system. In the Mel'nyk and Kondratiuk formations this age group accounted for 77.9 percent and 82.7 percent, respectively.[97] In a largely rural area that went through one of the harshest collectivization and Terror drives, this gap was a bad omen.

An effort to overcome alienation from the local scene at the initial stages of the war was evident in the decision of commissars of detachments to promote local people to command positions in order to avoid arousing antagonism.[98] Under such conditions some partisan leaders chose to avoid mobilization, thinking that this would only end up in a loss. They preferred to limit enrollment to resolute volunteers among the verified locals.[99] Often

---

[93] TsDAVOVU, f. 4620, op. 3, d. 102, l. 21; TsDAHOU, f. 128, op. 1, d. 1, l. 131.

[94] Martin C. Dean, "The German *Gendarmerie*, the Ukrainian *Schutzmannschaft*, and the 'Second Wave' of Jewish Killings in Occupied Ukraine: German Policing at the Local Level in the Zhitomir Region, 1941–1944," *German History* 14, no. 2 (1996): 173.

[95] Kurt Meyer, *Grenadiere/Panzermeyer* (Munich: Schild, 1956), 82–83.

[96] Dallin, *German Rule in Russia*, 412–14; HURIP, #548, 1. The discriminatory policy in favor of the Ukrainian POWs was abandoned in early November 1941, under pressure from both the German civilian administration and army commanders, who sought to use the POWs as auxiliary laborers. For an interesting reflection on the devastating impact these policies had in the ethnically mixed and culturally Russified Kiev, see the memoirs of Lev Dudin, *Velikii mirazh*, Hoover Archive, Nicolaevsky Collection, series 178, box 232, folders 10–11, p. 73.

[97] TsDAVOVU, f. 4620, op. 3, d. 102, ll. 28, 38. The figures applied only to partisans for whom such data existed, which makes it likely that the percentages were higher.

[98] IIAN ORF, f. 2, r. II, op. 9, d. 3, l. 2.

[99] Ibid., l. 6.

the draft to partisan units was a terrorizing process for the locals. Carried out forcefully at night, as one recruitment was recorded by the Germans, the villagers were led by armed partisans to a registration point and simply assigned to units. Protests against the forced drafting were brushed aside by the commissar, who kindly suggested that anyone who did not wish to go merely say so—an offer no one dared accept. Those who managed to escape after being recruited put their families in mortal danger.[100]

The spring of 1943 marked a noticeable shift in the attitude and conduct of the local population. Partisan leaders noted that complicity with the occupation authorities was dissolving. Villagers began to hand over collaborators to the partisans and to assist them with food supplies.[101] A similar though somewhat more reserved impression was conveyed in the accounts of two of the major formations in the region that were established late in the war. "Regardless of the fact that information about the actual situation in the Soviet Union and the successes of the Red Army passes through irregularly and scantily," Burchenko wrote to Khrushchev in August 1943,

> the population deeply believes in the return of Soviet power and does not believe the Germans in anything. The population, however, is extremely frightened and politically inactive because of the endless repression, deportations to Germany, and the espionage system. Many of the supporters of Soviet power were arrested in 1943. Many of them were executed; others were sent to concentration camps. The nationalists who made their way into the local organs help the Germans to unmask Soviet activists. There is no wide partisan movement in the region. Conditions for it are extremely difficult. Nevertheless, all sympathies are entirely with the Soviet side.[102]

Vasyl' Nyzhnyk, Burchenko's colleague in the obkom and the commissar of the Lenin Mounted Brigade, echoed the population's image of the unshaken pro-Soviet sentiments. The peasants, he wrote, maintained their belief in the Red Army all along and supported the partisans.

Yet the change in the population's conduct was not matched among partisan and party leaders. Even when these two prominent officials were striving to protect their "own turf," they felt a sense of isolation, if not betrayal, by the region they had left and to which they were about to return. The shift in the peasants' attitude did not result from a change of heart but rather from sheer opportunism. The peasants were on the fence

---

[100] Armstrong, *The Soviet Partisans in World War II*, 153–54.

[101] IIAN ORF, f. 2, op. 9, d. 3, ll. 19–20. Similar impressions of the popular mood in the villages were expressed by Kondratiuk, the commander of the brigade (d. 1, ll. 10–11).

[102] PAVO, f. 425, op. 2, d. 11, l. 6.

until the tide of the war was decided. Only the Red Army's victories and the increased partisan activity served as catalysts for shifting the peasants' mood. "Realizing the successful activities of the partisans, the peasants willingly informed [the partisans] about the number of enemy garrisons in the surrounding villages and towns, and many enrolled in the detachments," wrote Nyzhnyk.[103] The negative Soviet assessment of the local population was striking in comparison with that of the nationalists regarding the impact of Nazi terror on political loyalties. The latter viewed the population's paralysis as a natural reaction to Nazi unmitigated terror. Nationalist activists in Vinnytsia noted that, along with the failure to dissolve the collective farms, the Germans took indiscriminate revenge on the population, publicly hanged innocent people, mistreated POWs, recruited forced labor into Germany, and infused racial theory into everyday life, all leading to quick disenchantment with the Germans.[104] For Communist partisans, on the other hand, the fear of Nazi terror merely triggered either complicity or, at best, demoralization and paralysis, both inexcusable reactions.[105]

Probably most detrimental was the indictment handed down by Sydir Kovpak, Ukraine's most celebrated partisan and a persistent advocate of the peasantry. The peasants, remarked Kovpak, chose life and safety over the risk of death. Family and property ties, endangered by the prospects of German reprisals, made the peasants reluctant to take an active part in the partisan detachments.[106] At a time when they were needed most, the peasants chose not to rise to the occasion. In a polity built on the premise of transforming familial and regional loyalties into the socialist messianic crusade and its organizational embodiment—party-state institutions—this failure was indeed detrimental.[107]

---

[103] TsDAHOU, f. 128, op. 1, d. 1, ll. 7, 21, 39–40, 60–61.

[104] HURIP, #542, 9. According to an insightful activist: "The peasants saw how the convoy guards were hitting us with their rifle butts, and promptly people began saying that 'these were not the Germans we had expected.' Next came the liquidation of the Jews, and then the whole *Untermensch* propaganda; even those who did not know the 'theory' behind it felt its effect in the attitude. A friend of mine saw how a Ukrainian was being beaten for having entered a latrine marked 'Nur für Deutsche.' People talked a lot about such incidents" (ibid., #548, 3–4).

[105] The brigade commissar told the commission representatives that the Germans scared off the population when they posted everywhere a fixed toll for their losses: twenty-five people would be shot for every German killed, one hundred for every officer, and only twenty for a *starosta* (IIAN ORF, f. 2, r.II, op. 9, d. 3, l. 4).

[106] Sydor Kovpak, *Ot Putivlia do Karpat*, 34.

[107] On the transformation of loyalties to the ideological domain as the essence of the modern ethos, see the insightful observations of Michael Walzer, *The Revolution of the Saints: A Study in the Origins of Radical Politics* (Cambridge, Mass.: Harvard University Press, 1965).

Soviet reactions to this situation were harsh. Those who dared to speak against the Soviet cause were marked and punished. "If we heard that someone complained about Soviet power or the partisans and the Red Army, we found him and punished him," related Kondratiuk.[108] "The population of the surrounding villages and districts was 90 percent pro-Soviet, since we shot all the hostile elements," wryly noted the commissar of the Stalin Second Partisan Brigade.[109] By the time of liberation such sentiments were abundant in Vinnytsia and, given the identity of the local leadership, were bound to prevail. The transition of party personnel in the partisan detachments into key positions in political organs guaranteed that this resentment would have implications for the postwar scene. The mayor of neighboring Uman, a former partisan leader who operated in the Vinnytsia region, remarked to Alexander Werth that "it was a hard and grim life. They [the Germans] were merciless, and so were we. And we shall be merciless with the traitors now. It's no use crying in wartime."[110]

The Criminalization of Passivity

The criminalization of passivity in the armed struggle was a key feature in the war ethos. Even more than the figure of the collaborationist, the bystander was the prototype against which the identity of the ideal citizen was articulated. The juxtaposition of those who chose life and safety versus those who opted for risk and sacrifice has been a core Bolshevik theme, and the equation of passivity with hostile activity tapped into a long-standing and fundamental component of party life. By now it was being applied to the population at large and with harsher consequences. On 30 July 1942 a *Pravda* editorial reminded readers that "during the civil war, Lenin used to say: 'He who does not help the Red Army wholeheartedly and does not observe its order and iron discipline is a traitor.'" And Lenin's dictum was carried out regardless of the circumstances. The lives of civilians who were forced to work under the Germans were expendable. The words of Grigorii Linkov, a partisan commander who operated in western Belorussia, applied the same principle to the Ukrainian scene:

> I understood, of course, that the Hitlerites might send a punitive expedition to the village, accuse its citizens of contacts with the partisans, and cruelly avenge themselves on the peaceful population. But I also understood that the population that was driven to repair the enemy's roads, whether voluntarily or involun-

[108] IIAN ORF, f. 2, op. 9, d. 1, l. 11.
[109] Ibid., d. 3, l. 3.
[110] Werth, *Russia at War*, 792.

tarily, delayed the hour of victory for a while. But who can determine what a minute of military activity costs? . . . The party sent me to the rear to wreck the enemy's measures, to undermine his communication in every possible way. Could I have tolerated these nonvolunteers restoring communication?[111]

In some cases partisans intentionally provoked German reprisals as a punitive measure against a passive peasantry. Responding to the grumbling of peasants who complained that it was they who had to bear the consequences of Kovpak's presence among them, his deputy retorted in his memoirs that it evidently did not occur to these comrades that SS men existed in this world only to be killed and not to be hidden from in the bogs.[112]

The severity with which the returning Soviet power viewed passivity was marked by the identity of one particular group that fell within this category: Red Army soldiers who survived German captivity. With captivity already criminalized regardless of circumstances, the best hope for released POWs was to be categorized as passive in the struggle against the invaders. Alexander Werth, a British correspondent who was present in Kharkiv in February 1943, witnessed the practice of this policy. The neglect of those who survived German captivity, and who Werth describes as "weird ghostlike figures in terrible rags . . . [with] breath [that] smelled of death," seemed to be officially ordained but nonetheless carried out in a receptive environment. When Werth approached a Russian soldier, the soldier cynically remarked: "Don't you get het [*sic*] up about them. For all we know, they may have been left here by the Germans as spies or diversionists." "They don't look like it, do they?" asked Werth. "Maybe not," replied the soldier, "but one cannot be too careful these days. The NKVD had better find out who they are."[113]

For much of the war, Soviet Ukrainian partisans were starved for military seasoned personnel and could have used the escaping POWs. Nevertheless their judgment of Red Army servicemen who escaped captivity was equally harsh. A sardonic yet typical assessment was offered by Aleksei Fedorov, a prominent partisan leader and veteran party member. "There were all kinds of escaped POWs," recalled Fedorov.

Some had voluntarily surrendered to the Germans. Later, when they had been eaten by the lice in the camps and became sick of being punched in the jaw, they repented and escaped to join the partisans . . . some of the formerly encircled men who joined us had been "hubbies" [*primaki*] . . . Among the "hubbies"

---

[111] Grigorii Lin'kov, *Voina v tylu vraga* (Moscow: Gos. izd-vo khudozhestvennoi literatury, 1951), 92.

[112] Vershyhora, *Liudi s chistoi sovest'iu*, 245.

[113] Werth, *Russia at War*, 617.

were specimens who would have been glad to spend the war behind a woman's skirt, but the Germans would have either forced them to work in Germany or to join the police. Having considered this, such a guy would come to the conclusion that joining the partisans is better after all.[114]

In light of the relative preferential treatment of Ukrainian POWs by the Germans during the initial stage of the war, tensions flared when escaping prisoners joined partisan detachments or formed their own.[115] Within the partisan detachments the escaped or released POWs were viewed with deep suspicion. According to one partisan leader from Vinnytsia:

> We verified prisoners of war especially strictly. Only after they had described the circumstances of their falling into captivity, and how they escaped, did they receive assignments. After they fulfilled the assignment, and sometimes several assignments, they were included in the partisan detachment. If a group of POWs arrived, they were not placed in one company but were dispersed among three and were closely watched.[116]

Demonization and Excision

"Soviet leaders' rule is anchored in ideology, as was the divine right of kings in Christianity," reflected Milovan Djilas, "and therefore their imperialism, too, has to be ideological or else it commands no legitimacy. This is why the men in the Kremlin can lose no territory once acquired, why they cannot abandon friends and allies no matter how objectively they may have become to them . . . or admit alternative interpretations of the true faith."[117] In the concrete realm of nationality policy, this ideology meant that while the national or ethnic otherness had a right to exist in some form or another, it could do so only within the boundaries of the Soviet polity. Soviet presence in any given ethnonational region was perceived as natural and integral to the historical development of the group and the region.[118] Hence any notion that a Soviet presence in the newly annexed western Ukraine was foreign or that the struggle against nationalist forces was a war with external power were rejected unequivocally. As

---

[114] Fedorov, *Podpol'nyi obkom deistvuet*, 405–6.

[115] Vershyhora, *Liudi s chistoi sovest'iu*, 69; HURIP, #542, 9.

[116] IIAN ORF, f. 2, op. 9, d. 3, l. 6. Dmitrii Medvedev held similar views on the escaped POWs whom he termed collectively as a drunken and undisciplined lot. In some cases he resorted to executions (Medvedev, *Sil'nye dukhom* [Moscow, 1951]).

[117] Milovan Djilas, "Christ and the Commissar," in George Urban, ed., *Stalinism: Its Impact on Russia and the World* (Aldershot: Wildwood, 1982), 197.

[118] See the insightful discussion by Yuri Slezkine, "From Savages to Citizens: The Cultural Revolution in the Soviet Far North, 1928–1938," *Slavic Review* 51 (spring 1992): 56–76.

an internal problem, the solution to the conflict with the Ukrainian nationalist movement would be subjected to the rules of the Soviet domestic purification drive. Their very existence was a violation of the natural order, and hence there would be no mitigating circumstances in assessing their crimes. Nor would utilitarian considerations play a role in the fight against them. They would have to be excised from the Soviet Ukrainian body.

The demonization of the nationalists becomes clearer when considered along with the hate campaign against the German invaders. The nationalists' association with the Nazi satanic enterprise became a pillar in demonizing the nationalist cause, but representations of each differed substantially. The Nazis were relentlessly dehumanized in Soviet wartime propaganda, yet their very being as the external enemy meant that however horrifying their atrocities were, the fight against them was reactive, retaliatory, and subjected to the *Realpolitik* calculus of the international arena. At no point was the anti-Nazi crusade a part of the purification drive of the Soviet polity.

Indeed, the Axis invaders were publicly dehumanized and their lives regarded as expendable. And, for the most part, during the war no distinction was made between Germans and Nazis. "The Germans are not human beings," Ehrenburg, the spearhead of the anti-Nazi propaganda, informed the Red Army soldiers.

> Don't let us waste time talking or feeling indignant. Let us kill! If you haven't killed a German in the course of the day, your day has been wasted . . . If you can't kill a German with a bullet, kill him with your bayonet! If you have killed one German, kill another. Nothing gives us so much joy as German corpses.[119]

When Milovan Djilas mentioned during a conversation with Stalin that the Yugoslav partisans did not take German prisoners "because they killed all our prisoners," Stalin responded with this anecdote:

> One of our men was leading a large group of German prisoners and on the way he killed all but one. They asked him, when he arrived at his destination: "And where are all the others?" "I was just carrying out the orders of the commander in chief," he said, "to kill every one to the last man—and here is the last man."[120]

Still, the reactive and differentiated nature of the Soviet anti-German campaign was visible even at the height of the hate campaign. Stalin pursued this line in his various wartime addresses to the Soviet public. "If the Germans want to have a war of extermination, they will get it," promised

---

[119] Anatol Goldberg, *Ilya Ehrenburg: Revolutionary, Novelist, Poet, War Correspondent, Propagandist. The Extraordinary Epic of a Russian Survivor* (London: Weidenfeld and Nicolson, 1984), 197.

[120] Djilas, *Conversations with Stalin*, 76.

Stalin on 6 November 1941. But, followed the correction on 23 February 1942, the Soviet side did not approach the war as a racial clash, which meant that it was only reacting to external aggression. "The foreign press sometimes jabbers that the Soviet people hate the Germans just as Germans; that the Red Army exterminates German soldiers just as Germans out of hatred of everything German; and that therefore the Red Army does not take German soldiers prisoners. This, of course, is a similar stupid lie and a foolish slander against the Red Army. The Red Army is devoid of sentiments of racial hatred," declared Stalin and continued:

> Of course the Red Army has to destroy the German-fascist occupiers inasmuch as they wish to enslave our motherland; or, when being surrounded by our troops, they refuse to lay down their arms and surrender. The Red Army annihilates them, not because of their German origin but because they want to enslave our motherland. The Red Army, like any other people's army, has the right and is obliged to annihilate the enslavers of its motherland, irrespective of their national origin. . . . war is war.[121]

Even Ehrenburg and Konstantin Simonov, who urged the Red Army soldiers to kill the Germans anytime and anywhere, explained their rage by pointing to the unprovoked atrocities the Germans inflicted on the Russian people.[122] The record of the Lenin Partisan Brigade in Vinnytsia was somewhat less humorous than Stalin's quip to Djilas, but it also underlined the retaliatory nature of the practice. Revenge was indicated as the prime motive behind the execution of foreign prisoners. "In the village of Sleha a total of 56 Romanians were executed for the fallen commanders and soldiers in Chernivtsi," wrote the commander and commissar of the brigade. During a single raid into occupied Vinnytsia, the special department (*osobyi otdel*) of the brigade reportedly executed 291 German and Romanian prisoners.[123] Other commanders displayed before their troops the recovered and disfigured bodies of partisans who were tortured by their captors, so that everyone would know what awaited him if taken prisoner.[124]

The abrupt curtailment of the hate campaign toward the end of the war underlined its subjugation to Soviet objectives in the international arena. The campaign was brought to a sudden halt when the war was still raging and the Germans still offered a ferocious resistance to the advancing Red Army. With an eye already set on the postwar order, Ehrenburg's lack of differentiation between good and bad Germans turned from a virtue to a vice, and Stalin and Georgii Aleksandrov, the head of the agit-prop depart-

---

[121] Stalin, *Sochineniia* 15:24, 43–44.
[122] Werth, *Russia at War*, 412–14, 416–17.
[123] TsDAHOU, f. 128, op. 1, d. 1, ll. 69, 109.
[124] IIAN ORF, f. 2, op. 9, d. 3, l. 7.

ment of the Central Committee, could inform the Soviet people that Hitlers come and go, but the German people were there to stay.[125] By then, the redrawing of the borders of postwar Germany required the distinction between the German people and the Nazis.

But no such concessions were reserved for the nationalists. Neither circumstances nor redemption would play out in the representation of the Ukrainian nationalists and the exterminatory fight against them. The Soviets were well aware of the rapid deterioration in the relations between the Nazis and the nationalists. Intelligence reports on the situation in German-occupied Vinnytsia referred to this development in a matter-of-fact tone. "During the first days of the occupation of the Vinnytsia region, Ukrainian nationalists widely agitated among the population in favor of the creation of 'Independent Ukraine' with the help of Germany, and argued for the kinship of the Ukrainian people with the Germans." However, the reporter, the head of the Ukrainian NKVD, proceeded to describe the fallout between the two sides:

At the beginning of 1942 nationalist leaflets appeared in the town of Vinnytsia and its periphery. The leaflets stated that the Germans disavowed the OUN, arrested about sixty activists of the OUN in Kiev, and summoned to Berlin Stepan Bandera, one of the leaders of this party, where he was arrested. As a result, the Ukrainian population was called to fight the Germans and organize underground work. Moreover, after that it was pointed out in the leaflets that Germany is the eternal enemy of the Ukrainians.[126]

Knowledge, however, did not imply recognition. Notably Soviet reports took care to emphasize that the shift in the nationalist policy did not result from a change of heart or convictions but merely from the disappointment at their treatment by the Germans. Yet neither a circumstantial cause nor ideological change mattered. For the Soviets, the very existence of the nationalists was the bone of contention, not their tactics or alliances.

And so the ostracization of the nationalists only gathered momentum in the postwar years and was insinuated into all levels of Soviet political culture. In a polity that posited itself as the only viable alternative to fascism, the depiction of a Ukraino-German separatist movement was the ultimate representation of alienation. The identification of the nationalists as the "German-Ukrainian Fascists" had become a self-propelled dogma on the

[125] *Pravda*, 14 April 1945; On 1 May 1945 Stalin emphasized that the Allies do not aim at the liquidation of the German people but only at the destruction of fascism and German militarism. War criminals will be severely punished but peaceful German citizens will not be harmed. Stalin repeated this message in his 9 May radio speech (Stalin, *Sochineniia*, 15:191, 198).

[126] TsDAHOU, f. 1, op. 23, d. 685, ll. 36–37. Significantly the antagonistic relations between the Germans and Ukrainian nationalists in the region had already been noted in an earlier report dated 30 September 1942 (ibid., d. 124, ll. 26–27).

Soviet political scene even before the complete liberation of Ukraine.[127] Hence, in a mass circulated political poster by Koziurenko, "Two Boots Make a Pair," the nationalist movement was presented as the demonic co-culprit of the SS who thrives on the blood and destruction of the Ukrainian nation. Holding a knife dripping with blood, a crooked-faced nationalist was portrayed arm in arm with an SS henchman against the background of a burning village— their mutual accomplishment (Figure 3.1).[128]

The total alienation of the nationalist cause was captured in a colorful passage by Dmitrii Medvedev, the partisan leader-turned-writer. Referring to his own contacts with the nationalist leader "Bul'ba" (Borovets) and his entourage, Medvedev explained the national and linguistic alienation of the latter:

> The speech of the "hetman" was incomprehensible, a barbarian mixture of Ukrainian and German words. It was a language, as we later realized, broadly used by those Ukrainian nationalists brought up in the pubs of Berlin and in the taverns of Ottawa and Chicago, persons without a passport, without a homeland, subjects of the international black market, rascals, ready to sell themselves to the Gestapo or the Intelligence Service or the Federal Bureau of Investigation or any other bourgeois espionage organization.[129]

National ostracization was augmented by a touch of class alienation. In another meeting with the nationalists, Medvedev's representative noted that,

> almost all of [Bul'ba's entourage] arrived from abroad. The "editor" lived in Czechoslovakia, the "adviser" arrived from Berlin. They spoke in this Ukraino-German language, as did "Bul'ba," and differed from the "hetman" only in their clothing. Whereas the latter wore a *zaporozhtsa* (a Zaporozhian Cossack shirt), the former preferred a European suit, a colorful tie, and manicured fingernails, which were considered a sign of special refinement among the bandits (Figure 3.1).[130]

The total alienation of the nationalist cause was driven home through its exclusion from the core of the myth of the war in Ukraine, the unification of the Ukrainian lands and people for the first time in history. When the

---

[127] Lev Shankovs'kyi contends that Khrushchev himself coined the phrase "Ukrainian-German nationalists" in his speech in Kiev on the occasion of the liberation of the city on 27 November 1943 (Lew Shankowsky [Shankovs'kyi], "Soviet and Satellite Sources on the Ukrainian Insurgent Army," *The Annals of the Ukrainian Academy of Arts and Sciences in the U.S.* 9, nos.1–2 [1961]: 248).

[128] The poster was produced in L'viv in 1945 and ten thousand copies were circulated. It soon became the main visual representation of the Ukrainian nationalist movement in the Soviet Union and was reproduced in several editions of *Ukrains'kyi politychnyi plakat* (Kiev: Politvydav Ukrainy, 1957; rev. ed., 1981).

[129] Medvedev, *Sil'nye dukhom*, 84.

[130] Ibid., 86.

Figure 3.1. Two Boots Make a Pair. L'viv, 1945. A Soviet poster condemning the Nazi-Ukrainian nationalist alliance.

tenth anniversary of the unification was celebrated throughout the Union, Vinnytsia residents were reminded that "the most evil enemies of the Ukrainian people, the Ukrainian nationalists, who have always used the national flag to deceive the masses and conceal their counterrevolutionary plans, faithfully and truthfully served the German, French, Anglo-American, and other foreign oppressors and helped them in the evil business of oppressing and enslaving the toilers of western Ukraine."[131]

An equally biting tone was used by Nikita Khrushchev in a key speech to the Ukrainian Central Committee. Khrushchev's target audience was the population of the western Ukrainian provinces, Vinnytsia included, where the struggle with the nationalists was quickly turning into a civil war.[132] Khrushchev's speech was an artful preparation for the exterminatory campaign. The Ukrainian nationalist cause and its representatives were persistently delegitimized even when their forces were fighting the Germans or when Soviet power celebrated common themes such as the unification of the Ukrainian land. Although the focus was on the wartime and postwar activities of the nationalists, Khrushchev made sure to emphasize that the roots of the Soviet-nationalist clash were independent of the war. Armed clashes with nationalist forces had already commenced before the break of the German-Russian war, Khrushchev noted, thus making the struggle an internal affair with all that implied.[133]

The nationalists were de-individualized, portrayed as an undifferentiated collective, detached from any specific domestic intimate environment, and often referred to as animals. Killing them was not to involve any sense of guilt.[134] Thus members of the Soviet polity should engage in systematic elimination of the "snakelike, slavish dogs of the Nazi hangmen," the "Ukrainian-German fascists" or the "agents of foreign intelligence services," rather than mere "Ukrainian nationalists." "The Ukrainian bourgeois nationalists are a miserable band of adventurers who sold out to the German and Polish intelligence services," Khrushchev told his audience.

> When the Germans invaded our country, the Ukrainian-German nationalists assisted the Fascists in every possible way. They killed themselves trying to please their master, Hitler, and to get only a small portion of the loot for their doggish

---

[131] *Naddnistrians'ka zirka* (Vinnytsia), 24 September 1949.

[132] The speech repeated, if only in a more colorful terminology, the call from 12 February 1944 to the nationalists to surrender unconditionally. The address was circulated in the press, and, in addition, some three hundred thousand leaflets were distributed throughout Vinnytsia and the western provinces (TsDAHOU, f. 1, op. 6, d. 757, ll. 15–24; d. 715, ll. 37–38).

[133] Ibid., op. 1, d. 664, l. 263.

[134] See the suggestive insights of Ofer Zur, "The Love of Hating: The Psychology of Enmity," *History of European Ideas* 13, no. 4 (1991): 345–69, esp. 362–64; and James A. Aho, *This Thing Called Darkness: A Sociology of the Enemy* (Seattle: University of Washington Press, 1994).

service. The German invaders shed the blood of Soviet Ukraine, shot hundreds of thousands of Soviet people—women, the elderly, children. The Ukrainian-German nationalists assisted and at present [continue to] assist the Germans in these bloody crimes, fulfilling the role of hangmen.[135]

To make things worse, while the German component of the evil duo was beaten and driven out of the homeland, its Ukrainian counterpart continued the destructive mission. The efforts to sabotage the restoration of the economy were seen as the fulfillment of German instructions. Hence the internal enemy remained foreign even when its foreign ally invader was expelled from Soviet territory. Khrushchev dismissed the nationalists' efforts to disassociate themselves from their alliance with the Germans as a ploy in the face of inevitable defeat.[136]

Hence repentance did not necessarily buy rehabilitation. Rather, it bought an invitation to the Soviet purgatory. Following unconditional surrender and denunciation of their "anti-people cause," repenting nationalists were to be enrolled into combat service in the Red Army to defend the people.[137] The invitation to baptism by fire, however, was limited to nonactive nationalists. OUN members, especially the so-called security services, were destined for extermination. "These most inveterate cutthroats" should be fished out and exterminated, exclaimed Khrushchev.

Finally, the severity with which association with the Nazi cause was held in postwar Soviet Union was anchored in the realities of the occupation. But the realities and consequences of the Nazi occupation exceeded all expectations. With the outbreak of hostilities the local party apparatus paraded an unrestrained confidence in the outcome of the war. In the Chernivtsi district, a young enthusiast allegedly declared that "Hitler became full of himself, rejoicing with the successes in the war with the little powers. But the USSR is neither Belgium nor Greece. We'll crush the fascist hounds even faster than we crushed the White Finns." Comforting his parents, who apparently were less excited with the prospects of war,

---

[135] TsDAHOU, f. 1, op. 1, d. 664, l. 262–63. Khrushchev, it should be noted, was informed that the Germans also persecuted the Ukrainian nationalists, if only occasionally. A report submitted to Khrushchev by the Communist underground in the Bar district on 2 February 1945 stated that in early 1943 the Gestapo arrested and executed many of the nationalist activists (TsDAHOU, f. 1, op. 22, d. 166, l. 12).

[136] Ibid., ll. 265, 267. The association of the nationalist cause with foreign powers persisted throughout the Soviet period, with the identity of the foreign patron changing according to the contemporary geopolitical calculations. Thus when the authorities intensified the campaign against the Ukrainian Greek Catholic Church in western Ukraine, it was the Vatican that was blamed for financing and actively guiding the operations of the Ukrainian Insurgent Army (Bohdan R. Bociurkiw, *The Ukrainian Greek Catholic Church and the Soviet State (1939–1950)* [Toronto: Canadian Institute of Ukrainian Studies Press, 1996], 204–7, 238–39; Luka Kyzia and M. Kovalenko, *Vikova borot'ba Ukrains'koho naroda proty Vatikanu* [Kiev: Vyd-vo Kyivs'koho universiteta, 1959], 200–207, 221–29).

[137] TsDAHOU, f. 1, op. 1, d. 664, ll. 270–72.

another draftee was said to have exclaimed: "Parents! Why are you crying for us? There's nothing to cry for. Our valiant Red Army is so strong that soon we'll return from Berlin to our home villages."[138]

As great as the bravado was, so was the shock. Four weeks later, Vinnytsia was occupied and remained so for nearly three years. The extent of destruction in Vinnytsia was staggering. By 1 January 1950 the total population of the region was 2,012,452, a decline of 12 percent from the prewar total.[139] In 1956, some twelve years after the region was liberated, its overall population was still 6.3 percent less than the 1940 level.[140] The official estimate of human losses was fixed at 101,139, and some 64,076 were deported for forced labor in Germany. At the time of liberation, the twenty-three to twenty five thousand residents of Vinnytsia accounted for a quarter of the ninety-eight thousand on the eve of the war. Entire villages were burned down and their populations shot wherever partisan detachments operated.[141] The loss of property was colossal as well. The industrial, agricultural, and educational systems of the region were practically decimated, as were most of the theaters and hospitals and much of the housing.[142] Moreover, the destruction of the war continued even after the war had ended with the breakdown of the sanitation system, the outbreak of a raging typhus epidemic, and a negative birth-death ratio.[143] If the Soviet drive for purity made any compromise with the nationalist cause obsolete, regardless of the circumstances, the magnitude and endurance of destruction with which the nationalists were associated practically guaranteed relentless and merciless punishment. And residents of Vinnytsia, like those in all other regions, were constantly reminded not to forget and not to forgive (Figure 3.2).[144]

---

[138] PAVO, f. 136, op. 3, d. 392, l. 144. The scarcity of documents from the eve of the war and the initial stage of the German invasion are a major obstacle in the way of reconstructing the political atmosphere and reaction to this cataclysmic event. The author was told by archivists in Kiev and Vinnytsia that the two main reasons for this scarcity were the destruction of contemporary documents in the face of the rapid advance of the Germans and the Soviet bureaucratic procedure. When the Germans invaded, most of the documents from that period had not yet been deposited in the party archives but were in the possession of the various bodies. At this stage it is still unclear as to how many documents survived and how many were destroyed in the various archives.

[139] PAVO, f. 136, op. 30, d. 186, l. 3.

[140] *Osnovni pokaznyky rozvytku narodnoho hospodarstva Vinnyts'koi oblasti: Statystychnyi zbirnyk* (Vinnytsia, 1957), 7.

[141] TsDAHOU, f. 128, op. 1, d. 1, ll. 7, 45–46.

[142] TsDAVOVU, f. 4620, op. 3, d. 253, ll. 97–99. For the breakdown of population losses by individual districts, see ibid. d. 349; and TsDAHOU, f. 1, op. 50, d. 1, l. 13; *Prestupnye tseli—prestupnye sredstva: dokumenty ob okkupatsionnoi politike fashistskoi Germanii na territorii SSSR (1941–1944 gg.)* (Moscow: Gos. izd-vo polit. lit-ry, 1963), 137.

[143] In November 1944, seven months after liberation, twelve districts registered only 845 births as opposed to 1,210 deaths, including 190 babies younger than one year old (PAVO, f. 136, op. 13, d. 11, ll. 8–12).

[144] Vasyl' Nyzhnyk, "Ne zabuemo, ne prostymo," *Vinnyts'ka pravda*, 8 October 1944.

Figure 3.2. A monument overlooking the mass graves of several thousand locals and prisoners of war executed by the Nazis following the completion of construction of Hitler's headquarters nearby.

But wartime circumstances alone could not account for the qualitative shift in the Soviet purification drive. The meaning of these wartime events for contemporaries, as well as their impact, could not be detached from the preceding Soviet experience and treated as universal. The endurance and institutionalization of state revenge against those identified as internal enemies set the Soviet Union apart from other European countries and the United States, and pointed to another explanation. Wartime circumstances were read into the progressing narrative of the Revolution, which was itself undergoing change at the time.

The Logic and Practice of Excision

No matter what your ideology may be, once you believe that you are in the possession of some infallible truth, you become a combatant in a religious war. There is nothing to prevent you from

robbing, burning, and slaughtering in the name
of your truth, for you are doing it with a perfectly
clear conscience—indeed the truth in your possession makes it your duty to pursue it with an iron
logic and unwavering will . . . ideology demands
the liquidation of your enemies, real or imagined.
(Milovan Djilas, *Christ and the Commissar*)[145]

Reflecting on his wartime experience in Yugoslavia, Milovan Djilas, then
a Communist partisan leader, rationalized the execution of the leadership
of a certain clan whose members were friendly to the Communist partisans
with the failure of some of its members to subject their "primeval clan
ties" and loyalties to that of their political organization. The agitated
members of the Tadic clan were executed together with royal officers "not
merely for [the sake of] economy but to associate the fate of party enemies
with that of outside enemies." This ideological commitment, noted Djilas,
allowed for summary dealing with opponents whoever they might have
been.[146] With the inspiration of revolutionary idealism, neither mass brutality in general nor the killing of individuals in particular was considered
regrettable or detrimental. Indeed, while the Soviet practice of violence
was triggered by specific circumstances such as military necessity, its logic
was anchored in ideology. Violence was applied within a well-defined ideological framework that earmarked certain groups based on preconceived
biases and was incorporated into an all-encompassing drive to purify the
socionational body. Any potential restraints on how the exterminatory
campaign against the nationalists were neutralized by the appeal to higher
loyalties. Brutalities were committed as the ultimate expression of loyalty
to the socialist drive and its administrative embodiments: the Communist
Party and the Soviet Ukrainian nation.[147]

On the battlefield, therefore, the campaign against this alien body assumed an exterminatory character. Between February 1944 and March

---

[145] Milovan Djilas, "Christ and the Commissar," 207.

[146] Milovan Djilas, *Wartime* (New York: Harcourt, Brace, Jovanovich, 1977), 164–65;
Djilas, "Christ and the Commissar," 203–8.

[147] See Alexander Alvarez, "Adjusting to Genocide: The Techniques of Neutralization and
the Holocaust," *Social Science History* 21, no. 2 (summer 1997): 139–78, esp. 152–53. For
suggestive observations on the analogous Nazi understanding and practice of violence, see
Omer Bartov, *The Eastern Front, 1941–1945: German Troops and the Barbarisation of Warfare* (New York: St. Martin's, 1986); Bartov, *Hitler's Army: Soldiers, Nazis, and War in the
Third Reich* (New York: Oxford University Press, 1991); and notably in areas not subjected
to the anti–Bolshevik-Slavic crusade, see Mark Mazower, "Military Violence and National
Socialist Values: The Wehrmacht in Greece, 1941–1944," *Past and Present* 134 (February
1992): 129–58; Mazower, *Inside Hitler's Greece: The Experience of Occupation, 1941–1944*
(New Haven: Yale University Press, 1993).

1945 alone the NKVD claimed to have killed in battles no fewer than 81,520 guerrillas and arrested another 83,367. By 1 January 1946 the figures rose to 103,313 nationalists killed and 110,785 arrested. By May of that year the number of nationalists killed climbed to 110,835 (114,706 by January 1947) and those detained to 250,676—this within a territory inhabited by fewer than nine million ethnic Ukrainians. Notably Soviet casualties between February 1944 and May 1946 numbered 14,128 killed or missing in action.[148] Concentrated sweep operations accounted for the vast accrual of deaths. In one such operation between 10 January and 23 February 1945 more than 11,000 nationalists were killed and 26,000 were arrested.[149] Simultaneously, deportations assumed colossal magnitude. In the thirteen years between the annexation of western Ukraine and Stalin's death, some 570,826 people were deported from the Soviet Ukrainian Republic without permission to return, of whom 328,011 were sent to special settlements.[150] A close look at the deportation figures, however, highlighted the exterminatory character of the antinationalist campaign in the field. Between February 1944 and January 1946 the NKVD claimed to have detained 110,785 bandits (50,058 were convicted), but only 8,370 people were arrested as OUN members and 15,959 as active insurgents. The 182,543 nationalists deported from the seven western regions between 1944 and 1952 included family members of the OUN and the UPA and their supporters, nonadults, and families of those killed in clashes. Simply put, most of the active nationalist guerrillas were killed on the battlefield.[151]

In Vinnytsia this practice had already become a defining aspect of the battle scene since the early days of the war. When the Vinnytsia party leaders began to chronicle their wartime experiences, any reference to the practice of "take no prisoners" was made in the most casual manner. In an interview with members of the Commission for the Compilation of the Chronicles of the Great Patriotic War, Anatol' Kondratiuk, the commander of the Stalin Partisan Brigade, recalled that during the first days of the war his battalion consisted solely of western Ukrainians and people who worked in western Ukraine. "There were many nationalists. On the road we executed many. We shot those who refused to go to war," Kon-

[148] GARF, f. 9478, op. 1, d. 349, ll. 1, 5, 9; d.764, l.1; TsDAHOU, f. 1, op. 23, d. 2967, l. 25. Ivan Bilas, *Represyvno-karal'na systema v Ukraini, 1917–1953* (Kiev: Lybid, Viisko Ukrainy, 1994), 1:181.

[149] TsDAHOU, f. 1, op. 23, d. 3872, l. 37. See also the report of the Central Committee's November plenum (ibid., op. 1, d. 664, ll. 195–204).

[150] Nikolai Bugai, *L. Beriia-I. Stalinu*, 6, 212.

[151] Quite tellingly people who were categorized as kulaks along with their family members accounted for merely 12,135 of the 203,662 individuals deported during an intense collectivization drive in the western provinces (Bilas, *Represyvno-karal'na systema*, 181; Ihor Vynnychenko, *Ukraina 1920–1980-kh*, 82; and GARF, f. 7523, op. 109, d. 195, l. 49).

dratiuk calmly recalled.[152] Referring to the relations with Vlasovite forces, the commissar of the same brigade related that "some of the Vlasovites came to us, but they were all shot since there was no trust in the Vlasovites. The people demanded to execute them. We did not take prisoners as a rule. If we did take prisoners, we shot them after a preliminary interrogation."[153] In the same vein, a smaller detachment that operated in the Bar district claimed to have executed the sixteen nationalist guerrillas it captured following an armed clash.[154]

The return of Soviet power to the region and the resurfacing underground forces turned extermination into a policy. The intentional escalation was constantly driven home to the party ranks in the region. It was poignantly captured in an exchange in May 1944 between Havrylo Mishchenko, the first secretary of the Vinnytsia obkom, and Nikita Khrushchev.

> *Mishchenko*: Regarding grain delivery. By the twentieth we fulfilled 69.1 percent [of the requirement]. True enough, there is bread in nine of our districts, but the Banderites cause problems.
> *Khrushchev*: We ought to cause them problems. Watch out that they won't smoke you out of Vinnytsia.
> *Mishchenko*: Nikita Sergeevich, they won't smoke us out, but they can cause problems.
> *Khrushchev*: How many Banderites are there in Vinnytsia? There are not any Banderites there. Surely you borrowed them from Ilf and Petrov. (*laughter*) Where are Banderites? You don't have any. How many did you kill?
> *Mishchenko*: We killed a total of eight and captured sixteen.
> *Khrushchev*: And they hold up the region? (*laughter*)
> *Mishchenko*: Not over the whole region but over individual districts.
> *Khrushchev*: That is simply a disgrace. Don't tell that to anyone; they will laugh. What would you say about the Germans if eight Banderites can tie your hands?[155]

Eight bodies were not enough, and sixteen prisoners were too many. The present situation was deemed unacceptable, and the solution entailed concentrated brutalization of the fight against the nationalists. The message was not lost on Mishchenko and the Vinnytsia leadership. When commanders of the military units of NKVD Ukraine summed up the results of a sweep operation of three battalions against nationalist insurgents in Vinnytsia between 25 May and 30 June 1944, no fewer than 141 nationalists were killed and 42 captured, roughly estimated as two-thirds of active

[152] IIAN ORF, f. 2, op. 9, d. 1, l. 1.
[153] Ibid., d. 3, l. 5.
[154] TsDAHOU, f. 1, op. 22, d. 166, l. 20.
[155] Ibid., op. 1, d. 652, ll. 86–87.

Figure 3.3. The grave at Lityn's central square of an NKVD officer who was killed in a skirmish with a Ukrainian nationalist unit in the region in June 1944.

nationalists in the three districts where they were concentrated. NKVD losses totaled just 7 killed and 7 wounded (Figure 3.3).[156] However, the numerous reports on individual clashes with nationalist forces substantiate the impression that on the battlefield this was a war with no prisoners. In early May 1944 the NKVD pursued the liquidation of the largest nationalist band in the region, which was reported to have 138 fighters at the time. On 6 May 1944 the NKVD forces in the Khmil'nyk district succeeded in initiating contact with a large segment of the detachment. Following a two-and-a-half-hour battle, no fewer than 67 nationalist guerrillas were killed, the 20 wounded managed to escape to the forests, and only 1 individual was taken prisoner.[157] In another large clash with a nationalist force estimated at 50 men on 9 June 1944, 14 rebels were killed, but no prisoners were taken and no Soviet casualties were reported.[158]

---

[156] TsAVVMVDRF, f. 488, op. 1, d. 51, ll. 14, 16.

[157] Notably the NKVD forces suffered only two deaths and five wounded. The total arms captured from the eighty-eight men of the nationalist detachment was just twenty rifles, four machine guns, twenty hand grenades, and five horses (ASBUVO, d. 26674, ll. 37, 46, 51; and TsAVVMVDRF, f. 488, op. 1, d. 51, l. 10).

[158] TsAVVMVDRF, f. 488, op. 1, d. 51, l. 11. At this point, previous coordination with nationalist forces in the face of the common German threat had already been put to rest by both sides. According to intelligence reports of the Lenin Mounted Brigade the mood of the rank-and-file nationalists who arrived in Vinnytsia (about 510 armed people) was un-

Accordingly the public hanging of captured nationalist guerrillas became a didactic spectacle. Quite likely the ritual of hanging was intended to add an element of humiliation and terror, since the Soviet Criminal Code spoke only of shooting (*rasstrel*) as the exceptional measure of punishment for extremely serious crimes. Already in July 1943 eight Soviet citizens, convicted of collaboration, were hanged in the city square of Krasnodar in front of thirty thousand people, and newsreels of the trial and the hanging were shown in local cinemas.[159]

In Ukraine the ever brutish Khrushchev did not mince words regarding the need for this public ritual. In a letter to Stalin on 15 November 1944 Khrushchev proposed the formation of NKVD field courts-martial with special mandates. "To terrorize the bandits we should not shoot those condemned to execution by the field courts-martial, but hang them. The courts-martial must be conducted openly, with the local population in attendance," suggested Khrushchev.[160] Needless to say, in the localities where public hangings of suspected collaborators had already become commonplace, there were enough enthusiasts to undertake such an initiative.

---

compromising and utterly hostile to the Soviets. Following a barrage of protests against negotiating with the Red partisans, the nationalist commander was forced to apologize to his troops and to vow that from then on he would limit his contacts with the Red partisans to the battlefield (TsDAHOU, f. 128, op. 1, d. 5, l. 24). As noted earlier, nationalist commanders seemed convinced that "the population [wished] that the NKVD [would]be met with machine guns and resistance everywhere," and, accordingly, NKVD personnel who were taken prisoners were executed by nationalist forces in common with the NKVD practice, regardless of the sex of the condemned. See the interrogation of Il'ia Tkachuk, July 12, 1944 (TsAVVMVDRF, f. 488, op. 1, d. 51, ll. 32–33).

[159] See Article 21 of the 1926 Soviet Criminal Code, which remained in force until 1960 (with the exception of 1947–50 when the death penalty was abolished) (*The Russian Penal Code of the Russian Socialist Federal Soviet Republic* [London: Foreign Office, 1934], 10). Boris Levytsky claimed that in April 1945 the Presidium of the Supreme Soviet of the USSR decreed death by hanging as a deterrent to spies, deserters, and saboteurs. Levytsky, however, did not support this claim with any document (Boris Levytsky, *The Uses of Terror: The Soviet Secret Police 1917–1970* [New York: Coward, McCann, and Geoghegan, 1972], 167). Still, it seems that hanging was practiced not only in summary trials on the battlefield but also in more formal procedures against collaborators. For the Krasnodar hanging, see *Pravda*, 19 July 1943; and Aryeh Kochavi, *Prelude to Nuremberg: Allied War Crimes Policy and the Question of Punishment* (Chapel Hill: The University of North Carolina Press, 1998), 64–65. General Andrei Vlasov and his close associates were allegedly executed in this manner in Moscow after being convicted of treason and collaboration with the Germans. The same applied to captured émigré Cossack leaders (Catherine Andreyev, *Vlasov and the Russian Liberation Movement* [Cambridge: Cambridge University Press, 1987], 79); *Istochnik* 4 (1997): 135.

[160] Iurii Shapoval, "The Ukrainian Years, 1894–1949," in William Taubman, Sergei Khrushchev, and Abbot Gleason, eds., *Nikita Khrushchev* (New Haven: Yale University Press, 2000), 37–38. For visual documentation of these summary trials and public hangings, see

On 21 December 1944 the raikom secretary of Morochne district in the neighboring region of Rivne was reported to have conducted a meeting with the peasants of Zaliznytsia, where two OUN members were captured by the local NKVD operational group. The secretary told the peasants in advance that the nationalists would be hanged, and then organized a summary trial at which he served as prosecutor. After the sentencing the two nationalists were hanged in the village square.[161]

Incidentally, as the clashes continued, summary executions of suspects, regardless of established guilt, became a pattern in the fight against nationalists and probably a significant contribution to the growing list of the dead. In 1947, according to the MGB's own review, scores of people were interrogated for alleged nationalist activity, and their execution was falsely presented as "liquidation of armed groups of bandits."[162] By this time the execution of nationalist guerrillas and sympathizers had already become the rule.

Public executions of collaborators was something to brag about when party officials recorded their recent experience in the partisans' ranks. Vasyl' Nyzhnyk, the commissar of the Lenin Mounted Brigade, who was about to resume his post as an obkom secretary, was anything but reserved in his account of his wartime experience. His concluding report on the activity of the brigade openly celebrated the brutality. "According to the population," wrote Nyzhnyk, "the *starosta* of the village of Brytavka was wholeheartedly devoted to the German-Romanian power, mercilessly beat up the population, made a fortune out of plunder, and betrayed four paratroopers from the Second Ukrainian Front for four hundred marks. The command of the detachment ordered the special department to verify all the information and to hang the *starosta* at the central square of the village and attach a sign reading "TRAITOR." And so it was done."[163] Similarly, in the village of Demivka, the counterintelligence of the detachment arrested all the German-Romanian protégés. "Under investigation, they confessed to their crimes. At the request of the population and the decision of the command, 6 people were shot and 1 was hanged at the center of the village," reported Vladimirov and Nyzhnyk. In the same spirit, the brigade executed 56 prisoners from a Cossack regiment in the same village. During a raid into occupied Vinnytsia, the special department of the brigade shot and hanged a total of 84 people who were categorized as spies, nationalists, policemen, Vlasovites, and other counterrevolutionary elements.

---

the documentary *Russia's War: Blood upon the Snow* (IBP Films, 1995/PBS Home Videos, 1997), vol. 3.

[161] TsDAHOU, f. 1, op. 23, d. 1361, ll. 9–10.

[162] TsDAHOU, f. 1, op. 23, d. 4980, l. 154.

[163] Ibid., f. 128, op. 1, d. 1, ll. 41–42.

Overall, wrote Vladimirov and Nyzhnyk, the brigade executed 61 *starosty*, 182 policemen, and 582 other traitors.[164] There seemed to be no mitigating factors in punishing presumed collaborators. The Romanian-appointed *starosta* of the village of Nova Pryluka, who was even associated with the Soviet partisans and helped to rescue a young Jewish girl, was nevertheless executed.[165]

Once again, a comparison with other countries is telling. Estimates for the Netherlands were 3 or 4 deaths on the occasion of arrests and 40 deaths in the internment camps caused by resistance members acting as guards. In the significantly more violent Belgium, there were about forty extrajudicial executions.[166] Meanwhile, in the USSR, the special department of the Lenin Mounted Brigade, which operated briefly in the Vinnytsia region, was reported to have executed, often in public, no fewer than 825 collaborators. If the figures provided by the brigade's leaders are taken at face value, then the number of people executed by a single partisan brigade, not necessarily the largest one but one operating within a rather small region in Ukraine, amounted to 13.7 percent of the total number of summary executions before and during the liberation of France and 233 percent of those in Belgium.[167]

Finally, violence was exercised primarily for political rather than military reasons. Soviet authorities made extensive use of the destruction battalions while professing the negligible military value of these auxiliary troops in the pre-1939 Soviet territories. The value of these battalions, noted the deputy head of the Ukrainian NKVD, was the radicalization and proliferation of violence among the population at large, a key consideration in the Soviet Manichean worldview.[168]

---

[164] Ibid., l. 128.

[165] Another person in this village who served as a policeman and betrayed his Jewish friends was executed after the liberation (testimony of Elizaveta Borisovna Viner, Yad Vashem Archive, #03–4740, p. 6).

[166] Evidence gathered from personal communication with Luc Huyse. At present, there are still no official figures for the two countries.

[167] Marcel Baudot's careful study of summary executions in France arrived at a total of 6,029 people executed until the liberation in November 1944. Another 1,259 summary executions were carried out afterward when the jurisdiction of a legal purge went into full effect (cited in Henry Rousso, "L'épuration en France. Une histoire inachevée," *Vingtième siècle: Revue d'histoire* 33 [March 1992]: 82–83). For earlier and slightly higher estimates, see Peter Novick, *The Resistance versus Vichy: The Purge of Collaborators in Liberated France* (New York: Columbia University Press, 1968), 60–78, 202–8. In Belgium, according to a German account, some 353 executions of people in the German service, police, and fascist organizations were carried out between August 1942 and June 1944. After the war, partisans claimed to have executed about 1,100 collaborators (Etienne Verhoeyen, *België bezet, 1940–1945* [Brussels: BRTN, 1993], 416–22).

[168] TsDAHOU, f. 1, op. 1, d. 664, ll. 201–3.

And so, in spite of their professed uselessness, the battalions mushroomed in Vinnytsia. Thousands of locals were recruited and immediately engaged in bloody confrontations with nationalist forces. In 1944 some 46 battalions were operating in Vinnytsia, consisting of 3,436 people, of whom only 852 were party and Komsomol members. The battalions were assisted by 1,145 small auxiliary groups (*dopomizhni hrupy*), made up of 9,612 people, that helped to isolate individual enemy soldiers and deliver them to the NKVD. Over the course of nine months the Vinnytsia battalions captured 21 German paratroopers, 121 Ukrainian guerrillas, 239 collaborators, 1,550 deserters from the Red Army, and scores of escaping POWs.[169]

The concentration of Red Army veterans and partisans in the battalions' command guaranteed the escalation of the struggle. The notion of a unique blood feud between Soviet and nationalist partisans, which marked their recent wartime past, had now been extrapolated to the postwar scene. On the pages of the Republic's main newspaper, Vasyl' Behma, the first secretary of the Rivne obkom and a former partisan leader, pointed to the treacherous back-stabbing practices of the UPA by citing an order of a certain UPA commander to his troops to let the Red Army units cross the region and attack the isolated units of NKVD and Communist partisans.[170] The implications of such conduct were self-evident.

By the end of 1945 the fruits of the intense extermination drive were already evident. Numerous surveys indicated a qualitative and quantitative decline in nationalist activity in the region. During the third quarter of 1945 the military tribunals handed down 309 verdicts classified as "special jurisdiction," of which only 18 concerned nationalist activity. The majority of those charged were school directors and teachers who belonged to the nationalist educational organization *Prosvita*. The social profile of the accused could only be a source of satisfaction for the Soviet authorities. The high profile of the intelligentsia only highlighted the virtual absence of peasantry from the nationalist social pool. Whereas the politically sensitive position of these people—the education of the Soviet youth—could not be glossed over, it underscored the failure of the nationalists to expand their base of support among the peasantry, the embodiment of the Ukrainian nation.[171]

Similarly the campaign's imprint was evident in the regional profile of the hard-core guerrillas. Whereas the majority of guerrillas taken prisoner in the course of the sweep operation in May–June 1944 were locals, none

---

[169] Ibid., op. 23, d. 953, ll. 201–3.

[170] Vasyl' Behma, "Zakliatye vragi Ukrainskogo naroda," *Pravda Ukrainy,* 15 November 1944.

[171] PAVO, f. 136, op. 13, d. 48, l. 48.

of the twenty-one guerrillas captured by the NKVD between December 1944 and May 1945 came from Vinnytsia. Most of them came from two villages in the Ostroh district in the western region of Rivne.[172] When a group of three men was tracked down in the Teplyk district in March 1948 carrying nationalist literature addressed to local teachers, all three were identified as western Ukrainians.[173]

Increasingly the Vinnytsia landscape was cleared of nationalist activity. By late 1947 the nationalist armed struggle was confined to sporadic attempts on the lives of Soviet officials in the countryside. Six chairmen of kolkhozes and rural soviets were killed in various districts during that year, but, tellingly, the MGB formed ad-hoc detachments to liquidate the bands. By that time, standing MGB units and extermination battalions were no longer perceived as necessary.[174] Accordingly nationalist activity was being marginalized in official surveys of anti-Soviet activity. Of the 363 people arrested for hostile activity in Vinnytsia throughout 1947, only 43 were identified as members of the UPA or the OUN.[175] A survey of "anti-Soviet activity in the villages of the eastern regions of Ukraine" in mid-October 1947 underlined the numerical decline in nationalist activity. Of the 668 people who were arrested for anti-Soviet activity between 20 September and 10 October of that year, only 48 were categorized as Ukrainian nationalists.[176] Nationalist presence was still felt but in a somewhat unexpected form. Mykhailo Kucher, a twenty-six-year-old Komsomol member, was arrested for systematically writing anonymous letters to kolkhozniks in which he demanded food and money for an active nationalist group. "You well know," wrote Kucher, "that there is a special group of people who fight for an independent 'sovereign Ukraine.' You have to provide us with the food we now need. . . If you tell it to anyone, you will be punished mercilessly and your property will be set on fire."[177] Just two years after it reached its climax in the region, the nationalist struggle was up for grabs to petty criminals. Nationalist leaflets in the villages became ever more rare and desperate. One from August 1947 in the village of Tartak in the Chernivtsi district addressed the least likely audience of all, the Red Army servicemen: "Soldiers, Commanders of the Red Army! Stalin is the greatest enemy of the people. After Hitler it's Stalin's

---

[172] TsAVVMVDRF, f. 488, op. 1, d. 51, ll. 19–21; TsDAHOU, f. 1, op. 23, d. 1707, ll. 2–5.

[173] TsDAHOU, f. 1, op. 23, d. 5041, l. 22.

[174] Ibid., op. 46, d. 2285, ll. 187–89; PAVO, f. 136, op. 13, d. 134, ll. 22–24.

[175] PAVO, f. 136, op. 13, d. 134, l. 20.

[176] Most of the charges involved agitation against grain collection and attacks on Soviet officials in the wake of the recent famine (TsDAHOU, f. 1, op. 23, d. 4978, ll. 25–54; here, l. 29).

[177] Ibid., ll. 45–46.

time! Long live the will of the nations and people!"[178] Another leaflet that was posted in Iaryshiv on 26 April 1948 contained threats on the lives of individual Soviet activists, who allegedly oppressed the people during 1948, and was curiously signed by a "Heil Hitler" salute in the German language.[179]

At the March 1948 plenum of the obkom Mykhailo Stakhurs'kyi summed up the nationalist saga in the region, even as he referred to some spotted renewed activity in a single district:

> At one time OUN bands multiplied in our region. There were not so many of them, but they were not confronted. They went on unpunished in the districts of Haisyn, Khmil'nyk, Dashiv, and Lityn. In its own time the obkom bureau instructed the punitive organs to liquidate these bands, but they essentially did nothing. Once again it was time to address the issue to beat the culprits actively. All the bands were liquidated immediately.[180]

At the Eighth Conference of the Regional Party organization, in January 1949, the delegates were informed that with the exception of a single nationalist band in the Ulaniv district, the region was purged of nationalist guerrillas. During 1948 several groups were liquidated, such as the one in Haisyn that consisted of eleven members and was destroyed in September 1948.[181] In April 1949 the last major nationalist band of forty-one local members and active supporters was destroyed. The unit operated extensively for two years on the territory of three eastern oblasts. The Ministry of Internal Affairs (MVD) acknowledged the ideological motivation behind the band's activity, which indeed targeted party and Soviet activists.[182] But the random violence and the forced practice of living off the land, namely, robbing the kolkhozes, only punctuated the nationalists' desperate situation in the region. When the band took over a Soviet political gathering in the Zhytomyr region in early January 1949, the daring demonstration culminated in the killing of one of the participants who had tried to escape. In the intimate environment of the village, where family ties often reigned and cut across ideological divisions, random killings were not likely to secure political gains.[183]

---

[178] PAVO, f. 136, op. 13, d. 134, l. 14.

[179] DAVO, f. 2700, op. 7c, d. 132, l. 44.

[180] PAVO, f. 136, op. 12, d. 828, l. 155.

[181] Ibid., op. 29, d. 1, ll. 192–93.

[182] "We terrorized the population, threatening with execution those who attempted to inform on us. [But] we never touched rank-and-file kolkhozniks and systematically terrorized Soviet rural activists," the deputy commander told the MVD interrogators (PAVO, f. 136, op. 29, d. 185, l. 21).

[183] Ibid., ll. 19–22.

The latest reference to armed nationalist activity in the region concerned the implementation of a resolution of the obkom bureau of 7 June 1949, calling for the liquidation of political and criminal bands in the region. But three weeks later, when the MGB reported the liquidation of several small bands, their activity was not even classified as nationalist. According to the MGB, the bands engaged in systematic robberies rather than in nationalist agitation. The only reference to the nationalist character of a band that killed two party members was the contacts that one of its members had with active nationalists during the German occupation of the region. Only one individual was arrested on charges of membership in the OUN.[184]

Five years after the return of Soviet power the last vestiges of militant Ukrainian nationalism in Vinnytsia were eradicated. However, the purification of the Soviet Ukrainian nation from the contamination of wartime collaboration and nationalism was not merely a military exercise. Their excision was the cornerstone in the shaping of this ethnic community, by then already institutionalized and irreversible.

Irredeemability

As summary executions of presumed collaborators proliferated in the initial stage of liberation of the region, the returning Soviet power moved quickly to curtail this phenomenon. Random retributions that often bordered on anarchy were not merely a threat to state authority; for the latter, revenge was not necessarily the main motivation. The exercise of retribution only by Soviet power integrated it into the overall purification drive, which by now engulfed every layer of the polity. The return of the regime as the sole arbiter and executor of revenge meant that the purge would be conducted along lines that could hardly be imagined in a random, popularly initiated purge. But it certainly could build on and even cultivate the pervasive vengeful atmosphere following the German occupation. As Alexander Werth already noted with the liberation of Kharkiv in February 1943, no time was wasted in enacting the state-based purge.

> I saw two large letter boxes marked UNKVD—the Ukrainian Security Police—
> into which people were invited to drop denunciations and other relevant infor-
> mation. Here was scope for ugly vendettas. And at the former Gestapo prison,

---

[184] Bened Kolos, a forty-seven year old from the Pïyskiv district, was recruited to the OUN in October 1941. Kolos was accused of systematic nationalist agitation during the war, recruitment of villagers to the OUN, and participation in recruitment to forced labor in the Reich in his capacity as *starosta*. The MGB also cited individual OUN activists who were in hiding but whose identity was known (ibid., ll. 76–78, 81).

now burned out, I could see civilian prisoners being escorted into the basement for questioning by the NKVD.[185]

Extrajudicial justice operates as a cathartic moment, after which exhaustion, the desire to forget the imperfect past, and the impulse to reinstate a certain equilibrium combine to extinguish the flames of arbitrary acts. This, however, was not to happen. The transfer of the prosecution of alleged wartime collaborators and bystanders to the jurisdiction of the NKVD military tribunals signaled that the purge would become a permanent phenomenon in the political and social life of the liberated region. The report on the work of the NKVD Regional Military Court in Vinnytsia for the third quarter of 1945 cited that of the 309 verdicts it handed down during this period twenty-five concerned collective cases of former village elders and policemen.

Beyond that, the state absorption of punishment entailed several lasting principles. First, it ruled out the possibility of a complete rehabilitation even through the so-called baptism by fire. "Many of the cases involve traitors against the motherland," reported the chairman of the military tribunal, "who, during the initial days of the liberation of the Vinnytsia region, were enrolled into the Red Army ranks. Finding themselves at the front, they were wounded and in some cases received governmental awards. Whereas this situation did not change the essence of the case, it undoubtedly influenced the judicial repression of individuals who had returned from the front and were charged with criminal responsibility for the crimes they committed during the occupation."[186] One of those was Prokip Rybak, who betrayed two Soviet officials to the gendarmerie in August 1941. As a result, one of the officials was executed and the other beaten. After the Red Army returned, Rybak was drafted, served at the front, and was severely wounded. Rybak's life was spared, but he was sentenced nevertheless to ten years in prison, a light sentence according to the official NKVD report.[187]

The irreversibility of any form of collaboration was further underlined by the absolute denial of political or social rehabilitation, even in the face of a dire need for experienced personnel, a policy that set the Soviet Union further apart from other European countries that had been occupied by the Germans. In France the willingness of large segments of the population

---

[185] Werth, *Russia at War*, 617. An émigré informant, who had witnessed the Soviet return to Vinnytsia and Kharkiv, contended that by that time there was no sympathy left for the Germans. The mayor, policemen, and even cleaning women who worked for the Germans were shot. In Kharkiv, claimed this source, sixty thousand orders for arrest were issued (HURIP #542, 5).

[186] PAVO, f. 136, op. 13, d. 48, l. 48.

[187] Ibid., l. 53.

to accept certain acts of collaboration as legitimate, albeit undesirable, efforts to survive was taken by the authorities as a mandate for mass amnesty. In the Soviet Union, in contrast, the presence of similar sentiments worked to solidify the regime's resolve to excise collaborators, regardless of circumstances and the need for their services.[188] And unlike France, there was no political or social redemption for people known to have served under the occupation authorities.[189] There, noted Soviet commentators, the replenishment of the state and military apparatus with former Vichyites amounted to a conscious blurring of the distinction between victims and victimizers (Figure 3.4).[190] Nor could the stain of collaboration be removed by postwar performance. Soviet authorities continued to exact revenge on those suspected of collaboration with the occupiers down to the bottom of the social ladder. Professional and bureaucratic skills counted for nothing even in the face of severe shortages. Hence, on 13 October 1948, to cite one example, the MGB presented the obkom with a list of several dozen kolkhozniks and rural experts who had been recommended for governmental awards for their achievements in the 1947 harvest. Many of these people, argued the regional MGB chief, did not deserve the award because of their spotty wartime conduct. Some of these unworthy people served actively during the occupation period as policemen or as *starosty*, or they volunteered for work in Germany. Others were denied the award on the basis of passivity in the struggle against the occupiers. Petro Kushnir, a kolkhoz chairman from the village of Ivanivtsi, was recommended for

---

[188] Following President Vincent Auriol's call for national reconciliation in May 1949, opinion polls showed that 60 percent of the population supported a reconciliation bill. Several consecutive laws in 1951 and 1953 practically allowed for amnesty of the majority of convicts and the release of most detainees. Hence, in Belgium, by 1950 there were only 6,115 collaborators in prison (23.5 percent of the total number convicted), 6,715 in France (27.6 percent), and about 3,000 in the Netherlands (8.9 percent). By 1955 the numbers were 487 (1.9 percent) for Belgium, 424 (1.7 percent) for France, and 365 (1.1 percent) for the Netherlands (Huyse, "La reintegrazione dei collaborazionisti," 121).

[189] On the impressive comeback of Vichy officials, including the highest governmental offices, and the profound continuities in personnel and administrative patterns in postwar France, see Bertram Gordon, "Afterward: Who Were the Guilty and Should They Be Tried?" in Richard Golsan, ed., *Memory, the Holocaust, and French Justice: The Bousquet and Touvier Affairs* (Hanover, N.H.: University Press of New England, 1996), 179–98; Robert O. Paxton, *Vichy France: Old Guard and New Order, 1940–1944* (New York: Knopf, 1972), 330–57; and Philip M. Williams, *Crisis and Compromise: Politics in the Fourth Republic* (London: Longmans, Green, 1958).

[190] *New Times* (Moscow) 49 (3 December 1952): 19–20; *Izvestiia*, 7 December 1952. The contamination of postwar France was completed by allegations of forced recruitment of tens of thousands of German prisoners of war into the Foreign Legion, which was a conscious state act. Such an act was in line with the alleged release from prison of hundreds of "SS cutthroats" in the Federal German Republic and their draft into the new German army (*Izvestiia*, 22 and 28 January 1949; and *Pravda* 27 December 1952).

Figure 3.4. French Justice. Soviet mockery of the lenient treatment of wartime collaborators by the French government. Caption beneath reads: "Gentlemen, the bench is at your disposal. So, you are excused . . ." *Krokodil*, 30 January 1953.

the order of Hero of Socialist Labor. But during the war, argued the MGB, Kushnir refrained from enrollment into a partisan detachment despite being offered to do so by the commander of the detachment.[191] He was therefore rejected.

Crimes were attributed to a biological trait when the definition of irredeemable sins was extended to include collaborators' blood relatives, as was the rule with those marked as "enemies of the people." Scores of individuals were denied awards merely for being related to people who served as policemen or were in the Vlasov army. Among those were Anna Mel'nyk, whose father served with the Vlasov forces. Mel'nyk was denied the medal "For Labor Valor," as was Musii Bondar, whose brother worked for the occupation police.[192] Sons, it turned out, could be responsible for their fathers.

Another feature in the statization of punishment was the return to the core principle of individual occurrence and accountability. The bureau-

[191] DAVO, f. 2700, op. 7c, d. 136, l. 58.
[192] Ibid., l. 52.

cratic aspect of this feature could not be underestimated. The attempt to avoid collective guilt and punishment both helped to control the purge process and to establish its credibility. This proved to be difficult. The pervasive atmosphere of revenge, which the returning power so helped to cultivate, threatened to bring down the orderly process of verification. As Werth noted in early 1943, this was an invitation for a rumor mill, where denunciations settled personal vendettas. Volodymyr Prybeha, a kolkhoz chairman, was accused of membership in the nationalist organization OUN. The accuser was Aleksandrov, the chairman of the village soviet. The investigation that followed Prybeha's denial discovered that the source of this severe charge was quite mundane. Both Prybeha and Aleksandrov were in the same partisan detachment. On discharge, Aleksandrov took a horse which he sold, keeping the money for himself. Prybeha, in his capacity as kolkhoz chairman, demanded that the horse be returned to the kolkhoz and reported the illegal sale to the raikom. In turn, Aleksandrov, in his capacity as chairman of the village soviet, retaliated by evicting Prybeha's family from their apartment.[193] The case was returned for a further inquiry. Such a case, according to the chairman of the tribunal, was only one of many.[194]

The military tribunals often reversed the rulings of the lower courts or returned cases for further investigation that were found to be based on unverified rumors or exaggerated accusations. The tribunal returned for a second such inquiry into the charges against Ol'ha Kosyns'ka, who was accused of being a Gestapo informer while she was in forced labor in Germany. Kosyns'ka allegedly informed on other Soviet workers who engaged in anti-German activity. Since Kosyns'ka repudiated the charges in court and there was no other supporting evidence, the case was returned for further investigation.[195]

Nor was the charge of active collaboration applied en masse. In general, the number of those arrested and deported from Ukraine on charges of active collaboration was relatively low. In accordance with MVD directive no. 97 of 20 April 1946, "Concerning Former Policemen, Vlasovites, and Other Persons Who Served in German Uniformed Formations," some 4,216 people were deported from Ukraine to the GULAG by 20 May

[193] PAVO, f. 136, op. 13, d. 102, ll. 95b, 111–12.

[194] A similar case involved Ivan Rymar', who was charged with nationalist agitation and tormenting kolkhozniks during the occupation. The investigators not only failed to provide any concrete evidence but found evidence to the contrary. Rymar' apparently killed two Germans who scoffed at the villagers. As a result he was subjected to repression, and his house was burned down. At least some of Rymar's fellow peasants were not impressed by his wartime conduct. The case was returned for further investigation. See PAVO, f. 136, op. 13, d. 102, l. 94.

[195] Ibid., l. 16.

1948. Sixty-six such people were deported from Vinnytsia, all in 1946–47.[196] Of the 361 who were tried by the regional military tribunal of the NKVD in Vinnytsia during the third quarter of 1945, 8 were sentenced to death; of these sentences, only 3 were approved by the Supreme Soviet of the Republic. Similarly entire groups found to be falsely accused of membership in the UPA were acquitted.[197]

But purification continued relentlessly. And as European legislators were feverishly passing amnesty laws for convicted wartime collaborators, in the Soviet Union the search for and prosecution of alleged collaborators intensified. Throughout 1946 the MVD's military tribunal in the Vinnytsia region dealt with 704 cases, all falling under the category of "special jurisdiction." This category applied to those who served as *starosty* under the occupying rural administration, policemen, traitors against the motherland, and collaborators. Of the people in this category, 13 were sentenced to death, 186 to hard labor, and the rest to imprisonment for up to ten years; 340 verdicts were approved, and in 49 cases the prison term was reduced. However, none of the verdicts was considered too light.[198] Between 20 September and 10 October 1947 alone, 326 people were arrested in the eastern regions of Ukraine on charges of collaboration with the German occupation authorities, making them the single largest group of the 668 people who fell under the category of those involved in "anti-Soviet activity."[199] On 29 December 1949 the All-Union MGB circulated a list of ninety-nine individuals who were still on the loose. Five of them had recently deserted the Soviet Army and apparently had defected to the West; another thirty-seven had been jailed during the Terror of the late 1930s, had been released after the war, and then vanished without leaving a trace. The remaining fifty-seven on the list were sought for active collaboration with the German and Romanian occupiers, ranging from service in the SS and death camps to participation in the execution of Jews and Soviet citizens and in anti-partisan operations. The list was not for show only. When one of the men listed, Bronyslav Haida, was exposed during a trial in the United States in 1997 as an SS volunteer in Treblinka, Cracow, and Chenstokhova, the list was presented as supporting evidence.[200]

The 1955 amnesty decree of wartime collaborators excluded those convicted of the murder and torture of Soviet citizens, a rather fatal exception.

---

[196] Notably other eastern Ukrainian regions such as Luhans'k, Poltava, and Stalino accounted for 606, 524, and 507, respectively (Vynnychenko, *Ukraina 1920–1980-kh*, 63–64).

[197] At the same time, 120 were sentenced to hard labor and 233 to imprisonment (PAVO, f. 136, op. 13, d. 48, ll. 52–54).

[198] Ibid., d. 102, ll. 107–8.

[199] TsDAHOU, f. 1, op. 23, d. 4978, ll. 25–54; here, l. 29.

[200] "Orientirovka po rozysku no. 4/87," 29 December 1949, Arkhiv upravlinnia sluzhby bezpeky Ukrainy, Kiev (AUSBU), d. 19, ll. 207–22.

Whereas in France all those convicted of participating in the massacre at Oradour-sur-Glane, the single largest wartime massacre of a non-Jewish population, were released from prison by 1958, the Soviet regime continued to prosecute and execute similar cases well into the 1980s. At least one trial took place in Vinnytsia in the spring of 1961, where Emanuil Shul'ts (a.k.a. Vertogradov) and several others were accused of serving as guards in the Treblinka death camp. Notably one of the accused, Samiilo Pryshch, had already been sentenced to twenty-five years in 1950 for treason but managed to conceal his service in Treblinka. He was released under the 1955 amnesty but was arrested again when this aspect of his wartime record came to light.[201] As late as December 1984 a military tribunal sentenced to death individuals guilty of killing Soviet POWs, activists, Jews, and Communist partisans.[202]

Along with the revival of capital punishment for political crimes, the irredeemability of the Ukrainian nationalists was codified on 6 April 1950 by order no. 1398–508ss of the Council of Ministers of the USSR. This directive replaced shorter deportation terms for those exiled from Ukraine between 1944 and 1949 with permanent exile (*navechno*), most notably the 182,543 members and supporters of the OUN and UPA as well as their families.[203] By 1950 Ukrainian nationalists appeared beyond hope, and their exclusion from the Ukrainian body national was meant to be permanent. Accordingly families of nationalist activists who had either been arrested or killed were themselves deported. That their family members had been killed was not necessarily redemptive.[204] Thus the political-ideological movement finally joined the exclusive pantheon of irredeemable enemies, whose membership was limited to nationalities deported during and after the war, and to Baltic guerrillas.[205]

The irredeemability of the Ukrainian nationalist movement was further underscored even as the last vestiges of the GULAG system were being

---

[201] The trial was later moved to Kiev. AUSBU, d. 14, criminal file no. 66437.

[202] On France, see Sarah Farmer, *Martyred Village: Commemorating the 1944 Massacre at Oradour-sur-Glane* (Berkeley: University of California Press, 1999), 169. For a valuable, though incomplete survey of Soviet war-crime trials, see Lukasz Hirszowicz, "The Holocaust in the Soviet Mirror," in Lucian Dobroszycki and Jeffrey S. Gurock, eds., *The Holocaust in the Soviet Union: Studies and Sources on the Destruction of the Jews in the Nazi-Occupied Territories of the USSR, 1941–1945* (Armonk, N.Y.: M. E. Sharpe, 1993), 39–46.

[203] "O vypolnenii prikaza MVD SSSR no. 00248 ot 15 aprelia 1950 goda ob ob"iavlenii vyselentsam 'ounovtsam' ob ostavlenii ikh navechno v spetsial'nykh poseleniiakh," GARF, d. 9479, op. 1, d. 547, ll. 6–8; d. 896, l. 11.

[204] GARF, f. 7523, op. 109, d. 195, l. 49.

[205] For the 26 November 1948 decree by the Presidium of the Supreme Soviet on the permanent exile of nationalities deported during and after the war, see GARF, f. 7523, op. 36, d. 450, l. 87. For the 29 January 1949 decree on Baltic guerrillas, see GARF, f. 9401, op. 2, d. 10, l. 11.

dismantled. When the release of "accomplices of bandits and nationalists" from the special settlements was considered in Moscow in January 1958, the MVD of the three Baltic republics consented to the return of people of this category to their native republics, and, in the cases of Lithuania and Latvia, this included their former place of residence. In contrast, the Ukrainian MVD adamantly refused to adopt such measures. Instead, it opted for a ban on the return of accomplices of the OUN and UPA bands to western Ukraine and an exile of five years for those who returned without authorization.[206]

Nor did the post-Stalin amnesty signal rehabilitation. Ol'ha Shubert was seventeen years old when she joined the UPA in November 1943. Captured by the NKVD shortly thereafter, Shubert insisted, under interrogation, that she had joined the UPA detachment after the commander of the unit promised her protection from deportation to forced labor in Germany. Shubert was sentenced to twenty years in the camps but was released in February 1954. Only in April 1991, with the looming demise of the Soviet system, did she succeed in her quest for rehabilitation. Nearly fifty years after the event, Shubert was granted complete rehabilitation, on the grounds that "her hands were not stained with blood." The stain of nationalist activity, however, was almost irremovable.[207]

Soviet reluctance to rehabilitate the OUN and UPA persisted until the very eve of the Union's disintegration. Faced with persistent initiatives in western Ukraine to rehabilitate the OUN and UPA, the decaying regime mobilized for a final attack. Damning information from the KGB archives about the UPA atrocities was circulated in press conferences and published in the popular press. Graphic data on massacres of peaceful citizens, ethnic Poles, and Soviet activists, and close collaboration with the Nazis, were used to underline the essence of the nationalist movement as alien to the national body.[208] In response to pleas issued by the L'viv obkom secretary, the Central Committee in Moscow addressed the issue in a specific decree. The Central Committee made every effort to prevent the "justification of the crimes of the OUN bands under the guise of criticism of Stalinism." To counter the rehabilitation efforts by a variety of opposition groups in western Ukraine, it ordered the release of archival documents on the nationalist atrocities during and after the war, arranging meetings of victims of the nationalists with youth and organizing scholarly conferences on the "anti-people" deeds of the OUN and UPA. With

---

[206] Viktor Zemskov, "Prinuditel'nye migratsii iz Pribaltiki v 1940–1950-kh godakh," *Otechestvennye arkhivy* 1 (1993): 13–14; GARF, f. 9479, op. 1, d. 949, l. 119.

[207] ASBUVO, d. 26674, l. 72.

[208] See the article by Vasyl' Evtushenko, the deputy head of the Ukrainian KGB, in *Soiuz* 9 (February 1990): 14.

the fiftieth anniversary of the Great Patriotic War approaching, the treacherous nationalists were to be exposed.[209] As long as the myth of the war was the pillar of the polity's legitimacy, the excision of the nationalist cause was nonnegotiable.

However, the totalization of categories and practices in the struggle against internal enemies was far more than a radicalization of police and military methods against a stubborn opponent. The Soviet abandonment of differentiation, reform, and redemption of the enemy within appeared to challenge the Bolsheviks' belief in the primacy of nurture over nature. But was it so? The answer to this dilemma lay in the Soviet treatment of the Jewish minority.

[209] TsKhSD, f. 89, op. 20, d. 25, ll. 1–5.

Four

Memory of Excision, Excisionary Memory

> The dictatorship of the proletariat has once more
> earned the right to declare: " I do not fight to kill
> as does the bourgeoisie: I fight to resurrect toil-
> ing humanity to a new life. I kill only when it is
> not possible to eradicate the ancient habit of feed-
> ing on human flesh and blood."
>   (Maxim Gorky et al., *Belomor*)[1]

IT COMES AS NO SURPRISE that the totalization of Soviet practices in the quest for purity brought to the fore the inherent tension between the biological and the sociological categorization of the enemy within, and consequently the inevitable comparison to Nazi Germany, the other totalitarian enterprise. Nowhere else was this issue exposed more clearly than in the Soviet policy toward its Jewish minority. In the wake of the war and the trauma of the Holocaust, conducted extensively on Soviet soil with the implicit and often explicit approval of the local populace, as well as a wave of popular and official anti-Semitism that swept the immediate post-war era, ordinary Jewish citizens and activists began to ponder the unthinkable: Was there a logical affinity between the two ideologies?

For some there certainly was. In the small town of Nemyriv, Jews accused the local party leadership of deliberately impeding the evacuation of the Jewish community to the Soviet rear when the Germans were already at the outskirts. As a result, the majority of the community perished at the hands of the Nazis, whereas the local party officials lived out the war in safety at the rear. Insult was added to injury when, following the liberation of Nemyriv, the above-mentioned leaders, who never saw the front, returned to town and looted Jewish property. When Jews, who had survived the war in the villages, the forests, and the partisans detachments, returned and asked for their belongings, they were rebuffed. In addition, charged the Jews, the local leaders actively collaborated and participated in the extermination of the local Jewish community. Thus, they concluded, the party's policy toward the Jews did not differ from that of the Germans.[2]

---

[1] Gorky et al., *Belomor*, 338.

[2] Verification by an instructor of the obkom rejected most of the charges the Jews raised and claimed that in most cases Jews recovered their property: 119 of 147 claims were settled

On 4 September 1945 Kiev erupted. A Jewish NKGB officer named Rozenshtein got into a fight with two uniformed servicemen in Kiev. The two called Rozenshtein a "Tashkent partisan" (a derogatory term, reserved mainly for Jews, for people who lived out the war years in the safety of Tashkent) and beat him severely. Rozenshtein shot the two to death with his personal revolver. During the funeral procession for the two servicemen on 7 September, a mob diverted the procession to the Jewish market and a pogrom erupted. Approximately one hundred Jews were severely beaten, of whom thirty-six were hospitalized and five died of their wounds. The NKVD increased its patrols in the city after a group of servicemen and civilians prevented the removal of one of the instigators who had been detained, causing anti-Semitic agitation to spread across the city.[3]

The pogrom in Kiev took place in the wake of a series of similar, though less violent, episodes in eastern Ukrainian cities in the summer of 1944. Mobs of several hundred people in Dnipropetrov'k beat Jews to the shouts of "Death to the kikes" and "Thirty-seven thousand kikes had already been slaughtered, we'll finish off the rest," while, in Kiev, Jews swore to deal with the new incarnations of the Union of the Russian People [the prerevolutionary anti-Semitic organization] and to inflict an unforgettable "St. Bartholomew" [a reference to the massacre of the Huguenots in France in 1572] on Russians, if any of them touched a Jew.[4] The reactions from both sides to the killing and the subsequent pogrom in Kiev exposed their polarized views of the Jewish wartime experience. On the one hand, the two officers echoed a prevalent popular view of the role and place of the Jews during the war. At the same time, their actions instigated explosive expressions of uncontrolled popular rage. The regime's uneasiness and ambivalence toward manifestations of popular anti-Semitism was evident in the sentencing of Rozenshtein. He was sentenced to death, but in the honorable military fashion of a firing squad. Also, in spite of being stripped of his military rank, Rozenshtein's property was not confiscated, a measure meant to protect his family.[5]

---

in favor of Jews. However, the denials of the local NKGB chief, Timofeev, who himself was accused by the Jews in the confiscation of their property, could not conceal anti-Semitic undertones. Timofeev rejected all the charges as part of a vengeful agenda of a certain Jewish woman who was expelled from the party for passivity in the struggle against the invaders. He concluded, however, with a note that betrayed some traditional prejudices. Timofeev argued that the Jews categorically refuse to engage in any job except for commerce, and at the same time complain about "their humiliation" (PAVO, f. 136, op. 13, d. 186, ll. 224, 228–31, 236–39).

[3] TsDAHOU, f. 1, op. 23, d. 2366, ll. 4, 6–7, 21.

[4] TsDAHOU, f. 1, op. 23, d. 1363, ll. 5, 12.

[5] Ibid., l. 15.

The Jewish reaction to the pogrom was anything but ambivalent. A protest letter addressed to Stalin, Beria, and Pospelov (the editor of *Pravda*) from a group of local demobilized Jewish Communists delivered several scathing messages that touched on the deepest anxieties of both the regime and Jews. First, the Jewish veterans made accusations that drove to the core of the Communist ethos. The authors directly linked the German anti-Semitic propaganda and the current political mood in Soviet Ukraine. By emphasizing the pervasive and lingering impact of the Nazi ideology, they implicitly challenged the endurability of the Soviet experience. Twenty-five years of Soviet rule seemed to have been overwhelmed by only three years of German occupation. The disgrace to the party and the socialist motherland, asserted the authors, was all the more visible since the first pogrom under Soviet power took place after the victory over German fascism. The Germans, after all, may have lost the battle, but they won the war. "Here [in Kiev]," wrote the veterans,

> the impact of the Germans is still felt strongly. No fight whatsoever is conducted against the consequences of their political sabotage. There are all kinds of nationalists here, often with a party card in their pocket . . . The word "kike" or "beat the kikes," the favorite slogan of the German fascists, Ukrainian nationalists, and tsarist Black Hundreds, is heard with gusto in the streets of the capital of Ukraine, in the trollies, buses, stores, and markets, and even in some Soviet institutions. In a somewhat different, more veiled form it is heard in the party apparat, right up to the Central Committee of the Ukrainian Communist Party. The result of all this finally led to the pogrom of the Jews, which happened recently in Kiev.[6]

The willingness to risk a direct confrontation with the party was not a daily matter in the Soviet polity, particularly with such accusations and in such a tone. Instead of embodying the unity of the Soviet people, the Ukrainian Communist Party and government were stirring up national divisions among the peoples of the Soviet Union. Soviet power, charged the authors, actually adapted the agenda of the Ukrainian nationalists who are "equally prepared to step up against the Jews as well as the Russians or any other nationality residing in Ukraine."[7]

The Communist Party was outrightly equated with the Nazi Party. "There are Jewish-Communists who approached the raikoms and tore up their party cards or returned them, because they considered themselves unworthy to be in the ranks of a party that conducts racist politics, analogous to that of a fascist party," exclaimed the veterans. The reference to the "new course" of the Communist Party unmistakably echoed the Nazi

---

[6] Ibid., ll. 19–20.
[7] Ibid., l. 23.

New Order. " This 'course'," wrote the four veterans, " has much in common with the one that originated earlier from the chancery of Goebbels, whose worthy transmitters turned out to be in the Central Committee and the Council of People's Commissars of Ukraine."[8]

This point was also expressed bluntly by Vasilii Grossman in his epic *Life and Fate*, which he began writing at this time. For Grossman, there was nothing accidental or temporary about the barbarization of Bolshevism. It was ingrained in the core of the Bolshevik ethos, he argued. The war merely helped to bring this reality to the fore. Grossman chose none other than the triumphant moment and site of Stalingrad to underline the common ethos of the Nazi and Soviet enterprises. At a key moment in the novel, Victor Shtrum, the chief protagonist, fills out a party membership questionnaire. Reflecting on the articles of national and social origins, Shtrum notes to himself the change in priorities:

> 5. Nationality . . . Point five. This had been so simple and insignificant before the war; now, however, it was acquiring a particular resonance . . . 6. Social origin . . . This was the trunk of a mighty tree; its roots went deep into the earth while its branches spread freely over the spacious pages of the questionnaire: social origin of your mother and father, of your mother's and father's parents . . . The Great Revolution had been a social revolution, a revolution of the poor. Victor had always felt that this sixth point was a legitimate expression of the mistrust of the poor for the rich, a mistrust that had arisen over thousands of years of oppression.

This self-assurance, however, is shaken by the discomforting recognition that morality is neither universal nor absolute, and Shtrum ultimately scrutinizes the very principle of the search for purity of the body politic and its inherent genealogy. Grossman's protagonist is quick to draw a comparison to Nazi politics:

> Suddenly, probably because of the war, he began to doubt whether there really was such a gulf between the legitimate Soviet question about social origin and the bloody, fateful question of nationality as posed by the Germans . . . To me, a distinction based on social origin seems legitimate and moral. One thing of which I am certain: It's terrible to kill someone simply because he's a Jew. They are people like any others—good, bad, gifted, stupid, stolid, cheerful, kind, sensitive, greedy . . . Hitler says none of that matters—all that matters is that they're Jewish. And I protest with my whole being. But then we have the same principle: What matters is whether you're the son of an aristocrat, the son of a merchant, the son of a kulak; and whether you're good-natured, wicked, gifted, kind, stupid, happy is neither here nor there. And we're not talking about the

[8] Ibid., ll. 25, 27–28.

merchants, priests, and aristocrats themselves—but about their children and grandchildren. Does noble blood run in one's veins like Jewishness? Is one a priest or a merchant by heredity?[9]

Indeed, in the wake of the war, Soviet public representations increasingly identified Jews as inherently resistant to Soviet acculturation and, even more threateningly, as an undifferentiated entity. As early as December 1941, during a conversation with a visiting Polish delegation, Stalin found time to reflect on the martial qualities of the warring sides. The Slavs, observed the Soviet leader, are "the finest and bravest of all airmen. They react very quickly, for they are a young race that hasn't yet been worn out . . . The Germans are strong, but the Slavs will defeat them." He repeatedly referred to Jews, on the other hand, as "poor and rotten soldiers."[10]

The core message of the anticosmopolitan campaign in the late 1940s was that the Jew remained a Jew, an eternal alien to the body national, despite the circumstances. The term *cosmopolitan* appeared in public already during the war and with unmistakable reference to Soviet Jews. In the fall of 1943 Aleksandr Fadeev, already one of the most politically powerful Soviet writers, responded to an essay by Il'ia Ehrenburg by accusing him of misunderstanding Soviet patriotism, belonging to a well-known circle within the intelligentsia who "understands internationalism in a vulgar cosmopolitan spirit, and [fails] to overcome the servile admiration of everything foreign." But in November of that year, following the turn in the war and the Zionist conference in New York that called for the establishment of a Jewish state in Palestine, cosmopolitanism assumed a much more fateful meaning. In an article in *Pod znamenem marksizma*, Fadeev applied the term to a certain type of internal enemy. "Obviously, there is an insignificant chaff of people in our country who are hostile to our system," wrote Fadeev.

Besides, the enemy sends us its agents who can cause national rift in the brotherly community of the peoples of the Soviet Union by stirring up nationalist

---

[9] Vasilii Grossman, *Zhizn' i sud'ba* (Moscow: Knizhnaia palata, 1988), 542–43. In his letter to Khrushchev on 23 February 1962, pleading for the publication of his novel, Grossman noted that he had already started writing it during Stalin's life (*Istochnik* 3 [1997]: 133).

[10] Stanislaw Kot, *Conversations with the Kremlin and Dispatches from Russia* (Oxford: Oxford University Press, 1963), 153. Stalin's comments were actually triggered by the derogatory remarks of General Anders, who referred to the Jews as draft dodgers, deserters, and speculators, "who will never make good soldiers" (Kot, *Conversations*, 153). In his memoirs, Anders confirmed Kot's account of Stalin's anti-Semitic comments, although he made every effort to dispel the allegations of his own anti-Semitism by elaborating on the long history of anti-Semitism among the Bolsheviks in general and by Stalin in particular (Wladyslaw Anders, *Bez ostatniego rozdzialu: wspomnienia z lat 1939–1946* [Newtown, Wales: Montgomeryshire, 1950], 118, 124–25).

prejudices and vestiges among backward people, or undermine the feeling of national pride and honor in our peoples by slavish worship of everything that carries a foreign stamp. The sanctimonious preaching of groundless "cosmopolitanism" emanates from that all that counts for them are the "people in the world," while the nation and the motherland is an "obsolete idea."[11]

Several years later, at the height of the campaign, all inhibitions and code phrases were dropped. There, A. Fateev noted recently, some of the literary treasures of the prerevolutionary era were invaluable sources for the anticosmopolitan campaign. Ivan Goncharov's popular novel, *Fregat Pallada*, which he wrote in the mid-1850s, was one such source. In a section describing his experiences in the Cape Colony of South Africa, Goncharov portrayed a certain doctor Vederhead who spoke fluent French as no Englishman could "unless he had lived one hundred years in France." " Yes, he is a kike (*zhid*), Gentlemen," observed one of his companions, using a term that had already been recognized as pejorative for a Jew. "Who could have guessed! We observed him more intently," continued Goncharov.

> Pale face, fair hair, profile . . . a Jewish profile exactly. No doubt. However, in spite of this guess, some of us were still skeptical, questioning this opinion. Indeed, nothing about him was English: he does not look with his eyes wide open; his thought, reasoning, is not wedged in some kind of vise like an Englishman; he does not sift one word at the time, awkwardly, through his teeth. With this fellow thoughts flow so playfully and freely: obviously, his mind is not oppressed by prejudices; his views do not fit into the English cut, like a starched necktie. Well, in a word, everything was as it could be only with a cosmopolitan, that is, a kike.[12]

It was the editorial history, rather than the substance of this passage, that made it politically meaningful. Goncharov's tale enjoyed great popularity with Soviet readers. For most of the Stalinist era, however, they could not find this paragraph as it was omitted from various editions. Not until 1952 when the term "cosmopolitan kike" was reinstated in the Soviet lexicon with all the fatal implications for the Jewish community during this trying time. By then, Goncharov's "most amiable, educated, and obliging per-

---

[11] Aleksandr Fadeev, "O natsional'nom patriotizme i natsionl'noi gordosti narodov SSSR," *Pod znamenem marksizma* 11 (November 1943): 34–35, cited in A. V. Fateev, *Obraz vraga v Sovetskoi propagande, 1945–1954gg.* (Moscow: Institut rossiiskoi istorii RAN, 1999), 21–22.

[12] Ivan Goncharov, *Fregat "Pallada": ocherki puteshestviia* in *Polnoe sobranie sochinenii* (St. Petersburg: A. F. Marx, 1899), 5: 188–89; *Sobranie sochinenii* (Moscow: Pravda, 1952), 5: 130; compare with the 1949 edition of the novel (Gos. izd-vo. georg. lit-ry, p.190) where the above passage was omitted altogether. For the history of the term "zhid" in Russian culture, see John Klier, *"Zhid*: Biography of a Russian Epithet," *The Slavonic and East European Review*, 60, no.1 (January 1982): 1–15.

son" became a rootless, unpatriotic, and vile creature, just as the Jew
turned into a kike.

As such, the Jew had to be stripped of the false layers with which he
deceptively wrapped himself. In early 1949 the Soviet press violated one
of the taboos of Bolshevik revolutionary culture when it started disclosing
pseudonyms. Now the birth names of assimilated Jewish figures in the
arts were regularly attached to their assumed ones. Thus the literary critic
Il'ia Isaakovich Stebun learned, along with the readers of the republic's
main newspaper, that at day's end, after honorable service at the front and
a career of writing in the Ukrainian language, he was still Katsenelson.
Similarly the poet Lazar' Samiilovych Sanov found out that his own work
in the Ukrainian language and service as a war correspondent did not
change the fact that he was still Smulson, just as Zhadanov was still Livshits and Han remained Kahan.[13]

When the anti-Semitic campaign was reaching its climax in 1952–53,
the alleged Jewish resistance to Soviet acculturation called for the use of
uncompromising methods by the authorities. During the brutal interrogation of the leaders of the Jewish Anti-Fascist Committee (JAFC), the
chief interrogator frequently resorted to anti-Semitic slurs. "The Jews are
a base nation; Jews are swindlers, scoundrels, and scum; all opposition [to
Soviet power] was comprised of Jews; all Jews spit on Soviet power; and
the Jews wish to exterminate all Russians," Colonel Komarov told Solomon Lozovskii, one of the defendants.[14] Another defendant, Boris Shimeliovich, testified on the recurrent charge that "all Jews are anti-Soviet" and
"all Jews are spies."[15] Any doubts that the undifferentiated criminalization
of the Jewish community was only tactical or confined to a certain hot-
headed, anti-Semitic interrogator, were dispelled by Stalin himself. On
the eve of the announcement of the uncovering of the "Doctors' Plot,"
Stalin told members of the Presidium of the Central Committee that
"every Jew is a nationalist [and] an agent of the American secret services.
The Jewish nationalists think that the United States saved their nation
(there they can get rich, become bourgeois, etc.). They consider themselves indebted to the Americans."[16]

While exposing an accused Jewish embezzler in the town of Zhmerynka, who, needless to say, had relatives abroad and managed to avoid the

---

[13] "Do kontsa razgromit' kosmopolitov-antipatriotov!" *Pravda Ukrainy,* 6 March 1949;
"Bezridni kosmopolity—nailiutishi vorohy radians'koi kul'tury," *Naddnistrians'ka zirka,* 27
March 1949.

[14] *Nepravednyi sud,* 345.

[15] Shimon Redlich, *War, Holocaust, and Stalinism: A Documented Study of the Jewish Anti-
Fascist Committee in the USSR* (Luxembourg: Hardwood Academic Publishers, 1995), 147.

[16] Entry for 1 December 1952 in the diary of V.A. Malyshev, then a member in the Presidium and Minister of Shipbuilding Industry, *Istochnik* 5 (1997): 140.

front during the Great Patriotic War ("he fell ill precisely at the end of June 1941"), the satirical magazine *Krokodil* posed a rhetorical question: "To tell you the truth, we became tired of reading your decisions scattered there: 'to reprimand, to point out, to suggest,' etc. *Doesn't it seem to you, Comrades, that you overestimate the educational significance of these resolutions of yours? And, anyway, who are you trying to reeducate? With such touching forbearance, too?*"[17] The Jew, simply put, proved to be the anomaly in the Marxist premise of the primacy of nurture over nature. He was immune to reeducation. In early 1953, with the recent executions of the leadership of the JAFC, the unfolding Doctors' Plot, and rumors about the inevitable mass deportation of Jews dominating the day, the recommendation to transfer the case to the regional prosecutor, an office famed for meting out swift and harsh punishments, sent the unequivocal message that there was only one way to deal with such types.[18] As the living antithesis to the core Soviet myths of hard and honest socialist labor and the martyrdom of the recent war, the Jew was beyond redemption. His nature was immune even to the powerful acculturation of nearly four decades of Soviet life.[19] In line with this, portrayal of Jews in the press assumed an unambiguous racial character. In a biting feuilleton, which could easily be mistaken for Nazi prose, the true physical and psychological traits of an exposed Jewish embezzler came to light once he was caught and stood for

[17] Vasilii Ardamatskii, "Pinia iz Zhmerinki," *Krokodil* 8 (20 March 1953): 13 (my emphasis).

[18] In his memoirs, Aleksandr Nekrich claimed that he knew "for certain" of a brochure written by Dmitrii Chesnokov explaining the need for deporting the Jews. The brochure was ready for distribution when Stalin died (Nekrich, *Otreshis' ot strakha: Vospominaniia istorika* [London: Overseas Publications Interchange, 1979], 114). Nekrich's allegation was recently corroborated by Iakov Etinger, a former professor at the Institute of World Economics and International Relations at the Russian Academy of Sciences. According to Etinger, the book by Chesnokov argued that the Jews proved to be "unreceptive" to socialism. Etinger, along with Arkady Vaksberg, also claims that the regime began preparing pogroms, public executions of Jewish leaders, and mass deportation of the community (Etinger, "The Doctors' Plot: Stalin's Solution to the Jewish Question," in Yaacov Ro'i, ed., *Jews and Jewish Life in Russia and the Soviet Union* [Portland, Ore.: Frank Cass, 1995], 117–18; Arkady Vaksberg, *Stalin against the Jews* (New York: Knopf, 1994), 257–65. Throughout the Soviet Union, the secret police recorded the private conversations of both Jewish and non-Jewish citizens in which the deportation of Jews was accepted as a fait accompli. See the documents assembled by Mordechai Altshuler, "More about Public Reaction to the Doctors' Plot," *Jews in Eastern Europe* (fall 1996): 34, 45, 52, 55, 56–57.

[19] The impact of the events of January–March 1953 on popular perceptions was evident in the reactions to the announcement of Stalin's illness in early March. A Muscovite locksmith was recorded by the MGB declaring that "if Comrade Stalin does not get better, then we must go to Israel and destroy the Jews" (cited in "Pervaia protalina—pokhorony Stalina," *Komsomol'skaia pravda*, 5 March 1993). As a cosmopolitan entity, the Jew had to be excised not merely from the Soviet body politic but also from the universal body politic.

Figure 4.1. Footprints of Crimes 1953. Announcement of the uncovering of the "Doctors' Plot." The real (Jewish) face of the elusive enemy is unmasked, as well as that of his foreign patrons. *Krokodil*, 30 January 1953.

trial. The once "handsome, brown-haired [man] with a felt hat and well-cut overcoat" turned into a physically repulsive creature. "His long, fleshy nose points mournfully downward, his puffy lips tremble with fear, his small ratlike eyes roam uneasily. He only comes to life when he tells how he bought gold and concealed diamonds."[20] (Figure 4.1).

[20] *Komsomol'skaia pravda*, 12 February 1953.

Uncovering the *real* Jew, however, was not confined to the Stalin era. Several years later, it was the turn of the de-Stalinizing Khrushchev to warn other Communists against false hopes of acculturating the Jew. While attending a session of the Central Committee of the Polish Communist Party, Khrushchev urged the Poles to correct the "abnormal composition of the leading cadres" as the Soviets successfully had done. Staring hard at the chairman of the meeting, Roman Zambrowski, who was born Zukerman, Khrushchev exclaimed: "Yes, you have many leaders with names ending in 'ski,' but an Abramovich remains an Abramovich. And you have too many Abramoviches in your leading cadres."[21] The meeting with a delegation of the Canadian Workers' Progressive Party on 29 August 1956 provided Khrushchev with a forum in which to articulate another aspect of Jewish collectivity, one he alleged he had discerned through his wartime experience. Jews' contempt for manual labor, coupled with their understanding that this was the domain of "the other," appeared as an inherent trait of the group. "I would like to tell you about one incident that I witnessed myself," Khrushchev told the delegation. "When the town of Chernivtsi was liberated during the course of the Red Army offensive operations, it was extremely neglected and dirty. The task remained to clean the town. It should be mentioned that, during the occupation period, the Germans gave the town to the Romanians, and that's why its Jewish population escaped destruction. When we dealt with this issue, the town's Jewish population declared to us that after the Red Army arrived all the Ukrainians left for the villages, and so, they said, there was no one to clean the city."[22] Sometime later, while reflecting on the evident failure of the Jewish Autonomous Region of Birobidzhan to establish itself as a national homeland for Soviet Jewry, Khrushchev concluded that it was the result of historical conditions. Yet his description of the sociological was practically genealogical. "They [the Jews] do not like collective work or group discipline. They have always preferred to be dispersed. They are

---

[21] Joseph B. Schechtman, *Star in Eclipse* (New York: T. Yoseloff, 1961), 81. According to Benjamin Pinkus, this statement was authenticated by Jewish immigrants to Israel who held important posts in the Polish Communist Party and government (Pinkus, *The Soviet Government and the Jews 1948–1967: A Documented Study* [Cambridge: Cambridge University Press, 1984], 487 n. 38).

[22] *Istochnik* 3 (1994): 97–98, 101. Khrushchev's view of Jews and their attitude toward Ukrainians was in stark contrast to his portrayal of Russian-Ukrainian relations. There the Khrushchevian tale was one of harmony. Countering allegations of Russification in Ukraine, the story-telling leader told the Canadian delegation that when a Soviet delegation visited Canada, "Canadian nationalists arranged for it a 'hooting concert.' They yelled that the *moskali* oppress the Ukrainians. But the members of our delegation told them: Look at us, 'the oppressed.' We arrived as a delegation from all over the Soviet Union, but the majority of us are Ukrainians. This is how we are 'oppressed.' "

individualists," Khrushchev told *Le Figaro* in an interview in March 1958. Finally, in the crudest, officially ordained, anti-Semitic publication to emerge from the Soviet system—*Iudaizm bez prikras* (Judaism without embellishment) by Trohym Kychko, the very same pretender of the Vinnytsia underground and now an established expert on Judaism—Nazi-like vocabulary and illustrations drove home the message of alienation of everything distinctively Jewish from the tradition of progressive humanity in general, the Soviet family in particular, and, even more specifically, the Ukrainian nation. Portrayed as speculators hostile to manual labor, collaborators with the Nazis, and murderers of Symon Petliura, Jews were entirely excluded from the October Revolution, the Great Patriotic War, and Ukrainian aspirations for independence—all subjects of core myths within the Soviet milieu.[23]

But this complete exclusion concealed a crucial difference between the Nazi and Soviet enterprises. The class-based Soviet theory and practices of social engineering seemed to present an ominous obstacle to the application of uniform social targeting. Classes, strata, and layers were neither faceless nor homogeneous. Rather, they were variegated and arranged in a hierarchical order based on the services their members had rendered to the communist drive. Responsibility and accountability were assessed on the individual's merit, even though this principle was often compromised in the course of exercising the structuring acts. Moreover, as we have seen earlier, individuals maintained the right to appeal and often did so success-

---

[23] Trohym Kychko, *Iudaizm bez prikras* (Kiev: Vyd-vo Akademii nauk URSR, 1963), 160–61, 164–66. The book appeared in mass publication (twelve thousand copies) and was endorsed by the Academy of Sciences of the Soviet Ukrainian Republic. Adding insult to injury, such accusations came from one whose own wartime record was marred by allegations of collaboration. In his memoirs, the émigré journalist Leonid Vladimirov tells of his shock when he learned about the content of Kychko's book and the fact that a person accused of collaboration with the Germans rose to such academic status. When Vladimirov inquired about this from a friend, a prominent author in Kiev, his friend told him that the "colorful past of the rogue Kychko was well known in Kiev to all the proper people. However, there are services in Russia for which even collaborators are pardoned. Kychko understood this well and long ago, immediately after the war, "devoted himself" to anti-Semitic scientific research" (Leonid Vladimirov, *Rossia bez prikras i umolchanii*, [Frankfurt/Main: Possev, 1973], 279–81). Kychko's opportunism was underscored by another observer, a Canadian Communist who resided in Kiev when the storm broke out (John Kolasky, *Two Years in Soviet Ukraine* [Toronto: P. Martin, 1970], 102). That the Kychko affair was not an accidental slip was demonstrated by the belated Soviet reaction after the public storm had subsided. In 1968 the Supreme Soviet of Ukraine awarded Kychko with the Diploma of Honor "for his work for atheist propaganda," which followed the earlier reward of the Order of Lenin (Nora Levin, *The Jews in the Soviet Union since 1917: The Paradox of Survival* [New York: New York University Press, 1988], 2:621; Moshe Decter, "Judaism without Embellishment," in Ronald Rubin, ed., *The Unredeemed: Anti-Semitism in the Soviet Union* [Chicago: Quadrangle Books, 1968], 135).

fully.[24] And, above all, the fear of allowing biological-familial heredity to dictate the prospects of redemption continued to haunt the regime. Even at the height of cleansing campaigns, when entire families were often lumped together because of the alleged crimes of one of their members, concerns over the application of guilt onto children forced the authorities to differentiate their punitive measures. The 1930s were marked by consecutive resolutions on the rehabilitation and release of children of kulaks from the special settlements, starting as early as July 1930 with the permission to leave the settlements at the age of sixteen; continued by incentives for earlier release through shock work in 1934 and 1935; authorized enrollment in educational institutions outside the settlements in 1936; and culminating with above-mentioned ruling that granted internal passports in October 1938.[25] The anxiety over the children's fate persisted even after the totalization of enemy categories in the wake of the war. Barely nine months before the incarceration of Ukrainian nationalists and their families was converted into permanent exile, Nikita Khrushchev, the very one who presided over the extermination of the movement, appealed to Stalin in request for the release of some 161 youth who were convicted for nationalist activities between 1944 and 1946 and were sentenced to terms of five to twenty-five years of imprisonment. During their stay in the children labor colonies, argued Khrushchev, the youngsters who arrived there, who were twelve to fourteen years of age on average, acquired education and professions that made further imprisonment unnecessary. Moreover, Khrushchev recommended that the parents of some of the youth, who were exiled to eastern regions of the USSR following the conviction of their children, should be allowed to return to their former place of residence.[26] Even when weakened and worn out, the social-class paradigm still allowed for the coexistence of humanistic allusions and the harshest repressions.

No one could articulate this principle better than Stalin, and for good reason. In a series of speeches delivered as the Terror approached its climax, Stalin explained its guidelines. Concluding his remarks to the plenary session of the Central Committee, on 5 March 1937, Stalin warned the delegates not to confuse sworn and irredeemable enemies with those who recanted and redeemed themselves when they joined forces with the

---

[24] Thus the Supreme Soviet of the Ukrainian Republic commuted five of the eight death sentences passed by the NKVD's military tribunal in Vinnytsia during the third quarter of 1945 (PAVO, f. 136, op. 13, d. 48, ll. 52–54).

[25] Lynne Viola, "Tear the Evil from the Root: The Children of *Spetspereselentsy* of the North," in Natalia Baschmakoff and Paul Fryer, eds., *Modernization of the Russian Provinces*, special issue of *Studia Slavica Finlandensia* 17 (April 2000): 34–72.

[26] Volodymyr Serhiichuk, ed., *Desiat' buremnykh lit: Zakhidnoukrains'ki zemli u 1944–1953 rr. Novi dokumenty i materialy* (Kiev: Dnipro, 1998), 721–22.

Bolsheviks in the anti-Trotskyite campaign or those "who, at one point, happened to be walking along the street where this or that Trotskyite happened to be walking, too. ... In this question, as in all other questions, *an individual, differentiated approach* is required. We must not treat all alike," concluded Stalin.[27] Three months later, in a speech before the Military Council of the Defense Ministry on 2 June 1937, in the wake of the liquidation of the military leadership, Stalin reflected on the tension arising from the Soviet search for the enemy within. Reminding his audience of Lenin's noble origins and the bourgeois origins of Friedrich Engels, on the one hand, and, on the other, of the proletarian ancestry of Serebriakov and Livshits (former Central Committee secretary and deputy people's commissar of communications, respectively), who both turned out to be bad apples, Stalin concluded:

> Not every person of a given class is capable of doing harm. Individual people among the nobles and the bourgeoisie labored for the working class and not badly. Out of a stratum such as the lawyers came many revolutionaries. Marx was the son of a lawyer, not the son of a *batrak* [agricultural laborer] or of a worker. Among these strata, people can always be found who can serve the cause of the working class no worse, [but] rather better, than pure-blooded proletarians. That is why the general standard, that this is not a batrak's son, is an outdated one, not applicable to individual people. *This is not a Marxist approach . . . This, I would say, is a biological approach, not a Marxist one. We consider Marxism not a biological science, but a sociological science. Hence this general standard is absolutely correct with regard to estates, groups, strata, [but] it is not applicable to every individual who is not of proletarian or peasant origins.*[28]

And, indeed, the Soviets persistently rejected the primacy of the biological over the sociological. The principle of human heredity and its potential practices, whether exterminatory euthanasia or constructive eugenics, were

---

[27] "Zakliuchitel'noe slovo tovarishcha Stalina na plenume TsK VKP (b) 5 marta 1937 g.," *Bol'shevik* 7 (1937): 19 (my emphasis).

[28] "Rech' I. V. Stalina v Narkomate oborony, 2 iiunia 1937 g.," *Istochnik* 3 (1994): 73–74; emphasis added. For an intriguing analysis of the primacy of the individual in Soviet state violence, see Holquist, "State Violence as Technique." In this light, and without underestimating Stalin's anti-Semitism, Lenin could be recognized as a scion of the aristocracy but not as the grandson of the Jew Moishe Itskovich Blank. When Lenin's eldest sister, Anna Elizarova, reminded Stalin in 1932–33 that her grandfather was Jewish, her reasoning for publicizing this fact ran against the grain of the Marxist ethos. Lenin's Jewish origins "are further confirmation of the exceptional abilities of the Semitic tribe," she wrote Stalin in 1932. In another letter a year later, Anna wrote Stalin that "in the Lenin Institute, as well as the Institute of the Brain . . . they have long recognized the gifts of this nation and the extremely beneficial effects of its blood on mixed marriages." Stalin's refusal to publish a word about the matter became the rule for years to come (Dmitrii Volkogonov, *Lenin* [New York: Free Press, 1994], 8–9).

officially repudiated in the Soviet Union from the early 1930s on. More-over, the Soviet Union was practically alone among the major countries in the 1930s in its rejection of euthanasia or sterilization of the mentally retarded, a practice embraced, often enthusiastically, on both sides of the Atlantic. In such an atmosphere, Nobel Prize–winning doctor Alexis Car-rel could call on modern societies to do away with the mentally retarded and criminals who cost a fortune to maintain in asylums and prisons. "Why do we preserve these useless and harmful beings? why should society not dispose of the criminals and the insane in a more economic manner?" asked Carrel. The worst criminals (including the insane and people who misled the public in important matters), he concluded, "should be humanely and economically disposed of in small euthanasic institutions provided with proper gases . . . Modern society should not hesitate to organize itself with reference to the normal individual. Philosophical systems and sentimental prejudices must give way before such a necessity."[29] In Nazi Germany, as several scholars have recently reminded us, euthanasia was a key element in ideology and practice, and the forerunner of the persecution of the Jews, gypsies, and homosexuals, in sharp contrast to the Soviet purification drive, which at no point was anchored in genocidal ideology.[30] Without it, the operation of industrialized killing—the aspect that set the Holocaust apart from other genocides—was inconceivable.[31]

The same logic applied to eugenics, the constructive twin of euthana-sia. In his 1935 *Out of the Night: A Biologist's View of the Future*, Hermann Joseph Muller, the chief advocate of eugenics in the Soviet Union, argued

---

[29] Alexis Carell, *Man the Unknown* (London: Harper and Brothers, 1935), 318–19. On the wide approval of sterilization of the mentally ill in interwar Europe and the United States, see H. Friedlander, *Origins of Nazi Genocide*, 7–9, 18.

[30] Burleigh, *Death and Deliverance*; Friedlander, *Origins of Nazi Genocide*. There was, however, a single incident that accentuated the rule. In early 1938 about 170 invalid prison-ers in the Moscow oblast, who had already been tried and convicted for petty crimes such as theft and vagrancy, were tried again for the same charges, only this time they were sentenced to death. The operation was run by the special troika of the NKVD of the Moscow Region (the body that reviewed cases and passed sentences during the Terror). The motive behind the execution appeared to be the need to make room for the arrival of deported Germans, Poles, Latvians, and other ethnic groups. The chairman of the troika, Mikhail Ilich Semenov, was himself tried and executed in the summer of 1939 (*Soprotivlenie v Gulage: Vospominan-iia. Pis'ma. Dokumenty* [Moscow: Vozvrashchenie, 1992], 114–27).

[31] Ironically Grossman, who insisted on the commonality of the Soviet and Nazi polities, was also the first observer to recognize that the "conveyor-belt execution" was the distin-guishing feature of the Nazi exterminatory practices. See his description of Treblinka in Vasilii Grossman and Il'ia Ehrenburg, eds., *Hasefer Hashahor* (The black book) (Tel Aviv: Am Oved, 1991), 495–515, esp. 507. For a penetrating analysis of the Holocaust as milita-rized-industrial killing rooted in the ethos of the Great War, see Bartov, *Murder in Our Midst*.

that with artificial insemination technology, "in the course of a paltry
century or two . . . it would be possible for the majority of the population
to become of the innate quality of such men as Lenin, Newton, Leonardo,
Pasteur, Beethoven, Omar Khayyam, Pushkin, Sun Yat-sen, Marx. .. or
even to possess all their varied faculties combined . . . which would offset
the American prospects of a maximum number of Billy Sundays, Valen-
tinos, Jack Dempseys, Babe Ruths, even Al Capones."[32] But when Muller
forwarded a copy of his book to Stalin in May 1936, assuring him that
"it is quite possible, by means of the technique of artificial insemination
which has been developed in this country, to use for such purposes the
reproductive material of the most transcendently superior individuals, of
the one in 50,000, or one in 100,000, since this technique makes possible
a multiplication of more than 50,000 times," he practically sealed his fate
and the fate of eugenics in the Soviet Union for the next three decades.
Stalin read the book, and, although he did not respond either in writing
or verbally until June 1937, his actions spoke for themselves. Muller escaped the Soviet Union by the skin of his teeth, but every one of his
cohorts was shot. The Institute of Medical Genetics was disbanded, and
the era of Lysenkoism and its doctrine of acquired characteristics was
ushered in. In the long process of constructing a socialist society, acculturation prevailed over biology as the means both to expand and purify
the polity.

And certainly there was not, nor could there be, a highly placed Jew,
such as Lazar Kaganovich, in the Nazi leadership; nor could nearly half a
million Jews serve in the Wehrmacht or become members of the National
Socialist Party. It mattered not that they may have excelled in the ranks of
the German army in the Great War. There was one Jew only, and he could
not be Nazified. The Jew was an enemy not because of a role he played or
a position he represented. He was evil incarnate, irredeemable and unre-
constructed, and, as such, had to be exterminated. The basis on which the
extermination of the Jewish "lice" took place was neither that of religion
nor law, but the racial biopolitics of genetic heredity.[33] That was not the

[32] Mark B. Adams, "Eugenics in Russia, 1900–1940," in Adams, ed., *The Wellborn Science:
Eugenics in Germany, France, Brazil, and Russia* (New York: Oxford University Press, 1990),
194–95.

[33] Agamben, *Homo Sacer*, 114, 146–47. In this sense Saul Friedlander's recent introduction of "redemptive anti-Semitism" as the guiding logic of Nazi attitudes toward the Jews
requires some modification. Redemption implies a linear concept of historical time and a
certain finality, both alien to the Nazis' nihilistic violence and cyclical view of history, one
filled with nightmares of a possible defeat at the hands of the Jews (Friedländer, *Nazi Germany and the Jews*, 73–112). For a lucid analysis of the place of the Jew within the Nazi racial
hierarchy in theory and practice, see John Connelly, "Nazis and Slavs: From Racial Theory
to Racial Practice," *Central European History* 32, no. 1 (1999): 1–33.

case in the Soviet Union. True, living by the motto "sons are not responsible for their fathers" proved difficult. Just two years after Stalin's famous
dictum, NKVD and party investigators were busily plunging into the records of Communist Party members, resurrecting from oblivion the original sin of the wrong social origin to destroy scores of true believers and
their families. In the wake of the Terror, it appeared as if the stain of bad
social origin was indelible. It took the war to realize and institutionalize
Stalin's dictum in Soviet political life. Nevertheless, even at the height of
the officially endorsed anti-Semitic campaign, hundreds of thousands of
Jews remained in the ranks of the party, the army, and scores of other
political institutions. Restrictions on the number of Jews in state institutions (*Numerus clausus*) could and did coexist with Jewish high officers,
Heroes of the Soviet Union, and party activists.[34] The Nazi example was
still a powerful deterrent, especially regarding the Jews. The United Nations draft resolution of the Genocide Convention on 21 November 1947
provided the Soviets the opportunity to elaborate their own definition of
excisionary and exterminatory ideologies and practices. In his comments
on the treaty, Aron Trainin, then the leading Soviet authority on international law, agreed with the prevailing notion of genocide as extermination
of national or racial collectives. His points of disagreement, however, were
revealing. First, argued Trainin, however extreme the persecution of political opponents based on political motives may be, it does not constitute
genocide.[35] Second, the definition of genocide should not be confined to
physical extermination but applied to the curtailment of collective national-cultural rights as well. "Of course, in the land of the Soviets, where
the Leninist-Stalinist national politics triumphs and the cooperation of
nations is a political reality, there is no problem of national rights and
national minorities," wrote Trainin. It was a problem, however, in the
capitalist world, where class exploitation could be identified with national
oppression. Not only lynch trials but also a dense net of national-cultural
barriers separate Negroes in the United States from the white population,
Trainin continued.

---

[34] A rare admission by a Soviet official of a de facto *numerus clausus* for Jews was offered
by Ekaterina Furtseva, a Central Committee secretary, during an interview with *National
Guardian*, 25 June 1956. "The government had found in some of its departments a heavy
concentration of Jewish people, upward of 50 percent of the staff," said Furtseva. "Steps
were taken to transfer them to other enterprises, giving them equally good positions and
without jeopardizing their rights." These steps were misinterpreted as anti-Semitic, Furtseva
reassured the interviewer (Pinkus, *The Soviet Government and the Jews*, 58–59).

[35] Eventually the Soviets and their allies succeeded in omitting the category of political
groups from the draft in a deviation from an earlier resolution by the General Assembly
(Nehemiah Robinson, *The Genocide Convention: Its Origins and Interpretation* [New York:
Institute of Jewish Affairs, 1949], 15).

Accordingly, international law should struggle against both lynch trials, as tools of physical extermination of Negroes, and the politics of national cultural oppression. Therefore, along with physical and biological genocide, the notion of national-cultural genocide must be advanced, a genocide that sets for itself the goal of undermining the existence and development of national and racial groups.[36]

Essentially these were the twin pillars of Soviet population policies: the application of state violence anchored in political rationale and the simultaneous cultivation of ethnonational particularism. Without them, one could hardly understand the simultaneous eradication of entire national elites and intelligentsias along with the persistent delineation of particularistic identities.[37] In this light, total excision in the Soviet polity was not necessarily exterminatory nor did it operate by a racial-biological code. And this in turn shifts the focus of our discussion to another political arena within which the Soviet socioethnic body was delineated, that of commemorative politics of cataclysmic events.

Conventional wisdom points to the establishment of the state of Israel and the unfolding cold war as the primary causes for the deterioration in the status of the Jewish community within the Soviet polity. Indeed, the creation of the Israeli state transformed Soviet Jewry overnight into a diaspora nation with a highly active external homeland. In the 1930s a similar situation cost Polish and German minorities in the Soviet Union dearly. Often glossed over, however, is the centrality of the living memory of the war and the Jewish genocide in shaping the course of Soviet-Jewish relations and providing them with a constant point of reference in the years following the war. Soviet officials were aware of this juncture. Years after the war, when leading Israeli poet Avraham Shlonski visited the Soviet Union, Aleksei Surkov, the secretary of the Union of Writers, told him:

There were times when we thought that the process of Jewish assimilation was being intensified by dint of the historical logic of Soviet conditions, and that the Jewish problem was being solved by itself. Then came the war with its hor-

---

[36] Aron Naumovich Trainin, "Bor'ba s genotsidom kak mezhdunarodnym prestupleniem," *Sovetskoe gosudarstvo i pravo* 5 (May 1948): 4, 6. The official amendment offered by the Soviet delegation called for the extension of the definition of genocide to "national-cultural genocide," which included: "(a) ban on or limitation of the use of the national language in public and private life, and ban on instruction in the national language in schools; (b) liquidation or ban on the printing and distribution of books and other publications in national languages; (c) liquidation of historical or religious monuments, museums, libraries, and other monuments and objects of national culture (or religious) cult" (Trainin, "Bor'ba s genotsidom," 14).

[37] For a stimulating discussion of this duality in Soviet nationality policy, see Yuri Slezkine, "The USSR as a Communal Apartment; or, How a Socialist State Promoted Ethnic Particularism," *Slavic Review* 53 (summer 1994): 414–52.

rors, then the aftermath. All of a sudden Jews began to seek one another out and to cling to one another.[38]

If Surkov is to be forgiven for some self-righteousness, he was not off the mark. Ironically none other than Grossman pointed to memory as a key arena in shaping the postwar quest for purity. As the driving force behind the failed projects of the *Black Book* and the *Red Book*, the works celebrating Jewish martyrdom and heroism, respectively, which were never published in the Soviet Union, Grossman offered keen insight into a new mechanism for engineering the Soviet body social. The postwar construction of ethnic hierarchies of heroism and the simultaneous leveling of suffering underlined the power of commemoration in the shaping of an ideal community. This mechanism was particularly fateful for the Jews.

In his famous toast to the Russian people on 24 May 1945 Stalin made a point to single out the Russian people as the most loyal and selfless of the nations of the Soviet Union. Alluding to the behavior of some of the other nationalities, Stalin juxtaposed the Russian conduct during the trials of the war:

> Another people might have said to its government: You have not fulfilled our expectations, away with you, we shall establish another government that will conclude peace with Germany and bring us rest. But the Russian people did not do so, because it believed in the correctness of the policy of its government, and it sacrificed itself in order to guarantee the destruction of Germany. And this faith of the Russian people in its government became the decisive force that guaranteed the historic victory over the enemy of mankind—over fascism.[39]

Twenty years later, in March 1965, *Yad Vashem*, the Holocaust archival center in Jerusalem, requested documents from the Soviet government archives dealing with the fate of Soviet Jews. The Soviet authorities replied that the archives "relating to the crimes of German fascism in World War II are not organized according to the nationality of the victims."[40]

These seemingly unrelated incidents outlined the twin institutions of hierarchical heroism and universal suffering, the cornerstones of the Soviet ethnonational ethos of the war. Whereas the various nations of the Soviet Union were ranked in a pyramidlike order based on their alleged contribution to the war effort, their suffering was undifferentiated. More so than any other ethnonational community, these aspects of the Soviet ethos were

---

[38] Yehoshua A. Gilboa, *The Black Years of Soviet Jewry, 1939–1953* (Boston: Little, Brown, 1971), 88.

[39] "Vystuplenie tovarishcha I. V. Stalina na prieme v Kremle v chest' komanduiushchikh voiskami Krasnoi Armii," *Bol'shevik* 20, no. 10 (May 1945): 1–2.

[40] Nora Levin, *The Jews in the Soviet Union since 1917*, vol. 1, 424–25.

evident with regard to the Jewish community. Jewish participation in the trials of combat service were ignored in public and denied in private. By the time Stalin addressed the commanders of the Red Army, Jews had disappeared from public representations of the war. Similarly the Holocaust was incorporated into the epic suffering of the entire Soviet population, thus ignoring its uniqueness to the Jews.

One could hardly deny that the view of the Jew as an undifferentiated biological entity had deep roots in Russian anti-Semitism.[41] Yet to regard the exclusion of the Jews from the postwar Soviet body national as being exclusively rooted in traditional anti-Semitism is to risk teleological reductionism, which both ignores a rather complex environment and obscures the specific conditions and developments that turned a certain myth, one among several, into a hegemonic one.[42] To paraphrase David Nirenberg's apt insight, our task is to marry discourse and agency. Entrenched and prevalent as it was, the negative traditional discourse about Jews acquired force only when people chose to find it meaningful and useful, and it was itself reshaped by these choices.[43]

Universal Suffering

The Soviet authorities had been aware of the German extermination of the Jews. As early as October 1941 the murder of the Jews throughout Europe and the Soviet Union was publicly exposed. In one of the earliest wartime plays, Oleksandr Korniichuk's *Partizany v stepiakh Ukrainy* (Partisans in the steppes of Ukraine), the physician of a local partisan detachment is one Rosenfeld who volunteered to the unit after surviving German torture and witnessing the rape and murder of his two young daughters.

---

[41] On the eve of the First World War, Russian legislation on Jewish affairs increasingly assumed a racial undertone. In 1912 applicants to the Academy of Military Medicine and the Corps of Cadets had to prove that their families had not been Jewish for three generations. That year the Ministry of the Interior ruled that Jewish converts were not to be regarded as Russians and had to vote in Jewish electoral assemblies (Hans Rogger, *Jewish Policies and Right-Wing Politics in Imperial Russia* [Berkeley: University of California Press, 1986], 35–36).

[42] For two notable examples of the teleological explanatory paradigm that draw an uninterrupted monocausal link between traditional popular anti-Semitism and genocidal policies of the 1940s, see Norman Cohn, *Warrant for Genocide: The Myth of the Jewish World Conspiracy and the "Protocols of the Elders of Zion"* (New York: Harper and Row, 1967); and Daniel Jonah Goldhagen, *Hitler's Willing Executioners: Ordinary Germans and the Holocaust* (New York: Knopf, 1996).

[43] David Nirenberg, *Communities of Violence: Persecution of Minorities in the Middle Ages* (Princeton, N.J.: Princeton University Press, 1996), 6.

Rosenfeld, who commands the German language, reads to his partisan compatriots from the pages of a diary of a captured German colonel: "Fritz arrived and told us how he burned Jews alive in a synagogue in Rotterdam. I've never laughed so much in my life."[44] These references appeared among graphic and more detailed bragging by the Nazi officer over massacres of Poles and Ukrainians. There seemed to be nothing unique in such a representation for a multiethnic polity engaged in a desperate struggle for survival. Its ominous meaning for the Jews would become clearer only later. In the meantime the authorities continued to gather information on the unfolding genocide.

Communications of partisan units operating in Vinnytsia showed a clear understanding of the unique fate of the Jews under the Germans and the Romanians. Partisan leaders singled out the extermination of the Jews with respect to the persecution of other ethnic groups. A report by Savchenko, head of the Ukrainian NKVD beginning 26 January 1943, on the situation in occupied Vinnytsia, contained fairly accurate data on the extermination of the Jewish population in the city, referring to it as a distinct German policy. "The Jewish population that resided on the territory of the province has been exterminated almost entirely," Savchenko concluded.[45] Significantly, the victims were still recognized as Jews and not as the anonymous "peaceful civilians" they would later become. Referring to concentration camps in Ukraine, the commissar of the Stalin Partisan Brigade said in an interview on 5 March 1944 that "concentration camps in Ukraine confined Russians, Uzbeks and Georgians—all nationalities except Ukrainians. Of the Ukrainians, only Communists, Komsomol members, and Jews were impounded. The Jews were exterminated entirely; the other nationalities starved or were given the option to join the Vlasovite army."[46] Moreover, in certain forums, the Soviet authorities recognized the German treatment of the Jews, even in the most sensitive sphere of POW policy. During the first days of October 1941 the Germans executed 378 Jewish POWs in the Vinnytsia prisoners' camp, information that was forwarded to Vasilii Grossman and Il'ia Ehrenburg when the two

[44] The play was originally published in the Ukrainian Russian-language newspaper *Sovetskaia Ukraina* on 12 October 1941. Citation here is from the republication in *Novyi mir* nos. 1–2 (1942): 56–57.

[45] TsDAHOU, f. 1, op. 23, d. 685, l. 32.

[46] IIAN ORF, f. 2, op. 9, d. 3, l. 4. The report of the Communist underground in the Bar district, which was presented to Khrushchev and Mishchenko, specifically mentioned the persecution of the Jewish population in the district, "which was exterminated in various ways. Some were killed in the streets, others were forced to work and survive without food, and still others were decimated by the [intentional] avoidance of countering the epidemic" (TsDAHOU, f. 1, op. 22, d. 166, l. 11).

were compiling material for the *Black Book*.[47] Later, at the Nuremberg trials, the Soviets produced testimony by an SD official who bluntly stated that Jews and Communists in prisoners' camps on the eastern front were separated from their comrades and shot outside the camps.[48]

In addition, the regime pursued the punishment of perpetrators of anti-Jewish massacres from the moment of liberation until the very disintegration of the Soviet Union. NKVD military tribunals instantly began to try, on treason charges, both locals and Germans who participated in the massacre of Jews. On December 1944 fourteen employees at the local psychiatric hospital were arrested on charges of participating in mass executions of patients, including the shooting of four hundred Jewish patients in October 1941.[49] Early in 1946 the military tribunal in Vinnytsia sentenced to death one Herbert Lukes, a German who had served as a gendarme during the war. Lukes was accused of gathering about 100 "peaceful citizens," whom he then led to the site of their execution, ordering the shooting of a child who attempted to escape. The court also sentenced to death Serhii Iaremchuk, a local policeman from the Bar district, for personally participating in the massacre of Jews. In October 1946 the Odessa MGB arrested a group of 8 people charged with the massacre of 119 Jews and party members in the village of Terlitsa, the Monastyr' district, and in Vinnytsia in 1941. The victims had been buried alive in an anti-tank ditch, and the MGB insisted on exhuming the bodies in order to prepare the case against the group. When the oblispolkom in Vinnytsia delayed the act, the MGB urged the Supreme Soviet of Ukraine to order the local authorities to stop dragging their feet. In April 1948 the Vinnytsia MGB arrested one Andrii Prokopchuk, who had been trained as an SS guard in Trawniki and served there and in Maidanek.[50]

The authorities also offered material help to Jewish survivors. When the JAFC complained to Molotov and Beria about the indifference to the suffering of Jews still living in the ghettos established by the Romanians and about the obstacles that local authorities, especially in Vinnytsia, put in the way of those Jews who wished to regain their housing and property, the latter responded promptly. The Ukrainian Central Committee and government were ordered to offer the necessary help and to dispatch a plenipotentiary to the region to verify the circumstances. Beria's response

---

[47] Itzhak Arad, *Unichtozhenie evreev SSSR v gody nemetskoi okkupatsii (1941–1944): sbornik dokumentov i materialov* (Jerusalem: Yad Vashem, 1992), 301.

[48] The testimony of Otto Olendorf, 5 November 1945, reproduced in Arad, *Unichtozhenie evreev SSSR*, 285.

[49] GARF, f. 9401, op. 2, d. 92, ll. 146–47.

[50] PAVO, f. 136, op. 13, d. 102, ll. 19–20, 62, 94b–95, 109; DAVO, f. 2700, op. 7, d. 67, l. 82; TsDAHOU, f. 1, op. 23, d. 1364, l. 33; and PAVO, f. 136, op. 29, d. 185, l. 11.

was a rare official admission of the Jews' unique fate under the Nazis. He ordered the Ukrainian Central Committee and government, and Khrushchev personally, to take the necessary measures to assist in the working, housing, and domestic arrangements of Jews in the liberated territories "who were subjected to particular repressions by the German occupiers (concentration camps, ghettos, etc.)."[51]

At the same time the authorities made it clear that the surviving Jews were subjected to the same policies as the rest of the population, no matter how traumatic their experience had been. The Jews had to be mobilized at once for the postwar restoration effort, including the thousands of Romanian Jews who were deported to Transnistria during the war and were still stranded in the Vinnytsia region.[52] Knowledge of the Jews' fate under occupation did not necessarily convey recognition or empathy.

A leaflet of the underground obkom from January 1943 drew attention to the Jews' suffering. Addressing "Comrades, Kolkhozniks, fathers, brothers, and sisters on the temporarily occupied region!" the leaflet contained the following lines: "Ask yourselves, why? Why do the [Germans] shoot innocent people? Why did they exterminate the entire Jewish population?"[53] Ten months later, with liberation of the region already in sight, Jews were omitted entirely from the list of the suffering Soviet peoples. A leaflet distributed by Communist partisans in Vinnytsia on the occasion of the twenty-sixth anniversary of the October Revolution addressed only the "Brothers and Sisters! Russians, Ukrainians, Belorussians, Moldavians, Lithuanians, Latvians, and Estonians [who] are temporarily enslaved by the German-fascist scoundrels."[54] A few short months after the region's liberation Jewish losses were completely glossed over. In a public letter on 17 August 1944 from the population of Vinnytsia to Stalin, recording the Nazi atrocities, the massacres of Jews, which counted for the majority of human losses, were not mentioned. By then, the Jewish trauma had already been integrated into the epic suffering of the entire Soviet Union. As noted above, by the time the veterans complained to Stalin in the fall of 1945, the erasure of a distinct Jewish catastrophe had already become a fait accompli. "No other people experienced as much sorrow and misfortune as did the Jewish people during the Patriotic War. [Yet] not a single

---

[51] TsDAHOU, f. 1, op. 23, d. 3851, ll. 3–5.

[52] Between the spring of 1945 and the spring of 1946 an estimated forty thousand Romanian Jews, who were deported to Transnistria during the war, were repatriated to Romania (Joseph Schechtman, "The Transnistrian Reservation," *YIVO Annual of Jewish Social Sciences* 8 [1953]: 196; TsDAHOU, f. 1, op. 46, d. 329, ll. 1–8).

[53] TsDAHOU, f. 1, op. 22, d. 164, l. 102.

[54] TsDAVOVU, f. 4620, op. 3, d. 108, l. 151.

article was devoted in the press or in print to their situation [or] their needs," lamented the veterans.[55]

A major platform for the articulation of this commemorative canon of the war were the reports of the Extraordinary State Committee for the study of German-fascist atrocities. The stated goal of the committee was to chronicle the human and material losses at the hands of the Axis forces, which it did in the most detailed and graphic manner. Jewish victims figured highly in the reports, but only as individuals bearing Jewish names and not as a distinct group marked collectively by the perpetrators. The Jewishness of victims was not specified even in testimonies on massacres that were directed solely against Jews.[56] Thus the Committee outlined a long-standing pattern in establishing the myth of the war. The suffering of the civilian population at the hands of the invaders was universalized, ruling out any ethnonational distinction, in spite of the awareness of the Nazis' own racial hierarchies and practices. When certain space was allowed for the expression of ethnonational particularism, it was limited to a marginal, isolated, hardly visible tale such as that of the Romanian occupation.

The universal representation of suffering was punctuated by the authorities' reaction to the anti-Semitic wave that swept through Ukraine's major cities in the wake of liberation. Mob scenes, proliferation of anti-Semitic language in government and party circles, and aggressive Jewish reactions forced the NKVD to address the issue in a detailed investigation. The report of 13 September 1944 confirmed the prevalence of anti-Semitism, yet it was the politicized Jewish reaction, namely, the unmitigated militancy of a resurrected Jewish separatism, that drew the ire of the Ukrainian authorities. Thus the Jewish writer Hofshtein was singled out for stating that "what the Jews endure now is good. It resurrects their national consciousness, which had been lost."[57] The party's response to the report was revealing. Although the Ukrainian Central Committee's counter-report did not deny the occurrence of anti-Semitic incidents, it was reluctant to recognize their systematic nature. The party's concerns were clearly focused on the notion of the Jewish genocide as a catalyst for national consciousness. "The NKGB should better concentrate on the exposure of Ukrainian nationalist and Zionist organizations who seek to stir up national dissent," advised the authors of the counter-report. Indeed, the core of the Central Committee's investigation was a compilation of incriminating material about the na-

[55] TsDAHOU, f. 1, op. 23, d. 2366, l. 26.
[56] See the report by the Vinnytsia branch of the committee in TsDAVOVU, f. 4620, op. 3, d. 253.
[57] TsDAHOU, f. 1, op. 23, d. 1363, l. 11.

tionalist past and present of some Jewish public figures. "The NKGB seemed unaware of the effort of Zionist elements to organize a mass demonstration of the Jewish population in Kiev on the anniversary of the German massacre of Jews in Babyn Iar," charged the party officials.[58] They referred apparently to the recurring efforts of Jews throughout Ukraine to commemorate massacres by the Nazis. The MGB report of July 1946 on religious activity in the Vinnytsia region noted that "in September 1945, on the pretext of the anniversary of the execution of the Jewish population in the city of Vinnytsia by the occupiers, the *aktiv* of the [Jewish] community in Vinnytsia [organized] an illegal gathering in the Jewish cemetery in town in which two thousand people participated. This gathering turned into a demonstration, at which the community's activists delivered speeches that contained separatist Jewish nationalist rhetoric."[59]

The authorities' concerns were likely to be further fueled by the driving motivation of the local Jewish population, as well as the selection of commemoration sites. Within the Jewish community, the urge to commemorate their slaughtered brethren was an attempt to recast the memory of the war as one of particularistic historical suffering. In some cases, the survivors' drive to commemorate the war dead was conveyed in a religious manner. "It is obvious that God spared me so that I could immortalize all those murdered," a Jew from Lityn told his daughter, as they embarked on a lifetime project of commemorating the local dead. In the neighboring district of Bar, the urge to commemorate Jewish victimhood was explained as a commitment to the generation of the victims' children. The notion of a generational continuity of suffering was accentuated by placing the mass graves alongside the old Jewish cemetery whose desecrated tombstones would be a powerful reminder.[60]

Not surprisingly, the display of religious-national Jewish commemorative symbols was met with uncompromising resistance by the authorities who threatened to bulldoze every obelisk unless the six-cornered Jewish star was replaced by the five-cornered Soviet star.[61] The reluctance to commemorate particularistic suffering was captured in Khrushchev's memo-

[58] Ibid., l. 16.

[59] PAVO, f. 136, op. 13, d. 105, ll. 16–17. All-Union reports reflected similar concerns. The Jewish community was chastised (among other things) for its tendency to expand its function into activities of national character. The Soviet of Religious Cults was urged to repulse these attempts and limit the activities of the organized community strictly to the performance of religious duties. Nor did the community help itself when the leader of the Berdichev community told the plenipotentiary for religious affairs that even Communists who attended a synagogue during the Jewish High Holidays felt at that time they were Jews (RGASPI, f. 17, op. 125, d. 405, ll. 98–99).

[60] Yad Vashem Archive (YVA), #03–6401, testimony of Hanna Schwartzman, 15–16, 34; #03–4323, testimony of Mordechai Tkach, 4–7.

[61] YVA, #03–6401, testimony of Hanna Schwartzman, 15–16.

rable retort to Il'ia Ehrenburg. When the latter appealed to Khrushchev to intervene and stop the construction of a marketplace on the site of the massacre in Babyn Iar, Khrushchev advised him "not to interfere in matters that do not concern you. You had better write good novels."[62]

Ehrenburg may not have been aware that at the time the Soviet leader had already made plans and assigned a generous amount of money for the erection of a monument on the site. It is doubtful, however, that he would have been pleased with the plans. By mid-1945 the Ukrainian Council of Ministers approved the draft model designed by Kiev's chief architect, A. Vlasov. It ordered him to present his model and estimates by 1 August of that year and recommended an invitation to Vera Mukhina, the well-known sculptor, to join the project. Nearly two million rubles were allotted for the project. Already then, the resolution had no reference to Jewish victims but to the 140,000 citizens of Kiev who perished at the hands of the Fascists. And that was the way the monument was finally erected in 1976, fifteen years after Evtushenko's famous poem and thirty-five years after the massacre.[63]

Still, Jewish activists continued to pursue their right for a distinct memory of the genocide, often under the direst circumstances. During a heated exchange with the chairman of the court in the course of the JAFC leaders' trial, Itzik Fefer defiantly retorted that no other people suffered like the Jews. The extermination of one-third of their people earned Jews the right to mourn their loss, exclaimed Fefer. The chairman's response said it all. "This [loss] was not used for mourning but for anti-Soviet activity. The Committee became a center of nationalist struggle," he countered.[64] By then, not only were the Jewish leaders doomed, but so, too, were the prospects for official recognition of the community's right to observe its catastrophe.

The swan song of the attempt at public representations of particularistic ethnonational wartime suffering came in 1946 with the curtailment of publication of *The Black Book*, edited by Il'ia Ehrenburg and Vasilii Grossman. Intentionally or not, Grossman's preface cracked the wall of uniformity in the presentation of suffering. Beyond the troubling references to collaboration and participation of the local population in the extermination of Jews, Grossman repeatedly hammered to his readers that the Jews as a group were distinctly singled out by the Nazis. Grossman adhered to

---

[62] Abraham Sutzkever, "Il'ia Ehrenburg (A Kapital Zikhronot fon di Yaren 1944–1946)," *Di Goldene Keit* 61 (1967): 30.

[63] TsDAVOVU, f. 2, op. 7, d. 3939, l. 17. For a survey of the controversies surrounding the Babyn Iar monument, see William Korey, "A Monument over Babi Yar?" in Lucjan Dobroszycki and Jeffrey Gurock, eds., *The Holocaust in the Soviet Union: Studies and Sources on the Destruction of the Jews in the Nazi-Occupied Territories of the USSR, 1941–1945* (Armonk, N.Y.: M. E. Sharpe, 1993), 61–74.

[64] *Nepravednyi sud*, 34.

the Nazis' own hierarchy of brutality even when he paid tribute to the atrocities inflicted on the Russians, Ukrainians, Belorussians, prisoners of war, and partisans:

> The German race was declared to form the apex of this pyramid—a master race. They were followed by the Anglo-Saxon races, which were recognized as inferior, and then by the Latin races, which were considered still lower. The foundation of the pyramid was formed by Slavs—a race of slaves. [Then] the Fascists placed the Jew in opposition to all peoples inhabiting the world.[65]

Frustrated by the prolonged delay in publication of *The Black Book*, Ehrenburg, Grossman, and leaders of the JAFC appealed to Andrei Zhdanov, the Central Committee secretary, in November 1946. Zhdanov delegated the decision to Georgii Aleksandrov, head of the agitprop department. The latter's reaction to *The Black Book* sealed the project's fate. The authors, charged Aleksandrov, advanced a particularistic and inaccurate representation of suffering. "The preface written by Grossman," Aleksandrov wrote to Zhdanov,

> alleges that the destruction of the Jews was a particularistic provocative policy and that the Germans established some kind of hierarchy in their destruction of the peoples of the Soviet Union. In fact, the idea of some imaginary hierarchy is in itself incorrect. The documents of the Extraordinary State Committee convincingly demonstrate that the Hitlerites destroyed, at one and the same time, Russians, Jews, Belorussians, Ukrainians, Latvians, Lithuanians, and other peoples of the Soviet Union.[66]

Grossman's introduction proved to be the final official representation of singular wartime tragedy. *The Black Book* was never published in the Soviet Union.

Hierarchical Heroism: Where Have All the Jews Gone?

> *Petrenko*: "You grew up eating Russian bread, you
>   received an education paid for by the Russian
>   people, and now you betray your motherland?
>   For you and your whole people I fought at the
>   front for four years."
> *Shcharansky*: "My father also fought at the front.
>   He spent four years there as a volunteer. Per-
>   haps he did that for your son and your people?"

---

[65] Grossman and Ehrenburg, *Hasefer Hashahor*, 17.
[66] RGASPI, f. 17, op. 125, d. 438, l. 216.

Petrenko: "Your father? In the army? What division was he in?"
Shcharansky: "Artillery."
Peterenko: "Artillery?" He seemed genuinely
  amazed. "I also fought in the artillery, but I
  didn't see your sort there. What front was he
  on?"[67]

This exchange took place at the Lefortovo prison in the course of interrogation of the Jewish dissident Anatoly Shcharansky (Natan Sharansky) by
a KGB colonel named Petrenko. This conversation may have appeared
surrealistic had it not engaged a core issue in the myth of the war. Back
then, in a speech at the second meeting of the Jewish Anti-Fascist Committee held in Moscow on 20 February 1943, Il'ia Ehrenburg limited
himself to one, in his words, burning issue: the need to publish a book
that would detail Jewish heroism at the front. "Such a book is required,"
said Ehrenburg, "for the peace of mind of Jewish soldiers at the front who
received letters from their relatives in Uzbekistan or Kazakhstan telling
them that people there claim that one does not see Jews at the front because they don't fight." To illustrate this point, Ehrenburg told those attending the meeting the following story:

> I was visited by an old Jew, the father of a famous pilot, whose heroism was
> celebrated in the entire military press. He was this man's only son, and he loved
> him very much. He told me: "I spoke with a certain civilian official who said to
> me: 'Explain to me, please, why there are no Jews at the front? Why doesn't one
> see Jews in the war?' I did not answer him. I found it hard to speak. That was
> only four days after I had received from the commander the news of my son's
> death."[68]

What was the rationale behind these harsh and swift accusations? Such
comments defied the evidence and the contemporary official Soviet representations of the Jews in the war. The current affirmation and recognition
of the Jews' participation indeed pointed in the opposite direction. A recent and evidently conservative estimate points out that the number of
Jews in active combat during the war correlated to their share in the general population, and often exceeded it, especially among elite units, which
bore the brunt of fierce fighting at the fronts. Even as the percentage of
Jews declined with the mass influx of ethnic Ukrainians and Belorussians
into the Red Army after the liberation of the German-occupied territories,

[67] Anatoly Shcharansky, *Fear No Evil* (New York: Random House, 1988), 11–12.
[68] *Eynikayt*, 15 March 1943.

their overall share in the armed forces remained proportional to their number in the general population.[69]

Lack of awareness of Jewish losses at the front was practically impossible in an intimate environment such as Vinnytsia. In the small district of Bershad' alone, army records listed no fewer than 139 fallen Jewish soldiers.[70] The physical absence of these young men from the postwar local scene could not have been lost upon their non-Jewish neighbors, no matter how deeply they were immersed in their own losses. Yet awareness does not necessarily translate into recognition.

Moreover, throughout the war the Jewish contribution to the combat effort was recognized and rewarded publicly. Promotions or decorations for soldiers or officers of the fighting Red Army were bestowed on Jews and non-Jews without discrimination. Official publications celebrating the friendship of the peoples allegedly cemented under the trials of war allotted the Jews a respected place within the family of the fighting nationalities.[71] The Ukrainian staff of the partisan movement marked the Jews as the fifth largest ethnic group in its ranks, following the Russians, Ukrainians, Belorussians, and Poles, and the last publication in the Soviet Union dealing specifically with Jewish heroism in the war described the Jewish participation in the partisan movement.[72]

Early on, the exploits of a significant number of Jewish officers became public symbols of the Soviet resistance to the Nazi invasion. Jewish commanders such as Hayim Fomin, commissar of the Eighty-second Brigade which defended the Brest-Litovsk fortress in the first week of the war, became symbols of the myth to fight to the death.[73] Of even more enduring publicity was the case of Iakov Kreizer. Kreizer's meteoric rise led him from the command of the elite First Moscow Motorized Infantry Division

[69] Mordechai Altshuler, "Antisemitism in Ukraine toward the End of the Second World War," *Jews in Eastern Europe* 3 (winter 1993), 49–50 n. 29.

[70] YVA, 032/37 (5). These name lists and short biographies originated in the Central Archive of the Ministry of Defense (TsAMO).

[71] "Druzhba narodov SSSR—moguchii faktor pobedy nad vragom," *Bol'shevik* 23–24 (December 1944): 6. Overall 160,722 Jews won military awards, the fourth largest group after the Russians, Ukrainians, and Belorussians. These figures should be considered against the data from the 1939 population census that placed the Jews as the seventh largest ethnic group in the Soviet Union (Yossef Guri, "Yehudei Brit Hamoatsot Bamilhama Neged Hanazim," in *Lohamim Yehudim Bamilhama neged Hanazim* [Tel Aviv: Ha-Irgun Ha-Yisraeli shel hayalim meshuhrarim al yede Sifriyat Poalim, 1971], 41).

[72] O. Babishkin, *Osobyi sklad radianskikh partizaniv Ukrainy: Statystychnyi dani*, in TsDA-VOVU, f. 4620, op. 3, d. 102, l. 16; *Partizanskaia druzhba: vospominaniia o boevykh delakh partizan-evreev uchastnikov Velikoi Otechestvennoi voiny* (Moscow: Der Emes, 1948). The circulation of the book was curtailed almost immediately after its publication. An expanded edition in Hebrew was published in Israel in 1968.

[73] Yitzhak Arad, "Yehudei Brit Hamoatsot Bamilhama Neged Germania Hanazit," *Yad Vashem Studies* 23 (1994): 59–60.

at the rank of colonel to that of a general of the army. Kreizer became a
public symbol almost at the outbreak of war. Following his stubborn defense of the Borisov area, Kreizer was awarded Hero of the Soviet Union
as early as 22 July 1941. The following day a reporter for *Krasnaia zvezda*
(Red star), the official organ of the Red Army, wrote that "Iakov Kreizer
[is] the first of the courageous infantry commanders to be honored with
this high award for courage and heroism displayed at the front in the
struggle against fascism, for skillfully directing military operations, and
for setting a personal example in leading his units into battle." But in a
marked deviation from the Soviet rule for other nationalities, Kreizer was
not celebrated as the "faithful son" of his respective nationality, only as a
Soviet officer.

This tale of General Kreizer, however, foreshadowed things to come.
Kreizer's Jewish identity was well known, at least within the ranks of the
Red Army. The Nazis themselves reportedly tried to exploit Kreizer's Jewishness. German planes bombarded his division with leaflets urging soldiers to ask themselves: "To whom are you entrusting your lives? Your
commander is the Jew Yankel Kreizer. Do you really believe that Yankel
will save you from our hands?"[74] But within the Soviet political scene,
Kreizer's Jewishness was highlighted only within the narrow realm of the
Jewish community or for propaganda abroad. Kreizer became a leading
member of the JAFC, arguably one of the most effective tools of Soviet
wartime propaganda abroad, where he occasionally delivered ardent na-
tionalistic Jewish speeches.[75]

As the war drew to a close, Jews were no longer marked as a separate
group in either public presentations of war heroism or in confidential reports. Statistics of military awards bestowed on partisans in Ukraine by 1
January 1945 singled out a variety of nationalities, including non-Soviet
ones. Jews were not among them. They were incorporated into the category of "other nationalities."[76] Seven years later Jews were omitted altogether from the public celebration of combat heroism. In a mass-circula-
tion book from 1952, which specified the ethnic breakdown of recipients

---

[74] This account draws on Kreizer's biographical sketch in Gershon Shapiro, *Under Fire:
The Stories of Jewish Heroes of the Soviet Union* (Jerusalem: Yad Vashem, 1988), 271–305;
here, 275, 277, 303.

[75] Ironically, years later, Kreizer's Jewishness was to be paraded in public years, albeit in
utterly different circumstances. "If you go to Sverdlovsk, go and see Colonel-General
Kreizer. He is my friend, [and] he is an army commander. He is a Jew," Khrushchev told a
delegation of the French Socialist Party that had inquired about the state of anti-Semitism
in the Soviet Union in May 1956. So some of Khrushchev's best friends were Jews, and
Kreizer happened to be one of them (François Fejto, *Judentum und Kommunismus: Anti-
Semitismus in Osteuropa* [Vienna: Europa Verlag, 1967], 112).

[76] TsDAHOU, f. 1, op. 23, d. 1436, ll. 100–102.

of military awards in general and Heroes of the Soviet Union in particular, Jews were dropped from the list.[77] The nationality of some Jews was not even mentioned, as in the case of Yeidl Khaiat, one of the fallen heroes in the famous "Pavlov House"[78] at the battle of Stalingrad. In other cases, the nationality was simply altered. Thus the fallen Iakov Chapitzev, a Crimean Jewish poet and Hero of the Soviet Union, was identified as a *Krimchak*, but not as a Jew, in an interesting reversal of the 1939 census that abolished this category.[79]

The paradox of the large Jewish presence at the front and the industrious denial of Jewish heroism invited several explanations. For one, the notion of Jews avoiding military service seemed deeply rooted in both prerevolutionary and prewar Soviet society. The presence of approximately 350,000 Jews in the ranks of the Imperial Russian Army during the First World War, including a large number of decorated soldiers, did not prevent the military command from questioning the loyalty of these fighting men. On 27 April 1915 the General Staff of the Twelfth Army ordered all units to gather material on "(1) the attitude of Jews to our armies and the enemy; (2) their conduct in time of battle and in military operations in general; (3) the circumstances of surrender [to the enemy] of low-ranking Jews; (4) incidents of betraying duty and oath; and so on." These orders went hand in hand with the mass deportation of Jews from border regions and combat zones to the Russian interior on grounds of suspect loyalty to the Russian Empire, and in order to launch a spy mania in which Jews figured highly.[80] In June of that year the military censors issued a warning to a Minsk-based newspaper after it reported on the heroic exploits of a certain Jew named Appel. The censors demanded that the editorial board reveal the source of its information about Appel, since it had violated the policy against publishing any material on Jewish heroism at the front.[81] Notably this policy was most firmly established on Ukrainian territory,

---

[77] S. N. Golikov, *Vydaiushchiesia pobedy Sovetskoi armii v Velikoi Otechestvennoi voine* (Moscow: Gos. izd-vo polit. lit-ry, 1952), 187.

[78] A building named after Sergeant Iakov Pavlov whose heroic command of the post earned him the award of Hero of the Soviet Union.

[79] Arad, "Yehudei Brit Hamoatsot Bamilhama Neged Germania Hanazit," 77. *Krimchaki* was the name of Jews who lived in the Crimea for generations before the region became part of Russia. The Germans treated the *Krimchaki* as Jews and exterminated them with the rest of the Crimean Jews.

[80] *The Jews in the Eastern War Zone* (New York: American Jewish Committee, 1916), 54; "Dokumenty o presledovanii evreev," *Arkhiv russkoi revoliutsii* 19 (1928): 245–84; Peter, Gatrell, *A Whole Empire Walking: Refugees in Russia during World War I* (Bloomington: Indiana University Press, 1999), 17–18.

[81] GARF, f. 579, op. 1, d. 2011, l. 15. I thank Ben Nathans for providing me with this document.

Vinnytsia included, thus ensuring that the local population clearly understood that Jews were excluded from the patriotic family during the ultimate test—already named the Great War.

When the party surveyed its rank and file in the late 1920s it encountered, time and again, the prevalent perception of Jews as accomplished
draft dodgers and likely traitors in times of war. A decade later, during the
1939 campaign, a soldier felt free to utter, in the course of a political
educational discussion, that "if there are any Jews at all in the Red Army,
then there are very few. This is because the Jews are a cunning people who
know how to avoid the draft."[82]

The peculiarities of the warfare on the eastern front further advanced
the perception of "no Jews at the front." Jewish soldiers intentionally concealed their national identity, especially in combat units, as soon as it became clear that Jews faced summary execution by the Germans if taken
prisoner. According to some historians, right alongside the progressing
assimilation of Soviet Jewry, soldiers' denial of their Jewishness was a mass
phenomenon.[83] The problem of Jews intentionally concealing their identity was exacerbated by the intensive Nazi propaganda at the front that
played on traditional prejudices. The consequences were bluntly conveyed
by a Jewish colonel in a letter to Ehrenburg:

> We are all lying in the trenches. Soon I will have to give the command: "At-
> tack—up and out!" And then those devils with black crosses [German airplanes]
> start to fly by one after the other—just like locusts. We bury ourselves in the
> trenches and wait. The bombs will drop soon, and then we'll be in a really tight
> spot. But they keep flying and there are no bombs, only leaflets—a world of
> leaflets. Some made their way to me in the trenches. They contained only a few
> words, a message: "Look around you, Soldiers, are there any Abrahams or Israels
> around you?!" And that's all. And that was enough to make soldiers look around
> and, not knowing who was a Jew, to come to the poisonous conclusion: "There
> are no Jews at the front line."[84]

Another explanation for the popular perception that "there are no Jews
at the front" was that Jews indeed accounted for a relatively high percentage of the refugees and evacuees. The reason for this was twofold: The
Jews were engaged in a mass, disorderly flight because of the fear of exter-

---

[82] Iurii Larin, *Evrei i antisemitizm v SSSR* (Moscow: Gosizdat, 1929), 241; RGVA, f. 9, op. 39, d. 70, l. 97.

[83] Some cases indicated that this phenomenon was helped by the internalization of traditional stereotypes of Jewish appearance and characteristics by Jews themselves. "True, in my
unit they did not know that I was a Jew. I am strong and tall, a worker," wrote Mikhail
Shakerman to Ehrenburg and Khrushchev (PAVO, f. 136, op. 13, d. 184, l. 93).

[84] Hersh Smolar, *Vu Bistu Haver Sidorov?* (Tel Aviv: Farlag Y. L. Perets, 1975), 257–58.

mination, especially when reports of the German treatment of Jews reached Jewish communities; and, later, industries and bureaucracies containing a large concentration of Jews were evacuated.[85] This phenomenon, which saved the lives of hundreds of thousands of Soviet Jews, was unintentional, and many of the refugees and evacuees were eventually drafted into the Red Army. Nevertheless it helped to proliferate the notion of the Tashkent partisans.

The denial of Jewish combat heroism pointed to some deeper concerns and images with respect to Jews. The authorities fiercely resisted all attempts to carve out a particularistic Jewish space within the all-encompassing myth of the war. The Jews' self-perception of the uniqueness of their wartime experience threatened to undermine the universality of suffering and the ethnonational hierarchy of heroism, the twin pillars of the ethos of war. If the recollections of Jewish partisans are accepted at face value, then they went out of their way to exact a special revenge on the enemy. In the on-going process of brutalization of the public scene, Jews appeared determined to present themselves as active perpetrators and not merely passive victims. "Among the [captured] Germans we also found Vlasovites," recalled Zalman Teitelman, a Jewish partisan in the Chechl'-nyk district. "Granovskii, myself, and several other Jews consulted with the partisans and decided that all Vlasovites should be executed. We staged a military trial on the spot, and we mowed down ten Vlasovites, in the local dump, where the Jews were buried. With that we concluded our partisan activity."[86] Probably of more political weight were the attempts to parade this particularistic urge in public. In his appearance before the JAFC in the summer of 1945, David Dragunskii, the two-time Hero of the Soviet Union, described in detail the extermination of his entire family by the Germans in February 1942, and his visits to Babyn Iar and the concentration camps. The speech, however, was marked by Dragunskii's intense emphasis on his own special reckoning with the Germans as a Jew. "All of us hate the Germans!" he told the audience.

> But I hate them doubly. For one, because I am a Soviet man; for another, because I am a Jew! I was filled with hate because I saw what the Germans did to our people . . . I yearned to get to Germany. I got to Germany. I did my duty as a son of our motherland. I fought for all Soviet people. I fought for all Jewish people . . . The Germans knew that my brigade was headed by a Jew. They posted notices that they would flay me alive. They hated me twice over, for being a Russian and a Jew. That very night [in Berlin] we caught five hundred SS troops

[85] Mordechai Altshuler, "Escape and Evacuation of Soviet Jews at the Time of the Nazi Invasion: Policies and Realities," in Dobroszycki and Gurock, *The Holocaust in the Soviet Union,* 77–104.
[86] YVA, testimony of Zalman Teitelman, #03–3446, 20.

whose commander had posted that notice. We made *shashlik* and beef stroganoff of them all. We caught the colonel of the SS swine. He complained that someone had taken his watch. "Take care of his complaint," I commanded one of my men. The colonel is not around anymore.[87]

Sometime later, a group of Jewish veterans set out to reverse the prevailing order in the hierarchy of heroism. Jews, the veterans argued in a letter to Stalin, had more than a legitimate claim to share the glory of heroism with the rest of the Soviet people. After elaborating on the Jewish contribution to the October Revolution when the Jewish people "showed itself as the most revolutionary people," the veterans noted the Jewish contribution at the front, which, they argued, was exceptional: "During the Patriotic War tens of thousands of Jews fought heroically at the front. Many of them were killed in battles for their socialist motherland, and many became heroes. The percentage of decorated Jews in the Patriotic War is very high," they noted with pride.[88] Together with the rejection of the new Khmel'nyts'kyi order by scores of Jewish officers who viewed the now celebrated Cossack hetman as nothing but a *pogromshchik*,[89] Jews sought their own distinctive insignia. On 19 May 1947 *Dos Naye Lebn*, a Yiddish-language journal in Lodz, Poland, ran a short story by Itzik Kipnis, the Soviet Jewish writer. In the story, entitled *On Khokhmes, On Kheshboynes* [Without giving it a thought], Kipnis intimated a personal wish: "that all Jews walking the streets of Berlin, with a sure, victorious step, would wear bandannas with decorations and medals and also a small pretty *Magen David* (Star of David) on their chests. It would be our shameful mark. Everyone would be able to see that this is a Jew, and my Jewish and human worth is between loving citizens and cannot be diminished."[90]

The harsh reaction to Kipnis's story made it clear that, as a symbol of Jewish heroism, the Star of David needed a different place.[91] The establish-

---

[87] Raymond Arthur Davies, *Odyssey through Hell* (New York: L. B. Fischer, 1946), 206–7.

[88] TsDAHOU, f. 1, op. 23, d. 2366, ll. 23–24.

[89] Werth, *Russia at War*, 679.

[90] Significantly Kipnis did not include this paragraph in a shorter version of the story, which he published in June 1945 in Kiev under the title *Libshaft*.

[91] Kipnis was subjected to harsh criticism for the blasphemous idea of placing the Star of David, the Zionist symbol, side by side with the Soviet star, an "idea incompatible with being a Soviet writer," as the secretary of the Ukrainian Union of Writers concluded (*Literaturna hazeta*, 25 September 1947; Haim Loytsker, "Far ideyisher reynkeyt fun undzer literatur," *Der Shtern* [Kiev], no. 2 [1948]: 105–12). Kipnis's writings embodied the dual sin of the Jewish subversion of the Soviet myth of the war, namely, Jewish particularistic heroism and suffering. This could be traced back to his writings of the 1920s. In 1926 Kipnis published a novel, *Khadoshim un teg* (Months and days), that focused on the recent pogroms in Ukraine, a fact that was not lost on Loytsker. "Kipnis, so it turns out, has not forgotten his former *Khadoshim un teg*, although many years have passed. And he has learned nothing in all these years of Soviet rule," exclaimed Loytsker (112).

ment of the state of Israel in May 1948 was problematic enough for the already sensitive status of the Jewish community, transforming it overnight into a diaspora nation with a sovereign external homeland. The birth of the Jewish state amid a ferocious war instantly made it a living symbol of Jewish heroism at a time when the very notion of Jewish courage was being denied at home. A common thread throughout thousands of letters to the JAFC was the link drawn between the Jewish catastrophe in Europe and its redemption in Israel. Not only was the universalization of suffering rejected, its redemption could take place only outside the Soviet polity, in Israel. As one letter expressed it:

> I am sure that many of us are prepared to help Israel, not only with money but also by fighting personally in the Israeli army . . . At this time, when Jews have finally received their own state, to remain indifferent would be a crime and an act of betrayal of the millions of our brothers who perished in Auschwitz and Maidanek, Babi Iar, and thousands of other places . . . Let the image of our tortured brothers, fathers, and mothers guide your actions.[92]

The long process that began with attempts at integration and proceeded to carve a particularistic space for Jews was now laying the foundations for a break with the polity. The response to Jewish attempts to set their agenda was telling. Taking on Il'ia Ehrenburg, the Jewish high priest of the Soviet anti-German hate campaign, Oleksandr Dovzhenko, the famous film director, entered in his diary a conversation alleged to have taken place among Soviet soldiers:

> When I read him or listen to him being read, I start to feel very sorry for him. Why is that?
> Because he's so full of hatred. A bottomless abyss of hatred.
> Where does he get it all? He's covered with hatred like a horse with mange.
> Maybe he's just afraid that we don't have enough of those poisonous feelings.
> That's what I think. He doesn't believe in our anger and intelligence and aware-ness of history.
> He has no pity for us. We've knocked off four hundred battles all the way to Berlin, and now we've got to find the strength to start a new life.
> Strength for our women, friends, and for starting families. He has no pity for us, the living, only for the dead. That's why I don't want to read him. I have enough anger in myself and in all the pictures I've seen over the last four years. Never mind him. Let him write. It doesn't hurt us, but at least it annoys the Germans.[93]

---

[92] Redlich, *War, Holocaust, and Stalinism*, 383–84. See also Genadi Kostyrchenko, *Out of the Red Shadows: Anti-Semitism in Stalin's Russia* (New York: Prometheus, 1995), 103–4.

[93] Notebooks, entry on 30 November 1945 in *Alexander Dovzhenko: The Poet as Film-maker*, ed. Marco Carynnyk (Cambridge, Mass.: MIT Press, 1973), 137.

So even at the very moment when all Soviet men appeared as one undifferentiated whole fighting a common enemy, the Jew remained alien. And
it was not simply the additional devotion celebrated by Dragunskii and
Ehrenburg. It was the Jew's vindictive nature and his mistrust of his own
society that set him apart. Or maybe it was the enduring teachings of his
dead religion with its pretense to superiority and utter lack of compassion
that alienated his Christian brethren. Unfit for the tasks of war, the Jew
also had no place in the postwar milieu.

All these representations of the motives behind the troops' fighting
spirit actually outlined various degrees of resilience and subsequent
agendas within the Soviet family. The Jews had ulterior motives and plans.
This clearly was out of step with the Soviet hierarchical order of heroism.
In any case, Dragunskii's remarks could be related to his fellow Jews only
in a closed gathering. By then, any effort to break with the hierarchical
order of heroism in public was bound to be curtailed, as Ehrenburg
learned in the summer of 1944. When Ehrenburg tried to push forward
the so-called *Red Book*, the second part of the planned trilogy of the Jewish
fate in the war against the Nazis, which was supposed to tell the stories of
Jewish soldiers and partisans, he was bluntly told by a top official in the
Soviet Information Bureau that "there is no need to mention the heroism
of Jewish soldiers in the Red Army; this is bragging."[94]

By that time the refusal to recognize any trait of Jewish distinction
pervaded all spheres of Soviet society, notably the GULAG. When the
head of a cultural educational department in one of the camps drafted a
working paper that advocated methods of redemption for inmates toward
the end of the war, his exemplary cases included a Jewish inmate. Samuil
Goldshtein, whose ethnicity was not mentioned, was an exceptionally difficult case, refusing to work regardless of the consequences. Yet, instead
of resorting to harsh penalties, as others advocated, the author summoned
Goldshtein for a talk about the war. "Do you know what goals the fascists
pursue in the war against us?" Loginov asked Goldshtein. "I don't know,"
Goldshtein uttered quietly. "I explained to him who Hitler was and what
his goals were. I showed him several pronouncements of the fascist bandits
on world domination. I explained the essence of racial theory and the
Hitlerite new order in Europe," wrote Loginov. In all likelihood the
NKVDist did inform the Jewish inmate about the Jews' fate under the
Nazis, but in 1944 one certainly did not call a spade, a spade, nor was the
Jewish genocide mentioned explicitly. The tale, however, did not end
there. "The war will end. The happy life of our people will flourish once

---

[94] Il'ia Ehrenburg, *Sobranie sochinenii (Liudi, gody, zhizn')*, vol. 9 (Moscow: Sovetskii
pisatel', 1967), 377.

again. Every decent man will say: 'I shed blood and sweat fighting for this life.' What would you say? How would people look at you?" Loginov scolded the stubborn inmate and appeared to push his buttons. The conversation, claimed Loginov, was a turning point for Goldshtein, who, after digesting the information, turned into an exemplary worker in the camp and later volunteered for the front, where he heroically sacrificed himself in battle. Back in the camp, his combat exploits and letters from the front were paraded before the inmates. Loginov concluded with these words: "In eternal memory of Samuil Goldshtein"—but not the faithful son of the Soviet Jewish people, just one Goldshtein, a convict who redeemed himself by answering the motherland's call.[95] Like the rest of Soviet society, the GULAG world would recognize neither unique Jewish suffering at the hands of the Nazis nor a distinct contribution in the war against them. With the emergence of the war as the core legitimizing myth of the polity, Jews were separated as a *group* from the Soviet family.

"THERE ARE NO JEWS IN UKRAINE," lamented a horrified Grossman when he first encountered his liberated birthplace in 1943.

> Nowhere—Poltava, Kharkov, Kremenchug, Borispol', Yagotin—in none of the cities, hundreds of towns, or thousands of villages will you see the black, tear-filled eyes of little girls; you will not hear the sad voice of an old woman; you will not see the dark face of a hungry baby. All is silence. Everything is still. A whole people have been brutally murdered."[96]

Gabriel Temkin, a Jewish soldier in a Red Army unit entering Vinnytsia, was one of those who read Grossman's article. Together with other bits of information, he had already acquired a sense of the magnitude of the Jewish calamity. Still, the reality was more powerful than any words. "I did not know all these statistics [of Jewish communities exterminated by the Nazis] in the first days of March 1944 when we were moving southwest toward Romania. But passing through the many places known to have had large Jewish populations, and where we were presently being welcomed as liberators by the surviving inhabitants, I met not one Jew," recalled Temkin.[97]

True, soon after this lament, the Ukrainian terrain was filled again with returning Jews, albeit in significantly lower numbers and fewer places of

[95] GARF, f. 9414, op. 4, d. 145, ll. 11–12b.
[96] Vasilii Grossman, "Ukraina bez evreev," in Shimon Markish, *Vasilii Grossman. Na evreiskie temy*, vol. 2 (Jerusalem: Biblioteka-Aliia, 1985), 333–40; here, 334–35. This is a translation back into Russian from the Yiddish version that appeared in *Eynikayt*, 25 November and 2 December 1943. The original Russian-language version was apparently rejected by *Krasnaia zvezda*.
[97] Temkin, *My Just War*, 159–60.

concentration. But as early as 1943 Grossman's words rang true with regard to the future as well as the recent past, and in a way he could not envision at the time. The invisibility of Jews in the Soviet Union in general, and in Ukraine in particular, was not restricted to the physical. The surviving Jews indeed returned but rather as a mythical antithesis and into political invisibility.

At first glance this seemed not to be unusual in a polity whose official nationality policy envisioned at its final stage the merging (*sliianie*) of its various ethnic and national components into a single entity. The Jews, in this light, were leading the Soviet camp in terms of historical development. But there was an ironic twist in this instance. Whereas the means by which ethnic groups would merge included an intense cultivation of ethnic particularism, the Jews were to skip this stage in the wake of the war. And since the date of the final merging remained as elusive as ever, the erasure of Jewish collective identity from the new legitimizing myth of the polity bore grave consequences. Just two years after the region was liberated and, equally important, two years before the establishment of the state of Israel, the Jewish community in the Soviet Ukrainian Republic joined their German and Polish counterparts in the realm of political invisibility. The decision of the Vinnytsia oblispolkom, on 14 October 1946, to liquidate Jewish national soviets in the region and merge them with the Ukrainian soviets was critical to the shaping of the Soviet-Ukrainian-Jewish discourse. Local Jewish activists vehemently protested the decision claiming that, as a majority in the community, Jews were entitled to national soviets that offered services in their native language. When the regional authorities responded to the complaints in February 1947, they justified their decision by the recent demographic changes in these settlements. By that time, they argued, Jews constituted a small minority in these rural communities, leaving one to wonder about the gaps between the different estimates of the non-Jewish population in these villages. Further, the oblispolkom explained the liquidation of the national soviets and their merger with the Ukrainian soviets on the grounds of administrative efficiency. The small size of these units did not justify the maintenance of a separate apparat. It only created confusion in the leadership and added excessive personnel. The oblispolkom revealed that it had already petitioned the Presidium of the Supreme Soviet of the Republic to liquidate the national village soviets, and the latter responded positively in September 1946.[98]

The rationale the authorities offered for the liquidation of the Jewish soviets was firmly within the official policy. As crude as it may have ap-

---

[98] PAVO, f. 136, op. 13, d. 208, ll. 1–7.

peared to the local Jewish community, this was nothing but a translation
of the wartime demographic losses into the institutional power structure.
The sharp decline in the absolute and relative numbers of Jews in the
province warranted institutional adjustments. Second, the merger of the
rural soviets corresponded with the political agenda of the Republic's
leader, Nikita Khrushchev. Only three years later Khrushchev launched the
policy of amalgamation of kolkhozes into larger and more viable socioeconomic units. The merger of the sel'sovets appeared as the forerunner for
the larger scheme of administrative consolidation of Soviet power in the
countryside.

Yet the recent history of national soviets in the Union in general, and
in Ukraine and Vinnytsia in particular, offered another rationale, although
one that was not articulated as such. The Jewish sel'sovets were the anomaly in the prewar policy of liquidation of national soviets. Along with the
deportations of nonindigenous populations from the border zone in the
mid-1930s, their national soviets were abolished. The only direct restriction imposed on the Jewish settlements before the war was the ban on
foreign assistance, a policy that, in any case, was altered after the war broke
out.[99] Unlike the case of the prewar German and Polish sel'sovets, the
Jews had no external homeland to pose a potential threat of appealing to
its Soviet-based diaspora. There were, however, some hints in the oblispolkom decision that lent credibility to the suspicion that the liquidation of
the Jewish national soviets was long in the making and carried a certain
particularistic agenda. The oblispolkom decision did not even refer to the
discussed village soviets as national Jewish soviets but merely as village
soviet no.2, a point not lost on the Jewish activists.[100] Their very identity
was denied before their abolition.

The similarity to the Polish-German precedents of the 1930s was en-
hanced by the increased Jewish emigration from Vinnytsia to Birobidzhan. The erasure of Jews from the institutional space of the Soviet Ukrainian body national went hand in hand with the intensified decrease in their
physical presence in the republic in general and in the region in particular.
Whereas contemporary testimonies strongly point to Jewish self-initiative,
such an organized mass dislocation within the Soviet polity could not take
place without official sanction. Recall Khrushchev's admonition to Roza
Hudes in 1943: "And I believe that it would be advisable for Ukrainian
Jews who have survived Nazi extermination not to return to the Ukraine.

---

[99] On the 19 June 1938 ban on fund raising through exports, see GARF, f.5446, op.1,
d.500, 1.23. By 1944 the stream of packages from the United States was brisk enough to
become a bone of contention between disgruntled individuals and local leaders who enjoyed
better access to foreign donations. See the anonymous letter of complaint addressed to
Khrushchev in TsDAHOU, f. 1, op. 23, d. 2475, ll. 1–2.

[100] PAVO, f. 136, op. 13, d. 208, ll. 6–7, 10.

They would do better in Birobidzhan."[101] From late 1946 on, several thousand Jews from five Ukrainian provinces and Samarkand migrated to the Jewish Autonomous Region. Contemporaries actually referred to the migration as a redemption of sorts. "We wish to move to the region [Birobidzhan] in an organized manner, and found there a kolkhoz in the name of the victims tormented by the fascists in our town. We want to consecrate their memory through honest work for the further development of our socialist fatherland," wrote the leader of a group of demobilized servicemen on their way to Birobidzhan.[102] Redemption of Jewish particularistic suffering occurred right alongside socialist redemption. A profile of the settlers from Vinnytsia in 1948 revealed a concentration of manual laborers and collective farmers. The author of this report noted with pride that these figures indicated a shift toward a more productive community in agriculture and industry.[103] However, this also meant that the flip side of a more ideal socialist face for the Jews of Birobidzhan was their further deflation in Ukraine. For a community traditionally stereotyped as a nonproductive, parasitic collective, the socioeconomic composition of the emigration could only spell more of the same in one of the most tenuous moments of the Soviet-Jewish encounter.

Motivated either by a Jewish effort at socialist self-realization, frustration with the postwar hostility of the local community and authorities, or attempts by the authorities to defuse the explosive relations between Ukrainians and Jews by marginalizing the presence of the latter, the Jewish emigration from Vinnytsia underscored their growing exclusion from the body politic. In 1946–47 this process looked less brutal and conclusive than its Polish and German precedents. This was soon to change with the establishment of the state of Israel in May 1948 and the ensuing anticosmopolitan campaign. In the meantime, with the liquidation of Jewish institutional space and the state-sponsored emigration, the Ukrainian Jews were well on their way to political obscurity.

Deeply rooted popular anti-Semitism coincided with similar sentiments among the local and national leadership, but, more crucial, these attitudes were articulated within the powerful Soviet ethos of a simultaneous search for harmony and purity. A barrage of popular novels portrayed Jewish characters as draft dodgers who lived the war years in the safety of the rear—and on the blood—of their Soviet compatriots. It was a short step from the exclusion of Jews from the Soviet fighting family to their isolation from the Soviet family at large. The wartime stereotype of the Jew as

---

[101] Leon Leneman, *La Tragédie des Juifs en URSS* (Paris: Desclee de Brouwer, 1959), 178–79.

[102] GARF, f. 8114, op. 1, d. 8, l. 59.

[103] Pinkus, *The Soviet Government and the Jews*, 378.

evader of the front occupied a central place in the anticosmopolitan campaign as it assumed an increasing anti-Semitic character. This rootless cosmopolitanism was embodied by the worst antipatriotic act of all, the deliberate evasion of the front when the motherland needed the ultimate sacrifice of each and every one of its sons. The sons responded, except for the rootless cosmopolitans. They had lived the war in the safety of the Soviet rear, which did not prevent them from seeking medals for their "sacrifice" when the war ended. This representation reached its climax in the novel *Zhurbiny* by Vsevolod Kochetov.[104] The villain in this tale is one Veniamin Semenovich, a round-shouldered forty-year-old man with thinning, slick hair, and octagonal spectacles, a club director in a shipyard city on the Black Sea. Although Veniamin Semenovich had his moments in the early 1930s when he rushed from one construction site to another, the quarrelsome and treacherous character of this pseudo-intellectual led him to live the life of a constant wanderer. It is not accidental that *Agasfer* (The wandering Jew) is among the books that Veniamin carries with him in his suitcase wherever he goes. There was one more thing that set Veniamin Semenovich apart from his compatriots. Whereas they had shed their blood for the motherland in the various tests it confronted, Veniamin never came near the front. That, however, did not stop him from seeking some kind of order for his services.[105] For Veniamin, sacrifice could never be for the sake of the collective or an ideal. He concluded that there was no need for sacrifice where neither money nor fame were involved.

But Kochetov did not leave it at that. There was a way to deal with the Veniamins. A climactic encounter between Veniamin and Skobelev, the chief engineer of the shipyard, takes place in the train station when the former escapes the city, leaving behind his third and pregnant wife. On the surface, the two had much in common. Both had a solid reputation of being ladies' men, avid evaders of work, and dishonest. In a way, Kochetov noted, they even respected each other. But unlike Veniamin, Skobelev struggles to reconstruct himself and regain both his self-respect and the respect of his coworkers. The purifying moment arrives at the train station. Skobelev is exasperated by the judicial system's inability to deal with the Veniamins. They are too slippery for the system. After all, this was not the first time Veniamin had fooled the legal system. So Skobelev metes out a more primordial justice: He humiliates Veniamin by slapping him in public. And it is neither shame nor rage that overcomes Skobelev. Instead, after the incident, he "strode along proudly. He was pleased with himself. 'Well, he thought, the people will look into it. Perhaps they will disap-

---

[104] Vsevolod Kochetov, *Zhurbiny* (Leningrad: Sovetskii pisatel', 1952). The first edition of *Zhurbiny* alone enjoyed a circulation of forty-five thousand copies and was supplemented by subsequent editions.

[105] Kochetov, *Zhurbiny*, 225, 347, 349–50.

prove; perhaps they'll blame me. But then everyone will see that Skobelev acted honestly, as his conscience prompted him. Yes, Skobelev had a conscience; he had a sense of duty."[106]

And, indeed, his public slapping of the Jew becomes a cathartic moment in Skobelev's life. It actually reforms him both as a private and social person. Skobelev's entire demeanor is transformed from that of a parasite to that of a real worker. "Having stood up for Katia [Veniamin's abandoned wife]," Kochetov conveys Skobelev's feelings, "for the first time in his life Skobelev felt himself a real man. He was unaccustomed to the feeling of manliness; it filled him with pride. He no longer walked in his former soft catlike manner; he marched firmly and noisily down the pavement." Hence the public humiliation of the Jew turns into a vehicle for the physical and moral restoration of the Soviet male. Skobelev regains his true—as distinguished from his previously false—manhood. Exit Tarzan gigolo, enter *Homo Sovieticus*.[107] This resolve extends to the realm of performance at work, where Skobelev transforms himself and wins the respect of his co-workers.

And how does Kochetov have the party react to the recourse of violence? The party is of two minds. The official view considers the incident improper for modern Soviet society. "Comrade Skobelev," the party organizer, who deals with the incident, thoughtfully remarks, "the Stone Age was a good time. Primitive man picked up his club and went off to settle accounts with his neighbor." But then there is the private view, an understanding among men. "You know," the party organizer intimates to Skobelev, "as a man, I understand you. Such people deserve a slap in the face."[108]

If Kochetov's solution was not the outright sanctioning of pogroms, it was not far removed. The Jew might have succeeded in avoiding combat. He might have slipped through the legal formalities. But he could not escape basic justice at the hands of honest Soviet people. Yes, it was primitive, agreed the party, but it was also understandable.

In a polity that identified military service with local, national, and supranational Soviet identities, and sacrifice on the battlefield as a sign of true patriotism, exclusion from the myth of the war amounted to exclusion from the Soviet family. A similar outcome, if only through a different practice, emerged from the commemoration of wartime suffering. The mass murder of Jews was never denied in Soviet representations of the war, but

---

[106] Ibid., 328.

[107] Ibid., 329. It is hard to ignore the resemblance between Kochetov's archetypes and the archetype of Gogol's *Taras Bul'ba*. Saved from foreign invaders against whom he had not fought, Veniamin Semenovich rewards his saviors with betrayal, as did Yankel in the case of Taras. See Gary Rosenshield, "Socialist Realism and the Holocaust: Jewish Life and Death in Anatoly Rybakov's *Heavy Sand*," *Publications of the Modern Language Association of America* 111, no. 2 (March 1996): 243; and Judith Deutch Kornblatt, *The Cossack Hero in Russian Literature* (Madison: University of Wisconsin Press, 1992), 39–60.

[108] Kochetov, *Zhurbiny*, 335.

in the official accounts and artistic representations, memory of the Jewish catastrophe was submerged within the universal Soviet tragedy, erasing the very distinction at the core of the Nazi pursuit of racial purity.[109]

Such a policy certainly coincided with similar developments across the European continent. In the restored societies emerging from the Nazi occupation, memories of defeat and victimization were set aside in favor of intensive, state-sponsored cults of heroism and resistance. In the ravaged and humiliated societies burdened with the task of national revival, the mobilizing power of the myth of active heroism was undeniably greater than that of victimization anchored in the shame and guilt-ridden memory of defeat. Above all, memories of victimization bore the troublesome particularism associated with the Jewish minority. Jewish distinct suffering was integrated into an all-national paradigm of victimization and, in some cases, transformed into one of triumphant heroism.[110] The universality of the activist-triumphant myth was underscored by its predominance in the new Israeli state, where Zionism helped to reconstruct a series of cataclysmic defeats in Jewish history as redemptive triumphs, starting with the rebellions against the Romans in the first two centuries A.D. and culminating with the Holocaust. There the official commemoration of the Holocaust had been incorporated into the epic struggle for an independent Jewish state.[111]

Such a dilemma and solution were all too familiar to the Soviet scene, and for similarly compelling reasons. For one, the wave of pogroms that swept Ukrainian cities in 1944–45 marked a new development. For the first time in the Soviet era, violent anti-Semitism exploded as an open, urban phenomenon. In such a volatile environment and with the war still raging, identification with the traditionally resented minority was the last thing desired by the returning Soviet power. This was around the time of Khrushchev's alleged outburst: "Here is the Ukraine and it is not in our interest that the Ukrainians should associate the return of Soviet power with the return of the Jews."[112] Indeed, the industrious denial of Jewish contributions to the liberation of the Republic was in glaring contrast to the celebration of other nationalities. Sometime later, Georgian historians, for example, could publish a laudatory book on the contribution of the

---

[109] A good starting point is Zvi Gitelman, "Soviet Reactions to the Holocaust, 1945–1991," in Dobroszycki and Gurock, *The Holocaust in the Soviet Union*, 3–27.

[110] See Pieter Lagrou, "Victims of Genocide and National Memory: Belgium, France, and the Netherlands, 1945–1965," *Past and Present* 154 (February 1997): 191–222.

[111] Bartov, "Defining Enemies, Making Victims"; Tom Segev, *The Seventh Million: The Israelis and the Holocaust* (New York: Hill and Wang, 1993); James Young, *The Texture of Memory: Holocaust Memorials and Meaning* (New Haven: Yale University Press, 1993), part 3; Yael Zerubavel, *Recovered Roots: Collective Memory and the Making of Israeli National Tradition* (Chicago: University of Chicago Press, 1995).

[112] Leon Leneman, *La tragédie des Juifs en URSS*, 179.

Georgian people to the liberation of Ukraine, especially the role of Georgians in the ranks of the partisan movement.[113] Yet the wholesale deportations of alleged collaborationist minorities conveyed the message that the Soviet polity would not shy away from opening the Pandora's box of collaboration conceived in ethnic terms. This willingness to confront directly the ethnic face of wartime collaboration (in sharp contrast to other multiethnic polities), and the enduring denial of the unique Jewish fate under the Nazis long after the rest of Europe opted for such recognition, pointed to another motive, one that lay at the core of the revolutionary myth.[114]

The twentieth anniversary of the Great Patriotic War in 1965 marked the transition from a living to a historical memory of this cataclysmic event and a determined attempt to develop a commemorative canon and a sense of closure. The last vestiges of the socially alien element—the few remaining kulaks—were released and rehabilitated. Ethnic Germans deported en masse during the war received an official apology from the Supreme Soviet of the Soviet Union,[115] and, most notably, all limitations on former leaders and members of nationalist underground movements, the last category to win rehabilitation (and among whom Ukrainian nationalists were the largest component), were removed.[116] The reinstatement of the largest, best organized, and most persistent of the anti-Soviet separatist movements into the legitimate Ukrainian body national only fifteen years after it was singled out for eternal exclusion was indeed the most visible sign of reconciliation. Permission for individuals to return to their native places of residence was a display of confidence in both the efficacy of the punitive system and in its redemptive power.

But no olive branch was extended to the Jewish community. On the contrary, Jews were branded as traitors to the war effort. In a well-publicized speech to the political and artistic elite in March 1963, Khrushchev dwelled on the alleged treason by a Jew named Kogan, who served as an interpreter for Field Marshal Friedrich Paulus, the commander of the German troops at the Stalingrad front.[117] Whether or not Khrushchev was

---

[113] Mordechai Altshuler, "Jewish Warfare and the Participation of Jews in Combat in the Soviet Union as Reflected in Soviet and Western Historiography," in Zvi Gitelman, ed., *Bitter Legacy: Confronting the Holocaust in the USSR* (Bloomington: Indiana University Press, 1997), 157; referring to I. Babalishvili, *Voiny-gruziny v boiakh za Ukrainu v gody Velikoi Otechestvennoi voiny* (Tbilisi: Sabchota sakartvelo, 1969).

[114] For the shift in the Western European discourse on the Holocaust in the mid-1960s, see Lagrou, "Victims of Genocide," 215–20.

[115] For the decree of 28 August 1964 by the Presidium of the Supreme Soviet, see *Tak eto bylo*, 1:246–47.

[116] The rehabilitation was enacted in two resolutions of the Presidium of the Supreme Soviet on 6 December 1963 and 29 April 1964 (GARF, f. 7523, op. 109, d. 195, ll. 38–39).

[117] "Vysokaia ideinost' i khudozhestvennoe masterstvo—velikaia sila sovetskoi literatury i iskusstva," *Pravda*, 10 March 1963. Although Khrushchev went out of his way to emphasize

aware of the questionable character of his allegation, the charges promptly found their way into a mass-circulated historical novel published that year.[118] In his *Tuchi nad gorodom*, Porfyrii Havrutto elaborated on the treacherous acts of Kogan, referred to as the Judas, which, he claimed, were not limited to serving von Paulus. When the leaders of the Communist underground in occupied Kiev gather to discuss the possibility of treason from within the ranks, they—like the prospective reader—are perplexed by the traitor's identity. "A foul deed, you know, cannot remain secret for long. The whole of Kiev already knows of the betrayal. This foul crime was committed by a former Komsomol worker of the city, left behind for underground activities in the Kiev area, a certain Kogan by name," Andrei Kirilovich tells Kulik. "Il'ia and Pasechnik looked at each other in perplexity. 'I don't understand anything!' Kulik jumped from his chair and began pacing around the room nervously. 'The Hitlerites hate the Jews, destroy them. They make no exceptions for either children or old people. No, I don't believe it! A Jew could not do such a thing.'"

Well, a Jew could do such a thing, and did—as the thoughtful Andrei Kirilovich points out to his quick-to-judge comrade, who, not so incidentally, will soon die at the hands of the Gestapo. "That's up to you, brother," he tells Kulik. "But a fact is a fact. By his betrayal the scoundrel offered Hitlerites such a service that they even made an exception for him—they did not shoot him like they usually do with almost every Jew they arrest. He knew a lot, he was useful to the Germans, so they sent him to work as an interpreter in the military command of Poltava, and later, as a promotion, to the Sixth Army of the famous German commander Paulus. There Kogan has been quietly occupied till now. In short, the degenerate helps the Hitlerites to smash us."[119] And to remove any room for second-guessing, in the epilogue Havrutto assures the readers, in his own voice:

> There are no fictitious characters or incidents in the book. Everything related in the book really happened and those who betrayed our motherland and had been active in aiding the German invaders . . . were caught and severely pun-

---

his distinction between positive Jews—General Kreizer, as always, paraded as an example—and negative Jews, the detailed elaboration of this dubious affair, and its immediate translation into book form, left no doubt as to the officially endorsed view.

[118] Moisei Kogan was captured by the Germans when his Red Army unit surrendered near Kiev in September 1941. Pretending to be an Armenian, he worked under the Germans as a driver, until he escaped in December 1942. In early 1943 he was arrested by the security organs and sentenced to ten years' forced labor on charges of working for the Germans as an interpreter. For extensive documentation of the affair, including Khrushchev's speech, relevant segments from Havrutto's book, and rebuttals by Gromova and Kogan, see Pinkus, *The Soviet Government and the Jews*, 76, 127–33.

[119] Porfyrii Havrutto, *Tuchi nad gorodom* (Moscow: Molodaia Gvardiia, 1968), 165–66.

ished. The same fate overtook the foul traitor, the Judas Kogan, who had betrayed all the Kiev underground to the Germans. For almost two years the fallen man served Field Marshal Paulus, cleaned his boots, helped to interrogate Soviet prisoners-of-war, and even shot at his own compatriots.

The view of the affair as the official representation of the Jews' relations to the myth of the war was furthered by the proximity of the novel's publication to Khrushchev's speech and by the editorial note informing the readers that the novel was actually a documentary. Even when the Khrushchev-Havrutto account was refuted by the detailed investigation of the journalist Ariadna Hromova in a letter to *Literaturnaia gazeta*, it did not prevent a third mass edition of an even larger circulation that repeated the charges against Judas Kogan.[120] The coincidence of the upgrading of Kogan from a mere traitor in the 1963 edition to an accomplished Judas in the 1965 edition with the twentieth anniversary of the Great Patriotic War was neither accidental nor merely symbolic.

It was at this time that Stalin's daughter, Svetlana Allilueva, noted that already "with the expulsion of Trotsky and the extermination during the years of 'purges' of old party members, many of whom were Jews, anti-Semitism was reborn on new ground and first of all within the party itself."[121] Perhaps Allilueva got it right. The Bolshevik epic had to be purged of its association with the resented minority. By the eve of the war, popular identification of the Revolution with the Jews had already found its echo inside the party ranks. If the myth of the October Revolution was perceived as "Judaicized" beyond repair, then the new myth of the Great Patriotic War would not suffer the same fate.

---

[120] Ariadna Hromova, "V interesakh istiny," *Literaturnaia gazeta*, 9 August 1966; reprinted in Pinkus, *The Soviet Government and the Jews*, 128–29. Hromova, a non-Jew herself, was married to a Jew who was murdered in Babyn Iar. Whereas the first edition had a circulation of sixty-five thousand copies and the second seventy-five thousand, circulation of the third edition was increased to one hundred thousand copies. The 1968 edition modified some of the rhetoric on the one hand but vulgarized it on the other. It omitted the phrases: "who had betrayed to the Germans all the Kiev underground" and "cleaned his boots." These changes appear to be a response to Hromova's rebuttal. At the same time, the 1968 epilogue added that Kogan was promoted by the Germans, implying a career built on betrayal rather than an ad-hoc act under wartime conditions. See Pinkus, *The Soviet Government and the Jews*, 493, nn.. 113, 114.

[121] Svetlana Allilueva, *Only One Year* (New York: Harper and Row, 1969), 153. Ironically this was also the view in Berlin in early 1937. "Again a show trial in Moscow," Goebbels noted in his diary on 25 January 1937. "This time once again exclusively against Jews. Radek, etc. The Führer still in doubt whether there isn't after all a hidden anti-Semitic tendency. Maybe Stalin does want to smoke the Jews out. The military is also supposedly strongly anti-Semitic" (cited in Friedländer, *Nazi Germany and the Jews*, 185–86).

Part III

THE MAKING OF A POSTWAR SOVIET NATION

Five

Integral Nationalism in the Trial of War

REFLECTING ON the attempt of Ukrainian nationalists and Nazis to impose their ethnocentric agendas on Vinnytsia, an editor of *Vinnyts'ki visti*, the local wartime newspaper, noted that,

> passive dissatisfaction grew for a variety of reasons—including the inequality accorded to various nationalities: a concept entirely alien to Soviet men. In the end, everything could be reduced to "better our own," i.e., better even the Soviets than the Germans. The people's attitude toward the *uprava* [local administration] was likewise one of preferring "our own" institutions.[1]

Surely this was a remarkable assessment from a person who had done time in a Soviet labor camp on the eve of the war before being drafted to the soon-to-be-crushed Red Army. But what exactly did the elusive phrase "our own" mean?

If by "our own," locals expressed the desire to be left alone, this was a futile hope. The magnitude of events taking place before their eyes excluded neutrality from the menu. In a world of total war, any response, including inaction, assumed critical significance. Moreover, none of the political forces that operated in the region held a pluralistic vision of social order, and none thought of leaving society as is. Hence "our own" was not used in a permanent sense. People struggled to adjust their predispositions to the constantly changing circumstances. Hopes were dashed, new expectations arose, and the excruciatingly harsh present made it possible to compromise with the brutal, yet familiar, past. Further, the articulation of self-identities was shaped to a large degree by a unique, if obscure, feature of the Soviet totalitarian enterprise: the investment of power in both community and individuals to execute key policies decreed by the political power. Public deliberation, awareness, and active involvement in acts such as mass extermination, denunciations, or the selection of people for deportation established a myriad of practices that challenged daily the presumption of an autonomous, apolitical existence.

Any discussion of identities on the local landscape must certainly begin with the peasantry, and not necessarily because of the predominantly rural population of Vinnytsia but rather because all powers competing for

---

[1] HURIP #548, 5.

dominance in the region focused on this constituency. The very group that had been marked by Soviet power as the locus of the Great Transformation found itself celebrated by the nationalist movement as the backbone of the independent Ukrainian nation. In this light, the social and political arena of the peasantry became the site of a clash between conflicting assumptions about the nature of the peasantry and rival expectations for its political allegiance. More visibly than any other group, the local peasantry was a litmus test for the efficacy of three decades of Soviet power through the trial of war and was the key to understanding the fundamental transformation triggered by this cataclysmic event.

The choices locals made were largely shaped by the conflicts between the nationalist alternative and the new Soviet legitimizing myth of the war. There were three main arenas of discord: first, the encounter between the ideas and practices of ethnocentrism, including its most radical form of racially based genocide, and the Soviet legacy of sociologically driven excisionary policies; second, the clash between the nationalist revisionist view of the socioeconomic rural order and its main constituency, the precollectivization elite in the village, on the one hand, and the continuous sovietization of village culture and politics, with the rising constituency of Red Army servicemen and their families, on the other; and, third, the collision between nationalist separatism and the ritualized inculcation of Soviet Ukrainianhood via the tale of unification of the Ukrainian land and its people.

Ukrainian nationalist activists arriving from the western regions may have been unfamiliar with the local scene into which they followed the invading German army, but they certainly had a clear, well-articulated vision of what it should be. The nationalist world was an ethnic mosaic arranged in a hierarchical order of groups that had their own distinctive identities and agendas. By the late 1930s the German and Polish intellectual and political environment within which the nationalists operated before the 1939 partition of Poland was dominated by ethnocentrism. Practically all the major components of the post-Pilsudski Polish polity adopted exclusionary, violent ideologies that viewed the world as comprised of biologically constructed nations, each competing violently with the other. In this environment the physical removal and even destruction of ethnic groups who violated the desired harmony of the national body was acceptable. On the eve of World War II the view of ethnic minorities in Poland, most notably the Jews as a "foreign body, dispersed within our organism so that it produces a pathological deformation" had been absorbed into dominant ideologies and practices.[2]

---

[2] Cited in William W. Hagen, "Before the 'Final Solution': Toward a Comparative Analysis of Political Anti-Semitism in Interwar Germany and Poland," *The Journal of Modern*

The pursuit of ethnic purity and belief in aggression as the natural state of human relations constituted the core of the officially endorsed ideology of integral nationalism (*natsiokratiia*). The reading of the nation was unapologetically racial. Nationalist ideologues tried to draw the line between the Nazi blood-based concept of race and their own, which sought the spiritual and biological revival of the nation, but the result was nothing more than a semantic splitting of hairs with an ideology to which they confessed their affinity in any case. "The problem of race in Ukraine must be solved by cleansing Ukraine of the superfluous multiethnic elements of *moskali* [a derogatory term for Russians], Jews, Poles, Madiars, Tatars, and others," declared Maksym Orlyk in 1940. "In the wake of the Soviet-Muscovite chaos, Ukraine must mobilize and develop all its biological strength and shape itself racially in order to fill up and occupy the entire Ukrainian ethnographic space, rid itself of all other national elements, and defend itself from the chaotic mixture with the racial elements of *moskali*, and the Turkish and Caucasian peoples," continued Orlyk.[3] Dmytro Dontsov, the chief ideologue of Ukrainian integral nationalism, vehemently rejected all supra-national ideologies and associations espousing "humane feeling," "proletarian brotherhood," "peasant brotherhood," "Slavic brotherhood," or the Jewish-dominated international fronts. "Our Tolstoy-type 'patriots' call 'the idolizing cult' of the nation 'zoological nationalism,' " exclaimed Dontsov. "What do they mean by this not-so-much-terrible as stupid phrase? According to them, zoological nationalism applies to everyone who, for example, is not dragged into a united front with world Jewry for the struggle against Hitlerism; he who does not shiver with delight to the very sound of Pushkin's name; he who does not contribute to *Signal* [an ultra right-wing Russian émigré journal in the late 1930s] . . For our chatterers of humanity, every person who is not of our race is not a stranger but a brother."[4]

Avoiding the deadening, amorphous supra-national ideologies was only one way to maintain the purity of the nation. Ruthless, violent struggle against the contaminating elements was another. The world was divided into "master" and "plebeian" nations, and the preservation of purity was a precondition for preventing the sliding of the nation from the former

---

History 68 (June 1996): 351–81; here, 374 n. 43. For the politics of official anti-Semitism in Poland on the eve of the war, see also Edward d. Wynot, "A Necessary Cruelty": The Emergence of Official Anti-Semitism in Poland, 1936–1939," *The American Historical Review* 76, no. 4 (October 1971): 1035–58.

[3] *Ideia i Chyn*, no. 4 (1940), in RGASPI, f. 17, op. 125, d. 339, ll. 38–39.

[4] Dmytro Dontsov, *De shukaty nashykh istorychnykh tradytsii* (L'viv: Ukrainske vyd-vo, 1942), 49–50, 104. For a brief review of Dontsov's pamphlet, see John Armstrong, "Collaborationism in World War II: The Integral Nationalist Variant in Eastern Europe," *Journal of Modern History* 40 (1968): 403–4.

state to the latter. The Italian example, from the humiliating defeat of Adowa at the hands of African tribes in 1896 to the glorious fascist present, amply demonstrated that this was a viable mission. Restoring the Ukrainian nation to its glorious Cossack past entailed a ruthless eradication of the contaminating elements from the body national beginning with the alienated intellectual elite infected by international liberal traditions.[5] Dontsov scornfully rebuffed objections to "zoological nationalism." "The modern humanists predict the quick demise of all those who strengthen and develop their fighting instincts and intolerance," he lashed out. "But 'zoological nationalism,' this 'predation' that they condemn as a divine punishment, was in the past nothing but the normal foundation of every entity and race in the eternal struggle for [their] place under the sun," he wrote.[6] Such a world had no room for the ill-conceived liberal notion of harmony and equilibrium. It was time to bury the "so-called traditions of the nineteenth century, the traditions of liberalism, democracy, belief in harmony, belief in the disarming power of humanism, belief in 'crocodile tears,' belief in any illusion except in yourself," declared Dontsov.[7]

And this worldview was carried into the Eastern territories where ethnonational heterogeneity and centuries of coexistence may have diminished the alertness of Ukrainians and warranted double vigilance at every step. The war only demonstrated once more the inherent unreliability of the supra-national pseudo-alliances. After all, the working classes of Moscow and Berlin failed to come to the aid of their Ukrainian counterparts in this time of distress. "The Jewish-Muscovite proletarians, while fleeing from Ukraine, ruined your homes, factories, industries, and shops, and destroyed the cities in order to condemn you to famine and poverty so you would perish as did the Ukrainian peasantry in 1932–33. And this was done by your 'brothers,' the Muscovite proletarians and the Jews!" exclaimed the leadership of OUN-B in eastern Ukraine in April 1942 in an effort to incite Ukrainian workers.[8] By now, the brochure concluded, it was clear that the German proletarians proved to be as disastrous to the Ukrainian people as were the Muscovites and the Jews.

Ethnicity, indeed, took priority over all other factors in deciding membership in the renewed Ukrainian nation. The door was left open to landowners and Communists who sought to redeem themselves. "The landowner, the lord [*pan*], the Communist, if they are Ukrainians and want to work, they will get their share like any other person. JEWS WILL NOT HAVE THE RIGHT

---

[5] Ibid., 101–3.
[6] Ibid., 55.
[7] Ibid., 106.
[8] TsDAHOU, f. 57, op. 4, d. 347, l. 27.

TO OWN LAND. They will work as common laborers. If not—as forced labor," the OUN-M newspaper *Selians'ka dolia* informed the peasants.[9]

Purity had to be maintained at all costs and all levels. In the process, Russians, Poles, and Jews had to be removed from the Ukrainian scene. The message was rather blunt: "He who does not speak your language, who does not call himself a Ukrainian, or does the peasant wrong—this person is a *zaida* [a derogatory term for an outsider] and your enemy and must leave your land or die on it. The Muscovite, the Pole, and the Jew were, are, and will always be your enemies!"[10] But expulsion and elimination of the alien bodies was only one method in the struggle for purity. Purifying the nation required an all-out continuous effort down to the most intimate level. And so Ukrainian boys and girls were urged "not to marry foreigners because then you will betray your faith, your people, and your land." And this referred not only to Poles but also to Muscovites, as Taras Shevchenko wrote:

> You, the black-browed [Ukrainian], fall in love but not with the Muscovites
> Because the Muscovites are alien people who bring you misery."
> PEASANTS! YOU ARE THE POWERFUL UKRAINIAN PEOPLE, DO NOT BETRAY ITS
> BLOOD! PURE UKRAINIAN BLOOD RENDERS YOU THE RIGHT TO THE UKRAI-
> NIAN LAND! UKRAINE FOR THE UKRAINIANS—FOR YOU, PEASANT![11]

In the cities the cosmopolitan, assimilationist environment had to disappear, and the first step was to rearrange the ethnic categorization blurred by Russian Soviet rule. Reporting from neighboring Kamianets' in July 1941, one "marching group" (*pokhidna hrupa*) described the local population as consisting of 60 percent Jews, 20 percent Russified Ukrainians (*pomoskovtsi Ukraintsi*), 10 percent good Ukrainians (*dobri Ukraintsi*), and 10 percent Russians (*moskali*).[12] The use of the derogatory terms carried implications for the remaking of the urban administration. After securing leading posts in the regional administration such as chief of the administration, head of the Security Service, head of the propaganda department, head of the school system, and editor of the newspaper, according to OUN people and "competent urban [local] Ukrainians," the activists allowed for lower positions to be filled by "local good Ukrainians." Neither Russified Ukrainians nor local Russians had a role in the newly established administration.

Another report from Zhytomyr on 20–27 July 1941 conveyed the view of an urban society constituted of demonic enemies with distinct ethnic

[9] Ibid., d. 369, l. 63.
[10] Ibid., l. 60b.
[11] Ibid., ll. 66b–67.
[12] TsDAVOVU, f. 3833, op. 1, d. 14, l. 15.

faces, on the one hand, and atrophied masses, on the other. The city's population declined by 60 percent because of the mass flight of Jews and those Ukrainians associated with Soviet power: "After the Germans arrived, the Bolsheviks, with the help of agents whom they could find primarily among the Jews, burned many houses in the city," wrote the young activists. The remaining population was extremely frightened and, during the first days, had not shown up in the streets; it took a great effort to revive signs of life in the city. The passivity of the local population in this eastern city was seen as a consequence of the Bolshevik terror. "No one is sure that the Bolsheviks won't return," they concluded.

With Bolshevik power chased out of Ukraine, the reconstruction of Ukrainian society shifted gears, as did the translation of rhetoric to action. Violent attacks on various groups were openly admitted by the Kamianets'-Podil's'kyi marching group on 31 July 1941. The liquidation of NKVDists, Communists, and other bastards continues, came the laconic report.[13] The nationalist identification of Russians and Jews with the NKVD and the Communist Party, as we shall see below, made this terse statement rather meaningful. In any case, by the fall of 1941 all rhetorical inhibitions and vagueness disappeared. "All elements residing in our cities, whether Jews or Poles who have been brought here, must disappear. The Jewish problem is currently on the way to being resolved and will be resolved in accordance with the general reorganization of the new Europe . . . The Ukrainian city is now a clean page," declared the editor of *Volyn'*.[14] At this point in both time and place, there was nothing vague about the meaning of the statement. The nationalist movement was pursuing the physical removal of all foreign elements from the national body.

Of all nonindigenous groups residing on eastern Ukrainian territory, it was ethnic Russians who posed the greatest difficulties for integral nationalism in practice. Only 106,061 Russians were counted in Vinnytsia in the 1939 census—a mere 4.5 percent of the population.[15] But unlike the western Ukrainian theater where ethnic Russians and culture were recent arrivals and markedly alien to the population at large, in the east Russians constituted an integral part of the social, political, and cultural fabric. For nationalist activists and guerrillas streaming in from the west, it was an agonizing reality that they vowed to change. However, not in 1941 nor anytime later did the nationalists have the capacity to carry out the desired level of ethnic

---

[13] Ibid., l. 13.

[14] Ulas Samchuk, "We Shall Conquer the Cities," *Volyn*, 1 September 1941, as cited in Shmuel Spector, *The Holocaust of Volhynian Jews, 1941–1944* (Jerusalem: Achva, 1990), 239.

[15] Poliakov, *Vsesoiuznaia perepis' naseleniia 1939 goda*, 68.

purification; nevertheless the will was there and, when the opportunity to pursue such purification presented itself, the nationalists seized it.

In the culturally Russified and ethnically mixed Vinnytsia it was crucial at the start to expose the artificial dichotomy between Bolshevism and Russian imperialism. Bolshevik ideology had a distinct ethnic face and nationalist propagandists set to reveal it. Under the editorship of the young student Nofenko, *Vinnyts'ki visti* hammered out repeatedly that, regardless of its various incarnations, Red or White, Muscovite imperialism in Ukraine was one and the same.[16] More ominous to ethnic Russians was the overt connection of being Russian to the menace of the Jews, whose fate had already been decided. "[These] cynical Jews," lashed out the paper,

> tried to present the Russian-Jewish terror to the world as a holy crusade to lift the individual to the heights of human happiness. All this happened under the sun of the Stalin constitution, the most democratic constitution in the world, one that promised full rights to everyone . . . These Jewish-Russian criminals are too many to count. The Ukrainian people have learned very well about the baseness of the Jews. All the Jews held hands with our worst enemies—Russia and Poland. Together with the *moskali*, they tortured our people, starved them, and deported them as far as Siberia and Solovki. But the unavoidable end has caught up with them. There will be no tortures and persecutions in the new Ukraine, and the world will get rid of the Jews forever.[17]

Rhetoric was supported by action. In the fall of 1941 nationalist forces attacked urban Russian populations in eastern Ukrainian regions and executed Red Army POWs who were released back to their villages.[18] When the Ukrainian police in Kiev were ordered to secure hostages after an explosion occurred in the city in the fall of 1941, they arrested only Russians, scores of whom were then shot.[19] The German order excluded Ukrainians from being taken hostage, and, for die-hard activists, this was a green light for carnage. Lev Dudin, referring to the incident, recalled that the Ukrainian police were ordered to round up three hundred hostages for retribution following the destruction of a public building by the anti-German underground in October 1941. The police forces, consisting

---

[16] "Ukraina i Moskva," *Vinnyts'ki visti*, 15 October 1941; and "Bil'shovyzm i ukrains'ka natsiia," 18 December 1941.

[17] *Vinnyts'ki visti*, 9 November 1941. According to Aletiiano-Popivs'kyi, the local ethnic Russians succeeded in pressuring the Germans to get rid of Nofenko (Aletiiano-Popivs'kyi, *Z ideieiu v sertsi*, 33, 162).

[18] Armstrong, "Collaborationism," 409; Phillip Friedman, "Ukrainian-Jewish Relations during the Nazi Occupation," *YIVO Annual of Jewish Social Science* 12 (1958/1959): 269–70.

[19] Armstrong, *Ukrainian Nationalism*, 167 n. 18.

mainly of radical nationalists from the Subcarpathian region, set road-blocks and, through the examination of passports, picked up only ethnic Russians.[20]

During the initial phase of the German occupation, the Ukrainian-manned militia and administration were instrumental in proliferating an acute sense of fear and discrimination among local ethnic Russians. Differences that had appeared until recently as strictly cultural now assumed new political weight, and Russians became the first casualties. With nationalist posters declaring Jews, Poles, and Russians the mortal enemies of the Ukrainian people, using derogatory terms such as *Moskovshchyna* for *Rossiia*, *moskal'* for *russkii*, and *zhyd* for *evrei*, the Russian language retreated from public use to the domestic scene.[21]

In Vinnytsia, nationalist anti-Russian sentiments were further fueled by the solid presence of ethnic Russians in local administration and the modus vivendi between the latter and the German-occupation authorities. Not only was the Russian professor Aleksandr Sevastianov the German-appointed mayor of the city, but his deputy was the ethnic German Kezar Bernard, who enjoyed the support of some pro-Soviet Russified priests. And when the editor of the regional newspaper spoke out against the *moskali* and the *Volksdeutschen* (ethnic Germans), he was arrested by the Germans.[22] This only inflamed the situation. Nationalist surveillance reports on the sociopolitical situation in the Romanian-held districts of Vinnytsia portrayed Russians as the principal danger to Ukraine. Referred to as *katsap*, a derogatory term, Russians were claimed to pose a threat by their sheer existence and position on Ukrainian territory. "The Jewish problem in Ukraine, as a pillar of Bolshevism, has been resolved by the Germans," one survey declared.

> The principal Bolshevik strength in the eastern and central Ukrainian lands is [now] based on the *katsap* element. Its vigor should not be underestimated. Even when the Bolsheviks as such are destroyed the *katsapy* will still be a threat to us, and we should not underestimate this threat. The *katsap* feels himself superior to the Ukrainian and, in any case, he is a Muscovite patriot. He believes in the power and the mission of the Muscovite people. He is even more dangerous because he is in the city, the factories, and in all locations decisive for a revolution. The *katsap* language, lifestyle, and even political thought are dominant in the city. Even when the Bolsheviks vanish as a real force, the *katsapy* will still be in Ukraine and will always look to Moscow for support.[23]

[20] Lev Dudin, *Velikii mirazh*, Hoover Archive, Nicolaevky Collection, series 178, box no. 232, folder 10, 130–31.

[21] Ibid., 115–16, 125.

[22] Aletiiano-Popivs'kyi, *Z ideieiu v sertsi*, 33, 39, 48, 125, 162.

[23] TsDAHOU, f. 57, op. 4, d. 347, l. 38.

In the short run, the *katsap* peril was even more concrete. Despite its current low profile, warned the survey, the katsap-Bolshevik underground is capable of stabbing the Ukrainian cause in the back. The report also referred to the Old Slavonic Church [Orthodox] that operated in the southern parts of Ukraine as a bastion of the *katsap* elements and as an expression of Muscovite rule over Ukraine.[24] The implications of the inherent qualities of the *katsap* required no further clarification.

Still, the eastern Ukrainian condition did force a certain modification in dealing with the Russian problem, if only a tactical one. Not surprisingly a change in attitude toward ethnic Russians originated from within the UPA ranks. The prolonged period of activity on the ethnically heterogeneous territory of the east and the enrollment of young eastern Ukrainians into the ranks forced a reevaluation of policy. The first sign of moderation appeared in the spring of 1943 in a single leaflet that referred positively to ethnic Russians who were born in Ukraine and were not inherently opposed to Ukrainian independence. At the same time, the leaflet adhered to linguistic purity and the exclusiveness of the Ukrainian language in public life. The contamination of the Ukrainian language by the "Ukrainian-Russian jargon" spoken in Kharkiv was strongly condemned.[25] A more generous concession was offered by the Supreme Command of the UPA in June 1943. An address to ethnic Russians in Ukraine distinguished between the Bolshevik regime and the Russian people. The solution of the national problem lay in the struggle against foreigners and one's own imperialists, but not in imperialism that triggers the resistance of all neighboring nations. Russians were called on to establish a national government on Russian ethnographic territory, while Russians in Ukraine were invited to create Russian national units under the UPA to fight Hitlerite and Bolshevik imperialism.[26] Although the invitation remained, for the most part, on paper, some ethnic Russians did enroll in the ranks of the nationalist guerrillas.[27]

The only known attempt to articulate a coherent reevaluation of the nationalist Russian policy was made by Iosyp Pozychaniuk, a native of Vinnytsia who was brought up in the Soviet system. In a memorandum to the UPA leadership, Pozychaniuk drew the line between the Muscovite-Bolshevik empire and the Russian people. It was the latter, he wrote, who brought down the Romanov empire and the native Russian ultra-nationalism of the White generals.[28] Yet even this modest attempt at moderation

---

[24] Ibid., l. 37b.

[25] Armstrong, *Ukrainian Nationalism*, 117–19.

[26] TsDAHOU, f. 57, op. 4, d. 358, ll. 18–18b.

[27] Bilinsky, *The Second Soviet Republic*, 294.

[28] D. Shakhai, "Our Tactics with Regard to the Russian People," in Peter J. Potichnyi and Yevhen Shtendera, eds., *The Political Thought of the Ukrainian Underground, 1943–1951*

underscored the inability to part with the ethnocentric aspect of nationalist ideology. As Pozychaniuk himself admitted, the revision of the nationalist policy was merely tactical. "We have [so far] stressed unequivocally that our enemy is the Russian people, that we are struggling against the Russian people, Muscovite Russian culture, Russian imperialism, and the like. *Although essentially this is correct* from a tactical point of view, particularly at this time, it is sheer stupidity to identify the Russian people with Bolshevism."[29] Moreover, Pozychaniuk envisioned future relations between the Russian and Ukrainian states as inevitably antagonistic, although he believed this would not occur immediately. Elsewhere, Pozychaniuk was blatantly patronizing to the Russians: "Politically, the Ukrainian people (if one speaks of the whole) are more mature than the Russians. In addition, the Ukrainian people have a powerful ideal. The Russian people *lack an ideal of equal value*, except, perhaps, the ideal of a new social revolution."[30] Nor could Pozychaniuk bring himself to accept de facto the bilingualism of the Ukrainian polity. In the future Ukrainian state, wrote Pozychaniuk, the Russian national minority will enjoy the right to their own language, but only on the condition that the same rights are granted to Ukrainians throughout the Russian state. Critically, even this half-measured memorandum was not designated for general publication but rather as a memorandum to the leadership. Nevertheless these rare concessions came far too late, when the tide of the war had turned and the UPA was retreating from the eastern regions. The Russian pill was indeed bitter.

How viable was the anti-Russian message and practices in a place like Vinnytsia? Nationalist activists were quick to spot key groups, whom they believed espoused similar views. The local Ukrainian intelligentsia in town appeared to be a bastion of anti-Russian sentiments. In 1943, during his stay in Vinnytsia, Mykhailo Seleshko, a leading member in the OUN-M, was told by several Ukrainian intellectuals that the only solution to the Russification of Ukrainian cities was their demolition along with the population. The newly restored cities should be populated by Ukrainians only. If the danger of Russification is to be overcome, then the alien element (*chuzhyi element*) must once and for all be removed.[31] Such views were not

---

(Edmonton: Canadian Institute of Ukrainian Studies, 1986), 287, 289. Shakhai was Pozychaniuk's pseudonym.

[29] Ibid., 291.

[30] Ibid., 293.

[31] Mykhailo Seleshko, *Vinnytsia: Spomyny perekladacha komisii doslidiv zlochyniv NKVD v 1937–1938* (New York: Fundatsiia im. O. Olzhycha, 1991), 164. Seleshko was Andrii Mel'nyk's secretary and in 1943 served as an interpreter for the Nazi-sponsored international commission investigating the mass graves exhumed in Vinnytsia. Seleshko published a partial

anomalous among the young and best-educated. A strong sense that job discrimination favored the Russians fueled the identification of the most resented aspects of Soviet power with ethnic Russians. Members of this cohort blamed Russians more than any other ethnic group, including Jews, for the Bolsheviks' ascendance to power and for offering less opposition to collectivization. "Great Russians never opposed Stalin's policy," claimed one member of this group. "Great Russians find it impossible to fight the regime; Great Russians have no interest in an uprising. It would be silly to rise up against yourself."[32] Notably, however, members of this cohort did not necessarily support Ukrainian separatism.[33]

In any event, nationalists had greater expectations from the peasantry. Nationalist surveillance reports on occupied Vinnytsia conveyed the belief that the peasantry at large detested the Russians. "The village speaks in Ukrainian, the town speaks in "city" [Russian] language . . . They hate the *katsapy*.[34] Some nationalist activists saw what they considered to be exploitable friction between Ukrainians and Russians in daily life. There, argued Seleshko, the ethnic breach was augmented by class gaps. Ukrainian peasants who came to trade in the town markets were disadvantaged because of their poor command of the Russian language. The town dwellers (referred to as *mishchany*, a derogatory term for petty-bourgeois), who had a command of both languages, spoke Russian among themselves.[35]

As is often the case, Seleshko proved to be an astute observer but a poor analyst. The village, indeed, was perceived by many of those surveyed as a site of discord between Russians and Ukrainians and the lack of fluency in Russian in particular as creating an uproar among peasants.[36] But this negative reaction did not necessarily translate into political generalizations, not to mention endorsement of active persecution. At times, the sense of cultural inferiority inspired admiration and affection rather than resentment. Marriage to Muscovites was still considered a sign of worldliness, a trait in which peasants took great pride. "My lady, after all, is from Moscow!" proudly declared a peasant from the village of Byrlivka, referring to the qualities and achievements of his wife, a language teacher.[37] In the same vein, the young daughter of one of Seleshko's acquaintances in

---

account shortly after the war under the title "Vinnytsia—the Katyn of Ukraine," *The Ukrainian Quarterly* 5 (1949): 238–48.

[32] Sylvia Gilliam, "The Nationality Questionnaire," unpublished manuscript of the Project on the Soviet Social System, Harvard University, 1954, 123, 126.

[33] Ibid., xv.

[34] TsDAHOU, f. 57, op. 4, d. 347, l. 28a.

[35] Seleshko, *Vinnytsia*, 84.

[36] Gilliam, "The Nationality Questionnaire," 18, 51–52.

[37] Hanna Meller-Faust, *Me-ever la-nahar: Pikei Zikhronot Me-Transnistria*, (Israel: Kibbutz Lohamei Hagetaot Press, 1985), 149.

Vinnytsia viewed Moscow as "the center of the world, the pinnacle of all achievements, just like the song 'My Moscow' that was very popular in Ukraine." And in Stare Misto, a suburb of Vinnytsia referred to by Seleshko as a "big village," youngsters spoke Ukrainian at home with their parents, but once on the street and among themselves they switched to Russian, recalled an incensed Seleshko.[38] Moreover, peasants maintained a clear distinction between Soviet power and Russians. During the traumatic collectivization in the region, peasants distinguished between the "Russian militia," which treated them fairly and lawfully, and the "Jewish militia," which squeezed them mercilessly.[39] Equally important, peasants were inclined to blame the "Kremlin" twice as much as they blamed Russians for their position, and, overall, they did not envision a clash of interests with ethnic Russians.[40]

If anything, the people of Vinnytsia appeared puzzled by the venomous anti-Russian rhetoric of Ukrainian nationalists. Locals had little comprehension and acceptance of the nationalist insistence on excising ethnic Russians from the Ukrainian body. In mid-1943 Seleshko was dismayed to discover that in Vinnytsia even nationally conscious Ukrainians considered Russians "our own" (*svoi*). When Seleshko referred to Russians as *katsapy*, his audience corrected him, exclaiming that these were not Russians but some unpleasant people.[41] In his attempt to extrapolate the western-based ethnic demarcation onto the eastern scene, Seleshko, like so many other western Ukrainian activists operating in the eastern regions, found himself confronted not merely by three decades of Soviet acculturation but by three centuries of coexistence within the boundaries of the Russian Empire. It was an unlikely environment for an anti-Russian exclusionary message to gain widespread approval. While prejudice against Russians proliferated among the young, best-educated eastern Ukrainians, it was defused among the population at large. Indeed, a substantial minority of 39 percent countered with the view that Russians offered less opposition to collectivization than did other ethnic groups. An equal number, however, believed that Russians resisted collectivization as much as others did, and 20 percent even believed that Russians resisted more than other groups.[42]

[38] Seleshko, *Vinnytsia*, 150, 160.

[39] PAVO, f. 136, op. 3, d. 8, ll. 113–114.

[40] Gilliam, "The Nationality Questionnaire," 51–52. In their summary of the nationality questionnaire, Inkeles and Bauer plausibly attributed the absence of anti-Russian sentiments in the countryside to its relative homogeneity, which meant that peasants did not encounter direct competition by ethnic Russians (Alex Inkeles and Raymond Bauer, *The Soviet Citizen: Daily Life in a Totalitarian Society* [Cambridge, Mass.: Harvard University Press, 1961], 356–59).

[41] Seleshko, *Vinnytsia*, 150, 152.

[42] Gilliam, "The Nationality Questionnaire," 125.

Finally, 37 percent, a substantial minority, saw a community of interest between Ukrainians and Russians versus 31 percent who perceived a clash of interests between the two communities.[43] The Russian episode revealed some intriguing lessons for the resonance and viability of exclusionary messages and practices in a region like Vinnytsia. Indeed, people were seeing the world through ethnic glasses. Their world was made up of ethnic groups arranged in hierarchical order. They were also prone to blame their misfortunes on specific ethnicities. But, more often than not, they drew the line between holding prejudicial views and endorsing active persecution. Victimizing certain groups and excluding them from society often meant the preservation of Ukrainianhood, rather than an effort to destroy non-Ukrainians. In concrete terms, popular reactions meant that bias against Russians was not a viable mobilizing battle cry in Vinnytsia.

No such ambivalence was evident regarding the Polish community. The nationalists' unequivocal hostility toward this minority was spotted rather early by the Germans, who sought to make the most of it. While considering the option of establishing a nominally independent Galicia on the eve of the German invasion of Poland in September 1939, Wilhelm Canaris, head of the *Abwehr* (German Military Intelligence Service), noted in his diary that he "would have to make appropriate preparations with the Ukrainians so that, should this alternative become real, the Mel'nyk Organization [OUN] can produce an uprising that would aim at the annihilation of the Jews and the Poles."[44] Indeed, Poles figured highly in the nationalist hierarchy of enemies, and even more so for activists who came from the western regions. The interwar era in this territory was marked by ever radicalizing violence between the Polish government and Ukrainian nationalist activists. Polish oppression of the Ukrainian nationalist movement in Galicia and Volhynia was already avenged with the commencement of the German invasion, when armed Ukrainians attacked Poles in ethnically mixed areas with apparent approval from the Ukrainian auxiliary police. This situation was only bound to deteriorate as Stepan Bandera and his young cohort asserted increasing power within the nationalist movement. Years of terrorist attacks on Polish government officials, subsequent incarceration, and the violent Polish pacification campaign paved

---

[43] Ibid., 20, 154. Those conducting the survey defined "community of interest" as "the nationality with which an independent Ukraine might most easily become allied, according to popular attitudes. The question: In general, certain nationality groups have tended to band together with certain others because of a greater feeling of having common interests with these groups and not with others. We would like to know with which of the nationality groups listed below have the Ukrainians felt they have the most in common, and with which do they believe they have a clash of interests."

[44] Dallin, *German Rule*, 115

the way for a ruthless anti-Polish platform.[45] The vehemence of the anti-Polish sentiments surprised even the Germans, no fans of this group either. Complaining about the unruly conduct of the Ukrainian militia, an *Einsatzgruppe* report from 18 August 1941 noted that "Poles are equated with Jews and some have to wear [identification] armbands as well." This was accomplished under the slogans originating from L'viv that a "free and independent Ukraine must be created according to the motto "Ukraine for the Ukrainians, under the leadership of OUN."[46]

Equally revealing was the comparison nationalists drew between the fate of Poles and Jews under the Germans. The UPA never denied that the Germans engaged in a systematic extermination of the Jews, which they welcomed as a solution to the Jewish problem in Ukraine. But it made every effort to deny and mock Polish claims about German atrocities committed against the Polish population. The Polish government in exile called on the age-old Polish martyrdom in its attempt to win over world public opinion. It did not even shy away from imposing "Polish" identity on nearly thirty-five people who were executed by the Germans near Warsaw in January 1942, most of whom argued the UPA were "certainly Jews!" Polish claims about Bolshevik anti-Polish terror were similarly mocked for their inflated figures and worse, incorporating hundreds of thousands of Ukrainian victims into the fabricated myth of Polish victimhood.[47]

Nor did the systematic Soviet deportations of Poles from Vinnytsia in the mid-1930s tame the nationalists' resentment of this minority. Reflecting on Ukrainian-Polish relations in the region, Aletiiano-Popivs'kyi, a young nationalist activist in Vinnytsia could hardly muster a single good word for the Poles as he managed to do in his references to Jews. True, not all Poles were enemies of the Ukrainian nation. Actually there were some good ones who understood that their lot was with the people among whom they lived. But these were the exceptions. The Polish community in Ukraine consisted of nationalists who, during the revolution of 1917–19, sought the creation of a Poland "from sea to sea" in which there would be no place for Ukraine. Later, with the Bolsheviks' arrival, they converted effortlessly to Communist internationals. In both cases, concluded Aletiiano-Popivs'kyi, the Poles proved to be unrealistic dreamers. In 1937 the

---

[45] Armstrong, *Ukrainian Nationalism*, 37–38. On nationalist anti-Polish violence in interwar Poland, see Alexander Motyl "Ukrainian Nationalist Political Violence in Inter-War Poland," *East European Quarterly* 19 (March 1985): 45–55; and Bohdan Budurowiycz, "Poland and the Ukrainian Problem, 1921–1939," *Canadian Slavonic Papers* 25, no. 4 (1983): 473–500, esp. 486–90, 496.

[46] *Ereignismeldung UdSSR* (Operational Situational Report by the Einsatzgruppen in the USSR), no. 56 (18 August 1941), 3.

[47] TsDAHOU, f. 57, op. 4, d. 347, ll. 33–33b.

Dzierzynskis, Menzhynskis, and Markhelevskis woke up to find themselves labeled "Pilsudski's agents."[48] Later, directly addressing the Polish population, nationalist leaders emphasized that they had no quarrel with the Polish people as such, only with the imperialist aspirations of the Polish leadership that denied Ukrainian statehood and rights over western Ukraine. This modest claim, however, was followed by an inflammatory and graphic description of the massacres of thousands of Ukrainian villagers by Polish bands and the active collaboration of the Poles with the Germans.[49] The implications of such charges for the conduct of nationalist forces in the field were all too clear.

Indeed, the rhetoric and practices of both UPA leaders and the rank and file were less restrained. Mykola Lebed', a top commander of the UPA forces in Galicia, stated plainly that the goal of the 1943 campaign was to "clear the forests of foreign elements."[50] Just who these foreign elements were was clarified by a captured activist in neighboring Rivne. In the course of his interrogation by the NKVD on 31 January 1944, Vladimir Solov'ev recalled that, from the spring of 1943 on, the security services of UPA began cleansing the western regions of Poles. The population was told that the Poles were inveterate enemies of Ukrainians, an obstacle blocking an independent Ukraine, and, as such, must be exterminated. This policy was carried out ruthlessly. Entire villages and families were burned alive. Throughout May and June of 1943 several thousand Poles were murdered in the neighboring Rivne region alone. By then, the regions to the west of Vinnytsia sank into a bloodbath that stood out even by the standards of that era. Killing was personal, with neighbors who had lived together for decades, if not centuries, turning against each other with a ferocity that in rare moments of reflection astounded even themselves.[51]

[48] Aletiiano-Popivs'kyi, *Z ideieiu v sertsi*, 110–11.

[49] O. S. Sadovyi, "Kudy priamuiut' poliaky," RGASPI, f. 17, op. 125, d. 337, ll. 150–55.

[50] Mykola Lebed', *UPA, Ukrains'ka povstans'ka armiia* (1946), 76–79, cited in Friedman, "Ukrainian-Jewish Relations," 270–71 n. 19.

[51] TsDAHOU, f. 57, op. 4, d. 351, l. 8. Solov'ev claimed that the Germans encouraged the massacres of Poles. This seems rather doubtful. The Germans were indeed extremely hostile to the Poles but, as local Ukrainians were enrolling en masse in the UPA, they opted for the recruitment of Poles into the local administration and police, and even executed Ukrainians engaged in the killing of Poles (Armstrong, *Ukrainian Nationalism*, 110–12; idem, "Collaborationism," 409 n. 45). The literature on wartime Ukrainian-Polish conflict is highly tendentious and still awaits a thorough, even-handed investigation. A good start is Timothy Snyder, " 'To Resolve the Ukrainian Problem Once and for All': The Ethnic Cleansing of Ukrainians in Poland, 1943–1947," *Journal of Cold War Studies* 1, no. 2 (spring 1999): 86–120. See, also, Ryszard Torzecki, *Kwestia ukrainska w polityce III Rzeszy, 1933–1945* (Warsaw: Ksiazka i Wiedza, 1972); Lev Shankovs'kyi, "Ukrains'ka povstanska armiia," *Istoriia ukrains'koho viiska* (Winnipeg: Kliub pyiateliv ukr. knyzhky, 1953), 690–703; Mykolaj Terles, ed., *Ethnic Cleansing of Poles in Volhynia and East Galicia, 1942–1946*

Evidence substantiating the tone of the nationalist anti-Polish message among the people of Vinnytsia is scarce. For one, the Roman Catholic Church and monastery was part of the local scene from 1576 to 1918. Whatever affirmation existed was complicated by the legacy of three decades of Soviet power in the region. Nationalists were baffled by the malleability of national identification among people whom they unequivocally considered as Poles.[52] When asked for their nationality in 1943, Polish women in Vinnytsia defined themselves as "Catholic." Once the concept of nationality had been explained to them, the women redefined themselves as "Ukrainians," recalled Mykhailo Seleshko.[53] This, however, should have come as no surprise. By this time, the Soviet policy of allowing individuals a choice in selecting their national identity had taken root in practice. When the authorities recorded the reactions of local Poles to the massive conversion of Polish schools in the region into Ukrainian schools in the mid-1930s, the malleability of this ethnonational identity was evident. Needless to say, some categorically objected to the move. "[They] closed the school, but we remain Poles . . . I will still be a Pole for a long time," exclaimed one teacher. Others saw it as nothing but a reincarnation of the tsarist anti-Polish policies. According to one Iuzef Vytkovs'kyi from the village of Hutsulivka:

> First, they arrested the priests; then, under the pretense of renting the churches, they seized them; now they deprive us of schools; soon the time will come when they'll confiscate all literature; and later they may ban speaking in Polish altogether, and any printed or spoken word will land one in prison. There is no difference between the way we were persecuted under tsarism and our present situation.

In some villages parents persistently boycotted meetings that authorities set to address the new policy. Significantly, most of these individuals were identified as teachers in the converted schools, those most likely to be the first targeted for deportation. No less common were responses such as the

---

(Toronto: Alliance of the Polish Eastern Provinces, 1993); and Tadeusz Piotrowski, *Vengeance of the Swallows* (Jefferson, N.C.: McFarland, 1994). For a rare memoir of a perpetrator portraying his involvement in these atrocities, not in a report to superiors or under interrogation by captors, see Waldemar Lotnik, *Nine Lives: Ethnic Conflict in the Polish-Ukrainian Borderlands* (London: Serif, 1999), 54–79. Along with his comrades at the Polish Peasants' Battalion, eighteen-year-old Lotnik literally obliterated Ukrainian villages, murdering most people in sight, indiscriminately raping women, mutilating corpses, and burning villages to the ground.

[52] Some 55,610 Poles were counted in the region in the 1939 census; this accounted for about 15.5 percent of all Poles in the Soviet Ukrainian Republic (357,710) and 2.4 percent of the region's population (Poliakov, *Vsesoiuznaia perepis' naseleniia 1939 goda*, 68).

[53] Seleshko, *Vinnytsia*, 132.

following: "We don't need Polish schools. We are Catholics, not Poles. Our children study in Polish at school but speak Ukrainian at home"; or, "How come we are Poles when all our lives we and our children have spoken Ukrainian. Only since Polish schools were established were the children forced to learn the Polish language . . . We don't want to live in Poland. Our fathers and we grew up and lived in Ukraine. How come we are Poles?"[54] More concretely, following a decade of being targeted as an enemy nation by Soviet power, as *Untermenschen* by the Germans, and as deadly enemies by Ukrainian nationalists, Poles were less than forthcoming in declaring their nationality.[55] Still, this did not prevent Poles from insisting on reopening their churches (clearly identified as Polish and not merely Catholic) in the city after the Germans' arrival. Inferring from Polish history in general, and considering the absence of other institutional frameworks, the Catholic Church was regarded as the main preserver of a distinct Polish national identity, a fact recognized by Soviet power early on. During the mass deportations from Vinnytsia in 1935–36, the handful of priests and functioning churches (two and eight, respectively) were marked as centers of nationalist activity, operating under a religious mask and working for the separation of the Ukrainian Republic from the Soviet Union and its unification with Poland. In wartime, reasoned the authorities, these priests could provide leadership to anti-Soviet elements.[56]

Locals, it seems, had fewer problems distinguishing themselves from ethnic Poles. A nationalist activist, reflecting on wartime ethnic relations in the city, noted that indeed there were genuine anti-Polish sentiments. A survey of several hundred eastern Ukrainians immediately after the war showed a deep divide between the two communities. Only 12 percent considered Poles ready to assimilate into Ukrainian society, and barely 18 percent saw a community of interest between Poles and Ukrainians, a rate as low as that regarding the Jews.[57] Here, nationalists were in tune with the local scene. Unlike their attitude toward Russians, hardly any Ukrainians regarded Poles as their "own." In this light it is not surprising that one contemporary observer concluded that "Poles were a little worse off [than Russians and *Volksdeutschen*]"[58]—which leads us to another minority in the ethnic mosaic of Vinnytsia, the ethnic Germans.

[54] PAVO, f. 136, op. 6, d. 591, ll. 2, 3, 5, 7, 10–11.

[55] For intriguing samples of individuals who found themselves categorized as Poles in the 1939 census and tried their best to alter this identification, see Hirsch, *Empire of Nations*, 315–17. Being cast as members of an enemy-nation, people clung even to the hitherto contested and not so desirable Belorussian identity. At the same time, their stories displayed a genuine confusion produced by an ethnically heterogeneous society.

[56] PAVO, f. 136, op. 3, d. 371, ll. 5, 7.

[57] Gilliam, "The Nationality Questionnaire," 154, 160.

[58] HURIP #548, 6–7.

Few ethnic Germans were left in Vinnytsia when the German forces rolled into the region. Following the waves of deportations in 1935–36, merely 2,010 were counted in the region in the 1939 census.[59] The Germans' arrival, however, signaled a dramatic quantitative and qualitative reversal of this state of affairs. Ethnic Germans enjoyed a distinct and visibly privileged status in the Reichskommissariat Ukraine (RKU), and even more so in Vinnytsia where the town's deputy mayor was ethnic German and many other Germans assumed commanding positions in the localities. Despite initial reservations by Nazi purists regarding the racial quality and political reliability of the ethnic Germans, the latter obtained passports, were guaranteed a steady supply of food, enjoyed freedom of transportation, were not taxed, and, most important, were designated as the prime beneficiaries of the German resettlement plans and land reform.[60] Considered by Himmler as one of the key economic regions in the RKU, Vinnytsia was designated for colonization by *Volksdeutschen*. In November 1942 some forty-three thousand ethnic Germans had been settled in three villages between Zhytomyr and Vinnytsia, following the forced evacuation of the Ukrainian inhabitants.[61] According to some, resentment against the *Volksdeutschen* was minimal. Their integration into the German occupation structure was looked on as an attempt to save their lives.[62] At times, ethnic Germans who assumed positions of power in the localities clashed with the young militants arriving from Galicia.[63] Moreover, ethnic Germans were no different from other (former) Soviet nationalities in the malleability of their ethnonational self-identification. This pattern was only exacerbated by the prevailing conditions under German occupation, in which ethnic German identity was not merely desirable but was also accessible. Responding to Seleshko's inquiry, ethnic Germans defined themselves as Russians.[64] Hence the daughter of a Cossack officer was numbered among

[59] GARF, f. 9479, op. 1, d. 83, l. 3. The 1939 census did not even record Germans in the region as a separate category. Some 392,458 ethnic Germans were counted in Ukraine that year (Poliakov, *Vsesoiuznaia perepis' naseleniia 1939 goda*, 68).

[60] HURIP #542, 4; #548, 7; Dallin, *German Rule*, 288–93.

[61] Timothy Patrick Mulligan, *The Politics of Illusion and Empire: German Occupation Policy in the Soviet Union, 1942–1943* (New York: Praeger, 1988), 27; Dallin, *German Rule*, 286. Hardly any of these settlers remained after the war. They were evacuated along with the retreating German army with the collapse of the eastern front. Some 135,000 are said to have been evacuated from the territory of Transnistria alone (Fleischhauer and Pinkus, *The Soviet Germans*, 87).

[62] HURIP #542, 4.

[63] In Illintsi, one Dr. Heine, who had lived there since 1918 and was appointed mayor under the Germans, protected the local Jews from a pogrom by the Ukrainian police and nationalists (YVA, 03–2243, 14).

[64] Seleshko, *Vinnytsia*, 124, 133.

the ethnic Germans thanks to a German grandmother, just as others were included because of marriage relations.[65] The very fact that, in the German-occupied territories, one could obtain the beneficial *Volksdeutsche* identity easily defused much of the volatility inherent in this category. For locals, there was very little that was inherent in national identities, even regarding the celebrated German "superior blood" community.

But if the assumption of German identity was acceptable, the conduct that accompanied it was not. The separate stores for this group in Ukraine caused irritation and a growing hatred against the German colonists— something that had not existed before, claimed one émigré source.[66] New privileges, combined with the legacy of the past, encouraged many ethnic Germans to behave in a blatantly alienating manner. The anger, especially of youth, at the mistreatment of their families by Soviet power, manifested itself in preying on the rest of the population. For the latter, the war offered an opportunity to seek revenge for earlier personal misfortunes. Nearby Illintsi, the son of a German woman whose father had been repressed, quickly rose in the ranks of the police. His brutal manner was so excessive that he became the first to be marked for assassination by the local partisans. Not coincidentally, his mother was also killed.[67] On the eve of the German withdrawal from the region, ethnic German police regiments took part in anti-partisan mop operations, which meant burning down three villages.[68] Notably such actions applied to the population at large and not merely the persecuted Jews. By this time mutual alienation was beyond repair.

As the population was increasingly redefining itself along the lines of its wartime experience, especially with German occupation growing harsher by the day and the return of Soviet power looming on the horizon, the perception of willing, active collaboration with the Nazis severed ethnic Germans from the rest of the population. Ethnic Germans had already been stigmatized by Soviet power as a collaborationist group in the initial days of the war and were marked for total deportation. Notably the decree on the deportation of the Volga Germans also applied to the Ukrainian regions still unoccupied by the German army.[69] While this act could plausibly be interpreted as a continuation of the prewar policy of casting ethnic Germans as members of an enemy-nation, the removal of ethnic Germans

[65] HURIP #542, 4.

[66] Dallin, *German Rule*, 291.

[67] YVA, #03–2243, 45–46.

[68] Gerhard Lohrenz, *The Lost Generation and Other Stories* (Manitoba: J. Lohrenz, 1982), 67.

[69] An NKVD note from 12 December 1941 on the figures of ethnic Germans deported included some 79,611 people from the Ukrainian regions of Zaporizhzhia, Voroshilovhrad, Stalino, and Dnipropetrovs'k (GARF, f. 9479, op. 1, d. 83, ll. 51, 53).

from the ranks of the Red Army was much more critical. Even before the war, ethnic German servicemen were removed from the western border regions (Vinnytsia being one of these) or directed to nonmilitary service. Ethnic Germans were drafted into the Red Army following the German invasion, but, shortly thereafter, they were no longer mobilized, were removed from the ranks, and were sent to the rear for nonmilitary service.[70] In any case, ethnic Germans were kept out of the emerging Soviet patriotic pantheon. The handful of ethnic Germans who managed to stay in the Red Army did so under concealed identity. Ironically they found themselves in the company of Soviet Jewish veterans whose service was recognized and rewarded but on a personal basis, not as members of their respective ethnic community, as was the Soviet practice with all other nationalities. With families of Red Army servicemen emerging as the key political constituency in the region, the erasure of ethnic Germans from the fighting family was critical. They were cut off from the community of blood that had come to dominate the social and political landscape.

The other ethnic group targeted for excision by the nationalist quest for purity was the Jewish minority—a most explosive issue as the influx of nationalist forces to the eastern provinces approached. The shared desire of both Nazis and nationalists to see a Jew-free Ukraine spelled both promise and complications. The Ukrainian nationalists exercised more leverage in pursuing their goals with the Jews than with other ethnic minorities, but they also had to confront the implications of their exclusionary ideology, especially when compared and contrasted to the Nazi extermination machine that started rolling from the moment it crossed the Soviet borders. Although the nationalists' attitude toward the Jews was formulated well before the German invasion, the unprecedented magnitude of the war and genocide made it a time of choices. And chose they did.

Nationalist writers before and during the war consistently hammered out the inherent incompatibility between Ukrainians and Jews. One brochure, entitled "Ukraine in the Jewish Talons," informed the Ukrainian population that had been living under Soviet rule for the last two-and-a-half decades that,

> there is no other people in this world who suffered from the Jews as much as the Ukrainians. To write the history of the Jewry on Ukrainian lands would mean to retell the eternal horrifying exploitation and oppression of Ukrainian peasantry and workers by the Jews. It would make a thick volume [to record] the misfortunes that Ukraine had to go through in the millennium since her founding.[71]

[70] For the prewar removal, see Rittersporn, " 'Vrednye elementy,' " 115; for the wartime removal, see 150–51 in this work.

[71] "Ukrainia v zhydivs'kykh labetakh," TsDAVOVU, f. 3833, op. 2, d. 74, l. 3.

Throughout its history, the pamphlet continued, Ukraine has been constantly betrayed and tormented by the Jews who took it for a "New Palestine" and its people for their servants. During the fight for independence, Jews in Kiev shot Ukrainian Cossacks forced to retreat in face of the overwhelming Muscovite troops in the rear, joined both Denikin's forces and those of the Red Army, and later disproportionately populated all branches of Soviet power, especially its punitive organs.

But before the tale of horrors could be told, the unchanged and irredeemable nature of the elusive Jew had to be exposed. "The history of all peoples and scientific research testify that . . . a Jew is a Jew! Whether he is Red or White, reactionary or a democrat, he considers himself superior," decried the pamphlet.[72] This clarification was doubly necessary in a region such as Vinnytsia, where Soviet political culture had gone to great lengths to present a new kind of Jew, beginning with their very name. The pamphlet opened with this statement: "The Zhyds, who in Ukraine under the Soviets were called 'ievrei' belong to the worst enemies of the entire world!"[73] Tellingly, there was no pretense to conceal the offensive connotation of the term. True, in the formerly Polish-controlled territory, *zhyd* was the common word for a Jew. But nationalist propagandists made it clear that they were fully aware of the derogatory context of the word. By 1941, after two years of intensive Soviet propaganda in the newly annexed western territories, the derogatory meaning of the term was clearly understood.

There were, however, the author indicated, a few sources of consolation and hope for true Ukrainians. The Ukrainian peasant who knew the true and eternal nature of the Jew was not the one to be fooled by semantic changes. "In Zhmerynka," came the comforting example, "a Jew blocked the way for a kolkhoznik who was carrying a heavy load on his shoulders. 'Let me pass, Zhyd!' the villager shouted angrily, because it was muddy all around. The Jew promptly reproached the Ukrainian that he was not a Zhyd but *ievrei*. 'Fine, let me pass, *ievrei*—you former mangy [*parkhatyi*] Zhyd," responded the kolkhoznik.[74]

Further, history had shown that the Jewish crimes against the Ukrainian people and land could not and did not go unpunished. "The Ukrainian people did not always allow Jews to act with impunity. The history of Ukraine knows many eruptions of national and social anger against the Jews, [those] allies of Moscow and Warsaw. The Zaporozhian [Cossacks], the *Haidamaks*, and the Ukrainian army of the recent past had all duly punished the kikes for their evil wantonness in Ukraine," the brochure proclaimed. As short a time as three centuries ago the glorious hetman Bohdan Khmel'nyts'kyi, "the horror of the Jews," had tried to implement

---

[72] Ibid., l. 2.
[73] Ibid.
[74] Ibid., l. 11b.

a plan for the total exile of Jews from Ukraine, but this time the prospects for success were real. "This fight is not over yet. At the appropriate time the Ukrainian people will present the Jews with a long bill for *everything*. And they will be made to account in full for their culpability. Long will be the indictment. Swift will be the sentence," was the brochure's ominous concluding message to the Ukrainian population.[75]

Indeed, nationalist rhetoric and practices turned deadly when the opportunity arose in June 1941. As early as April 1941 a resolution of the Second General Congress of the OUN-B vowed to combat the Jews, whom it labeled the "vanguard of Muscovite imperialism in Ukraine." At the same time the resolution pointed out that the Muscovite-Bolshevik regime sought to exploit the "anti-Jewish sentiments of the Ukrainian masses to divert their attention from the true cause of their misfortune and to channel them in times of frustration into pogroms against Jews."[76] One might read this resolution as a wish, however ambiguous, to avoid the eruption of mass pogroms. Maybe. Yet, in light of the mayhem about to explode shortly thereafter, it was not only meaningless but instead an invitation for violence. The view of Jews as the most faithful Bolshevik constituency in Ukraine and the belief in the popularity of anti-Semitism were hardly a recipe for moderation. In any case, barely two months later, these fine distinctions evaporated. With the German invasion and the mass executions of Jews under way, nationalist statements on the Jewish issue assumed exterminatory goals. "The Jews help Moscow to consolidate its hold on Ukraine. Therefore I am of the opinion that the Jews should be exterminated and [see] the expediency of carrying out in Ukraine the German methods for exterminating the Jews," wrote Iaroslav Stets'ko, head of the Ukrainian government in July 1941.[77]

The excisionary rhetoric was put into practice by units of western Ukrainians who followed the German troops into the region. During the initial stage of the German invasion, nationalist units in western Ukraine massa-

---

[75] Ibid., ll. 3b, 12. Haidamak—a twist of the word *haydut* (robber in Turkish) and the name of a movement that spread in the Right bank throughout the second half of the eighteenth century, was comprised of a series of spontaneous revolts and several large-scale uprisings by Orthodox peasants and Cossacks against the Polish landed nobility, Jewish arendars, and the Roman Catholic and Uniate clergy. For a brief summary of the history of the movement that brings out the differences in Ukrainian, Polish, and Jewish historiographies, see Paul Robert Magocsi, *A History of Ukraine* (Toronto: University of Toronto Press, 1996), 295–300; and Jaroslaw Pelenski, "The Haidamak Insurrections and the Old Regimes in Eastern Europe," in *The American and European Revolutions, 1776–1848* (Iowa City: University of Iowa Press, 1980), 228–42.

[76] The text of the article on the Jews in the April 1941 Resolution is reproduced in Friedman, "Ukrainian-Jewish Relations," 265.

[77] The sentence had an unclear handwritten addendum "excluding their assimilation" or "including those assimilated" (TsDAVOVU, f. 3833, op. 3, d. 7, l. 6).

cred Jewish partisans and civilians, while Ukrainian municipal organizations issued anti-Semitic decrees.[78] Fresh from organizing and participating in a series of mass pogroms throughout the western regions, nationalist
formations, now enrolled in the police forces, took active part in massacres
in the eastern provinces, including Babyn Iar.[79] Their arrival to the town
of Brailiv signaled the beginning of unrestrained violence against the local
Jewish population,[80] while in Vinnytsia the *uprava* furnished rosters of
Jews in response to German requests.[81] On 4 August 1941 the commander
of the Ukrainian militia in the Shpykiv district ordered Jews seven years
and older to wear an armband displaying the Star of David and, on the
29th of that month, Jews were ordered to sweep the streets around their
houses twice a day, and were banned from walking on main streets and
appearing in public after 8:00 P.M.[82] Throughout the *Generalkommissariat*
Shitomir, which now included much of the Vinnytsia region, OUN activists recruited loyalists into the Ukrainian police (*schutzmannschaft*), an
organ that soon became an integral part of the extermination machine.[83]

Nationalist sources, both in wartime and the postwar era, offer little,
if any, information about their treatment of Jews. Aletiiano-Popivs'kyi,
who otherwise has nothing to say about Jews in his recollection of wartime Vinnytsia, tells of the rescue of a Jewish man who helped the OUN,
leaving one to wonder about the attitudes toward Jews who were not
useful to the cause. Moreover, the OUN district leader asked the young
nationalist activists, one of whom was Aletiiano-Popivs'kyi, not to succumb to German ideology that portrayed the Jews as the chief enemy and
the ones who should be destroyed. The real culprits, explained the leader,
were the Muscovite imperialists, and the Jews were merely going along
with them.[84] Mykhailo Seleshko also condemns the erroneous impression
that Jews constituted the main enemy of freedom-loving Ukrainians ("It
was not the Jews and their ideas who enslaved Ukraine but the Muscovites
and the Muscovite imperialist ideology") and tells of the participation of
the Ukrainian auxiliary police in the executions of Jews, Communists,

---

[78] Friedman, "Ukrainian-Jewish Relations," 268–69, 276–77; Yitzhak Arad, "The Holocaust of the Soviet Jewry in the Occupied Territories of the Soviet Union," *Yad Vashem
Studies* 21 (1991): 41–42.

[79] For the role of the so-called Bukovinian Battalion, an unofficial unit led by the OUN-
M and comprised of hundreds of OUN members and sympathizers from Galicia and Bukovina, at Babyn Iar, see Karel Berkhoff, "Hitler's Clean Slate: Everyday Life in the Reichskommissariat Ukraine, 1941–1944," Ph.D. dissertation, University of Toronto, 1998, 60.

[80] The testimony of Mikhail Kigis (YVA, #03–4067).

[81] HURIP, #548, 2.

[82] DAVO, f. 1417, op. 3, d. 1, ll. 2, 48.

[83] Martin Dean, "The German *Gendarmerie*, the Ukrainian *Schutzmannschaft*, and the
'Second Wave' of Jewish Killings in Occupied Ukraine," 171–72, 175.

[84] Aletiiano-Popivs'kyi, *Z ideieiu v sertsi*, 41, 63.

and Soviet partisans, providing such a detailed account of the executions that one wonders if indeed he had not been present at the site of the extermination.[85]

Not unlike the Nazis themselves, the nationalists were amenable to tactical adjustments, as long as the long-term goal of cleansing Ukraine remained intact. By April 1942 the political calculus dictated additional consideration to the international arena and the Second Conference of the OUN-B declared that,

> regardless of the negative attitude toward the Jews as a weapon of Muscovite-Bolshevik imperialism, we believe it is inexpedient at the present stage of the international situation to take part in anti-Jewish actions in order not to become a blind tool in foreign hands and not to divert the attention of the masses from the principal enemies.[86]

Moreover, the absence of the moral considerations that guided Metropolitan Sheptyts'kyi's call in Galicia ("Thou Shall Not Kill!") indicated that a change in the nationalists' Jewish policy was a bitter pill to swallow, and even more so to implement. In speeches to the indigenous population, the temptation to invoke demeaning stereotypes of the Jew could not be resisted. Jokes circulated in the nationalist *Ukrainskyi perets'*, in the section "Red Army Anecdotes," poked fun at the draft-dodging Jew even when the subject was the other side. "Abrasha, a relative of Lazar Kaganovich, writes to his sister: Dear Sarah! I'm on the front line, behind Tashkent. And as the motherland and Comrade Stalin demand, I will go even further, to Chita," went one of these anecdotes.[87] When the Germans and nationalists marked the second anniversary of the deliverance of the region from the Bolshevik yoke, it was also an opportunity to remind the locals about the inherent unreliability of the Jew at a time of need. With the tide of war turning, the locals had to be reminded of the ethnic face and true core of the regime only two years ago. One could expect the Jew to fight to the death for his cherished cause of Bolshevik power and against the German forces in the trying days of July 1941. That, of course, was too much to expect, intimated a columnist of *Vinnyts'ki visti*. Their first reaction to the outbreak of the war was to raid the stores and buy everything

---

[85] Seleshko, *Vinnytsia*, 136, 63–67, esp. 66–67. See also pages 86–87 for Seleshko's explanation for the tenuous relations between Ukrainians and Jews in the cities and villages.

[86] TsDAHOU, f. 57, op. 4, d. 346, l. 4; and Armstrong, *Ukrainian Nationalism*, 117. In mid-1944, with defeat in the war looking inevitable, none other than Himmler authorized negotiation with the Allies and Jewish organization for the sale of one million Jews, who had not yet been exterminated, for ten thousand trucks. The genocide, however, continued uninterrupted (Raul Hilberg, *Perpetrators, Victims, Bystanders: The Jewish Catastrophe, 1933–1945* [New York: Aaron Asher, 1992], 324–30).

[87] PAVO, f. 138, op. 5, d. 264, l. 30.

they could. And when the general mobilization order was passed on the evening of 22 June, the Jews pretended to run for weapons but disappeared in the rear. When the alarm was sounded, so, too, did the Jews disappear. They could be found in cellars and shelters.[88]

Probably more than any other organized group in German-occupied Ukraine, the nationalists were fully aware of the ongoing genocide of the Jews, nor did they try to conceal this awareness. At no point, however, did nationalist writers and activists refer to the state of Jews in wartime Ukraine as a moral dilemma. At most, it was a matter of tactical expediency. When the rift with the Germans reached its climax in the second half of 1943 and the UPA found itself under both German and Soviet pressure, it began to enroll surviving Jewish specialists into its ranks. "Recently the terror against the Jews stopped," informed a captured activist in early 1944. "The UPA started drafting doctors, shoemakers, tailors, and other specialists of Jewish nationality."[89] Expediency, however, proved fragile, and when circumstances changed it gave way to ideology and deep-seated resentments. As Soviet troops continued their advance into Ukraine and the armed struggle appeared beyond hope, these Jewish doctors were executed by the UPA.[90] In the villages and forests the extermination of Jews continued uninterrupted. "One day in 1942 a Jew came to us in the woods," a Ukrainian nationalist partisan told a fellow inmate in Vorkuta where they were imprisoned after the war. "He thought we were Red Partisans. 'I want to help you,' he said, 'I'll show you where the Germans are.' We put a rope round his neck and said, 'We're going to hang you.' He wouldn't believe it; he thought we were being funny. We gave him time to grasp the fact that his last hour had come and then hanged him from a tree."[91] Throughout 1943 nationalist guerrillas, wherever they gained control, continued to hunt down Jews who survived Nazi extermination. In neighboring Rivne, according to a captured activist, the Bandera troops "literally hunted for Jews, organizing round-ups and combing the forest paths, ravines, etc."[92] Another nationalist prisoner told the NKVD interrogator that the Security Services (SB) of UPA carried out

---

[88] *Vinnyts'ki visti*, 22 July 1943.

[89] TsDAHOU, f. 57, op. 4, d. 351, l. 52. For the tale of a Jewish doctor from L'viv who served in a UPA unit and died in battle in the Carpathians, see *Litopys ukrains'koi povstans'koi armii* 4 (Toronto: Vyd-vo Litopys UPA): 170–74; and Friedman, "Ukrainian-Jewish Relations," 285 n. 59.

[90] Friedman, "Ukrainian-Jewish Relations," 284–86; Shmuel Spector, *The Holocaust of Volhynian Jews*, 271.

[91] Joseph Scholmer, *Vorkuta* (New York: Holt, 1954), 109. Scholmer was a German Communist imprisoned after the war. His remarkable account of Vorkuta sheds light on the ethnonational composition and relations in the GULAG.

[92] See the interrogation of Vladimir Solov'ev in TsDAHOU, f. 57, op. 4, d. 351, l. 10.

the order of the local leadership to "physically exterminate Jews who were hiding in the villages."[93] One graphic account of this final cleansing, carried out by the *Gendarmerie* on 7 May 1943 near Pohrebyshche, conveyed its brutality. By this time the German-controlled territory of Vinnytsia was practically *Judenrein* (Jew-free) following the final waves of mass executions in the summer and fall of the previous year. "On 7 May 1943, 21.00 hours, 8 Jews being 3 men, 2 women, and 3 children, were flushed from a well-disguised hole in the ground in an open field not far from Pogrebichi [Pohrebyshche] by the post here due to a confidential report and all of them were shot while trying to escape," reported the head of the *Gendarmerie* to the command in Koziatyn. "In the case concerned they are Jews from Pogrebichi who lived in this hole in the ground for almost a year. The Jews did not have anything else in their possession except their shabby clothing. The few items of food which they had which were lying strewn around the camp were given to the poor of the township. The same applies to the clothing that was perhaps still useable [*sic*]. The burial was carried out immediately there and then," concluded the report.[94]

There was little room for change in such a world, and when it finally came it was too late and meant too little. By early 1944 hardly any Jews were left alive, and the UPA's attention turned to the Polish population and the advancing Red Army. The troops on the field were ordered to refrain from violent attacks on Jews based on a chilling rationale. With almost all Jews murdered, "the Jewish question ceased to be a problem (very few of them remain)," the UPA command stated plainly.[95] With no one left to put the declaration to test, the change was merely semantic, and, in any case, left no impression on local Jews. Jewish survivors appeared oblivious to the alleged change in nationalist policy toward them. As late as 1947 a group of Jews from the Zhmerynka district, who had enrolled into a technical secondary school in the neighboring region of Kamianets'-Podil's'kyi, still viewed the activity of nationalist guerrillas there as a threat.[96]

In the nationalist world the problem with the Jew went beyond his deeds or even his physical existence. The Jew continued to exert influence and inflict damage even when he seemed to disappear from the scene. When the Germans finally decided to exhume the mass graves of the Terror's victims in the spring of 1943 (most likely in the wake of the propa-

[93] See the interrogation of Ivan Kutkovets in ibid., l. 52. For identical testimonies of Jewish survivors, see Spector, *The Holocaust of Volhynian Jews*, 270.

[94] Dean, "The German *Gendarmerie*, the Ukrainian *Schutzmannschaft*, and the 'Second Wave' of Jewish Killings in Occupied Ukraine," 185.

[95] TsDAHOU, f. 1, op. 23, d. 931, l. 173; GARF, f. 9478, op. 1, d. 126, l. 234.

[96] YVA, #03–4067, 21.

ganda success of the Katyn graves just two months before), the event turned into the most ferocious anti-Semitic fanfare in wartime Vinnytsia, despite the fact that the local Jewish community had already been decimated. The Judeo-Bolshevik duality of evil took center stage more forcefully than ever before (Figures 5.1, 5.2). The opening verses of a poem by the commander of an entertainment unit in Vinnytsia in August 1943 read:

Vinnytsia, the town on the edge of the Bug,
is famed throughout the world.
Nobody could hear its name without terror.
Through murder and sadism at the hands of the Jews
the Ukrainian land was tainted.

These vile deeds were allowed to go on completely unhindered
as even the most courageous were afraid—
the same could happen to us.
But he who has seen this pest with his own eyes
stands firm forevermore.[97]

The exhumation under the auspices of an international medical commission received the utmost publicity inside and outside Vinnytsia. Throughout the summer and fall of 1943 the regional newspapers carried daily reports on the exhumation process, the mass funerals that followed, and names of identified bodies. The affair showed at least one organized constituency—the Ukrainian Autocephalous Church—favorable to the nationalist and Nazi agenda. Radically nationalist and ethnocentric, the leadership and rank-and-file parishioners of the Autocephalous Church were receptive to the persecution of the Jews.[98] When it was Bishop Hryhorii's

[97] Ernst Klee, Willi Dressen, and Volker Riess, eds., *"The Good Old Days": The Holocaust as Seen by Its Perpetrators and Bystanders* (New York: Free Press, 1991), 123–24. In a letter to her husband who was in the ranks of the Red Army, Anna Serga, from the village of Luko-Meleshkivs'ka, told him that "under the Germans I was told: 'Your husband went off to defend the Jews.' " (TsDAHOU, f. 1, op. 23, d. 1021, l. 56).

[98] Gilliam's "Nationality Questionnaire" revealed members of the Autocephalous Church as the single most ethnocentric group among the interviewees (164). On the history of the Autocephalous Church during the brief period of independence and the prewar Soviet era, see Bohdan Bociurkiw, "The Rise of the Ukrainian Autocephalous Orthodox Church, 1919–1922," in Geoffrey Hosking, ed., *Church, Nation, and State in Russia and Ukraine* (London: Macmillan, 1991), 228–49; idem., "The Soviet Destruction of the Ukrainian Autocephalous Orthodox Church, 1929–1930," *Journal of Ukrainian Studies* 12, no. 1 (1987): 3–31. On the politics of the Autocephalous Church in wartime Ukraine, especially its relations with the Nazi authorities and the nationalist movement, see Harvey Fireside, *The Icon and the Swastika: The Russian Orthodox Church under Nazi and Soviet Control* (Cambridge, Mass.: Harvard University Press, 1971), 86–87, 95–97, 146–60, 173–74.

Figure 5.1. *Vinnitsa.* Vinnytsia, 1943. A Nazi poster portraying the exhumation of mass graves of victims of Soviet terror in the region. A grotesque figure of a Jewish-Bolshevik commissar is shown presiding over the corpses.

Figure 5.2. *Vinnitsa: Do Not Forget What Happened!* Vinnytsia, 1943. A Nazi collage of photos of the exhumation of mass graves of victims of Soviet terror in the region.

turn to speak, the vehemence became more intimate and powerful. "My Dear Ones!" Hryhorii addressed the crowd of mourners at the second funeral procession:

> Put yourself, if only for a moment, in their [the victims'] position. Poor, without counsel within the four stone walls of the NKVD [cell], they found themselves in a miserable, helpless position. The Jews come in, tie their arms, twist them. They would like to cry for help. But there is no one to appeal to, no one would hear. And if someone tried to show any resistance, he was hit with a rifle butt and his head cracked. Having done with mocking, for a farewell they put a leaden bullet in his head.

In essence, the bishop charged on, this was only a reincarnation of the original crime, with the same culprits and victims. "When I look at the tortured remains lying in these graves," lamented Hryhorii, "before my eyes appears the image of suffering Christ who died for teaching the same truth at the hands of the same Jews." Finally, the tirade tied all things together:

> Well then, my dear ones, rise up at once and, like Christ, ask the bloodswollen torturer, "the father of all workers," Stalin, for which of the good deeds that we have done for you and your Jews throughout our lives, you torture us so much? Maybe for our hard labor in the kolkhoz fields, where we worked without straightening our backs, growing high wheat, so that your Jews would have a tasty roll for *shabbas* and Passover? Or maybe for our filling our eyes with sweat as we worked on sugar beats so that your kikes would have sweet things?"[99]

From Kiev, *Nove Ukrais'ke slovo*, which was distributed in Vinnytsia as well, announced that "Europe is liberating itself from the Jews." The more that Europe realizes its power and is moving toward a united economic block, the more it needs a concord on decisive political questions. The Jews were already up in arms to prevent the European unification which impairs their dreams of conquering the world. "Hence," concluded the editorial, "it is impossible to resolve this question with compromises— here, decisiveness is needed."[100] By the end of July 1943, the date the editorial was published, hardly any Jews were left alive in Ukraine. In the Nazi and nationalist world, however, this was not a cause for celebration— at least not yet. As an elusive, omnipotent, and omnipresent enemy of European civilization in general, and of the Ukrainian nation in particular, the Jew had to be fought constantly and relentlessly as both a physical and metaphysical entity. Exterminated physically, the memory of the Jew

---

[99] *Vinnyts'ki visti*, 1 July 1943. Hryhorii was using the Hebrew words for Saturday (*Shabbat*) and Passover (*Pesakh*), and, interchangably, Jews (*zhydy*) and Hebrews (*iudei*).

[100] *Nove Ukrains'ke slovo*, 31 July 1943.

also had to be destroyed. Indeed, in postwar Ukrainian nationalist my-thology, by then forced into emigration, the Jew reincarnated himself in even more satanic ways. The 12 July 1950 issue of the Ukrainian-language daily *Svoboda* carried an essay on the Soviet reaction, on their return to Vinnytsia, to the exhumation of the mass graves. Based allegedly on eye-witness accounts, the paper claimed that the Soviets gathered the local population around the graves and then shot those who were identified as relatives of the victims, their bodies falling in the very same ditches. The rest were sent unarmed to the front, only to perish under German fire. The MVD commissar who commanded the procedure was identified by the Jewish name, Rapaport.[101] Adding more Ukrainians to those he had slaughtered, the eternal Jew had the last morbid laugh.

So how did the ordinary men and women of Vinnytsia react to the actual implementation of the excisionary rhetoric? Tracing the response of by-standers, anywhere, to the unfolding Holocaust is the historian's night-mare, especially in Eastern Europe. The population, in whose midst the mass extermination took place, rarely left testimonies. The information on popular reactions to the genocide of the Jews derives mainly from contem-porary impressions of the perpetrators and later recollections of survivors. Not surprisingly, evidence is often politically motivated and always emo-tionally charged. Moreover, survival, which was possible only with help of bystanders, already rendered survivors' testimonies somewhat exceptional. Those who were turned away by locals and were subsequently killed did not record impressions of their surroundings. Certain reactions to the event appear almost universal regardless of ethnic, religious, and social makeup. Human generosity surfaced side by side with barbarism, compas-sion with greed, sacrifice with indifference, and heroism with cowardice. The Eastern European theater, however, bore certain unique features. It was here where the Nazi extermination machine was put to practice in its full capacity and venom. Marked by the Nazi leadership as a clean slate, to borrow Karel Berkhoff's apt phrase, Ukraine, in particular, became the site of Nazi population policies, of which the Holocaust was only a part, albeit a unique one. In this light, response to the unfolding Jewish catas-trophe cannot be detached from the non-Jewish population's own sense

---

[101] Anthony Dragan, *Vinnytsia: A Forgotten Holocaust* (Jersey City N.J.: Svoboda Press, 1986), 49–50. It is sufficient to comment here that, by this time, hardly any Jews were in the internal security apparat. The command of the NKVD-MVD in Vinnytsia was entirely Ukrainian and Russian and the head of the local NKVD was Kasatkin. On 1 January 1945 Jews accounted for 579 of the total 12,888 NKGB cadres in Soviet Ukraine. Of these, 7,881 were Russians, 3,853 were Ukrainians, and 138 were Belorussians. The largest group among the Jews was employed in the censorship department (TsDAHOU, f. 1, op. 23, d. 2425, ll. 2–3).

of victimization at the hands of the Nazis. "A disoriented population, uncertain of its future under German occupation, scrambled for morsels to stay alive. In this integration, the Jews were perceived as a different people whose misfortune, deserved or undeserved, was not a Ukrainian concern and still less a Ukrainian responsibility," was Raul Hilberg's insightful observation.[102]

The repetitive nationalist references to the prevalence of anti-Semitism among the populace invites a look at the reception of their rhetoric and practices. It is revealing that, in nationalist surveys, popular resentment against the Jews was viewed as a pillar of the viability of the cause in the region and the hostility against Soviet power.[103] Indeed, Ukraine was a place where anti-Semitism had been a traditional, integral component of social, economic, and political life. Supplemented by the legacy of equating Bolshevik power with Jews and three years of constant exposure to relentless, exterminatory, anti-Semitic rhetoric and practices, this profound sentiment became a crucial component of popular views of the genocide. At issue, however, was more than the resonance of traditional anti-Jewish sentiments. The practice of genocide raised the Jewish question to an unprecedented new level, one that forced every person in the region, and elsewhere in the German-occupied territories, actively to confront it from the onset of the German invasion.

Scholars pointed out the low number of Jews who survived the massacre in western Ukraine. The 17,000 survivors counted for merely 2 percent of the prewar total. In neighboring Vinnytsia extermination was almost absolute as well. Executions by *Hilfswillige* (Ukrainian auxiliary troops) continued to the very final moments when the German and Romanian forces were already withdrawing from the region.[104] Of the nearly 142,000 counted in the region in 1939, only 15,000–20,000 survived, most of them in the Romanian-controlled territory of Transnistria and not necessarily natives of the region. The estimated figures of survivors in Transnistria included the city of Odessa and deportees from Romania and Moldavia.[105] The Nazis were keen on launching the genocide in any case, argues Aharon Weiss, yet such a low rate of survival as that in western Ukraine could not be reached without the activities of the nationalist

[102] Hilberg, *Perpetrators, Victims, Bystanders*, 200.

[103] TsAVVMVDRF, f. 488, op. 1, d. 51, l. 43b.

[104] Meir Teich, "The Jewish Self-Administration in Ghetto Shargorod (Transnistria)," *Yad Vashem Studies* 2 (1958): 248–49.

[105] The figures from the 1939 census are in Mordechai Altshuler, ed., *Distribution of the Jewish Population of the USSR, 1939* (Jerusalem: Hebrew University, Center for Research and Documentation of East European Jewry, 1993), 23. The estimated number of survivors are from Arad, "The Holocaust of Soviet Jewry in the Occupied Territories of the Soviet Union," 44–45.

forces and the attitude of large segments of the population.[106] However, one cannot ignore that the Holocaust was carried to its extreme in societies that were bereft of entrenched anti-Semitic tradition and even organized mass rescue operations, as Mark Mazower showed in his study of wartime Greece.[107] Still, the various low numbers of those rescued did point to key differences in the mode of popular reactions, which were critical in a region like Vinnytsia.

One could hardly fault the Ukrainian nationalists for misreading popular perceptions. Anti-Semitism was a steady presence on the regional scene if only in alternating cycles. Popular resentment of eastern Ukrainians against Jews appeared rather entrenched. A survey of several hundred people immediately after the war showed that anti-Semitism was prevalent at rates twice those of anti-Russian sentiments and was often unrelated to nationalist expressions. As many as 69 percent would exclude Jews from marriage compared to 29 percent who would do the same to Russians. And along with Poles, Jews were the ethnic group with whom most Ukrainians did not see a community of interest. Not least important, these views were prevalent among a key group—the young and the middle-educated, that is, the bulk of the rank-and-file activists. This cohort was also the most likely one to identify Jews with the Bolshevik regime.[108]

The evolution of Soviet ethnic policies in the decade before the German invasion left an intriguing legacy. The ethnicization of the body social was not translated instantly into a conscious worldview by large segments of society, especially in the ethnically mixed regions like Ukraine, as Lev Dudin observed from occupied Kiev. But they did provide a framework for reading events, one that was set in motion when the Nazis made racial ethnicity the fundamental principle in the lives of the occupied societies. With Soviet policies during the prewar decade shifting from the abandonment of the fight against anti-Semitism to tacit approval, it appeared that anti-Jewish rhetoric and practices would be a viable mobilizing policy in

[106] Aharon Weiss, "Jewish-Ukrainian Relations in Western Ukraine during the Holocaust," Howard Aster and Peter Potichnyi, eds., *Ukrainian-Jewish Relations in Historical Perspective* (Edmonton: Canadian Institute of Ukrainian Studies, 1988), 409–20. Also on popular pogroms in western Ukraine on the retreat of Soviet troops, and often without incitement by the Germans, see Andrzej Zbikowski, "Local Anti-Jewish Pogroms in the Occupied Territories of Eastern Poland, June–July 1941," in Dobroszycki and Gurock, eds., *The Holocaust in the Soviet Union*, 173–79; Friedman, "Ukrainian-Jewish Relations, 274–77.

[107] Mazower, *Inside Hitler's Greece*, 235–61. Fewer than ten thousand Greek Jews survived out of seventy to eighty thousand at the outbreak of the war (idem., 256).

[108] Fifty-nine percent did not see a community of interests between Ukrainians and Jews, and 60 percent saw none between Ukrainians and Poles. Of the respondents, however, 97 percent saw a community of interests with the Belorussians (Gilliam, "The Nationality Questionnaire," 19, 126).

the fight over the souls of the locals. This was even more the case in Vinnytsia, where anti-Jewish violence had a long tradition. Earlier we noted
how the relentless violence that seized the region since the mass deportations of World War I entailed further ideological approach to the Jewish
issue and the consequent radical methods meted out to solve the problem.
During the civil war, Vinnytsia was the site of several brutal pogroms.[109]
By then, anti-Semitism completed its evolution from a religious and socioeconomic phenomenon into a political one. Jews figured highly as the
arch-enemy in the burgeoning anti-bourgeois campaign, which by that
time had already turned into the defining motif of the revolutionary political culture of both the Right and the Left.[110] Cast as Communists by
Whites, Cossacks, Directory's troops [the administration of the short-
lived Ukrainian People's Republic], and anarchists, on the one hand, and
as reactionaries by the Reds, on the other, Jews, during the civil war, were
fair game for all.[111] The consolidation of Soviet power signaled some major
changes, however. Anti-Semitism, later characterized by Stalin as "the
most dangerous vestige of cannibalism,"[112] was outlawed: Jews were integrated into the legitimate power structure of the new polity, their assimilation gathered momentum, and, finally, this extraterritorial minority was
allotted a region, bringing it into the family of legitimate Soviet nations.
Not surprisingly, Jews who came of age during this period, especially in
the towns, claim that they had not encountered anti-Semitism before the
war.[113] Still, popular identification of the resented Nepmen as synonymous

[109] The pattern of these pogroms were similar to the rest, with external forces—Cossacks,
Directory's troops, and anarchists—instigating and leading the attacks, and the local mob—
usually peasants from neighboring villages—following by looting property and carrying out
random killings. See the special issue "Pogroms and Self-Defense in Ukraine, 1919–1920,"
He-Avar 17 (1970): 3–136. For estimates of the number of people killed and injured in
several localities in the region, see Volodymyr Serhiichuk, ed., *Pohromy v Ukraini: 1914–
1920: Vid shtuchnykh stereotypiv do hirkoi pravdy, prykhovuvanoi v radians'kykh arkhivakh*
(Kiev: Vyd. im. Oleni Telihy, 1998), 452–55.

[110] Boris I. Kolonitskii, "Antiburzhuaznaia propaganda i "antiburzhuiskoe" soznanie,"
Otechestvennaia istoriia 1 (1994): 17–27; here, 20; Henry Abramson, *A Prayer for the Gov-
ernment: Ukrainians and Jews in Revolutionary Times, 1917–1920* (Cambridge, Mass.:
Ukrainian Research Institute, Harvard University, 1999), 30–32; for the place of the Jew in
White ideology, see Peter Kenez, "Pogroms and White Ideology in the Russian Civil War,"
in John Klier and Shlomo Lambroza, eds., *Pogroms: Anti-Jewish Violence in Modern Russian
History* (New York: Cambridge University Press, 1992), 293–313.

[111] In the town of Tul'chyn, any Jew caught by the Whites on the road was "promptly
informed that he was a Communist and was killed on the spot," while in Khmil'nyk in the
Lityn district Bolshevik forces cast the Jews as rightist reactionaries and subjected them to
constant confiscations and searches (Pinhas Gilter, "Ha-Pogrom be- Tul'chyn, Pelekh Po-
dolia"; and Zeev Igeret, "Pirkei Zikhronot," *He-Avar*, 80–82, 159–74, respectively); Abramson, *A Prayer for the Government*, 79–83, 109–40.

[112] Stalin, *Sochineniia*, 13:28.

[113] A native of Mohyliv-Podil's'kyi, who was born in 1929, states in her recollection that
"we never experienced anti-Semitism before the war" Felicia (Steigman) Carmelly ed., *Shat-*

with Jews, and of Jews as those getting the best jobs and avoiding manual labor, which worked on both traditional images of the Jewish profiteer and the one who benefited most from the new Communist order, kept the issue alive.[114]

As the Great Transformation gathered momentum, so did the popular identification of Soviet power with the Jews. The epoch of collectivization in the region witnessed outbursts of anti-Semitic violence. On 5 May 1932 in Krasne, in the Tyvriv district, a potato requisition raid turned into a mass display of anti-Semitism. An old man carrying a cross and a bible instigated a crowd of approximately five hundred people by telling them that "one has only to cry *gewalt* and nobody will rob you." When the chairman of the village soviet tried to arrest the old man, the chairman was beaten to the shouts of his attackers: "The Jews are stealing the cross and the Bible! Beat the Jews!" "The Russian militia knows the law well and that is why it takes care to give back potatoes and not to rob the peasant. But these Kikes know only how to go overboard."[115] Similar outbursts occurred in the midst of collectivization in the small town of Staryi-Dashiv. The ten Jewish families residing in town were constantly terrorized by a group of young Ukrainian kolkhozniks opposing collectivization. On the night of 7–8 January 1932 a group of nine men surrounded the Jewish huts and, to shouts of "Beat the Jews, Save Ukraine," smashed windows and set several huts on fire. It was irrelevant that the Jews, including those in the neighboring town of Novyi-Dashiv, where Jews constituted 90 percent of the population, were subjected to the similar process of collectivization or were later dying of hunger like the rest of the peasants. In the popular imagination, the Jews belonged to the other side.[116]

As noted above, that one of the great moments in the emerging Soviet mythology was resentfully identified with the Jews was not lost on the authorities nor was it detached from party life. As the 1930s progressed, the regime abandoned its unswerving battle against anti-Semitism, which had crept back into local politics. Explaining the meaning of the tsarist tricolor flag, a teacher in a workers' faculty in the Zaslavs'kyi dis-

tered! 50 Years of Silence: History and Voices of the Tragedy in Romania and Transnistria (Ontario: Abbeyfield, 1997), 249; Boris Halfin, interview, 18 February 1994, Kiryat Gat, Israel.

[114] Alan M. Ball, *Russia's Last Capitalists: The Nepmen, 1921–1929* (Berkeley: University of California Press, 1987), 100; Larin, *Evrei i antisemitizm v SSSR*, 241, 243. On the profound sense of victimization of Jews embedded in these lingering stereotypes, see the complaint letter by a group of Jews from the Podillia province (later Vinnytsia region) addressed to the All-Union Central Executive Committee in 1924, in A. Livshin and I. Orlov, eds., *Pis'ma vo vlast', 1917–1927. Zaiavleniia, zhaloby, donosy, pis'ma v gosudarstvennye struktury i bol'shevistskim vozhdiam* (Moscow: ROSSPEN, 1998), 393–98.

[115] PAVO, f. 136, op. 3, d. 8, ll. 113–14.

[116] Ibid., f. 136, op. 3, d. 131, ll. 1–2. In April 1933 some forty-five starving Jews and thirty-five who had already died were counted in Ulaniv alone (d. 80, l. 66).

trict, a party member since 1926, told the students that "the white, blue, and red makes a beautiful combination. Beat the Jews—beat and don't spare the rubber."[117] Significantly this teacher found supporters among his colleagues. Yet probably more consequential was the lavish use of anti-Jewish stereotypes by at least one speaker in the Third Plenum of the Vinnytsia obkom on 20–21 June 1934 in which Jews were portrayed either as the old generation's speculators or as the young power holders, populating the institutions of the new Soviet order.[118] The authorities still categorized such incidents as "counterrevolutionary ramblings of clerical and kulak-Petliurite elements," but, in the intimate environment of a small region like Vinnytsia, anti-Jewish anecdotes that peppered some speeches in party conventions could not remain within the plenums' halls. Anti-Semitic incidents were still condemned at the Tenth Plenum of the obkom on 17 January 1936, but barely three years later the not-so-tacit removal of Jews from visible posts at the All-Union level was already under way.[119]

This development was built on a concrete social and economic base that underlined the community's isolation from the rest of the population. On the eve of the war, the state of the local Jewish community resembled that of so many other Jewish communities across Europe. It was largely urban. In 1939 the 91,006 Jews in towns constituted 33.6 percent of the region's urban population. In some of the smaller towns of the districts' centers, Jews were in the majority.[120] Language was a key factor in determining the status of the community: 73.5 percent of the 141,825 Jews declared Yiddish as their native language whereas only 16.6 percent declared Russian and 9.9 percent Ukrainian.[121] In a predominantly rural and ethnically Ukrainian region such as Vinnytsia, these figures spelled cultural, and most likely social, isolation. In one respect, however, Vinnytsia was unique.

---

[117] Ibid., f. 136, op. 3, d. 219, l. 126.

[118] Ibid., f. 136, op. 1, d. 96, ll. 25–26.

[119] Ibid., f. 136, op. 1, d. 185, l. 160. According to Hitler's "table talk," Stalin told Ribbentrop in 1939 that he was only waiting for the emergence of a broad enough indigenous intelligentsia to finish off the Jews as a ruling elite (*Hitlers Tischgespräche im Führerhauptquartier, 1941–1942* [Bonn: Athenaum-Verlag, 1951], 119; cited in Pinkus, *The Jews of the Soviet Union*, 336 n. 88). In his memoirs, Molotov confirmed the long-held rumors about the purge of Jews in the government. According to Molotov, Stalin indeed ordered the removal of Jews from leading positions in general and from ambassadorial posts in particular (*Sto sorok besed s Molotovym*, 274).

[120] In Vinnytsia, the largest town in the region, 33,150 Jews accounted for 35.63 percent of the population; in Bershad 4,271 Jews comprised 73.57 percent of the population; and in Khmil'nyk 4,793 accounted for 63.8 percent of the total (Altshuler, *Distribution of the Jewish Population*, 23).

[121] Notably 45.3 percent of the Jews in Soviet Ukraine declared Yiddish as their native language, 49.4 percent Russian, and 5.3 percent Ukrainian (ibid., 9, 17).

The 50,819 Jews living in the countryside (35.8 percent of the community) counted for merely 2.45 percent of the rural population, but that was more than double the average in the Ukrainian Republic and the highest rate in the Soviet Union. Although Jews did not count for more than 4.83 percent of the total rural population in any of the region's districts, in some villages they were a majority or a substantial minority.[122] Jews, in a sense, were not socially alien to the Vinnytsia countryside. Exposure to similar experiences, such as collectivization and famine, did not necessarily convey a sense of empathy, as the above tales show. By 1939, however, the Ukrainian and Jewish rural communities had been subjected to the same routine of Soviet conditions for more than a decade. Jewish collective farms not only challenged deeply rooted stereotypes of the community. They would prove critical to the rescue of the few remaining Jews when the Nazi extermination machine began spinning.

More than anything else, it was the unprecedented scale and endurance of the genocide that shaped people's responses. At no point before the genocide were Jews slated for total removal from the public scene, and certainly not for complete physical destruction. This was the harsh reality that the Nazis and nationalists presented to the local population. But the deep resentment against the Jewish minority, the identification of Bolshevik power with the Jews, and the actual extermination of Jews by the Nazis blurred together basic greed for the property of the vanquished and the attractive proposition of a Jew-free landscape. It was left to individuals to weigh their greed and resentment against the trauma of living in the midst of an ongoing genocide.

In light of the complex relations between Ukrainians and Jews, it is important to examine the unmitigated reaction of local rural activists to the withdrawal of Soviet power from the region and the declaration of Ukrainian independence on 30 June 1941 following the German invasion. The First Congress of peasants and employees in the Nemyriv district on 8 August 1941 drew together no fewer than 793 delegates. The resolutions of the gathering were unequivocally anti-Soviet. The Congress strongly condemned the Muscovite Red yoke for the centuries-old oppression of freedom-loving Ukrainians and the Bolshevik murder of the best sons of Ukraine. It passed a resolution to erect a memorial in honor of the brothers who sacrificed their lives in the fight for a free Ukraine. Although the resolutions referred more than once to "we/us Ukrainians" and saluted the leadership of the Ukrainian nationalist movement, the absence of anti-Russian or anti-Jewish rhetoric stood out, especially in light of

---

[122] In the village of Monastyrshche the 1,398 Jews constituted 74.36 percent of the population; in Ulaniv, 70.5 percent (1,188); and in Chechel'nyk, 66 percent (1,327) (ibid., 46–47).

what was to follow. Moreover, the names of members of the presidium contained several non-Ukrainian ones, most likely ethnic Germans.[123] Jews were not at the top of the local agenda.

This was also the Germans' impression during the initial phase of their arrival in the region. It appeared that, unlike in the Baltics and the western Ukrainian regions, there was no popular anti-Semitic violence in the region all set to go nor was the persecution of Jews at the forefront of the local population's plans. In Vinnytsia, complained *Einsatzgruppe C*, the NKVD had left the region eleven days before the arrival of German troops and had either taken or destroyed all essential documents. Locals, it seems, did not rush to denounce Jews, and the *Einsatzkommando* was forced to conduct house-to-house searches for Communist functionaries and Jews, which yielded hardly anything. Hence the unit resorted to more innovative tactics to trap and liquidate the local Jews. The town's "most prominent rabbi" was ordered to gather the Jewish intelligentsia within twenty-four hours on the grounds that they were required for registration work. Since not enough Jews showed up, the group was sent back home twice with the order to gather the remaining intellectuals. This process was repeated three times until enough Jews were assembled for a mass shooting.[124]

It seemed the local population needed to be actively incited to be drawn into a more active role in helping to solve the Jewish problem. The Germans then employed a method that had worked well in L'viv, where the discovery of corpses of NKVD victims was used to launch a massive pogrom. The living memory of Soviet terror in Vinnytsia was seen as a viable tool to mobilize the population against the Jewish-Bolshevik menace. Initial and partial exhumation of mass graves of victims of the 1937–41 Terror commenced upon the Germans' arrival in Vinnytsia. According to one cursive report from the chief of the Police and the SS Security and Intelligence Service on 9 August 1941, "In Vinnytsia, 30 murdered bodies were found under a layer of top soil; 146 Jews were liquidated, among them [one] member of the NKVD."[125] A month later the issue was again addressed in a somewhat more detailed manner. This time the report cited the exact location of the graves (the backyard of the NKVD building), where twenty-eight bodies were exhumed. Following an autopsy, some of the bodies were identified, and the victims were ceremonially buried in a mass procession, with thousands of locals attending.[126]

---

[123] DAVO, f. 1311, op. 1, d. 5, ll. 1–2.

[124] *Ereignismeldung UdSSR*, no. 47, 9 August 1941, 7–9.

[125] Ibid., 13.

[126] Ibid., no. 81, 12 September 1941, 11. The reporter noted that the victims were of modest classes and origins, and not of the privileged strata. Relatives told the Nazi officers that people were picked up by the NKVD in 1937 or 1938. Somewhat later they received a

In spite of the general impression that "the population is always grateful for our treatment of the Jewish question [and that] the executions of Jews are understood everywhere and accepted favorably," there were problems in various regions. In the "old Jewish" districts west of Zhytomyr and Berdychiv, observed *Einsatzgruppe C*, "a greater passivity and accommodation to the association with Jews took over the course of centuries . . . Almost nowhere could the population be induced to take active steps against the Jews" because of the still prevailing fear in many circles that the Bolsheviks might return, as occurred in 1918 with the Germans' sudden withdrawal. To break this fear and to impress the population with the finality of the present measures, the *Einsatzkommando*, in several instances, marched the Jews through the town, under guard, before their execution. It was also deemed important to have men from the militia (the Ukrainian auxiliary police force) participate in the execution of Jews. Sometimes the execution of Jewish Soviet officials was public entertainment, involving the beating of the condemned by the gathering crowd before their hanging.[127] There was also a carrot to encourage the evacuation of Jews, a sort of genocidal upward mobility. When the *Einsatzkommando* discovered the "oddity" of a considerable number of Jewish kolkhozes whose workers had not been evacuated to the Soviet rear, it liquidated only the Jewish managers (so as not to interfere with the work of the kolkhozes) and replaced them with Ukrainians.[128]

There was no refuge for bystanders from the unfolding genocide. The unprecedented magnitude of Nazi policies ultimately brought to the fore the distinction between ideology and practice, between holding onto anti-Semitic views and pursuing anti-Semitic policies to their maximum. Although the rampant popular anti-Semitism was critical in producing a favorable atmosphere for the removal of Jews from the public scene, still the actual extermination left many horrified. Like most Europeans, including the Germans themselves, locals wanted to see the Jews diminished, isolated, even removed, but in a sterile way that would not further unnerve an already ravaged society. In other words, it was the form rather than the intent of the anti-Jewish measures that disturbed the locals.[129]

Nonetheless there was little subtlety in the removal of the local Jewish community from the public eye. The initial mass executions in late Sep-

---

note that the arrested person was sentenced to ten years of forced labor for anti-Soviet views, with no right to correspondence.

[127] For such a spectacle in Zhytomyr on 7 August 1941, see Klee et al., "The Good Old Days," 107–18.

[128] *Ereignismeldung UdSSR*, no. 81, 12 September 1941, 13–15.

[129] For the way Germans coped with the tension between racist views and the implementation of racial policies, see David Bankier, *The Germans and the Final Solution: Public Opinion under Nazism* (Cambridge, Mass.: Blackwell, 1992), esp. 67–88, 116–52.

Figure 5.3. The Holocaust in Vinnytsia. Massacre of local Jews by an *Einsatzgruppe* unit.

tember 1941 were carried out with no attempt either to screen the intent or the process itself. By *Einsatzgruppe* standards, the liquidation of Vinnytsia's Jewish community was not unique. The Jews were forced to dig the graves, were lined up in groups of fifteen to twenty people, were "positioned with their backs to the firing squad at the edge of the ditch and killed with a shot in the back of the neck from a submachine gun. . . When the Jews saw how easy it was to be executed, they ran to be shot of their own accord. They even pushed in front of one another to get there sooner," recalled a German official who was present at the time.[130] This scene was repeated daily over the following weeks, and the death toll rose to several thousand—enough even to unsettle some of the German observers (Figure 5.3).

The locals, with all this slaughter occurring before their eyes, were fully aware of the fate awaiting their Jewish neighbors, especially after the initial executions and the establishment of ghettos in every town. People talked

---

[130] Klee et al., "The Good Old Days," 119–21.

about the executions, about "the trembling soil where many half-dead, including children, were buried alive."[131] Some were horrified by the consequences. "They kill the Jews in vain. I wish they had not started, but once they started they'd kill them until dusk. [The Jews] will take revenge on us," one woman told another when executions near Illintsi erupted.[132] Most watched their Jewish neighbors being led to their graves. In Illintsi people watched a twelve-year-old boy dragged from the hospital and marched to his death. "The Christians who watched when [the Germans] led the children through the town told us later that my brother cried hard and begged them to let him go. He said repeatedly: 'My Dad paid you for me,' " recalled Eva Shliapobevarskaia.[133] The son of Rakhil' Fradis-Milner was blond and blue-eyed, which prompted a Ukrainian woman in Nemyriv to offer to adopt the child. "They'll kill you in any case. Have pity for the child. Give him to me," she told the mother.[134] Others stripped an old woman of her shawl on the way to her execution: "Give up the shawl; in any case you are going to die."[135] Often locals witnessed not only the round-up of Jews but the actual extermination. Sometimes they were ordered to collect clothes from the victims' corpses and transfer them to the authorities; some were simply there on their own initiative.

By the time the next massacre took place in April 1942 the town was in shock. No longer could the locals remain oblivious to the events unfolding before them, the enactment of the "final solution" to the Jewish problem. Although one cannot ignore the likely motives behind the identical descriptions by both émigré Ukrainian sources and the regional branch of the State Extraordinary Commission for the Study of Nazi Crimes—both having an invested interest in presenting a community with an affinity for Jews—it appears that the event unnerved the locals. The second wave of exterminations "produced a depressing morale among the population . . . In town, horrible scenes took place: Husbands or wives, though non-Jews, accompanied their Jewish mates voluntarily to their deaths. I was instructed by the municipal government to inspect a children's colony [orphanage] in a former noble's estate; among the orphans there I found an eighteen-month-old Jewish girl being hidden," recalled a nationalist journalist in wartime Vinnytsia, whose testimony is corroborated by that of Jewish survivors.[136]

---

[131] YVA, #03–5241, 8.

[132] Ibid., #03–2243, 29.

[133] Ibid., 22.

[134] Grossman and Ehrenburg, *Hasefer Ha-shahor*, 100.

[135] YVA, #03–2243, 33.

[136] See HURIP, #548, 2, and the almost identical testimony of M. I. Sokolov before the State Extraordinary Commission in TsDAVOVU, f. 4620, op. 3, d. 253, l. 12; see also YVA, #03–5241, 7–8.

Others were either in a state of denial or simply could not comprehend the relentless, systematic massacre. Hanna Meller was astounded to learn that in the village where she found shelter there were those who knew virtually nothing about the massacres of the Jews. "Vasia responded with disbelief when I told him how we were deported," recalled Meller. "And once, in the meadow, while we were walking behind the cows, he stopped suddenly, fully astounded: 'Say, Niura,' he said and pointed with excitement at the cows: 'That was how they led you, too?' "[137]

The dividing line that ran through both popular collaboration in the genocidal enterprise and rescue of Jews was between an improvised, reactive, and individually based action, on the one hand, and an initiated, planned, organized mass effort, on the other. One organized group we have already encountered was ethnic Ukrainians who participated actively in the various extermination waves of the local Jewish community from September 1941 to December 1942; their involvement was mainly as members of the auxiliary police in charge of rounding up the Jews, leading them to the execution sites, and occasionally taking part in the shooting. Survivors who recorded encounters with the Ukrainian police noted the latter's sadistic treatment of the Jews. In one of the earliest executions in Radomyshl' in September 1941, the Ukrainian militia shot 561 young Jews in addition to the 1,107 adults shot by the Germans. By 1943, with the intensification of partisan warfare in the region, the number of local policemen was estimated at four to five thousand men, a rather substantial number in a small region depleted of many young males who were either in the ranks of the Red Army, in forced labor in Germany, or in the various partisan forces.[138] Nevertheless their brutal conduct assumed a particularistic ethnic face, especially when compared to other non-German units who accompanied the Germans into Vinnytsia. In the town of Illintsi Hungarian soldiers warned Jews of a coming *aktion*, and, in Vinnytsia, one of them slapped a boy and berated him in public for informing on a Jewish schoolmate.[139]

Throughout the centuries the Ukrainian countryside gained an almost mythical reputation for anti-Jewish violence, most recently during the col-

[137] Hanna Meller-Faust, *Me-ever La-Nahar*, 153.

[138] YVA, #03–3446, 16. "The Ukrainian police in Vinnytsia guarded the execution sites but did not participate in the actual killings. In other places, we learned, the police participated in the executions," said a member of the editorial board of *Vinnyts'ki visti*, in reference to the mass executions in the city in April 1942 (HURIP, #548, 2; Dean, "The German *Gendarmerie*, the Ukrainian *Schutzmannschaft*, and the 'Second Wave' of Jewish Killings in Occupied Ukraine," 175). In 1943 the *Generalkommissar* Shitomir put the strength of local police at 16,400 people, including around 7,000 firemen. Since the Vinnytsia region formed about one-quarter of the *Generalkommissariat*, a figure of four to five thousand local policemen in this area is reasonable. I thank Martin C. Dean for this information.

[139] YVA, #03–2243, 16; #03–5241, 4–5.

lectivization drive.[140] Nor did the homogeneous socioethnic environment appear favorable for the outsider. There was nothing unusual in a suspicious neighbor confronting a Jewish girl who sought refuge in one village: "You have such snow-white hands, you are so white, you are so milksoap, you must be a Jewess; you are a little kike, for sure."[141] During the war years, however, these very same villages became the main sites for the rescue of Jews. In prewar Vinnytsia, as noted above, Jews were somewhat more familiar with peasant communities than was the average Jewish community in the Ukrainian Republic.[142] More dispersed than the urban communities and closer to the forests, villages served as temporary shelters for Jews who were accepted by individual peasants. Indeed, most of the survivors of the extermination in Vinnytsia spent a significant time in peasant huts, especially during German liquidation operations.

Some incidents appeared to have violated the peasants' sense of basic justice and prompted ad-hoc collective mobilization to help persecuted Jews, even risking direct confrontation with the occupation authorities. In mid-November 1941, recalled the leader of the Jewish ghetto in Sharhorod, a group of almost nine hundred deportees arrived from the district of Dorohoi, under orders to leave the next day. Nearly all of them were women with children, and a few were elderly. With a snowy winter already set in, their journey would have meant certain death. "We interceded with the (Romanian) praetor for permission to leave them with us for a few days until the weather improved, but our attempt was in vain," recalled a Jewish community leader.

> He ordered the immediate departure of some in the group the very next day. However, when the people set out for the march, many of the Ukrainian peasant women who had come to the market crowded around the deportees and gave them food for their journey. Arriving in front of the praetor's office, the women knelt down and blocked the road. The praetor, furiously cursing, arrived at the scene but could not change the situation. The peasant women cried, screamed, raised their fists against him, and shouted: "You *Burzhui*. How can you be so hard on human beings?"[143]

[140] For the prevalence of popular violent anti-Semitism in the Ukrainian countryside in the late Imperial period, see Theodore R. Weeks, *Nation and State in Late Imperial Russia: Nationalism and Russification on the Western Frontier, 1863–1914* (DeKalb: Northern Illinois University Press, 1996), 41. For a nuanced survey of the evolution of both this popular image and of Ukrainian anti-Semitism until the watershed of the Ukrainian Revolution, see Abramson, *A Prayer for the Government*, 30–32.

[141] YVA, #03–5241, 14.

[142] For tales of Jews rescued by peasant friends in the region, see YVA, #03–5241, 8, 20; #03–2243, 23, 28, 39–40.

[143] Teich, "The Jewish Self-Administration in Ghetto Shargorod," 231–32.

The transport was returned, and eventually all the deportees remained in Sharhorod. Local Jews who fled the German-occupied territory and found shelter in the ghetto were sent to the villages when the gendarmerie raided the ghetto.[144] In other localities, active participation in the genocide was perceived as a violation of a fundamental social contract that applied to the Jews as well, and people reacted in kind. Rather than delivering collaborators to the Soviet courts, villagers opted for a social boycott. After Samiilo Khasids'kyi betrayed the Schwarzman family and looted their property, he found himself cast as a social pariah, reproached by his neighbors and shunned by his own family. The Schwarzmans declined suggestions to take Khasids'kyi to court and instead took satisfaction in the hostile environment surrounding him; ultimately they lived to see him dying, alone and impoverished.[145]

The bravery of such actions cannot be measured by friendly or even familial connections alone. As one moved eastward in Nazi-occupied Europe, retaliation against those sheltering Jews turned more draconian. Decrees distributed in the towns and villages warned the local population that, if they were caught hiding Jews, not only would they be shot and their house burned down but the same would happen to their neighbors.[146] In the village of Noskivtsi, a peasant who helped a wounded Red Army soldier into a hospital was beaten wildly, forced to dig his own grave, and then shot in front of his wife.[147] In October 1943 the SS reported the execution of some one hundred Ukrainians, mainly peasants, who rescued Jews in the Galicia district.[148] The message for those who sheltered Jews was unequivocal.

Against the fatal choices with which the Nazis confronted the population, blood ties often ran thin. Even the Jewish community broke down. As deported Romanian Jews pored into the newly created Transnistria, local communities bribed the Romanian gendarmerie to keep the Jews out of town. Besides fearing the spread of disease, they worried that they would be confused with the refugees and possibly deported themselves.[149] Unlike the policy in non-Slavic territories, where the offspring of mixed marriages were often salvageable by Aryan blood, in the Soviet Union the combination of Jewish and Slavic blood doomed such families to extinction.[150] Those who chose to stand up for Jewish relatives, in public or in

---

[144] Ibid., 236.

[145] YVA, #03–6401, 32–33.

[146] Ibid., #03–2243, 28.

[147] TsDAVOVU, f. 4620, op. 3, d. 253, ll. 17–19.

[148] Friedman, "Ukrainian-Jewish Relations," 288.

[149] YVA, #03–3446, 6–8; #03–6061, 7.

[150] For a decree in this spirit in Rostov, on 11 August 1942, see Arad, *Unichtozhenie evreev SSSR*, 220.

private, did so with full awareness of the consequences.[151] The profound brutalization of public life was evident even in cases of rescue. Several hundred Jews in Vinnytsia survived execution for a while because of their professions. One of them was told by a Ukrainian commissar and friend of the family who had rescued her several times: "You think that you'll be able to save yourself from execution if you go to the village of Raiky. In the end, however, the Germans will issue a decree to kill [all] the Jews. But a human being is a human being. He needs to buy things, to wash. There's nowhere to hide. But don't you worry, specialists like you we don't kill."[152] At most, Jewish life in the German-occupied territory was a commodity. The choices locals made reflected the harsh dilemma. In Bohdanivka, a Jewish convert was nevertheless locked up in a camp as a Jew. His Russian wife and children did not join him, nor did they visit him. Another Russian teacher led his Jewish wife to the camp where she was later shot.[153] Yet there were some who risked their lives by refusing to give up their spouses and others who joined them in death.[154]

Most rescuers operated as individuals and, in some cases, initiated the rescue. Hanna Schwarzman and her father were rescued by a friend who hid them in his village. The friendship between the two men dated back to the Great War, when they served together, and continued to the end of their lives.[155] Other survivors benefited from improvised rescue networks. Rakhil' Fradis-Milner was a medical nurse who often visited sick peasants in the villages around Nemyriv. Her son was saved by several friends who transferred him from one to the other whenever they sensed danger of a search or denunciation.[156] A common military background was often crucial. While in a German prisoners' camp, Gabriel Temkin could only pray that his Jewish identity would not be revealed by some of his fellow prisoners who helped the Germans to sniff out Jews, stripping them of their boots before they were led to execution. But none other than a rabid Ukrainian anti-Semite saved Temkin himself. "Did you really think, you motherfucker, that I would be after you for a loaf of bread," the Ukrainian reproached Temkin, forging an unexpected friendship. A certain universal sense of dignity overpowered entrenched animosities.[157] Jewish Red Army servicemen, who escaped from German captivity, were in a somewhat bet-

---

[151] For a nuanced evaluation of this delicate dilemma, see Mordechai Altshuler, "The Unique Features of the Holocaust in the Soviet Union," in Yaacov Ro'i, ed., *Jews and Jewish Life in Russia and the Soviet Union* (Portland, Ore.: F. Cass, 1995), 180–81.

[152] YVA, #03–2243, 27, 32–33.

[153] Ibid., #03–3827, 9.

[154] Altshuler, "The Unique Features of the Holocaust in the Soviet Union," 180.

[155] YVA, #03–6401, 32–33.

[156] Grossman and Ehrenburg, *Hasefer Hashahor*, 104–5.

[157] Temkin, *My Just War*, 60.

ter position, if only marginally. Here, families of servicemen, especially ethnic Russians, who were already emerging as a key group on the local scene, were critical to their rescue. In Haisin, Iakov Talis was hidden by the wife of one of his fellow officers, who also provided him with false Ukrainian documents. A similar fate befell Solomon Lozinskii in Kiev.[158]

More often, rescues were improvised following encounters with individual Jews in locations out of public sight. Compassion for the lost individuals, whose fate was already familiar to the locals, seemed to be the overriding motive. For some it was their duty as Christians, especially to save the innocent children. Oscar Shmarian from Brailiv was hidden by a peasant woman who was standing by the open grave at the time of the executions. The woman pushed the boy under a pile of the victims' clothing and sheltered him for a few days until he joined a partisan unit.[159] Some adopted Jewish orphans as emotional compensation for a child who had recently died; others needed someone to take care of their younger children.[160] But piety could work both ways within the same person. The peasant woman who risked her life sheltering Eva Shliapobevarskaia could turn on her parents in a moment of grief and expel them from her hut just as "the Lord ordered her."[161] Material needs, exacerbated by the impoverished occupation, played a significant role in the decision to risk hiding Jews. Under the conditions of occupation, there was a thin line between the rescuers' demand to be paid with food or to be given valuables and gold.[162]

The same was true in the case of betrayal and indifference. The motivation here was often a combination of greed for the victims' property and utter fear of German retaliation. But choices were also made unrelated to German pressure. Zoia Melamud, a twelve-year-old girl who escaped being shot in April 1942 by convincing the police that she was Ukrainian, was betrayed by the woman who occupied her parents' house. Earlier, while waiting her turn to be shot, Melamud, who eventually escaped, saw another woman collecting the possessions of people who had just been executed.[163] Indeed, people were making choices.

Like the rest of the German-occupied territories, the absence of organized networks of rescue symbolized the situation in Vinnytsia. Under wartime conditions, such networks could operate only through the Soviet partisans and the churches. Although Jews did make it to the ranks of the local partisan detachments, and, as noted above, in larger numbers than

[158] YVA, #03–5159, 5; #03–6061, 3–4.
[159] Grossman and Ehrenburg, *Hasefer Hashahor*, 61.
[160] Meller-Faust, *Me-ever la-nahar*, 142; YVA, #03–5241, 8.
[161] YVA, #03–2243, 39–40.
[162] Ibid., 23; #03–3446, 8.
[163] DAVO, f. 138, op. 4, d. 73, ll. 3–7.

in other locations, they did so on an individual basis. At no point was the rescue of Jews a goal of the Soviet partisan movement. In Chechel'nyk a Red Army officer, who was dispatched to supervise partisan operations, informed the local Jewish underground that Jewish affairs as such do not concern him. He'll take care of their concerns, but only as part of the general population.[164] In any case, when the partisan movement gathered momentum in Vinnytsia in early 1943, the Jewish population under the German-controlled territory was already decimated. The existing churches were even less likely to provide a rescue network for the Jews. In Vinnytsia, it was not merely the absence of infrastructure of monasteries following three decades of the Soviets' relentless antireligious campaign. At issue was the will to extend help, as demonstrated by the rescue activities of Metropolitan Sheptyts'kyi, head of the Uniate Church in Eastern Galicia.[165] The two dominant churches in the region, the Ukrainian Orthodox and the Autocephalous, had no intention of rescuing Jews. Closely associated with the nationalist cause and movement, the leadership of the Autocephalous Church displayed the kind of vehement anti-Semitism we met in Hryhorii's sermons.

The key to the rare communal rescue efforts lay in the specific social fabric. The rescue of Hannah Meller-Faust in the village of Byrlivka was a case in point. The young refugee from Romania was taken in by a couple of peasants after she told them her history and with an understanding that at the end of the war she would be free to return to her surviving family. Right from the start, neither she nor her saviors pretended not to know she was Jewish. The couple maintained contact with the surviving members of Meller's family, who were in the Bershad' ghetto, and provided them with food. Unlike almost all other sheltered Jews, Meller did not spend her days in a bunker nor was she forced constantly to change her location. Rather, she lived in daylight, led the cows of her protectors to the meadow in the company of other youth, and enjoyed evenings of dancing and singing with the young lads of the village. On Sundays, she joined everyone in church. She was presented as the daughter of her rescuers, relying on

[164] Notably the witness, Zalman Teitleman, describes the Red Army officer, Timoshenko, as a sympathetic person (YVA, #03–3446, 18). Ukrainian partisans also tried to lure Mikhail Mortkov from the ghetto into their ranks telling him that the Germans are determined to exterminate all Jews. They did not attempt, however, to liberate the ghetto. The partisans were too busy in their struggle to survive, said Mortkov (YVA, #03–6870, 6). See also Mykhailo Koval', "Natsysts'kyi henotsyd shchodo ievreiv ta ukrains'ke naseleniia (1941–1944 rr.)," *Ukrains'kyi istorychnyi zhurnal* 2 (1992): 25–32.

[165] Shimon Redlich, "Metropolitan Sheptyts'kyi and Ukrainian Jewish Relations," in Zvi Gitelman, ed., *Bitter Legacy: Confronting the Holocaust in the USSR* (Bloomington: Indiana University Press, 1997), 61–76. Of the vast literature on Sheptyts'kyi, see especially the excellent volume by Paul Robert Magocsi, ed., *Morality and Reality: The Life and Times of Andrei Sheptyts'kyi* (Edmonton: Canadian Institute of Ukrainian Studies, 1989).

the fact that the occupation authorities only knew that the couple had a daughter but had never seen her. This was a major risk, since the couple's daughter was a partisan executed by the Germans only ten days before they took Meller in. The couple, Andrii and Kateryna, were well known in the village. Andrii was already the kolkhoz chairman before the war, and Kateryna was a language teacher in Bershad'. Hence everyone in the village knew her true identity. In conversations with the village youngsters, Meller spoke of the murder of her people, which was raging not far from there.[166] How was this possible?

Rescue tales of Jews in Vinnytsia, as elsewhere in German-occupied Europe, defy generalizations. The ferocity of extermination and the German retaliation for helping Jews narrow the search for motives as to why individuals would extend a hand despite the enormous risks. Such individuals certainly existed in the village of Byrlivka, but under what conditions could their desire to help translate into action? One prerequisite was the presence of a pragmatic, nonfanatic occupation commander. Just like the German commander in the southern French village of Chambon-sur-Lignon who knew about the sheltering of thousands of Jews but turned a blind eye, or the German officer who deliberately avoided countercepting Danish ships carrying Jews to Sweden, so did Byrlivka gain from the cooperative Romanian commander Fantonel, who, unlike his predecessor, chose not to interfere in village matters.[167] Furthermore, a careful look at the village revealed a common thread in the very few European communities engaged in rescue operations. If the example of Bishop Fuglsang-Damgaard in Denmark, Metropolitan Sheptyts'kyi in Galicia, and Pastor André Tocme in Chambon-sur-Lignon lent meaning to these rescue missions, it was the presence of a powerful moral authority constantly preaching to the flock, in both words and deeds, its moral obligation to its Jewish neighbors.[168] Byrlivka's strong moral authority was in the person of the local priest, whose Sunday sermons evolved around human relations. At

---

[166] Meller-Faust, *Me-ever la-nahar*, 141–55.

[167] Ibid., 151. On Le Chambon-sur-Lignon, see Phillip Hallie, *Lest Innocent Blood Be Shed: The Story of the Village of Le Chambon and How Goodness Happened There* (New York: Harper and Row, 1979); Susan Zuccotti, *The Holocaust, the French, and the Jews* (New York: Basic Books, 1993), 228–31. On Denmark, see Leni Yahil, *The Rescue of Danish Jewry* (Philadelphia: Jewish Publication Society of America, 1969), 234–35.

[168] Following the massacres in November 1942, Sheptyts'kyi threatened with "divine punishment" all those who "shed innocent blood and make themselves outcasts of human society by disregarding the sanctity of man." Against the background of Nazi occupation and the entrenched anti-Semitism of nationalist forces, Sheptyts'kyi's call could have only a limited impact. His network of monasteries, however, rescued several hundred Jews. See Phillip Friedman, *Their Brothers' Keepers* (New York: Crown, 1957), 133–36; and Aharon Weiss, "The Holocaust and the Ukrainian Victims," in Michael Berenbaum, ed., *A Mosaic of Victims: Non-Jews Persecuted and Murdered by the Nazis* (New York: New York University Press, 1990), 112.

these sermons he would cite repeatedly, "Love thy neighbor as you love thyself."[169] Second, organized communal rescues took place within ideologically and socially cohesive communities with an ethos of persecution. Such a legacy appears to motivate action. If this were so in the Huguenot Presbyterian Le Chambon-sur-Lignon, so, too, was the case in Byrlivka. The village had several key constituencies, the most important being a large number of families of Red Army servicemen and partisans. These families were subjected to reprisals by the occupation authorities and fellow villagers who suffered under Soviet power and assumed positions of authority during the war. It was mainly a Russian-speaking community, certainly not the rule in the Vinnytsia countryside, and it had a large number of *Subbotniki* (Seven-Day Adventists), a staunch Protestant sect with a long tradition of persecution dating back to the tsarist era. Members of the sect displayed a remarkable affinity to the Jews and were especially friendly to the young Jewish girl.[170]

What was the lasting impact of the Jewish genocide on the private world of individuals? By the time of liberation the Jewish fate under the Nazis had already come to symbolize suffering among all the peasantry. When K. M. Sokatniuk, a peasant from the Teplyk district, complained about the miserable conditions in the village, she compared her situation to that of the Jews. "It would simply be better to dig a ditch and kill me, like the Germans killed the Jews," she wrote in May 1945 to a relative in the Red Army.[171] Similarly spirited, if less gracious, one Chumak, a kolkhoznik from the village of Maidano-Stasiv, Lityn district, told the Communist school director: "It is a pity that the Germans did not deal with you the way they dealt with the Jews."[172]

Victimization often breeds more victimization rather than empathy, and the pogroms in the summer of 1944 are a case in point. Several years after the war a nationalist activist from Vinnytsia observed that, under the Germans, anti-Semitism had been transformed from being religious-based to having racial underpinnings. The exposure to a lengthy, relentless barrage of Nazi anti-Semitic policies left unmistakable imprints on various segments of the local population. As the war progressed and the Nazi occupation became intrinsic in the local political scene, so, too, did anti-Semitic expressions become ever more racialized. A somewhat colorful example could be found in the collection of patriotic poems by one Ivan

[169] Meller-Faust, *Me-ever la-nahar*, 151.

[170] The *Subbotniki* observed *Shabbat* (Saturday) as a holy day, revered the Old Testament like all other Baptist sects, and regarded the Jews as the true children of biblical Israel (Meller-Faust, *Me-ever la-nahar*, 149–50, 152–53). For the rescue of Jews by *Subbotniki* in Volhyn, see Spector, *The Holocaust of Volhynian Jews*, 244.

[171] DAVO, f. 2700, op. 7c, d. 34, l. 53.

[172] PAVO, f. 136, op. 29, d. 243, l. 47.

Mazur of the village of Iukhymovo in the Kirovohrad region. Hand-written in a small notebook, the poems of this amateur poet combined unbounded love for Ukraine along with unrestrained hatred for Jews. In Mazur's world there were two sworn enemies of the Ukrainian nation: Stalin and the Jews. Neither the party nor Communists figured in Mazur's tirades. If the Jews actually played the role of the Communist Party, they also had their own distinctive antagonistic identity. Referred to as individuals or as a collective, Mazur's Jews were both impersonal and inhumane. In the poem "The Kremlin Flayer," Stalin and the Jews comprised an evil duo that joined forces to inflict misery on the Ukrainian nation.

> O you, Stalin, the flayer,
> What have you done to us now?
> You expelled Ukrainians from their huts,
> And Jews became the rulers.
> We spend the nights under fences,
> We have no fathers, we have no mothers,
> Because you, Stalin, a cruel beast,
> Drove them as far as Siberia,
> And to the Jews you gave medals,
> So that they could torture us.[173]

In another of Mazur's poems, entitled "To Adolph Hitler," Jews were portrayed as the willing tormentors of the Ukrainian peasant long before Stalin's arrival onstage.

> From country to country
> The accursed Jews
> Caused ruins,
> But in my Ukraine
> There is not enough of our blood
> To satisfy the Jews.
>
> Stalin sat down in the Kremlin,
> Had a drink with the Jews.
> They had red blood
> Poured into their glasses
> And then they feasted on human flesh.[174]

The beastial metaphor was not limited to nationalist circles. The portrayal of the Jew as a parasitic organ living off the blood of decent patriotic people could be found in expressions of local Red Army servicemen as

---

[173] TsDAHOU, f. 57, op. 4, d. 356, l. 186.
[174] Ibid., ll. 188–89.

well. "There are five to seven thousand Jews [in Vinnytsia]," two officers wrote to Khrushchev, while they were vacationing in Vinnytsia in the summer of 1944.

> They are like worms. A Jew controls the housing administration . . . In the military-trade store—a Jew. In the office—a Jew, that Kaminskii type. In other commercial establishments it is filthy.[175]

Five years later, but in a similar spirit, another veteran took on the local Jews. In April 1949 Volodymyr Krynyts'kyi, a thirty-eight-year-old decorated veteran of Polish origin, was arrested by the Vinnytsia MGB on charges of addressing anonymous anti-Semitic letters to Khrushchev and a local plant manager. The letter to Khrushchev from July 1948 complained about Jewish control of housing and commerce, and, in general, that they held the best jobs in Vinnytsia. Krynyts'kyi concluded his letter with an open threat:

> Patience is getting short. I am asking you to consider and take the most urgent measures or else I will be forced to declare a patriotic war against [anti-Semitic expression]. I have with me a sufficient number of well-trained soldiers. The entire Russo-Ukrainian simple people [masses] support us. I studied well the mood of the people. . . We love our power, but without the [anti-Semitic expression]. Assign them a single oblast and deliver the Russians and Ukrainians from the oppression, servitude, scoffing, and mockery that [the Jews] inflict on the Russo-Ukrainian people.[176]

The author then gave Khrushchev two months to think it over or else he would declare a patriotic war under the slogan "For Soviet power, without the Z[hids]. Beat the Z[hids] and save Russia and Ukraine." Krynyts'kyi's second letter to the plant manager contained harsh anti-Semitic statements and a threat on his life. After a long interrogation in which he stubbornly denied writing the letters, Krynyts'kyi confessed to the MGB that indeed he was the author. Apparently Krynyts'kyi held a grudge against the plant manager, whose wife happened to be Jewish. This trivial motivation behind the letters underlined the extent of anti-Semitic sentiments. The plant manager had aroused Krynyts'kyi's anger when he ordered him, instead of his Jewish assistant, to do a certain job.[177]

By the end of the war Soviet Ukrainian society was not free of Jews, but it had come to accept the "Jewish problem" as a legitimate one and to reflect on it increasingly in racial terms. The Jew was thought of as an

---

[175] TsDAHOU, f. 1, op. 23, d. 1385, ll. 4–5.
[176] PAVO, f. 136, op. 29, d. 185, ll. 72–73. The phrase "anti-Semitic expression" was interjected into the MGB report.
[177] Ibid., ll. 63–70b.

inherently alien biological organ whom people wished to see removed from their midst. Soviet Ukrainians may not have had the exterminatory intentions that made Nazi anti-Semitism unique but they were open to its arguments. And this tension between arguments and the pursuit of their logic suddenly came to the fore in January 1953 with what came to be known as the "Doctors' Plot."

The Doctors' Plot, as Mordechai Altshuler pointed out, differed from previous anti-Semitic acts in its dimensions and publicity. For nearly three months before Stalin's death, the affair dominated domestic news and public life in a way that resembled the Great Terror of the late 1930s. Following the announcement of the arrest of several Jewish doctors accused of killing Zhdanov and Shcherbakov, and plotting to eliminate the rest of the Stalinist leadership in the service of American, British, and Zionist agencies, the regime solicited popular reaction to the affair.[178] At issue, however, was not the prevalence of anti-Semitism in postwar Soviet society, which as we have seen was substantial. Rather, the affair provided focused insight into the way the Soviet body social was being delineated through both governmental and popular perceptions and practices. Reactions of non-Jewish citizens to the matter and its conclusion captured the essence and complexities of the Soviet purification drive in the postwar era and highlighted a society actively engaged in shaping the course of events.

At the outset, local party organizations seemed puzzled by the unfolding affair. The avalanche of announcements from Moscow emphasized that most of the culprits were Jews but made certain distinctions among members of the group. This ambiguity was captured in meetings that were held to arouse vigilance and in investigations of Jewish doctors conducted by local party organizations at medical institutions often bearing the name of none other than Lazar Kaganovich, the single most powerful Jew in the Soviet high echelons.[179]

Maintaining differentiation, however, was an uphill struggle. By 1953, as indicated by the treatment of enemy nations and nationalist guerrillas, the extension of guilt to entire collectives was the norm rather than the exception in the purification drive, conducted in a brutal and ever zealous manner. From the narrow aspect of political control over the citizenry, the unfolding affair threatened to get out of hand. Outside the realm of party cell meetings, in leaflets and personal conversations, people hardly differentiated between bad and good Jews. As a rule, guilt in these domains

---

[178] All the following citations refer to documents from TsDAHOU, f. 1, op. 24, d. 2773, assembled and translated by Mordechai Altshuler in "More about Public Reaction to the Doctors' Plot," *Jews in Eastern Europe* (fall 1996): 24–57.

[179] Ibid., 42.

was extended to all members of the ethnic group, which also appeared beyond redemption. Calls for violent actions against the Jews were common. Following a meeting with factory workers convened to address the announcement of the affair, during which the secretary of the Bar raikom, Pavel Lukovskii, stirred up anti-Semitic sentiments, the town descended into an anti-Semitic rampage. Jews were physically harassed, posters calling for people to "Beat the Jews, Save Russia" appeared in a school whose principal was Jewish, and one worker announced that "the Germans knew how to kill the Jews. When the Americans arrive, I'll show you how to slaughter the Jews." Baffled, the secretary called for a second meeting and read the workers a lecture on the friendship of the peoples.[180] Similarly, the charges of alienation and foreign connections found a receptive audience. Jews were viewed as alien leaches who thrive materially with the help of their rich brethren in America. "There are more than three thousand Jews in the town of Bershad', and 75 percent of them have relatives in America," complained an unsigned letter from a kolkhoz in the Bershad' district. The authors proceeded with a meticulous calculation of the lifestyle of the Jewish chairman of the town soviet. The latter's monthly salary was 350 rubles in support of a family of eight people, but his daily [sic] expenses on food alone exceeded 400 rubles. In addition, the Jew purchased furniture for 10–12 thousand rubles and clothing for another 5–6 thousand, bringing his annual expenses to about 1 million rubles.[181] Elsewhere party officials often explained to participants in the vigilance-raising meetings that the campaign does not target honest Jewish physicians and that the police were ordered to uncover and arrest the authors of the illegal anti-Semitic pamphlets.[182]

But when we shift the focus from the direct, narrow solicitation of a specific response, the picture that emerges from the hundreds of people cited in the reports is one of a society deeply entrenched in a Manichean ethos, accustomed to viewing itself as composed of both righteous citizens, on the one hand, and mortal enemies, on the other. Notably, in intimate settings and anonymous leaflets, individuals appeared to operate on assumptions embodied in the official postwar Soviet view of the enemies within. First and most visibly was the totalization of categories. Many had no qualms with extending the charges against the eleven doctors to the entire Jewish community. Their statements stressed the elusive and beastly nature of this group. The Jews were alienated from Soviet society by their very nature. "Unfortunately, it took us a long time to understand

[180] PAVO, f. 136, op. 36, d. 298, ll. 20–22.
[181] TsKhSD, f. 5, op. 15, d. 407, l. 104. I thank Frank Grüner for providing me with this source.
[182] Altshuler, "More about Public Reaction to the Doctors' Plot," 29, 54.

that these people can in no way be trusted," a chief designer told workers at the Kiev Industrial Design Institute.

> They live like wolves, only for themselves, and are capable of any betrayal that is in their selfish interest. Many of them are party members. They are universally honored, [well] clothed, and well provided for. They all go to the resorts and have received [state-funded] higher education. Despite all this, their actions know no bounds. They would have murdered us all if they had not been found out. One wonders why our government allows them to join the party, to occupy important posts, and to serve in important state institutions.[183]

Thus the government needed help from its more righteous citizens. "In order to strengthen the Soviet regime and to improve people's lives," read one leaflet,

> both among the collective farmers and among the workers, we have to fight the terrible and hated enemy, the enemy that hates ordinary people, that kills the innocent as well as the outstanding leaders of the Soviet state. This is not a people but the anti-people called the "kikes." . . . They are not human beings but traitors who sell innocent Soviet victims to America for dollars.[184]

This message was certainly in the spirit of the time. As the Soviet Union was marching toward communism, the polity should be totally cleansed of the internal enemy. The leaflet called for the Soviet state "to exile all Jews to Palestine or America" and concluded with the slogan, "Forward to the victory of Communism!"[185] Another leaflet posted in Kiev immediately after the announcement of the affair called to kick out all the kikes and "hustle them out by the scruff of their necks so that our land stops stinking from them," while another declared that "all Jews are our enemies and traitors to our beloved motherland."[186]

The totality of the distinct ethnic face of the enemy within and its alienation was viewed by both believers and skeptics in light of the recent war. "The time has come for the working class and for the working peasantry," read leaflets in the city of Smila in the Cherkasy region,

> to unite as one for the elections to local soviets of workers' deputies around the single demand: Get rid of all Jews from the southeast and southwest territories of the Soviet Union, i.e., from Ukraine, since these people have sold themselves to American imperialism. Thereby we shall be protected from a fifth column in

[183] Ibid., 39–40.
[184] Ibid., 29. The leaflet posted in Kiev in late February 1953 was issued by a group of youngsters claiming to be members of the Ukrainian Socialist Communist Populist Party, which included several Komsomol members among its number.
[185] Ibid.
[186] TsKhSD, f. 5, op. 15, d. 407, l. 93.

our rear . . . The party and government will fulfill the wishes of the people. In order to convince people, let us remind them [of the parallel betrayal] of the Crimean Tatars during the war years, as well as that of the Chechens in the northern Caucasus.[187]

The author of an anonymous letter to the secretary of the Sumy obkom traced Jewish anti-Soviet treachery to Judas-Trotsky and Fania Kaplan and requested the expulsion of all Jews from the province to remote places in the Soviet Union where they should "expiate themselves before the Soviet people and the motherland through honest work." Since all Jews were enemies and a fifth column, "they are like the Kalmyks, Ingushetians, and Crimean Tatars," one author charged. "They are American spies, our vilest enemies, and there should be no forgiveness. Blood for blood! They deserve this; there is and there should be no mercy for them."[188] Even Jews themselves seemed to believe that inevitably the next step in the unfolding affair would be deportation. "[The Jews in Izmail] think that the Jews might be resettled in the Jewish Autonomous Region," one Jew speculated in a conversation with acquaintances; "I believe that the government will adopt some resolution to resettle all the Jews," stated another Jewish worker in Kiev. "Now we all may be sent to Siberia. There's nothing to be done. We'll simply have to go," observed another from Kherson.[189]

The reference to enemy nationalities deported during and after the war on charges of collective guilt highlighted the internalization of the other pillar of the postwar purification drive: the abandonment of belief in the prospect for redemption of the enemy within. However brutal, exile and officially endorsed migration were meant as corrective measures, key components in the rehabilitation and sovietization of those social and ethnic groups who had strayed. The Jews, however, managed to turn even the new sites into contamination centers. "The Jews have gone too far with their outrages," exclaimed one Pleshakova, an assistant at an agricultural institute.

> For example, by moving from Kherson to Birobidzhan they made tremendous amounts of money. They sold their apartments and arrived in Birobidzhan with train compartments full of all kinds of goods. There they sold them at inflated prices and then quietly returned to Kherson where they bought better homes in the city center. The whole center of the city is in the hands of the Jews.[190]

Army servicemen continued to figure highly in the onslaught on the Jews, which underlined once more the army as the ultimate incubator for

[187] Altshuler, "More about Public Reaction to the Doctors' Plot," 45.
[188] Ibid., 56–57.
[189] Ibid., 52, 34, 55.
[190] Ibid., 54.

anti-Semitic sentiments. Even more important, the servicemen's young age guaranteed that the problem would not fade away any time soon. In Moscow, one such soldier complained that the administration of the Moscow Military District is populated by scores of Jews who "changed their surnames to Russian and Ukrainian ones, and occupy high positions in military institutions," not least, the housing management department.[191] The echoes of the servicemen from Vinnytsia in 1944 notwithstanding, the addition of the elusive nature of the Jew, now capable of worming his way even to the holiest of the holy—the Soviet army—was critical. Uprooting elusive enemies called for the harshest measures.

Not only did ordinary citizens appear to accept the principle of elusive enemies in their midst, but they also accepted the worst charges. The treacherous wartime conduct of the Kalmyks and the Chechens was accepted at face value, and, in the wake of the announcement of the arrest of the doctors, scores of people refused to be treated by Jewish physicians.[192] Some went further and filed charges of criminal negligence against Jewish doctors, which, according to one allegation, caused the death of an ill child, and, in another, led to the death of a woman who was in labor.[193] When news of Stalin's illness was broadcast, it was clear, at least for scores of Red Army servicemen, that the Jewish "murderers in the white gowns" got to *him*, too. "What a pity that he became so ill! Did the Jews not lay their hands on him?" wondered a civilian worker on a military base in Moscow. "The doctor-murderers are guilty in Comrade Stalin's serious illness. Evidently they prescribed a delayed-action poison to Comrade Stalin," observed another. The required antidote for the Jewish venom was familiar. "If Lenin were alive, they would not be here. He would have deported them all to Palestine," stated the head of a cafeteria who wondered why there were no Jews in the collective farms and only in high posts. That was not enough for a locksmith who threatened that "if Comrade Stalin does not recover, we'll have to go to Israel and rout the Jews."[194]

Even more telling were the reactions to the 4 April 1953 announcement by the MVD that the entire affair was a fabrication and that the doctors were fully rehabilitated. Issued only a month after Stalin's death, the laconic statement turned upside down nearly three months of relentless, ferocious announcements. But if the rehabilitation statement was meant as the first signal that the era of mass terror had come to an end, it did not

---

[191] TsKhSD, f. 5, op. 15, d. 407, l. 103.

[192] Altshuler, "More about Public Reaction to the Doctors' Plot," 33.

[193] Ibid., 41–42, 46–47.

[194] "Posledniaia bolezn' Stalina: Iz otchetov MGB SSSR o nastroeniiakh v armii vesnoi 1953 g.," *Neizvestnaia Rossiia. XX vek* (Moscow: Istoricheskoe nasledie, 1992), 2:253–58; here, 254, 255, 256.

land on fertile soil. The sample of forty letters, admittedly limited, to *Pravda* and governmental organizations by non-Jewish individuals following the rehabilitation statement revealed a population whose absolute majority was still receptive to the principle of elusive enemies, even when it doubted the specific identity of certain targets.[195] True, 15 percent of the letter writers lashed out at the internal security organs and *Pravda* for concocting such outrageous libel, publicizing it, and then reversing themselves without bothering to provide any explanation. As one group of Communist workers wrote:

> For two or three years the paper has waged a pogromlike anti-Semitic campaign in its articles and feuilletons, relishing in Jewish names and trying to prove, like fascist leaflets, that they deserve what they are getting. And now you print editorials on the Soviet ideology of friendship of the peoples. Who will believe you? You are prostitutes and beasts . . . Fascists . . . must be kept out of *Pravda*, which our people regard as infallible. Quit before it's too late and surrender your positions to staunch and honest Communists."[196]

Such sentiments, however, were in the minority. About 10 percent of the letters endorsed the "just, honest, and human act of our dear, beloved government," as one letter stated, without any further reflections.[197] The largest single group, some 40 percent of letter writers, demanded information on the reasons behind both the doctors' arrest and their rehabilitation. "Has everything published in the newspaper on 13 January 1953 been refuted, or are there still some valid facts? In what light should we view the activities of the Zionist organization 'Joint'?" inquired an army captain. Others lashed out at the "autonomous state of the MGB and MVD," which was above criticism. Such an outrageous affair could not have occurred in England, where access to information is not the domain of a single, corrupted, and hermetically closed group, concluded one individual from Leningrad.[198] Yet the matter-of-fact attitude of such letters only accentuated the lack of reflection on principles that made the affair possible in the first place. Undoubtedly displeased with the entire matter, the authors of these letters were concerned with the way their world operated, not with the worldview that shaped it. These individuals' world still consisted of righteous men and evil-doers. One had only to make sure that the eradication procedures were conducted with strict adherence to legality so as not to persecute innocent people.

[195] A. Lokshin, "Delo vrachei": "otkliki trudiashchikhsia," *Vestnik evreiskogo universiteta v Moskve* no. 5 (1994): 52–62, based on the sample of fifty-nine letters (forty by non-Jews) assembled in *TsKhSD*, f. 5, op. 30, d. 5.

[196] Ibid., 56.

[197] Ibid., 54.

[198] Ibid.

The remaining 35 percent of the letters' authors refused to accept the rehabilitation. The rhetoric of these letters was unmistakably anti-Semitic, but there was more to them than merely hatred for this specific group. By 1953 Soviet anti-Semitism had already been molded by the overarching purification drive of the postwar era. Once again, righteousness was judged in light of one's wartime experience. More than one letter expressed anger at the official admission of "impermissible investigation methods strictly forbidden by Soviet law." "Were they subjected to torture like those staunch and true patriots Zoia [Kosmodem'ianskaia] or Liza Chaikina?" cried one Savelev from Moscow in reference to the two young partisans who became the symbols of martyrdom after being tortured and executed by the Germans. "Even terrible torture did not break the spirit of heroic Komsomol members and did not provide the Fascists with the confessions they sought," wrote a group of students from Iaroslavl. "And what about our ordinary citizens who stood their ground when stars were being branded on their bodies or when parts of their bodies were being amputated. They revealed nothing," wrote another from Moscow. The Jews, in this light, were not only guilty based on their confessions. Just as they had done during the war, once again they "managed to get off scot-free." The Soviet view of the war was regenerated even when specific actions were rejected. This also made clear that this was a world in which perpetrators and victims alike had a distinct ethnic face. "Our government has taken a great step," read one of them.

> It made clear that biased investigation of cases took place in the past, and showed the people that it wants to change its domestic policy. But why did this act of global significance have to begin with exalting a pack of Jews and humiliating Russians? So many victims of the unjust repressions of 1933–34 and 1937–38 are still languishing in the camps; yet they are not the first to be rehabilitated, but a pack of Jews! . . . The Russian people have no use for this kind of international prestige that is based on the humiliation and insult of Russians for the sake of the Jews.[199]

And in such a world, the only cure was the physical removal of the culprits from the healthy body to the remote areas of the Soviet Union. "We ask you to publish an article on the Jewish Autonomous Republic," wrote a group of Komsomol members from Leningrad Secondary School No. 210 to *Pravda* and the Central Committee.

> Neither our geography teachers nor our other teachers tell us anything about this republic. Where is this republic? What is its geographical position and population? Who runs the republic and what is the name of its administrative center?

---

[199] Ibid., 59.

What natural resources and industry are there? How many Jewish workers, peasants, and scientists are there? Is it possible to settle there?

The students may not have known much about Birobidzhan. But they did
know that it was a remote place, a place for their Jews.

By the spring of 1953, on the eve of a new era, one encountered a
society struggling to make sense of an abrupt about-face. But it was not
simply a passive, reactive body. Rather, it was a society constantly reiterat-
ing itself into the unfolding revolutionary narrative. The appropriation of
the official line, the pursuit of an agenda beyond the regime's expressed
wishes, and the reluctance of a substantial portion of the citizenry to accept the change in course showed a society both deeply entrenched and
actively engaged in the shaping of the totalitarian ethos. Given the predisposition of people toward the totalitarian aesthetic enterprise, the weeding out of undesirable elements in particular, what, then, was the ideal
image they aspired to achieve through this lengthy and violent process?
In what terms did the residents of this mostly rural and ethnic Ukrainian
region define themselves in the wake of the most cataclysmic event in their
lives? Once again, the answer was to be found in the countryside.

Six

Peasants to Soviets, Peasants to Ukrainians

IN NATIONALIST IDEOLOGY the nation was embodied by a single socioethnic group: the Ukrainian peasantry. Tested by recurrent destruction inflicted by a host of foreign occupiers, the peasantry was believed to have preserved its ethnic, religious, and linguistic purity. Moreover, it was the peasantry that held the keys to victory in the cataclysmic struggle for independence. "The time has come when our entire people stands up to fight for new life and a better fate," exclaimed *Selians'ka dolia*, an OUN-M journal directed solely at the peasantry.

> Success and victory will depend on you, the peasant . . . Ukraine, her power and wealth—that is you . . . Who feeds the entire Ukraine? The village. Who gives Ukraine a healthy and guiding intelligentsia—soldiers of the national revolution? The village. The Ukrainian peasant is a fighter and martyr for the freedom and happiness of Ukraine. For centuries, his blood and sweat watered the Ukrainian land.[1]

In stark contrast to the Soviet cult of the urban working class, a sovereign Ukraine would be a peasant state. The free farming community had not only been the sole glimmer of hope in the past, it was now the backbone of the future socioeconomic order. "The Ukrainian state is a state of the conscious toiling peasant masses. Its laws will be issued in order to strengthen the peasantry stratum, to deepen its national consciousness, and render it the proper place at the stirring will of the state. The land in Ukraine is the land of our peasantry. It [the peasantry] owns it," declared the journal. "We shall abolish the exploitation by international capital and international communism, restore private ownership of the land, and abolish collective and state farms. The land will be divided among the Ukrainian peasantry. There will be no capitalists in Ukraine, no Muscovite Skoropads'kyis servants, no Poles, and no Jews. Any hopes for the restoration of large estates will be crushed under the blows of peasant hands under the banner of the Organization of Ukrainian Nationalists," concluded the author.[2]

---

[1] TsDAHOU, f. 57, op. 4, d. 369, ll. 60, 61, 61b.
[2] Iu. Iosenko, "Osnovy zemel'noi polityky orhanizatsii Ukrains'kykh nationalistiv," in ibid., l. 61b.

For wartime nationalist language regulators, it was the often belittled language of the village that embodied Ukrainianhood. As one of them wrote, in 1943:

> There is a tendency generally [to consider] that the development of a language begins with the town, not with the village, despite the fact that some linguists are glad to direct writers en masse to the village. And though the rural language does provide the profusion of expression for contemporary writers, [it] is still very important and we still need to examine it closely; it controls the literary language, since the Ukrainian literary language is somehow based on the language of the village.[3]

Moreover, despite the Soviets' return to the region in the spring of 1944, circumstances in the immediate postwar era stirred hope among nationalists. Nature appeared to play into their hands—or so it seemed. The postwar restoration of the resented collective farming system was accompanied by the disastrous famine of 1946–47, and nationalist writers saw the event both as evidence to the unchanged criminal nature of Soviet policies in Ukraine and an opportunity for the nationalist cause. In a brochure entitled *New Famine Catastrophe in Ukraine*, Iaroslav Starukh advanced the nationalist version of the disaster. Starukh insisted on calling the recent development a famine as distinguished from its Soviet official designation as a drought, or "dryness." A drought indeed had occurred, but it built on the more fundamental cause of the collective farm system. "That best colonial exploitation system" enabled the regime to squeeze grain from the peasantry regardless or despite the drought. Consequently the famine was viewed as a deliberate punitive method by the Soviet regime *directed against the peasantry in general, but, above all, against Ukraine.*"[4] The present famine was a repetition of 1921–23 and 1932–33, argued Starukh. "When we consider that at any time, against the growing wave of liberating fight of the Ukrainian people Moscow always organized her *counteraction* by help of a hunger, then we shall see that the hunger, this the greatest mass murder of millions of men, *is a conscious plan, organized action of Bolshevik Muscovy which considers the famine as an instrument and weapon of her imperialist policy for enslaving and exterminating the other nations!*"[5] Such an intent by the Soviet side was evidenced by the continuous export of grain to France, Yugoslavia, Poland, and other countries at a time when millions were starving at home.

[3] Paul Wexler, *Purism and Language: A Study in Modern Ukrainian and Belorussian Nationalism (1840–1967)* (Bloomington: Indiana University Press, 1974), 174.

[4] Iaroslav Starukh, "The New Catastrophe in Ukraine," *Litopys Ukrains'koi Povstans'koi Armii* 17 (1988): 81.

[5] Ibid., 74. I have quoted directly from the English text and have retained any grammatical errors that were in the original.

Starukh reserved his most intriguing observation for the collective farm system, which he perceived as the root of evil. The 19 September 1946 decree that ordered the restoration of communal land and work discipline was interpreted as nothing more than a "sensational avowal" by the Soviet government that "the peasant masses, i.e., 70% of the entire population of the USSR population, do not accept the Soviet collective farm system, are boycotting it, and openly objecting to it. And that happens now, after 30 years of Soviet rule, after a victorious end to the war." This active resistance by the peasants, the author concluded, "denotes the passage of the masses from the passivity to revolutionary forms of resistance and struggle."[6]

If Starukh's predictions were somewhat upbeat, his reading of the entrenched hostility to the collective farming system was not entirely misguided.[7] The Soviets themselves were quick to recognize the dire state of affairs in the countryside. Although they could count on the resumption of grain deliveries immediately after liberation, since "everybody had plenty at that time and partly because they felt patriotic," ironically it was the bounty that made the regime nervous.[8] In wartime Vinnytsia conditions were relatively better than before the war compared to other regions. The peasants, according to those who lived out the war years in the region, had quantities of fruit, fowl, bacon, and cheese. In Romanian-ruled Transnistria, where no mass deportations of working men took place and one could obtain practically everything, life seemed almost "normal."[9] The belligerent mood of the returning Soviet power toward the Ukrainian peasantry could hardly be concealed. "They [the Ukrainian peasants] lived reasonably well under the occupation," Alexander Werth was told by his companion, the famous writer Boris Polevoi.

> For the sly Ukrainian peasant is the greatest virtuoso in the world at hiding food. He always hid it from us; you can imagine how much better still he hid it from the Germans! And now that the Germans have disappointed them, they hope that maybe we shall scrap the kolkhozes. But we won't.[10]

[6] Ibid., 62, 64.

[7] Scrapping the collective farm system was by far the most frequent answer to the question, "What would you be sure to change?" posed to displaced Soviet citizens in the immediate aftermath of the war (Inkeles and Bauer, *The Soviet Citizen*, 352).

[8] Fedor Belov, *The History of a Soviet Collective Farm* (New York: Praeger, 1956), 23. Belov was a young demobilized officer who was elected chairman by the members of a kolkhoz in his native village in 1947. He served in this capacity until the end of 1949 when he was recalled to the Soviet army. Belov defected to West Germany in 1951. His diaries and recollections are the basis of the book.

[9] HURIP #542, 7, 8–9; #548, 1–2.

[10] Werth, *Russia at War*, 799–800.

More so than the futile German land reform of 1942–43, it was the relative prosperity in the wartime Vinnytsia countryside that highlighted the deficiencies of the collective farm system. True, the chaotic conditions under Romanian occupation did not amount to an articulated, positive alternative to the Soviet system, but, for most, it was a first crack in the hitherto impenetrable totality of the collective farming system. Hence, throughout the liberation period, the regime publicly voiced alarm at the state of affairs following three years of exposure to Nazi propaganda. "During the occupation," warned *Pravda* on 17 October 1944,

> the German invaders tried by every method to poison the consciousness of Soviet men and women and to confuse them . . . Particular attention must be paid to the question of implanting in the population a socialist attitude toward labor and public property, strengthening state discipline, and overcoming the private property, anticollective farm, and antistate tendencies planted by the German occupiers.[11]

In June 1945 Vasyl' Nyzhnyk, the second secretary of the obkom, reported to the plenary session that in almost every village in the Bershad district,

> you can hear from the kolkhoznitsy that there won't be kolkhozes when the war ends. England and America presented the Soviet Union with an ultimatum to dissolve the kolkhozes. In the village of Topokakh in the Teplyk district, a seventy-year-old kolkhoznik says "you know why it is bad here in the kolkhoz, because no one talks to us, no one assembles us, issues are not discussed." It is being said in the village that clearly there won't be kolkhozes after the war. As a result, some of the kolkhozniks pilfer property. Who will take home the wheel? Who will take home the yokes? Twelve yokes were found in the possession of one kolkhoznik.[12]

The raging famine of 1946–47 further inflamed the belligerent mood in the countryside. As hunger spread, large numbers of peasants fled to the newly annexed western regions, which suffered significantly less than their eastern counterparts. This was a major cause for alarm to the authorities since these strongholds of the nationalist movement had not yet been collectivized. "The hunger started in Zhmerynka," recalled Ol'ha Lytvyn. "I went to the Ternopil' region. People were well off. They supported us. They were asking us about the collective farms. We did not hide anything. Peasants gave us food. Sometimes they gave us slices of bread." The regime retaliated with mass arrests of thousands of peasants traveling illegally out

---

[11] Cited in John Curtis and Alex Inkeles, "Marxism in the USSR: The Recent Revival," *Political Science Quarterly* 61, no. 3 (September 1946): 358.

[12] RGASPI, f. 17, op. 45, d. 1999, l. 147.

of the region.[13] Two years later, the regime recorded a practically identical mood. In a conversation with fellow peasants in the village of Skytka in July 1948 Paraska Rachek complained: "Here we are gathering the crops this year, but we won't eat them, because the government takes them all and gives it to the French and the English. And we, the kolkhozniks, sow, harvest, but we won't eat. They'll feed us with their agitation."[14]

But it was not only the peasants' hostility to the collective farms that troubled the Soviet authorities. In some villages the war years witnessed the transformation of passive resentment into political activity. In the immediate aftermath of liberation, party leaders admitted that nationalist literature and folk songs were still abundant in the villages.[15] Writing in August 1945 about nationalist activity in two villages, the NKVD chief in the Lityn district identified the former de-kulakized peasants as the nationalists' primary sociopolitical base. The population of the Rozhok and Mykulyntsi villages was almost entirely Ukrainian. Before the establishment of Soviet power in these villages in 1920–21, peasants, who hired labor and engaged in private farming, comprised about 10 percent of the population. Collectivization in 1929–30 liquidated this stratum and established a kolkhoz structure allowing for some individual plots. In 1932 the population of the two villages was resettled in other locations in the districts, and all the land was transferred to the state. In 1941, however, the Germans allowed the population to work on the villages' original lands. Thus, wrote the NKVD chief, these two villages became a source of material and moral support for Ukrainian nationalists. The latter even succeeded in enrolling locals into an active UPA unit, which accounted for thirteen of the thirty-eight members.[16]

This impression was echoed in a detailed account by a *Pravda* correspondent who visited the kolkhozes of the Mohyliv-Podil's'kyi district in the summer of 1944. In a letter addressed to the Central Committee, the correspondent identified two groups in the collective farm kolkhozes that lived in mutual hostility: de-kulakized peasants, who returned to the villages during the war and assumed leading roles in the local scene, and their bitter antagonists, the families of Red Army servicemen. "The kulak elements, who were exiled at the time, returned to the village and raised

[13] Ivan Shul'ha, "Holodomor 1946–1947 rokiv na Podilli," *Derzhavnist'* 3 (1991): 53. On the postwar famine in the region, see also idem., *Holod na Podilli* (Vinnytsia: Vyd-vo Kontynent-PRYM, 1993), 150–90; Amir Weiner, "The Politics of Natural Disaster: The Famine of 1946–1947 in Eastern Ukraine," unpublished paper presented at the International Conference on Hunger and Famine in History, New York University, May 1995.

[14] DAVO, f. 7c, op. 7, d. 132, l. 82.

[15] TsDAHOU, f. 1, op. 50, d. 1, l. 210.

[16] The NKVD also identified twenty-seven locals who provided material support to nationalist guerrillas (PAVO, f. 136, op. 13, d. 50, ll. 13–15).

their heads. They spread rumors that the kolkhozes would be scrapped after the war," wrote Muliar.[17] Whereas the returning kulaks preyed on the kolkhoz property and occupied the best housing, alleged the correspondent, many families of Red Army soldiers remained with no cows and received no help at all, not even to rebuild their houses.[18] Moreover, many of the returning kulaks in the Subotnyk collective farm had served under the Germans, some of them in the punitive detachments. Muliar continued:

> Who are the leaders of the villages and kolkhozes who allow such an outrage? They are basically people who worked under the Germans and the Rumanians, and served the occupiers body and soul. The chairman of the village soviet, Iakym Sotnychenko, made a career with the Germans. He and Mykola Skorodyns'kyi, the current assistant manager of the artel, delivered to the occupiers all the weapons that were kept in the village and intended for the partisans.[19]

The party organizations, Muliar concluded in his long tirade, "did not remove the traitors and betrayers from the leading jobs in the villages and the kolkhozes, [and] hardly promoted those young workers who proved themselves in the struggle against the occupation regime to the leading posts."[20] Indeed, letters from peasants indicated that the returning authorities bore an almost visceral hostility toward the families who had remained on the occupied territory. Complaining to his father in the Red Army, a young peasant from the village of Kurenivka in the Chechel'nyk district wrote that the family was denied aid despite the father's military service. "Mother went there yesterday to demand the document, but they beat her and the prosecutor himself said: 'Let Hitler pay you for three years, but we'll take even more taxes from you. We'll rob you better than the Romanians did," wrote the son.[21] By all accounts, the countryside appeared ready for the nationalist message.

But the countryside did not explode in rebellion. The collective farming system did not collapse, and the local peasantry did not flock en masse to the nationalist camp. Rather, the opposite occurred. At meetings not intended for outside consumption, the Vinnytsia party leaders conveyed confidence in the political reliability of the peasantry.[22] Herein lay arguably

---

[17] PAVO, f. 136, op. 13, d. 5, l. 42.

[18] For similar charges from the Iampil' district, see DAVO, f. 2700, op. 7c, d. 34, ll. 51–51b.

[19] PAVO, f. 136, op. 13, d. 5, ll. 44–45.

[20] PAVO, f. 136, op. 13, d. 5, l. 45.

[21] DAVO, f. 2700, op. 7, d. 7, l. 85.

[22] See the speech of the secretary of the Khmil'nyk party raikom before the obkom's plenum in December 1944 (TsDAHOU, f. 1, op. 50, d. 1, ll. 156–57).

the most intriguing consequence of the war: the profound transformation of the countryside. Instead of an entrenched, nationalist, anti-Soviet constituency or an exhausted, passive body, an active Sovietized community was emerging.

To be sure, the returning Soviet power showed no signs of concessions regarding the kolkhoz system. Credited by Stalin in his election speech on 9 February 1946 as one of the main sources of the victory and a validation of the superiority of the Socialist economy, the system was there to stay.[23] Whatever crisis emerged it would have to be worked out within this system. Moreover, the regime held an incredible amount of coercive power to impose its agenda on the countryside and did not hesitate to use it. A series of decrees issued between 1946 and 1948 aimed to restore and revitalize the system. On 19 September 1946 the government issued the decree "On measures to liquidate breaches of the kolkhoz statute," which was forcefully implemented. The authorities were in for a surprise, however. They were the first to learn that the collective system's profound lack of popularity by no means meant that the system had disintegrated. Upon launching their campaign to recover kolkhoz land that had been seized, the extent of land reclaimed proved amazingly small. Figures from March 1947 indicated that the 4,700,000 hectares of land recovered throughout the USSR accounted for a mere 4 percent of the total area under cultivation in 1938. Moreover, peasants returned barely 521,000 hectares, and other unspecified persons another 177,000 hectares, which meant that various industrial organizations had encroached on most of the land.[24] The figures in Vinnytsia were equally meager. The collective farms in the region recovered some 38,498 hectares, comprising barely 2.5 percent of the sown land in 1940. The actual percentage was probably lower when taking the entire kolkhoz land into account.[25] The drive to recover the kolkhoz land continued well into 1949–50. Although the authorities prosecuted and imprisoned dozens of people who had seized the collective land, the actual amount of land recovered again was insignificant. In 1949, only 518 hectares had still not been returned to the kolkhozes.[26]

---

[23] "Rech na predvybornom sobranii izbiratelei Stalinskogo izbiratel'nogo okruga goroda Moskvy," in I. V. Stalin, *Sochineniia* 3 (16): 15–16.

[24] Barrington Moore, *Soviet Politics: The Dilemma of Power* (Cambridge, Mass.: Harvard University Press, 1950), 346–47. RGASPI, f. 17, op. 122, d. 291, l. 138.

[25] Figures for animal husbandry were quite low, probably because of the war, the Red Army mobilization, and the famine of 1946. Only 406 horses were returned, 137 cattle, 272 pigs, and so on (TsDAHOU, f. 1, op. 23, d. 4212, l. 91; d. 3505, ll. 33–46; d. 3508, ll. 24–25; *Osnovni pokaznyky rozvytku narodnoho hospodarstva Vinnyts'koi oblasti: Statystychnyi zbirnyk*, 50).

[26] PAVO, f. 136, op. 29, d. 793, ll. 1–23; op. 30, d. 173, ll. 28–41, 47–56. Vinnytsia was singled out as a region that lagged behind in recovery of kolkhoz property because of the alleged liberal attitude of its local leadership. A report by the prosecutor of the USSR of 1

In public, Soviet authorities did not spare condemnations of the so-called Land Reform introduced by the Germans in 1942–43. Their internal communications, however, betrayed much less anxiety over the impact of these measures, and for a good reason. Never intended to be anything but the core of Lebensraum for the German people, more specifically for discharged army veterans, and the grain basket for the Third Reich, Ukraine could not and did not experience a genuine agrarian reform. The collective farm system remained practically unchanged. The New Agrarian Order issued on 15 February 1942 and revised several times throughout the spring and summer of 1943 merely renamed the kolkhozes "joint-farming establishments" (*Gemeinwirtschaften*) and granted the peasants property rights over a private plot, which they already had under Soviet power. When the decision to privatize the land finally came in June 1943, it was trumpeted by local papers as the regeneration of the Ukrainian peasantry. Unlike the collectively inclined Muscovite peasantry, declared *Uriadovi Dunaievets'ki visti*, Ukrainians never approved of the kolkhozes which they regarded as a form of serfdom.[27] Private ownership of land would be extended to all who suffered at the hands of the Bolsheviks, including those who were evacuated from Ukraine or mobilized into the Red Army, announced *Vinnyts'ki visti*.[28] Few were surprised, however, when the transition to farm cooperatives (*Landbaugenossenschaften*), which foresaw a significant increase in the land allotted to each family (ten to twenty acres), was watered down, a result of continual feuds among Nazi bureaucracies, the decision to reward only politically reliable peasants, and increasing pressure applied by the growing Soviet partisan activities. In this light it was hardly unexpected that, by August 1943, Ukrainians who were allotted private farmsteads rejected the offer.[29]

This outcome also owed much to the intimate yet profound changes in the wartime villages. Families of Red Army servicemen were a key group in this development. Concern for dear ones (many had several relatives in service), discrimination at the hands of the Germans and collaborators, and, most important, at the hands of "former people" who returned from exile and assumed positions of power especially in the villages forged a cohesion that developed into loyalty to Soviet power. Gabriel Temkin experienced this phenomenon while in Cossack and Ukrainian villages after

---

January 1947 called attention to the fact that chairmen of kolkhozes and activists of the rural economy accounted for 60.5 percent of people who were tried for violating the kolkhoz decree (TsDAHOU, f. 1, op. 23, d. 4804, ll. 37–44).

[27] *Uriadovi Dunaievets'ki visti*, 1 July 1943.

[28] *Vinnyts'ki visti*, 27 June 1943.

[29] For a concise and thorough discussion of the German agrarian reform, see Mulligan, *The Politics of Illusion and Empire*, 93–105, here, 93–94, 98; Dallin, *German Rule*, 308–13, 316–75, esp. 344–47.

his escape from a German prisoners' camp and before reuniting with the Red Army forces. Above all, observed Temkin, the Red Army was the army of their husbands, fathers, and sons. "More than once," recalled Temkin, in reference to the numerous occasions when he was saved from inquisitive local policemen or the Germans, "I saw a mother looking at me tenderly, as holding back tears or shedding them profusely she would whisper: 'Perhaps your mother is now taking care of my boy.' " When more acute political issues came to the fore, mainly the dismantling of the collective farm, this largely female group offered the fiercest resistance. Faced with the probable outcome of such an act, when they were passed over in favor of dekulakized members in the division of property (in this case a single horse), they opted for delaying any decision until the men were back. "*Bez khoziaina dom sirota*" (in the absence of the master the house is an orphan), said one of these women, while others giggled cheerfully in agreement.[30] But even in villages where the peasants effectively dismantled the collective farm, this did not necessarily mean a return to the precollectivization past. The prewar transformation of the village was especially evident in the status of "former people" whom the Germans allowed to return to their native village. Endorsed by the Germans as the most likely sympathizers and anti-Soviet constituency, returning kulaks strove to regain their former possessions and authority, and at times even demanded privileged positions and treatment. While the Germans generally showed favoritism toward former people by appointing many of them as village elders and by issuing decrees that encouraged the restoration of property, peasants were less enthusiastic about this blast from the past.[31] In Fedor Belov's village, the peasants had already taken the initiative before the Germans' arrival and literally dismantled the collective farm. Under the supervision of a former church deacon and special commission, implements, machinery, and harnesses were divided among the peasants. But the key to the village wartime politics lay in the land question and the personnel in charge of it. The allotment of the land, noted Belov, was overseen by a temporary committee elected by a special village assembly. The composition of the committee (two schoolteachers, the former secretary of the village soviet, and several peasants who were most likely associated with Soviet power and were the main beneficiaries of its prewar policies) was not particularly promising for former people. Thus, even when they were allowed to return to their old homes, land was left out of the equation.[32] In other villages, the returnees were even said to suffer discrimination and to be squeezed for higher taxes and grain deliveries. When

---

[30] Temkin, *My Just War*, 67–68, 71, 81–82.
[31] HURIP #542, 2; #548, 3.
[32] Ibid., 6; Belov, *The History of a Soviet Collective Farm*, 19–20.

they received plots, these were significantly smaller than the average.[33] When Soviet power returned in early 1944, it cleansed these aberrations immediately. The returned former people were forcibly evicted from their old homes, and the forty-odd deserters, who had settled in the village during the war, were executed.[34] Such measures were in line with the Soviet purification drive; that they were unnecessary only underlined the intemperate aspect of the Soviet ethos. Already by 1941 the social and political makeup of the Soviet village was irreversibly changed. Neither former people nor deserters from the Red Army could sway the profound sovietization of the countryside.

A careful reading of the eastern Ukrainian scene on the eve of the war reveals that, by that time, Soviet power had made significant inroads into village life, creating a substantial reserve of support or at least a reluctance to change. The eastern Ukrainian village comprised a new administrative strata trained under Soviet power with a more favorable view toward collective farming. One testimony, and not necessarily by a pro-Soviet source, showed that when the newly established system of collectivized agriculture promoted stability and some popular consent, it was able to produce capable and popular managers. Reflecting on the relatively prosperous years of 1934–41 in the kolkhoz he led in the postwar period, Fedor Belov credited the chairman of the farm during these seven years with making the kolkhoz prosperous and winning over the peasants following the calamitous 1932–33 famine. According to Belov, Dmitrii A., the chairman in question, assumed his post in the wake of a series of corrupt drunkards, who had not lasted long in this position. His strict and authoritative manner, abstinence from drinking, bribes, and profane language in addressing the peasants won him their respect and love, and granted him leverage with the district authorities, who did not disrupt his lengthy job tenure. Hand in hand with the chairman's leadership, the peasants exercised a greater say than usual in the actual running of the farm.[35]

Both Soviets and nationalists celebrated youth as an ideological metaphor and a key sociological cohort for their respective enterprises. And both were aware that the outcome of their struggle would largely be decided by the local youth. One could not ignore the attraction of nationalist ideas for some young local activists, especially after the annexation of the western regions in 1939. Rumors of demands for Ukrainian sovereignty emerging from L'viv and the restrictions on traveling into the western region imposed on former people, only increased the thirst among local youth for more information and contact with the western-based OUN,

---

[33] Seleshko, *Vinnytsia*, 99.
[34] Belov, *The History of a Soviet Collective Farm*, 21.
[35] Ibid., 14–18.

argued Aletiiano-Popivs'kyi. By June 1943, *Uriadovi Dunaievets'ki visti* voiced alarm that among the "forest people," that is, criminal bandit elements of Bolsheviks and surviving Jews, there are also young Ukrainians who believe that they serve the Ukrainian national interest by fighting the Germans.[36] As late as December 1944, school-age youngsters in Vinnytsia were still drawn to the risky business of organizing a nationalist cell in the city.[37]

Nevertheless it was nationalist activists in the region who recognized that local youth were a considerably sovietized cohort. Too young to be traumatized by collectivization and the famine of 1933, unlike the older generation, they had been molded by the system they were born into. "In general," lamented Mykhailo Seleshko, who spent part of 1943 in Vinnytsia, "[the youth] did not consider that the situation in Ukraine under the Soviet regime was abnormal, as did the older people, for the youth knew no other life and had nothing to compare it with." Whereas the older generation could look to the pre-Bolshevik era—either the tsarist or the brief independence of 1918—as a living memory and a reference point, the youngsters born into the Soviet system had, for comparison, only life under the Nazi New Order. And, as they took care to tell Seleshko, the latter was even more horrifying than the Bolshevik propaganda portrayed it.[38] Worse still, from the nationalists' angle, was the young people's utter lack of national hatred and their reluctance to "delineate national differences." Seleshko's observations appear even weightier considering that these conversations took place in the midst or shortly after the exhumation of the mass graves of victims of Soviet terror on the outskirts of the town. In the world of Seleshko and his cohort, this represented the very pillar of national consciousness. Its outright rejection by the Vinnytsia youth led him to conclude, with unconcealed bitterness, that "to them, their stomach, that is, social affairs, came first."[39]

This observation was plausible enough if the notion of ideological commitment was confined to the nationalist camp alone. However, this was also a time of massive enrollment of local youth into the Soviet underground and partisan movement. Many underground cells consisted of

[36] *Uriadovi Dunaievets'ki Visti*, 4 June 1943; Aletiiano-Popivs'kyi, *Z ideieiu v sertsi*, 159–60.

[37] TsDAHOU, f. 1, op. 50, d. 1, ll. 208–10.

[38] Seleshko, *Vinnytsia*, 146, 164.

[39] Ibid. Some nationalist writers, apparently less familiar with the situation in the eastern regions, were more optimistic. In 1943 Iu. M. Khersonets was still confident that the war abruptly ended the socialization of Ukrainian youth into the Soviet system. The war confronted the Bolshevik system with an insurmountable challenge, concluded Khersonets. See Iu.M. Khersonets, "At the Turning Point," in Potichnyi and Shtendera, *The Political Thought of the Ukrainian Underground*, 229–38.

youngsters thirteen to sixteen years of age. The Komsomol underground in the village of Zhadano in the Dashiv district, to cite only one of many examples, had in its ranks Volodymyr and Hanna Mykytiuk, both born in 1928; Ol'ha Chekerlan', born in 1929; Zinaida Zhurbenko, born in 1930; and several others of similar age.[40] Undoubtedly fear of deportation to forced labor in Germany played a role in these youngsters' decisions. Yet they were aware of the fate of those the Germans caught and charged with partisan activity, which would indicate that their joining the Soviet underground displayed a certain degree of commitment on their part, one that Seleshko's theory of "stomach first" failed to explain.

Sovietization of the countryside was evident in a least likely realm, that of religion. True, on the eve of the war, state and church relations appeared fixed and popular belief in irreversible decline (if not as fast as the authorities wished). However, these assumptions were turned upside down by the German policy toward the church in occupied territories and the shift in Soviet policy in unoccupied regions. Ultimately the spontaneous religious revival on the former, and hitherto inconceivable concessions on the latter, have long been perceived as signs of a fragile sovietization of the populace, the regime's awareness of this fragility, and its subsequent decision to turn from socialist revolutionary to more traditional sources of legitimization for the polity.

The Germans' arrival certainly signaled a religious revival in the region. Some 840 churches, mainly Autonomous Orthodox and Ukrainian Autocephalous, were reopened in Vinnytsia, a rather impressive increase in comparison with the recent past, yet a meager third of the number of functioning churches before the Revolution.[41] Attendance at services, and baptisms in particular, significantly increased when compared to the Soviet era. Yet the opening of 4,500 churches for the nearly 17 million people residing in the Reichskommissariat Ukraine resulted in one church per 3,750 people, a rather low ratio. Equally important was participation in religious ceremonies. True, large crowds showed up for major religious events, as thousands did in Vinnytsia where victims of Soviet terror were reburied, or as some sixty thousand people did for the more festive Water Blessing (*Vodokhreshchi*) in Dnipropetrovs'k in 1943. Such events, however, were rare opportunities for mass celebration during the dark days of the brutal German occupation, concludes Karel Berkhoff.[42]

Paradoxically, a certain momentum was initiated by the shift in the Soviet regime's policy on the nonoccupied territories, epitomized by Stalin's

---

[40] PAVO, f. 138, op. 4, d. 196, ll. 9–10.

[41] Soviet postwar report counted 215 Ukrainian Autocephalous churches and 230 Autonomous Slavonic churches reopened on German-controlled territory, and some 400 churches under the Romanians. PAVO, f.136, op.13, d.105, ll.1–2.

[42] Berkhoff, *Hitler's Clean Slate*, 265–69.

meeting with Orthodox Church leaders in September 1943 and the opening of churches in regions under Soviet rule. Vinnytsia would be liberated
within seven months of this rapprochement and faced with its consequences. But what did the regime have in mind in sacrificing the tenets
of the revolutionary creed? For one, this was not an act of a desperate
regime. The shift occurred well after the wartime crisis was over and not
during the low point of 1941–42. One possible explanation may be the
intriguing coincidence of the accord with the articulation of the theory
of "no conflict" in the arts, befitting a society that had just prevailed in
its Armageddon and embarked on the transition to its ultimate goal of
communism. The integration of this event into the unfolding revolutionary epic was complemented by believers' own expectation of the emergence of a more harmonious society. Although believers clearly wished for
a thorough religious revival, their dreams were not articulated as a desire
to return to the prerevolutionary era. By the outbreak of the war, the
Soviet state had already become a fixture in their world, and the aspiration
was for a harmonious, organic society in which the Soviet state and the
church would come together after having weathered the Nazi menace.
Sometimes this wish created comic situations such as the one in the Vinnytsia district where a priest asked the secretary of the Komsomol to lend
twelve *komsomol'tsy* with good voices for the church choir, or genuine
expectations from the local authorities to provide material aid for the construction of new churches.[43] More often, they encountered stiff resistance
from the local party cadres and ended up petitioning Moscow for help.
Occasionally they succeeded. In February 1948 six hundred local Catholic
parishioners managed to reverse the closure of the church by the Regional
Executive Committee two years earlier by bombarding Moscow with peti-
tions. In the process, they found themselves, like so many petitioners before them, locked in a familiar game, where the only available channel was
the same Soviet bureaucracy.[44]

The change in policy was not without cost. None was more shocked
than Communist activists in the localities. These people were the core of
Communist true believers with a greater personal stake in the implementation of socialist atheism. The result was confusion among the ranks of
Communist true believers who suddenly found themselves bombarded
with requests by local parishioners for the construction of new churches or
negotiating the return of kolkhoz clubs converted to belfries and churches
during the war. The authorities went out of their way to reassure the activists that no change in the party's religious policy and Marxist worldview

[43] RGASPI, f.17, op.45, d.1999, l.188.
[44] PAVO, f.136, op.29, d.215, ll.8–9.

occurred in the wake of the war.[45] These people, still at the helm of power in the countryside, effectively held excessive expectations and activities of religious believers in check, until the relaxation was put to rest in 1948.[46] But there was more to it.

The regime seemed well aware that, however painful this temporary shift in religious policy might be, this was a risk it could afford without bringing down the (Soviet) house. Twenty-five years of antireligious campaigns and cultivation of new modes of association effectively diminished the role of religion in the lives of Soviet citizens, something that even the experience of the magnitude of the war could not shake. If anything at all, wartime experience both reflected and accelerated the secularization of the countryside. Here, too, youth held the keys to any meaningful development. This was already evident in the 1937 census where religious belief was recorded. While 57 percent of the entire population identified themselves as believers, the results for the sixteen to twenty-nine year olds were exactly the opposite, with 57 percent declaring themselves nonbelievers.[47] On his collective farm, wrote Fedor Belov, cultural life in its Soviet form remained fairly active and popular. The impact of the closure and subsequent demolition of the local church, which had been the center of spiritual life in the community, was offset by the formation of an active village club. The atheist group that made extensive use of the club consisted mostly of young people.[48] Religious affinities were expected to revive when the Germans reopened churches and priests took over teaching in many of the region's schools. In any case, the opening of the churches did not translate into a mass revival of belief. Soviet activists took comfort in incidents such as that in the village of Pechera in the Shpykiv district, where fourth-grade students challenged the priest to demonstrate the existence of God. The evidence the priest provided was so unconvincing that the students stopped attending the school, rejoiced a Soviet intelligence re-

[45] RGASPI, f.17, op.45, d.1999, ll.188–89. On the impact of the shift in religious policy on local activists in Russia, see Daniel Peris, "God Is on Our Side": The Religious Revival on Unoccupied Soviet Territory during World War II," *Kritika* 1:1 (Winter 2000): 97–118; and Elena Zubkova, "Mir mnenii sovetskogo cheloveka. 1945–1948 gody," *Otechestvennaia istoriia* no.3 (1998):34–36.

[46] A slight decline in the number of open churches in the region from 840 to 827 was registered already in 1946. PAVO, f.136, op.13, d.105, l.2. For the regime's return to antireligious policies after 1948, see Zubkova, "Mir mnenii sovetskogo cheloveka," 36.

[47] Sheila Fitzpatrick, *Stalin's Peasants: Resistance & Survival in the Russian Village after Collectivization* (New York: Oxford University Press, 1994), 204; Valentina Zhiromskaia, et al., eds., *Polveka pod grifom: Vsesoiuznaia perepis' naseleniia 1937 goda* (Moscow: Nauka, 1996), 98.

[48] Belov, *The History of a Soviet Collective Farm*, 56–57.

port from September 1942.[49] The Germans' own surveys were just as blunt. Shortly after their arrival in Vinnytsia, the Germans concluded that the majority of church attendants in the countryside were elderly, while the youth and those who were middle-aged displayed sheer apathy. Another survey estimated that about half the youth were atheists.[50] While in town two years later, Mykhailo Seleshko noted that youngsters who were brought up in the Soviet educational system and were accustomed to different forms of popular culture, such as movies, publicly displayed their displeasure with the tedious sermons when they did bother to attend service. By then, even the elderly stopped attending services regularly.[51]

Nor did preaching for victory of the "light-haired knights" [Germans] over the "enemy" [Bolsheviks] by Autocephalist priests of strong nationalist convictions endear the church to many locals, old and young alike, with relatives in the ranks of the Red Army. "At first, even the youth reached out to the church, mainly out of curiosity, but it quickly became disappointed. Gradually adults also started to cool down and lose respect for the church, especially in connection with appeals by priests to [G]od to help defeat the Red Army and to let the Germans win," noted a Communist underground activist in Kiev and Kirovohrad.[52]

Not least important, religious revival did not penetrate the ranks of the largest Soviet institution, the Red Army. By late 1939, young servicemen groomed in the Soviet system were already baffled by the religiosity they encountered in the newly annexed regions. "As to the situation with girls," one serviceman in western Ukraine informed his friend, Sasha:

The girls here are cute. There are Polish, Ukrainian, and Jewish girls. Their faces are very pretty, but alas they are very religious. They are so sure that there is a God that it's impossible to dissuade them. You invite her to the movies and she drags you off to church. No matter how many villages we passed, we saw a booth on every street and in it a clay image of God. But, in general, we saw many Gods here of all kinds! The Poles have their own God, the Jews have their own God, and the Russians have their own. You tell a girl that they all have different Gods and that all of them are not worth a farthing, and she replies: *ia nytz, nytz nerazumiiu* [I don't understand anything at all]. The hell they don't understand.[53]

[49] "Razvedsvodka no.11: O polozhenii v okkupirovannoi protivnikom Vinnitskoi oblasti, po sostoianiiu na 30.9.42 g." TsDAHOU, f.1, op.23, d.124, l.24.
[50] *Ereignismeldung UdSSR*, 45 (7 August 1941), 6; 120 (21 October 1941), 10.
[51] Seleshko, *Vinnytsia*, 102.
[52] Berkhoff, *Hitler's Clean Slate*, 272–73, n. 165.
[53] Vladimir Zenzinov, *Vstrecha s Rossiei: Kak i chem zhivut v Sovetskom Soiuze. Pis'ma v Krasnuiu Armiiu 1939–1940* (New York: L. Rausen, 1944), 332.

Later, during the war, young peasants going into battle whispered the Lord's Prayer and crossed themselves repeatedly, and the dying yelled or murmured "Gospodi pomilui" [Lord, have mercy]," recalled Gabriel Temkin, but there were no services in the field, nor priests to give absolution, and no requiems for the departed souls. "Ours was still the Red Army," Temkin concluded.[54] Like so many other wartime trends and policies, the fate of religion depended, to a large degree, on the course taken in the Red Army. And there, the prospects were slim.

By the outbreak of the war, the peasants of Vinnytsia viewed themselves and their surroundings through Soviet-tinted glasses. In private conversations, kolkhozniks under Romanian occupation referred to representatives of Soviet power as *nashi* (ours).[55] As seen in an incident cited in the previous chapter, when Ukrainian peasant women confronted the Romanian praetor in Sharhorod protesting the scheduled deportation of Jews, they cursed him as nothing other than "You *Burzhui*." Despite the traumatic experience of collectivization and famine, peasants had internalized this terminology, and not only in their contact with Soviet power.

The nationalists' growing frustration with the current affairs in the countryside and with their failure to spread the nationalist idea beyond the intelligentsia was evident in their addresses to the peasantry, as seen in one such lament:

> Ukrainians, we are a mighty people. There are fifty million of us. But we don't have unity and we don't listen to our leader, the Organization of Ukrainian Nationalists, our intelligentsia. We would rather believe the Muscovite tsar, the Bolshevik Jew, or the Polack [liats'kyi] Polish pan, than our own intelligentsia which originates from the same village and most of all wishes it the best.[56]

As time went on, hopes of winning over the countryside seemed dashed forever. As we have seen, these hopes were anchored, on the one hand, in the peasantry's hostility toward the collective farm system, which had resulted in the great famine of 1933, and, on the other, in their disillusionment with the German land reform of 1942. But, by the spring of 1942, the outlook had changed. The peasants of Vinnytsia began to realize that the Germans' terror overshadowed the half-hearted concessions they offered, and, in public meetings, the peasants openly compared the German policies to their Bolshevik precursors.[57] Viewing the Bolshevik menace in

---

[54] Temkin, *My Just War*, 132.

[55] Meller-Faust, *Me-ever la-nahar*, 142–55.

[56] D. Zahirs'kyi, "Shcho to e Ukraina ta shcho zrobylo ukrains'ke selo dlia Ukrainy," TsDAHOU, f. 57, op. 4, d. 369, l. 60b.

[57] The disbelief in the German proposals was recognized by the German authorities themselves. Nevertheless, in September 1942, German experts on the local scene advised against

relative terms and recognizing that no viable alternative was in the offing took the edge off the nationalist message. Moreover, the majority of local youth knew only the Soviet system, and most of them feared losing the communal safety net in favor of the unknown. Thus drastic change was not in the cards. This dreary situation was admitted quite early by those activists familiar with the eastern Ukrainian scene. A painful concession made by OUN-M in May 1942 was to drop the denunciation of the kolkhoz and allow the members to decide whether to retain or abolish the collective farm.[58] The resolutions of the Third Extraordinary Grand Assembly of the OUN, from 21–25 August 1943, explicitly stated that in the future independent Ukraine, "the Ukrainian national regime will not impose on farmers any one method of working the land. In the Ukrainian state, both individual and collective work on the land will be permitted; the method chosen will depend on the will of the farmers."[59] For all practical purposes, the anti-kolkhoz message, expected to have been the winning battle cry on Soviet territory, was dropped.

It was the postwar era, however, that witnessed the thorough Sovietization of the countryside largely through the new powerful and dynamic agency of Red Army servicemen and their families. The criteria for legitimacy and belonging in the rural community were delineated by Soviet veterans of World War II who were taking over and insinuating their images of the war into the local scene. The yardstick for political recognition in the countryside was no longer the traumatic experiences of collectivization and famine, but rather that of the recent war. In the world of these peasant-soldiers, the war had become an autobiographical point of departure. It erased the pain and humiliation of collectivization and famine, and the stains of social categorization that accompanied these events. And it was the war that finally connected the ordinary peasant in the small collective farms of this remote region to a Soviet myth in which he (rarely she) was not the culprit but the hero. By January 1946, more than 88,000 demobilized servicemen returned to the region. Of the 75,588 who were working, the majority (63,507) labored in the countryside. Five months later, the number had already grown to 120,381.[60] Veterans were quick to assume leading roles, enjoying both political and popular endorsement.

---

any further concession in light of the peasants' expectations for restoration of individual land ownership that would cause social chaos (TsDAVOVU, f. 3206, op. 1, d. 26, l. 27). For a nationalist survey of the peasantry's attitudes toward the German and Bolshevik agrarian order that reached a similar conclusion, see TsDAHOU, f. 57, op. 4, d. 347, ll. 37, 38.

[58] Armstrong, *Ukrainian Nationalism*, 92.

[59] Potichnyi and Shtendera, *The Political Thought of the Ukrainian Underground*, 343, 378.

[60] TsDAHOU, f. 1, op. 23, d. 2981, ll. 4, 26.

Figure 6.1. *We Were Triumphant in Battle—We Shall Be Triumphant on the Labor Front.* Kharkiv, n.d. War veterans are called on to transfer the zeal of the front to the harvest campaign.

By January 1946, more than 700 demobilized servicemen were already working as chairmen of kolkhozes, and in some districts they formed an almost absolute majority at this post. At the end of the year demobilized servicemen accounted for 33 of the 64 chairmen in Bar, 32 of the 50 in Lityn, and 29 of the 46 in Mohyliv-Podil's'kyi.[61]

The veterans were expected to transform the devastated countryside by transferring their front-line zeal to the civilian front. The war, for these young men, was far from over. "We were triumphant in battle—we shall be triumphant on the labor front. Demobilized soldiers of the war, be the leaders in the fight for a model collection of the harvest," read a slogan on a poster depicting a decorated veteran operating a threshing machine in the field (Figure 6.1). In Babaevskii's popular novel discussed above, an army general advised his protégé, a young officer who was about to embark on a civilian career as chairman of a raispolkom, not to survive on his past glory alone.

[61] PAVO, f. 136, op. 21, d. 118, l. 1; d. 165, ll. 1, 45, 48.

You'll have to renew your military glory every day in your work, so it will not be tarnished and appear corroded with conceit. They say that the decorations on a soldier's chest are the mirror of his soul. That's probably quite right. But in that mirror people see only our past and our present; the future must find its reflections in our deeds. So my wish for you . . . is that, in a year or two, a decoration for heroism in labor may appear beside those you have for heroism in war.[62]

On the occasion of the announcement of the first wave of demobilization, the press was already praising veterans for living up to the wishes of Babaevskii's fictitious general. Tempered at the front, these young men were claimed to combine the necessary balance between authoritarianism and patience, discipline and compassion. "Recently our paper wrote about Comrade Dluhunovych a demobilized Communist front-line soldier, who was directed by the Kiev raikom to the Berezan' kolkhoz, one of the backward kolkhozes in the district," an editorial of *Pravda Ukrainy* informed the readers.

> The kolkhoz was lagging behind, slow to make grain deliveries, dragging out work in the fields. The Communist-warrior rolled up his sleeves and started to instill order in the kolkhoz, helping the inexperienced chairman to understand the economics of the farm. He made suggestions on how to improve the organization of labor, allocated taxes, and assigned the kolkhozniks [work]. Comrade Dluhunovych went to each of the kolkhoz huts and explained at great length to the individual kolkhozniks, as well as to the general meeting, the great importance of grain procurement in the first year after the war. He talked in detail about political events in the country and abroad. Results were soon evident. The backward kolkhoz pulled itself up and climbed to the leading ranks.[63]

Earlier we pointed to the criticism leveled at this rosy scenario that owed more to veterans' self-image and the regime's desires than to the grim reality of the postwar countryside. But there was more to it. Veterans who assumed positions of power often triggered dissatisfaction, not least among women who filled these jobs during the war. While touring the Kursk countryside in 1947, Osip Chernyi recorded one of the last few kolkhoz chairwomen in the region passing the verdict on the returning veterans whose work habits, she told him, were inferior to women.[64] Sometime later, in her novel *In an Average District*, Iuliia Kapusto portrayed an old Communist woman complaining about the demobilized servicemen who either shunned work or were satisfied only with the post of

---

[62] Babaevskii, *Kavaler zolotoi zvezdy*, 334.

[63] *Pravda Ukrainy*, 23 September 1945. For a similar tale that occurred a while later, this time from Kherson province, see the 17 April 1946 issue.

[64] Osip Chernyi, "Na kurskoi zemle," *Znamia* 1 (1948): 138, 140.

a chairman.[65] And Viktor Nekrasov, ever resentful of the regime saddling the tormented veterans ("the Soviet lost generation") with big causes, summed up the job skills they acquired at the front: "Haven't we had enough young boys who left for the front straight from school and returned home to ashes—no house, no parents, no friends . . . And, as a rule, no profession either. In their seventeen or eighteen years they learned two things: to kill and to avoid getting killed, and nothing else. And what is there for them now, when this is no longer necessary?" Yes, there were those, who, as in the popular version, returned from the front with a medal-covered chest, itching with desire to work, and who, by their sheer energy, transformed their ruined native kolkhoz into a flourishing, well-run collective. But there was also more complexity, wrote Nekrasov.[66]

Indeed, the long-term significance of mass demobilization for the countryside lay elsewhere than in the capacity of veterans to mobilize peasants to work in the fields of the collective farms. The ongoing process both reflected and shaped the transformation of the Bolshevik ethos in the postwar countryside. As the myth of the war was being integrated into the Bolshevik master-narrative, the latter was being molded in the mirror of the former. By 1947 this development came to the fore throughout the entire union. At about this time Barrington Moore observed that the political necessity for strict control produced excessive bureaucratic structures and practices, which, in turn, brought about a diminution of the enthusiasm the regime depended on, and often led to some kind of opposition. "At this point," noted Moore "the regime typically [engaged] in a campaign of re-democratization in which the democratic aspects of its ideology are given not only lip service, but receive additional realization in practice."[67] Such a point was reached in early 1947. Early on, party leaders began to express anxiety over the evident failure of the local leadership to build on the enthusiasm that had swept the villages in the initial days of liberation.[68] In a speech to the obkom's plenary session on 28 March 1945, the Vinnytsia gorkom secretary complained that party leaders in the localities treated collective farmers with excessive bureaucratism

---

[65] Iuliia Kapusto, *V srednem raione* (Moscow: Sovetskii pisatel', 1950), 129. I thank Ann Livschiz for bringing this source to my attention.

[66] Nekrasov, "Slova 'velikie' i prostye," 58.

[67] Moore, *The Dilemma of Power*, 339–40.

[68] Evidently such enthusiasm did exist in the countryside in the immediate aftermath of liberation. According to Fedor Belov, the peasants in his village donated large amounts of grain to the Red Army, "partly because everybody had plenty at the time and partly because they felt patriotic." German atrocities drove many peasants to the ranks of the partisans, while others awaited with impatience the return of the Russians (Belov, *The History of a Soviet Collective Farm*, 21, 23). Belov explained the relatively large stocks in the hands of the peasants by pointing out that the Germans distributed among the peasants all the grain they could not take with them when they withdrew.

(*administrirovanie*) and "failed to talk the kolkhozniks into following them by stirring up the patriotic elan and enthusiasm that had existed in the first days after liberation and that still exist in large part because of the victories of the Red Army."[69] By early 1947 stagnation had reached a point where the regime felt compelled to order the gathering of kolkhoz assemblies throughout the Soviet Union by 15 February.[70] What took place on that date demonstrated the transformation of village politics in the wake of the war.

When the kolkhoz assemblies were convened in February 1947 during the campaign to revitalize kolkhoz life and the economy, the peasants forced district authorities to conduct an election for new leadership positions rather than submit to an imposed appointment by the raikom. They managed to do so mainly by appealing to recently demobilized officers. That was how one of them, Fedor Belov, found himself and his army comrades as the embodiment of kolkhoz democracy. Referring in his diary to the meeting at which he was elected, Belov noted that,

> he didn't know the kolkhoz members could criticize not only B. [the outgoing chairman] but also the raion authorities so fearlessly and angrily as they are doing. It is obvious that democracy is not yet crushed in the kolkhozes . . . The kolkhoz members were in full control of the meeting and did not even consider the suggestions of the representatives of the raion party committee . . . [they] elected me chairman unanimously. To my great surprise, they allowed me personally to elect the board of managers.[71]

At the end of the day all the top posts in the village passed into the hands of former front-line officers. In a given situation, the peasants' particularistic urge to belong and participate in the political process joined with the

---

[69] RGASPI, f. 17, op. 45, d. 1998, l. 109. The relations drawn between the war, suffering, and performance in work were celebrated in the kolkhozes. The rite of thanking the party, the army, and Stalin for the victory over Germany was celebrated in mass meetings on the occasion of V-Day. As many as 2,119 such meetings were organized in 1,938 kolkhozes. A sixteen year old from Sytkov district declared: "Through my labor I will avenge the German bandits for the murder of my mother. I pledge to overfulfill the norms in the autumn harvest and to work qualitatively." And a sixty-year-old kolkhoznik from the Plyskiv district stated: "A year ago the German monsters shot and tormented Soviet people. Now the Red Army has thrown the German robbers out of Ukraine. In honor of the great celebration of the complete liberation of Ukraine, I pledge to give the Red Army reserve more than the required plan" (TsDAHOU, f. 1, op. 23, d. 885, ll. 6–7).

[70] For complaints of kolkhozniks against the excessive bureaucratic practices of the raikoms and the kolkhoz chairmen, see TsDAHOU, f. 1, op. 46, d. 2285, ll. 57–60.

[71] Belov, *The History of a Soviet Collective Farm*, 27. In some instances, highly decorated veterans who were elected to head the kolkhozes did not hesitate to take on raikom officials who encroached on their managerial authority (TsDAHOU, f. 1, op. 46, d. 2284, l. 17). On popular elections of veterans by kolkhoz assemblies, see I. M. Volkov, "Kolkhoznaia derevnia v pervyi poslevoennyi god," *Voprosy istorii* 1 (1966): 29.

officers' personal bonding to institutionalize the myth of the war in the Soviet system. The elections highlighted the fact that the war was rapidly becoming the main prism through which the revolutionary ethos was viewed.[72] Here, the negotiation between the universal and particular visions accelerated the remodeling of the Bolshevik master-narrative after its new legitimizing myth.

The investment of power in the community was equally evident when the collective farm assemblies were assigned the task of cleansing themselves of internal weeds. Herein lay arguably one of the most powerful features of the Soviet ethos. The community did not have the authority to change the deportation decree, but every single member was attached to its execution through public discussion, suggesting potential deportees, and voting. Here, too, the experience of the recent war loomed as the main prism for categorization and action, enabling the regime to push its rural constituency further toward the ultimate goal of self-policing, a policy it had had difficulties implementing during the prewar cleansing campaigns. Addressing the chronic problem of poor work discipline in the collective farms, Nikita Khrushchev, in a memorandum to Beria on 10 February 1948, recommended giving the kolkhoz or village assemblies the power to exile the most dangerous elements from the villages. In what would later become the trademark of his tenure at the helm, Khrushchev sought to draw the peasants into the ongoing drive to purify their own milieu. Referring to nothing else but the tsarist past, when a law gave peasant communities the right to "pass sentences on removing from the village individuals 'whose further existence in the milieu threatens local welfare and safety' (Russian Empire Code of Laws, vol. 9, article 683)," Khrushchev indicated the usefulness of an analogous law for the Soviet Ukrainian countryside. In order to protect socialist property in the Soviet era, reasoned Khrushchev, it would be beneficial to issue a law that invests "the general assembly [of collective farms] with the right to pass sentences on the eviction beyond the borders of the [Ukrainian] Republic of the most dangerous, antisocial, and criminal elements who stubbornly refuse to participate in socially useful labor."[73] Khrushchev may have been a poor student of the very history that only recently he had helped to shape, for the method he proposed had already been practiced during collectivization and the prewar annexation of the western territories.[74] Moreover, his

[72] Some 10,000 demobilized soldiers were employed as agitators during the election campaign of January–February 1946, regardless that only 1,146 of them were party members and candidates, and only 1,199 were Komsomol members (TsDAHOU, f. 1, op. 23, d. 1776, ll. 22, 24–25).

[73] "Neizvestnaia initsiativa Khrushcheva (o podgotovke ukaza 1948 g. o vyselenii krest'ian)," *Otechestvennye arkhivy* 2 (1993): 35–36.

[74] Already in the initial wave of collectivization, the assemblies of collective farms and poor peasants were assigned drawing lists of kulaks of the second category who were de-

rationale was a logical extension of Stalin's own initiative at the height of the Terror. On 3 August 1937 Stalin ordered secretaries of obkoms and kraikoms [territorial party committees] throughout the Union to extend the struggle against enemies of the people from the closed channels of the NKVD into the public domain with the explicit goal of mobilizing kolkhozniks. "Considering the political mobilization of kolkhozniks around [the struggle] to crush the enemies of the people in the rural economy to be absolutely necessary," wrote Stalin,

> The Central Committee obliges the obkoms, kraikoms, and the Central Committees of the National Communist Parties to organize in every region throughout the districts two to three public show trials of the enemies of the people, saboteurs of the rural economy who found their way into the district party, soviet, and land organizations . . . and report extensively on the course of the trials in the local press.[75]

Eleven years later, Khrushchev took Stalin's order one step further. "We have laws," he continued,

> to punish thieves, plunderers of social property, and other criminals. We exile individuals who are found guilty of crimes, but we do all this through administrative channels, through the court or other organs of Soviet power. The promulgation of a law on assigning the right to pass sentences on the exile of criminal elements will be useful because the mass of kolkhozniks will participate actively in the fight against the antisocial and criminal elements, and, even more, the kolkhoz *aktiv* will be rallied and tempered.[76]

On 21 February 1948 the Presidium of the Supreme Soviet SSR issued the accompanying decree, entitled "On the exile from the Soviet Republic of Ukraine of people, who persistently evade work in the rural economy and those who conduct an antisocial, parasitic way of life." The dictum ordered

---

ported to other districts within the Republic. The lists were subjected to the approval of the raispolkoms and okrispolkoms. See the Politburo decision of 30 January 1930 in *Istoricheskii arkhiv* 4 (1994): 150. Not surprisingly, at this early stage the procedure was chaotic, and the OGPU often took charge of both selection and deportation (Merle Fainsod, *Smolensk under Soviet Rule* [Cambridge, Mass.: Harvard University Press, 1958], 247–51). The practice was repeated in 1939–40 in the newly annexed territories (Gross, *Revolution from Abroad*, 199–202).

[75] TsKhSD, f. 89, perechen' 48, dok. 12, l. 1. For reports in the local press of such trials, some of which preceded Stalin's order, see Fitzpatrick, *Stalin's Peasants*, 296–312.

[76] "Neizvestnaia initsiativa," 36. The decree was not published in the Soviet press, although in his report to the Ukrainian Central Committee on 9 March 1948 Khrushchev called for the intensification of the struggle against the vestiges of private property, which he identified as a major source for the poor performance of the backward collective farms in the Republic (Nikita Khrushchev, "O vosstanovlenii i pod"eme sels'kogo khoziaistva i partiino-politicheskoi rabote na sele," *Partiinaia zhizn'* 5 [March 1948]: 16).

the exile of those in the above category from sixteen eastern Ukrainian regions to Komi, Arkhangel'sk, Tiumen', Kirov, and the Karelo-Finnish territory. Every kolkhoz was ordered to gather its general assembly and select those people considered parasitic elements. The MVD was ordered to arrest those denounced immediately and hold them for seven days to prevent their escape. Those who were exiled had the right to take their families and some property with them. The term of exile extended to eight years, but the exiled had the right to appeal to the obkom and the kolkhoz assembly after five years to return to their locality.[77]

The implementation of the decree resulted in the exile of only a small number of peasants. By 31 March the assemblies of 1,932 kolkhozes decided on the exile of merely 589 kolkhozniks and warned 1,325 others.[78] The protocols of the assemblies revealed both support for the decree as well as resentment and apathy. There were some who were enthusiastic to denounce individuals who hampered the work of the collective and engaged in speculation in the surrounding towns. Others were hostile to the proposal. One Fedir Kushnir from the village of Antonivka in the Tomashpil' district told fellow peasants, after the assembly dispersed, that "[they] exile us from the kolkhoz not because [we] did not fulfill the minimum quota of labor days, but because our government likes work for free and so that we work as donation. The Romanians were here for three years, and it was better than thirty years of Soviet power."[79] In the Chernivtsi district, the MGB recorded threats on the kolkhoz chairman's life following a meeting where it was decided that some individual should be exiled.[80] The comments of still other peasants showed utter indifference. "There were many other decrees before, and nothing was done. And now they won't exile anyone either," snapped Mykhailo Chyzhyk, a peasant from the village of Stryzhavka in the Vinnytsia district.[81] And then there were those like Olena Halatfutnik. "It's like the days of collectivization again," Halatfutnik told fellow kolkhozniks in the village of Voronovitsa. "[The authorities] would get angry with someone and deport him. Someone would arrive from the district, testify against someone else, and the latter would be arrested on the spot. They only say that the kolkhozniks themselves decide the fate of those who avoid work in the kolkhoz. In reality they exile whoever they want."[82] One is left to wonder whether it was the policy of exile or the practice of usurping the peasants' right to decide who should stay and who should go that elicited Halatfutnik's ire.

[77] PAVO, f. 136, op. 13, d. 152, ll. 1–8.
[78] DAVO, f. 2700, op. 7c, d. 133, l. 25.
[79] Ibid., l. 27.
[80] PAVO, f. 136, op. 13, d. 152, ll. 157–58.
[81] Ibid., l. 116.
[82] DAVO, f. 2700, op. 7, d. 133, l. 16.

Nonetheless the assemblies' deliberations and the identity of those selected for exile revealed an intriguing pattern. The most aggressive denunciations were voiced by war invalids and veterans using images drawn directly from the front. The enemies of kolkhoz life were identified as those who had not shared their wartime ordeal. The mood was so volatile that, in the assembly of the Bushynka village in the Nemyriv district, one war invalid felt compelled to plead with his fellow veterans for restraint:

> We know that the people of Bushynka lived under occupation and that this left a strong impact. We cannot consider as enemies those who had worked for the Germans but now work well. And when they work, we watch and control them. This decree undoubtedly helps us greatly in the tightening of discipline if we ourselves study it. When order 227 [the imposition of draconian penalties on unauthorized retreat from the battlefield] was issued, some officers said that it was permitted to shoot [panicked or deserting soldiers], and they almost did. This method, too, is wrong.[83]

His voice, however, was a lone one. The kolkhoz agronomist inflamed the mood against all peasants who had remained on the occupied territory. "The decree of the Presidium of the Supreme Soviet of the USSR is essential," he told the gathering. "We know that during the Patriotic War, especially in the localities occupied by the Germans, some people got used to making their living by stealing, etc. And especially when the kolkhozes began to be restored, they treated the kolkhoz structure badly, not in the interests of strengthening the kolkhozes themselves."[84] Other veterans at the gathering, who addressed the lack of initiative in the maintenance of kolkhoz animal husbandry, drew analogies from their experience at the Leningrad front where such problems were overcome by the sheer power of innovation. Others who called for the tightening of work discipline pointed out to their fellow kolkhozniks that, "had there not been severe discipline in our army, it is possible we would not have defeated the enemy. When we heard about the decree formulated by Stalin we cried, and this order compelled us to stand firm against the enemy."[85] Eighteen years after the rural community was first assigned the task of cleansing itself, it became fully involved in this key feature of Soviet socialization. With the help of the war, it was now a Soviet community par excellence.

The impact of the wartime experience was further substantiated when the MGB drew up lists of candidates for exile on 5 March 1948. Those who had served under the Germans and those who had no relatives in the Soviet army figured more prominently than any other category in the list

---

[83] PAVO, f. 136, op. 13, d. 152, l. 26.
[84] Ibid., l. 12.
[85] Ibid., ll. 50, 25.

of "people who, during 1947, did not fulfill the minimum work days, broke down labor discipline among the kolkhozniks, or did not work at all in the kolkhozes." For example, Havrylo Koval'chuk, a peasant from the village of Pyliava in the Tyvriv district, was cited as one who "resided in Germany during the war. None of his family serves in the Soviet Army." Others, such as Dorofei Handzii and Kharyton Svets', served during the occupation in the rural administration or as policemen. This was true of Hnat Tsurkan, whose brother, moreover, had been an officer in the Vlasov army.[86]

By the time the Presidium of the Supreme Soviet extended the deportation decree to all other Soviet republics on 2 June 1948, some 5,180 people had already been exiled from eastern Ukraine, along with 1,672 family members who joined them voluntarily. Both decrees accounted for 9,438 individuals exiled to special settlements and 2,929 who left the Ukrainian republic voluntarily.[87] Singled out by Khrushchev for their meager performance during the critical harvest of 1947, the collective farms' assemblies in Vinnytsia contributed 1,042 exile sentences, of which only 32 were overturned, and another 168 volunteers, second only to the Kam'ianets'-Podil's'kyi region.[88]

The 1948 episode offers a glimpse into the fundamental change that was taking place in the villages. By then, the war had already turned into a prism through which to view the surroundings, form alliances, and rewrite communal and individual autobiographies in which the prewar passive and defective rural object was replaced by a dynamic and active subject. Writing to the Supreme Soviet of the Soviet Union to request that his home in the Lipetskii district of the Voronezh region be returned, a recently demobilized serviceman had no qualms about presenting himself as a member of a dekulakized family. "In 1933 our entire family was deported to Karelo-Finnish SSSR, where we lived until 1941," wrote F. Ia. Anan'ev.

> Later we were evacuated to the Komi ASSR. In 1941 my father, elder brother, and me were drafted to the Red Army. My father and brother were killed at the front. My mother, as a member of a family of servicemen, was released and received documents. In 1944 she returned to our native village to settle there permanently. I was demobilized according to the 4 February 1947 decree and also returned to the village. Mother and I wander in other people's homes and live in poverty, because our home is now used as a first-aid station. I appealed to the district prosecutor and he advised me to write to you. I ask you, Comrade

[86] Ibid., ll. 94–100.

[87] GARF, f. 9479, op. 1, d. 458, ll. 34–35. Another estimate was slightly lower: 12,265 removed of whom 9,275 were sentenced to exile and 2,990 left voluntarily (ibid., d. 406, l. 371).

[88] GARF, f. 9479, op. 1, d. 458, l. 40.

Chairman, to help in returning my father's home to us since I do not have the means to purchase [the house] or to build a new one.[89]

A barrage of similar letters from villages were written by peasants who were formulating their identities not merely around the recent war. They were literally rewriting their lives from the moment of their own or a family member's enrollment in the ranks of the Red Army on the eve of the war or from June 1941 on. Life in these narratives commenced with the war, consisted of daily battles, and culminated with expectations to resume a more privileged civilian life on discharge from the army. "Our Dear People's Deputy in the Supreme Soviet of the USSR, Comrade Bazhan!" read one such letter by Fedor Morozov from the Tul'chyn district, who complained about the bureaucratic delays of his wartime pension.

> I am compelled to lay out to you my entire story, to wit: On 5 January 1938 I was drafted ahead of schedule to the Red Army in the ranks of the NKVD SSSR force in the capacity of a Red Army soldier. Since I had a high school education I was sent in October 1938 to the regular academy of border troops of the NKVD SSSR in Leningrad, and later to Partalm. I graduated ahead of schedule and with distinction in 1940 and was appointed to the military rank of lieutenant. I was then appointed the commander of the eighteenth border unit of Outpost no. 4 at the western border.
>
> On 22 June 1941 at 3:30 A.M., when our entire people were still asleep, me and my soldiers stepped into the defense of the socialist motherland against the German-fascist invaders. On the first day of the war at 4:55 I was seriously wounded. I remained in the battlefield and continued to command the outpost until the arrival of reinforcements.[90]

Morozov then went on to describe his experiences, in the most minute details, from his recovery, exploits in the battles of Moscow and Stalingrad, repetitive injuries, return to the NKVD ranks in Vinnytsia through his demobilization as an invalid of the second degree suffering from a head injury and traumatic epilepsy. "The above enumeration conveys my short life history," wrote Morozov. There was no mention of social origin, class status, or date of enrollment into the party in this autobiographical sketch of a veteran NKVDist and Communist. Life commenced with the war, and all that followed originated from that event.

---

[89] Cited in Veniamin Zima, *Golod v SSSR 1946–1947 godov: proiskhozhhdenie i posledstviia* (Moscow: Institut Rossiiskoi Istorii RAN, 1996), 88–89. Anan'ev's plea was turned down but, interestingly, not because of his class origins but on the grounds that too much time had passed, making it impossible to review the case.

[90] Tsentral'nyi derzhavnyi arkhiv-muzei literatury i mystetstva Ukrainy (TsDAMLMU), f. 535, op. 1, d. 149, ll. 46–48; for an identical letter by one Pliushkin, see l. 96. Morozov's letter is dated 12 August 1946.

The centrality of the war in the lives of individuals in the countryside was not limited to self-representations. The war was literally transforming the social and political landscape by the day, and a key constituency until the commencement of mass demobilization was that of families of Red Army servicemen. By the end of 1944 there were already 336,832 families of Red Army servicemen in Vinnytsia, including 16,036 families of officers, 13 generals and 53 Heroes of the Soviet Union.[91] By 1 July 1946 there were about 136,000 families of Red Army servicemen in Vinnytsia and 76,913 families of fallen soldiers.[92] A close look at this large community reveals hundreds of thousands of peasants defining their political and social identity on the basis of their sacrifice for the Soviet motherland and in juxtaposition to those who had not gone through the same ordeal of war or did not identify themselves with the Soviet cause. Their reading of the wartime experience was constantly insinuated into the village politics, they consciously sought to shape the local political arena after their own image of this cataclysmic event. At the time when nationalist guerrillas intensified their persecution of Red Army servicemen and families, the latter were taking over the village.[93]

The role of wartime experience in shaping village politics was particularly evident in personal letters that were intended to be private and not meant to be read by the authorities. Letters from the villages to relatives in the Red Army revealed an emerging Soviet constituency that vied for recognition and privileges both inside and outside the rural community.[94] The intimate domain and language in these letters underlined the personalization of the war's legacy that significantly intensified the prospective retribution against those who were marked as the "others."

In the pauperized postwar countryside, the slightest material differentiation assumed political significance, and, indeed, many of the letters focused on material deprivation. By this time, Red Army families had already been accustomed to preferential treatment that turned economic hardship into political divisions. "We distributed among the population the bread we confiscated from the Germans," a local Soviet partisan leader recalled

---

[91] TsDAHOU, f. 1, op. 23, d. 953, l. 206.

[92] Ibid., d. 2981, ll. 4, 26.

[93] Throughout the regions under its control, UPA was said to hunt down and execute Red Army stragglers and escaping POWs—including ethnic Ukrainians, according to one source—who sought refuge in the villages. In early summer 1943 some one hundred Red Army POWs were killed in the Goshchansk district alone. People identified with Soviet power were executed regardless of their position and family situation, such as a former store clerk and mother of four in the village of Simonov in the Goshchansk district (TsDAHOU, f. 57, op. 4, d. 351, ll. 9–10).

[94] The letters were opened by the military censors under the NKVD, which transferred to the party those segments that dealt with complaints about the material conditions of families of servicemen in the countryside.

immediately after the war. "We arranged that the wives of Red Army soldiers and partisans received bread first."[95] Similarly, after liberation, special
support was offered to native war heroes, such as the family of Hero of
the Soviet Union S. Iu. Oliinyk, who received aid for the renovation of
their home and barn, and were guaranteed fuel for the winter.[96] Hence,
when individuals felt they were overlooked, their grievances assumed a
distinctly harsh political undertone. The blame for past and present misery
was laid at the door of those had lived out the war years in the villages
and who, in the absence of the Red Army servicemen, held local power,
or, in the colorful words of one writer from the village of Hlyns'k in the
Kalynivka district, those "who were hiding in the bushes [*sideli po bur'ia-
nakh*] while you have been fighting already three years, defending us all."[97]
Others were even less gracious attaching the nickname Fritzes (Germans)
to those who evaded the front (l. 21). From the village of Lypivka in the
Tomashpil' district, Iryna Zatula wrote:

> Who's the war for? Who's the motherland for? Take Muldovan. He enjoyed
> authority under the Germans, had reserves then, and still has reserves now. They
> drink, have a good time, and I don't have my sons, my husband, my son-in-law,
> and they still torment us. To whom shall I talk. God is high, and Stalin is far. (l.
> 24b)

The resentment for the front dodgers was coupled with a strong sense of
entitlement. "They sent [our] husbands to fight, and then sat home and
filched the government property. Their wives live luxuriously and receive
aid, but I, who have been sick all that time and whose husband has been
fighting for three years, receive no help at all," wrote Maria Drobazha
from the village of Khvostivtsi (l. 20b). Her tirade was echoed by a kolkhoznitsa from the Pishchanka district in a letter to her brother:

> It is already the fourth year that you defend the country but you could not imag-
> ine how your parents have been suffering. And this is not the Romanian power,
> but the Soviet. Only under the Germans was Father told: "Your son is a com-
> mander, you don't have a place here." All the people drank, had a good time,
> and only we shed tears. Then came the Soviet power, and we got a certain selfish
> one as chairman of the village soviet. Those men who were home for three years,
> drank, and had a good time have now sent documents to their wives so that they
> can receive firewood. But when I went to the village soviet I was told: "Maybe
> your brother is having a good time with the Germans, how can I know?" (l. 83)

[95] IIAN ORF, f. 2-II, op. 9, d. 1, l. 11.
[96] TsDAHOU, f. 1, op. 23, d. 953, l. 211.
[97] DAVO, f. 2700, op. 7c, d. 7, l. 23.

Sacrifice at the front was not enough, however. Timing and motives were equally important. Peasants were intent on distinguishing between those who joined the patriotic cause from the very beginning and those who jumped on the bandwagon only when the tide of war changed in favor of the Soviets. "You, my son, went off to shed your blood," Iryna Kolotus', from the village of Tashlyk in the Dzhulyn district, wrote to her son on 31 August 1944:

> I now have to pay all the taxes that existed before the war, but I decided not to pay and said that my sons defend Soviet power . . . Prosha, you have been serving for five years in the army, you have shed your blood, but your wife and baby have nothing. The families of those who were home for three years and only now joined the army already receive help.[98]

Sometimes the contempt for those who pretended to be on the Soviet side found livelier expression. "Our kolkhoz chairwoman is a certain Russian," wrote Vira Shestyryna from the village of Norylivka in the Haisyn district to a relative in the Red Army on 2 September 1944.

> She formed a brigade and started robbing the village, saying it was for the Red Army. Later she threw the kolkhoz over to her brother, Stepan, threshed our wheat, and went to Russia to speculate. She returned after a month for the beginning of the harvest . . . [and] replaced the head of the economic department with Mykola Kuprian, who was the head of the kolkhoz under the Germans . . . The chairman of the village soviet, Shokhrai, calls himself a partisan. At night he takes a rifle and goes after the apples and pears . . . That is who they fight against in the village, and not against the German enemy . . . Shokhrai was not wounded; he is healthy and fights the old grannies in the village.[99]

To be sure, this sense of antagonism and entitlement was echoed in the urban scene. "Those who lived under the Germans, the German 'dolls,' have beautiful apartments. But the families of Red Army servicemen, partisans, and invalids of the Great Patriotic War stand in line for months to receive apartments," wrote Sonia Kurolap from the city of Vinnytsia (l. 20b). Also from the city came the following letter:

> Did I fight and liberate the brothers, sisters, and mothers so that my sick mother would be thrown violently from work, my mother who survived the torture thanks to her sons who fought in the ranks of the Red Army, three of whom were killed [and only] one survived? Where is their care for the parents of a twice-decorated officer who was wounded four times? Could it really be that

[98] TsDAHOU, f. 1, op. 23, d. 1021, l. 64b.
[99] DAVO, f. 2700, op. 7c, d. 7, l. 81.

there behind the desk sit leaders who have not seen and have not smelled gunpowder. You see, Hero, you fight for them, shed blood for them, and mother, father, and sister, who live at my expense, suffer. It is simply angering what we are fighting for. (ll. 20–20b)

The passage of time did not calm passions. "There is war there, and there is war in the village," read one letter from the village of Liubomyrka in the Ol'hopil' district (d. 34, l. 53b). With mass demobilization still in the future, the local leadership in many of the villages was slow to change, and tensions ran high. "Mikhail Popov was the kolkhoz chairman under Romanian power. He handed people over to the gendarmerie, lived well, built himself a house, and now he is the kolkhoz chairman again," wrote one Lashchuk from Iaryshiv (l. 53). A. I. Remeniak from the village of Zharapanovka in the Kryzhopil' district echoed this tension:

> The brigadier of the kolkhoz A. I. Phil' simply torments us . . . That is how the families of the front-line soldiers are being tormented. Phil' himself had worked as a brigadier under the Germans, beat people, taunted them as much as he could, and locked them in cellars. And now he again works as a brigadier and again torments us. He added two years to his age to avoid being drafted into the army. He dodged mobilization. Write to the prosecutors that the traitors will not torment us. (l. 79)

Resentment against village officials who avoided the front was unrestrained. "You are suffering there and I am tormented here. [They] threw me and the baby out of the hut to the street. Refused to look at the document from the Military Committee. You defend the motherland, and those who hid behind your back here taunt us," wrote M. G. Latkovs'kyi from the village of Khomutyntsi in the Kalynivka district (l. 53). The tension between the two groups was evident in a letter from the village of Mar'ianivka in the Bratslav district of 15 May 1945, which also recounts the abusive behavior of some local officials:

> The chairman of the kolkhoz Kvasnevs'kyi gave us a deadline of fifteen minutes to evacuate the apartment. Once he came in drunk, smashed all the dishes, and even beat the baby for no reason. I go to work in the kolkhoz. I tie my daughter to the stove, and she cries out all day long. I sent a note to the district, the prosecutor arrived, but Kvasnevs'kyi gave her something to drink, gave her the kolkhoz wheat, and she said that he was right, it is not our business where we shall live. He lived under the Germans and saw off the Romanians, called them "brothers," and now he lives and torments the families of the Red Army soldiers. He even told me: "Get out *kulachka*! Your husband is not at the front. He serves in a gang." (l. 54)

Judging from letters written well over two years since liberation of the region, feelings seemed not to have changed, as demonstrated in this letter from Pohrebyshche in July 1946:

> I should have been proud that my sons are in the army. But you know here they don't care for the families of the servicemen and for your awards. Kachura says: *"In war you can either win decorations or get killed."* Yesterday when father stayed home to gather in the crop from the kitchen-garden, Chmiriuk wanted to beat him and said: "Don't even think of eating this bread." Under the Germans he betrayed people, collected cows from them and now he sends people to the Donbas. He has condemned many. They know about it in the district and even Khrushchev knows. (d. 67, l. 25)

The war's central role in village life was accentuated by the frequent identification of Soviet power with the Red Army. An old kolkhoznitsa from the village of Berezivka in the Chernivtsi district complained that she had been intimidated by the local authorities and dragged into court. "They told the court that they sued me because I had denounced him [a local official] in my complaint as an enemy of the people," wrote the peasant. She continued:

> But I was not wrong about it because during the war he tore down my fence, entered my home, and threatened me with a knife. The kids ran away from home. He did this to create dissatisfaction with the Red Army . . . Last year he collected money from the kolkhozniks for the state loan and took it for himself, but the raikom covered it all up. Tell your command to verify this directly because the tormenting of your mother is already intolerable. (l. 42)

The Red Army, in this sense, was the Soviet institution to which the peasant looked in the hope of remedying injustices in the villages. Servicemen, in turn, expected their families to obtain the status and privileges they earned in blood. "I am indignant at your treatment of my family," read a letter addressed to the chairmen of the kolkhoz and village soviet of Puzyrky in the Koziatyn district.

> I have served three years in the war, was wounded four times, and received a governmental award. I [expected] that the local power would treat my family humanely and help them. Perhaps the laws of the USSR regarding the army servicemen and the privileges of their families do not extend to you, but even the privileges of the decorated soldiers and families do not concern you. I think that the law of the USSR obliges you, unless there you have other laws and another power. Maybe there are still those among you who helped the German Fascists in their vile work and activity. They should be thrown out immediately. (d. 7, l. 25)

Equally forceful, if only more threatening, was Ivan Rudyi's letter to the local authorities about the alleged mistreatment of his family in the Nemyriv district. "When I received a letter from my sister Maria Arsenivna, I learned that at the present time she does not live as a family of servicemen should live," began Rudyi.

> As chairmen of the local power, you show absolutely no concern. [My sister's] cow was taken from her for reasons unknown to me. You do not guarantee her clothing, nor do you help her have food. That is why I am asking to check on all this and fix what is needed. One thing must be clear and the appropriate conclusion must be drawn. Her husband died for the motherland, her brother, Mykyta, fights the German invaders and destroys these bandits, her second brother died for the beloved motherland, and, finally, the third brother beats the hated, damned Huns and other German dogs for a fourth year. But relatives still suffer because of slipshods. Forgive me that I am writing in such frustration and cannot endure these facts of how my sister Maria came to such a state. Inform me about all the measures you take. If my sister complains to me once more and you do not offer help, I'll be obliged to write the district chief of the NKVD so that the guilty ones will be put in line. (ll. 87–88)

These letters exerted immediate impact on the molding of the postwar village. Censured by the NKVD, they were used by the authorities to weed out the final vestiges of the occupation in the countryside. Kolkhoz leaders, who remained on the occupied territory and had served under the Germans, were dismissed and sometimes prosecuted. Even by 1944 the appointment of people, who had remained on the occupied territory, to the post of kolkhoz chairman was considered a political error, as the first secretary of the Lityn raikom learned.[100] The district branches of the MGB continued to draw up lists of kolkhoz chairmen and brigadiers who managed to escape scrutiny well into 1950. In January of that year, for example, the MGB chief of the Komsomol district composed a list of alleged collaborators in individual kolkhozes, some of whom had already been sentenced to long prison terms.[101] The travails of the Soviet peasantry were far from over, and it continued to be a second class long after the war. Peasants were still deprived of internal passports, and the mass migration to the cities continued. Nevertheless the war paved the way for future improvement.[102] It ushered in a new village, dominated by vast networks

---

[100] RGASPI, f. 17, op. 45, d. 1998, l. 139.

[101] See the report on the "Zahal'na Pratsia" and the "Lenin" kolkhozes in the Komsomol district (PAVO, f. 136, op. 30, d. 211, ll. 7–12) and on the "New Life" kolkhoz in the Nemyriv district (ll. 118–23).

[102] Peasants were issued internal passports only in 1975, and even then only after nearly a decade of prolonged, equivocal deliberations at the higher ranks. By this time it seemed that

of Red Army veterans and their families for whom the war had erased past humiliation and heralded a new beginning as legitimate and more assertive members of the Soviet family.

Ukrainianhood

The focus on western Ukraine in the study of Ukrainian nationalism has left its eastern counterpart insufficiently studied and underestimated. The brand of nationalism that emerged in the western Ukrainian regions captured the imagination of contemporaries and historians alike, and for good reason. The greater ethnic and regional cohesiveness, the presence of an active separatist movement with an articulated program, and the magnitude of the guerrilla warfare attracted so much attention that Ukrainian nationalism came to be identified solely with the western regions.[103] Summing up the state of affairs in Soviet Ukraine, the author of the most meticulous study of Ukrainian national attitudes concluded that "in eastern Ukraine the regime has succeeded to some degree in emasculating Ukrainian nationalism by instilling cultural pride devoid of aspirations of national independence."[104]

Indeed, unlike the Galician and Volhynian village, which literally turned into nationalist bastions, the ethnonational identification of the eastern Ukrainian villager puzzled nationalist activists. The absence of a deterministic link between linguistic-ethnic homogeneity and national consciousness conveyed an entrenched sense of class-territorial identity rather than ethnic particularism. A dispirited Mykhailo Seleshko noted that all the (ethnic) Ukrainians he encountered in wartime Vinnytsia regarded themselves as Ukrainians but "this consciousness was territorial, not internal, not spiritual." While visiting a friend, Seleshko learned that her mother considered him a "Galician" and did not refer to the language he spoke as Ukrainian. He went to great length to explain to the old woman the concept of linguistic dialect, but his portrayal of the encounter conveys

---

bureaucratic inertia, more than the principled Bolshevik distrust of the peasantry, forestalled the immediate removal of this epitome of the "Great Transformation," whose usefulness and ethics were challenged long before it was abolished. Significantly the discontent of demobilized soldiers was cited as a major reason to reform the passport system. For the Politburo decision to deprive the peasantry as a whole of passports (with few exceptions) on April 1933 and the various initiatives to do away with this restriction from 1967 until its final removal in August 1974, see *Istochnik* no. 6 (1997): 106, 113–21.

[103] Such is the line of reasoning in the still authoritative studies of Armstrong, *Ukrainian Nationalism*; and Yaroslav Bilinsky, *The Second Soviet Republic*.

[104] Gilliam, *The Nationality Questionnaire*, 47.

an unbridgeable gap between these two Ukrainian populations, which ran along educational, cultural, and, most likely, class lines as well.[105] Seleshko's experience was not unique. While in Vinnytsia the population termed all nationalist activists *zakhidniki* (westerners), and, in the Russified Donbas, the western dialect of members of the OUN "marching groups" who followed the German troops was often mistaken for Polish.[106] Nor was the relatively high educational level of the young activists and their belief in the elitist role of the intelligentsia likely to bring them closer to the kolkhoz peasantry.[107] Even to a sympathetic crowd, such as the editorial board of the *Vinnyts'ki visti*, the ferocious ideological conflict between nationalist factions was incomprehensible and resembled a petty feud among boys.[108]

A nationalist reporter, who visited a village in the Taganrog district on the lower Don in early 1942, noted that all the inhabitants spoke pure Ukrainian and retained Ukrainian customs. However, the peasants objected to being addressed as Ukrainians, insisting that the "Ukrainians" lived across the border in the west. When the reporter pointed out the similarity of their speech and manners to those of the western population, the peasants agreed that the westerners were their brothers but still they were not Ukrainians.[109] Several years later, in Vinnytsia, by then under Soviet power, the story repeated itself in the village of Hrabarivka in the Pishchanka district. Until 1940 the village, whose entire population was ethnically Ukrainian, was in the territory of the Moldavian Republic. The following year it was transferred to the Ukrainian Soviet Republic on the grounds that its population was exclusively Ukrainian. On 19 May 1945 the assembly of the Molotov kolkhoz requested that the Supreme Soviet of the Ukrainian Republic allow them to return to Moldavian jurisdiction. The reason given by the kolkhozniks could hardly have pleased any nationalist activist in the region. The kolkhozniks explained that the distance from the village to the center of the Pishchanka district in the Vinnytsia region was twelve kilometers farther than to the center of the Kamenskii district in Moldavia, and for that reason alone they wished to return to Moldavia.[110]

Equally baffling for nationalist activists was that victimization at the hands of the Soviet regime did not necessarily breed separatist nationalism, and was often offset by Soviet nationality policy. Reflecting on his

---

[105] Seleshko, *Vinnytsia*, 150.

[106] HURIP, #548, 6; Zynovii Matla, *Pivdenna pohidnia hrupa* (Munich: Tsitsero, 1952), 17.

[107] Lev Shankovs'kyi, *Pohidni hrupy OUN* (Munich: Ukrains'kyi samostiinyk, 1958), 71–72.

[108] HURIP, #548, 6. Similarly German surveillance reports concluded that the population was interested mainly in the land reform, in which, in any case, it had little confidence (TsDAVOVU, f. 3206, op. 1, d. 26, l. 27).

[109] Armstrong, *Ukrainian Nationalism*, 190–91.

[110] PAVO, f. 136, op. 13, d. 68, l. 5.

own and his family's fate at the hands of the Bolsheviks, a professor of
physics recalled, immediately after the war, that his brother's head had
been broken against a wall in 1920 and that "they [the Bolsheviks] destroyed me and all the intelligentsia because I had a Ukrainian name . . .
accused me of separatism, and condemned me to death . . . Finally, my
sentence was suspended." Nevertheless, the professor insisted,

> [It] can't be said that the Soviet government leans toward one nationality in
> particular or that some nationalities received special privileges . . . [There have
> been] some good achievements as far as the nationality question in the Soviet
> Union is concerned . . . In tsarist times everything was done by Russians. Under
> the Soviets the cultural level of each nationality was raised, and there are no
> differences between them.[111]

Nationalist writers were at a loss to explain this situation. A review of
this issue in 1943 attributed the absence of proper nationalist sentiments
in Soviet Ukraine to the "philosophical and spiritual deformation that
resulted from the long, one-sided influence of Moscow on Ukraine." Russification, argued Dmytro Maivs'kyi, invaded every sphere of life, the language of conversation, the ethical and moral outlook of society and domestic customs.

> The spirit of Tolstoy, Dostoevsky, Gorky and a long succession of others have
> weakened and even totally emasculated the principle of national primacy; they
> heaped derision on the sacred values of the nation. As a result the circle of spiri-
> tual cripples has constantly widened. For some of our countrymen, Moscow and
> its territory gradually became the "fatherland"; the Russian nation came to be
> regarded as a joint patrimony, first because it was Russian, then Orthodox, Slavic
> and proletarian, and now Soviet. The sense of belonging to one's own nation
> was reduced to a narrow, territorial, regional feeling and thus deprived of all its
> political force. Included among the symptoms of this state of mind is also the
> desire, which exists primarily among the lower strata of society, to reduce every-
> thing to their own level—the level of nothingness.[112]

This is true enough, if nationhood is understood as a strictly ethnocentric
institution, confined to a full-blown political sovereignty and historical

---

[111] Gilliam, *The Nationality Questionnaire*, 32–33. The authors of the report considered
such a response, along with several other similar responses, the outcome of extreme pressure
that led people to give up convictions that seemed too dangerous. Bear in mind that the
interview was conducted beyond the reach of the regime, several years after the complete
break with the Soviet Union and the subsequent exposure to alternative views on the Soviet
situation.

[112] P. T. Duma, "Internal Obstacles to the Ukrainian National Liberation Struggle," in
Potichnyi and Shtendera, *The Political Thought of the Ukrainian Underground*, 247–48.
(Duma was Maivsky's pseudonym.)

past constituted by a chain of heroic events. More often, however, nation-hood is a mundane, banal institution that is concentrated in a barrage of daily activities, rituals, and signs. The subtleties of nationhood should not be confused with innocuous representations. They are powerful tools in demarcating the boundaries of the community and categorizing legiti-macy and belonging. Not least, their constant presence enables society to mobilize itself in a rather smooth fashion for extreme acts and sacrifice.[113] More than others, notably outside observers, contemporary Ukrainians were well aware of this feature of the Soviet polity.[114]

Herein lay the immense power of Soviet Ukrainianhood. The focus on locals' primary identification with their immediate geographic vicinity missed the entrenchment of a powerful national identity in the region whose Soviet component could not, and did not, stamp out its Ukrainian counterpart. Mykhailo Seleshko himself noted that when ethnic Ukraini-ans in Vinnytsia referred to an association larger than the immediate local-ity they had in mind the existing political structure within which they lived. When they spoke of "our rich country," they were referring to the Soviet Union.[115] Indeed, peasants' identity neither began nor ended with the village boundaries. It was molded into a Soviet Ukrainian constitu-ency, and playing a key role is this process was the war that engulfed the region from 1939 on. The articulators, representatives, and transmitters of Soviet Ukrainianhood were not only intellectuals but also ordinary ap-

---

[113] Michael Billig, *Banal Nationalism* (London: Sage, 1995), 175. See also the pioneering study of George Mosse, *The Nationalization of the Masses: Political Symbolism and Mass Move-ments in Germany from the Napoleonic Wars through the Third Reich* (New York: Howard Fertig, 1975).

[114] Reflecting on wartime concessions to Ukrainians, some of which were withdrawn after the war, Vasyl' Kostenko, then secretary of the Komsomol of the Ukrainian Commu-nist Party, noted that Ukrainian Communists were savvy enough to dismiss gestures such as the creation of the Ukrainian Ministry of Defense as a charade, yet they genuinely wel-comed the symbolic gestures to Ukrainian nationhood as signs of recognition of their con-tribution to the war effort (interview with Vasyl' Kostenko, 23 March 1993, Kiev, Ukraine). On Soviet wartime concessions, see John Armstrong, *The Politics of Totalitarianism: The Communist Party of the Soviet Union since 1934* (New York: Random House, 1961), 150–51. Interestingly, Western politicians' and academicians' identification of Ukrainian nation-alism with the ethnocentric brand that emerged from the western Ukrainian regions led to a complete ignorance of the power of Soviet Ukrainianhood. Most memorably, this igno-rance was reflected in the speech of President George Bush before the Supreme Soviet of the Soviet Ukrainian Republic on 1 August 1991, in which the American president warned the delegates that "Americans will not support those who seek to replace a far-off tyranny with a local despotism. They will not aid those who promote a suicidal nationalism based upon ethnic hatred" (*New York Times*, 2 August 1991). Three weeks after Bush's speech came the attempted putsch, followed three months later by the smooth break with the Soviet Union.

[115] Seleshko, *Vinnytsia*, 132, 144, 153.

paratchiks and Red Army servicemen and veterans, many of whom transmitted a powerful narrative of the Ukrainian nation with the unification of all Ukrainian lands and peoples for the first time in history as its core. This tale was written into the lives of every community and individual through a myriad of rites and rituals that reordered the loyalties and priorities of postwar society.

The war did not mark the advent of Soviet Ukrainian particularism, however. By the late 1930s such identities had already been entrenched. Early in the Soviet era the regime made peace, albeit reluctantly, with the existence of the ethnopolitical unit of Ukraine,[116] and then went on to cultivate particularistic ethnonationalism through a myriad of institutions such as passports, territorial borders, and linguistic reforms. Notably the accompanying brutality of the 1930s did not halt or even slow down the Ukrainization of the sociopolitical body in the republic, a fact not lost on eastern Ukrainians. Indeed, along with the widely shared belief among eastern Ukrainians that the regime actively sought the supression of national-cultural expressions was the recognition that the regime was sincere in its wish to promote internationality, peace, and harmony, if only on its own terms. Eastern Ukrainians displaced in the postwar period were still impressed by the fact that all Russian schools in Ukraine were forced to teach Ukrainian for a specified number of hours a week to all their students and that Ukrainian became the official language of some governmental agencies, for example, the departments of health, welfare, and education as well as the agency regulating theaters. Commenting on the encounter between eastern and western Ukrainian inmates in the GULAG, one observer noted that the former still credited the Soviet regime with the introduction of Ukrainian language to public schools.[117] By the outbreak of war, people's reactions to the avalanche of events and newcomers were informed by nearly three decades of effective Soviet writings of the Ukrainian social and national narrative. When western Ukrainian nationalists arrived in Kiev, they found that even those who had no clue about their ideological debates and nuances nevertheless had firm perceptions of

[116] This valid, yet often glossed over point made by Jurij Borys in *The Sovietization of Ukraine, 1917–1923: The Communist Doctrine and Practice of National Self-Determination* (Edmonton: Canadian Institute of Ukrainian Studies, 1980), was recently revived in Stephen Kotkin's "1991 and the Russian Revolution: Sources, Conceptual Categories, Analytical Frameworks," *Journal of Modern History* 70 (June 1998): 409.

[117] Gilliam, *The Nationality Questionnaire*, xiv–xv, 10–11; Bilinsky, *The Second Soviet Republic*, 297. For this intriguing dimension of Soviet nationality policy, see the thought-provoking essay by Yuri Slezkine, "The USSR as a Communal Apartment; or, How a Socialist State Promoted Ethnic Particularism," *The Slavic Review* 53 (summer 1994): 414–52; and George Liber, *Soviet Nationality Policy, Urban Growth, and Identity Change in the Ukrainian SSR, 1923–1934* (Cambridge: Cambridge University Press, 1992).

them. Thus they found themselves referred to as the incarnations of Hetman Skoropads'kyi, the German puppet, heirs of the civil war *pogromsh-
chiki* and White Guard traitors, Petliura, Konovalets, and the Ukrainian
Central *Rada*, and associates of bandits such as Makhno and Zelenyi.[118]

It was the war, however, that provided Ukrainians with a powerful myth
that both integrated them into the larger Soviet epic and allowed for particularistic appropriation. To be sure, the Ukrainian particularistic narrative still acquired its meaning from the larger framework of Soviet patriotism. "The Ukrainian people has its own historically established traits of
national character, reflected in its songs, language, literature, and tradition
of courageous struggle for freedom against the foreign, Tatar-Turkish and
Polish-noble oppression. It is essential to maintain and develop these better traditions on a new, Soviet basis," wrote a Soviet theoretician in
1948.[119] And these better traditions resided securely under the holy trinity
of one Soviet motherland, state, and culture. "Soviet patriotism," continued Vyshinskii, "assumes the love of Russians for their great national culture, for their language, for their national traditions; the love of Ukrainians for their nation and their culture; the love of Georgians for Georgia,
for the national culture of the Georgian people, and so on. But, above all,
Soviet patriotism is about the love of Russians, Ukrainians, Belorussians,
Georgians, Armenians, and other peoples of the Soviet Union for their
common socialist motherland, for the Soviet state, and for a single socialist
culture."[120] Probably more important, the viability of this patriotism
evolved around the recent epic of the war which meant that Ukrainians,
who by and large felt they were specifically victimized by the revolutionary
ethos, chiefly the 1932–33 famine, were now placed in the vanguard of a
triumphant myth, almost on a par with the Russian people. Trying to
explain to a delegation of Russian émigrés the distinction between Imperial Russian patriotism and Soviet patriotism, the Soviet ambassador in
Paris emphatically noted:

> There is a vast difference between the Russian patriotism of the émigré and the
> Soviet patriotism of the peoples of the Union. The Union, as such, is higher
> than Russia, and Union patriotism is higher than Russian patriotism. The Union
> has united 120 nationalities. A new status, unheard of in history, has been cre-
> ated for the nationalities, and, in this titanic struggle, the peoples have demon-
> strated heroic devotion to the great common motherland—the Soviet Union
> . . . The confusion of the concepts of Russian and Soviet patriotism is common

---

[118] Dudin, *Velikii mirazh*, 124.

[119] P. E. Vyshinskii, "Sovetskii patriotizm," in F. Konstantinov et al., *O sovetskom sotsialisticheskom obshchestve*, 447.

[120] Ibid.

now . . . but the émigrés must find the strength of spirit and understanding to rise to the concept of Soviet patriotism.[121]

Together the unification of the Ukrainian land and its people ordained the myth of the war with a tangible sense of generational continuity in the life of that community. The war has been represented as the event that helped realize the historical necessity of bringing together a previously fragmented family. At times the Soviet component was emphasized. Addressing the unification at the plenum of the obkom in December 1944, the first secretary of the Vinnytsia obkom, Havrylo Mishchenko, addressed the issue by referring to a Siberian peasant tale. A *muzhik* became so ill that his neighbors, who thought he was dying, set their eyes on his property. But the *muzhik* recovered and decided to reclaim his possessions. He asked the neighbors to return his property, but they responded with threats. So he hit one neighbor in the teeth, and the latter returned his cow. Then he hit the other on the back of his head and recovered his horse. The third returned the calf of his own will. Our government, explained Mishchenko to those who still did not get it, was too weak during the imperialist war, the Revolution, and the civil war to guard the integrity of its borders. But when it gained strength, the Soviet Union, just like that *muzhik*, recovered what was hers.[122] At other times the Ukrainian component was the focus. "It means a great deal for the Ukrainian people that thanks to the wise Stalinist policies of the Bolshevik Party and the Soviet government, the unification of all the Ukrainian lands was realized and the entire Ukrainian people [lives] in one Soviet Ukrainian state," the secretary of the Vinnytsia obkom told the plenary session in February 1949.[123] Soviethood and Ukrainianhood were synonymous.

In folk songs the unification of the western and eastern sisters of the Ukrainian family was celebrated as an act of restoration and a new beginning. "There will be happiness, there will be joy / In all of Ukraine / Free sisters in a union / From now and forever," read a verse of one of many poems composed for the occasion.[124] The plots of popular memoirs and novels took place in the newly acquired territories of western Ukraine, thus familiarizing readers with the new areas of the unified Republic. When Petro Vershyhora commemorated the fallen "Chusovitin [who]

---

[121] The meeting took place on 14 February 1945 when a delegation headed by V. A. Maklakov came to the Soviet embassy in Paris to pay tribute to the Russian "national government" for its role in the war (*Novoe Russkoe Slovo*, 7 March 1945, 1–2, as cited in Towster, *Political Power in the USSR*, 102 n. 30).

[122] TsDAHOU, f. 1, op. 50, d. 1, ll. 269–70.

[123] PAVO, f. 136, op. 29, d. 8, l. 23.

[124] "Brat'iam galichanam" (To the Galician brothers), in Grigorii Litvak, ed., *Pesni i dumy Sovetskoi Ukrainy* (Moscow: Gos. izd-vo khudozh. lit-ry, 1951), 119.

rests on Hill 1613 in the Carpathians, in a rocky tomb formed by giant boulders at an altitude frequented only by mountain eagles, [and] four-teen-year-old Mykhailo Kuzmovych Semenis'tyi sleeps on the Hungarian frontier," the melodramatic obituary celebrated the blood bond of Ukrai-nians to their unified native land.[125]

The leading role that the Ukrainian Republic commanded in the evolu-tion of the Soviet cult of World War II did not go unnoticed. The centrality of the memory of the war in Ukraine was punctuated both by some dis-tinctive rituals and by the overtly elaborated manner and number of com-memorative symbols. From the early aftermath of the war, Ukraine set the tone and pace for integrating the cult of the war into the fabric of private and public life throughout the Union. The early and intensive incorpora-tion of the war's memory into public life in Ukraine pointed to its key role in the fight over the shaping of identities of this particular region. Whether as a counter image of the prewar calamities of collectivization and famine or nationalist separatism, a balance for the haunting impres-sion of mass wartime collaboration, an intuitive response to the calamities of war that hit Ukraine the hardest, or a transmission of the memory of a defining event in the life of a crucial segment of the body politic, the cult of the war was zealously pursued in Soviet Ukraine.

In the highly stylized Soviet system one could hardly be surprised that the authorities took the initiative in institutionalizing the myth of the war and framing its acceptable rituals. Writing in *Pravda Ukrainy* on the occa-sion of the announcement of the first wave of mass demobilization, the writer Iurii Ianovs'kyi conveyed the urge for an immediate historicization of the fresh memory of the war.

> We must hurry with this [task], because time blurs memory, people forget de-tails, they lose documents. We are obliged to write about all that has to do with the history of the struggle of our youth with the German occupiers—in every village, town, mine, and factory. The ghosts of the youth, tortured for the moth-erland, have the right to demand remembrance from us. We dare not forget them.[126]

But such a plea was scarcely needed in the liberated localities where the industrious commemoration of the war had already been set in motion, often at the initiative of locals. There, the integration of the war into the calendar of Great Moments started upon liberation. It was in the small towns and villages where the cult resonated most powerfully as a blood

---

[125] Vershyhora, *Liudi s chistoi sovest'iu*, 45–46.
[126] *Pravda Ukrainy*, 23 September 1945.

bond between the community and the all-Union cause.[127] Barely two weeks after liberation of the region, a Central Committee representative instructed the Vinnytsia raisovets and raikoms to take care of burial sites in such a way that "the population would see how the Soviet power takes care of people who fought for our Soviet motherland."[128] Regardless of the meager financial resources in late 1945, the oblispolkom assigned about half a million karbontsy for the construction of monuments honoring fallen soldiers and commemorating the victory over Germany and the liberation of the region. Some of these monuments carried a plaque with Stalin's declaration of the liberation of Vinnytsia.[129] That year the oblispolkom also ordered that memorial obelisks be erected on sites of partisan battles and that the graves of fallen partisans be put in order.[130] Following a directive of the Ukrainian Council of Ministers on 26 March 1946, the oblispolkom instituted a systematic survey of the state of military cemeteries and of mass and individual graves of fallen Red Army soldiers, officers, generals, and partisans located in Vinnytsia.[131]

Throughout 1944–50 some thirty-eight monuments were erected in the region. Some honored fallen native sons, others honored Red Army soldiers who died fighting for the district's liberation. Some of the memorials were financed by the government, such as those in the district of Zhmerynka. Others, notably, were built at the expense of villages, such as the one in the village of Kupchyntsi in the Dashiv district that was erected in memory of two Red Army officers and twenty-five unidentified soldiers. The monuments were also financed occasionally by the selsovet, such as the mass grave on the Petrov kolkhoz in the district of Illintsi. At a time of financial constraints of the immediate postwar years, that was no small sacrifice.[132] Twenty years later the region was literally plastered with some 523 mass graves of more than 145,000 servicemen, prisoners of war, partisans, and civilians who died during the war, covering practically every population point in the region (Figure 6.2).[133] Erected, as a rule, at the

[127] For the efficacy of a similar phenomenon in Europe, especially during the interwar period, see George L. Mosse, *Fallen Soldiers: Reshaping the Memory of the World Wars* (Oxford: Oxford University Press, 1990).

[128] TsDAHOU, f. 1, op. 22, d. 161, l. 9.

[129] DAVO, f. 151, op. 9, d. 71, l. 5.

[130] PAVO, f. 136, op. 13, d. 38, l. 35.

[131] DAVO, f. 2700, op. 7c, d. 80, ll. 12, 14. By 1 July 1947 the oblispolkom recorded some 1,881 mass graves and 2,574 individuals, of whom there were 6 Heroes of the Soviet Union, 1,155 officers, 4,165 sergeants and soldiers, and 343 partisans. The survey recorded not only the number in each category but also the type of tombs: 106 graves had granite tombs, 49 had wooden tombs, and 2,137 had wooden pyramids.

[132] DAVO, f. 4971, op. 1, dd. 40, 41, 63.

[133] Ibid., f. 138, op. 4, d. 28, ll. 1–33.

Figure 6.2. The monument and eternal flame honoring fallen soldiers in the center of Vinnytsia.

village's central square with lists of the fallen native sons inscribed on marble plaques, these humble monuments were ever visible in village life (Figure 6.3). The naming of locations and activist groups after fallen heroes established an uninterrupted chain in the life of the community. "Each of these is a living memorial to those who, with weapons in hands, fought the Fascists bravely and joined the immortals," read one of the many manuals for rituals in the late 1980s. Pioneer groups and local school museums were named after fallen soldiers, like the museum in the Pratsia kolkhoz honoring Bonzi Sordia, a Georgian Hero of the Soviet Union

Figure 6.3. An obelisk commemorating the fallen native sons of the village of Bahrynivtsi. Of the 846 villagers who served at the front in World War II, 210 were killed.

who was killed in the fight over the village of Frontivka. Probably more intimate were the memorials of local boys, such as the one honoring the three Pustovitov brothers from one village in the Orativ district.[134]

There were also the living reminders of the war—the local veterans. Their constant presence, enduring prestige, and grip on local positions of power guaranteed that the myth of the war would endure. Just three weeks after liberation of the region, and one week before a similar decree came from the Central Committee in Kiev, the bureau of the Vinnytsia obkom ordered the Department of Agitation and Propaganda to circulate information in the press on the partisan struggle in the region, and the regional museum was told to create a permanent exhibition on the theme, "The Partisan Struggle against the German Aggressors."[135] On 12 December 1947 the Ukrainian Council of Ministers admitted that a large number of servicemen had not received any awards or medals for their heroism. Since most of them had already been discharged and were back at work, the oblispolkom was obliged to "order the chairmen of gorispolkoms and raispolkoms to use theater halls, clubs, and palaces of culture for the presentation of government awards in ceremonial decor [and] to use the occasions of visits of chairmen of raispolkoms and raivoenkoms to large settlements where more than ten decorated people reside in order to present them with awards at their place of residence."[136] The election campaign in January–February 1946 provided an additional stage for the celebration of veterans and the cultivation of the war myth. Although by no means a measure of efficacy, reports glorifying the military exploits of local and national party leaders, such as Mykhaylo Stakhurs'kyi, Dmytro Burchenko, and Timofei Strokach, were read in mass meetings that had been organized as cultural gatherings. It was reported that 713,000 people attended 120 such gatherings. The presentations were followed by concerts, films, and artistic performances that guaranteed large attendance.[137]

The highly stylized commemoration of the dead and the living did not diminish the spontaneous and intimate nature of the event. Soviet com-

[134] *Imeni geroev: iz praktiki sozdaniia imennykh polei i ikh ispol'zovaniia v voenno-patriot-icheskom internatsional'nom vospitanii, sovershenstvovanii sotsialisticheskogo sorevnovaniia v Oratovskom raione* (Vinnytsia, 1988).

[135] RGASPI, f. 17, op. 44, d. 1652, ll. 18–20.

[136] DAVO, f. 2700, op. 7c, d. 80, ll. 36–38. The republic press simultaneously paraded on its front pages long lists of servicemen and partisans who were decorated with various awards, the most prominent of which was the recently introduced Order of Bohdan Khmel'-nytskyi, the seventeenth-century legendary Cossack leader. In the exceptional case of Hero of the Soviet Union, the papers dedicated a large amount of space to individual biographies of the commanders (*Pravda Ukrainy,* 8 August 1944). In a speech at a mass gathering, Khrushchev proudly announced that nearly twenty-three thousand Ukrainian partisans received various awards, including thirty-two Heroes of the Soviet Union (21 October 1944).

[137] PAVO, f. 136, op. 13, d. 75, l. 32.

memorative acts lent themselves for appropriation by individuals who embodied the orchestrated rituals. The proximity of Victory Day on 9 May to 1 May, the other pillar in the revolutionary calendar, only underscored the growing remoteness of the latter date and its tedious, imposing character. Metaphorically speaking, there were no unknown soldiers in the villages and small towns of Vinnytsia, and the tombstones carrying lists of the fallen native sons and daughters offered a constant, powerful reminder of the familial nature of wartime sacrifice. Referring to the commemoration of the new focal event in the Soviet calendar in the early 1950s, a former educator in Vinnytsia, himself a veteran, recalled:

> The ninth of May was celebrated beautifully and with vast enthusiasm. On this day I led the students [approximately eight hundred], with wreaths of flowers, to the mass graves. It was moving. The children listened to stories of those invited to speak, people who were sometimes illiterate and simple but who tried to piece together who was buried there and how they got there . . . Veterans drank vodka, embraced and kissed one another, remembered the war, danced and cried. They all wore decorations and military uniforms [those who had them]. Victory Day was celebrated in a much more spiritual and better way than November 7th or May 1st. The holiday had an intimate character. Officers in reserve kissed soldiers in service; everyone recalled memories from the war and was amazed to still be alive . . . It was a genuine celebration, and it was not shameful to be drunk.[138]

The cult of the war seemed only to intensify as the Soviet polity moved away from both the October Revolution and the war itself. This development went hand in hand with the denunciation and removal of such key elements of the Stalinist regime as the cult of personality and the mass terror, the partial acknowledgment of the crisis of the command economy, and the routinization of other fundamentals of the revolutionary ethos.[139]

The war was present in the lives of locals from the onset of their socialization well into the twilight of their lives. Through the continual, routine commemorations, those who participated in the war continued to live it long after it was over, and those who happened to be born after the war became de facto participants.[140] The commemoration of the war was inte-

---

[138] Boris Halfin, letter to the author, 29 April 1995. Identical events took place in every district center and collective farm (DAVO, f. 4597, op. 1, d. 78, ll. 3, 7: op. 9, d. 164, l. 45). See also Christel Lane, *Rites of Rulers—Ritual in Industrial Society: The Soviet Case* (Cambridge: Cambridge University Press, 1981), 140–52.

[139] See Christopher A. P. Binns, "The Changing Face of Power: Revolution and Accommodation in the Development of the Soviet Ceremonial System," *Man* 15, no. 1 (1980): 171–72.

[140] For an intriguing analogous case of socialization in Israel, see Asher Arian, Ilan Talmud, and Tamar Hermann, *National Security and Public Opinion in Israel* (Jerusalem: *Jeru-*

grated into virtually every component of ordinary citizens lives, including
the most intimate ones. From elementary school to coming-of-age rites
such as the passport ceremony, to the induction of newly enlisted men
into the Soviet army, to wedding processions and holidays honoring the
older generation, the war was omnipresent in various ways: the choice of
location (war monuments, the eternal flame in honor of the fallen soldiers); the participation of war veterans in the rituals; youths hiking to
battle sites and pilgrimages to monuments of local heroes; and countless
meetings with army and partisan veterans who romanticized the war to
the successive generation with tales from the battlefield. The personalization of the myth abolished the distinction between actual experience and
memory, between participants and successive generations.

As time passed, the Soviet revolutionary ethos was increasingly read
through the prism of the war. The calendar of sacred events and ceremonies that marked the lengthy procession of baptism into Soviet citizenry
was conveyed in terms of this cataclysmic event. Several decades later, with
another war turning into an open wound, the need to hold on to the
memory of the "good war" became even more meaningful.[141] By now, the
Great Patriotic War was intricately woven into every layer of the upbringing of future defenders of the motherland. In the Zabolotnyi Medical
School, the Komsomol cell launched a game entitled *Orliatko*, engaging
several hundred youngsters in a competition over military operations, tactical maneuvers, and marches to revolutionary, military, and labor sites of
glory. The game was played on two dates, Soviet Army Day and Victory
Day, following a year-long preparation that included meetings with Heroes of the Soviet Union, veterans of the Great Patriotic War, and former
partisans and underground activists. The participants were commended
for helping in the search and gathering of material for the regional museum dedicated to former school graduates who had fought at the Great

---

salem Post, 1988), esp. chap. 5. In their discussion of the impact of military service and
political socialization, the authors conclude that "Israelis have internalized within themselves
service in a spiritual army long before actual service in the real army begins. Since the process
starts so early and is so over-arching, values are securely in place before exposure to the
physical army commences. The society is geared to the army experience: Nursery school
children fantasize army life and high school students train for the army while still in school.
It [military service] does not signify breaking with the past or being introduced to new
values. Rather, it is being initiated into an institution of adult practices and rituals that you
have been familiar with from a very young age" (67). See also Steve Knapp, "Collective
Memory and the Actual Past," *Representations* 26 (1989): 134–47.

[141] In a similar vein, observers of the American scene noted that the perception of World
War II as a "good war" owes more to the perceptions of the Vietnam generation than those
of the World War II generation (Howard Schuman and Jacqueline Scott, "Generations and
Collective Memories," *American Sociological Review* 54 (1989): 378).

Patriotic War.[142] The Komsomol cell of the pedagogical institute came up with another rite—the Starry Tours (*Zoriani Pokhody*). The focus of the rite was familiarization of the local youth with the war generation in the villages. Visits to homes of veterans and war widows included offering material help to the aged and recording their wartime exploits. The Komsomols were assigned to write the biographies of local veterans, especially those who fought for the liberation of the region, and compose albums that were displayed on Victory Day.[143]

During a single academic year, one school in Vinnytsia arranged no fewer than three meetings with Heroes of the Soviet Union and twenty-eight sessions with veterans of the war. The familiarization with the war's legacy was supplemented by an honorary guard of Komsomol members at the Eternal Flame by the Memorial to Glory and expeditions to famous battle sites such as the Hero-City of Kiev and the Brest fortress.[144] Youth also figured in increasing number in V-Day celebrations. By the early 1980s, May 9 involved the march of thousands of veterans and youth to the site of the Eternal Flame accompanied by a brass band of reportedly close to one thousand players. The festivities concentrated especially on streets named after fallen local heroes such as Ivan Bevz and Lialia Ratushna.[145] The increasing mass character of May 9 was softened as well by the intimate and painful legacy of wartime widowhood. In some villages, commemoration centered on the many wartime widows. One such celebration, said to be a model for the upcoming fortieth anniversary of the victory over Germany, took place one evening in 1982 in the village of Tin'ky in the neighboring region of Cherkasy. As many as 115 war widows received invitations in the standard military envelop to an evening of celebration at the village's cultural club. Other invitees included their families, surviving veterans, and conscripts to the Soviet army. At the club they were met by popular tunes from the war years and a recording of Iurii Levitan reading the Soviet Information Bureau's announcement of the defeat of fascist Germany.[146] To these sounds the crowd was led to the

---

[142] *Nikto ne zabyt, nichto ne zabyto: iz opyta raboty komiteta komsomola Vinnytskogo meduchilishcha imeni akademika D. K. Zabolotnogo po voenno-patrioticheskomu vospitaniiu uchashchikhsia* (Vinnytsia, 1986).

[143] *Nikto ne zabyt, nichto ne zabyto: iz opyta raboty komsomol'skoi organizatsii peduchilishcha po organizatsii i provedeniiu "zvezdnykh pokhodov"* (Vinnytsia, 1989).

[144] *Vospityvat' patriotov: iz opyta raboty Vinnytskogo SPTU-11 po voenno-patrioticheskomu vospitaniiu uchashchikhsia* (Vinnytsia, 1986).

[145] A. D. Didkovs'kyi, "Vazhlyvyi vykhovnyi zasib," in *Novi zvychai, dobri traditsii* (Odessa: Maiak, 1983), 57.

[146] Iurii Levitan was the news broadcaster of the All-Union Radio of the USSR from the early 1930s. His deep and authoritative voice while delivering official announcements during

Obelisk of Fame, where they laid wreaths of flowers at the feet of the monument on which, carved in gold letters, were the family names of fallen fellow villagers. The celebration then continued at the club where the tune "Wide Is This Homeland of Mine" was played. When the song subsided, the silence was broken by the sound of "Holy War" by Aleksandrov. The famous poster "The Motherland Calls" was shown on the screen followed by segments from the documentary "The Great Patriotic War" by Karmen.[147] The widows were then thanked for their heroic sacrifice, received notification on the increase of their monthly pension, and were honored by the customary loaf of bread.

The women were celebrated not only as widows but even more as mothers. In the Ivan Franko collective farm in the Sharhorod district, a commemoration focused on the six children of Maria Andriichuk whom she raised alone after her husband's death at the front in 1944. The loss suffered by the elderly widow took a back seat to the six lives she gave to the community. All six children, it was emphasized, were model workers in the collective farm. The widows, as mothers of war orphans, were immediately elevated to the status of living symbols of the unvanquished spirit of the community, its will to survive, and its ability to overcome the greatest of challenges. In such an intimate environment, even the grandiose rhetoric of the chairman of the kolkhoz regarding its postwar reconstruction assumed a familial touch, anchored in the living experience of so many members of this small community. The national and communal survival and triumph were very personal experiences.[148]

The war resonated visibly for youth in the coming-of-age rites, starting with the presentation of a passport at the age of sixteen. An authoritative manual of Soviet rites recommended that the procession be held either at a war memorial or at the Palace of Ceremonial Events. There the future citizens paid homage to the fallen soldiers, who in their death had given them life, with a moment of silence before a symbolic alcove of the eternal flame displaying the words: "In memory of the heroes who died in battles for the motherland, sacred for the descendants."[149] The presence of war veterans, especially those highly decorated, was integral to the ceremony. A living example of model citizenry, the veterans were there to inspire the new citizens.[150] On receiving their passports, the youth of Vinnytsia were

---

the war became one of the memorable symbols of the time, and is still well remembered by contemporaries.

[147] V. K. Sobchenko, "Trudovye traditsii, prazdniki i obriady truzhenikov sela," in V. A. Zots, ed., *Traditsii, obriady, sovremennost'* (Kiev: Izd-vo polit. lit-ry Ukrainy, 1983), 158–60.

[148] *Vshanuvannia saldats'kykh vdiv (Vinnytsia, 1980); Kolhospnyk,* 28 March 1981.

[149] *Sovetskie traditsii, prazdniki i obriady: opyt, problemy, rekomendatsii* (Moscow, 1986), 252; Binns, "The Changing Face of Power," 174–75.

[150] A. D. Didkovs'kyi "Vazhlyvyi vykhovnyi zasib," 63.

told by the state official to "remember the commandments of the great Lenin, to solemnly preserve the conquest of all generations of the Soviet people who under the leadership of the Communist Party stormed the Winter Palace, defended the fatherland in the Great Patriotic War, and built a developed socialist society."[151] Often the attending veteran talked briefly about his heroic past and his present field of activity and participated in handing out passports.[152]

The induction procession of newly enlisted men into the Soviet army highlighted the continuity of the heroic tradition of the Great Patriotic War, bridging the small rural community to the supra-national legend. Drawing on the prerevolutionary tradition of a collective farewell for the conscripts, the elaborate ceremony involved the entire community.[153] On one Sunday in late 1965, in Reshetylivka in the Poltava region, the new recruits gathered in the court of the local military committee accompanied by their relatives and friends. Dressed in their best suits, they marched to the stadium where the local population assembled; war veterans who were present wore their decorations and medals, others their civilian decorations. The recruits and their parents then watched an allegorical portrayal of heroic moments in the history of the Soviet people. A brief display of civil war heroes, such as Frunze, Chapaev, Shchors, and Kotovskii, was followed by a review of "unforgettable episodes from the Great Patriotic War":

> With her head held high, Zoia Kosmodem'ianskaia hurls words of hatred to the Hitlerite hangmen. The young guards of Krasnodon swear the oath of allegiance to the motherland. The participants in the celebration recognize their compatriots in the pantomimes played out on other floats: Marina Maienko, the runner for the partisan formation of General Naumov; Nikolai Krivoshta, the sailor from Sevastopol' whose heroic exploits are exhibited in the Simferopol' museum.

The ceremony concluded with the recruits marching to a brass band and saluting the gallery of portraits of Heroes of the Soviet Union who came from the Reshetylivka district.[154] In villages in Vinnytsia veterans delivered

---

[151] *Ia hromadianyn Radians'koho Soiuzu: Z dosvidu roboty po vruchenniu pasportiv iunym hromadianam v Staromis'komu raioni m. Vinnytsi* (Vinnytsia, 1980).

[152] Lane, *Rites of Rulers*, 101.

[153] For a brief portrayal of induction ceremonies in Ukrainian villages between 1950 and 1956, which closely resembled the prerevolutionary rituals, see H. Iu. Stel'makh, "Formuvannia novykh zvychaiv v ukrains'komu kolhospnomu seli," *Narodna Tvorchist' ta Etnohrafiia* 1 (1957): 93; O. F. Kuven'ova, *Hromads'kyi pobut Ukrains'koho selianstva: istoriko-etnohrafichnyi narys* (Kiev: Naukova dumka, 1966), 122–23.

[154] *Sotsialistychna kul'tura*, 11 (1965): 14. In Rivne the conscripts swore allegiance to the Soviet motherland in front of the monument of the Hero of the Soviet Union (Nikolai

passionate recollections, exclaiming how the "blood of their generation that watered the grateful land, [was] now handed over to the sons' generation."[155] Although the new inductees had been born long after the war, noted a columnist from the village of Mykhailivtsi, in their hearts they forever carried the unfading legacy of the Soviet people's achievements in the Great Patriotic War, the exploits of their fellow villagers who had fallen, and of Captain Bohdan, Hero of the Soviet Union, who died heroically in the struggle to liberate the village and whose memory remains alive in people's minds and in the portraits decorating the House of Culture.[156]

The war followed young citizens into the next, and arguably one of the more intimate, rituals of one's life: the wedding procession. Marking generational and communal continuity, couples were encouraged to get married at the site of the Eternal Flame and lay wreaths of flowers for those who had died to give them life.[157] In a neighboring region, during the reception, the wedding host (*tamada*) would propose a toast in honor of the couple, their families, and the various guests, particularly those who fought in the war. At some weddings that were attended by veterans of the Great Patriotic War, the host would ask the guests to greet them, and, addressing all of them, would announce: "At our celebration today are those who, during the terrible days of the war, spared no effort and risked their health and their lives to win the victory over the enemy. We are indebted to these heroic people, the war veterans, for our peaceful working days, for our own happiness. We wish them many more years!" Often the public singing included popular war songs such as "Katiusha," "In the Forest at the Front," and "Victory Day."[158]

The tale of unification of the Ukrainian land and people was integrated into the Soviet master-narrative and, as such, reflected the evolution of this narrative. Starting with the downgrading of a class-based ethos, the story of unification moved on to a distinct ethnonational reading and

---

Kuznetsov. P. P. Kampars, and N. M. Zakovich, *Sovetskaia grazhdanskaia obriadnost'* [Moscow: Mysl', 1967], 189). Veterans of World War II attended practically every ceremonial induction into the army at which time they told the conscripts tales from their past. For such a scene in a large factory in Khmel'nyk in the early 1980s, see P. Ia. Slobodianiuk, "Osobennosti organizatsii novykh prazdnikov i obriadov v usloviiakh goroda," in Zots, *Traditsii, obriady, sovremennost'*, 144.

[155] *Lenins'kym shliakhom*, 12 November 1981.

[156] *Slovo khliboroba*, 29 October 1981; *Nove zhyttia*, 13 March 1980.

[157] Iu. N. El'chenko, *Novomu cheloveku-novye obriady* (Moscow: Izd-vo polit. lit-ry, 1976), 39–40; V. G. Sinitsyn, ed., *Nashi prazdniki* (Moscow: Politizdat, 1977), 140; *Sovetskie traditsii, prazdniki i obriady: opyt, problemy, rekomendatsii* (Moscow: Profizdat, 1986), 318–20.

[158] V. K. Borisenko and A. V. Kurochkin, "Kul'tura svadebnogo zastol'ia v sovremennom gorode," in Zots, *Traditsii, obriady, sovremennost'*, 177, 180–81.

then, along with the rest of the Soviet polity, into the era of socialist harmony. The goal of unification of the Ukrainian lands was promoted well before the pact with Nazi Germany. As early as 1935, this message was articulated in the film *Granitsa* (Border) where the story takes place in a western Ukrainian village four kilometers from the Soviet border. At the time, the expressed desire for ethnonational unification was still overshadowed by class rhetoric. Brutalized by the police and local capitalists, hopeless impoverishment and anti-Semitism, the village poor cannot avoid comparing their lot with Jewish brethren across the border. "Why do people live like human beings in a kolkhoz only four versts from here, but here we starve? Why?" cry out the oppressed. Some of the heroes end up fleeing to the Soviet Union. "This is a fine film," applauded a reviewer in *Pravda*. "It will particularly be familiar and understood in Ukraine and Belorussia, near the borders beyond which beat the hearts of the heroes of this film."[159] Accordingly, before the war the Bolshevik Party had been credited with the historical achievement. A poem from 1940, *Spasibo vam, bol'sheviki*, read like an oath of allegiance to the party:

Thank you, Bolsheviks,
For the freedom you gave us,
For the slavery you smashed,
And unchained us!

We vow to thee, that we will be
faithful sons,
No one will separate us—
We are forever with you.

Glory to the honest toilers
Of the Soviet land,
Eternal congratulations, beloved Stalin,
Dear Party![160]

Eastern Ukrainians responded enthusiastically to the unification of Ukraine in its Soviet mold. Pavel Negretov from Kirovohrad was sixteen years old at the time of the annexation. His Soviet convictions were sufficiently entrenched to outweigh the difficulties posed by the great famine of 1933. He saw people dying of hunger and heard rumors about cannibalism. But there were no doubts in this youngster's world, a world that had been shaped by the revolutionary romanticism of "The Red Devils" and

---

[159] Pravda, 28 April 1935.
[160] "Spasibo vam, Bol'sheviki," (Thank you, Bolsheviks), in Litvak, *Pesni i dumy Sovetskoi Ukrainy*, 126–27.

"Chapaev." When installments of the *Short Course* were published in *Pravda*, the tenth-grader swallowed every word. "We were not blood-thirsty," recalled Negretov,

> but when western Ukraine and the Baltic Republics were annexed, we were glad about the successes of our policy. I remember that at that time one of my school-mates said: "Well, now the NKVD will clean things up there." And none of us spoke against him. Our *Stalinjugend* were molded just as successfully as our peers in Germany were molded in their *Hitlerjugend*.[161]

Negretov was not off the mark. The letters and diaries Vladimir Zenzinov gathered from the bodies and belongings of Soviet fallen soldiers in Fin-land paraded a remarkably cohesive Soviet Ukrainian pride informed by the progressing revolutionary ethos. Class enemies were increasingly eth-nicized, and Soviet patriotism was colored with the more particularistic nationalism of the non-Russian nationalities. Poles were almost unani-mously referred to as "Pans" and Finns as "white samurais" and, in a less complementary way, as treacherous swines and scoundrels who attacked the peaceful Soviet motherland with the blessing of capitalist Britain, France, and the United States.

The unification of the Ukrainian and Belorussian lands and peoples seemed to draw the most enthusiastic reactions. As one serviceman, Ev-teev, stationed in western Ukraine, wrote to a close friend in the Soviet rear:

> Our Red Army was assigned with the liberation of the Ukrainian and Belorus-sian peoples from the yoke of the landowners under which they have lived for twenty years . . . It was our fate to help these peoples and take them under pro-tection, liberate them from the oppression of the Polish landowners and officers. The Red Army fulfilled this task with honor. [We] freed forever those who were condemned to starvation and death. [We] united western Ukraine with Soviet Ukraine and established there the power of the workers and peasants—the power of the soviets.

And if the international situation demands so, Evteev assured his friend, then we are ready to defend our sacred borders and even proceed to liber-ate the toiling masses of any country that aspires for a peaceful life.[162] With similar bravado, one Mitia from Zhytomyr wrote to his friend Boris Karpov, who was at the Finnish front at the time, that "from your letter

---

[161] Pavel Negretov, *Vse dorogi vedut na Vorkutu* (Benson, Vt.: Chalidze, 1985), 24–25, as cited in Karel Cornelis Berkhoff, *Hitler's Clean Slate, 339.*

[162] Zenzinov, *Vstrecha s Rossiei*, 331–32. It should be noted that the correspondence Zen-zinov collected from fallen Soviet soldiers were private letters between friends and family members.

it is clear that you are happy to defend the border of our immense Union. I am proud, Borek, that you are on the borders, and I wish you success at a time that calls for a Bolshevik answer to the enemy who tries to breach our border." Mitia himself took part in the Polish campaign: "This year I, too, joined the ranks of the invincible glorious Red Army and liberated our Ukrainian and Belorussian brothers from the landowners' yoke. Borek, you cannot imagine the burst of joy in meeting those who, until very recently, were dependent on the Polish lord but now have become completely independent."[163]

In a textbook published by the Ukrainian Academy of Sciences on the eve of the war, credit went largely to the working masses. Having suffered the assault on their cultural existence, the Ukrainian toilers led the heroic struggle for the unification of the Ukrainian people in one state, wrote the authors. "The eyes of the working people of western Ukraine turned with hope to the USSR, where their blood brothers live in freedom and happiness, where the Ukrainian socialist state of the workers and peasants develops and gets strong under the sun of the Stalin Constitution." Some nuances, however, pointed in a new direction. The textbook paraded the Soviet narrative of unification as a historical necessity to bring together blood relatives and to reach unity through purification. The weeds, however, had distinct ethnic faces, namely, the Polish landowners and their faithful lackeys, the counterrevolutionary bourgeois nationalists. The toilers of western Ukraine with great joy met the liberating Red Army that helped them to "cleanse their land of the Polish pans." Tellingly the section that dealt with the unification was entitled "The Unification of the Great Ukrainian People in One Ukrainian Socialist State."[164]

By then, the adjective *velykyi* (great), usually reserved for the Russian people, had already become a common currency in references to the Ukrainian and Belorussian peoples, the two ethnic groups incorporated into their Soviet counterparts in September 1939. Repeatedly evoked from the early days of unification,[165] it dominated the call to arms with the onset

---

[163] Ibid., 356.

[164] *Istoriia Ukrainy: korotkyi kurs* (Kiev: Vyd-vo AN URSR, 1941), 390–91.

[165] For the frequent use of "Great Ukrainian people" and "Great Ukraine" by the arriving representative of Soviet power in the newly annexed western regions in the fall of 1939, see B. M. Babii, *Vozziednannia zakhidnoi Ukrainy z Ukrains'koiu RSR* (Kiev: Akademiia nauk Ukrains'koi RSR, 1954), 174, 183; Serhy Yekelchyk, "Stalinist Patriotism as a Contested Discourse: Reconciling the Ukrainian and Russian 'Heroic Pasts,' 1939–45," a paper presented at the Thirty-first Annual Conference of the American Association for the Advancement of Slavic Studies, St. Louis, 21 November 1999. For the Soviet application of the adjective in reference to Belorussians, see the 14 November 1939 annexation decree by the Presidium of the Supreme Soviet of the Belorussian Republic, in Vladimir Picheta, *Osnovnye momenty istoricheskogo razvitiia zapadnoi Ukrainy i zapadnoi Belorussii* (Moscow: Gos. sots.-eko. Izd-vo, 1940), 136.

of hostilities. On 6 July 1941 Nikita Khrushchev addressed his constituency with a marked particularistic tone: "Comrades, workers, peasants, and intelligentsia of the great Ukrainian people! Brothers and sisters! Sons and daughters of great Ukraine! . . . To live in a free Ukraine or to fall into the slavery of the yoke of Hitler—this is the question now facing the Ukrainian people . . . Forward! For our native Ukraine, for the Great Soviet Union!"[166] On the occasion of the twenty-sixth anniversary of the October Revolution and with the complete liberation of Ukraine in the offing, Aleksandr Fadeev, the prominent Soviet writer, highlighted the unique status of the Ukrainian people, sharing a pedestal only with their Russian "elder brother." Celebrating the great friendship between the two great peoples (and betraying a certain anxiety over Ukraine's attachments to the Union in the wake of German occupation), Fadeev's ode presented the entire revolutionary epic as an enterprise undertaken solely by Russians and Ukrainians. Dating back to the days of Volodymyr of Kiev, Danylo of Halych, and Bohdan Khmel'nyts'kyi, the two peoples forged a revolutionary alliance that culminated with the establishment of the Great Soviet Ukraine, whose present culture and civilization are far superior to that of many western European countries.[167] The war and the ensuing reunification would be read through an increasingly ethnonational lens.

The following year the party was scarcely mentioned on the debt list of the Ukrainian nation. With the war still raging, political posters flirted with Ukrainian nationalist sentiments without the slightest mention of Soviet power or even the Red Army. A poster by R. Mel'nychuk celebrated the liberation and unification of Ukraine. The poster showed a determined young female in plain clothes holding a rifle and a flag against a background of stormy skies and the cavalry on the attack (Figure 6.4). A poem by Mykola Tereshchenko below the scene read:

> The sun has fully risen
> It is liberation day for Ukraine.
> In the liberated expanse once again
> The fields rustle, the factories buzz.
>
> Gone is the poisonous fume.
> United and indivisible,
> Beneath the flag of triumphant host
> Ukraine is free forever!

---

[166] TsDAHOU, f. 1, op. 23, d. 17, ll. 11–15.
[167] Aleksandr Fadeev, "O sovetskom patriotizme i natsional'noi gordosti narodov SSSR," *Pod znamenem marksizma*, no. 11 (November 1943): 25.

Figure 6.4. *The Sun Has Fully Risen—It Is Liberation Day for Ukraine!* Kiev, 1944. A poster celebrating the liberation of Ukraine.

Other poems celebrated the unfolding liberation from the German occupation by repeatedly referring to "Ukraine, My Motherland," with no reference at all to the Soviet motherland, the Red Army, or Stalin.[168] Another poster incorporated the poetry of Taras Shevchenko, the national bard, into the war effort, again with no mention of Soviet power. The lines of the great nineteenth-century poet appeared under his portrait and above a sketch of a destroyed German tank and a pile of German corpses (Figure 6.5):

> Thistles and nettle—and nothing else,
> will grow up over your corpses,
> and piled in heap upon heap
> Stinking feces—and all of this,
> the wind will scatter bit by bit . . .

The incorporation of Shevchenko into the myth of the Great Patriotic War continued in the postwar years. When *Pravda Ukrainy* announced the erection of monuments honoring heroes of the Patriotic War, including the legendary Kovpak, the text opened with a note that they were manufactured by the same factory that produced the Shevchenko monument in front of Kiev University. Shevechenko begot Kovpak.[169]

By now the cult of Ukrainian history reached the point where party ideologues were alarmed at what they viewed as a monster of their own making. The balancing act between a counter to the separatist message of Ukrainian nationalists in the occupied territories and a mobilizing battle cry for Ukrainians in the ranks of the Red Army (and, to a lesser degree, for those under German occupation) proved to be more delicate than ever. For some Ukrainian intellectuals, including prominent figures in the Soviet cultural establishment, the delicate balance within the Soviet Ukrainianhood formula tilted heavily toward the latter, as Serhy Yekelchyk's study of Ukrainian historians at war demonstrates convincingly. Tolerated and even endorsed during the war, repeated literary references threatened to drop the Soviet component from the equation altogether. Maksym Ryl's'kyi, the officially ordained poet, heralded "the freedom-loving Ukrainian people [who] have always strived toward the unification [of the Ukrainian lands], toward the creation of their mighty state on the banks of the Dniester and the Dnieper." Mykola Bazhan's 1942 poems celebrated Danylo of Halych, the great Galician-Volhynian medieval prince, as the "first warrior in Ukrainian fields," and in 1944 the historian Kost' Huslys'tyi observed that the prince was "one of the great ancestors of the Ukrainian people in the same way as Aleksandr Nevskii was one of the great

---

[168] "Zdravstvui, Ukraina!" in Litvak, *Pesni i dumy Sovetskoi Ukrainy,* 165.
[169] *Pravda Ukrainy,* 17 April 1946.

Figure 6.5. A poster featuring the poetry of Taras Shevchenko, the nineteenth-century Ukrainian national bard, who was mobilized to the Soviet war effort. Kiev, 1944.

ancestors of the Russian people." Emphasis on the historical, brotherly
relations with the Russian people was, at best, a partially successful solution. The Soviet component had to be reinstated, if only to curtail the
mistaken assumption by these intellectuals that Ukraine was liberated
from the Nazis "under the banner of [Taras] Shevchenko and [Pantelei-
mon] Kulish," as Kost' Lytvyn, the Secretary for Ideology of the Ukrainian Central Committee warned Ukrainian writers in late August 1946.[170]

However, by the time Lytvyn issued his stern warning, this correction
was already well under way. It was pursued in a subtle and peculiar manner
by which the Red Army towered over the party and Stalin as the embodiment of Soviet power in the liberated Ukrainian territories. A gradual shift
toward combining Ukrainian national and Soviet pride was traced in a
poster, entitled "Ukraine Is Free!" that celebrated the pride in unifying
the Ukrainian lands under the auspices of the victorious Red Army. The
poster portrayed a towering figure of a Red Army soldier marching east.
Holding a rifle in one hand, the soldier points with his free hand to a large
red-colored map of western Ukraine (Figure 6.6).

The following year the harmonious triangle of Ukrainian nationalism,
Soviet power, and the Red Army again emerged on the horizon. While
the determined look remained, the grim solitary figures in the foreground
of political posters were replaced by harmonious collectives of optimistic
faces bursting with health. The stormy tempestuous scenes of war that
served as background for wartime posters were replaced with calm pastoral
scenes of the Ukrainian heartland. A poster by Myronenko, "Long Live
and Forever Flourish Soviet Unified Ukrainian Land, Liberated by the
Red Army!" portrayed a familylike image of Ukrainian society. It showed
a female figure in traditional eastern Ukrainian dress holding a red flag.
At her side, carrying a young daughter, stands a man in traditional western
Ukrainian dress. Behind the young family stands a Red Army soldier,
holding a rifle in one hand and, with his other, supporting the woman
holding the flag. The Soviet Ukrainian coat of arms looms over the symbolic collective (Figure 6.7). Pride in the unification of the Ukrainian
land received an even more explicit expression in a poster from L'viv, the
center of western Ukraine. The poster shows two female figures celebrating the unification, while adhering to a fundamental principle that underlined the Soviet view of the union. This was not a marriage of equals, at
least not for the time being. Western Ukraine was the infant daughter,
catching up fast but still in need of guidance. The unification with its
eastern mother brought western Ukraine the fruits of Soviet civilization,
notably a modern health care system. "The question arises," wrote Aleksandr Fadeev sometime earlier, "who arrived here as the more advanced,

---

[170] Yekelchyk, "Stalinist Patriotism as a Contested Discourse."

Figure 6.6. *Ukraine Is Free!* Kiev, 1944.

Figure 6.7. *Long Live and Forever Flourish Soviet Unified Ukrainian Land, Liberated by the Red Army!* Kiev, 1945.

cultured European state: Soviet Ukraine or prewar Poland ruled by the very same circles who still dream of subjugating the western regions of Ukraine?"[171] In line, the unequal status between western and eastern Ukraine is demonstrated by having the woman in traditional eastern Ukrainian dress in the forefront. She holds the flag and coat of arms of Soviet Ukraine in one hand and, with the other, leads her western counterpart (Figure 6.8). Below the illustration is a poem by the well-known poet Pavlo Tychyna:

Beautiful Ukraine—
United, united!
The sun shines above her,
The land is full of plenty.
And the people are all heroic,
As if of iron—everlasting.

Iron forges itself within us,
It does not submit to the enemy
and never will:
In unification we find happiness!
In Soviet Ukraine
We are strong and united.

By 1946 the harmonious Ukrainian family, along with the rest of the Soviet brethren, moved into the realm of plenty and dignity. Decorated war veterans were still at the core of the family, but now they dressed in respectable suits. In a popular poster, "The Best Sons and Daughters of the Ukrainian People," they were joined by a woman in traditional national dress, holding a volume of Stalin's work and an old *intelligent* with a civilian award attached to the lapel of his suit. The quartet radiated respectability, culture, and a sense of achievement (Figure 6.9). By then harmony was achieved with the return of *Bat'ko* Stalin as the father of the Soviet Ukrainian family. In the poem *Zakarpatskaia pesnia* Stalin was credited with familial reunification:

From Moscow Stalin dropped us a line to the Carpathians:
Carpathian Ukrainians, dear brothers,
Wait in the Subcarpathians
Soon the army of the Soviets will be with you . . .
Soon we will give you freedom and happiness.

[171] Fadeev, "O sovetskom patriotizme i natsional'noi gordosti narodov SSSR," *Pod znamenem marksizma*, 26.

Figure 6.8. *Beautiful Ukraine—United and Indivisible!* L'viv, 1945.

Figure 6.9. *Vote for the Best Sons and Daughters of Our People to the Supreme Soviet of the Ukrainian Soviet Republic!* 1946. Poster depicting the ideal postwar Soviet Ukrainian Family.

And the Carpathians, as true sons, responded in kind: They formed partisan detachments and started beating the fascist barons. "Our Ukrainian brothers," concluded the ballad, "began to sew the red standard."[172] On Soviet Army Day, years after the war had ended, school children in Vinnytsia commemorated the event by reciting poems such as the following:

> Throughout the centuries the rough Carpathians have sadly called to
> The roar of the speeding current of the Dnieper:
> We have one language, We have one mother
> Our fate must be one.
> The sunny dream of the people was realized
> Stalin warmed the Carpathians with his kindness.
> Praise, friends, the long desired freedom,
> Praise, friends, the unification of brothers.
> In Poltava the silver poplars rustle

---

[172] "Zakarpatskaia pesnia" (A subcarpathian song), in Litvak, *Pesni i dumy Sovetskoi Ukrainy*, 185; in the same collection, see also *Rodnye Karpaty*, 175.

In L'viv the music of the chestnuts echoes
From now and forever we have one fate
We have one leader and one path.[173]

The war would not change the image of Vinnytsia as a remote and tranquil
provincial town. In Moscow the announcement of the liberation of the
city by the Red Army was greeted by a gun salute and, on the radio, Volodymyr Sosiura, the very poet who wrote "Love the Ukraine," read a poem
entitled "Sun over Vinnytsia."[174] But the town did not enter the Soviet
pantheon of Hero Cities, nor would it occupy a special place in the cult
of the war. It was this very anonymity, however, that made the war such a
powerful link to the national scene and a watershed in the identities of its
residents. However redundant Sosiura's lines were, they still had meaning.
Especially in Vinnytsia. "A crimson sea is rising, sea of light and liberation
floods more towns and villages of suffering Ukraine / The regiments of
victory have chased the bloody fascist night out of one more of the ancient
towns of our motherland / our star-studded warriors have filled the hearts
with sunny hymns of joy and great love to our immortal Stalin / the sun
of victory is over Vinnytsia," read Sosiura.[175] In this same spirit, Liberation
Day on March 20, a new addition to the calendar of sacred events, would
be commemorated with one eye focused on local veterans of the Soviet
Army and partisans and the other on distinct Ukrainian national features.
When the town celebrated the twenty-fifth anniversary of its liberation
from the Germans, the ceremony opened with the traditional presentation
ritual, in which veterans who had participated in the liberation of the city
were offered bread and salt, wrapped in Ukrainian towels and carried by
three girls dressed in Ukrainian national costumes. The anniversary was
also an occasion to honor servicemen and local underground fighters with
the title Honorary Citizen of Vinnytsia; those honored included all-Union
figures such as the marshal of the Soviet Union, Kyryl Moskalenko, who
had commanded the Thirty-eighth Army that liberated Vinnytsia, and
even the fallen Ivan Bevz, previously disgraced by the prewar revolutionary ethos but now restored as a legitimate hero.[176] Embroiled in Soviet
patriotism and Ukrainian national pride, the residents of the region were
able to set aside the shadow of the Great Terror and join the triumphant

---

[173] The scenario was composed by the local ethnographer Maria Prisianiuk (DAVO, f.
5105, op. 1, d. 115, ll. 2–25; here, l. 9).

[174] *Po obe storony fronta/Auf beiden Seiten der Front: pis'ma sovetskikh i nemetskikh soldat
1941–1945 gg.* (Moscow: Sol', 1995), 67.

[175] TsDAMLMU, f. 44, op. 1, d. 432, l. 1.

[176] DAVO, f. 151, op. 9, d. 2357, l. 1; d. 2257, l. 50.

march toward Soviet Ukrainianhood. Vinnytsia was neither a Hero-City nor the symbol of a place once overcome by enemies of the people. As members of the new Soviet Ukrainian family, they were no longer the backward peasant mass nor a bastion of ferocious separatist chauvinism. They were on equal footing with the Soviet vanguard, assuredly marching on the path to the paradise of communism.

A Soviet World without Soviet Power,
a Myth of War without War

For the residents of Vinnytsia, like the rest of the Soviet population, World War II was the culmination of a chain of cataclysmic events, each one enough to warrant a lifetime of reflection. It was also their most challenging and pervasive experience, one that knew no class, ethnic, or territorial boundaries. The war visited every community, family, and individual in the Union in a manner and magnitude that tested existing commitments, loyalties, and associations. People struggled to make sense of the war and the trials it had in store for them: combat and captivity, occupation and liberation, collaboration and resistance, total mobilization and disintegration, mass extermination and deportations, famine and the further pauperization of an already impoverished existence. For most, the wartime encounter with Ukrainian nationalism and Nazism was also the first exposure to articulate alternatives to the ethos in which they had lived all or most of their lives.

In their attempt to rationalize what they had experienced, men and women were informed by their preconceived biases and the world that shaped these beliefs. This world was very much a Soviet one. The war, not surprisingly, meant different things to different people. For the true believers, this was the apocalyptic Armageddon they had been expecting, although not wanting, for three decades. When it came, they were ready to accept it, if not the actual painful events, then their rationale. In their world the war helped to uncover the elusive and most dangerous enemies who had managed to survive the political and social purgatory thus far. "We purged and purged, yet it turns out that rightists still sat in the Politburo! It is impossible to understand this only by figures and formal criteria," reasoned Molotov some thirty years after the war.[1] This final cleansing act would homogenize the socialist polity and bring it within reach of communism, the final station of history.

This logic resonated in an equally powerful way in the world of those ridden with doubts, whose lives had been shaken by the destruction of the pantheon of heroes and the bloodletting of the 1930s. The blood of this world war, in the words of Vasilii Grossman, the most eloquent

---

[1] Feliks Chuev, ed., *Sto sorok besed s Molotovym*, 464.

representative of these men, would redeem the blood that was shed during collectivization and the Terror. Having gone through Revolution, civil war, and collectivization, they turned to the war as their new formative experience, one that overshadowed and often erased its predecessors. This also meant that society would resume its march toward communism on a more just path, but nevertheless one with the same destination.

Those who felt victimized by Soviet power, mainly peasants, were not only integrated for the first time into a Soviet triumphant epic, but now it was not as the embodiment of backwardness but as heroes, often finding themselves entangled in a myriad of rituals and practices that transformed the war experience into a major vehicle of their own sovietization. Assigned with the cleansing of social and political weeds from their midst, peasants turned to their wartime experience as the prism through which they defined the "other" and ordered their surroundings.

And all were constantly grappling with the infusion into their midst of racial ideology and practices. For some, this was nothing but a logical extension of the thorough ethnicization of the Soviet world before, during, and after the war. For others, the racialization of the social and political habitat marked the collapse of a sacred tenet of Soviet civilization, namely, the belief in differentiated, reformable, and redeemable individuals and collectives. Both, however, had to grapple with the complete brutalization of public life in the wake of the war. As communist regimes shifted gears in their pursuit of homogeneous and harmonious societies, their belief in the malleability of human nature seemed to wane. In the Soviet Union, those the party-state marked as internal enemies after the establishment of socialism were deemed irreducible, unreformable, and irredeemable. Similarly, in the heyday of China's Cultural Revolution, the "blood pedigree theory" was practiced under the slogan: "If the father's a hero, the son's a good chap; if the father's a reactionary, the son's a bad egg."[2] Did nurture finally succumb to nature? Not necessarily. Excision, even when carried out to completion, did not emanate from a genocidal ideology and was not practiced through exterminatory institutions. Hence Communists repeatedly turned their attention to groups and individuals they had already engaged previously, an inconceivable practice had these entities been stigmatized a priori as racially, biologically unfit. Purification did not engage collectives as such but rather the individuals who comprised them. As the ticking of the Soviet eschatological clock grew louder, they bore the brunt of an increasingly urgent quest for purity.

But true believers, doubters, and victims alike, assessed this fundamental experience in juxtaposition to the Soviet ethos which offered itself as an exclusive framework for conceptualizing all political experiences by Soviet

---

[2] Lynn T. White III, *Policies of Chaos*, 222.

citizens. If the war was an all-pervasive experience, so, too, was the Soviet experience that overlooked no one and politicized all facets of life. But was there a way out? Could one have experienced the war and made sense of it outside the Soviet prism? On the surface, the war seemed to offer itself as a catalyst for a profound change in this very world. After all, the various individuals and communities we have encountered were keen on establishing the war as a watershed in their autobiographies, regardless of their political affiliation. Moreover, Soviet authorities publicly displayed concern for the impact of the hitherto unfamiliar temptations of the outside world on their subjects. They even went as far as to invoke the ghost of the Decembrist uprising in 1825. Even if Nazism and East-Central European fascism were hardly attractive for Soviet citizens as were revolutionary America and France for young aristocrats over a century before, the metaphor was very much present in the mind of a regime still shaken from the blows of war.[3] Indeed, in some cases, the war led individuals, and remarkably even high-ranking officers, to question the fundamentals of the entire system.[4] These, however, were isolated incidents and still beyond the comprehension of most contemporaries who lacked, among other things, viable channels to disseminate their discontent. Red Army servicemen were, by and large, products of the Soviet system and one could not in good faith expect most of them to question the high politics and philosophical dimensions of the polity that raised them. The transformation of personal assessments into political generalization and articulation of political identities and agendas outside the Soviet realm would wait much longer, owing more to the dismantling of physical terror after Stalin's death, and would not necessarily emerge from the ranks of the veterans, cautions Elena Zubkova.[5]

Yet something else was taking place in the trenches. The prolonged experience of warfare created a unique mode of association and a sense of

---

[3] Indeed, the regime did not conceal its anxiety over the potential trappings of capitalist seduction for Soviet soldiers. In September 1944 Leonid Sobolev warned, in the pages of *Pravda*, that "we shall yet pass through many foreign countries. Soldiers! Your eyes will often be dazzled; but do not be deceived by these outward signs of their so-called civilization! Remember, real culture is that which you carry with you" (Werth, *Russia at War*, 947). For the authorities' warnings against the Decembrist temptation, see Elena Seniavskaia, *Frontovoe pokolenie, 1941–1945: Istoriko-psikhologicheskoe issledovanie* (Moscow: Institut rossiiskoi istorii RAN, 1995), 90–93.

[4] In private conversations, two of these individuals, retired generals Fillip Rybal'chenko and Vasilii Gordov, went as far as challenging the premise of collectivized agriculture which, they argued, should be replaced by the market and a "true democratic system." The two, along with Marshal Grigorii Kulik, were surveilled by the MVD, arrested in early 1947, and executed in August 1950. Neither recanted despite several years of harsh interrogation (Nikolai Smirnov, *Vplot' do vysshei mery* [Moscow: Moskovskii rabochii, 1997], 179–89).

[5] Elena Zubkova, *Obshchestvo i reformy*, 23–24.

self that did not run through the socialization channels provided by the regime. And this experience, argues Elena Seniavskaia, was critical for the fate of the Soviet system:

> The generation of the front returned from the war triumphant and insightful. [Its members] discovered through their huge losses [that they had gained] moral power, setting in motion, as a matter of fact, the phenomenon of the Twentieth Congress . . . The peoples of the former USSR especially owe to the generation of the front not only their independence and their very existence but also the first spiritual and political assault on totalitarianism, which we now call "the Thaw," during the second half of the 1950s.[6]

One might be skeptical about the assertion of a direct link between the spirit of the front-line generation and the post-Stalinist "Thaw." Such an interpretation, not unlike those advanced later for Gorbachev's reforms, tends to inflate the weight of popular pressure and marginalize party-state power, the single indispensable source for a shift of this magnitude within the Soviet system. The question remains whether the experience of war altered the ABCs of Soviet totalitarianism? Were structures overpowered by the impact of this cataclysm? Did the newly discovered self-assertiveness influence the regime's policies? After all, it was still a ruthless power that proved it would stop at nothing when challenged or in implementation of full-blown sovietization, as entire nationalities and Baltic and Ukrainian nationalist guerrillas learned during that era. Nor can we ignore the regime's role in creating venues for self-assertion. The redemption of past sins through wartime exploits, particularly the stain of wrong social origin, was ordained by the regime itself, as evidenced by hundreds of thousands of "former people."

Whereas the front did not breed Western-style democrats, it did produce an assertive Soviet individual who held tight to his (and it was mostly his and not her) newly earned-in-blood right to define his identity and status based on his wartime exploits. Returning soldiers displayed uncompromising reluctance to let others—the regime included—articulate for them the defining moment of their lives. Front-line assertiveness pervaded every realm of the Soviet polity, even the GULAG. The waves of strikes that swept the Soviet penal system during the last six years of the Stalinist era were instigated and led by new inmates who built on their wartime experience and utilized their military organizational skills. Former Red Army servicemen, Ukrainian nationalist guerrillas, and Vlasovites spearheaded the wave that eventually contributed to the crumbling of the penal

---

[6] Elena Seniavskaia, "Dukhovnyi oblik frontovogo pokoleniia: istoriko-psikhologicheskii ocherk," *Vestnik Moskovskogo Universiteta*, series 8, *Istoriia* 4 (1992): 50–51; idem, *Frontovoe Pokolenie*, 93, 158.

system. But even then, the protests within the GULAG echoed those outside. Demands for improvement of the brutal regime were often articulated within an orthodox Soviet frame, challenging the authorities to live up to their proclamation of legality, and, in some rebellions led by Communist Red Army officers, sought to uproot an "anti-Soviet and counter-revolutionary spirit."[7]

In the final analysis, one must examine the world of those who claimed to have turned the war into a vehicle for a conscious break with the system. Recently historians started paying attention to the internalization of the Soviet belief system by large segments of society, including victims of the regime.[8] These pioneering works examine a variety of individuals who have established their own viable subjectivity through persistent efforts to integrate themselves into the unfolding Soviet enterprise. The clear imprint of the system on the lives of its citizens, and especially its victims, invites an examination of this system and its resonance in the world of individuals who tried to step out of the Soviet realm, those who crossed the threshold from discontent into active opposition.

A study of the value system of dislocated eastern Ukrainians, who chose not to return to the Soviet Union at the end of the war, has revealed the coexistence of hostility to certain aspects of the Soviet political system along with acceptance of some of its fundamental socioeconomic principles. A detailed survey in 1950–51 of some 459 ethnic Ukrainians who had lived within the pre-1939 borders of the Soviet Union and who, as evidenced by their age, were mostly products of the Soviet educational system, revealed a society in which resentment for the arbitrary use of terror and hyper-centralization of economic and political life resided alongside the internalization of some key attitudes of the Soviet order. These included firm support for the welfare state and a strong tendency to qualify support for personal freedom and civil liberties by affirming the government's right to protect its interests and prestige, and to preserve order and public morality. Ukrainians displayed a strong sense of victimization as a result of the regime's policies. Of the respondents in the survey, 91 percent answered negatively to the question of whether Soviet nationality policy improved the position of Ukrainians, and 65 percent

---

[7] Andrea Graziosi, "The Great Strikes of 1953 in Soviet Labor Camps in the Accounts of Their Participants: A Review," *Cahiers du Monde russe et soviétique* 33:4 (October–December 1992): 419–46.

[8] For illuminating treatments of the struggles of ordinary citizens to define themselves culturally and politically within the Soviet system and operating within the public realm, see Kotkin, *Magnetic Mountain*, chaps. 5–6; and Igal Halfin, "From Darkness to Light: Student Communist Autobiography during NEP." On individuals operating within the most intimate realm, that of personal diaries, see Jochen Hellbeck, "Laboratories of the Soviet Self," and his "Diary of Stepan Podlubnyi (1931–1939)."

believed that their intelligentsia was more prone to arrest than other national intelligentsias. Some had a clear notion of being targeted by the social policies of the 1930s. "To be Ukrainian often meant having been designated a kulak," remarked one respondent.[9] At the same time, a substantial majority of collective farmers (84 percent) replied that the government should guarantee employment and own heavy industry (83 percent).[10] Moreover, a key cohort of young and highly educated eastern Ukrainians exhibited extreme antiseparatist views on Ukrainian history, more so than any other age group or group at a different educational level and twice as frequently as the older well-educated cohort.[11] These individuals accepted the Soviet version of Ukrainian history, a factor made more relevant by the following story.

The travelogue of a twenty-year-old woman journeying on a train from Luts'k to Kiev on 18 October 1945, entitled "The Life and Worries of the Citizens of Soviet Ukraine," was apparently submitted as a report to her superiors in an OUN underground cell.[12] It is impossible at this point to discern whether the travelogue followed a standardized form. The author declares that she intended both to provide information on the social and political affairs in postwar Ukraine and to explain to herself how she came to break with the Soviet world she was raised in. While the prevalence of this specific mixture of surveillance and confession among nationalist activists is not known, one is struck by the powerful resemblance to a similar Soviet genre. Just as the nationalist surveillance reports were patterned identically after their Soviet counterparts, so the confessional component of this travelogue echoed communist autobiographies. Constantly weaving together her personal past, contemporary political events, observations about fellow passengers, and Soviet society in general, the author of this account offers insight into the way Soviet individuals struggled to make sense of a life made up of endless cataclysmic events and the interpretations offered them by no fewer than three rival totalitarian movements. Life had unexpected challenges and setbacks, but it proceeded in a straight path from the darkness of unquestioning ignorance to the light of revelation. Although the ultimate awakening was allegedly built on seeds of

[9] Gilliam, *The Nationality Questionnaire*, 14, 27, and ix, respectively.

[10] Inkeles and Bauer, *The Soviet Citizen*, 348–49.

[11] Answering the question, "Which description conforms most closely to the existence of the Ukrainian nation?" 36 percent of this young and highly educated group stated that the existence of the Ukrainian nation cannot be separated from Russia (against 17 percent of the older group) (Gilliam, *The Nationality Questionnaire*, 44–45). The overall share of those who did not see a separate existence between Russia and Ukraine was 19 percent (22).

[12] L.F., "Zhizn' i zaboty grazhdan Ukrainskoi SSR," GARF, f. 9478, op. 1, d. 643, ll. 103–20. The document was seized by the NKVD and submitted to the command of the organization.

suspended skepticism, it materialized into a worldview only in the wake of a single cataclysm that shook long-held conventions. It was a Manichean world, divided between the righteous and the opportunists, in which the yardstick for meritocracy was an uncompromised devotion to the cause. It was a Soviet world par excellence, even when one was struggling to do away with this world.

Identified only as L.F. by the NKVD translator, this young woman immediately turns to the recent war as the focus of her narrative. This may come as no surprise given her age and immediate surroundings—the train is full of demobilized servicemen and dislocated persons traveling home for the first time since the outbreak of war. But in L.F.'s world, wartime experience has a dual purpose: it is a prism through which one observes both the past and present, while it shapes the lives of ordinary Soviet Ukrainians.

L.F.'s upbringing was a traditional Soviet one. In school she studied the lives of Lenin and Stalin, led a pioneers' detachment, and followed the example of Pavlik Morozov to search out counterrevolutionaries. Then, she says, along came the genuine interest in communism as the ultimate truthful idea. It was a closed and safe environment, guaranteed to be stable by the shared common experience of all and lack of familiarity with another life. "The difficult material conditions at home explained why my father and mother could not survive. But none of my friends and comrades lived any better."[13]

A window to a different past was occasionally offered by the older generation in the intimate surrounding of the family. In Ukraine, in particular, this meant familiarization with national myths and the living memory of the brief period of independence. "Sometimes the elders told us about the prosperous life before the Revolution," she recalls. Her mother read her poems of Shevchenko, and her father sobbed when she herself recited the national bard. Her mother also provided information on the work of *Prosvita*, the enlightenment societies, during the brief period of independence in 1918.[14] It was interesting, writes L.F., but "we did not believe them, because at school they taught us not to believe our own parents, to regard all of this as fairy tales and fabrications [and] I sought to overcome this interest, because everything that had to do with the [Ukrainian] revolution of 1917, I considered hostile."[15] For so many of L.F.'s generation, home was an important source of historical education but one that seemed

---

[13] Ibid., 107–8.

[14] Gilliam cites identical expressions (*The Nationality Questionnaire*, 59). "Mother told me about Petliura; she taught me the Ukrainian national anthem," stated one respondent.

[15] GARF, f. 9478, op. 1, d. 643, ll. 107–8.

overwhelmed by the intense Soviet formal education.[16] Nor did the ban on certain books in school leave deep imprints at the time. In fifth grade she was baffled when a teacher confiscated the works of Storozhenko and burned them in front of the students[17]—a bizarre and mystifying incident but nothing to trouble the stability of a happy Soviet childhood.

L.F.'s world appeared secure and safe until the summer of 1941, although a series of earlier events left her, for the first time in her life, with unanswered questions. First came the war with Finland, with its expansionist goals and tortured conduct that complicated the hitherto unproblematic world of the youngster. She derived information about the outside world from the press and lectures, yet the unprecedented justification and nature of the war was unclear. "What right does the Soviet government have to treat the Karelians as its subjected slaves? To what end did thousands of our countrymen, relatives, and acquaintances freeze and perish in Finland?"[18] Even less comprehensible was the announcement of Ribbentrop's arrival in Moscow. "We felt that we did not understand something as we should have. Today's reality contradicts what we were taught yesterday. Yesterday we were taught to hate fascism but today to take it for a friend," was L.F's bewildered reaction, similar to that of so many of her fellow countrymen.[19] Significantly, however, no such confusion arose from the events in Poland and Bessarabia. Eastern Poland, now renamed the western Ukrainian regions, was a backward, oppressive prison for Ukrainians who had been liberated by Soviet power. The stream of prisoners arriving from Poland were the first people from abroad she had ever

---

[16] Only 33 percent of the young, well-educated respondents to the questionnaire cited the home as the most important source of cultural indoctrination. The share of the least-educated was 67 percent (Gilliam, *The Nationality Questionnaire*, 61).

[17] GARF, f. 9478, op. 1, d. 643, l. 108. One of the respondents to the questionnaire also recalled that, in art class in elementary school, one of the boys dabbed together for his picture the gold and blue colors (the colors of the Ukrainian flag) completely innocently and without nationalist deviation in mind. The teacher, greatly agitated and horrified, snatched the offending emblem, tore it to bits, and sent the children home (Gilliam, *The Nationality Questionnaire*, 57).

[18] Ibid., 108–9. From the Finnish territory, P. P. Liakovskii, a soldier and Komsomol member, complained to his comrades in the Fourteenth Army: "We liberated eleven million Ukrainians and Belorussians, but a similar number of our people lie on the territory of Finland. The USSR does not conduct the war in order to liberate the Finnish people but in order to occupy Finland. These actions of the Soviet government cannot be justified. This is a policy of aggression" RGVA, f. 9, op. 39, d. 86, l. 129b). Letters of fallen Red Army soldiers at the Finnish front conveyed a similar diminished enthusiasm as the invasion was botched and turned into a massive disaster (Zenzinov, *Vstrecha s Rossiei*, passim).

[19] Ibid., 109. "Why do our newspapers not scold Goebbels nowadays? Did he become a Bolshevik?" were questions thrown at Soviet agitators at the time (RGASPI, f. 17, op. 125, d. 46, l. 7).

met and talked with. "Many of them were Ukrainians who described life in feudal Poland, which was a fairy tale to us."[20] For the young nationally minded Ukrainian, the unification of Ukrainian land and people struck a chord even if the Soviet sponsorship of this event made her reluctant to admit it.

These misgivings, however, did not shake L.F's fundamental belief in the Soviet cause. By the time she joined the Komsomol in 1940, she writes, "I was not as much in love with the idea of communism as I had been in 1937–38. Nevertheless, until the arrival of the Germans, I still believed in the necessity of the Soviet Union and its just politics."[21] Given L.F.'s carefully measured words, there was surely more to this statement than its laconic nature suggests. Although by 1940 the Komsomol more than doubled its membership to nine million youths between the ages of fifteen and twenty-six, enrollment was still voluntary. Moreover, after a special resolution of the Eighteenth Party Congress in March 1939 formalized the position of the Komsomol as the party's assistant in all party tasks, it was evident for the newly enrolled that it was a stepping stone for a party career.[22]

Similarly, the subdued reflection on the years of the Great Terror as the apex of belief in the communist idea cannot be glossed over. By the time of her writing, L.F., like most wartime Dnieper Ukrainians, had been exposed to the avalanche of information on the Terror in Vinnytsia emanating from the Ukrainian-language press throughout the spring of 1943. Yet the focus of Nazi and nationalist propaganda on Ukrainians as the main victims is absent from L.F.'s recollections. Quite likely, the memory of the Terror was overshadowed by the much more devastating and fatal collectivization and famine of 1932–33. Squeezed between 1933 and 1941, the impact of the Terror was marginalized by the magnitude of collectivization and famine, and World War II. Moreover, for Ukrainian nationalists the essence of the Terror lay somewhere else. Having consumed the lives of so many die-hard Ukrainian Communists, the Terror was the final proof, if indeed any confirmation was needed, that Stalinism and Ukrainianhood were inherently antagonistic. But there seemed to be another line of reasoning, one that was especially relevant to L.F. and her contemporaries. For one who was born into the system and raised as a member of its future leading cadres, the Terror was a logical, albeit brutal, stage in the continuous purification of society. As the Terror was reaching its climax in February–March 1938 with the trial of Nikolai Bukharin, Komsomolites were called on to help unmask the elusive enemies who had

[20] GARF, f. 9478, op. 1, d. 643, l. 109.
[21] Ibid.
[22] Towster, *Political Power in the USSR*, 139–41.

survived thus far.[23] With no familiar pantheon of revolutionary heroes other than the Stalinist one, L.F. was not bound to the confusion that rattled the world of so many of the older generation. For many, the Terror was an event relegated to oblivion, erased from memory. For some, it was a cathartic moment of rebirth. For others, it was a shattering blow from which they would not recover.[24] And for a great many, the ensuing war would be a point of departure, the key moment in the rewriting of their communist autobiographies.

L.F.'s moment of crisis and revelation, however, came at a different time, and in a way that paradoxically underscored her entrenched communist world. For her, the critical moment came on 14 August 1941. "On that day I saw Germans for the first time. I was choked, and tears rolled from my eyes. A short, strongly built German approached me. 'Crying? Cry for the Russian soldier. The German soldier is better than the Russian soldier." But the German simply did not understand, continues L.F. in one of the most revealing passages of her narrative. It was not for the Russian soldier that she was crying. Rather, it was the overwhelming sense of humiliation in the face of completely unexpected defeat. "The belief in the invincibility of the Soviet Union collapsed, the gilded facade fell away, and falsehood showed its real face. What was the point in fortifying the defense for such a long period and all the talk about the invincibility [of the Soviet Union], when everything collapsed in one month?"[25]

L.F.'s focus on the humiliation of defeat is revealing. Only in the wake of the unfolding catastrophe did L.F. begin her tortured break with the Soviet cause and her flirtation with the Ukrainian nationalist movement. Shattered myths are hard to restore. Their collapse, however, does not necessarily trigger a coherent alternative, as was evident in the German-occupied countryside. What distinguished L.F's story from those of most of her contemporaries was that she had an opportunity to act on the crisis set in motion by the Soviet collapse and chose to do so. Her immediate social surrounding was critical, as she herself noted. At the medical institute she was surrounded by equally young, urban, and single-minded nationalist enthusiasts. In such an environment, nationalist literature offered a positive alternative. Still, the Soviet system was judged on its own terms and merits. It was the regime's failure to live up to its own claims that

---

[23] Ralph Talcott Fisher Jr., *Pattern for Soviet Youth: A Study of the Congresses of the Komsomol, 1918–1954* (New York: Columbia University Press, 1959), 212.

[24] See Hellbeck's excellent treatment of those who sought a spiritual rebirth throughout the course and wake of the Terror, as did the playwright Aleksandr Afinogenov, and those who were shattered by the message of rejection and their own incurable impurity, as were the independent-minded peasant Andrei Arzhilovskii and the engineer Iuliia Piatnitskaia (Hellbeck, *Laboratories*, chaps. 3, 7).

[25] GARF, f. 9478, op. 1, d. 643, l. 109.

shook the world of the young believer, not the seduction of an external alternative, veritably incomprehensible up to that point.[26] For this young eastern Ukrainian, the slide toward Ukrainian nationalism was the outcome of the system's crisis, not the cause of her dissent. As such, the discredited system would continue to exert enormous influence on shaping the world of the dissatisfied and the skeptical.

When she turns from contemplating the social and political aspects of her surroundings to intimately and painfully examining her soul, trying to understand how she came to depart from the Soviet world, her tale bears all the trademarks of the Soviet-style confession so familiar to her as a Komsomol member. L.F. scolds herself and her comrades in the nationalist camp for losing heart and spirit. "Before my eyes, people changed, lost their belief," she laments.[27] Arrested by the NKVD, having apparently been betrayed by close comrades, she was forced to work as an informant, which brought her to the brink of desperation. "At the worst moments, I wanted to commit suicide. Twenty years of life had lost their importance for me, and I became indifferent." A life of compromise was not worth living. Yet this was also her moment of redemption. Since life derived its meaning from its attachment to a larger cause, she realized she was not solely in possession of her life. "Only that, which I learned in such moral torture, kept me alive. I alone did not have the right to cut it short."[28] She faced the temptation, succumbed, but then regained her faith in the cause and ultimately broke with the NKVD.[29] And not unlike so many Soviet-geared youngsters, even at the moment of moral triumph L.F is consumed by fear of contamination and the desire to cleanse herself of her compromised past.

> What lies ahead? All the same, if only they would believe in my sincerity; if only my comrades would understand me; if only they would entrust me with any task in the service of the organization. [Can they] believe me after I have already broken down once and betrayed the people? The question of how I can justify myself before the organization and at the same time before the people remained unanswered for me.[30]

This was a world composed of enemies with a distinct ethnic face and arranged hierarchically based on their wartime experience. Ethnic Rus-

---

[26] For a similar response of shock by Soviet citizens of various nationalities at the sight of German troops rolling into their towns and villages, see YVA, #03–2243, 10; and Berkhoff, *Hitler's Clean Slate*, 46–47.

[27] GARF, f. 9478, op. 1, d. 643, l. 112.

[28] Ibid., l. 112–13.

[29] An almost identical dilemma and evasion was encountered by the young Stepan Podlubnyi in his struggle to become a proper Soviet citizen (Hellbeck, *Fashioning*, 369).

[30] GARF, f. 9478, op. 1, d. 643, l. 114.

sians were identified as such and were often scolded for their arrogant conduct and meddling in Ukraine, but L.F maintained a careful differentiation between good and bad Russians. Russian soldiers and officers on the train are recorded with either affection or indifference. No judgment is passed on one soldier from Kursk who complained that it was impossible to bring home more booty from Germany, nor on a Russian serviceman residing in the western city of Lutsk, nor even on an officer stationed in western Ukraine, most likely involved in the pacification of nationalist insurgents.[31] The brunt of scorn is reserved for the new class of Russian officers' wives, those uncultured, crude parasites who made the most of the wartime sacrifices of the others. A series of popular anecdotes mock these women who shamelessly parade the new wealth their husbands brought from the West. As L.F. recounts: Two fancily dressed women are walking along the street. Among the dull, ordinary mass of people in the street were many servicemen who commented: *Ot krali* [Look at these queens, but, also, stolen]. This provoked a great uproar by the two women: "We did not steal them; our husbands did and sent them to us." Or the standard joke about a certain Glasha, who noisily shows off the entire wardrobe her husband brought from Prague, Bucharest, Berlin, and Vienna before the audience at a concert. "Quiet, overture," hissed another woman. Unfamiliar with the operatic term, Glasha retorts harshly: "You yourself are an overture, and your father is an overture, and your mother, too."[32] Probably unknowingly, L.F. was recounting an all-Union genre of mocking the officer cast's malapropisms, a genre that quite likely was politically orchestrated.[33] In her version, the class aspect of mockery was forcibly ethnicized. But the appropriation of the Soviet value system also left the unmistakable imprint of the very system she wished to defy.

Yet no such humor is reserved for another, treacherous group: the Jews—but she speaks of them in a rather surprising way, given her confessed adherence to nationalist teachings. The frequent reference to Jews as *zhydy* (kikes) by a Soviet-educated eastern Ukrainian woman was probably an import from the western regions. But the bulk of L.F.'s tirade was well within the Soviet discourse.

> An "immigrant from Birobidzhan" started a conversation with me. This is a local kike from Volodymyr-Volyns'ka. He is curious why I don't carry anything to trade in Kiev. He is amazed how someone can skip an opportunity to make

[31] Ibid., ll. 105, 106, 120.

[32] Ibid., ll. 115–16.

[33] In Moscow, Alexander Werth recorded the very same anecdote. Werth suggested that the sudden buzz of anecdotes on the officers' wives was orchestrated by the party in order to put down the overly confident Red Army leadership. The technique, he argues, was a familiar one in Russia (Werth, *Russia at War*, 1003).

a profit. He has worked in the trade system for a long time. Now, after returning from central Asia, where he had been evacuated between 1941 and 1944, he holds a leading position in the trade system in Volodymyr-Volyns'ka. He has a good income but has no wish to stay in the USSR after the war is over. He wants to leave for America at the first opportunity.[34]

The Jew, simply put, spent the war years in the safety of the rear sharpening his trading skills, while his compatriots shed their blood at the front or languished under German occupation. And after being saved by the Soviets, his only wish was to break with the motherland. Here L.F., unbeknownst to her, was actually articulating the Soviet stand regarding the Jews during and after the war. Not recognized as members in either the community of suffering or the community of heroism, Jews were the ultimate outcasts. But the tirade does not stop there. Toward the end of her account, L.F. seeks to highlight the Russian imperialist nature of Bolshevism in Ukraine. She demonstrates it with a tale of the housing problem that plagued Kiev after the war. She proceeds to recount in detail a story she heard from a friend about the pogrom that took place in Kiev early in September 1945, which was described earlier. "After the war ended," she writes,

> A pilot, twice Hero of the Soviet Union, received an apartment in [the district] of Stalinka, which, until 1941, belonged to a kike who had been evacuated somewhere in central Asia. The pilot lived there with his old mother quietly and peacefully, ignoring the poverty. He could do so as long as the kikes who fled to the Far East and central Asia during the war had not started to flee back to the West, this time because of the Japanese threat. Shortly thereafter, the former owner of the apartment arrived and demanded that the apartment, which once belonged to him, be returned. He threatened to throw the pilot out in the street. Pointing to the two golden stars and medals he earned, the pilot declared that he had no intention of vacating the kike's apartment. Was the kike unaware to whom he was talking? The kike responded with irony, "What are these pieces of tin to me? If I want, I can get even more than you by tomorrow!"and he poked his finger reproachfully at the pilot's medals. The pilot then punched him in the nose. The kike did not think twice, pulled out a pistol (he was working in the NKGB or NKVD), and shot this Hero of the Soviet Union. A second pilot, who lived nearby, rushed to the scene. The kike, without hesitation, killed this one, too. The mother of the Hero died of a heart attack when she heard what happened.[35]

And so, in this version of the incident, the two servicemen who, according to the NKVD investigation we encountered above, had preyed on the Jewish policeman and beaten him up, now turned out to be pilots with

---

[34] GARF, f. 9478, op. 1, d. 643., l. 106.
[35] Ibid., ll. 117–18.

the highest decorations, just as Rozenshtein, the Jewish officer, turned out to be the evacuated homeowner. And in this version, Rozenshtein, who was promptly tried and executed for the shooting, was declared insane and sent to the Crimea for rehabilitation until he could stand trial.[36] Nor was the Russian ethnicity of the servicemen residing in Kiev held in scorn by the young nationalist. More people attended the funeral than that of the fallen general Vatutin (the Soviet general reputedly killed by Ukrainian nationalist guerrillas), reports L.F.

Notably the repetitive references to Jews established a single archetype of the Jew: a speculative draft dodger and cosmopolitan living off the blood of his compatriots. There were no good, bad, or even ordinary Jews and no distinction between alleged Jewish objectives and the conduct of individual Jews. The pogrom that erupted during the funeral procession, she concluded, was organized by Russian chauvinists in order to deflect the people's antagonism from the government to the Jews, as the Black Hundreds had done in tsarist times.[37] Directed against the Russian meddling in Ukraine, L.F.'s venom was, in the end, very much a product of Soviet postwar policies. The status of righteousness was won by exploits at the front; that of evil was gained by draft dodging in the rear.[38] Ethnic and class antagonism were articulated in the most Soviet fashion.

Could such resentment toward the regime materialize into a viable alternative? It could, argues L.F., but in a rather intriguing way. By the time L.F. wrote down her observations, she had developed a deep antagonism toward the political class of all sides involved, including her own. Her comrades in the nationalist underground seemed to ride an emotional roller coaster between exhilaration and despair, trust and suspicion of one another. In any case, the NKVD penetrated the ranks almost effortlessly.[39]

Communists are obviously discarded as well, but not necessarily because of their views and policies. Rather, it is the mechanical dullness, the lack of independent views, and mainly the detachment of the communist political class from the living experience of the war that alienates the young woman. In Kovel', L.F. watches a stream of hundreds of thousands of people repatriated from forced labor in Germany all going eastward. "The slogans posted on the walls of the Kovel' station welcome them with joy and friendship," she notes. But this is not the attitude of her fellow passengers, mostly officials and representatives of Soviet power. "The 'Commies' refer to those who return to their homeland with arrogance

---

[36] For the NKVD investigation of the incident, see TsDAHOU, f. 1, op. 23, d. 2366, ll. 4, 6–7, 21.

[37] GARF, f. 9478, op. 1, d. 643, l. 118.

[38] Moreover, claimed L.F., the fiercest anti-Jewish expressions came from war invalids (ibid., l. 118).

[39] Ibid., f. 9478, op. 1, d. 643, ll. 113–14.

and hatred through which fear creeps in. In their opinion, they all went to Germany voluntarily. Therefore, they are 'traitors against the motherland,' an anti-Soviet element," she claims (ll. 1034). But where were these higher-ups during the war? One of them, a former deputy to the Supreme Soviet of the Soviet Ukrainian Republic attracts L.F.'s ire in particular. "During the entire conversation, she has not expressed one thought or opinion of her own, only foreign [other people's] words she heard somewhere or that were simply ready-made." In such a turbulent, dynamic time, this dullness can only be acquired under conditions of total detachment from true-life experience in the safety of the rear. Pointing to the repatriates, the Communist utters wryly that they won't be at home for long. There is also a place ready for them in Kazakhstan, where she herself languished in the war years, in evacuation (ll. 104, 107).

The key for salvation, then, lay with groups and individuals whose wartime experience gave them the opportunity to taste a different life and compare it to the Soviet situation. But it was not the repatriates from forced labor in Germany to whom she looked with hope. Rather, and as an intriguing note, she stakes her hopes on the unlikely alliance of Red Army servicemen and veterans, and western Ukrainians. Glossing over the reputed hostility of Red Army troops toward the nationalist movement and its cause, she views the former as a potential anti-Soviet bastion and a bridge to the nationalist movement. For one thing, "the front-line soldiers [*frontoviki*] are very different from the men of the party and the rear. They, who have seen the West and a different life, express their views much more freely and closer to the truth than the latter [party people]," L.F. writes. And this brings them together with the *zapadniki* (western Ukrainians). The latter, she observes, are very different from the *vostochniki* (eastern Ukrainians), not so much in their language and clothing but in their topics of conversation and their political education. "It is not surprising," she continues, "that, in debates, the truth is basically on the side of the 'Westerners.' They had the opportunity to see a different life and compare it to the present" (l. 106).

But it is not only the exposure to an alternative way of life that draws the two hostile groups together. Both constitute a community of blood, a fighting family, that overpowers ethnic and ideologically imposed divisions, argues L.F. At times, their violent encounter even helped to dispel the official propaganda that portrayed the nationalist movement as murderous and beastly. She concludes with an apocryphal tale of one Major Sokolov, a Russian officer in the tank forces. In the process of capturing Ternopil', Sokolov told her, his unit ran out of food. Their service unit was delayed somewhere, and it was impossible to get anything from the countryside, which was under the Banderovites' control. After a third group that had been dispatched to gather food in the countryside disappeared without a trace, Sokolov was ordered there with fifty of his soldiers. The mission failed, and he was captured by the Banderovites. He was released after three days, despite his being a Russian. "He now views the insurgents with the highest regard. "If I had had such merry and determined lads in my unit,' Sokolov tells L.F. in Russian, "I would have turned the world upside down" (l. 120).

L.F was certainly not what the Soviet system expected to produce. Her discontent crossed the threshold from lingering doubts to enrollment into the most vehement anti-Soviet movement at the time. Her dissent, however, was far more complex than her Manichean worldview may suggest. Hers was a world that closely resembled the one she rebelled against. The individuals and groups she envisioned as agents bringing freedom of spirit and thought were the least likely to play this role. More often than not, wars do not breed pluralism and tolerance, which was aptly recognized by Soviet power.[40] The very same veterans who symbolized for L.F. free spirit and thought were the ones expected to transfer their front-line zeal into the postwar arena, to cleanse the villages and towns of the weeds of occupation, and to restore discipline in the countryside—all of which they were anxious to do. Their counterparts, the Ukrainian nationalist underground activists, who rounded up L.F's imagined sovereign national community, were the least prone to a pluralistic worldview. Most intriguing, however, was that L.F.'s articulation of a particularistic, anti-Soviet agenda built on the appropriation of Soviet tools and a Soviet framework. Thus, ironically, L.F. regenerated the Soviet ethos. The Manichean reading of the world, the linear concept of personal and historical time, the contempt for private economic activity, the nature and face of the internal enemy, and, finally, the view of the recent war as a prism for interpreting the intimate and political environment—all were the essentials that constituted the world of the Soviet citizen in the postwar era. As was true for so many of her generational peers, the world of this young anti-Soviet activist was very, very Soviet.

Together, the aspiration for an ethnonational community built upon cross-ideological wartime suffering and heroism, including the adversity

---

[40] Referring to the impact of the wartime experience on the conduct of a kolkhoz chairman who had been a veteran, an editorial from 1968 described the former veteran as one who "brought from the war strictness and discipline. He decided to overcome the savage devastation with a desperate attack, as he had recently taken the enemy entrenchments. His ears sometimes became deaf to the innumerable human complaints and requests that he could in no way satisfy. The word *do* became the most frequent in his lexicon" (*Sovetskaia Rossiia*, 6 February 1968, cited in Jerry Hough "The Changing Nature of the Kolkhoz Chairman," in James Millar, ed., *The Soviet Rural Community* [Urbana: University of Illinois Press, 1971], 106–7). Historians of post–World War I Europe noted the correlation between veteran movements and the rise of authoritarian movements (Robert Wohl, *The Generation of 1914* [Cambridge, Mass.: Harvard University Press, 1979]); Mosse, *Fallen Soldiers*.

and bravery of those who remained on German-occupied territory, was a form of Ukrainianhood that outlived all other forms of national identification. Fifty years after L.F. put her thoughts on paper, General Petr Shuliak, a product of the Soviet military system and now a general in the army of newly independent Ukraine, drew an important lesson from the war. As the general remarked in a lead interview for a special issue of *Panorama*, the regional newspaper: "We have no right to forget our own history, the heroic sacrifice of those who fought for a sovereign state. The glorious tradition of older generations must be regenerated in the deeds of the present defenders of the young Ukrainian state." The fight against fascism was a fight for national sovereignty and independence, said Shuliak, lumping together the Soviet and nationalist causes.[41] The wartime ideological divisions and the Soviet cause have all but evaporated from the reconstruction of the memory of the war in the hands of this fine product of the Soviet system. L.F. would have agreed.

The myth of the war, then, was driven by a narrative which, hand-in-hand with its rise to dominance within the Soviet polity, lent itself for appropriation by particularistic visions. The cult of the war seemed only to intensify as the Soviet Union moved away from both the October Revolution and the war itself, and as some key elements of the Stalinist regime were being denounced, for example, the cult of personality and mass terror, the partial acknowledgment of the crisis of the command economy, and the routinization of other fundamentals of the revolutionary ethos. But it also increasingly became a foundational Ukrainian myth, and not by default.

A walk through the cemetery of the small town of Lityn is also a journey through various lives of the myth of the war. The sixteen undistinguished mass graves in the small plot are the site of three generations of commemorative politics. The dead are memorialized by a grim stone obelisk from the late 1940s, marked only by the Soviet Star at the top (Figure A.1 [*left*]. Facing it is the towering figure of a soldier with a machine gun. The statue, erected in the mid-1960s, is made of bright shining stone and is further distinguished by a plaque with golden letters that reads: "Eternal Glory to the Fallen Soldiers of the Great Patriotic War, 1941–1945" (Figure A.1 [*center*]). This typical Soviet monument faces nothing other than a large, simple wooden cross, erected recently by local parishioners (Figure A.1 [*right*]). And not far from the celebrated mass graves rest their Jewish alter egos. In an open field lay the ruins of desecrated tombstones from the early twentieth century, ravaged by the passage of time, neglect, and sheer vandalism. Alongside the ravaged tombstones is a faceless monument commemorating the murdered local Jewish community: a four-cornered con-

---

[41] *Panorama*, 11 May 1995.

Figure A.1. Three generations of memorials to war victims (1945, 1965, 1991) at a cemetery in Lityn.

crete surface with a modest obelisk at its center (Figure A.2). With no
inscription on the stone, one had to consult some of the aging residents
and the local archive to find out what the nameless concrete monument
memorialized. Erected in 1945–46, the obscure identity of the monument
is now punctuated by its other neighbor, the new Jewish cemetery, which
displays headstones with photos of the deceased and inscriptions of their
personal data. For nearly five decades the bleak monument bore no mark
at all. In this small Ukrainian town, like other former Soviet sites, the
Jewish tragedy was not denied; its memory was merely anonymous. But
in 1991 Hanna Schwartzman, whose efforts in 1945 to inscribe the Star
of David on the grave were met by the authorities' threat to bulldoze the
tombstone, finally reinstated the Jewish national symbol, along with two
crosses honoring the Romanians, Czechoslovaks, and Communists who
were also buried there.[42] Although the rituals and the power with which
they are associated have changed, the memory of the war as the heart of
this community's identity has remained intact.

More often than not, national epics evolve around bloody defeats that
ordain the nation with a new beginning. The death of the sons and daughters is neither final nor without purpose. "We will die in order to live
forever," Lazar, the Serbian prince defeated at Kosovo in 1389, is said to
have declared on the eve of battle, and the crushing defeat became a major
triumph by placing it on eschatological reading of the Serbian national
destiny.[43] Similarly a series of cataclysmic defeats in Jewish history, not
least of all the Holocaust, were reconstructed as redemptive triumphs in
the Zionist writing of the national myth. With several such triumphs—a
handful of Jewish partisans taking center stage as the forerunners of the
Israeli army, the official day of remembrance being named "The Day of
Holocaust and Heroism," and the national shrine being called "Yad Vashem Heroes' and Martyrs' Memorial"—the passive, fatalistic, and defense-
less Diaspora Jew was converted into a fighting Israeli.[44] Nor was the suffering of Vinnytsia's residents in vain. When one proceeds from Lityn to
nearby Ivanivtsi, the clue to the remarkable endurance of the myth offers
itself at the town's center. Above a long list of fallen native sons and daughters emerges the figure of a maidenlike nurse comforting the Christlike
figure of a dying soldier (Figure A.3). Whatever the female figure was
initially meant to represent, this small-scale Ukrainian *Pieta* conveys a
sense of continuity and purpose, turning death into a stage rather than a

---

[42] YVA, #03–6401, 15–16.

[43] Ralph Bogert, "Paradigm of Defeat or Victory? The Kosovo Myth vs. the Kosovo Covenant in Fiction," in Wayne Vucinich and Thomas Emmert, eds., *Kosovo: Legacy of a Medieval
Battle* (Minneapolis: University of Minnesota Press, 1991), 186.

[44] Segev, *The Seventh Million*; Young, *The Texture of Memory*, part 3.

Figure A.2. Jewish cemetery in Lityn. Note the unmarked obelisk for victims of the Holocaust and the desecrated tombstones.

Figure A.3. A Soviet Ukrainian *Pieta*. Commemoration of fallen native sons in the village of Ivanivtsi.

finality. As Christ has risen from the dead so will the Ukrainian nation.[45] Herein lay the power of the Soviet myth of the war. Victimization and fatalism gave way to the celebration of activity and continuity; the traumas of collectivization, famine, and terror gave way to the triumphant war; collaboration to common suffering; and civil war to unification of the national family.

---

[45] Similarly the Christ metaphor figured highly in national commemorations in Europe during and after World War I (Mosse, *Fallen Soldiers*, 70–106, 126–81).

In this spirit the town of Vinnytsia commemorated the fiftieth anniversary of World War II. The thrust of commemorative acts and reflections was the establishment of continuity between the sacrifice and heroism of the Ukrainian war generation, and the creation and defense of the newly independent Ukraine. Here, too, the words of General Shuliak were illuminating. The horrendous sacrifice of Ukrainians during the war was not in vain, the general repeatedly emphasized. Eight million (!) Ukrainians were killed in the war, said Shuliak, but "we cannot forget that after the conclusion of the Great Patriotic War Ukraine became a member of the United Nations and other organizations."[46] The war had been fully Ukrainianized.

When the Communist Party finally withdrew its all-Union claims and powers in Ukraine, as elsewhere across the Union, more than an ethnonational, administrative, territorial unit remained. There was also a viable and enduring epic that, considering the unique Soviet nationality policy, offered itself for appropriation by various nationalities touched by the war. Indeed none other than the children of the war, those party *apparatchiks* who thrived on the wartime legacy of a unified Ukraine, were the ones to lead Ukraine into sovereignty.

The myth of World War II, in this light, occupies a unique place between the formation and disintegration of the Soviet polity. On the one hand, the supra-class, cross-ethnic aspect of the myth provided the polity with a previously absent integrating theme and folded large groups previously excluded into the body politic. At the same time, the symbolic space for the articulation of particularistic, albeit nonantagonistic, visions, delineated by the primacy of personal bonding and the deliberative character of the Soviet polity, paved the way for the articulation of particularistic identities. Through its various incarnations, the myth of the war has outlived the polity itself.

[46] *Panorama*, 11 May 1995.

Bibliography

Archives

Arkhiv upravlinnia Sluzhby bezpeky Ukrainy, Kiev (AUSBU), Kiev
files 14 and 19 (war crimes trials)

Arkhiv upravlinnia Sluzhby bezpeky Ukrainy po Vinnytskoi oblasti (ASBUVO), Vinnytsia
file 26667 Ukrainian nationalists

Bakhmetev Archive, Columbia University, New York
Harvard University Refugee Interview Project (HURIP)

Derzhavnyi arkhiv Vinnyts'koi oblasti (DAVO), Vinnytsia
f. 151, op. 9, Vinnytsia City Council
f. 1311, Wartime occupation administration in Vinnytsia
f. 1417, Wartime occupation administration in the Shpykiv district
f. 2700, op. 7, Vinnytsia Regional Executive Committee
f. 4971, Vinnytsia Regional Administration for Culture
f. 5105, Maria Prisianiuk Collection
f. 5243, Iavdokha Horb Collection

Gosudarstvennyi arkhiv Rossiiskoi Federatsii (GARF), Moscow
f. 5446, Council of Peoples' Commissars
f. 7523, Supreme Soviet
f. 8114, Jewish Anti-Fascist Committee
f. 9401, Stalin's MVD Special Files
f. 9414, GULAG Central Administration
f. 9478, NKVD and Nationalist Guerrilla Movements
f. 9479, GULAG Special Settlements

Hoover Institution Archives, Stanford, California
Nicolaevsky Collection
Lev Dudin Collection

Institut Istorii Rossii (IIR), Moscow
f. 2, State Commission for Chronicling the Great Patriotic War

Partiinyi arkhiv Vinnyts'koi oblasti (PAVO), Vinnytsia
f. 29, Vinnytsia Regional Committee (pre-1932)
f. 136, ops. 13, 29, Special Department of the Vinnytsia obkom
   op. 16, Obkom Personnel Department
f. 138, Vinnytsia obkom
f. 425, Soviet partisan movement in Vinnytsia

Rossiiskii gosudarstvennyi voennyi arkhiv (RGVA), Moscow

f. 9, Main Political Administration

Rossiiskii gosudarstvennyi arkhiv sotsial'no-politicheskoi istorii (RGASPI), Moscow

f. 17, Central Committee:
  ops. 44, 45, Vinnytsia obkom
  ops. 114, 122, Orgburo
  op. 125, Agitation and Propaganda Department
  op. 162, Politburo

Tsentral'nyi arkhiv vnutrennikh voisk ministerstva vnutrennikh del Rossiiskoi Federatsii (TsAVVMVDRF), Potichnyi Collection, Robarts Library, University of Toronto

f. 488, NKVD and Nationalist Guerrillas in Postwar Ukraine and Belorussia

Tsentral'nyi derzhavnyi arkhiv hromads'kykh ob'iednan Ukrainy (TsDAHOU), Kiev

f. 1, Ukrainian Central Committee:
  op. 6, Central Committee Resolutions
  op. 16, Protocols of Sessions of the Politburo, Orgburo, and CC UKP (Central Committee of the Ukrainian Communist Party)
  op. 22, Special Department—Partisan Movement in Ukraine
  op. 23, Special Department
  op. 46, Personnel Department
  op. 50, Vinnytsia obkom
f. 57, op. 4, Communist Party of Ukraine in Wartime
f. 128, Soviet Partisan Detachments in the Vinnytsia region

Tsentral'nyi derzhavnyi arkhiv-muzei literatury i mystetstva Ukrainy (TsDAM-LMU), Kiev

f. 44, Volodymyr Sosiura Collection
f. 535, Mykola Bazhan Collection

Tsentral'nyi derzhavnyi arkhiv vyshchykh orhaniv vlady ta upravlinnia Ukrainy (TsDAVOVU), Kiev

f. 3206, Reichskommissariat Ukraine
f. 3833, Ukrainian Nationalist Movement
f. 4620, op. 3, Collection of Documents on the History of World War II

Tsentr khraneniia sovremennykh dokumentov (TsKhSD), Moscow

f. 5, General Department of the Central Committee
f. 6, Communist Party Control Commission
f. 89, Trial of the Communist Party

Yad Vashem Archive (YVA), Jerusalem
Testimonies of Jewish Survivors of the Holocaust

United States National Archives, Washington, DC
Microcopy T-175, rolls 233–36; Records of the Reich Leader of the SS and Chief of the German Police (Operational Situational Reports by the *Einsatzgruppen* in the USSR)

Newspapers
Eynikayt (Mosow)
Izvestiia (Moscow)
Kolhospnyk (Vinnytsia)
Komsomol'skaia pravda (Moscow)
Lenins'kym shliakhom (Vinnytsia)
Literaturna hazeta (Kiev)
Literaturnaia gazeta (Moscow)
Naddnistrians'ka zirka (Vinnytsia)
New Times (Moscow)
Nezavisimost' (Kiev)
Nove Ukrain'ke slovo (Kiev, 1941–43)
Nove zhyttia (Vinnytsia)
Novoe Russkoe slovo (Kiev, 1941–43)
Panorama (Vinnytsia)
Pravda (Moscow)
Pravda Ukrainy (Kiev)
Slovo khliboroba (Vinnytsia)
Uriadovi Dunaievets'ki visti (Kiev, 1943)
Vinnyts'ka pravda (Vinnytsia)
Vinnyts'ki visti (Vinnytsia, 1941–43)

Books and Articles
Abramov, Fedor. "Liudi kolkhoznoi derevni v poslevoennoi proze." *Novyi mir* 4 (1954): 210–31.
Abramson, Henry. *A Prayer for the Government: Ukrainians and Jews in Revolutionary Times, 1917–1920*. Cambridge, Mass.: Ukrainian Research Institute, Harvard University, 1999.
Adams, Mark B. "Eugenics in Russia, 1900–1940." In Mark B. Adams., ed., *The Wellborn Science: Eugenics in Germany, France, Brazil, and Russia*. New York: Oxford University Press, 1990.
Agamben, Georgio. *Homo Sacer: Sovereign Power and Bare Life*. Stanford: Stanford University Press, 1998.
Aho, James. *This Thing Called Darkness: A Sociology of the Enemy.* Seattle: University of Washington Press, 1994.
Aletiiano-Popivs'kyi, Ievhen. *Z ideieiu v sertsi—zi zbroieiu v rukakh*. London: Ukrainska vydavnycha spilka u V. Brytanii, 1980.
Allilueva, Svetlana. *Only One Year.* New York: Harper and Row, 1969.
Altshuler, Mordechai. "Antisemitism in Ukraine toward the End of the Second World War." *Jews in Eastern Europe* 3 (winter 1993): 40–81.

————, ed. *Distribution of the Jewish Population of the USSR, 1939.* Jerusalem: Hebrew University of Jerusalem, Centre for Research and Documentation of East European Jewry, 1993.

————. "Escape and Evacuation of Soviet Jews at the Time of the Nazi Invasion: Policies and Realities." In Lucjan Dobroszycki and Jeffrey S. Gurock, eds., *The Holocaust in the Soviet Union: Studies and Sources on the Destruction of the Jews in the Nazi-Occupied Territories of the USSR, 1941–1945.* Armonk, N.Y.: M. E. Sharpe, 1993.

————. "More about Public Reaction to the Doctors' Plot." *Jews in Eastern Europe* (fall 1996): 24–57.

————. "The Unique Features of the Holocaust in the Soviet Union" In Yaacov Ro'i, ed., *Jews and Jewish Life in Russia and the Soviet Union.* Portland, Ore.: F. Cass, 1995.

————. "Jewish Warfare and the Participation of Jews in Combat in the Soviet Union as Reflected in Soviet and Western Historiography." In Zvi Gitelman, ed. *Bitter Legacy: Confronting the Holocaust in the USSR.* Bloomington: Indiana University Press, 1997.

Alvarez, Alexander. "Adjusting to Genocide: The Techniques of Neutralization and the Holocaust." *Social Science History* 21, no. 2 (summer 1997): 139–78.

American Jewish Committe, ed. *The Jews in the Eastern War Zone.* New York: American Jewish Committee, 1916.

Anders, Wladyslaw. *Bez ostatniego rozdzialu: wspomnenia z lat [1939–1946].* Newtown, Wales: Montgomeryshire, 1949.

Andreyev, Catherine. *Vlasov and the Russian Liberation Movement.* Cambridge: Cambridge University Press, 1987.

Arad, Yitzhak. "The Holocaust of the Soviet Jewry in the Occupied Territories of the Soviet Union." *Yad Vashem Studies* 21 (1991): 1–47.

————. *Unichtozhenie evreev SSSR v gody nemetskoi okkupatsii, 1941–1944.* Jerusalem: Yad Vashem, 1992.

————. "Yehudei Brit-Hamoatzot Bamilhama Beged Germania Hanazit." *Yad Vashem Studies* 23 (1994): 51–89.

Ardamatskii, Vasilii. "Pinia iz Zhmerinki." *Krokodil* 8 (20 March 1953): 13.

Arendt, Hannah. *The Origins of Totalitarianism.* New York: Harcourt, Brace, 1951.

Arian, Asher, Ilan Talmud, and Tamar Hermann. *National Security and Public Opinion in Israel.* Jerusalem: *Jerusalem Post,* 1988.

Arkhangorodskaia, N. S., and A. A. Kurnosov. "O sozdanii komissii po istorii Velikoi Otechestvennoi voiny AN SSSR i ee arkhiva." *Arkheograficheskii ezhegodnik za 1981 god* (Moscow: Izd-vo Akademii nauk SSSR, 1982): 219–29.

Armstrong, John. "Collaborationism in World War II: The Integral Nationalist Variant in Eastern Europe." *Journal of Modern History* 40, no. 3 (1968): 396–410.

————. *The Politics of Totalitarianism: The Communist Party of the Soviet Union since 1934.* New York: Random House, 1961.

————. *The Soviet Bureaucratic Elite: A Case Study of the Ukrainian Apparatus.* New York: Praeger, 1959.

———, ed. *The Soviet Partisans in World War II*. Madison: University of Wisconsin Press, 1964.

———. *Ukrainian Nationalism*. New York: Columbia University Press, 1990.

Babaevskii, Semen. *Sobranie sochinenii*. Moscow: Khudozhestvennaia literatura, 1979.

Babii, B. M. *Vozziednannia zakhidnoi Ukrainy z Ukrains'koiu RSR*. Kiev: Akademiia nauk Ukrains'koi RSR, 1954.

Babin, A. I., et al. *SSSR v gody Velikoi Otechestvennoi voiny (iun' 1941-sentiabr' 1945)*. 3 vols. Moscow: Nauka, 1977–1981.

Baczko, Bronislaw. *Ending the Terror: The French Revolution after Robespierre*. Translated by Michel Petheram. Cambridge: Cambridge University Press, 1994.

Ball, Alan. *Russia's Last Capitalists: The Nepmen, 1921–1929*. Berkeley: University of California Press, 1987.

Bankier, David. *The Germans and the Final Solution: Public Opinion under Nazism*. Cambridge, Mass.: Blackwell, 1992.

Barber, John, and Mark Harrison. *The Soviet Home Front, 1941–1945: A Social and Economic History of the USSR in World War II*. New York: Longman, 1991.

Barnes, Steven. "All to the Front, All for Victory! The Mobilization of Forced Labor in the Soviet Union during World War II." *International Labor and Working Class History* 58 (fall 2000).

Bartov, Omer. "Defining Enemies, Making Victims: Germans, Jews, and the Holocaust." *American Historical Review* 103 (June 1998): 771–816.

———. *The Eastern Front, 1941–1945, German Troops and the Barbarization of Warfare*. New York: St. Martin's, 1986.

———. *Hitler's Army: Soldiers, Nazis, and War in the Third Reich*. New York: Oxford University Press, 1991.

———. *Murder in Our Midst: The Holocaust, Industrial Killing, and Representation*. New York: Oxford University Press, 1996.

Bauman, Zygmunt. *Modernity and the Holocaust*. Ithaca: Cornell University Press, 1991.

Becker, Carl. "What Are Historical Facts?" In Phil L. Snyder, ed., *Detachment and the Writing of History: Essays and Letters of Carl L. Becker*. Ithaca: Cornell University Press, 1958.

Beevor, Antony. *Stalingrad*. London: Penguin, 1998.

Belov, Fedor. *The History of a Soviet Collective Farm*. New York: Praeger, 1956.

Benes, Eduard. "The Organization of Post-War Europe." *Foreign Affairs* (January 1942).

Berlin, Isaiah. "Marxism and the International in the Nineteenth Century." In Isaiah Berlin, *The Sense of Reality*, 116–67. Edited by Henry Hardy. London: Chatto and Windus, 1996.

Bidlack, Richard. *Workers at War: Factory Workers and Labor Policy in the Siege of Leningrad*. Pittsburgh: University of Pittsburgh Center for Russian and East European Studies, 1991.

Bilas, Ivan. *Represyvno-karal'na systema v Ukraini, 1917–1953*. 2 vols. Kiev: Lybid, Viisko Ukrainy, 1994.

Bilinsky, Yaroslav. *The Second Soviet Republic: The Ukraine after World War II*. New Brunswick, N.J.: Rutgers University Press, 1964.

Billig, Michael. *Banal Nationalism*. London: Sage, 1995.

Binns, Christopher. "The Changing Face of Power: Revolution and Accommodation in the Development of the Soviet Ceremonial System." *Man* 15, no. 1 (1980): 170–87.

Bociurkiw, Bohdan. "The Rise of the Ukrainian Autocephalous Orthodox Church, 1919–1922." In Geoffrey Hosking, ed., *Church, Nation, and State in Russia and Ukraine*. Basingstoke, England: Macmillan, 1991.

———. "The Soviet Destruction of the Ukrainian Autocephalous Orthodox Church, 1929–1930." *Journal of Ukrainian Studies* 12, no. 1 (1987): 3–31.

———. *The Ukrainian Greek Catholic Church and the Soviet State (1939–1950)*. Toronto: Canadian Institute of Ukrainian Studies Press, 1996.

Boemeke, Manfred, et al. *Anticipating Total War: The German and American Experiences, 1871–1914*. Cambridge: Cambridge University Press, 1999.

Bogatyr', Zakhar. *V tylu vraga*. Moscow: Sotsekgiz, 1963.

Bogert, Ralph. "Paradigm of Defeat or Victory? The Kosovo Myth vs. the Kosovo Covenant in Fiction." In Wayne Vucinich and Thomas Emmert, eds., *Kosovo: Legacy of a Medieval Battle*. Minneapolis: University of Minnesota Press, 1991.

Bonnell, Victoria. *Iconography of Power: Soviet Political Posters under Lenin and Stalin*. Berkeley: University of California Press, 1997.

Borisenko, V. K., and A. V. Kurochkin. "Kul'tura svadebnogo zastol'ia v sovremennom gorode." In *Traditsii, obriady, sovremennost'*. Kiev: Izd-vo Polit. lit-ry Ukrainy, 1983.

Borkovskii, P. A. "Vosstanovlenie i organizatsionnoe ukreplenie partiinykh organizatsii zapadnykh oblastei USSR (1944–1945 gg.)." *Voprosy istorii KPSS* 11 (1971): 64–74.

Borys, Jurij. *The Sovietization of Ukraine, 1917–1923: The Communist Doctrine and Practice of National Self-Determination*. Edmonton: Canadian Institute of Ukrainian Studies, 1980.

Breitman, Richard. *The Architect of Genocide: Himmler and the Final Solution*. Hanover, N.H.: University Press of New England, 1991.

Broberg, Gunnar, and Mattias Tyden. "Eugenics in Sweden: Efficient Care." In Gunnar Broberg and Nils Roll-Hansen, eds., *Eugenics and the Welfare State: Sterilization Policy in Denmark, Sweden, Norway, and Finland*. East Lansing: Michigan State University Press, 1996.

Brody, Richard. *Ideology and Political Mobilization: The Soviet Home Front during World War II*. Pittsburgh: University of Pittsburgh Center for Russian and East European Studies, 1994.

Brubaker, Rogers. *Nationalism Reframed: Nationhood and the National Question in the New Europe*. Cambridge: Cambridge University Press, 1996.

Brzezinski, Zbigniew. *The Permanent Purge: Politics in Soviet Totalitarianism*. Cambridge, Mass.: Harvard University Press, 1956.

Buchsweiler, Meir, ed. "A Collection of Soviet Documents concerning Germans in the USSR." Research Paper No. 73, The Marjorie Mayrock Center for Soviet and East European Research. The Hebrew University of Jerusalem, 1991.

Budurowiycz, Bohdan. "Poland and the Ukrainian Problem, 1921–1939." *Canadian Slavonic Papers* 25, no. 4 (1983): 473–500.

Bugai, Nikolai. *L. Beriia-I. Stalinu: "Soglasno Vashemu ukazaniiu . . ."* Moscow: AIRO XX, 1995.

————. "40–50-e gody: posledstviia deportatsii narodov (Svidetel'stvuiut arkhivy NKVD-MVD SSSR)." *Istoriia SSSR* 1 (1992): 122–43.

Burchenko, Dmytro. *Reid k iuzhnomu Bugu*. Kiev: Politizdat Ukrainy, 1978.

Burleigh, Michael. *Death and Deliverance: "Euthanasia" in Germany 1900–1945*. Cambridge: Cambridge University Press, 1994.

Burrin, Philippe. "Political Religion: The Relevance of a Concept." *History and Memory* 9, nos. 1/2 (fall 1997): 321–49.

Carel, Alexis. *Man the Unknown*. London: Harper and Brothers, 1935.

Carmelly, Felicia (Steigman), ed. *Shattered! 50 Years of Silence: History and Voices of the Tragedy in Romania and Transnistria*. Ontario: Abbeyfield, 1997.

Carynnyk, Marco, ed. *Alexander Dovzhenko: The Poet as Filmmaker*. Cambridge, Mass.: MIT Press, 1973.

Chang, Gordon. "Social Darwinism versus Social Engineering: The Education of Japanese Americans during World War II." In Amir Weiner, ed., *Landscaping the Human Garden*. Stanford: Stanford University Press, forthcoming 2001.

Chesnokov, Dmitrii. *Sovetskoe sotsialisticheskoe gosudarstvo*. Moscow: Gos. Izd-vo polit. lit-ry, 1952.

Clark, Katerina. *Petersburg: Crucible of Cultural Revolution*. Cambridge, Mass.: Harvard University Press, 1995.

————. *The Soviet Novel: History as Ritual*. Chicago: University of Chicago Press, 1981.

Cohn, Norman. *Warrant for Genocide: The Myth of the Jewish World Conspiracy and the "Protocols of the Elders of Zion."* New York: Harper and Row, 1967.

Connelly, John. "Nazis and Slavs: From Racial Theory to Racist Practice." *Central European History* 32, no. 1 (1999): 1–33.

Conquest, Robert. *Power and Policy in the USSR*. London: Macmillan, 1962.

Conway, Martin. *Collaboration in Belgium: Leon Degrelle and the Rexist Movement*. New Haven: Yale University Press, 1993.

————. "Justice in Post-War Belgium: Popular Passions and Political Realities." *Cahiers d'histoire du temps present* 2 (1997): 7–34.

————. "The Liberation of Belgium, 1944–1945." In Gill Bennett, ed., *The End of the War in Europe 1945*. London: HMSO, 1996.

Cooper, Matthew. *The Phantom War*. London: Macdonald and Janes, 1979.

Corney, Frederick. "Rethinking a Great Event: The October Revolution as Memory Project." *Social Science History* 22, no. 4 (1998): 12–28.

Curtis, John, and Alex Inkeles. "Marxism in the USSR—The Recent Revival." *Political Science Quarterly* 61, no. 3 (September 1946): 349–64.

Dallin, Alexander. *German Rule in Russia, 1941–1945: A Study of Occupation Policies*. London: Macmillan, 1957.

Davies, Raymond Arthur. *Odyssey through Hell*. New York: L. B. Fischer, 1946.

Deák, István. "Civil Wars and Retribution in Europe, 1939–1948." *Zeitgeschichte*, 7–8/25/Jahrgang/1998: 244–52.

————. "Trying to Construct a Productive, Disciplined, Monoethnic Society: The Dilemma of East Central European Governments, 1914–1956." In Amir Weiner, ed., *Landscaping the Human Garden*. Stanford: Stanford University Press, forthcoming 2001.

Dean, Martin C. "The German *Gendarmerie*, the Ukrainian *Schutzmannschaft*, and the 'Second Wave' of Jewish Killings in Occupied Ukraine: German Policing at the Local Level in the Zhitomir Region, 1941–1944." *German History* 14, no. 2 (1996): 168–92.

Decter, Moshe. "Judaism without Embellishment." In Ronald Rubin, ed., *The Unredeemed: Anti-Semitism in the Soviet Union*. Chicago: Quadrangle, 1968.

Didkovs'kyi, A. D. "Vazhlyvyi vykhovnyi zasib." In *Novi zvychai, dobri traditsii*. Odessa: Maiak, 1983.

Djilas, Milovan. "Christ and the Commissar." In George Urban, ed., *Stalinism: Its Impact on Russia and the World*. Aldershot, Hants, England: Wildwood, 1982.

———. *Conversations with Stalin*. New York: Harcourt, Brace and World, 1962.

———. *Wartime*. New York: Harcourt Brace Jovanovich, 1977.

"Dokumenty o presledovanii evreev." *Arkhiv russkoi revoliutsii* 19 (1928): 245–84.

Donchenko, V. N. "Demobilizatsiia sovetskoi armii i reshenie problemy kadrov v pervye poslevoennye gody." *Istoriia SSSR* 3 (May–June 1970).

Dontsov, Dmytro. *De shukaty nashykh istorychnykh tradytsii*. L'viv: Ukrainske vydvo, 1941.

Dragan, Anthony. *Vinnytsia: A Forgotten Holocaust*. New Jersey: Svoboda, 1986.

"Druzhba narodov SSSR—moguchii faktor pobedy nad vragom." *Bol'shevik* (December 1944).

Duma, P. T. "Internal Obstacles to the Ukrainian National Liberation Struggle." In Peter J. Potychnyi and Yevhen Shtendera, eds., *The Political Thought of the Ukrainian Underground, 1943–1951*. Edmonton: Canadian Institute of Ukrainian Studies, 1986.

Dunham, Vera. *In Stalin's Time: Middleclass Values in Soviet Fiction*. Cambridge: Cambridge University Press, 1976.

Dunmore, Timothy. *Soviet Politics, 1945–1953*. Basingstoke: Macmillan, 1984.

Dyck, Harvey. *Weimar Germany and Soviet Russia, 1926–1933*. New York: Columbia University Press, 1966.

Dzhigurda, Olga. "Teplokhod 'Kakhetiia': zapiski voennogo vracha." *Znamia* 1 (1948): 3–86; 2 (1948): 22–79.

Ehrenburg, Il'ia. *Sobranie Sochinenii*. Vol. 9: *Liudi, gody, zhizn'*. Moscow: Sovetskii pisatel', 1967.

Eisfeld, Alfred, and Victor Herdt, eds. *Deportation, Sondersiedlung, Arbeitarmee: Deutsche in der Sowjetunion 1941 bis 1956*. Cologne: Verlag Wissenschaft und Politik, 1996.

El'chenko, Iu. N. *Novomu cheloveku-novye obriady*. Moscow: Izd-vo polit. lit-ry, 1976.

Ellis, Frank. *Vasiliy Grossman: The Genesis and Evolution of a Russian Heretic*. Providence, R.I.: Berg, 1994.

Etinger, Iakov. "The Doctors' Plot: Stalin's Solution to the Jewish Question." In Yaacov Ro'i, ed., *Jews and Jewish Life in Russia and the Soviet Union*. Portland, Ore.: F. Cass, 1995.

Fadeev, Aleksandr. "O sovetskom patriotizme i natsional'noi gordosti narodov SSSR." *Pod znamenem marksizma* 11 (November 1943): 16–35.

Fainsod, Merle. *How Russia Is Ruled*. Cambridge, Mass.: Harvard University Press, 1953.

————. *Smolensk under Soviet Rule.* Cambridge, Mass.: Harvard University Press, 1958.

Falasca-Zamponi, Simonetta. *The Fascist Spectacle: The Aesthetics of Power in Mussolini's Italy.* Berkeley: University of California Press, 1997.

Farmer, Sarah. *Martyred Village: Commemorating the 1944 Massacre at Oradoursur-Glane.* Berkeley: University of California Press, 1999.

Fedorov, Aleksei, *Podpol'nyi obkom deistvuet.* Kiev: Izd-vo politicheskoi lit-ry Ukrainy, 1986.

Fejto, François. *Judentum und Kommunismus: Anti-Semitismus in Osteuropa.* Vienna: Europa Verlag, 1967.

Fireside, Harvey. *The Icon and the Swastika: The Russian Orthodox Church under Nazi and Soviet Control.* Cambridge, Mass.: Harvard University Press, 1971.

Fisher Jr., Ralph Talcott. *Pattern for Soviet Youth: A Study of the Congresses of the Komsomol, 1918–1954.* New York: Columbia University Press, 1959.

Fitzpatrick, Sheila. "Ascribing Class: The Construction of Social Identity in Soviet Russia." *Journal of Modern History* 65 (December 1993): 745–70.

————. "Postwar Soviet Society: The 'Return to Normalcy,' 1945–1953." In Susan J. Linz, ed., *The Impact of World War II on the Soviet Union,* 129–56. Totowa, N.J.: Rowman and Allanheld, 1985.

————. "Stalin and the Making of a New Elite." *Slavic Review* 38 (September 1979): 377–402.

————. *Stalin's Peasants: Resistance and Survival in the Russian Village after Collectivization.* New York: Oxford University Press, 1994.

Fleischhauer, Ingeburg, and Benjamin Pinkus. *The Soviet Germans: Past and Present.* Jerusalem: Hurst, 1986.

Friedlander, Henry. *The Origins of Nazi Genocide: From Euthanasia to the Final Solution.* Chapel Hill: University of North Carolina Press, 1995.

Friedländer, Saul. *Nazi Germany and the Jews.* Vol. 1: *The Years of Persecution, 1933–1939.* New York: HarperCollins, 1997.

Friedman, Phillip. *Their Brothers' Keepers.* New York: Crown, 1957.

————. "Ukrainian-Jewish Relations during the Nazi Occupation." *YIVO Annual of Jewish Social Science* 12 (1958/1959): 259–96.

Gallagher, Matthew P. *The Soviet History of World War II: Myths, Memories, and Realities.* New York: Praeger, 1963.

Garthoff, Raymond. *Soviet Military Doctrine.* Glencoe, Ill.: Free Press, 1953.

Gatrell, Peter. *A Whole Empire Walking: Refugees in Russia during World War I.* Bloomington: Indiana University Press, 1999.

Gavrutto, Porfirii. *Tuchi nad gorodom.* Moscow: Molodaia Gvardiia, 1963.

Gelb, Michael. "An Early Soviet Ethnic Deportation: The Far-Eastern Koreans." *The Russian Review* 54 (July 1995): 389–412.

Gellately, Robert. *The Gestapo and German Society.* Oxford: Clarendon, 1990.

Gentile, Emilio. *The Sacralization of Politics in Fascist Italy.* Cambridge, Mass.: Harvard University Press, 1996.

Getty, J. Arch. "The Politics of Repression Revisited." In J. Arch Getty and Roberta Manning, eds., *Stalinist Terror: New Perspectives.* Cambridge: Cambridge University Press, 1993.

————, et al. "Victims of the Soviet Penal System in the Pre-War Years: A First Approach on the Basis of Archival Evidence." *American Historical Review* 98 (October 1993): 1017–49.

Geyer, Michael. "The Militarization of Europe, 1914–1945." In John Gillis, ed., *The Militarization of the Western World*. New Brunswick, N.J.: Rutgers University Press, 1989.

Gilboa, Yehoshua A. *The Black Years of Soviet Jewry, 1939–1953*. Boston: Little, Brown, 1971.

Gill, Graeme. *The Origins of the Stalinist Political System*. Cambridge: Cambridge University Press, 1990.

Gitelman, Zvi. "Soviet Reactions to the Holocaust, 1945–1991." In Lucjan Dobroszycki et al., eds., *The Holocaust in the Soviet Union: Studies and Sources on the Destruction of the Jews in the Nazi-Occupied Territories of the USSR, 1941–1945*. Armonk, N.Y.: M. E. Sharpe, 1993.

Gladkov, Teodor. *Ostaius' chekistom!* Moscow: Izd-vo politicheskoi literatury, 1987.

Glantz, David, *When Titans Clashed: How the Red Army Stopped Hitler*. Lawrence: Kansas University Press, 1995.

Glezerman, Georgii. *Likvidatsiia ekspluatatorskikh klassov i preodolenie klassovykh razlichii v SSSR*. Moscow: Gos. Izd-vo polit. lit-ry, 1949.

Goldberg, Anatol. *Ilya Ehrenburg. Revolutionary, Novelist, Poet, War Correspondent, Propagandist: The Extraordinary Epic of a Russian Survivor*. London: Weidenfeld and Nicolson, 1984.

Goldhagen, Daniel J. *Hitler's Willing Executioners: Ordinary Germans and the Holocaust*. New York: Knopf, 1996.

Goliakov, T. "Ocherednaia vekha na puti k kommunizmu." *Sovetskoe gosudarstvo i pravo* 11 (1950).

Golikov, S. N. *Vydaiushchiesia pobedy sovetskoi armii v Velikoi Otechestvennoi voine*. Moscow: Gos. izd-vo polit. lit-ry, 1952.

Goncharov, Ivan. *Fregat "Pallada": ocherki puteshestviia*. In *Polnoe sobranie sochinenii*. Vol. 5. St. Petersburg: A. F. Marx, 1899.

Gordon, Bertram. "Afterward: Who Were the Guilty and Should They Be Tried?" In Richard Golsan, ed., *Memory, the Holocaust, and French Justice: The Bousquet and Touvier Affairs*. Hanover, N.H.: University Press of New England, 1996.

Gorky, Maxim. *Untimely Thoughts: Essays on Revolution, Culture, and the Bolsheviks, 1917–1918*. Translated by Herman Ermolaev. New Haven: Yale University Press, 1995.

————, et al. *Belomor: An Account of the Construction of the New Canal between the White Sea and the Baltic Sea*. New York: H. Smith and R. Haas, 1935.

Graziosi, Andrea. "The Great Strikes of 1953 in Soviet Labor Camps in the Accounts of Their Participants: A Review." *Cahiers du Monde russe et soviétique* 33, no. 4 (October–December 1992): 419–46.

Gross, Jan. *Revolution from Abroad: The Soviet Conquest of Poland's Western Ukraine and Western Belorussia*, Princeton, N.J.: Princeton University Press, 1988.

Grossman, Vasilii. "Ukraina bez evreev." In Shimon Markish, *Vasilii Grossman. Na evreiskie temy*. Jerusalem: Biblioteka-Aliia, 1985.

————. *Zhizn' i sud'ba.* Moscow: Knizhnaia Palata, 1988.

————, and Il'ia Ehrenburg, eds. *Hasefer Hashahor.* Tel Aviv: Am Oved, 1991.

"Gulag v gody Velikoi Otechestvennoi voiny. Doklad nachal'nika GULAGa NKVD SSSR V.G. Nasedkina. Avgust 1944 g." *Istoricheskii arkhiv* 3 (1994): 60–86.

Guri, Yossef. "Yehudei Brit-Hamoatzot Bamilhama Neged Hanazim." In *Lohamim Yehudim Bamilhama neged Hanazim.* Tel Aviv: ha-Irgun ha-Yisreeli shel hayalim meshuhrarim al yede Sifriyat Poalim, 1971.

Gusarov. "O rabote s kadrami v Ukrainskoi partorganizatsii." *Partiinaia zhizn'* 1 (November 1946): 39–45.

Gutin, M. L. "Vosstanovlenie partiinykh organizatsii na osvobozhdennoi territorii v gody Velikoi Otechestvennoi voiny." *Voprosy istorii KPSS* 9 (1974): 77–87.

Hagen, William W. "Before the 'Final Solution': Toward a Comparative Analysis of Political Anti-Semitism in Interwar Germany and Poland." *Journal of Modern History* 68 (June 1996): 251–81.

Halfin, Igal. "From Darkness to Light: Student Communist Autobiography during NEP." *Jahrbücher für Geschichte Osteuropas* 45 (1997): 210–36.

Hallie, Phillip. *Lest Innocent Blood Be Shed: The Story of the Village of Le Chambon and How Goodness Happened There.* New York: Harper and Row, 1979.

Hellbeck, Jochen. "Fashioning the Stalinist Soul: The Diary of Stepan Podlubnyi." *Jahrbücher für Geschichte Osteuropas* 44 (1996): 344–73.

Hilberg, Raul. *Perpetrators, Victims, Bystanders: The Jewish Catastrophe, 1933–1945.* New York: Aaron Asher, 1992.

Hirsch, Francine. "The Soviet Union as a Work-in-Progress: Ethnographers and the Category *Nationality* in the 1926, 1937, and 1939 Censuses." *Slavic Review* 56, no. 2 (1997): 251–78.

History of the Communist Party of the Soviet Union (Bolsheviks): The Short Course. New York: International, 1939.

Holquist, Peter. "Conduct Merciless, Mass Terror: Decossackization." *Cahiers du Monde russe,* 38, nos. 1–2 (1997): 127–62.

————. "Information is the Alpha and Omega of Our Work: Bolshevik Surveillance in its Pan-European Context." *Journal of Modern History* 69 (September 1997): 415–50.

————. "State Violence as Technique." In Amir Weiner, ed., *Landscaping the Human Garden.* Stanford: Stanford University Press, forthcoming 2001.

Holubnychy, Vsevolod. "Outline History of the Communist Party of the Ukraine." *The Ukrainian Review* 6 (1958): 68–125.

Horn, David. *Social Bodies: Science, Reproduction, and Italian Modernity.* Princeton, N.J.: Princeton University Press, 1994.

Hough, Jerry. "The Changing Nature of the Kolkhoz Chairman." In James Millar, ed., *The Soviet Rural Community.* Urbana: University of Illinois Press, 1971.

Huyse, Lucien. "La reintegrazione dei collaborazionisti in Belgio, in Francia e nei Paesi Bassi." *Passato e presente* 16, no. 44 (1998): 113–26.

————, and Steven Dhondt. *La repression des collaborations 1942–1952. Un passé toujours present.* Brussels: Centre de recherche et d'information socio-politique, 1993.

Ia hromadianyn Radians'koho Soiuzu: Z dosvidu roboty po vruchenniu pasportiv iunym hromadianam v Staromis'komu raioni m. Vinnytsi. Vinnytsia, 1980.

Imeni geroev: iz praktiki sozdaniia imennykh polei i ikh ispol'zovaniia v voenno-patrioticheskom internatsional'nom vospitanii, sovershenstvovanii sotsialisticheskogo sorevnovaniia v Oratovskom raione. Vinnytsia, 1988.

Inkeles, Alex, and Raymond Bauer. *The Soviet Citizen: Daily Life in a Totalitarian Society.* Cambridge, Mass.: Harvard University Press, 1961.

Istoriia mist i sil URSR: Vinnyts'ka oblast'. Kiev: Hol. Red. Ukrainskoi rad. Entsyklopedii AN URSR, 1972.

Istoriia Ukrainy: korotkyi kurs. Kiev: Vyd-vo Adademii nauk URSR, 1941.

Iurchuk, V. I. "Vosstanovlenie i ukreplenie partiinykh organizatsii na Ukraine v 1945–1953 godakh." *Voprosy istorii KPSS* 6 (1962).

Iwanov, Mykolaj. *Pierwszy Narod Ukarany: Polacy w Zwiazku Radzieckim w latach 1921–1939.* Warsaw: Panstwowe Wydawnictwo Naukowe, 1991.

Johnson, Eric. *Nazi Terror: The Gestapo, Jews, and Ordinary Germans.* New York: Basic Books, 1999.

Kaganovich, Moshe. *Der Yidisher Ontayl in Partizaner-bavegung fun Sovet-Rusland.* Rome: Oysg. fun der Tsentraler historisher komishe baym Partizaner farband P.H.H. in Italye, 1948.

Kamenetsky, Ihor, ed. *The Tragedy of Vinnytsia: Materials on Stalin's Policy of Extermination in Ukraine during the Great Purge, 1936–1938.* Toronto: Ukrainian Historical Association, 1989.

Kammari, M. D. *Marksizm-Leninizm o roli lichnosti v istorii.* Moscow: Gos. izdvo polit. lit-ry, 1953.

Kapusto, Iuliia. *V srednem raione.* Moscow: Sovetskii pisatel', 1950.

Kedar, Benjamin. "Expulsion as an Issue of World History." *Journal of World History* 7, no. 2 (1996): 165–80.

Kenez, Peter. "Pogroms and White Ideology in the Russian Civil War." In John Klier and Shlomo Lambroza, eds., *Pogroms: Anti-Jewish Violence in Modern Russian History.* New York: Cambridge University Press, 1992.

Kertzer, David. *Politics and Symbols: The Italian Communist Party and the Fall of Communism.* New Haven: Yale University Press, 1996.

Kharkhordin, Oleg. *The Collective and the Individual in Russia: A Study of Practices.* Berkeley: University of California Press, 1999.

Khersonets, Iu. M. "At the Turning Point." In Peter J. Potychnyi and Yevhen Shtendera, eds., *The Political Thought of the Ukrainian Underground, 1943–1951.* Edmonton: Canadian Institute of Ukrainian Studies, 1986.

Khrushchev, Nikita. *Khrushchev Remembers.* Translated and edited by Strobe Talbott. Boston: Little, Brown, 1971.

——. "O vosstanovlenii i pod"eme sels'kogo khoziaistva i partiino-politicheskoi rabote na sele." *Partiinaia zhizn'* 5 (March 1948).

Klee, Ernst, Willi Dressen, and Volker Riess, eds. *"The Good Old Days": The Holocaust as Seen by Its Perpetrators and Bystanders.* New York: Free Press, 1991.

Klier, John. "*Zhid*: Biography of a Russian Epithet." *The Slavonic and East European Review* 60, no.1 (January 1982): 1–15.

Knapp, Steve. "Collective Memory and the Actual Past." *Representations* 26 (1989): 134–47.

Kochavi, Aryeh J. *Prelude to Nuremberg: Allied War Crimes Policy and the Question of Punishment.* Chapel Hill: University of North Carolina Press, 1998.

Kochetov, Vsevolod. *Zhurbiny.* Leningrad: Sovetskii pisatel', 1952.

Kolakowski, Leszek. *Main Currents of Marxism.* 3 vols. Oxford: Clarendon, 1978.
———. *The Presence of Myth.* Chicago: University of Chicago Press, 1989.
Kolasky, John. *Two Years in Soviet Ukraine.* Toronto: P. Martin, 1970.
Kolonitskii, Boris. "Antiburzhuaznaia propaganda i 'antiburzhuiskoe' soznanie." *Otechestvennaia istoriia* 1 (1994): 17–27.
Komarov, P. "O trebovatel'nosti i chutkosti." *Partiinaia zhizn'* 17 (December 1954): 20–25.
Kornblatt, Judith Deutch. *The Cossack Hero in Russian Literature.* Madison: University of Wisconsin Press, 1992.
Korniichuk, Oleksandr. *Front.* Moscow: Gos. izd-vo khudozh. lit-ry, 1942.
Kostiuk, Hryhory. *Stalinist Rule in the Ukraine: A Study of the Decade of Mass Terror (1929–1939).* New York: Praeger, 1960.
Kostyrchenko, Genadi. *Out of the Red Shadows: Anti-Semitism in Stalin's Russia.* New York: Prometheus, 1995.
Kot, Stanislaw. *Conversation with the Kremlin and Dispatches from Russia.* Oxford: Oxford University Press, 1963.
Kotkin, Stephen. "1991 and the Russian Revolution: Sources, Conceptual Categories, Analytical Frameworks." *Journal of Modern History* 70 (June 1998): 384–425.
———. "In Search of the Nomenklatura: Yesterday's USSR, Today's Russia." *East European Constitutional Review* 6:4 (December 1997): 104–20.
———. *Magnetic Mountain: Stalinism as a Civilization.* Berkeley: University of California Press, 1995.
Koval', Mikhail. "Natsysts'kyi henosyd shchodo ievreiv ta ukrains'ke naselennia (1941–1944 rr.)." *Ukrains'kyi istorychnyi zhurnal* 2 (1992): 25–32.
Kovpak, Sidor. *Ot Putivlia do Karpat.* Moscow: Gospolitizdat, 1945.
Kraus, Richard Curt. *Class Conflict in Chinese Socialism.* New York: Columbia University Press, 1981.
Kravchenko, Victor. *I Chose Freedom.* New York: Scribner's, 1946.
Kulynych, Ivan, and Nataliia Kryvets. *Narysy z istorii nimets'kykh kolonii v Ukraini.* Kiev: Natsionalna akademiia nauk Ukrainy, 1995.
Kurnosov, A. A. "Vospominaniia-interv'iu v fonde komissii po istorii Velikoi Otechestvennoi voiny akademii nauk SSSR." *Arkheograficheskii ezhegodnik za 1973 god,* 118–32. Moscow: Izd-vo Akademii Nauk SSSR, 1974.
Kuromiya, Hiroaki. *Freedom and Terror in the Donbas: A Ukrainian-Russian Borderland, 1870s-1990s.* Cambridge: Cambridge University Press, 1998.
Kuven'ova, O. F. *Hromads'kyi pobut Ukrains'koho selianstva: istoriko-etnohrafichnii narys.* Kiev: Naukova dumka, 1966.
Kuznetsov, Nikolai, P. P. Kampars, and N. M. Zakovich. *Sovetskaia grazhdanskaia obriadnost'.* Moscow: Mysl', 1967.
Kychko, Trohym. *Iudaizm bez prikras.* Kiev: Vyd-vo Akademii nauk URSR, 1963.
Kyzia, Luka, and M. Kovalenko. *Vikova borot'ba Ukrainskoho naroda proty Vatikanu.* Kiev: Vyd-vo Kyivskoho universiteta, 1959.
Lagrou, Pieter. "Victims of Genocide and National Memory: Belgium, France, and the Netherlands, 1945–1965." *Past and Present* 154 (February 1997): 191–222.
Landes, Richard. "Lest the Millenium Be Fulfilled: Apocalyptic Expectations and the Pattern of Western Chronography, 100–800 C.E." In Werner Verbeke et al.,

The Use and Abuse of Eschatology in the Middle Ages. Leuven, Belgium: Leuven University Press, 1988.

Lane, Christel. *Rites of Rulers. Ritual in Industrial Society: The Soviet Case.* Cambridge: Cambridge University Press, 1981.

Larin, Iurii. *Evrei i antisemitizm v SSSR.* Moscow: Gosizdat, 1929.

Lebed', Mykola. *UPA, Ukrains'ka povstans'ka armiia.* Vydannia Presovoho biura UHVR, 1946.

Lefort, Claude. *The Political Forms of Modern Society: Bureaucracy, Democracy, Totalitarianism.* Cambridge, Mass.: Polity Press, 1986.

Leneman, Leon. *La Tragedie des juifs en U.R.S.S.* Paris: Desclée de Brouwer, 1959.

Leonov, Leonid. "Nashestvie." *Novyi mir* 8 (1942): 50–85.

Levin, Nora. *The Jews in the Soviet Union since 1917: The Paradox of Survival.* New York: New York University Press, 1988.

Levytskyi (Lewytzkyi), Boris. "Besonderheiten der sowjetukrainischen Entwicklung." *Osteuropa* 11 (October 1962): 669–75.

———. "Kommunistychna partiia Ukrainy—1955 rik." *Ukrains'kyi zbirnyk* 3 (1955): 100–31.

———. *Die Sowjetukraine, 1944–1963.* Cologne, 1964.

———. *The Uses of Terror: The Soviet Secret Police 1917–1970.* New York: Coward, McCann, and Geoghegan, 1972.

Lew, Roland. "Grappling with Soviet Realities: Moshe Lewin and the Making of Social History." In Nick Lampert and Gabor Rittersporn, eds., *Stalinism. Its Nature and Aftermath: Essays in Honor of Moshe Lewin.* Armonk, N.Y.: M. E. Sharpe, 1992.

Lewin, Moshe. *The Gorbachev Phenomenon: A Historical Interpretation.* Berkeley: University of California Press, 1988.

Liber, George. *Soviet Nationality Policy, Urban Growth and Identity Change in Ukrainian SSR 1923–1934.* Cambridge: Cambridge University Press, 1992.

Linderman, Gerald. *The World within War: America's Combat Experience in World War II.* Cambridge, Mass.: Harvard University Press, 1997.

Lin'kov, Grigorii. *Voina v tylu vraga.* Moscow: Gos-izd-vo khudozhestvennoi literatury, 1951.

Lipkin, Semen. *Stalingrad Vasiliia Grossmana.* Ann Arbor: Ardis, 1986.

———. *Zhizn' i sud'ba Vasiliia Grossmana.* Moscow: Kniga, 1990.

Livshin, A., and I. Orlov, eds. *Pis'ma vo vlast', 1917–1927. Zaiavleniia, zhaloby, donosy, pis'ma v gosudarstvennye struktury i bol'shevistskim vozhdiam.* Moscow: ROSSPEN, 1998.

Lohrenz, Gerhard. *The Lost Generation and Other Stories.* Manitoba: J. Lohrenz, 1982.

Lotnik, Waldemar. *Nine Lives: Ethnic Conflict in the Polish-Ukrainian Borderlands.* London: Serif, 1999.

Lokshin, Aleksandr. "Delo vrachei": "otkliki trudiashchikhsia." *Vestnik evreiskogo universiteta v Moskve* 1, no. 5 (1994): 52–62.

Loytsker, Haim. "Far ideyisher reynkeyt fun undzer literatur." *Der Shtern* (Kiev) 2 (1948): 105–12.

Magocsi, Paul Robert. *A History of Ukraine.* Toronto: University of Toronto Press, 1996.

————, ed. *Morality and Reality: The Life and Times of Andrei Sheptyts'kyi.* Edmonton: Canadian Institute of Ukrainian Studies, 1989.

Malia, Martin. *The Soviet Tragedy: A History of Socialism in Russia, 1917–1991.* New York: Free Press, 1994.

Mannheim, Karl. *Essays on the Sociology of Knowledge.* London: Routledge and Kegan Paul, 1952.

Markish, Shimon. "A Russian Writer's Jewish Fate." *Commentary* 81, no. 4 (1986): 39–47.

Martin, Terry. "The Origins of Soviet Ethnic Cleansing." *Journal of Modern History* 70 (December 1998): 813–61.

Matla, Zynovii. *Pivdenna pohidnia hrupa.* Munich: Tsitsero, 1952.

Mazower, Mark. *Inside Hitler's Greece: The Experience of Occupation, 1941–1944.* New Haven: Yale University Press, 1993.

————. "Military Violence and National Socialist Values: The Wehrmacht in Greece, 1941–1944" *Past and Present* 134 (February 1992): 129–58.

McDaniel, Tim. *The Agony of the Russian Idea.* Princeton, N.J.: Princeton University Press, 1996.

Medvedev, Dmitrii. *Na beregakh iuzhnogo Buga.* Moscow: Molodaia gvardiia, 1957.

————. *Sil'nye dukhom.* Moscow: Voennoe Izdatelstvo Voennogo Ministerstva Soiuza SSR, 1951.

Meller-Faust, Hanna. *Me-ever la-nahar: Pikei Zikhronot Me-Transnistria.* Israel: Kibutz Lohamei Hagetaot, 1985.

Meyer, Kurt. *Grenadiere/Panzermeyer.* Munich: Schild, 1956.

Milova, O. L., ed. *Deportatsii narodov SSSR (1930-e—1950-e gody).* Moscow: Rossiiskaia Akademiia Nauk, 1995.

Moore, Barrington. "The Present Purge in the USSR." *Review of Politics* 9, no. 1 (1947): 65–76.

————. *Soviet Politics: The Dilemma of Power.* Cambridge, Mass.: Harvard University Press, 1950.

Moore, Bob. *Victims and Survivors: The Nazi Persecution of the Jews in the Netherlands, 1940–1945.* London: Arnold, 1997.

Mosse, George. *Fallen Soldiers: Reshaping the Memory of the World Wars.* Oxford: Oxford University Press, 1990.

————. *The Nationalization of the Masses: Political Symbolism and Mass Movements in Germany from the Napoleonic Wars through the Third Reich.* New York: H. Fertig, 1975.

Motyl, Alexander. "Ukrainian Nationalist Political Violence in Inter-War Poland." *East European Quarterly* 19 (March 1985): 45–55.

Müller, Ingo. *Hitler's Justice: The Courts of the Third Reich.* Cambridge, Mass.: Harvard University Press, 1987.

Mulligan, Timothy Patrick. *The Politics of Illusion and Empire: German Occupation Policy in the Soviet Union, 1942–1943.* New York: Praeger, 1988.

Naiman, Eric. *Sex in Public: The Incarnation of Early Soviet Ideology.* Princeton, N.J.: Princeton University Press, 1997.

Naimark, Norman. "Ethnic Cleansing between Peace and War." In Amir Weiner, ed., *Landscaping the Human Garden.* Stanford: Stanford University Press, forthcoming 2001.

Naumov, Vladimir, ed. *Nepravednyi sud: poslednii stalinskii rasstrel. Stenogramma sudebnogo protsessa nad chlenami evreiskogo antifashistskogo komiteta.* Moscow: Nauka, 1994.

―――. "Sud'ba voennoplennykh i deportirovannykh grazhdan SSSR. Materialy Komissii po reabilitatsii zhertv politicheskikh repressii." *Novaia i noveishaia istoriia* 2 (March–April 1996): 91–112.

Nazi Conspiracy and Aggression. Office of the United States Chief of Counsel for the Prosecution of Axis Criminality. Washington, 1946.

Negretov, Pavel. *Vse dorogi vedut na Vorkutu.* Benson, Vt.: Chalidze, 1985.

"Neizvestnaia initsiativa Khrushcheva (o podgotovke ukaza 1948 g. O vyselenii krest'ian)." *Otechestvennye arkhivy* 2 (1993): 31–38.

Nekrasov, Viktor. "Slova 'velikie' i prostye," *Iskusstvo kino* 5 (1959): 55–61.

―――. "V rodnom gorode." *Novyi mir* 10 (October 1954): 3–65; 11 (November 1954): 97–178

Nekrich, Aleksandr. *Otreshis' ot strakha: Vospominaniia istorika.* London: Overseas Publications Interchange, 1979.

―――. *The Punished Peoples: The Deportation and the Fate of Soviet Minorities at the End of the Second World War.* New York: Norton, 1979.

Nikto ne zabyt, nichto ne zabyto: iz opyta raboty komiteta komsomola Vinnitskogo meduchilishcha imeni akademika D.K. Zabolotnogo po voenno-patrioticheskomu vospitaniiu uchashchikhsia. Vinnytsia, 1986.

Nikto ne zabyt, nichto ne zabyto: iz opyta raboty komsomol'skoi organizatsii peduchilishcha po organizatsii i provedeniiu "zvezdnykh pokhodov." Vinnytsia, 1989.

Nimtsi v Ukraini 20–30-ti rr. XX st.: Zbirnyk dokumentiv derzhavnykh arkhiviv Ukrainy. Kiev: Institut Istorii Ukrainy, 1994.

Nirenberg, David. *Communities of Violence: Persecution of Minorities in the Middle Ages.* Princeton, N.J.: Princeton University Press, 1996.

Novick, Peter. *The Resistance versus Vichy: The Purge of Collaborators in Liberated France.* New York: Columbia University Press, 1968.

Osnovni pokaznyky rozvytku narodnoho hospodarstva Vinnyts'koi oblasti: Statystychnyi zbirnyk. Vinnytsia, 1957.

Ovechkin, Valentin. *Z frontovym pryvitom.* Kiev: Ukrainske derzhavne vyd-vo, 1946.

Overy, Richard. *Russia's War: A History of the Soviet War Effort, 1941–1945.* New York: Penguin, 1998.

Ozerov, V. "Obraz bol'shevika v poslevoennoi sovetskoi literature." *Bol'shevik* 10 (May 1949): 54–70.

Partizanskaia druzhba: vospominaniia o boevykh delakh partizan-evreev uchastnikov Velikoi Otechestvennoi voiny. Moscow: Der Emes, 1948.

Paxton, Robert O. *Vichy France: Old Guard and New Order, 1940–1944.* New York: Knopf, 1972.

Pelenski, Jaroslaw. "The Haidamak Insurrections and the Old Regimes in Eastern Europe." In Jaroslaw Pelenski, ed., *The American and European Revolutions, 1776–1848.* Iowa: University of Iowa Press, 1980.

Peris, Daniel. "God Is on Our Side": The Religious Revival on Unoccupied Soviet Territory during World War II." *Kritika* 1, no. 1 (winter 2000): 97–118.

Pesni i dumy Sovetskoi Ukrainy. Moscow: Gos. izd-vo khudozh. lit-ry, 1951.

Petliak, F. A. *Partiinoe rukovodstvo sovetami na Ukraine v gody Velikoi Otechestvennoi Voiny (1941–1945).* Kiev: Vyshcha shkola, 1986.

———. "Vosstanovlenie i ideino-organizatsionnoe ukreplenie partiinykh organizatsii Ukrainy posle ee osvobozhdeniia ot nemetsko-fashistskoi okkupatsii, (1943–1945 gg.)." In F. P. Ostapenko, ed., *Voprosy istorii KPSS perioda Velikoi Otechestvennoi Voiny.* Kiev: Izd-vo Kievskogo universiteta, 1961.

Peukert, Detlev. "The Genesis of the 'Final Solution' from the Spirit of Science." In Thomas Childers and Jane Caplan, eds., *Reevaluating the Third Reich.* New York: Holmes and Meier, 1993.

Picheta, Vladimir. *Osnovnye momenty istoricheskogo razvitiia zapadnoi Ukrainy i zapadnoi Belorussii.* Moscow: Gos. sots.-eko. Izd-vo, 1940.

Pick, Daniel. *Face of Degeneration: A European Disorder, c. 1848–1948.* Cambridge: Cambridge University Press, 1989.

Pinkus, Benjamin. *The Jews of the Soviet Union.* Cambridge: Cambridge University Press, 1988.

———. *The Soviet Government and the Jews,* Cambridge: Cambridge University Press, 1984.

Piotrowski, Tadeusz. *Vengeance of the Swallows.* Jefferson, N.C.: McFarland, 1994.

Po obe storony fronta/Auf beiden Seiten der Front: pis'ma sovetskikh i nemetskikh soldat 1941–1945 gg. Moscow: Sol, 1995.

"Pogroms and Self-Defense in Ukraine 1919–1920." *He-Avar* 17 (1970).

Pohl, J. Otto. *The Stalinist Penal System.* Jefferson, N.C.: McFarland, 1997.

Poliakov, I. A., ed. *Vsesoiuznaia perepis' naseleniia 1939 goda: Osnovnye itogi.* Moscow: Nauka, 1992.

Pomerantsev, Vladimir. "Ob iskrennosti v literature." *Novyi mir* 12 (1953): 218–45.

"Posledniaia bolezn' Stalina: Iz otchetov MGB SSSR o nastroeniiakh v armii vesnoi 1953 g." *Neizvestnaia Rossiia. XX vek,* 2:253–58. Moscow: Istoricheskoe nasledie, 1992.

Prestupnye tseli—prestupnye sredstva: dokumenty ob okkupatsionnoi politike fashistskoi Germanii na territorii SSSR (1941–1944 gg.). Moscow: Gos. izd-vo polit. lit-ry, 1963.

Redlich, Shimon. "Metropolitan Sheptyts'kyi and Ukrainian Jewish Relations." In Zvi Gitelman, ed., *Bitter Legacy: Confronting the Holocaust in the USSR.* Bloomington: Indiana University Press, 1997.

———. *War, Holocaust, and Stalinism: A Documented Study of the Jewish Anti-Fascist Committee in the USSR.* Luxemburg: Harwood, 1995.

Rich, David. *The Tsar's Colonels: Professionalism, Strategy, and Subversion in Late Imperial Russia.* Cambridge, Mass.: Harvard University Press, 1999.

Rigby, Theodore H. *Communist Party Membership in the USSR, 1917–1967.* Princeton, N.J.: Princeton University Press, 1968.

————. "Crypto-Politics." *Survey* 50 (1964): 183–94.

Rittersporn, Gabor. " 'Vrednye elementy,' 'opasnye men'shinstva' i bol'shevistskie trevogi: massovye operatsii 1937–38 gg. i etnicheskii vopros v SSSR." In Timo Vikhavainen and Irina Takala, eds., *V sem'e edinoi. Natsional'naia politika partii bol'shevikov i ee osushchestvlenie na Severo-Zapade Rossii v 1920–1950-e gody.* Petrozavodsk: Izd-vo Petrozavodskogo universiteta, 1998.

Robinson, Nehemiah. *The Genocide Convention: Its Origins and Interpretation.* New York: Institute of Jewish Affairs, World Jewish Congress, 1949.

Rogger, Hans. *Jewish Policies and Right-Wing Politics in Imperial Russia.* Berkeley: University of California Press, 1986.

Rogovin Frankel, Edith. *Novy Mir: A Case Study in the Politics of Literature, 1952–1958.* Cambridge: Cambridge University Press, 1981.

Rokossovskii, Konstantin. *A Soldier's Duty.* Moscow: Progress, 1985.

Rosenshield, Gary. "Socialist Realism and the Holocaust: Jewish Life and Death in Anatoly Rybakov's *Heavy Sand.*" *Publications of the Modern Language Association of America* 111 (March 1996).

Rousso, Henry. "L'épuration en France. Une histoire inachevée." *Vingtième Siècle: Revue d'histoire* 33 (March 1992).

The Russian Penal Code of the Russian Socialist Federal Soviet Republic. London: Foreign Office, 1934.

Schechtman, Joseph. *European Population Transfers, 1939–1945.* New York: Oxford University Press, 1946.

————. *Population Transfers in Asia.* New York: Hallsby, 1949.

————. *Postwar Population Transfers in Europe, 1945–1955.* Philadelphia: University of Pennsylvania Press, 1962.

————. *Star in Eclipse.* New York: T. Yoseloff, 1961.

————. "The Transnistrian Reservation." *YIVO Annual of Jewish Social Sciences* 8 (1953): 178–96.

Scholmer, Joseph. *Vorkuta.* New York: Holt, 1954.

Schuman, Howard, and Jacqueline Scott. "Generations and Collective Memories." *American Sociological Review* 54 (1989).

Scott, James C. *Seeing Like a State: How Certain Schemes to Improve the Human Condition Have Failed.* New Haven: Yale University Press, 1998.

Seaton, Albert. *The Russo-German War, 1941–1945.* New York: Praeger, 1971.

Segev, Tom. *The Seventh Million: The Israelis and the Holocaust.* New York: Hill and Wang, 1993.

Seleshko, Mykhailo. *Vinnytsia: Spomyny perekladacha komisii doslidiv zlochyniv NKVD v 1937–1938.* New York: Fundatsiia im. O. Olzhycha, 1991.

————. "Vinnytsia—The Katyn of Ukraine: A Report by an Eyewitness." *The Ukrainian Quarterly* 5 (1949): 238–48.

Sella, Amnon. *The Value of Human Life in Soviet Warfare.* London: Routledge, 1990.

Seniavskaia, Elena. *Frontovoe Pokolenie, 1941–1945: istoriko-psikhologicheskoe issledovanie.* Moscow: Institut rossiiskoi istorii RAN, 1995.

————. "Dukhovnyi oblik frontovogo pokoleniia: istoriko-psikhologicheskii ocherk." *Vestnik Moskovskogo Universiteta, series* 8 Istoriia (1992).

Serhiichuk, Volodymyr. ed. *Desiat' buremnykh lit: Zakhidnoukrains'ki zemli u 1944–1953 rr. Novi dokumenty i materialy.* Kiev: Dnipro, 1998.

———. *Pohromy v Ukraini, 1914–1920: Vid shtuchnykh stereotypiv do hirkoi pravdy, prykhovuvanoi v radians'kykh arkhivakh.* Kiev: Vyd. imeni Oleni Telihy, 1998.

Shakhai, D. "Our Tactics with Regard to the Russian People." In Peter J. Potychnyi and Yevhen Shtendera, eds., *The Political Thought of the Ukrainian Underground, 1943–1951.* Edmonton: Canadian Institute of Ukrainian Studies, 1986.

Shankovs'kyi (Shankowsky), Lev. *Pohidni hrupy OUN.* Munich: Ukrainskyi samostiinyk, 1958.

———. "Soviet and Satellite Sources on the Ukrainian Insurgent Army." *The Annals of the Ukrainian Academy of Arts and Sciences in the United States* 9, nos. 1–2 (1961): 234–61.

Shapiro, Gershon. *Under Fire: The Stories of Jewish Heroes of the Soviet Union.* Jerusalem: Yad Vashem, 1988.

Shapoval, Yuri. *Ukraina 20–50-kh Rokiv: Storinky nenapysanoi istorii.* Kiev: Naukova dumka, 1993.

Shcharansky (Sharansky), Anatoly. *Fear No Evil.* New York: Random House, 1988.

Shul'ha, Ivan. *Holod na Podilli.* Vinnytsia: Vyd-vo Kontynent-PRYM, 1993.

———. "Holodomor 1946–1947 rokiv na Podilli." *Derzhavnist'* 3 (1991).

Simmel, Georg. "Soziologische Aesthetik." *Die Zukunft* 17 (1896): 204–16.

Simonov, Konstantin. "Zadachi sovetskoi dramaturgii i teatral'naia kritika." *Novyi mir* 3 (1949).

Sinitsyn, V. G., ed. *Nashi prazdniki.* Moscow: Politizdat, 1977.

Slezkine, Yuri. *Arctic Mirrors: Russia and the Small Peoples of the North.* Ithaca: Cornell University Press, 1994.

———. "From Savages to Citizens: The Cultural Revolution in the Soviet Far North, 1928–1938.' *Slavic Review* 51 (spring 1992): 56–76.

———. "The USSR as a Communal Apartment, or How a Socialist State Promoted Ethnic Particularism." *Slavic Review* 53 (1994): 414–52.

Slobodianiuk, P. Ia. "Osobennosti organizatsii novykh prazdnikov i obriadov v usloviiakh goroda." In *Traditsii, obriady, sovremennost'.* Kiev: Izd-vo polit. lit-ry Ukrainy, 1983.

Smirnov, L. "Neustanno povyshat' politicheskuiu bditel'nost' sovetskikh liudei." *Bloknot agitatora* 3 (January 1953): 11–22.

Smirnov, Nikolai. *Vplot' do vysshei mery.* Moscow: Moskovskii rabochii, 1997.

Smolar, Hersh. *Vu Bistu Haver Sidorov?* Tel Aviv: Farlag Y. L. Perets, 1975.

Snyder, Timothy. " 'To Resolve the Ukrainian Problem Once and for All": The Ethnic Cleansing of Ukrainians in Poland, 1943–1947." *Journal of Cold War Studies* 1, no. 2 (spring 1999): 86–120.

Sobchenko, V. K. "Trudovye traditsii, prazdniki i obriady truzhenikov sela." In *Traditsii, obriady, sovremennost'.* Kiev: Izd-vo polit. lit-ry Ukrainy, 1983.

Soprotivlenie v Gulage: Vospominaniia. Pis'ma. Dokumenty. Moscow: Vozvrashchenie, 1992.

Sovetskie traditsii, prazdniki i obriady: opyt, problemy, rekomendatsii. Moscow: Profizdat, 1986.

Spector, Shmuel. *The Holocaust of Volhynian Jews, 1941–1944.* Jerusalem: Achva, 1990.

Stalin, I. V. "O nedostatkakh partiinoi raboty i merakh likvidatsii trotskistskikh i inykh dvurushnikov. Doklad na Plenume TsK VKP (b) 3 marta 1937." *Bol'shevik*, no. 7 (1937): 1–17.

———. "Otchetnyi doklad XVII s"ezdu partii." In *Sochineniia*, 13:282–379. Moscow: Gos. izd-vo polit. lit-ry, 1951.

———. "Rech' I.V. Stalina v Narkomate oborony, 2 iunia 1937 g." *Istochnik* 3 (1994): 72–88.

———. "Rech' na predvybornom sobranii izbiratelei Stalinskogo izbiratel'nogo okruga goroda Moskvy." In *Sochineniia*, 3 (16): 1–22. Edited by Robert McNeal. Stanford: Hoover Institution on War, Revolution, and Peace, Stanford University Press, 1967.

———. "Vystuplenie tovarishcha I.V. Stalina na prieme v Kremle v chest' komanduiushchikh voiskami Krasnoi Armii." *Bol'shevik* 20, no. 10 (May 1945): 1–2.

———. "Zakliuchitel'noe slovo tovarishcha Stalina na plenume TsK VKP (b) 5 marta 1937 g." *Bol'shevik* 7 (1937): 18–27.

Starozhilov, Nikolai. *Partizanskie soedineniia Ukrainy v Velikoi Otechestvennoi voine*. Kiev: Vyshcha shkola, 1983.

Starukh, Iaroslav. "The New Catastrophe in Ukraine." In *Litopys ukrains'koi povstanskoi armii*. Vol. 17. Toronto: Vyd-vo Litopys UPA, 1988.

Steiner, John. *Power Politics and Social Change in National Socialist Germany: A Process of Escalation into Mass Destruction*. Atlantic Highlands, N.J.: Humanities Press, 1976

Stel'makh, G. Iu. "Formuvannia novykh zvychaiv v ukrains'komu kolhospnomu seli." *Narodna Tvorchist' ta Etnohrafiia*, 1957.

Stepanian, Tsolak. "Usloviia i puti perekhoda ot sotsializma k kommunizmu." In F. Konstantinov et al., *O sovetskom sotsialisticheskom obshchestve: sbornik statei*. Moscow: Gos. izd-vo politicheskoi literatury, 1948.

Stites, Richard., ed., *Culture and Entertainment in Wartime Russia*. Bloomington: Indiana University Press, 1995.

Sto sorok besed s Molotovym: iz dnevnika F. Chueva. Moscow: Terra, 1991.

Stolleis, Michael. *The Law under the Swastika: Studies on Legal History in Nazi Germany*. Chicago: University of Chicago Press, 1998.

The Stroop Report. Translated by Cybil Milton. New York: Pantheon, 1979.

Sutzkever, Abraham. "Il'ia Ehrenburg (A Kapital Zikhronot fon di Yaren 1944–1946)." *Di Goldene Keit* 61 (1967).

Swayze, Harold. *Political Control of Literature in the USSR, 1946–1959*. Cambridge, Mass.: Harvard University Press, 1962.

Szöllösi-Janze, Margit. "'Pfeilkreuzler, Landesverräter und andere Volksfeinde' Generalabrechnung in Ungarn." In Klaus Dietmar Henke and Hans Woller, eds., *Politische Saüberung in Europa: Die Abrechnung mit Faschismus und Kollaboration nach dem Zweiten Weltkrieg*. Deutscher Taschenbuch Verlag GmbH, 1991.

Tak eto bylo: natsional'nye repressii v SSSR 1919–1952 gody. 3 vols. Moscow: Rossiiskii mezhdunar. fond kul'tury, 1993.

Talmon, Jacob. *The Myth of the Nation and the Vision of the Revolution*. London: Secker and Warburg, 1981.

————. *The Origins of Totalitarian Democracy.* London: Secker and Warburg, 1952.

————. *Political Messianism—The Romantic Phase.* London: Secker and Warburg, 1960.

Teich, Meir. "The Jewish Self-Administration in Ghetto Shargorod (Transnistria)." *Yad Vashem Studies* 2 (1958).

Temkin, Benjamin. *My Just War: The Memoir of a Jewish Red Army Soldier in World War II.* Novato, Calif.: Presidio, 1998.

Terles, Mykolaj, ed. *Ethnic Cleansing of Poles in Volhynia and East Galicia, 1942–1946.* Toronto: Alliance of the Polish Eastern Provinces, 1993.

Tikhonov, Nikolai. *Pered novym pod"emom: Sovetskaia literatura v 1944–45 gg.* Moscow: Literaturnaia gazeta, 1945.

Timasheff, Nikolai. *The Great Retreat: The Growth and Decline of Communism in Russia.* New York: E. P. Dutton, 1946.

Tolstoy, Aleksei. "Strannaia istoriia." *Krasnaia zvezda,* 28 August 1942.

Torzecki, Ryszard. *Kwestia ukrainska w polityce III Rzeszy, 1933–1945.* Warsaw: Ksiazka i wiedza, 1972.

Towster, Julian. *Political Power in the USSR, 1917–1947.* New York: Oxford University Press, 1948.

Trainin, Aron Naumovich. "Bor'ba s genotsidom kak mezhdunarodnym prestupleniem." *Sovetskoe gosudarstvo i pravo* 5 (May 1948).

Trainin, I. "Kommunizm i gosudarstvo." *Sovetskoe gosudarstvo i pravo* 2 (1939).

Trotsky, Leon. *Nashi politicheskie zadachi.* Geneva, 1904.

————. *The Revolution Betrayed.* New York: Doubleday, Doran, 1936.

Tumarkin, Nina. *The Living and the Dead: The Rise and Fall of the Cult of the War.* New York: Basic Books, 1994.

Urban, Michael. *An Algebra of Soviet Power: Elite Circulation in the Belorussian Republic 1966–1986.* Cambridge: Cambridge University Press, 1989.

Vasil'ev, Valerii. "Krest'ianskie vosstaniia na Ukraine, 1929–30 gody." *Svobodnaia mysl'* 9 (1992): 70–78.

————, and Lynne Viola, eds. *Kollektivizatsiia i krest'ianskoe soprotivlenie na Ukraine (noiabr' 1929-mart 1930 gg.).* Vinnytsia: Logos, 1997.

————, ed. *Politychni represii na Podilli (20–30-i rr. XX st.).* Vinnytsia: Logos, 1999.

Verhoeyen, Etienne. *België bezet, 1940–1945.* Brussels: BRTN, 1993.

Vershyhora, Petro. "O 'byvalykh liudiakh' i ikh kritikakh." *Zvezda* 6 (1948).

————. *Liudi s chistoi sovest'iu.* Moscow: Moskovskii rabochii, 1946.

————. "Zhizn' v bor'be." *Literaturnaia Gazeta* 17 (December 1957).

Viola, Lynne. *Peasant Rebels under Stalin: Collectivization and the Culture of Peasant Resistance.* New York: Oxford University Press, 1996.

————. "Tear the Evil from the Root: The Children of *Spetspereselentsy* of the North." In Natalia Baschmakoff and Paul Fryer, eds., *Modernization of the Russian Provinces, Studia Slavica Finlandensia* (special issue) 17 (April 2000): 34–72.

Vladimirov, Leonid. *Rossiia bez prikras i umolchanii.* Frankfurt/Main: Possev, 1973.

Vladymyrov, Mykhailo. *Vohnenna zona.* Kiev: Vyd-vo polit. lit-ry Ukrainy, 1982.

Volkogonov, Dmitrii. *Lenin*. New York: Free Press, 1994.

Volkov, I. M. "Kolkhoznaia derevnia v pervyi poslevoennyi god." *Voprosy istorii* (1966): 15–32.

Von Geldern, James. *Bolshevik Festivals, 1917–1920*. Berkeley: University of California Press, 1993.

Von Hagen, Mark. "Soviet Soldiers and Officers on the Eve of the German Invasion: Towards a Description of Social Psychology and Political Attitudes." *Soviet Union/Union Soviétique* 18, nos.1–3 (1991): 79–101.

Vospityvat' patriotov: iz opyta raboty Vinnitskogo SPTU-11 po voenno-patriot- icheskomu vospitaniiu uchashchikhsia. Vinnytsia, 1986.

Vynnychenko, Ihor. *Ukraina 1920–1980-kh: deportatsii, zaslannia, vyslannia*. Kiev: Vyd-vo "Rada," 1994.

Vyshinskii, P. E. "Sovetskii patriotizm." In F. Konstantinov, M. Kammari, and G. Glezerman, eds., *O sovetskom sotsialisticheskom obshchestve: Sbornik statei*. Moscow: Gos. izd-vo politicheskoi literatury, 1948.

Walicki, Andrzej. *Marxism and the Leap to the Kingdom of Freedom: The Rise and Fall of the Communist Utopia*. Stanford: Stanford University Press, 1995.

Walzer, Michael. *The Revolution of the Saints: A Study in the Origins of Radical Politics*. Cambridge, Mass.: Harvard University Press, 1965.

Watson, James L., ed. *Class and Social Stratification in Post-Revolution China*. Cambridge: Cambridge University Press, 1984.

Weeks, Theodore R. *Nation and State in Late Imperial Russia: Nationalism and Russification on the Western Frontier, 1863–1914*. DeKalb: Northern Illinois University Press, 1996.

Weisberg, Richard. *Vichy Law and the Holocaust in France*. New York: New York University Press, 1996.

Weiss, Aharon. "The Holocaust and the Ukrainian Victims." In Michael Berenbaum, ed., *A Mosaic of Victims: Non-Jews Persecuted and Murdered by the Nazis*. New York: New York University Press, 1990.

———. "Jewish-Ukrainian Relations in Western Ukraine during the Holocaust." In Howard Aster and Peter Potichnyj, eds., *Ukrainian-Jewish Relations in Historical Perspective*. Edmonton: Canadian Institute of Ukrainian Studies, 1988.

Werth, Alexander. *Russia at War*. New York: Avon, 1964.

———. *Russia: The Postwar Years*. New York: Taplinger, 1971.

Werth, Nicolas, and Gael Moullec, eds. *Rapports secrets soviétiques: la société russe dans les documents confidentiels, 1921–1991*. Paris: Gallimard, 1994.

Wexler, Paul. *Purism and Language: A Study in Modern Ukrainian and Belorussian Nationalism (1840–1967)*. Bloomington: Indiana University Press, 1974.

White III, Lynn T. *Policies of Chaos: The Organizational Causes of Violence in China's Cultural Revolution*. Princeton, N.J.: Princeton University Press, 1989.

Williams, Philip M. *Crisis and Compromise: Politics in the Fourth Republic*. London: Longmans, Green, 1958.

Wohl, Robert. *The Generation of 1914*. Cambridge, Mass.: Harvard University Press, 1979.

Wortman, Richard. *Scenarios of Power: Myth and Ceremony in the Russian Monarchy*. 2 vols. Princeton, N.J.: Princeton University Press, 1995.

Wynot, Edward D. " 'A Necessary Cruelty': The Emergence of Official Anti-Semitism in Poland, 1936–1939." *American Historical Review* 76, no. 4 (October 1971): 1035–58.

Yack, Bernard. *The Longing for Total Revolution: Philosophic Sources of Social Discontent from Rousseau to Marx and Nietzsche.* Princeton, N.J.: Princeton University Press, 1986.

Yahil, Leni. *The Rescue of Danish Jewry.* Philadelphia: Jewish Publication Society of America, 1969.

Young, James. *The Texture of Memory: Holocaust Memorials and Meaning.* New Haven: Yale University Press, 1993.

Zbikowski, Andrzej. "Local Anti-Jewish Pogroms in the Occupied Territories of Eastern Poland, June–July 1941." In Lucjan Dobroszycki and Jeffrey S. Gurock, eds., *The Holocaust in the Soviet Union: Studies and Sources on the Destruction of the Jews in the Nazi-Occupied Territories of the USSR, 1941–1945.* Armonk, N.Y.: M. E. Sharpe, 1993.

Zemskov, Victor. "Prinuditel'nye migratsii iz Pribaltiki v 1940–1950-kh godakh." *Otechestvennye arkhivy* 1 (1993): 4–19.

———. "Spetsposelentsy (po dokumentatsii NKVD-MVD SSSR)." *Sotsiologicheskie issledovaniia* 11 (1990): 1–17.

Zenzinov, Vladimir. *Vstrecha s Rossiei: Kak i chem zhivut v sovetskom soiuze. Pis'ma v Krasnuiu Armiiu 1939–1940.* New York: L. Rausen, 1944.

Zerubavel, Yael. *Recovered Roots: Collective Memory and the Making of Israeli National Tradition.* Chicago: University of Chicago Press, 1995.

Zhiromskaia, Valentina et al., eds. *Polveka pod grifom: Vsesoiuznaia perepis' naseleniia 1937 goda.* Moscow: Nauka, 1996.

Zima, Veniamin. *Golod v SSSR 1946–1947 godov: proiskhozhdenie i posledstviia.* Moscow: Institut Rossiiskoi Istorii RAN, 1996.

Zubkova, Elena. *Obshchestvo i reformy 1945–1964.* Moscow: Rossiia molodaia, 1993.

———. "Kadrovaia politika i chistki v KPSS (1949–1953)." *Svobodnaia mysl'* 4 (1999): 97–110

Zuccotti, Susan. *The Holocaust, the French, and the Jews.* New York: Basic Books, 1993.

Zur, Ofer. "The Love of Hating: The Psychology of Enmity." *History of European Ideas* 13, no. 4 (1991): 345–69.

Unpublished Dissertations and Manuscripts

Berkhoff, Karel Cornelis. "Hitler's Clean Slate: Everyday Life in the Reichskommissariat Ukraine, 1941–1944." Ph.D. dissertation, University of Toronto, 1998.

Bone, Jonathan. "Asia Stops Here: Border-Zone Slavicization and the Fate of the Far Eastern Koreans, 1925–1937." Paper presented at the Thirty-first Annual Meeting of the American Association for the Advancement of Slavic Studies, St. Louis, 18–21 November 1999.

Deák, István. "Collaboration/Accommodation/Resistance." Paper presented at the conference on "Remembering, Adapting, Overcoming: The Legacy of World War II in Europe." Remarque Institute, New York University, 24–27 April 1997.

Gilliam, Sylvia. *The Nationality Questionnaire.* Unpublished manuscript of the Project on the Soviet Social System, Harvard University, 1954.

Hellbeck, Jochen. "Laboratories of the Self: Diaries from the Stalin Era." Ph.D. dissertation, Columbia University, 1998.

Hirsch, Francine. *Empire of Nations: Colonial Technologies and the Making of the Soviet Union, 1917–1939.* Ph.D. dissertation, Princeton University, 1998.

Holquist, Peter. "To Count, to Extract, to Exterminate: Population Statistics and Population Politics in Late Imperial and Soviet Russia." Paper presented at a workshop entitled "Empire and Nation in the Soviet Union." University of Chicago, 24–26 October 1997.

Lagrou, Pieter. "Heroes, Martyrs, Victims: A Comparative Social History of the Memory of World War II in France, Belgium, and the Netherlands, 1945–1965." Ph.D. dissertation, The Catholic University of Leuven, Belgium, 1996.

Lohr, Eric. "Enemy Alien Politics in the Russian Empire during World War I." Ph.D. dissertation, Harvard University, 1999.

Weiner, Amir. "The Politics of Natural Disaster: The Famine of 1946–1947 in Eastern Ukraine." Paper presented at the International Conference on Hunger and Famine in History, New York University, May 1995.

Yekelchyk, Serhy. "Stalinist Patriotism as a Contested Discourse: Reconciling the Ukrainian and Russian 'Heroic Pasts,' 1939–1945." Paper presented at the Thirty-first Conference of the American Association for the Advancement of Slavic Studies, St. Louis, 21 November 1999.